1000 DRESSES

THE FASHION DESIGN RESOURCE

TRACY FITZGERALD
ALISON TAYLOR

FOREWORD BY STEPHEN FAERM

Thames & Hudson

First published in the United Kingdom
in 2014 by
Thames & Hudson Ltd
181A High Holborn
London WC1V 7QX

Copyright © 2014
Quarto Publishing plc

British Library Cataloguing-
in-Publication Data
A catalogue record for this book
is available from the British Library

ISBN: 978-0-500-29144-3

Colour separation in China by PICA
International Pte Ltd

Printed by 1010 Printing
International Limited, China

To find out about all our
publications, please visit
www.thamesandhudson.com.
There you can subscribe to our
e-newsletter, browse or download
our current catalogue, and buy any
titles that are in print.

On the cover: Dress by Carolina
Herrera from her autumn/winter 2011
collection, WireImage/Getty Images

1000 DRESSES

THE FASHION DESIGN RESOURCE

Contents

Foreword

Whether you are a student, a professional or considering a career in the fashion industry, *1000 Dresses* offers a comprehensive overview of one of fashion's primary – and highly popular – areas of apparel design: the dress. Following a historical and contextual overview of the dress, individual chapters showcase the key silhouettes employed throughout modern history. Readers may review each chapter's categories and sub-categories sequentially, or in any order that fits their needs. No matter where in the book the reader lands, they will find extensive information about the world of dresses, including design inspiration, textile knowledge and detail development, seasonal variations, styling considerations, diverse aesthetics and many other informative areas about dresses. Each category provides readers with historical examples for context alongside a wide range of traditional and interpretive design examples of the silhouette. Throughout *1000 Dresses*, the versatility and timelessness of the dress is fully illustrated.

To succeed in today's competitive and highly accelerated fashion industry, students and professionals must acquire a tremendous amount of knowledge and skills quickly and thoroughly. *1000 Dresses* contributes significantly to this knowledge by giving readers a deeper understanding and literacy of fashion design, thus supporting the ability to solidify one's own unique and innovative vision for fashion design.

STEVEN FAERM
Assistant Professor, Fashion Design
Parsons The New School For Design

About this book

This is an indispensable source of inspiration for the practising fashion designer, stylist, fashion buyer, fashion and textiles student, dressmaker and anyone with an interest in the creative side of the fashion industry. The book offers a dictionary of ideas that can be used as a springboard for your own unique dress designs.

Each chapter focuses on a different dress genre, explained in articles that place the garment in its fashion and social context, and ones that identify its key design features. The dress genre is then organized into a multitude of variations – for example, the coatdress includes the subcategories tailored, housecoat, wrap and cape. Each subsection contains a multitude of images that comprise the directory.

DIRECTORY

The directory is beautifully illustrated with a wealth of photographic images that enable comparisons, aid understanding and inspire creative design thinking. Captions to each dress analyse, contextualize and, above all, nail what it is about a particular design that makes it desirable.

IN CONTEXT

Each style is introduced with historical information on the development of the cut, and key historic events, designers or dresses are discussed.

In context

Historic photographs of iconic dresses

Tabs on the right-hand side indicate the section

DESIGN CONSIDERATIONS

Design considerations – such as silhouette, length, fabrics, fastenings, embellishment, necklines, sleeves, lining, details and shaping – are clearly explained, and simple annotated artworks show the dress construction.

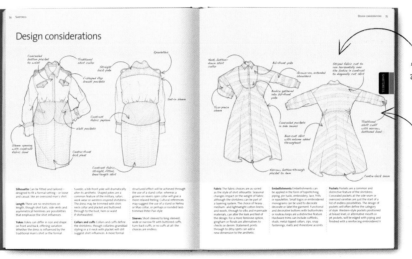

Design considerations

Annotations point out technical details

Illustrations showing the front and back of two extremes of the style

Boho

Enlargements give a close-up view of garment details

Drawings show design alternatives inspired by dress

Beautiful colour photographs of 1000 dresses

Captions for every dress analyse each design

Key characteristics of the style are called out in bullet points

Use this book as inspiration for silhouettes, fabrics and details.

Create a mood board to commmunicate your inspiration and vision.

The design process

The design process is centred on research, experimentation and innovation, combined with analysis and development. Trial, error and intuition are all part of the equation. Taste, aesthetics, trend and who is wearing the dress and why must also be negotiated. Understanding the customer and market is crucial to getting the right balance between creativity, wearability, innovation and commerciality.

To create a collection you need a solid foundation in design practices and an understanding of construction and make. You will also need to communicate effectively with the customer who, in turn, buys into the look. This originates from your inspiration – based on theme, muse and defined trend – and develops into a creative narrative that tells the story of your brand. Understanding what other designers have done successfully in the past and exploring a variety of possibilities is vital to jumpstarting your own design process.

To help you do this, this book consists of a comprehensive directory of dress silhouettes. Easy-to-navigate text discusses style, form, cut, proportion and construction and informative artworks illustrate these. Catalogued and presented in straightforward, accessible sections – including a useful glossary for easy reference – the information is intended to provide the means to broaden design knowledge and technical understanding.

Use the book as a starting point, as a reference for ideas. You may wish to concentrate on the specific categories, though mixing and matching design details across other dress styles is also an option. Altering the neckline, changing the length of the skirt or adding volume can dramatically alter a look. Varying the textile can also change the aesthetic, for example, transforming a day dress into evening wear.

1,000 Dresses is intended as a starting point for your own unique interpretations. Discover the myriad of design possibilities and use this book as a library of sources to assist you in your design process.

Customer profile Have an idea of who you want to create your work for. Who is your customer? What does she do and why does she need your garment? Navigate this book to help pinpoint what your customer might want to wear and use this to originate or bounce ideas.

Muse Your chosen muse is the ideal person who you are designing for. She can be a well-known personality or simply the ideal figure or style icon that would wear your dress. This gives you a focus, and you and your customer will both find the muse inspirational.

Market research Investigate what competitors in your market are doing so that you do not replicate what is already out there and can authoritatively predict what should be offered next. This book presents alternative dress styles by a wide range of designers, across numerous categories.

Inspiration Gather inspiration from a number of sources as a starting point for design development. Use this book, along with the Internet, magazines, books, exhibitions and film, to gather relevant images that fit with your theme, customer, muse and market. Your own photographs and drawings, fabric swatches, vintage garments, found objects and ephemera are also good foundations for ideas. See the list (opposite) of other sources of inspiration.

Fabric sourcing Collect swatches of fabrics that fit with your collection and best express your theme. In the initial stages this might be snips for colour referencing. You may wish to create small samples of

Use rough sketches to generate ideas and troubleshoot problems.

Final drawings are used to sell your idea to your customer.

seams or pockets with certain fabrics to fully understand the performance qualities and allow you to construct the look you want. Use this book to help you understand what fabric is best suited for any silhouette.

Colour stories Decide what colour palette suits your collection and fits with the story and mood that you want to create. You may wish to consult a colour-forecasting company to help you predict the trends for the particular season in mind. Colours can be developed through your research, looking at nature or vintage textiles, for example. Use Pantone references to communicate and match your chosen colours. Look through this book to see how other designers use colour to communicate ideas.

Mood boards Create a mood board to set the scene for your ideas. Collect fabrics, magazine tears, photographs, postcards, etc. – anything that fits your theme, and can motivate and inspire you to further design development. The mood board is a good form of communication, in order to make sure that the design team are on the same page.

Drawing To generate and communicate ideas, drawing is an important part of the design process. From recording and generating original research and inspiration, through to the development of design ideas and the creation of rough sketches of garment silhouettes and details. Final illustrations can communicate and promote your collection to your customer.

Design development Decide what sketches work best and refine and edit, cutting out elements that don't work and designing into gaps within the collection. Fabric choices, colour and pattern balance are all important considerations. Finishings, fastenings and trims must all function, as well as aesthetically balance.

Edit final choices The collection must work as a whole, and therefore the final edit will prioritize the collection and help to build range, allowing for coordinated looks.

Working drawings Create flat drawings showing back and front views, as well as complicated side views or detailed areas, such as pockets. The drawings will communicate construction details, finishing requirements and final fabric selection. These specifications will give accurate, detailed measurements that will help you to create your toile and form the basis for the specification packs sent to the manufacturer when going into production.

Toile development Create prototypes in calico or muslin, translating the paper designs into a three-dimensional garment using the working drawing as a blueprint for measurement and scale. Working on the stand or tailor's dummy allows you to check for fit and analyse the overall silhouette and finishing details. The toile should always be worn on the body for the final fit to check for ease of movement. Any adjustments can be resolved at this stage in the process before making the sample in final fabrics.

Final garment samples Cut in final fabrics using authentic fastenings and trims. Garment samples are now ready for the fashion show, photo shoot and saleroom!

OTHER SOURCES OF INSPIRATION

- ☑ Historical garments
- ☑ Fashion shows
- ☑ Street fashion
- ☑ Fine art
- ☑ Popular culture
- ☑ Craft techniques
- ☑ Other cultures
- ☑ Nature
- ☑ Technology

DAY DRESS

The essential of any woman's wardrobe, casually worn
for leisure and comfort or formally dressed for boardroom
and status, the day dress comes in many guises,
serving a multitude of functions.

Diagonal lines are
emphasized by the sash
inserted into parallel
raglan-styled seams.
Contrast textures are
achieved by utilizing both
sides of the silk satin.

In context

This elegant yet understated fitted day dress by Christian Dior features a square neckline that shows off the feminine collarbone and neck. The curved neckline forms the sleeves, which are kept short and semifitted. The neckline also mirrors the proportion of the hat.

n the early 1900s, Paul Poiret abandoned tailoring and pattern cutting for a more experimental draped silhouette, inspired by a more natural female form. This paved the way for the changes in women's clothing in the 1920s, when women were liberated by the silhouette of the day dress, which elongated the body's proportions by dropping the waistline and shortening the length to midcalf. By the 1930s, the day dress was becoming more practical as women led more active lives, a phenomenon that Coco Chanel exploited by developing sports-inspired, easy-to-wear jersey dresses. The austerity measures necessary during World War II resulted in fabric shortages. Manmade fabrics, such as rayon and synthetic jersey, took over from luxury cloth at a time when wool was used for uniforms and silk for parachutes. The unadorned silhouette was cut narrower and shorter for cost and economy. Post-war, ordinary women were able to find employment outside of domestic service, and the day dress adapted to suit their new roles, with ready-to-wear dresses making style affordable and accessible and allowing women to keep up to date with new fashion trends.

In 1947, Dior launched his New Look, with its glamorous nipped-in waist and longer, fuller skirts, which women embraced. Modern kitchen appliances allowed women to shake off their domestic ties and free their time for more fulfilling roles in the workplace. Givenchy introduced the sack dress in 1958, liberating women from the cinched waist and hourglass figure and paving the way for the shift dress and mini of the 1960s. The silhouette softened and lengthened in the 1970s, to midi and maxi. Laura Ashley, Bill Gibb and Perry Ellis explored a more ethnic and romantic styling, as did Ossie Clark and Celia Birtwell with their floral prints. The padded-shouldered power dressing of the aspirational 1980s epitomized that decade's obsession with status and success and translated easily into the day dress through formal business and office wear.

The iconic model Suzy Parker jauntily wears this fitted white linen dress. A novelty neckline calls attention to her collarbone and softly sloping shoulders, while a matching belt emphasizes her small waist.

Design considerations

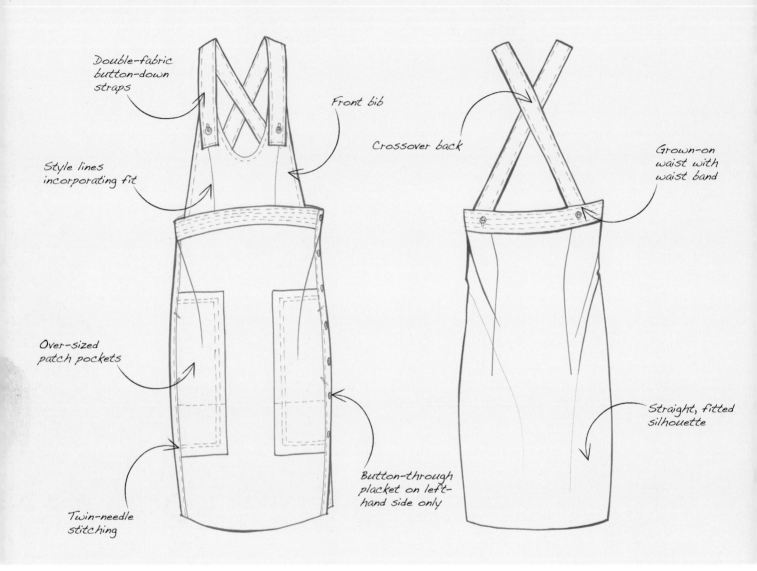

Double-fabric button-down straps

Front bib

Crossover back

Style lines incorporating fit

Grown-on waist with waist band

Over-sized patch pockets

Straight, fitted silhouette

Twin-needle stitching

Button-through placket on left-hand side only

Versatility The day dress is defined by the intention that it is worn during the day. However, it is a versatile piece of clothing that can be dressed up or down depending on the event and can transcend into evening. As an alternative to casual wear separates, the day dress can function as a single item of clothing that can be 'thrown on' as an easy-to-wear no-fuss option. Alternatively, the pinafore can be teamed with a shirt or fine-gauge knitwear for a relaxed,

informal aesthetic. Choice of fabrics, dress length, sleeve style, neckline and silhouette determine its character.

Style The broad array of day-dress styles means there is one for any situation. Typically, the formal day dress can be worn in the workplace and provides a more feminine alternative to power dressing. Often teamed with a jacket, the dress can be softened by a cardigan and accessories and worn during a night out.

Silhouette The figure-enhancing fit-and-flare silhouette translates well with the wrap styling, and it suits casual and formal dresses. Less formal circumstances require comfortable, unstructured dresses that are less figure hugging.

Length Length may be the obvious indicator of the day dress, traditionally at knee length, it works well with flat pumps, heels or boots; however, there

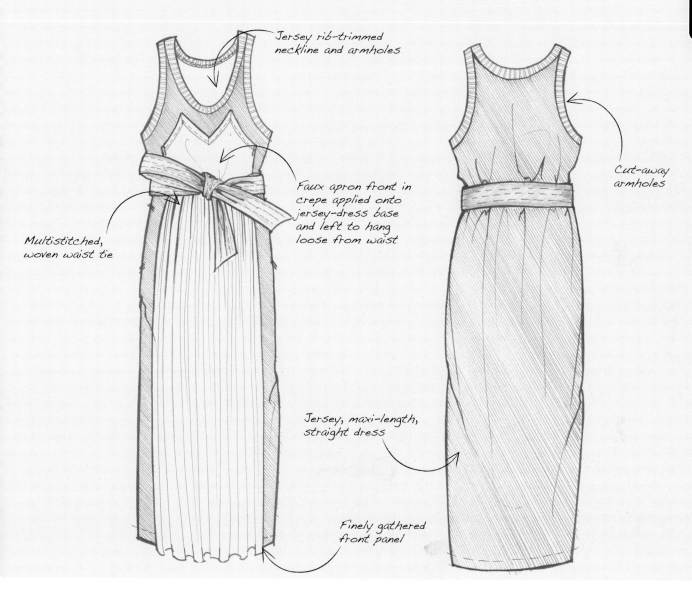

Jersey rib-trimmed
neckline and armholes

Faux apron front in
crepe applied onto
jersey-dress base
and left to hang
loose from waist

Multistitched,
woven waist tie

Cut-away
armholes

Jersey, maxi-length,
straight dress

Finely gathered
front panel

are no rules, and from maxi through to mini the variations are endless.

Fabrics Spandex combinations and new synthetics offer easy-care, crease-free options that are particularly useful for the busy working woman, and also good for travelling. Sportswear fabrics such as wool and cotton jerseys and sweats offer ease of movement and are great for layering for home and weekend living.

Fastenings The opportunity to select from a broad range of fastenings allows for diversity of styling and detailing. Contrast-colour thread, multistitch detail and contrast-colour piping inserts can also provide design interest. Fastenings and hardware can be prominent features on casual dresses with chunky metal or plastic zips and elaborate zip pulls. Buckles and braces, rivets, eyelets and press-studs reflect work-wear references and can be seen on pinafores and overalls.

Functionality and convenience demand pockets, which can be concealed within the garment seams or applied for a more decorative effect.

Formal

Every woman needs a dress that is sophisticated, maybe understated, and possibly practical, which she can effortlessly wear in order to create an impression. This dress has a polished aesthetic, which means it can be worn at an interview or business meeting. Semifitted, tailored and structured in woven fabrics or gathered and flared in softly draping fabrics, the formal day dress sends out a strong message of authority, capability and glamour. Minimal lines and neutral colour tones with interesting yet subtle detailing exploit femininity yet, at the same time, mean business.

Modern blended, easy-care fabrics are an ideal choice, making the dress hardwearing and crease resistant and able to withstand the rigours of the working day, while maintaining the appearance of effortless chic.

Often designed to be worn with a matching jacket or coat, the formal day dress can be short-sleeved or sleeveless, though long or three-quarter-length sleeves provide a more covered look more suited to the working environment. The formality of the dress suggests a longer length to just above knee level, varying in length to the calf. A shorter length, within reason, can be acceptable, however, for a younger market. Necklines seldom offer exposed cleavage, and range from the simplicity of a round neck to the exploitation of a variety of collars. Shoulder pads and strong shoulder lines echo the power dressing of the 1980s and emulate a masculine silhouette.

KEY CHARACTERISTICS

- ☑ Sophisticated, smart, functional
- ☑ Semifitted, tailored, structured
- ☑ Minimal lines and neutral colours
- ☑ Easy to wear, hardwearing, practical

The black side panels flatter the body shape, while the white vertical **centre-front panel** elongates the body, giving the impression of a slimmer silhouette. The **front** neck has a simple placket opening.

Alternative neckline and sleeves: funnel neck and set-in short sleeves

The simplicity of the sleeveless round-neck, knee-length fitted dress with centre-front and -back seams is the perfect shape for the bold monochromatic animal print.

1 Grown-on, cap-sleeved day dress with a high V-neck and a tulip-shaped peplum over a fitted pencil skirt. 2 Body-conscious, cap-sleeved dress. The high, square neckline reflects the angular cut and three-dimensional detail on the hips. 3 Semifitted dress with a square neckline and stand collar that sits away from the neck. Darts to the waist and bustline create shape and fit.

4 Vertical and horizontal black-on-white detailing of inset panels establishes a graphic symmetry to this semifitted, Op Art-inspired dress. 5 Slash-neck, pinafore-style dress with hourglass-shaped centre-front panel that accentuates the curves of the body. The fluoro-green piping defines the outline of the shape. 6 Fine wool dress with grown-on boatneck. The bodice is fitted to just

above the bust point, where a circular-cut flared skirt is attached. 7 Elbow-length magyar sleeves, a simple rounded neckline and a tied waist – this day dress is cut to give minimal flare at the hemline. 8 Fluid silk jersey with a bodice cut generously to give a blouson effect above the waist seam. Long fitted sleeves and a tighter cut in the skirt contrast to give a more body-conscious effect.

> The graphic white and sheer **cutouts** of the dress are the primary attraction on the otherwise simple **slash-neck**, semifitted dress with straight sleeves. The look is at once athletic and feminine.

Alternative
neckline, sleeves,
and panelling:
scooped round
neckline and
cap sleeves

A slash-neck, semifitted dress with
raglan short sleeves that have a
wide **turn-back cuff** opening, which
is wrapped and cut higher at the
front to form a **cape effect** at the
back. The simple silhouette of the
main body allows the interesting
sleeve detail to be the main focus.

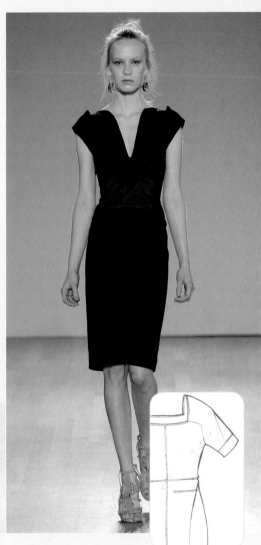

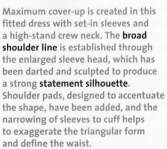

Maximum cover-up is created in this fitted dress with set-in sleeves and a high-stand crew neck. The **broad shoulder line** is established through the enlarged sleeve head, which has been darted and sculpted to produce a strong **statement silhouette**. Shoulder pads, designed to accentuate the shape, have been added, and the narrowing of sleeves to cuff helps to exaggerate the triangular form and define the waist.

Knee-length fitted **little black dress** with deep waistband in **contrast satin**, suggesting a cummerbund and defining the waist. The sculpted silhouette, created at the shoulder profile and neckline, interrupts the formality of the dress.

Alternative neckline, armhole and sleeves: square neck, saddle shoulder and short sleeves

The **white piping** contrasts with the black to create vertical and horizontal lines that dissect the dress at centre front and waist. The round neck and armholes are faced, in keeping with the simple, uncomplicated shape. Falling just above knee length, the dress is fully lined. Piped pocket openings at the hip reflect the **horizontal waistline** and continue the monochromatic effect.

> The use of varying weights of white woven fabrics in panels creates contrasting density. Deep shoulder straps create a **halter neck** that stands around the neck edge; contrast binding is used to face and trim the armhole. The high **sweetheart neckline** is accentuated by the deep split at centre front.

Quirky, printed, soft-woven dress, which has the main bodice and sleeves cut in one piece. Fit has been achieved through the addition of **horizontal tucks** along the neck edge and shoulders, which form the sleeve head. The sleeve hem is shaped, cut away at the front and left to drape loosely at the back. In contrast to the feminine style, the main focus of this dress is a **bold eye-like appliqué** exposing the torso. The appliqué is also reflected in the contrasting trim on the skirt hem.

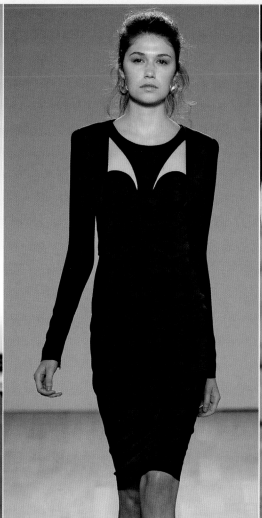

Fitted to the **body contours** and simply finished with facings at the round neck and armholes, this is the perfect dress to transcend occasions. The **side split** at hemline breaks up the monotony of the black, creating a sexy and sophisticated aesthetic, perfect for accessorizing.

A long, lean silhouette is created in this long-sleeved dress, which hits just above the knee. The **squared padded shoulders** give a severe masculine appearance, which is feminized in the **cutout keyhole panels** at the bust with sweetheart neckline. Though revealing some flesh at the chest, the look is still demure and so maintains an aspect of formality.

A strong silhouette with **curve-cut, three-quarter-length sleeves**, tulip-shaped knee-length skirt and cowl-front neckline. The leather tie belt adds interest to the expanse of solid-colour fabric. All elements of this design use exaggerated curved seams to highlight the **drapery in the neckline**.

Alternative neckline and sleeves: low cowl neck and grown-on cap sleeves

1 The symmetry of this V-neck dress is emphasized by the contrasting colour side panels and prominent centre-front seam. 2 Body-conscious dress with pencil skirt and empire-line bodice. Bust suppression is achieved through tucks on the bodice that are left open at the neck edge. 3 An extended shoulder line creates a broad V-shaped silhouette that is mirrored in the A-line knee-length skirt. The centre-front stripe and contrasting shoulder yoke and pocket flaps accentuate the shape. 4 The exaggerated tulip-shaped skirt is constructed from multiple layers of laser-cut shapes that are stitched at one edge to a foundation skirt, creating a three-dimensional effect. 5 Tabard-style, sleeveless dress with button fastening at the shoulders. 6 Layers imitate separate garment pieces: a fine cotton overlayer is gathered at the side seams then brought forwards with a tie belt. 7 A dipped-dye effect tops and tails this silk fitted column dress. The neckline is almost off the shoulder but high above the cleavage. 8 The design interest of this understated sheath dress is focused on the deep U-shaped neckline and capped sleeves.

The **magyar sleeves** are the focal point of this dress, with self-fabric tucks inserted into the seam of the sleeve and running continuously from elbow to centre-front neckline. This creates the split collar, which stands from the neckline, and silhouettes the curve of the sleeve, creating an **exaggerated sweetheart shape**. The cuff and underarm sleeve gusset are cut in one piece, as are the side dress and top of the sleeve.

The dress is fitted to the contours of the body with gathered fabric at the bust dart, **accentuating the curves** and giving a softer shape. The bodice yoke, in aubergine latex, provides a sharp contrast and an unexpected **contemporary twist**.

Alternative neckline and sleeves: V-neck and saddle shoulders with short sleeves

The dress has a minimalist quality, with a **heavy duchess-satin base** contributing to the formal aesthetic. With references from **Japanese geisha**, the front contrast panel at the centre of the bodice has decorative embroidered and appliquéd graphic floral motifs. The high waistline, three-quarter-length sleeves and neckline continue the strong, feminine-yet-puritanical look.

Pinafore

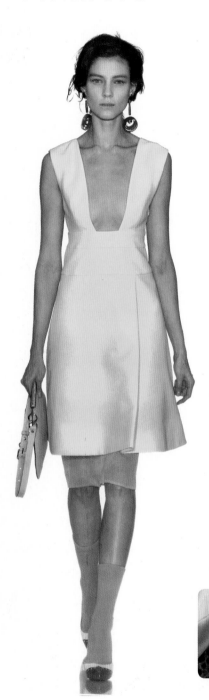

A sleeveless dress designed to be worn over a blouse or sweater, the pinafore dress is derived from the apron, which is worn to protect the garments underneath it.

The pinafore dress can be opened and fastened at the back with buttons or a zip, which mirror the traditional apron. It can, however, be opened and fastened at the shoulder, by a front placket of variable length, or buttoned or zipped through the front from neck to hem. It can also double as a shift and be pulled over the head, but is defined by the fact that it is worn over other layers. For ease, the dress may have a side zip fastening or symmetrical underarm placket and buttons on both sides. The neckline would generally be low enough to reveal the blouse or sweater underneath, with variations from V to round neck, or perhaps a sweetheart shape.

Due to the work wear and protective connotations of the apron, the pinafore dress will invariably have pockets, whether patched on the front or invisible at the side seam. Lining is essential, but some designs with a yoke might be faced at the yoke and unlined at the skirt.

The wide shoulders extend into the fitted bodice, creating a **wide, low neckline**. The bodice is attached to an underbust band, which forms part of the **deep waist yoke**. Extra flare is created in the A-line skirt with the addition of a full-length pleat on the left side. A sheer organdie underskirt contrasts with the solid-colour fabric.

The shaped waist, in contrasting **leather panels**, leads the eye to the metal chain strap that supports the skirt, forming a **halter-neck style**. The shaped hemline, with curved border, and the self-fabric band, left to hang from the skirt hem, reflect the shaped waistline and chain strap.

KEY CHARACTERISTICS

- ☑ **Derived from the apron**
- ☑ **Worn over other layers**
- ☑ **Sleeveless**
- ☑ **Reveals garments underneath**

1 Shift-style pinafore dress giving a sporty feel. The multiple colour-blocked linen panels are defined by a strong outline of black tape and allude to the traditional apron shape. 2 Pinafore dress cut under the bustline with integrated bra cups threaded through the dress to form the shoulder straps. 3 Inserts of mesh are outlined by swirls of three-dimensional corded embroidery on this ditsy tie-print dress. The combination of fabric and shape gives an athletic twist. 4 Trapeze-shape pinafore dress pleated into a band above bust level, with shoulder straps. The deep border at the hem spreads the pleats to increase the volume. 5 Asymmetrical bodice styling, two different capped sleeves, a soft, flared A-line skirt, and a fitted waistline. 6 Simple colour blocking in a 1960s-inspired pinafore dress with deep, circular cutout armholes from shoulder to hipline. 7 A round neckline and deep cutaway armholes. The heavy embellishment softens the look and contrasts the black with the white underlayered accessories. 8 This fitted-bodice, sleeveless dress has an exaggerated envelope neckline that complements the knee-length flared skirt.

Overalls

From classic Great Depression styling through to World War II army girls, the overalls dress is a derivative. Following the styling details of the bib-and-brace denim work-wear tradition, originally worn to keep garments underneath clean, the overalls dress copies the same durable vibe, creating a casual statement. Since the 1960s, different colours and patterns have been adapted into the dress, often with one of the straps worn loose or unfastened along the side and under the arm. The skirt is tight with a back split for ease of movement, and commonly worn above the knee for a younger look.

The bib-overalls fashion trend among American youth culture peaked in the latter half of the 1970s, and again in the late 1990s. Ralph Lauren, in particular, adopted this trend, which has been adapted and translated over many years.

Traditionally, this style of dress has five pockets and crossover back straps that pass over the shoulders to buckle to rivets on the bib front. Diagonal side openings with rivet-buttoned fastenings reinforce the dungaree function. Denim-jean style seaming and topstitching are common features. Fabrics include denim, corduroy and cotton twill. Sanding techniques give wear and tear to areas of the garment for a distressed look, and other treatments, such as sandblasting, creasing and stone washing, are also employed. Dyeing and bleaching add to the well-worn look.

Often worn over T-shirts or checked or plain cotton shirts, the dress can also be teamed with a more feminine white blouse for a prairie feel.

High-shine and paper-thin, this **plastic-coated fabric** has been translated into a **dropped-waist minidress** with deep V-notched neckline and metal dungaree clip fastenings on the shoulder straps. The skirt has been gathered into the waist seam, giving a softer feminine feel to this usually more aggressive fabric.

Wide straps buttoned onto the bodice form the focal point of this design, creating a deep, scooped V-neckline. The loose-fitting, straight-cut dress is easy to wear and uses **colour blocking** to define the body's proportions. A large contrast-colour pocket creates an informal asymmetric style.

KEY CHARACTERISTICS

☑ Derived from denim work-wear overalls

☑ Bib front, crossover back straps, diagonal side openings

☑ Tough, durable casual look

1 Needle-cord dungaree dress with deep waistband and A-line skirt with centre-back fastening. The bib front has wide straps that cross over the back and button at the back waistband.
2 A shirt has been deconstructed to inspire this quirky minidress. The main body of the shirt has been taken away, leaving only the lower part of the sleeves, collar and placket. **3** The crossover bib front is extended from the grown-on waist skirt with origami-like folds and tucks that give volume and drape to the wrap skirt. **4** Wide, short straps that end in a pronounced angle function as a visual emphasis on the shoulders. **5** The bodice has no shaping, creating an androgynous feel, though the buttons, binding and motif give a more feminine aesthetic. **6** Textured straps reinforce the delicacy of the print and call attention to the full width of the shoulder.
7 The delicate two-colour straps suggest a slip and bra, the bare essentials for a hot summer day.
8 Authentic 'bib-and-brace' buckles support this shift-like bodice. The inverted V inserts reflect the V-shaped dropped waistline, to which a contrast fabric skirt has been attached.

Wrap

The wrap dress was made popular by American designer Diane von Fürstenberg in the 1970s, and DvF still produces variations of it today. Although categorized as a day dress, the relaxed, longer version – reminiscent of the housecoat – can be grouped with the kaftan style. The shape is flattering and suits the hourglass figure: The skirt is fitted into the waist, then tapered over the hips and flared to the hem.

A jersey or stretch fabric gives the dress a fluid drape, but equally a crepe or woven fabric with a spandex mix gives a similar effect. Traditionally, the wrap dress has no buttons or zips. Instead, the internal wrap is tied to the right-hand seam inside the dress, then tied at the left side as the dress crosses over. Sometimes the ties are taken through a buttonhole opening at the left side, then wrapped around the body and tied at the front. It is a simple and chic style that can be worn to any occasion, day or night.

The sleeve would normally be fitted to the body to continue the fitted upper-body silhouette, although sleeveless or capped sleeves are options. A drop armhole shape and shorter turned-back deep sleeves can be applied to give a more relaxed look. The wrap will generally create a V-neck, the depth of which can be determined by the cross of the wrap.

This style works best to the knee or just above, but is also flattering at calf length. A longer maxi length takes this style into the evening, where choice of fabrics can change the look from understated sophistication to full-on glamour.

Effective use of **colour blocking** is underlined in this simple wrap style. The sleeveless garment has wide shoulders that continue into the bodice and wrap across the body to a dropped waistline, to create a **low V-neckline**. The uncomplicated fitted miniskirt reflects the overall modern feel.

Soft jersey wrap-over dress that fastens at the right hip with a tie, then buttons at the left-hand side. The front wrap facing conceals the buttonhole, giving the below calf-length dress a **streamlined** appearance.

KEY CHARACTERISTICS

☑ **Front panels wrapped and often secured with ties or buttons to one side or belted**

☑ **V-neckline**

☑ **Fabrics with fluid drape**

1 A 1920s-inspired, sheer silk-chiffon wrap dress with kimono-style elbow-length sleeves. The loose wrap-front bodice is secured into a dropped-waist seam. 2 Charming wrap-front minidress with a young, fresh appeal belying its vintage inspiration. 3 Mini-length, loose-fit halter-neck sundress with a plunging V-neckline. The tie, at hip level, creates soft drapes across the body.

4 The silk satin fabric has a metallic foiled print that drapes to give a soft, liquid effect. Deconstructed finishes, such as the overlocked edges and the open underarm seam, give a lingerie styling. 5 The wrap ties of this silk satin dress create shape and drape to otherwise rectangular shapes. Circular flared sleeves echo the soft drape at the hemline. 6 Two separate

contrast-print garment panels wrap around the body and attach at the hip, forming a low V-neck. 7 The wrap is secured by double-breasted buttons on a deep-fitted dropped waistband. The fitted waistband contrasts with the softly gathered skirt and the drape of the magyar sleeves. 8 The deep scallop-edged V-neck gives detail and decoration to an otherwise plain dress.

> With no shoulder seams, this dress is cut in **one piece** from front to side panel, draped around the neck to form the **draped cowl** at the back, then continued to the other side panel. The front wrap panels are pleated at the ties and tied at the left-hand seam to provide further draping.

Alternative sleeves: raglan armhole with butterfly sleeves

Maxi-length wrap dress constructed from **scarf squares** in fine cotton lawn, to give a tiered, layered effect, making the loose kaftan shape ideal for summer. The scarf squares are fixed at the shoulder by a fine shoestring strap and again at the cuff, leaving the top of the sleeve open to **expose shoulders** and upper arms. The bodice is wrapped to form a V-neckline and a self-fabric belt defines the waist and closes the wrap.

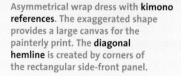

Asymmetrical wrap dress with **kimono references**. The exaggerated shape provides a large canvas for the painterly print. The **diagonal hemline** is created by corners of the rectangular side-front panel.

An elegant wrap-front dress that finishes just below knee length. The inherent drape in the fabric is shown to its best advantage with **fluted, tiered short sleeves**. The wrap creates a low, plunging V-neckline that leads to a contrasting tied belt, which defines the waistline. The stylized tulip print achieves a **contemporary feel** with its expansive use of background colour.

This relaxed pinafore wrap is constructed in a woven tartan cotton. The bodice is cut on the bias, and excess fabric is softly pleated into the shoulder seam and the armhole facing. The **additional fabric** is wrapped across the waist and extended in a loop before returning. The skirt is **pleated** at the hip into a deep yoke from the waist seam.

Alternative sleeves and neckline: elbow-length dolman sleeves with asymmetric revers collar

Fitted-and-flared

The fitted-and-flared day dress is a feminine, pretty and often flirty style that has a semifitted bodice and waist that gradually flares out from the hip level to create a fuller skirt at the hem. Modified from the A-line shape, the flare of a fitted-and-flared dress is usually evenly distributed around the body, creating a softer and less dramatic silhouette. It flatters the figure, accentuating the waist and is a versatile style that works just as well for special occasions as for day wear.

Often able to absorb the latest prints or garment details, the fitted-and-flared style can be translated easily into most fashion trends and is continually reinvented by designers every season. Style variations are endless, depending on the source of inspiration, with necklines ranging from V, scooped and horseshoe to those with collars. Lengths are variable, from mini through to knee length and maxi. It is often designed with front button-through fastenings or concealed side zips, though the options are limitless.

Soft woven fabrics that have drape work best for this style because they maintain the gradual flare of this silhouette, though more structured versions in heavier-weight fabrics will create a defined, strong shape.

The **print design** is integral to the shape, and mimics the centre-front yoke panel, defines the waist and edges the hemline. The bodice is darted to fit, disguised within the print, and the deep return side pleats create the **A-line flare** of the skirt.

The dramatic use of **monotone jersey stripe** creates an avant-garde silhouette. The addition of volume and flare to the skirt changes the direction of the stripe, accentuated by the uneven hemline, which dips at the side views. The **solid-colour, square neckline** provides structure.

KEY CHARACTERISTICS

- ☑ Semifitted or fitted bodice
- ☑ Skirt flares out from hip level
- ☑ Varied lengths, necklines, details

1 Strapless dress to midcalf length in lightweight woven fabric. Cut as a separate bodice and skirt, both on the bias to create stretch and flare.
2 The yellow neck detail and inserts into the bodice add interest to the neat fitted-and-flared dress. 3 A flirty fitted-and-flared strapless sundress with built-in-apron effect in contrast stripe and floral print. 4 The heart-shaped neckline forms a wrap opening and reinforces the pretty and feminine shape of the fitted waist and flared skirt.
5 An exaggerated shoulder detail sits on top of a traditional set-in sleeve and extends past the natural shoulder line, forming a grown-on stand collar at the back and leaving the front neckline exposed. 6 Cute fitted-and-flared dress layered over petticoats. A sash emphasizes the waistband and establishes the 1950s silhouette. 7 The bodice design gives the impression of a strapless dress, but remains appropriate for day wear when combined with the shirting neck feature.
8 The complex embroidery and shapes within the pattern have been placed to define the fitted bust, the waist and the flare of the skirt.

Body conscious

The body-conscious day dress represents female strength and power. This potent style defines body contours, often creating an hourglass figure, and making the most of the bustline, waist and hips. Its pedigree is in the long, lean, sheath-like silhouettes that skimmed the contours of the body in the 1950s, where complicated construction produced the appearance of simplicity. The contemporary body-conscious dress also cleverly incorporates fit and shaping in style lines and panelling that flatter the figure, concealing curves where they are not needed and accentuating those that are. Fabrics are usually medium- to heavyweight structured woven, and often have an elastic content to help achieve a perfect fit and comfort. Style lines and panelling can be highlighted with contrast-colour piping to create a sportier vibe and are often colour-blocked for a more youthful feel.

An empowering style, bringing confidence to the wearer, the versatility of the body-conscious day dress makes it an ideal choice for office wear in black, greys and more muted tones, as personified by the much-imitated Galaxy dress by Roland Mouret in 2005. The very fitted silhouette defines this style, although the neckline, sleeve styles and skirt lengths can vary depending on the design influence. Wide, open square necklines exposing the chest area work well, with short and capped-length sleeves and interestingly cut sleeve heads to soften the overall look. Lengths work best at around the knee, either finishing slightly above or below.

This figure-hugging dress to the ankle gives an elongated **column appearance** with a split up the centre front to thigh. The front panel has a separate piece that has been stitched to side seams after being twisted to form a **draped effect** that flatters the stomach area.

Body-hugging sheath dress. A side slit allows for ease of movement and reveals a **show of leg.** The diagonal white abstract print breaks up the column of black. A **cutout insert** strategically integrated into the print, with set-in power mesh, shows a flash of body.

KEY CHARACTERISTICS

☑ **Fitted, hourglass silhouette**

☑ **Style lines and panelling that flatter the figure**

☑ **Woven fabric with stretch combinations**

1 Cutout, raglan-shaped armholes and a round neckline create a sporty feel. Curved dart shaping from armhole to waistband create style lines that emphasize the contours of the bodice. 2 Body-contouring panels are trimmed with neon yellow. Curved seams that extend from front to back panels avoid the need for side seaming. 3 Contrast-colour fabrics combined with a mesh print define the panels and trims within this body-conscious minidress. 4 A plain-black shift-shape dress is enhanced with black-and-white and rainbow body-conscious style lines. 5 Leather piping trims the shoulder, the armhole and the bodice seam, which mirrors the boatneck. 6 Strips of tie-dyed fabric run horizontally around the body, fixed by vertical knitted loops that continue to form a halter neck and shoulder straps. 7 Excess fabric is draped and gathered into the seams of the skirt to create a ruching effect. The soft gathers are contrasted by angular points that overlap the shoulder. 8 Panelled sections emphasize the curves of the body. The print reinforces the style lines and create a visual play with the lacing at the shoulders and thigh.

SHIFT DRESS

The shift dress is a versatile wardrobe staple, with universal appeal that transcends all seasons. Androgynous and ageless, the shift can be styled up or down for casual and evening wear, adapting easily from office to party.

White shift dress with short, set-in sleeves and V-neck. The printed, graphic image of a sundress with a chevron stripe caricatures the body, giving the illusion of a slimmer silhouette.

In context

The shift can be sophisticated and elegant, as exemplified by this white linen tunic and underskirt by Givenchy, worn by Audrey Hepburn.

The shape of the shift dress allows for freedom of movement, making it easy to 'shift' around in. However, the term also signifies a shift in culture and attitude, reflected in the radical changes in fashion in the 1920s, when the emancipation of women demanded a more flexible style of clothing. The 1920s flapper or Charleston dresses evolved through the revolutionary designs of Coco Chanel. The shift style became popular with American youth culture in the 1950s, then translated into the sack dress shown in Cristóbal Balenciaga and Hubert de Givenchy's 1957 Paris collections. In the 1960s, reflecting the age of space travel, new technology and the sexual revolution, the shift was popularized by Mary Quant, Pierre Cardin and André Courrèges. Icons such as Jackie Onassis, Audrey Hepburn, Twiggy and Jean Shrimpton have famously worn the shift.

The mood of the photograph, the setting and the fashion are all stereotypically 'swinging sixties'. Young women wanted to emphasize their youthful exuberance, not look like their mothers. These shift dresses, in bright bold colours and graphics, are shapeless, creating a girlish figure with a flat chest and no hips.

Design considerations

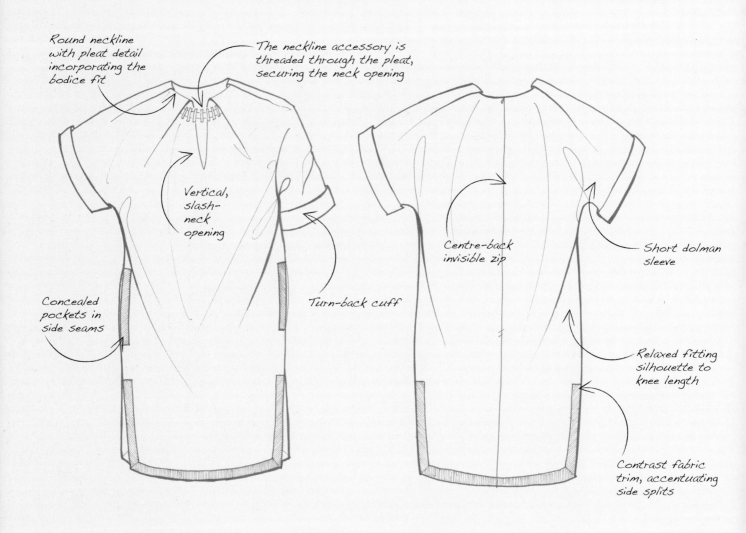

Round neckline with pleat detail incorporating the bodice fit

The neckline accessory is threaded through the pleat, securing the neck opening

Vertical, slash-neck opening

Concealed pockets in side seams

Turn-back cuff

Centre-back invisible zip

Short dolman sleeve

Relaxed fitting silhouette to knee length

Contrast fabric trim, accentuating side splits

Versatility The timeless silhouette is extremely versatile. It can be adapted to fit a variety of shapes and sizes and is suitable for all ages. The easy-to-wear attributes of the shift dress make it an ideal garment for casual wear. The shift can transcend day into evening, can be dressed up or down and is an ideal blank canvas for accessorizing or for showing off large and colourful print stories.

Silhouette Its loose and easy cut allows the shift dress to hang from the shoulders, though it can be adapted to allow for back and front yokes. The silhouette can be straight or A-line, permitting ease of movement. There is minimal or no waist definition, with the dress often concealing the shape of the body. If sleeveless, the loose shape can be worn over a sweater or T-shirt.

Length Usually sits above the knee, with variations at knee length or below. The mini length epitomizes the shift-dress style.

Sleeves Sleeveless or short-sleeved and rarely below three-quarter length. Armholes offer design variations from set-in to raglan, and sleeve heads also provide scope for styling possibilities.

Neckline Typically a high round neck or boatneck, though neckline variations, such as V, can be considered. Assorted collars, such as a Peter Pan or Nehru, can also be applied.

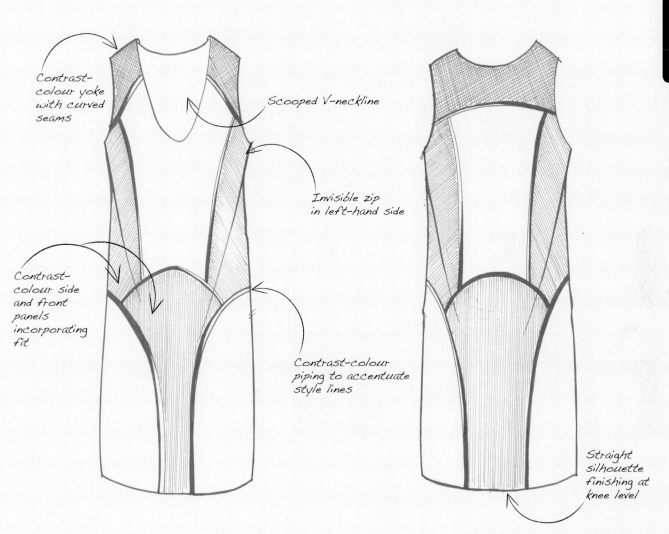

Contrast-colour yoke with curved seams

Scooped V-neckline

Invisible zip in left-hand side

Contrast-colour side and front panels incorporating fit

Contrast-colour piping to accentuate style lines

Straight silhouette finishing at knee level

Fastenings Depending on the design of the shift, openings and fastenings can include side, centre-back and front zips, or alternatives such as buttons or popper-stud fastenings.

Darts and seams The shift normally requires fit around the bust in the form of darts, which can be manipulated to form style lines. The dress also has side seams, unless design considerations dictate otherwise.

Fabric Fabric choices are key to this style. The shift works best with a structured woven, heavyweight jersey or stretch woven fabric in order to stand away from the body. The fabric consideration can often dictate the usage of the dress; for example, day wear/work wear or occasion/evening wear. The simplicity and versatility of the shift, however, can often transcend categorization.

Lining The shift can be lined or unlined, depending on the choice of fabric, occasion and season.

Details Historically, the shift is plain, to conform to its work wear origins, though design details and functionality considerations, such as concealed or patch pockets, can be applied.

Shift

The shift dress signifies youth culture; however, because its style flatters a range of figure types, it has been adapted and worn by women of all ages.

Choice of fabric can dramatically affect the look. Plain black or white fabric can provide a sophisticated canvas to dress with accessories. In contrast, the simple shape is an ideal background to show off vibrant, colourful prints.

The easy cut allows the shift dress to hang loose with little waist definition, designed to conceal feminine contours yet expose legs and arms. Traditionally simple, short and above the knee, it can be sleeveless or short-sleeved, often sporting a high neckline or typical boat-neck collar. Various modifications to length can reinvent the youthful aesthetic to give a more sophisticated, grown-up appeal. The bust is usually fitted with darts, and the skirt is either straight or A-line, with shoulder and side seams.

For formal day wear the androgynous shift is an ideal substitute for the masculine trouser suit, worn under a jacket for power dressing. The dress can be worn straight from the office to evening events and restyled for a more glamorous and feminine vibe.

A classic sleeveless shift in a large tweed with contrast **Peter Pan collar**. **Fabric roses** are applied to form a deep textured hem.

The **column effect** of this monochrome dress is accentuated by the black-and-white striping running **horizontally** around the bodice. The binding on the neck and armholes also runs down the side seam and matches the dimension of the stripe.

KEY CHARACTERISTICS

- ☑ Fitted bust
- ☑ Little waist definition, skimming the body
- ☑ Straight skirt above or to the knee level
- ☑ Sleeveless or short-sleeved

1

2

3

4

5

6

7

8

1 Contrast fabric and colour blocking give the suggestion of a pinafore style. **2** The dress is pleated to the yoke, controlling the fullness above the bustline, then tapers to the short hemline. The bold print, square neckline and three-quarter-length sleeve create a 1960s aesthetic. **3** The metallic sheen of the silver fabric and interesting asymmetrical keyhole cutout add glamour to an otherwise simple dress. **4** Horizontal contrast panels of floral cotton and chintz brocaded prints set against nude seersucker give a ribboned bandeau effect. The placement of the bands is designed to edge the hemline and cuffs and to define the yoke and bustline. **5** Geometric vertical and horizontal colour blocking gives definition to the shift and the illusion of a dropped waistline. **6** Straight vertical and horizontal asymmetrical panels juxtapose with the organic curves of the black-and-grey tonal brocaded print. **7** Studs are used to control the pleating on the neckline and to reinforce and define the strong, curved, dropped shoulder line. **8** Contrast matt and shine add interest to a simple yet strong shape. Laser-cut edging and minimal detailing create a sharp look.

> Short and sleeveless red dress with an abstract print. The styling emphasis is on the neckline, where a bias-cut, **self-fabric scarf tie** knots around the neck and drapes down the centre front. The abstract diagonal shards of the print work with the **bias of the cut**.

Grecian styling is created using **two different fabric layers**. The body-conscious underlayer forms the foundation for the shift, which is established by the bias cutting of the second layer of soft fabric draping as a **cowl at the front**. The cowl is attached to the raglan-shaped neckline, which defines the straps of the sleeveless yoke.

Evoking 1950s styling, this sophisticated shift has a grown-on **funnel collar** and short set-in sleeves. The simplicity of the uncluttered shape is a perfect blank canvas for the bold jewelry-motif print, designed with a **strategic border** running around the hemline.

Alternative sleeves: short puff sleeves, gathered into fixed bands

The rounded front panel **crosses and intertwines** with the rounded neckline then curves to the underarm. This is mirrored in the **curved hemline**, which scoops to the side seams towards the hipline. The full sleeves softly gather to the cuff and again at the armhole shoulder.

Alternative neckline and sleeves: funnel neck and raglan short sleeves

The bold, photographic enlarged floral print on a **semitransparent fabric** is the main feature of this simple shift. The cuffs of the full sleeves are gathered into a binding that is also used to edge the neckline. One sleeve is left unprinted to give an **asymmetrical twist** to the story.

1 Organdie layers are used to create a colour-blocked, geometric, large placement pattern. The shapes are defined by a combination of French seams, decorative stitching and bindings. 2 Soft suede and black leather panels contrast in colour and texture. The inserted V-yoke panel is mirrored by the hemline. 3 A twist on a simple shift with deep, asymmetrically placed double pockets on the left hip. 4 Diagonal panels in contrast fabric, with a drop shoulder and deep, round neck, are designed to mimic a separate garment. 5 The placement of the bold pattern emphasizes the cut of the dress. The kangaroo pocket forms an envelope shape and places focus at the front of the dress. 6 A beautifully understated shift dress that allows the detailing of the finish to become the focal point. The bound neckline curves through to the dropped armhole, which translates into a capped sleeve. 7 The diagonal of the raglan armhole continues into the neckline, which enables a green yoke to be inserted for contrasting interest. 8 This archetypal, uncomplicated shift shape enhances the heavily bead-encrusted and embroidered fabric.

In contrast navy and white, this shift has **nautical references**, reinforced with a boatneck. Falling just above knee level, the design emphasis is placed on the front **placket opening** at the hemline in contrast topstitching. The navy capped sleeves, edged with a deep white binding, echo the theme of straight and curved shapes.

The large mirror-image **placement print** with heraldic references sits on an ombré background, which fades to the hemline. Elbow-length sleeves have inverted pleats to cuff and set-in armholes, which help to reinforce the symmetry of the print. The simple square neckline, cuffs and hemline emphasize the **uncomplicated cut** and give prominence to the print.

Monochrome blocked panels give **architectural influence** to a shape that has clean, formal lines. The lack of symmetry is reinforced in the side-split front. The **decorative seaming** incorporates darts and shaping and cleverly conceals the pocket openings. The asymmetrical colour blocking on one sleeve distorts the balance of the dress.

The fabrication of the dress is **layered and sculpted** to define the suggestion of body contours, and incorporates shaping and style lines without compromising the traditional shift silhouette. Laser-cutting and bonding – cleverly forming and stitching together contours – connect vertices with flat, triangulated and curved shapes, which almost create a **three-dimensional surface** and give the impression of articulated joints.

Contrasting fabrics are used to distinguish the yoke panel of this simple shift. The bust suppression has been incorporated into the seam and the grown-on stand collar and capped sleeves keep additional seams and **style lines to a minimum**.

Oversized shift dress with a wide **dropped shoulder** and deep armhole, which can be belted through the front to create waist definition. The scale of the dress provides a **large canvas** to showcase the dynamic placement print. Contributing to the kaftan-like style of the dress, the back hangs loose to create volume.

1 Placement of the print is completely mirrored to create perfect symmetry. The padded shoulders give definition to an otherwise simple silhouette. 2 A chic sleeveless shift with black-and-white contrast accentuating the cut. The bust suppression is disguised within the bib-front panelling. 3 Cream-and-black contrast blocking cuts the dress at the waistline. Pattern is created by bold graphic black panelling down the front bib. 4 The lace bib yoke trims the silk satin shift dress. Full rounded sleeves gathered at the cuff and sleeve head help create a soft cocoon silhouette. 5 Crew-neck, felted-knit, raglan-sleeved mini-length shift. The softness of the fabric and the rounded silhouette counterbalance the geometry of the asymmetric pattern. 6 The simple shape is a perfect canvas for displaying the painterly, geometric print, which graduates in tone towards the hemline. 7 Short-sleeved shift dress in Aertex fabric creating a sportswear feel. 8 The graphic, colour-blocked centre-front panel of this shift is softened by the lighter side panels. With its wide boatneck and elbow-length split sleeves, this simple shape achieves a feminine feel.

1 Knee-length shift dress with monochromatic tessellated shapes, patchworked to give a dynamic pattern with a three-dimensional effect. 2 A simple shift with a patch pocket – perfect for accessorizing. 3 The placement of the geometric print creates borders at the hemline and gives the illusion of side panels. Interest is focused on the bodice, where the zigzag seam is accentuated with embellishment. 4 An enlarged placement print of botanical florals is the centrepiece of the front panel of the dress. The contrasting white deep shoulder straps mimic a pinafore style. 5 The pared-down, clean simplicity of the white dress is interrupted by a contrast bib-fronted panel, layered from the yoke seam. 6 Simple shift with high round neck and grown-on cap sleeves, and trimmed with gold zip-fastened pocket openings at hip level. 7 The matt wool skirt contrasts with the sheen of the leather drop-waisted bodice, creating a pared-down aesthetic. 8 Generously cut gathered sleeves and deep side pockets accentuate the curve of the silhouette of this pretty minidress.

9 Geometric patterns and different densities of tone and colour are created through multilayering of organdie, leaving some single layers for transparency. **10** Almost clashing two garments, the right- and left-hand sides differ in fabric, colour and proportion. The staggered geometric panelling tapers in steps towards the shoulder and drops lower at the hemline. **11** This shift is traditional in styling, made in a textured stone linen for a simple aesthetic. **12** The asymmetrical styling is created by contrasting panels of colour and mixing different weights and textures of cloth. **13** The subtle double layering of white fabric implies an overalls shape that integrates with the neck facing and is inserted behind the yoke panel. **14** A panel of contrasting fabric inserted down the centre front, intersecting with jagged seams that are echoed at the hemline, gives the impression of an apron with a bib. **15** Heavy duchess satin gives weight to this shift, which is divided by a dropped waist. The neckline is edged with metallic binding. **16** Featuring a round neck and drop shoulder with short, wide sleeves, the generous silhouette is gathered at the hemline with a drawstring.

A-line

The A-line shift shape is easily recognized. The silhouette is flared from a narrow shoulder line to the hemline, with the increase in dimensions occurring at the side seams, rather than distributed equally around the circumference, as seen in the trapeze shift dress. Courrèges defined the A-line dress in the 1960s as the triangular shape we associate with the term, which was widely used as a silhouette by Mary Quant. The style represents the 1960s ideology of space age, and can be seen in a number of sci-fi movies of the time, characterized as the dress of the future.

The shape is flattering and easy to wear for a number of body shapes since it doesn't hug but skims the body. It works well with fabric that has a medium- to heavyweight structure, and is ideal for heavier jersey or wovens. The simplicity and geometry of the style make it ideal for minimal use of colour, or strong, bold geometrics.

The dress works best with a simple collarless neckline and sleeveless armholes cut as rounded or scooped, or accentuating the geometry as a V or a square cut. Variations and subversions with collars and sleeves can be added to create diversity. Fastenings and trims, such as pockets, zips or buttons, can be used to break up the blank canvas of the simple shape. It is traditionally worn above the knee to mini length.

KEY CHARACTERISTICS

- ☑ Triangular or A-shape: narrow shoulder line, wide hemline
- ☑ Flared silhouette increasing at side seams
- ☑ Knee to mini length

Microgeometric-patterned, **jacquard**, sleeveless shift with contrast-fabric centre placket, collar and underbust band. The white **contrasting colour** and scalloped edge of the collar feminizes this traditionally menswear jacquard pattern.

The simplicity of the round neckline and deep armholes creates a sophisticated feel. The A-line of the skirt from **empire-line** seam is helped by the deep inverted box pleat at centre front. The contrast of **transparent fabric** at the hemline and centre insert creates interest.

1 Printed, round-neck, mini-length A-line shift with contrast-fabric full sleeves, which are gathered into the sleeve head. The long sleeves have a deep shirred cuff. **2** Dropped-shoulder, mini-length shift with centre-front inverted box pleat, which creates fullness in the skirt. The short sleeves are heavily gathered and flared. **3** Checks, stripes and colour blocking define the bodice and create a deep border at the hemline. The A-line shift is created from back and front panels of heat-set pleating, which excludes the need for bust suppression. **4** A 1960s-inspired shift, with an oversized Peter Pan collar, detailed bodice trim and button front. **5** Simple, 1960s mini-length A-line shift with a slightly wide round neckline. The full-length, set-in sleeves have buttoned shirt cuffs. **6** The graphic impact of the main dress is complemented by the solid-colour collar and deep hem band. **7** This simple shape has a slightly flared hem and a large self-fabric bow placed diagonally across the chest at the neckline. **8** Mini-length shift with contrast piping that accentuates the A-line shape and pockets. Shoulder piping directs the eye to a corsage.

1 An oversized-check shift dress with short puffed sleeves. The wide round neck, hem and underbust band have been cut on the bias to contrast the direction of the check. 2 This exaggerated, structured A-line silhouette combines contrasting fabrics of solid and transparent to create design interest on the bodice and hem. 3 Mini-length, structured shift dress with a wide scooped neckline and narrow sleeveless shoulders. Double rows of solid-black trim run along the underbust seam and hem. 4 Sleeveless dress with a grown-on stand-funnel neck. Jet pockets are trimmed with black binding, and black piping runs down each side of centre front and along the hemline. 5 The deep V-shaped neck yoke and vertical style lines on the bodice draw the eye to the box-pleated skirt. The horizontal waistband accentuates the dropped waist. 6 The mix of fabrics with contrasting sleeves and curved neckline is designed to mimic a pinafore dress. 7 The lace, drop-waisted bodice suggests a two-piece, but a pleated skirt is attached and layered to create a day dress. 8 A simple A-line shape incorporates the shaping into the bodice panel.

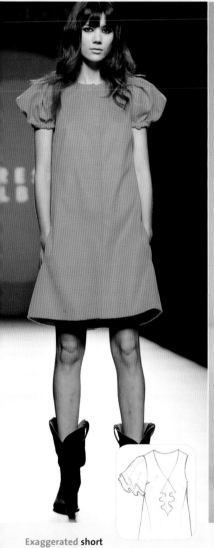

Exaggerated short puffed sleeves are gathered at the cuff and pleated into the armhole to create maximum volume. The hot pink reinforces the **feminine aesthetic**. The side seam pockets help to define the trapezoid shape.

Alternative neckline and sleeves: V-neckline with jabot frill and double-layer, fluted sleeves

‹ Quintessential 1960s-inspired sleeveless shift. The wide neckline and armholes are highlighted with a **contrast binding**, which frames the uncomplicated A-line silhouette. The strong style lines and **large pocket details** are also emphasized by the binding.

1920s-inspired shift with dropped waist, featuring **colour-blocked**, rectangular, diagonal-stitched and appliquéd fabrics on the bodice with a square neckline and short capped sleeves that continue the geometric theme. The layered skirt again reinforces the **flapper inspiration**.

The **cutwork and appliquéd** large-scale pattern creates a **scalloped edge** and defines the profile of the neckline, capped sleeves and hemline. **Contrast fabrics** and stitching help to outline the pretty, floral-inspired motifs.

The combination of **vertical and horizontal lines** is the distinctive feature of the sleeveless trapeze dress in a black-and-white geometric textured fabric with a **shirt collar** and placket in contrast black. The yoke and top of the patched pocket are edged with the black fabric, and the dress is cut short to reveal the black underskirt.

1 A-line sleeveless dress with a no-frills aesthetic. The centre-front opening has invisible fastenings. Deep inset pockets, cut diagonally, are attached at the side seam. 2 Enlarged broderie anglaise A-line shift dress in sugary pastels. The oversized embroidered collar contrasts with the plain white organdie yoke and sleeves. 3 Emphasis is placed on the deep-plunge V-neck, cut to reveal a shaped, curved undercorset. Volume is created in the exaggerated A-line skirt. 4 The fabric has been heat-set in fine pleats to create movement and give structure to the simple boatneck and A-line silhouette. 5 The angles created by the stand shawl collar inserted into the square neckline and the diagonal of the capped sleeve counterbalance the A-shaped skirt. 6 The A-line shape is created partly on the bias, with diagonal panels bonded together using needle-punched felting. 7 The bejewelled V-neckline creates a point at the centre of the waistline. The points of the folded origami panels also join at centre front, creating an envelope effect. 8 Transparent black layers of organdie create a two-tiered A-line effect. The black is punctuated by the deep V-neckline.

The dress is simple, with the focus on the **hemline and cuff**. The black lining is visible where the back of the dress is longer than the front, and in the binding at the front hemline. Long set-in sleeves, with a little fullness at the head on a slightly dropped shoulder line, taper to the petal-style wrap cuff, also exposing a **black lining**.

The perfect canvas for a bold **1970s-inspired print**, this archetypal trapeze minidress has a number of **traditional features**. With a wide funnel neck and set-in three-quarter-length sleeves with a turned-back cuff, the dress is also embellished with reflective silver discs that decorate the front panel and collar.

Black and white contrast panels give a modern feel, while the satin silk fabric is more formal, allowing the dress to **transcend day to evening**. The round neckline and armhole suggest a prim aesthetic, but the **V-insert** at the bustline offers a glimpse of cleavage and adds an element of sensuality.

Alternative neckline and sleeves: slash neckline with extended shoulder seam and wide cap sleeves

The wide, **deep V-neck** plunges at the bust and is cut wide towards the armhole, almost giving a strap effect at the shoulder, with the front panel designed to give the illusion of a **slimmer silhouette**.

< The trapeze is combined with the shirtdress, evidenced in the hemline with a **shirt-tail** effect. This also creates the suggestion of layered garments, where the hemline dips lower at the back to reveal the **black lining**. The black also borders the front hemline and the armhole.

Trapeze

In contrast to the basic shift dress, where the shaping is added to the side seams to create an A-line shape, the flare of the trapeze shift is increased throughout the dress by dividing, slashing, opening and spreading, thus enhancing the width of the hemline of the front and back pattern pieces to create volume. Like the A-line shift, the trapeze is narrow at the shoulder and flares out towards the hem and does not define the waistline. The volume in the dress creates drape and allows the hemline to swing freely. Contemporary versions can be customized with belts and gathered to create a soft, blouson look.

The term *trapeze* is taken from the geometric shape known as the trapezoid. The trapeze shape is often favoured in maternity and children's dresses, with baby-doll dresses a derivation of this shape. The trapeze shape became a major fashion trend after the launch of Yves Saint Laurent's 1958 collection for Dior, and was a distinct contrast to Dior's previous heavily structured New Look garments. The trapeze shape found its way into mainstream fashion in the 1960s with the shorter minidresses of Mary Quant, and has remained a core garment silhouette ever since.

A long-sleeve, jersey, turtle-neck trapeze shift with a very wide skirt hem. The **weight and drape** of the fabric increases the movement and impact of this style. This pattern has been slashed from the hem to the bust and **fullness added**, keeping the shoulder and cross-chest area fitted to maintain a flattering shape.

A formal, sleeveless wool shift that finishes just above the knee. The centre-front panel is grown-on at the neckline to create an unusual **semifunnel shape**. Fullness has been added on the dress panels from below the bustline, gradually increasing to the hem to create the trapeze shape.

KEY CHARACTERISTICS

- ☑ **Trapezoid shape: narrow shoulder line, very wide hemline**
- ☑ **Flared increase in silhouette throughout dress to create volume**
- ☑ **Unstructured look without waist definition and free hemline**

1 A casual trapeze with long sleeves that are full and flared at the hem, reflecting the flare of the dress hem. 2 A bold style, maximizing graphic impact with opposing-direction black and white stripes. The fluidity of the solid-colour fabric helps to balance the strong shoulder line. 3 This sunray-pleated silk trapeze, with short balloon sleeve and an open, slotted neckline, is a feminine interpretation of the shift style. 4 This archetypal trapeze has a young, retro feel. The high round neck balances the flirty short hemline and small cap sleeve. 5 An unusual trapeze shift, with a wide stand collar, cape-effect sleeves and a modern self-fabric bow. The cape sleeves are left loose, wrapping around the arm into a centre-front yoke. Flare has been created in the skirt from below the yoke seam. 6 The printed geometric border adds interest to this simple knee-length trapeze. The gathered round neckline is reflected in the cuffs. 7 Florals and tartans in a wool fabric are mixed to create a border print. 8 The solid, wide straps of this dress help to highlight the trapeze shape. The fitted bodice is a stark contrast to the full mid-thigh-length skirt.

> Abstraction of shape and **disproportionate cutting** subvert the notion of the trapeze. Circular cutting is implemented, wrapping the body, mixing gathered **tiered borders** of varying depth that attach on top and underneath the main dress panel.

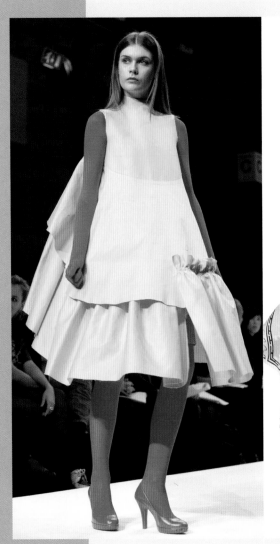

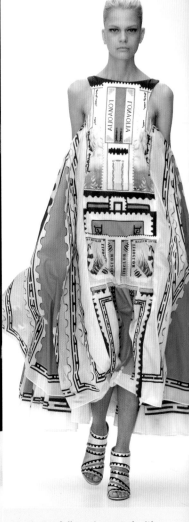

Maximum fullness is created with the combination of **circular cutting** and yards of lightweight silk habotai, which enable **fluidity of movement.** The manipulation of placement prints, derived from postage stamps, adds a touch of **humour.**

Blue **leather** cut in panels integrates the shaping to create a distinctive trapeze silhouette. The **side curved vent openings** have a contrast orange gusset, adding to the sporty feel.

Alternative neckline and sleeves: keyhole neckline and low, raglan cap sleeves

The high, round neck and slightly extended, sleeveless shoulders of this trapeze create an informal balance with the **diagonal dissecting panelling** and asymmetric hemline. The contrasting sheer-and-matt stripe chiffon fabric accentuates the diagonal style lines, creating a delicate **cobweb-like effect** that complements the full, uneven hem.

The trapeze shape is accentuated by the **horizontal panel** above the bust and the **braided fabric** detail that expands in width towards the hem. The braided fabric straps at the shoulder and the fitted knit sleeves only serve to emphasize the voluminous hem.

Tent

Voluminous layers of black transparent-over-solid fabrics shroud the body, disguising the contours. Flesh-coloured power mesh set into four rows of **V-shaped banding** stripe through the negative space of the neckline, keeping the shoulders of the dress from falling.

Circular cutting rounds the short hemline of the kaftan shape. The black-and-white tribal print is engineered around the body, defining and mocking a yoke and creating borders around the hemline and cuffs. The soft fabric and volume combine to create **movement and drape**.

The tent dress has similarities with the A-line and trapeze shift dresses, but is recognizable for having greater volume. The silhouette can also be called a pyramid flare. The tent flares out from the chest and envelops the whole body, achieving a smock effect. This is a difficult style to wear for women with large busts, since these can push the dress farther away from the body, causing it to resemble maternity wear; however, it can be worn with a skinny belt to cinch the waistline. The dress can incorporate gathered tiers, creating even more fullness. Strategically placed pleats or sunray pleats are a popular feature.

Fabric choices are generally lightweight, to accentuate the movement of the dress. Large prints work well and plain colours offer scope for costume jewelry. The tent has potential for voluminous asymmetrical shapes and is favoured by avant-garde designers who want to envelop, rather than accentuate, the body. This is an ideal shape for hot weather, since it doesn't stick to the body.

The dress can be styled with or without sleeves, and although an ideal shape for spring/summer, it can work well for winter, with solid tights or leggings. The length works best to the knee or several inches above it. Too short and the dress would be classified as a baby-doll. The tent also works well as maxi length, falling into the realms of the kaftan.

KEY CHARACTERISTICS

☑ Tent shape: narrow shoulder line, extremely voluminous hemline

☑ Envelops the body

☑ Lightweight fabric

SHIFT DRESS

1 The body is enveloped in this knee-length dress cut with magyar sleeves. Shoulder padding creates a straight, strong shoulder line. 2 Colour-blocked stripes emphasize the geometric cut. Chiffon pleating softens the hard lines. The dress is fixed at the waistline, giving some definition to the shape. 3 With drop shoulders and wide set-in sleeves, volume is added to the already overblown cocoon-like shape. 4 Floor-length dress with an austere feel and a robe-like quality, broken by the deep V-neckline. 5 A printed panel at the front of the dress suggests a slim column silhouette. This is contradicted by pleated chiffon side panels flaring at the hemline, making a tent-like shape. 6 Folded handkerchief triangular shapes are created from rectangular panels to create sleeves and armholes integrated into front and back panels of the dress. 7 Enveloping the body, abstract pleated shapes create asymmetrical pattern pieces. Edged with strapping, the dress has a deconstructed look. 8 Circular cutting is evident, and gathering into the bodice creates a trapeze silhouette, but turning back on itself, the hemline transforms into a tulip shape.

The oversized shapes are created by cutting rectangular pieces of contrasting silk satin, which are **folded and seamed** into corners and joined at the centre front and back. The striped fabric gives an indication of the **grain** and helps to explain how the pieces have been cut. The excess fabric is allowed to form the drape at the front, adding to the volume of the dress.

Many features of the dress suggest a **kaftan shape**, such as the round neckline split at the bodice, and the volume and length. The shapes, however, are more rounded, and circular cutting, rather than rectangular shaping, is evident. The overall aesthetic is **cocoon-like**, particularly apparent at the armholes and the cape effect at the back.

The dress is cut with greater volume at the left-hand side, which **pleats** at the shoulder, creating drape at one side. The side of the dress seemingly folds into the hemline, giving the impression of a **continuous** piece of fabric.

1 Abstract shapes are achieved through the crossover wrapping effect, where two halves of different-shaped garments seemingly collide. 2 Coloured stripes in varying proportions punctuate the oversized tent shape. The horizontal band at the waist gives a slimming effect. 3 Silk is gathered into a contrasting knitted-rib panel, which divides the dress at the bodice to give a blouson effect. The deep V-neckline and the side split reveal the body. 4 Lightweight sunray-pleated chiffon fabric is held in place with a brass neckpiece, then cascades down the body. 5 Circular shapes at front and back are joined at the top of the sleeve to create a kaftan shape. The deep, slashed neckline is grown on from the front panel. 6 Simple oversized dress in wool and linen mix. The neck and opening are trimmed with a black leather binding, which is also used for the lacing down the front. 7 Generously proportioned shift with turned-back kaftan sleeves, button-through side panel and shoulder seam. 8 Oversized tent dress with wide sleeves, which are pleated into the dropped shoulder, creating a curved silhouette.

Tunic

The tunic shift dress is usually worn over layers of other garments such as leggings, thick tights, a sweater or a shirt. Simple in style, reaching from the shoulders to a length somewhere between the thighs and the ankles, it is based on an Ancient Roman garment worn by both men and women. A tunic describes military and ecclesiastical garments, and the term is often used to define protective garments that are worn over other clothes. The tunic dress is generally sleeveless, if designed to be worn over a T-shirt or a sweater, and may have front, back or shoulder fastenings. If the dress is cut loose, then it can be pulled over the head with no need for fastenings. The neckline needs to accommodate the undergarment, and so a round, scooped, V or square-cut neckline is an ideal choice.

Variations to a neckline, such as asymmetrical cutting or scalloped edgings, may also be echoed in the armhole shaping. Zipped or buttoned centre or side-front panels with a split hemline can be applied to reveal an underlayer of leggings or thick tights, and statement feature pockets can add to the work-wear aesthetic of the tunic dress.

A slightly oversized, relaxed-fit, sleeveless check shift with a wide round neckline that complements the **front yoke seam**. Finishing at knee length, the dress has a deep **inverted pleat** that starts from the yoke seam and continues to the hem.

A very loose-fit dress, with grown-on shoulder seams that allow the garment to hang from the shoulders. The front neck yoke extends to the armholes, which accentuates the **boxy feel**. The dress has a concealed centre-front button placket, which develops into a pleat at skirt level to create more fullness to the hem. **Deep pockets** are inserted into the long diagonal bust darts.

KEY CHARACTERISTICS

- ☑ **Derived from ancient military and ecclesiastical clothing**
- ☑ **Designed to be worn over other garments**
- ☑ **Generous, loose fit**
- ☑ **Knee length or shorter**

1

2

3

4

5

6

7

8

1 Loose-fitting, sleeveless, ankle-length dress. Piping highlights the neckline and thigh-high side splits. **2** Heavy cotton dress, with wide round neck, elbow-length sleeves, self-fabric belt and jet side pockets giving a utilitarian air. **3** This tabard-style shift has a wide boatneck with sheer, contrast-fabric shoulder straps. Sheer fabric side panels are inserted to create fit. Side splits and a deep border hem accentuate the large side pockets.

4 Combining tunic and coatdress styling with a deep V-neckline and button-through centre-front opening. Large patch pockets and pocket flaps are positioned at the side hips. **5** Rectangular cutting, influenced by the kimono, breaks up the dress into sections of monochromatic print and solid black with coloured horizontal stripes accenting the bodice, waist and hemline. **6** This shift displays traditional shirting references, which include the curved shirt-tail hem and traditional shirt cuffs. **7** Navy-on-white diagonal panels create a wrapped stole effect. The shapes are defined by contrasting topstitching. **8** Loose-fitting tunic dress with minimal shaping. The wide boatneck gives a deconstructed look.

SHIRTDRESS

The shirtdress is a good fashion basic for building a wardrobe and, because of its potentially simplistic nature, is an ultimate standard for layering with other garments or mixing with accessories. The crossing of boundaries between masculine and feminine allows for versatility of shape and style.

The flat shirt collar and layered shirt tails define this dress, placing it firmly in the shirtdress category. The exotic stamp-inspired design has been carefully placed for maximum impact. The sharp, crisp cotton lends itself well to the oversized silhouette and large kimono sleeves.

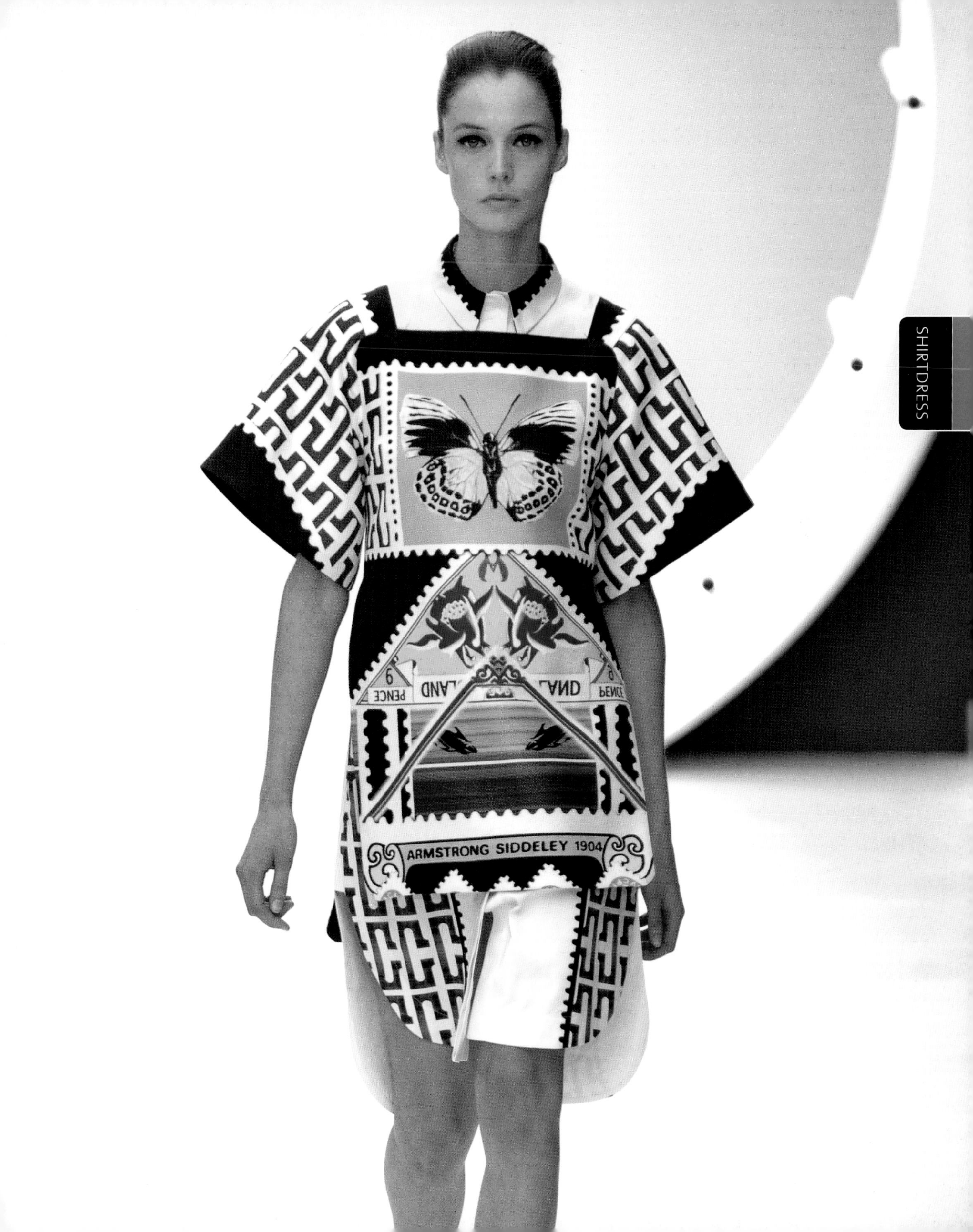
ARMSTRONG SIDDELEY 1904

In context

The iconic 1960s model Twiggy wears a shirtdress with an exaggerated Henley collar and flap pockets. The effect of the shapeless shift on the petite model is one of a child wearing an adult shirt. Youthful exuberance and naiveté characterized this decade of exploration.

The shirtdress, as the term implies, is derived from a traditional man's shirt, with separate button placket, double-layer back yoke and collar stand, through to the more formal dress shirt with the winged collar, bib front and turned-back cuffs and cufflinks. The dress gives the impression of a lengthened shirt and can be oversized and worn loose or belted. The dress can also be seamed at the waist, with a separate bodice and skirt, otherwise known as a shirtwaister. The shirtdress can be androgynous and masculine or, by sharp contrast, feminine and pretty, as seen in the shirtwaisters of the 1950s, typically worn by Doris Day.

Dior's post-World War II New Look defined the shirtdress, where the silhouette included very full skirts and a nipped-in waist, and often featured a notched collar and elbow-length sleeves with cuffs. In the 1950s, American popular culture adopted the shirtdress as part of its uniform, and housewives made their version of the housecoat dress respectable. Influences have also been derived from military, uniform, safari and work wear, with a revival of the shirtdress in the 1980s.

As women entered the workforce in earnest throughout the 1970s and 1980s, they needed clothes that they could feel comfortable in and would look great. This shirtdress by Calvin Klein has a dirndl skirt, sashed waist and a jacket-like collared neckline that is both sexy and reminiscent of the man's dress shirt it is imitating.

Design considerations

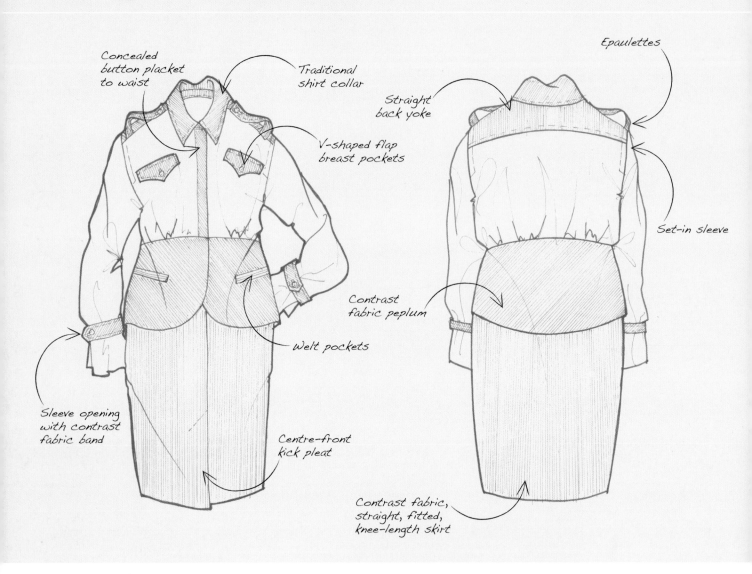

Concealed button placket to waist

Traditional shirt collar

V-shaped flap breast pockets

Welt pockets

Sleeve opening with contrast fabric band

Centre-front kick pleat

Epaulettes

Straight back yoke

Set-in sleeve

Contrast fabric peplum

Contrast fabric, straight, fitted, knee-length skirt

Silhouette Can be fitted and tailored – designed to fit a formal setting – or loose and casual, like an oversized man's shirt.

Length There are no restrictions on length, though shirt tails, side vents and asymmetrical hemlines are possibilities that emphasize the shirt influences.

Yokes Yokes can differ in size and shape on front and back, offering variation. Whether the dress is influenced by the traditional man's shirt or the formal

tuxedo, a bib-front yoke will dramatically alter its aesthetic. Shaped yokes are a common feature of the military, safari, work wear or western-inspired shirtdress. The dress may be trimmed with shirt-neck collar and placket and buttoned through to the bust, hem or waist if shirtwaisted.

Collars and cuffs Collars and cuffs define the shirtdress, though collarless granddad styling or a V-neck with placket will still suggest shirt influences. A more formal

structured effect will be achieved through the use of a stand collar, whereas a grown-on revers open collar will give a more relaxed feeling. Cultural references may suggest the use of a stand or Nehru or Mao collar, or perhaps a rounded lace-trimmed Peter Pan style.

Sleeves Short-sleeved to long-sleeved; wide or narrow fit with buttoned cuffs; turn-back cuffs, or no cuffs at all: the choices are endless.

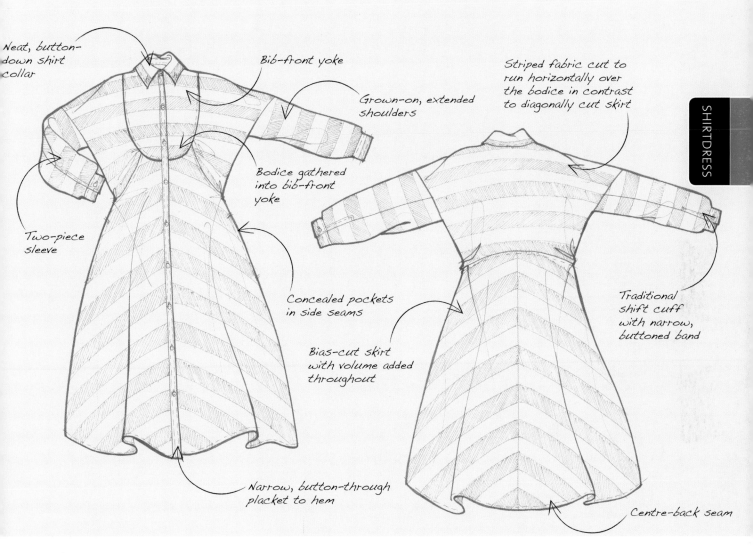

Neat, button-down shirt collar

Bib-front yoke

Grown-on, extended shoulders

Striped fabric cut to run horizontally over the bodice in contrast to diagonally cut skirt

SHIRTDRESS

Bodice gathered into bib-front yoke

Two-piece sleeve

Concealed pockets in side seams

Traditional shift cuff with narrow, buttoned band

Bias-cut skirt with volume added throughout

Narrow, button-through placket to hem

Centre-back seam

Fabric The fabric choices are as varied as the style of shirt silhouette. Seasonal changes impact on the weight of fabric, although the shirtdress can be part of a layering system. The choice of heavy-, medium- and lightweight cotton linens and wools, through to silks and manmade materials, can alter the look and feel of the design. For a more feminine option, gingham or florals are alternatives to checks or denim. Statement prints through to ditsy spots can add a new dimension to the aesthetic.

Embellishments Embellishments can be applied in the form of topstitching, piping, pin tucks, embroidery, lace, frills or epaulettes. Small logos or embroidered monograms can be used to decorate decorate or label the garment. Functional and decorative buttons with buttonholes or rouleau loops are a distinctive feature. Hardware trims can include cufflinks, studs, metal-tipped collars, zips, snap fastenings, rivets and rhinestone accents.

Pockets Pockets are a common and distinctive feature of the shirtdress. Concealed pockets at the side seam or oversized varieties are just the start of a list of endless possibilities. The design of pockets will often define the category of style. Western-style pockets positioned at breast level, or alternative mouth or jet pockets, will be edged with piping and finished with a reinforcing embroidered V.

Shirt

The shirtdress derives from numerous sources of inspiration, such as safari, lumberjack, western, regatta and rugby shirts. It is rooted in tradition, born out of the menswear classic shirt, and can be reworked to provide a versatile, utilitarian and often simple chic appeal in their classic form, combining utility and elegance.

This classic dress style is usually defined by time-honoured design features, such as back yokes and, sometimes, front yokes, depending on the inspiration; double-needle stitching on the side seams and underarm sleeve seam; collars that can set the tone of the style and can range from rounded, button-down and straight point to wing and Nehru; shirt tails topstitched with a rolled hem, often with a gusset in the side seams; and cuffs that can be buttoned or cufflinked.

The shirtdress is a hard-working basic that can be dressed up or down, and is often accessorized with a self-fabric belt, usually tied, not buckled. For formal wear, the collars and cuffs can be cut in contrasting colour fabric. Suitable for all climates and occasions, the shirtdress can be made in traditional lightweight woven cotton poplin and broadcloth, or be adapted in silk for evening wear, and wools for autumn and winter.

Soft, relaxed, oversized long-sleeved shirtdress to calf length with **side splits** to the knee and bound edges. The two-piece collar has a classic broad spread and top-button fastening. Other details include a forward shoulder seam and a **square pocket** applied at the left breast.

This dress combines a **trapeze-style** shift with shirt-style collar and front placket opening. The white cotton summer dress has a **sportswear feel** with contrast blue collar and V-shaped patch pocket and short sleeves. The piped front placket is fastened with rouleau and small buttons.

KEY CHARACTERISTICS

- ☑ **Traditional men's shirt detailing**
- ☑ **Sometimes back and front yokes and placket**
- ☑ **Collars and cuffs**
- ☑ **Pocket features**
- ☑ **Run-and-fell seams on side seams and underarm sleeve seam**

1 Drop-waisted shirtdress with box-pleat skirt. The bodice is seamed for fit with a two-piece 1970s-inspired pointed collar. 2 Silk and chiffon shirtdress, softly gathered to the waist seam with belt tabs. The stand collar is cut on the bias and ties at the front neckline opening. 3 Contrast colour neck stand and centre-front placket. Details include front-pleated panels and side-seam pockets. 4 Sleeveless shirtdress with Peter Pan collar. The skirt is attached to a dropped waist and is cut from rectangles that extend the width of the waist measurement, falling as a handkerchief hemline. 5 High-waisted shirtdress with an A-line skirt. Full sleeves are gathered to the sleeve head and to a narrow, buttoned cuff. 6 Equal proportions balance the contrasting collar, cuffs, placket and inverted V-shaped waistband. The matt dress contrasts with the shine sleeves. 7 Gingham shift dress with transparent sleeves and starched flat collar and cuffs. A wide V-neck allows the collar to stand at the shoulder. 8 Fit-and-flare minidress with front placket opening to below bust. The front bodice darts split the shoulder into a keyhole opening.

> Panels of ditsy floral prints are mixed together in this pretty shirtwaisted dress. Fullness is controlled at the bust, hip and cuffs by a **smocking effect** using dirndl elastic. The large, pointed flat collar lays flat against the garment. The front placket is faced with a **contrast print**.

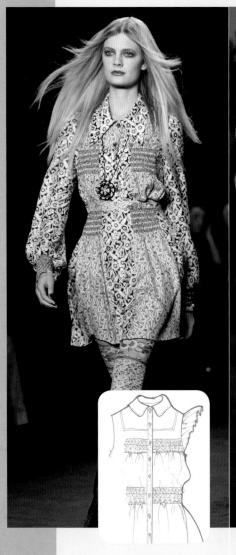

Alternative sleeves: gathered cap sleeves

A bold hexagonal print with a **vintage feel** is contrasted with a black collar, cuffs and **patch pockets**, then finished with a black belt and decorative vintage-inspired buckle. The pockets and collar are embellished with lace panels that are in keeping with the retro feel of the dress.

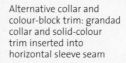

The **slim-line silhouette** of the shirtdress is exaggerated by the floor length, which elongates the body. Worn **unbuttoned to thigh** and again at the deep V-neckline to give a sophisticated edge, this is an ideal garment to wear into evening or over separates for a more casual look.

The **lightweight fabric** of the spot print is an ideal choice for the shirtwaisted dress. The skirt is cut on the bias to create **volume and flare** to below the calf. Sharp contrast-colour stripes edge the cuff and collar and run down to form the placket of the dress from neck to hem, and are used again to create the tie-belted waist.

Alternative collar and colour-block trim: grandad collar and solid-colour trim inserted into horizontal sleeve seam

Crisp, white cotton shirtdress with an **irregular cut**. The bodice is shaped diagonally to create two different silhouettes either side to the placket. The right-hand skirt is pleated and gathered into the waist seam on the lower side and forms a sharp A-line from the left side seam. The **asymmetrical hemline** and colour blocking on one sleeve and opposite hemline help to create a shirtdress with a split personality.

1 Crisp, oversized boyfriend shirt with traditional attributes, such as two-part stand collar and patched breast pockets. **2** Sundress with a deep armhole and V-neck tapering to shoulder straps with a flat shirt-neck collar. Worn layered over a contrasting print as a pinafore. **3** Maxi shirtdress in a floral chintz with contrasting collar and placket to the waist. A self-fabric rouleau cord is threaded through the shoulder, waistband and hemline. **4** A traditional, button-through, shirtwaisted dress that flares out to the hemline. **5** The brocaded fabric, deep V-neck, raglan armhole and curved-to-pointed hemline suggest an elongated waistcoat. Worn layered over a chiffon blouse to create a pinafore style. **6** The oversized pinstripe and starched white collar are subversions of a traditional man's shirt. Back to front in appearance, the collar forms a boatneck. **7** Sleeveless shirtdress with halter neck to stand collar. The skirt is cut on the circle with excess pleated into the waist seam. The hemline is split at the side seams, forming a classic scoop shirt tail. **8** Maxi-length shirtdress with a bold placement print from waist to hem.

Positioned **off-centre** on the left-hand side of the dress, the button-through placket is extended, turned back and held down by buttons and buttonholes. The overall styling is relaxed, with short sleeves and a self-fabric tie belt. The fabric is embroidered with rows of tiny florals that give a **raised-slub effect** to create a dress that can be dressed up or worn casually.

The small, one-piece collar is stitched flat to the neckline with a button-through placket down centre front with **numerous small buttons**. The wide waistband sits high below the bustline, falling at hip level. The bodice is gathered into a yoke panel and again at the waist.

Alternative sleeves and waist yoke: batwing sleeves with V-seam detail reflecting the V-shaped waist yoke

The textured seersucker woven fabric allows for a **structured design**. Much emphasis is placed around the shoulder and neckline with a high but wide V-neckline trimmed with a **shawl collar**. Yoke panels at armhole level incorporate two layers of sleeve with a capped sleeve layered over a short sleeve, giving an epaulette effect. The button-through separate placket runs to a dropped-waist seam, where the flare of the skirt is controlled by **large box pleats**.

Pretty, vintage-inspired shirtdress with a **bib-front panel** running from neck to hem, giving the impression of a placket opening where the buttons are purely decorative. Pleats run from the centre panel around the dress, suggesting a gymslip. Black piping and decorative trim are used to outline the front panel and waist seam and define the **large one-piece collar** sitting flat around the neckline, with black cuffs and a border around the hemline to complete the look.

Sleeveless silk dress with a small button-down collar on a separate stand and a front button-through placket to a **dropped-waist** seam. A mock waistband is tied with a leather cord. Pleats in the skirt are fixed into the waistband and again at the hem, and stitched into the inside facing, which binds the hemline and **deep scoop tail** with side splits.

The oversized shirt sports a **granddad collar stand** with a single button fastening at the neck. The centre-front placket facing is cut on the bias and opens to below the bust. The crisp cotton check is a perfect summer weight, and with **side openings** and a deep-scooped tail, this is an ideal garment for layering over trousers.

Alternative front fastening: bib panel with button-through placket and Nehru collar

The inserted contrast red fabric **bib-front yoke panel** is the main focus of this dress with a large Peter Pan collar and decorative beads, jewels and embroidery embellishing the seam. Three-quarter-length sleeves are edged with a cuff to pick up the collar detail. The striking large-scale subverted tartan and warm colours in **fine wool fabric** help to create an ideal dress for autumn/winter.

< Panelled dress fitted to the waistband with an **A-line skirt**. The shirt collar is an **additional accessory**, separate from the dress, which is sleeveless with a V-neck. Heavily embellished with red discs, the panels vary between solid and transparent.

Uniform/military

Inspiration from a wealth of sources can inform this style, including military, police, work wear and school uniforms. Uniforms were designed to standardize dress, creating a distinctive garment intended for identification, belonging and display, while providing an air of authority and organization. Decadent and colourful for ceremonial occasions, through to functional and utilitarian for practicality, the looks can vary in aesthetic.

Key shapes are double-breasted with stand collars; single-breasted with large revers collars; shearling collars, Nehru or Mao collars; fitted waists and full skirts, pencil skirts with back vents; pleated skirts and peplums; and A-line with inverted box pleats, dropped waistlines or knife pleats.

Design features centre around collars, pockets and buttons, as well as epaulettes, embroidered insignia, badges and ribbons. Multipockets are a strong theme, often with a mixing of styles and sizes. Reinforced areas, such as quilting and leather patches, will replicate the protection of armour, and self-fabric or leather belts and belt loops can emphasize form and add to the feeling of constraint.

Literal translations into fabrics such as wools, gabardine, cotton twill and cotton drill are obvious choices, but silks, linens, finer cottons and manmade fabrics can also accommodate the styling features. Colours such as navy, black, red and khaki illustrate the theme, but subversions will take the dress into a less obvious realm. Stripes, camouflage, geometrics and image prints will give added interest.

The **basic shape** has the features of military uniform, with shirt collar and front placket opening, breast pockets inserted into the yoke seam and diagonal side pockets with stand. The **digital print** is strategically engineered to trim and define the pattern pieces.

This luxury, sanded-silk, **maxi-length** dress has an asymmetric button fastening on the left side, which continues to the floor. There are oversized patch pockets at hip level, smaller patch **pockets** with flaps at the bust, a soft shawl collar and long and lean set-in sleeves.

KEY CHARACTERISTICS

- ☑ Traditional military uniform detailing
- ☑ Collar, pocket, button and epaulette design features
- ☑ Decorative embellishments, badges, insignia and topstitching

1 Cotton shirtdress with inverted-pleat patch pocket with flap and exposed side pocket bags. The pinafore skirt panel and pockets are trimmed with mitred corners in contrasting colours.
2 Double-breasted dress with inverted-pleat pockets with flaps on the breasts and hips, epaulettes, strapping and a double-buckle belt.
3 Collarless shirtdress with dirndl waist and front placket opening concealing button fastenings. The inverted-pleat pocket and flap and shoulder epaulettes are trademark military features.
4 A fitted shift style with concealed-button placket on a high, round neckline, contrasting leather epaulettes and belted waist. **5** Multiple pockets in varying shapes are an eclectic mix, held together by the solid colour of the fabric. **6** Shirtdress with pared-down uniform styling. The front body is extended to form a concealed fly front, with a single button revealed at the neck stand of the two-piece collar. **7** A short centre-front zip and low-lustre fabric yoke and sleeves contrast with a suiting-fabric main body and white collar. **8** The applied breast pockets, with an inverted pleat and button-down flap, are distinctly military in feel.

Safari

The safari-style shirtdress is a classic that has been reinterpreted by a range of designers. It transcends fashion trends. While Yves Saint Laurent developed the safari dress in the 1960s, it was made fashionable in the 1980s by Ralph Lauren and Calvin Klein. The style is ideal for summer travelling and hot climates and was popularized by Meryl Streep in the 1985 film *Out of Africa*.

Fashion takes the image of the romantic explorer and reinterprets it for the modern traveller, using traditional linens, khaki cottons, poplin or twill, or contemporary performance fabrics. Muted khaki, olive or stone, with perhaps a camouflage print, are used to create an authentic safari look, although white is an ideal alternative. The use of a bright, trend-led summer palette can update the look, and a modern camouflage-inspired or animal print can also help to confirm the style.

Traditionally, the safari shirtdress is a cross between a military field jacket and a shooting jacket, with four bellow pockets, a belt across the middle and a traditional point collar with epaulettes on the shoulder. Pockets were designed to carry ammunition, compass, map and knives. The contemporary equivalent survival kit might consist of a mobile phone and laptop computer, credit cards, passport and sunglasses, and may be the blueprint for designing the size and shape of the pockets. Alternatively, they can remain purely for decoration.

Loose-fit, georgette shirtdress, taking inspiration from camouflage prints. It has a button-through centre-front placket leading to a traditional shirt collar. A belt creates a **softly gathered waist**. The **dropped shoulder** complements the relaxed style and the wide short sleeves are loosely secured back.

The left side of this dress has a **fitted bodice**, using princess seams to create shaping and fit over the bust into a nipped-in waist. In contrast, the right side has a **draped silk jersey** panel that creates soft folds as it wraps to the left, creating a deep wrap opening at the hem.

KEY CHARACTERISTICS

- ☑ Cross between military field jacket and shooting jacket

- ☑ Four bellow pockets, belt across the middle, traditional point collar, epaulettes

- ☑ Khaki, olive, stone or white colour or camouflage print

1 The oversized breast pockets and wide dropped-shoulder sleeves match the generous proportions of this ankle-length dress. 2 The formal feel of the suiting fabric is offset by the self-fabric waterfall frill, which begins under the collar on the right side and is inserted into the side seam. 3 Loose, short-sleeve shirtdress with front placket buttoned from neck to hem. The inverted-pleat patch pockets with flap fulfil the safari look. 4 This cool linen shirtdress has short sleeves, side splits, a grown-on collar, centre-front placket and inverted-pleat pocket with flap. 5 The loose-fit bodice has symmetrical patch pockets with box-pleat detail and button-down flaps. A full skirt is created by ample tucks at the waistline. 6 Button-through shirtdress with set-in sleeves with turn-back cuffs. The bodice and skirt are separated by a waistband that gives definition to the waistline. 7 The use of khaki fabric and animal-print trim strongly suggest safari references. The asymmetrical design details and peplum subvert the traditional safari shirt. 8 This wide, horizontal stripe in high-shine silk satin creates a bold design, offset by the simple A-line shape and military-inspired pockets.

> **Body-conscious**
shirtdress with
traditional safari
detailing, which has
been enhanced by
the addition of a
metallic belt and
metal epaulettes.

Safari and trench-style shirtdress
with off-set button-through,
double-breasted placket opening,
which continues around the hem
with a mitred corner. **Double-needle
topstitching** features around pockets
and collars with a double storm-flap
feature on one side. Three **applied
pockets**, two at the hip and one on
the breast, have box pleats, mitred
corners and contrast-colour buttoned
V-flaps.

A self-fabric **drawstring tie** at the waist adds slight definition to the relaxed shape of this dress. The soft drape of the silk complements the **cape-effect shoulders**, while the sheer contrast-fabric chiffon sleeves add a subtle twist to the design.

Double-breasted button-through **trench-style safari dress** with storm flaps. The tie-dyed fabric suggests dappled sunlight, giving a **camouflage effect**. A leather belt defines the waist and adds to the utility aesthetic.

V-neck collarless and sleeveless shirtdress with button-through front placket opening. **Safari styling** is created with the application of deep applied pockets with curved flap at the hip and mitred pockets at the breast. A self-fabric belt is threaded through decorative leather **belt tabs** and tied at the waist.

Alternative pocket: rounded bellow pocket with button-down flap

Tuxedo

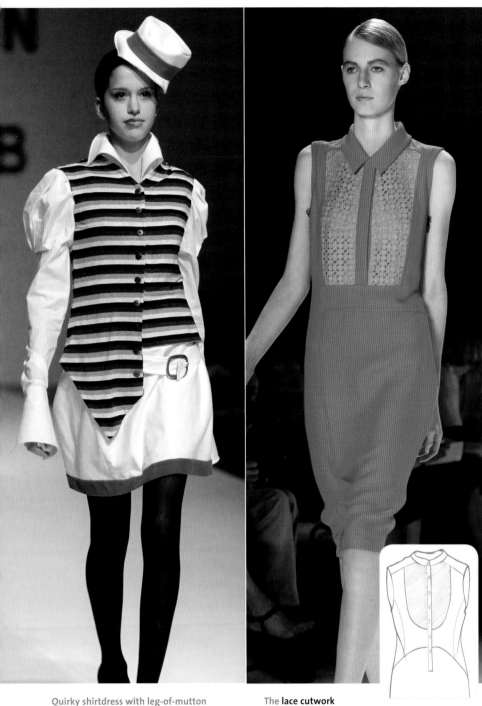

Derived from a formal man's dress shirt, the tuxedo-style shirtdress borrows from its distinctive design features. The style evokes formality and dress codes, although it can still maintain a relaxed vibe, suggesting boyfriend-borrowed chic. Strong features are the starched bib-fronted yoke and turned-back cuffs. Long sleeves may be rolled up to achieve a more casual feel. With the addition of a collarless stand left open, or with a wing collar added and buttoned to the neck, the effect will still be created.

Dickey front, detachable wing collar, cufflinks and button studs can help to authenticate the look. Pleats, pin tucks or lace braid can be used to decorate the dickey front, and a pull-on tab can be added at bottom centre front of the bib panel. Rumba frills can also adorn the front shirt panel either side of the placket. Embroidery can be used for a decorative effect and monograms can replace the logo.

Long, curved shirt tails and side vents can be used to vary the hemline, and lengths can be short and sexy or long and voluminous, maximizing cover-up. Pinstriped fabrics and white starched linen or cotton fabrics help to recreate the aesthetic, though shaping and details mixed with vibrant colours and patterns can also help to realize a subverted version. Styling combinations that integrate the tuxedo jacket with the shirt can develop a less traditional and more abstracted form.

Quirky shirtdress with leg-of-mutton sleeves that extend into an **exaggerated cuff**. The contrasting horizontal-stripe fabric gives the illusion of a separate vest. The **revers collar** stands high and curls away from the neckline. The mini-length hem has side splits and a solid-colour border.

The **lace cutwork panels** on the bodice are inspired by traditional dress shirts and give a feminine feel to an otherwise formal style.

Alternative collar and front panel: grandad collar, curved bib front and shaped waist seam

KEY CHARACTERISTICS

☑ **Derived from male formal dress shirts and dinner jackets**

☑ **Starched bib-fronted yoke**

☑ **Turned-back cuffs**

1 Shirting collar details synthesize with oversized tailored jacket lapels on the bodice. This extends into a draped panel at the hip that continues into a straight skirt. **2** Shift-shape shirtdress with a low, curved neckline and contrasting cuffs. A detachable stand collar and bib wraps and fastens at the neck. **3** Transparent undershirt with solid cuffs, collar and bound hemline. A tuxedo layered-vest front has a circular-cut peplum and waterfall frill that cascades from the centre placket. **4** Black and white suit and shirt details reference masculine formal dress. The faced collar and revers define the V-neck, while the mock jacket revers forms a capped sleeve. **5** A dickey fly-front with pleated tucks and a placket that extends to a pull-on tab define this drop-waisted, sleeveless dress.

6 A fitted, sleeveless bodice with a contrast-colour, bib-effect panel with button-through opening to the waistline. **7** Wrapped shirtdress with revers collar and low front neck drop. Vertical welt pockets sit high on the loose-fit bodice and echo the tailoring influences. **8** Dickey bib-front yoke and rounded shirt tails reflect a masculine dress shirt. Contrasting stand collar, placket and cuffs.

> An asymmetrical, masculine dress shirt with **opposing features** on each side of the centre-front placket. The left side is **exaggerated in scale**, no longer fitting the body, falling off the shoulder and reaching the floor, creating a look that questions proportion and fit.

Elements of the shirt have been subverted to create a waisted dress in sharp cotton. The **bib front** crosses the waistband, extending to patch pockets with flap, front placket and stand collar. The use of flesh-coloured power mesh as a base gives **transparency** to the back and shoulders. The deep, plunging cleavage combines feminine and masculine features.

Traditional tuxedo design details have been subverted and applied in **multiples** to different areas of the body to create this interesting garment. The **layering** of the contrasting sheer and solid fabric is integral to the design.

This duchess satin, **shift-shape** dress has contrasting sheer inserts that accentuate the style lines, reflecting the **oversized wing collar** detail.

Deconstructing the shirt and abstracting and layering have created an innovative statement dress. Although breaking with convention, recognizable elements of the shirt remain. The use of repetition reinforces the iconic value of the traditional man's shirt. Starching, bonding and a clever use of interfacing have been employed to achieve a **sculptural silhouette**.

SUNDRESS

This versatile wardrobe essential transcends occasions, making it an ideal style for day and evening wear. With a multitude of design options, there is a sundress for every taste. It is an important inclusion in all spring/summer collections.

This digitally printed sundress has a fitted bra-cup bodice, wide shoulder straps forming a sweetheart neckline and a full, gathered dirndl skirt. The bra cups are sandwiched into the skirt's waistband at the side views, exposing the centre-front torso. The deep, solid-colour horizontal band inserted in the skirt breaks up the busy print.

In context

So much of what was popular in the 1960s was about bright colours and bold graphics. These two Lilly Pulitzer shift sundresses were just that, yet they were also appropriate for wealthy socialites on vacation in warm climates. Their matching bandanas perfectly finish off the look.

A must-have for every warm-weather holiday, the sundress is a practical and easy-to-wear garment that can be worn all day in a warm climate. Worn long or short, it can be a great canvas for bold prints or for solid colours with accessories for evening wear. Designed to keep you cool in hot weather, the sundress is typically produced in lightweight jersey and woven fabrics, often in natural fibres appropriate for spring/summer. It can be worn strapless for an even tan during the day and combined with a shoulder cover for cooler evenings. The extensive range of styles, with varying hemlines, necklines and sleeves, make it suitable for most occasions.

It is said that the origins of the sundress began in Palm Beach in the 1950s. American socialite Lilly Pulitzer is believed to have invented the sundress to disguise the juice stains on her clothes after making orange juice. The dresses were very colourful so that the stains would not show. They became admired and much sought after, leading Lilly into a new career in fashion.

Iconic American designer Claire McCardell also had functionality at the heart of her design ethos. The ready-to-wear designer produced simple, affordable clothes suited to most forms from the 1930s to the 1950s. Her celebrated bright, cotton chequered sundress, a basic tent dress with a halter-neck top and belted to give shape, accentuated the female form, but could also be worn unbelted to accommodate different body types.

In the UK, ready-to-wear fashion company Horrockses came to epitomize the quintessentially British sundress of the 1950s. The dresses reflected the optimism of the time, with bright floral and bold stripe cotton prints, fitted bodices and full skirts. In contrast, Emilio Pucci took the fashion world by storm with his lightweight textiles and dazzling psychedelic prints, abandoning the heavy fabrics and traditional floral prints that were familiar at the time. These revolutionary new designs were ideal for his lightweight silk jersey and silk chiffon high-summer beach- and evening-wear dresses, which became an essential component of resort wear for the international smart set, and were favoured by film stars such as Elizabeth Taylor and Marilyn Monroe.

Emilio Pucci became known in the 1960s for his brightly coloured graphic prints, which were easy to wear and comfortable. This kaftan sundress is ideal for a hot day on the beach or in town, all the while looking exotically chic.

Design considerations

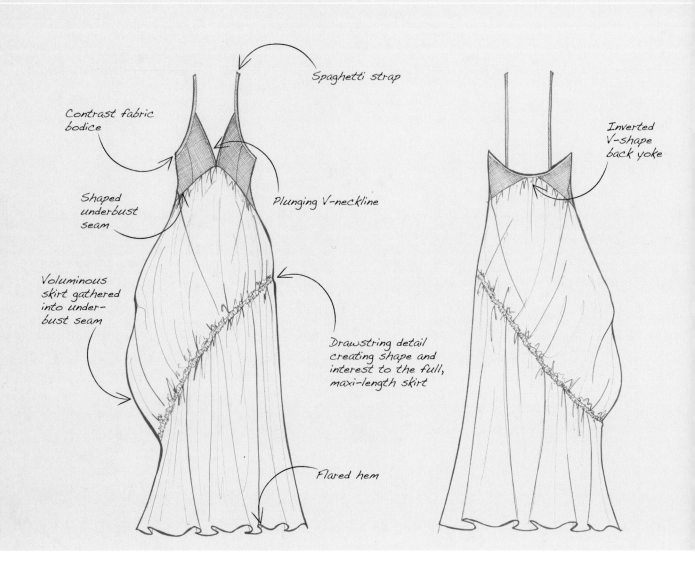

Contrast fabric bodice

Spaghetti strap

Shaped underbust seam

Plunging V-neckline

Voluminous skirt gathered into under-bust seam

Inverted V-shape back yoke

Drawstring detail creating shape and interest to the full, maxi-length skirt

Flared hem

Influences The sundress draws upon a diverse range of exotic travel influences, such as the kaftan, kimono and sari, all worn by cultures in hotter climates.

Practicality Functionality is the crucial design consideration because the sundress must be comfortable to wear in warm weather. Ideal for holidays, the sundress is a versatile garment that can pack easily, produced in a crease-resistant fabric or intentionally creased for effect.

The sundress can be dressed down for day and accessorized for evening.

Silhouette Generally sleeveless, strapless or with fine spaghetti straps, the sundress can be mini or maxi length, with variations in between. Taking inspiration from petticoat styles, the sundress is often bias cut, skimming the body and allowing for the natural stretch inherent in the woven fabrics. Alternatively, it is often loose and oversized, allowing for air circulation, and sometimes intended as a cover-up from the sun, hanging loosely to avoid contact with the body contours. Gathers and tiers are a common feature, creating volume and silhouette.

Fastenings Fastenings are often kept to a minimum, with the intention that the dress be thrown on over swimwear. Fit can be achieved through shirring, smocking or drawstring ties.

Traditional grandad collar

Extended centre-front button-through placket

Drawstring detail creating a relaxed front yoke

Straight back yoke

Vertical drawstring with self-fabric tie giving shape to the hemline

Oversized, horizontal pleats at waist level

Full dirndl skirt gathered into horizontal pleat

Voluminous, loose-fitting silhouette

Deep hem band

Bodice Sundress designs are often influenced by foundation garments such as bras and corsets, accentuating the bust with integrated bra cups. Details such as eyelets and lacing or hooks and eyes are commonly used to define the bodice.

Fabrics Fabrics are often lightweight, soft wovens that can vary from transparent or translucent to solid. They have a mainly natural fibre content for breathability, such as linen cotton and silks, though new manmade fibres allowing for non-crease and permanent pleating are often used. New technology has developed fabrics with wicking properties and sun-blocking features, adding greater functionality to the styling.

Seasonal styling The seasonal aspect of the sundress demands bright colours and bold prints. Embellishments, such as embroidery, beading, lace and other trimmings, evoke the often bohemian feel of the sundress. The sundress can transcend seasons through layering over garments in pinafore styling or accessorizing with knitwear, jackets and tights.

Sun

The sundress is intended to be worn in warm weather, and is typically an informal dress made in print and solid-colour fabric, such as lightweight cottons or cotton combinations, and other natural fibres that are cool and breathable, such as linen. Associated with holidays and exotic travel, when the high levels of sunlight allow the wearer to be more ambitious with colour and print, the dress features fabrics ranging from delicate ditsy florals to bold, graphic geometrics. Embroidery and embellishment are also key design details that can recreate an exotic, ethnic theme.

Sleeveless or with fine or spaghetti straps, the sundress is usually open-necked, exposing the shoulders, back and arms, making it ideal for a walk on the beach or for pulling on over swimwear. It is frequently designed with a keyhole back fastening with a rouleau loop and button or invisible zip in the left side.

The neckline can be sweetheart, halter neck, wide scoop or V. Designed for easy care, comfort and ease of wear, shaping can be created through the use of darts, bias cutting or smocking, so the dress can be pulled over the head without the need for fastenings. Appropriate for all ages and body shapes, the sundress works in a variety of lengths, from mini to maxi.

A sleeveless, V-neck, shift-shape, mini-length dress. **This simple style** is an ideal canvas for very **detailed fabric.**

Alternative neckline: square neckline with wide straps and bow detail

1970s-style, hippie-inspired maxi sundress in fine cotton lawn. The high-waisted bodice is heavily embellished with **braiding and embroidery**, suggesting multicultural influence. The skirt is gathered into the waistband to create fullness, in keeping with the **boho aesthetic**.

KEY CHARACTERISTICS

- ☑ **Lightweight fabrics often in natural fibres**
- ☑ **Ambitious colours and prints**
- ☑ **Sleeveless, usually with fine straps**
- ☑ **Various lengths and necklines**
- ☑ **Loose and relaxed fit**

1 The volume of fluid silk creates impact. The straight neckline, simple shoulder straps and solid colour are balanced by the ornately embellished neck edge. **2** A-line, sleeveless shift with a boatneck. The underbust self-fabric band gives definition to the bodice. **3** An off-the-shoulder neckline with a contrast-fabric collar-effect detail. Darts from the waistline to the bust give shape. **4** Lively sundress with a fitted bodice and contrasting lace circular skirt. The horizontal style line above the bust creates a yoke-like detail and allows for two clashing colours to be used together. **5** The overlapping swags of fabric coupled with the warm colours reinforce the Indian-inspired jungle print for an exotic appeal. **6** The diagonal neckline is bound and extended to the shoulder strap, creating a sarong-inspired sundress with minimal structure. **7** Sleeveless sundress with a scooped front neckline. Shoulders that divide into two add interest to an otherwise simple style. **8** A vest-shaped bodice creates a casual, easy-to-wear garment. An intricate cutwork fabric adds interest to the full, flared skirt.

1 A length of cotton lawn is folded and gathered across the width and worn diagonally from armhole to shoulder strap. Excess fabric forms a draped sleeve. 2 Simple A-line shift minidress. The denim fabric suggests dungaree styling; however, the double-tiered frill at the bodice gives a softer feel. 3 High-waisted sundress with a sweetheart neckline and gathered skirt. Contrasting borders define the neckline, waistband, tie and hemline. 4 Easy-to-wear sundress with an empire line, wrap-over bodice and softly gathered, flared miniskirt. 5 Strapless sundress with curved bodice and integrated bust support. The simple shape allows the bold print to fill the dress panel. 6 Sleeveless minidress with tiered and gathered hemline. Circular keyhole cutouts around the neckline are trimmed with contrast ribbon. 7 Patchwork denim mini sundress, heavily inspired by western styling, including twin-needle stitching and contrast-colour thread. The dress has an open-ended centre-front zip and faux jean waistband on a dropped waistline. 8 A geometric stencil print is echoed in the cutout ladder straps at the back of the dress.

9 Fit-and-flare sundress with a wide, square neckline that forms the shoulder straps and yoke. Panel seams are accentuated with bright piping. **10** The peplum and fishtail hemline create a Victorian-inspired silhouette that enhances the hourglass figure. **11** Maxi tent dress with exaggerated volume increasing from the hip. Deep side pockets are in keeping with the oversized proportions. **12** Maxi dress in lightweight cotton. Built-in bra and cups with a sweetheart neckline give structure and shape to the strapless bodice. **13** A full skirt has been pleated into the bra-style bodice. Care has been taken throughout to cut the pattern pieces to maximize the print. **14** Fitted, strapless bodice and pencil skirt with a curved peplum. A front bib panel, inserted into the waist seam, creates a high neckline over the strapless bodice. **15** Chiffon halter-neck sundress with a deep V-neckline, which appears to extend around the arms to create a faux off-the-shoulder effect. The full skirt has godets to add more flare. **16** This sundress is based on simple sarong styling and handkerchief shaping, taking the corners of the rectangle to create the halter neck.

❯ Tiered, short **skater skirt** attached to a dropped-waist bodice gathered by a drawstring to create a soft, blouson effect. The **gathered frill** around the neckline and down one side of centre front to the waist accentuates the peasant look. The cotton muslin produces a fluted edge on the layered flounces.

The archetypal sundress with **fitted bodice** to the waist and gathered and flared hem. The sweetheart neckline, wide shoulder straps and shaped cups are all iconic features of the **1950s-inspired sundress**. The gathering has been confined to the hips and back, keeping the front panel flat to give a more flattering shape.

SUNDRESS

The full, gathered, tiered **prairie-influenced skirt** contrasts with the fitted, sleeveless bodice with wide **square neckline**. The waistline is accentuated by the addition of a short, gathered circular-cut peplum, and the busy print is balanced by tiers of larger-scale complementary prints at the hemline.

Fit-and-flare sleeveless sundress with V-neck and halter-neck straps that extend from underarm side seam and cross over to back neck. The **pussycat bow** at centre-front neckline creates a feminine decoration. The **lightweight** woven fabric flares to below the knee.

Diagonal seamed panels create structure and suggest origami-inspired pleating and folding. The **shibori-dyed print** continues the theme and complements the three-dimensional folded panels.

Pretty, lightweight cotton minidress with retro 1970s-inspired geometric print. The **crochet lace** of the collar and the front placket and pockets continue the **eclectic vintage feel**.

References to Japanese origami and **packaging** are evident in the design of this dress. Vertical and horizontal lines intersect the centre front and waistband, almost packaging the body with ribbons and ties. Shoulder ties in contrast colour strongly suggest a **dungaree style**.

Simple A-line sleeveless shift dress with separate bodice with round neck, centre-front placket and deep-cut armholes. The simple shape is subservient to the **bold floral print** of the cotton dress.

1

2

3

4

5

6

7

8

1 Contrast-colour blocking defines the proportions of the dress. The drop waistband elongates and disguises the contours of the body. 2 The dress is worn dungaree style over a sleeveless vest, which gives the body-contouring shape a sportswear feel. 3 Enveloping the figure, the oversized proportions are gathered at the yoke and drawn in at the hemline. The bodice suggests a bandeau-wrapped effect. 4 A large frill, gathered into the yoke above the bust, curves and dips lower at the back, creating volume, in sharp contrast to the closer-fitting, slimmer shape underneath. 5 Sophisticated sundress with zigzag silhouette cut into bodice seaming, giving strong suggestions of a tuxedo. This shape is echoed again at the hemline. 6 Lightweight, cotton, maxi-length sundress with Hawaiian print. Sleeveless with a deep round neck and drawstring waistline. 7 A floral print is cut on the bias, with a diagonal waistband and front yoke panel. Waterfall-draped panels, inserted from the waistband, hang to form draping. 8 Monochrome panelled dress with body-contour panels that give a slimming effect. The bra top is shaped into a deep sweetheart silhouette.

Smock

The smock evolved from traditional clothing worn by British shepherds and peasants as a protective work-wear garment. These smocks were decorated to achieve individuality, with design origins related to regions, families and the wearer's occupation.

Traditionally made in linen or wool, the smock is an oversized T-shape, finishing at the knee or calf, and often featuring a round flat collar or shirt collar with a short placket. The excess fabric at the shoulders and sometimes the bodice was pleated into unpressed folds and decorated with smocking embroidery in self-coloured heavy linen thread. The smocking embroidery allows for a degree of stretch, making the garment easy to pull on and off. The reversible features of the smock meant the garment could be worn inside out when dirty. The smock was adapted to serve other occupations, such as fishing and painting, with large pockets to accommodate tools.

The smock dress has featured extensively in children's wear and is traditionally used for christenings; it is also an ideal shape for maternity wear. In mainstream women's fashion, the smock has been translated into lightweight linens, silks and cottons and embroidered with more contemporary threads in contrasting colours. The smock dress has evolved through the decades, taking on a more bohemian look, adopted by the hippies of the 1970s. Smocking is now used to embellish other areas of the garment, such as sleeves and cuffs, where gathering is required.

KEY CHARACTERISTICS

☑ Oversized T-shape

☑ Knee or calf length

☑ Round, flat collar or shirt collar with short placket

☑ Pleated, unpressed folds at shoulders or bodice

☑ Gathering, shirring and smocking

Wide, elasticated neckline and **cap sleeves** that can be worn either on or off the shoulder. The dress has **two skirt layers** under the bust. The front of the outerlayer is left open to expose the contrast-printed underskirt.

Alternative bodice: spaghetti straps with elasticated, smocked empire-line bodice

The white bandana and long, flowing, smocked dress, with a **shirred neck** and side slits, suggests a Greek holiday and the **exotic peasant styles** popular in the late 1960s. One can imagine this dress against sun-bleached white buildings and a crystal-blue sky.

1 The yoke has been extended with fabric bands to give the impression of cap sleeves. The yoke finishes above the bustline and the skirt is gathered into the yoke seam. 2 Shift-shape sundress with a square neckline. A detailed vertical panel of fine pin tucks on the centre front continues to the dropped-hip seam. 3 The substantial fabric of this sundress is gathered and smocked into a single-shouldered band. 4 Extra volume is added with drawstring ties on the skirt's sides. A half-skirt with an oversized apple-catcher pocket is added at the waist. 5 Multiple vertical pin tucks on the bodice achieve fit to the waist and bustline. An exaggerated sweetheart neckline is created from twisting the bodice fabric to form straps. 6 An elasticated, gathered neck edge creates a flexible neckline. Voluminous raglan sleeves are gathered into an elasticated cuff and reflect the capacious body. 7 The pleats, which start at the neck, create shape and texture and manipulate the graphic print. 8 The voluminous silhouette is achieved by an A-line bodice and additional fullness from the dropped waist seam. The bell sleeves echo the silhouette.

Petticoat

Influenced by lingerie styles, the petticoat sundress is made of lightweight woven fabric, often bias cut in linen and cotton, with spaghetti straps and lace trims.

The petticoat style can convey a variety of historical design references, from the narrow, sheath-like sheer slips of the late 1920s to the full, ruffle-tiered, western-style prairie petticoats with broderie anglaise trim. Some subcultures have also adopted the petticoat style as part of their uniform, from the stiff layered net of the 1950s-inspired rockabillies and the romantic gathered flounces of Victorian-influenced New Romantics through to the macabre mourning dress worn by goths.

Every decade fashion designers reinvent the underwear-as-outerwear trend, which was popularized in the 1980s by Madonna, although now the originally garish designs have taken on a more subtle and romantic feel. Contemporary petticoat-dress styles now integrate lingerie features, such as fabrics, pattern cutting and trims, and are not defined by length, which ranges from very short to full length. Necklines, such as V, sweetheart and halter, expose the chest and can vary in feel from demure to seductive. This is an ideal style for layering and juxtaposing with masculine tailoring or knitwear.

Grecian styling is evident in this dress, with two circular necklaces used as a base to fold, wrap and thread lengths of fabric. **Layers of organdie** allow varying degrees of transparency and create different levels of hemline. The stitched waistband controls the fabric and creates fit to accentuate the waist.

This silk satin sundress is bias cut, creating a **body-skimming** fit. A contrast-colour, more-structured overlayer on the bodice softly curves around the body from the underbust level on the front view to a full-length panel on the back. Fine **spaghetti straps** discreetly support the dress.

KEY CHARACTERISTICS

☑ Influenced by lingerie styling

☑ Often bias cut in silk, linen or cotton

☑ Spaghetti straps and lace trims

1 Stripes run horizontally at the deep waistband and gathered tiered hemline. The direction of the fabric changes at the bodice and skirt, where the stripe runs vertically. **2** Body-skimming, bias-cut dress with a gradually flared skirt starting from hip level, a subtle cowl on the high neckline and spaghetti straps. **3** This maxi-length dress has a fitted bodice and wide sweetheart neckline.

The bra cups and shoulder straps are reminiscent of swimming-costume styles. **4** All-over lace sundress with a fitted bodice and full calf-length dirndl skirt. The skirt is panelled to accommodate flare from the hip through to the hem. **5** Shoulder straps extend to the waistband and outline a heart-shaped panel at centre-front bodice. **6** Delicate minidress with a wide, square neckline,

reflecting the horizontal, multistripe lace trim on the bodice. **7** The tubular shape of this simple mini sundress is emphasized by the vertically striped fabric. Compacted, circular-cut gathered frills at the hemline add interest. **8** A hand-painted image fills the canvas of the vintage petticoat; the surface decoration has been added after garment construction.

> Bias cutting and lace inserts accentuate the diagonal of the dress, creating a **V-shape** at centre front and back. The V-shaping is picked up at the neckline, where a **lace** insert is positioned at the yoke and trimmed with pink silk binding, and at the handkerchief hemline.

This ethereal calf-length sundress achieves impact through the use of a substantial amount of silk chiffon fabric. The simple, contemporary feel of the style is created by the **straight halter neck** and unusual diagonal direction of the spaghetti straps. The dress is circular cut from the neckline, with a **voluminous skirt** that falls longer at the back.

SUNDRESS

The dress is slashed from the hem to dropped waistline where bias-cut godets are inserted into the panels to create a **flared hemline**. The changes in the direction of the chequered fabric create additional design interest. The structured **braided trim** at the deep neckline and armhole emphasizes the petticoat styling.

Sunray pleating is stitched down at the hip to create a fitted waistband; the excess fabric at the bodice is folded over to create a blouson effect. The thin binding around the neckline and armhole also forms the fine **spaghetti straps**.

The handkerchief hemline with **fringed border** gives an asymmetrical appearance and, together with the bold print on silk fabric, suggests a **vintage shawl**. Bias cutting avoids the need for bust suppression, while facing at the bodice creates a streamlined neckline. Thin spaghetti straps are tied at the shoulder and left to drape, providing additional decoration.

Simple, **tabard-style** minidress with a contemporary floral-pattern fabric. **Laser-cut floral motifs** have been heat-sealed and sandwiched between layers of organdie to achieve an interesting and contemporary version of a floral print.

The bodice and shoulder straps are cut all in one with an **asymmetric** V-shaped neckline, emphasized by a self-fabric tied bow. The neckline is balanced with the diagonal underbust seam and asymmetric, deep, circular frill hem. An additional, smaller, circular **frill bow** echoes the neck detail.

A typical **baby-doll** style of sundress in a silk chiffon fabric. The bra-cup bodice has solid-colour straps reflecting the highlight colour in the print design. The dress is fully lined, and the **chiffon skirt** is lightly gathered into the underbust seam, finishing above knee level.

1 Lines of elastic detailing on the bodice define the body's contours. Elasticated to the top hip, creating a dropped waistline, the skirt is softly gathered and flared. **2** Sheer, body-skimming sundress. The embellished fabric is contrasted with solid-colour, circular-cut frills at the neckline, hip and hem to give a degree of modesty. **3** Uncomplicated, sleeveless maxi-length dress with a high V-neckline – an ideal canvas for the graduated border embroidery. **4** A bold placement print is the focal point of a simple shift-shape sundress. An elaborate beaded border trim complements the print. **5** Midi-length, sunray-pleated chiffon dress with delicate spaghetti straps and elasticated blouson waistline. **6** Broderie-anglaise lace dress with a scalloped hem and bodice. Cut as a shift, a deep ribbon is used to accentuate the high waist. **7** Supported by fine spaghetti straps, the neckline is fully gathered, forming draped cowls to hip level, with the underskirt draping to the hemline. **8** Sleeveless, scooped-neck sundress with asymmetric style lines incorporating volume in the panels to achieve drape in the bodice.

Sarong

The sarong can be traced to southern Asia, and the term originally describes the lower garment worn by both males and females in Malaysia, Indonesia and the Pacific Islands. It is usually formed from a length of fabric with a decorative panel of pattern or contrast colour woven or dyed into it. Patterns are often created through batik dyeing and ikat weaving. Similar to the Indian sari, it features a length of fabric wrapped around the body to create the garment. This style has been adapted for beach and après beach, as well as finding a place in mainstream high-summer fashion. Mimicking the tying and wrapping techniques of the sarong, designers engineer the construction through clever pattern cutting and draping devices.

The style is flattering, sometimes exposing bare shoulders or wrapped and open at the hem to create a split effect to expose the leg. Necklines vary from halter to strapless, and the length can be from knee to floor. Borders are engineered to echo the traditional styling, and bold patterns and striking colours often define the sundress version of this style.

The sarong style of sundress epitomizes holidays in the sun, and its versatility as a garment transcends day to evening. Statement jewelry and flat sandals can accessorize this look and glamorize an otherwise simple style.

This maxi-length, chiffon sarong style has an asymmetric **tied and knotted neckline** that exposes the shoulders and arms. The dress falls from the gathered neckline, with a gradually flared skirt. Definition to the shape is created by a **simple rouleau tie belt** around the waist.

The deep plunging neckline is emphasized with **metallic foil highlights**, and the animal-inspired pattern graduates from **small to large** at the hem, increasing in scale with the increased width of the skirt.

KEY CHARACTERISTICS

☑ Mimics tying and wrapping techniques of traditional sarongs

☑ Exposed shoulders and split leg

☑ Bold patterns and striking colours

1 A traditional twisted-and-knotted neckline and asymmetric knotted hip detail maximize sarong styling. **2** The garment design has become subservient to the print artwork, with the print defining the strapless bodice and A-line silhouette. **3** With no cutting or bust suppression, the dress doubles as a canvas for a digital print. The dress is pleated into a horizontal bodice supported by V-neck shoulder straps. **4** The solid-colour, wide shoulder straps wrap around the body and hold the unstructured fabric in place, creating a deconstructed look. **5** Devoré dress with semifitted bodice and full maxi-length skirt. A curved, strapless neckline is gathered into a deep, tucked neck stand. **6** An exaggerated cowl-front bodice is bias cut, creating drapery to the dropped waistline. The waistline has a contrast-colour drawstring band and supports large external pockets. **7** A halter neck and inverted V-shaped yoke support a voluminous floor-length skirt, panelled to create extra flare. **8** Halter-neck sundress with a length of fabric integrated into the seam, which is wrapped around the body to imply a sarong.

Skater

Mini in length and inspired by American ice-skating dresses of the 1950s, this style has a young appeal, with a pretty and flirty sensibility. The style is usually defined by a fitted bodice, a waist seam and a flared or pleated skirt; however, fit and flare can be achieved by inserting godets or circular cutting the skirt. Pleats can be constructed as box pleats, inverted box, sunray or knife pleats inserted into a waist seam or yoke. Permanent pleating can be achieved through heat-pressing on manmade fabrics. Soft gathers are also an option, with varying length tiers a possibility. The style of bodice and necklines is limitless, and though generally sleeveless, the dress can have short or three-quarter sleeves.

This sundress is often designed with underpetticoats that accentuate the fullness of the skirt and create a more exaggerated silhouette. Soft wovens or jersey knitted fabrics are ideal for this style. Although the silhouette is predominantly feminine, it can also have a sportier vibe, as typically seen in the Norma Kamali 1980s version.

The fitted bodice, cinched waist and short flared skirt are typical of the skater style. The curved **sweetheart neckline** is cut high and is accentuated by the deep split at centre front. The wide **box pleats**, fixed sharply to the waistband, soften as they reach the hemline, owing to the unpressed folded edge that doubles back as lining.

High-waisted **strapless bodice** with shaped panels at centre front and inserted bows at neckline. The fullness of the gathered skirt is increased by a **layered petticoat**. Vintage-style printed florals with border hemline contrast with a tartan petticoat and braided trim.

KEY CHARACTERISTICS

☑ Fitted bodice with flared or pleated skirt

☑ Mini length

☑ Underpetticoats to accentuate the fullness of the skirt

1 Pinafore bib front with halter neck and waistband that amplifies the hourglass figure. The sharp box pleats sewn into the waistband contradict the unstructured folded hem. 2 The bodice is gathered into the waistband, and cutout panels at the side seam exaggerate a slim waist. The gathered skirt and layered petticoat hemline complete the skater look. 3 Micro-minidress with flared skirt cut on the bias. The fitted bodice is faced with an integrated bra to create bust support and enhance cleavage. 4 A stripe print runs horizontally, accentuating the fullness of the skirt. Style lines created by darts run on an angle from waist seam to bust. 5 Strapless drop-waisted bodice with boned panels, which incorporate bust suppression and provide added support. 6 The scooped neckline and dropped shoulder, with keyhole opening and ties, reinforce the retro look. 7 Sundress with a princess-seam fitted bodice and mini-length, full circular skirt. A vertical laser-cut design adds interest. 8 A busy microprint is used for a fitted bodice with open neckline, contrasting the larger-scale pattern used for the gathered full skirt.

Tea dress

Nothing epitomizes summer like a floral tea dress. Afternoon tea, a fashionable pursuit of the rich, was adopted as an aspirational activity of the lower classes of society. Taking tea required a new wardrobe, and the tea dress became an important symbol of this ritual. This style transcends fashion trends and is embraced and adapted by designers from season to season. Its versatility as a sundress and its wealth of historical references allows for reinvention while maintaining its vintage appeal. The tea dress is traditionally fit and flare, sometimes cut on the bias, and can have a variety of bodice styles and necklines and sport different collar shapes and styles. Hemlines are traditionally to the knee, or variations of calf length, but can be subverted to mini length for a younger market.

Feminine and pretty, the sundress version would be made from lightweight wovens, usually printed in floral patterns, though geometrics, paisleys and combinations of prints work well for a quintessential look. Embroidery and lace trims often embellish the bodice, with covered buttons and rouleau loops an additional feature. Gathered frills and circular-cut flounces can also add design interest. Bodice designs accentuate the feminine feel with pin tucks and underbust seams with softly gathered bra cups. Half-tie belts can be inserted into the side seams and tied in a bow to add interest to the back view. Side- and back-seam zipped fastenings are common features, ensuring the decorative interest on the front bodice and sleeve is not interrupted, since the dress is seen to its best advantage across a tea table.

Fitted bodice with dart suppression, wide V-neck, and set-in capped sleeves. Shaped from the waist seam, the **A-line skirt** ends at knee length and fastens at side seam by an invisible zip. The pretty print, in crisp medium-weight woven cotton, is complemented with an **asymmetrical belt** at the waist.

The V-neckline draws attention to the **centre-front seam** and the centre-front, thigh-length split. The skirt has a **curved yoke** that balances the neckline.

Alternative bodice and sleeves: wrap front with short kimono sleeves

KEY CHARACTERISTICS

☑ **Fit and flare or draped and gathered**

☑ **Feminine and pretty**

☑ **Knee or calf length**

☑ **Soft woven fabric, ditsy florals and polka-dot prints**

1 A basic semifitted shape with short, set-in sleeves and a subtle A-line skirt. Unusual oversized pocket openings add interest and drama. **2** Straps cross at the neck to create a halter neck. An opaque top layer of silk chiffon in a soft floral creates a feminine and fluttery look. **3** A simple fit-and-flare shape is offset by a geometric embroidered pattern and an elaborate beaded neckline. The colours are bright, feminine and summery. **4** Floral lace appliqué creates a delicate three-dimensional look that is balanced with the simplicity of a jewel neck and A-line skirt. The red-and-navy striped waistband reinforces the flag influence. **5** Deep V-neck, high-waisted sundress in cream silk with diagonally cut panels trimmed in red tape. **6** Ditsy-floral shirtdress with scallop-trimmed collar, decorative lace-panelled yoke and deep lace hemline border **7** Fit-and-flare dress with button-through front fastening, wide neckline and short puffed sleeves. The Peter Pan lace collar and lace appliquéd detail on the bodice and pocket trims add a quirky element. **8** Combinations of mismatched vintage prints create an eclectic layered effect.

KNIT DRESS

Whether figure-hugging or oversized, the knitted dress has become an important fashion staple, crossing the boundaries of sportswear through to evening glamour.

Heavy-gauge, double-breasted coatdress with short set-in puffed sleeves, fastened with a self-yarn tubular tie belt. An ornate ribbed revers collar is edged with a scalloped trim. The crinoline-style skirt creates volume to emphasize the small fitted waist. The garment shaping is created and disguised within the crochet-knitted stitch.

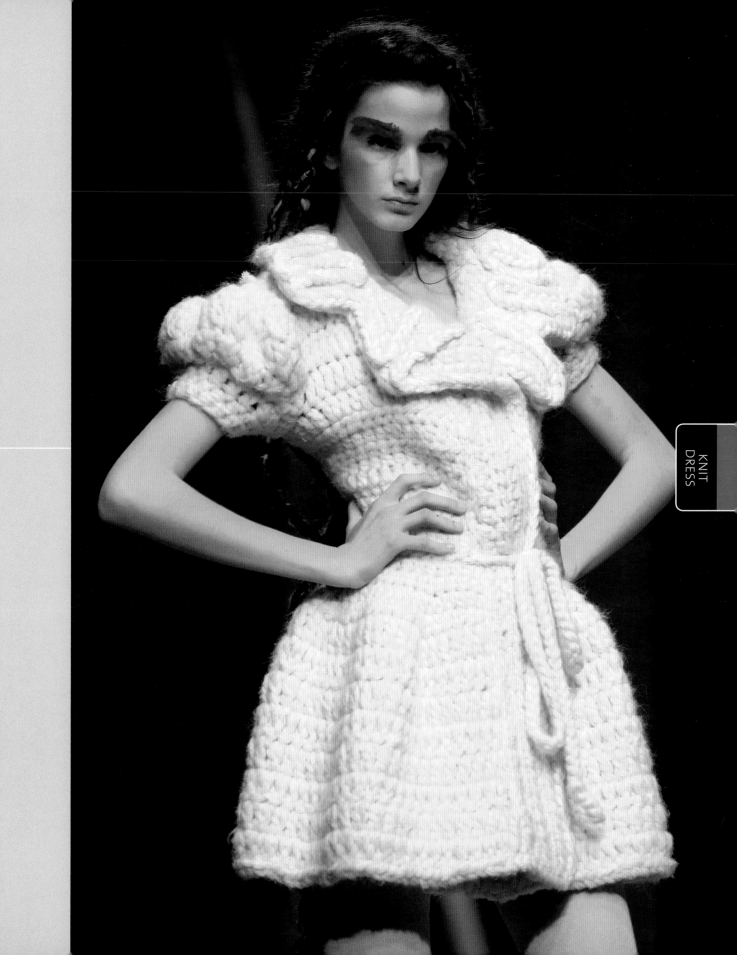

In context

The model Lauren Hutton epitomized the sexy 1970s, and Halston was an iconic designer known for his stunning yet simple knits. Here, silk jersey drips over Hutton in the form of a deep-V halter with a fabric twist under the bust, and a high slit from the front hem.

nnovations in technology and the creative potential of knit structures have allowed the knitted dress to evolve from the humble origins of underwear to the prominence of the mainstream fashion runway. Knit's inherent elasticity, enabling the fabric to stretch, expand and return to its original shape, allows for a relaxed ease of movement, which means that it can be worn casually in a sportswear context, meet the practical needs of office-to-home day wear or be dressed up for body-conscious evening glamour.

The more relaxed silhouette of the 1920s saw tunic-shaped knits emerging, and Madeleine Vionnet's bias cutting, showing the contours of the body, translated through to the knitted dresses of the 1930s. The make-do-and-mend era of the 1940s encouraged women to hand-knit dresses, the patterns for which were published in magazines, while, in contrast, Hollywood was inspiring the design of glamorous knitted full-length jersey dinner dresses. Coco Chanel came to epitomize the twinset, often including knitted dresses in her collection.

The skinny-rib sweaterdress of the Swinging Sixties was epitomized in Mary Quant's London collection, in parallel to Dorothée Bis and Sonia Rykiel in Paris. In the 1980s, the power dressing of body-conscious women in gyms encouraged designers such as Azzedine Alaïa to design body-conscious knitted dresses with references to corsets, and Norma Kamali to develop jersey-knit sportswear-inspired dresses. In the UK, Bodymap and Pam Hogg were designing dance-inspired jersey-knit dresses.

In the 1990s, Japanese designers from Rei Kawakubo of Comme des Garçons and Junya Watanabe to Kansai Yamamoto and Issey Miyake pushed the boundaries of the design of the knitted dress. Miyake's A-POC (A Piece of Cloth) range saw the construction of the garment from a single piece of cloth.

Comfort and agility are key attractions in knit dressing. While creating a slim and attractively clinging silhouette, the knit dress with Henley collar and slim, shawl-collar jacket allow for movement and ease.

Design considerations

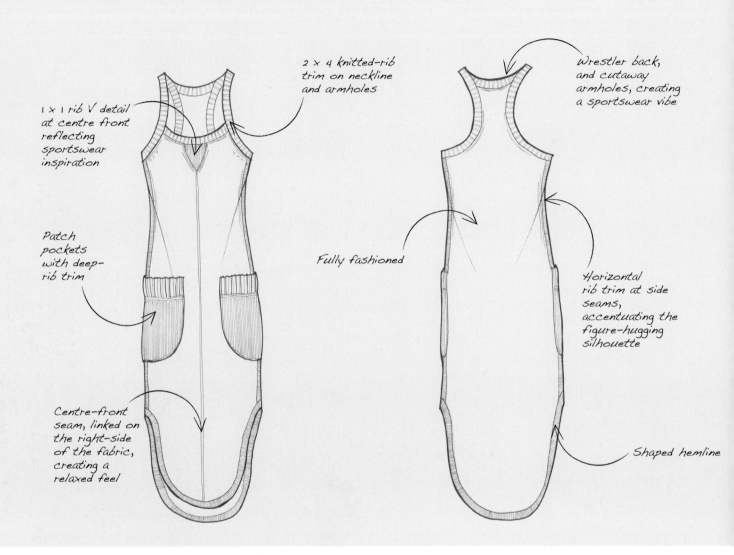

1 x 1 rib V detail at centre front reflecting sportswear inspiration

2 x 4 knitted-rib trim on neckline and armholes

Patch pockets with deep-rib trim

Centre-front seam, linked on the right-side of the fabric, creating a relaxed feel

Wrestler back, and cutaway armholes, creating a sportswear vibe

Fully fashioned

Horizontal rib trim at side seams, accentuating the figure-hugging silhouette

Shaped hemline

Versatility The versatility of the knit dress provides enormous scope for design expression, with the stretch-performance qualities allowing for greater possibilities than a less forgiving woven fabric. Shaping can be factored into the design detailing, surface, structure and decoration, removing the need for darts and other methods of compression.

Surface decoration Techniques such as intarsia, jacquard, Fair Isle, cable, lace, weave, Swiss-darning embroidery, crochet, macramé and dyeing offer design versatility in pattern and surface decoration.

Fabrics Diversity of knit processes, from hand to machine, means a variety of stitch structures and textures is available, forming fabric types such as felt, fleece, rib, double or single jersey, plain or purl, and cloque or blister fabrics.

Qualities A variation of gauges determines the weight of fabric and density of the knit structure. The breadth of yarn qualities, from manmade to natural fibres, with combination blends and different finishes, presents tremendous scope for texture, drape and handle. Bouclé or slub yarns can add texture and colour, and dyeing techniques such as ombré and space dyeing can give an ikat appearance when knitted.

Rib polo
neck

Saddle-shape full-
fashioned armholes

V-shape front
and back yoke

Cable stitch
detailing on
front view

Relaxed fitting
silhouette
finishing at
mini length

2 x 2 rib cuffs and welt

Fully fashioned Fully fashioned knitwear is engineered and shaped to size during knitting. The fashioning marks, or shaping, are evident at the point of increasing or decreasing. The welts and cuffs are integral, with only the collar or plackets added afterwards. Linking is used as a joining method for shoulders and collars, which is a stitch-per-stitch joint. The garment sides, sleeves and underarms are cup-seamed, stitching the edges of knit pieces together. This method decreases wastage and is used for high-end garments using more expensive yarns.

Cut and sew The cut-and-sew technique is the quickest and cheapest method of knit construction, where garment pattern pieces are cut to size from lengths of knitted fabric from a flat bed or circular cloth. Seams are overlocked prior to sewing or linking to prevent stitches from unravelling, but they can look bulky.

This method increases fabric wastage and is generally used in mass production.

Complete garment The complete-garment technique is the same as fully fashioned but without seams. Garment panels are knitted simultaneously on the machine together with cuffs, collars and welts, with the body tube in the middle and two sleeves either side, each with a separate cone of yarn. The garment leaves the knitting machine completed.

Knit

The knit dress crosses all categories, from casual to formal, and can be worn during the day through to evening. New and exciting yarn developments allow the knit dress to be designed for hot summer climates and adapted for cold winter months. The designer has control over all aspects of the design process, from textile development to garment silhouette, with huge potential for cutting-edge and creative masterpieces.

Experimenting with combinations of texture, stitch, colour and pattern, Kenzo and Missoni are examples of design labels known for their production of exuberant knitted collections. Creative and glamorous, the fine, weblike knitted structures of Julien Macdonald's signature dresses are fit for the red carpet. Mark Fast and Louise Goldin explore innovative techniques to develop exciting new garment shapes and stitch structures that continue to push boundaries. Celebrated for his originality and innovation, Azzedine Alaïa experiments with various manmade yarns to create ingenious, dense-yet-pliable knitted structures, described as perforated, blistered and pleated, which embrace complex tailoring techniques and enhance the female form.

Heavy-gauge jersey knit coatdress with scooped neckline, long sleeves and front-placket opening. Two breast patch pockets and **oversized pockets** at hip level are trimmed with **large press-stud fastenings** with reinforced topstitching. Bound edgings feature strongly, as well as the twin-needle topstitching.

Fine-gauge, knitted jersey, drop-waisted **1920s-inspired** dress falling just below the knee. The contrast-colour, bold **graphic banding** adds interest and gives definition.

Alternative neckline and sleeves: ribbed, knitted collar with raglan short sleeves

KEY CHARACTERISTICS

☑ **Fully fashioned or cut and sew**

☑ **Fine to heavy gauge**

☑ **Textured stitches, cables and ribs**

☑ **Fair Isle and intarsia patterns**

1   2   3   4   5   6   7   8

KNIT DRESS

1 Contrast chenille and rayon fit-and-flare dress. The dress is complemented by an exaggerated scarf-like striped neckline. 2 Exaggerated shoulders are further emphasized with a self-yarn waterfall frill. A similar frill creates a peplum effect on an otherwise body-conscious shape. 3 The fit-and-flare houndstooth knitted pattern suggests a woven cloth, but shaping and volume have been achieved through full-fashioned knit shaping. 4 Fine-gauge jersey, drop-waisted dress suggesting a two-piece outfit. The pressed knife-pleated skirt finishes just above the knee, epitomizing 'granny chic'. 5 Openwork-lace patterning creates changes in scale and patterning throughout the dress. A picot edging trims the hemline, sleeves and neckline. 6 Oversized shapes are created with a scooped neckline and dropped shoulder. Contrast exaggerated cuffs and patch pockets create graphic colour blocking. 7 Tucking gives a seersucker effect, with contrasting tensions creating a blistering relief over a simple T-shirt shape. 8 Ribbed pinafore dress with contrast-colour argyle-inspired pattern. The skirt is panelled to give flare.

> Gathered tiers in black-and-white striped horizontal bands, and contrasting **stocking stitch and rib**, mimic a two-piece. Binding at the neckline and armholes also creates the shoulder straps of the dress.

Gathered **knitted tiers** are created and layered to form the hemline of the dress, contrasting with an **eyelet patterned knit**. On a smaller scale the tiers are used horizontally around the bustline and to edge the neckline and form short sleeves.

Mimicking a two-piece, the horizontal **knitted rib** is gathered to form a double layer of tiers at the **dropped waistline**. The gathered rib also creates a tiered hemline and decorates the pocket openings.

Alternative bodice detail: square neckline with wide shoulder straps and knitted waterfall frill

Fine-gauge knitted dress shaped to fit and flare to knee length. The **scooped boatneck**, round armholes and **open-lace effect** stitch combinations make this an ideal summer-weight garment.

Graphic grey-and-black striping runs horizontally and contrasts with a thinner stripe running vertically at the sleeves and side panel. Wide magyar sleeves are cut into a **racer-style** armhole and a deep black rib **accentuates the waist**. A vertical panel is set into the side seams to give a peplum effect.

1 Skinny, ribbed turtleneck sweaterdress. The dress increases in volume at the hip towards the hemline, where it gathers into a knitted binding. 2 A plain jersey panel cuts diagonally through the middle of the dress from shoulder to hip, contrasting texture and colour. 3 Graphic colour blocking in panels give a body-conscious sportswear feel. The concealed pockets with zip openings accentuate the active, athletic vibe. 4 This dress is cut as separate pieces and joined at the high waist seam to create a fitted bodice and flared skirt. 5 Full-fashioned knitted minidress with use of diverse stitch textures to define panels. 6 Fine-gauge, voluminous, relaxed maxi-length dress with variegated stripe mixed with Fair Isle-patterned panels. Style definition is achieved by drawstring knitted tapes that outline the shapes. 7 A tiered-lace gathered skirt is joined seamlessly with a knitted sweater bodice with polo-shirt collar and placket. 8 Use of strong colour blocking delineates the drop-waisted silhouette. The stripe helps to create a sporty vibe, which is offset by the feminine lace-effect striped skirt.

KNIT DRESS

Mixing tucks, lace, Fair Isle and rib-knit patterns in multicoloured horizontal stripes in fine-gauge linen and cotton. The mini-length dress is shaped to **flare out** at the hem and cuffs, but the waist and sleeves are fitted. The knit increases again at the bust and the top of the sleeve to give a ruched sleeve head. The applied lace neck placket is cut wide to give a **dropped shoulder**.

Heavy-gauge bouclé yarn gives the appearance of hand-knitting, with four **cabled panels** running centre front on a stocking-stitch base. The cables split at the waist to suggest V-shaping, while ribbing at the waist provides fit. The cable outlines the raglan shaping to reinforce the full-fashioned detailing.

Hand-knitted and felted, the simple grey mélange sleeveless dress is **flared** to just above knee level. The cast-on hem, cast-off neckline and unbound armholes maintain the pared-down aesthetic. Large three-dimensional **knitted and crochet** stemmed daisies decorate the hemline.

Sweater

A sweaterdress is an elongated version of the sweater and can be worn as an oversized garment or as a semifitted, body-skimming version. Traditionally, the sweaterdress is an autumn/winter item in a heavy gauge, though finer-gauge versions are a consideration for spring/summer collections. Necklines and trims reflect the nature of the sweater, with versions such as the turtle, polo, crew or V-neck. Predominantly this style is long-sleeved with ribbed cuffs. Armholes and sleeve heads may be set-in, raglan, saddle shoulder, dolman, dropped shoulder or batwing. Knitted-stitch structures, such as cabling, Fair Isle and lace, can be applied, as well as intarsia and embellishment.

The sweaterdress made an appearance as far back as the 1920s, but was often worn as an oversized twinset. During the beatnik 1950s, the exaggerated proportions of the sloppy-joe sweater, often borrowed from boyfriends' wardrobes and usually worn to the knee with capri pants or slimline ski pants, was the forerunner of the contemporary sweaterdress. The statement skinny-ribbed sweaterdress, as epitomized by Mary Quant, Dorothée Bis and Sonia Rykiel in the 1960s, was worn well above the knee, sometimes belted and accessorized with tights or over-the-knee socks. The 1980s sweaterdress referenced the graphic impact of the 1920s styles and echoed the oversized silhouette of the 1950s, but with deeper armholes, wider sleeves and emphasized shoulders, often using shoulder pads. Pictorial images using intarsia and embellishment were prevalent.

KEY CHARACTERISTICS

- ☑ Elongated sweater
- ☑ Sweater necklines and trims
- ☑ Predominantly long-sleeved
- ☑ Heavy gauge

Body-conscious, mid-thigh bandage sweater dress. Individual bandages are knitted using the jacquard technique in alternating scales of **houndstooth pattern**. Hardware pieces are woven and sewn between each bandage, adding texture and dimension to the dress.

A bohemian feel is produced by the use of **braided fringing** knitted into the dress, running horizontally around the body. The bodice, turtleneck and short set-in sleeves are knitted in a tuck stitch, and chenille yarns are used to create a **soft feel**.

1 Fleece-back sweater minidress with self-colour 1x1-rib cuff and hem. A contrasting rib neck insert creates a turtleneckline. **2** This nautical-inspired boyfriend sweater with a deep V-striped front has rows of two different types of cable knits and a flirtatiously short hem. **3** Basket-weave, hand-knitted dress with a 3x2-rib turtleneck and stocking-stitch set-in sleeves. The uneven hem fringing is achieved by knitted rouleau lengths and knitted strips to give a 1920s flapper silhouette. **4** Garter stitch is used to trim the neckline and cuffs and in a deep band at the hemline, which extends the flare of the skirt. Inverted-V pointelle patterning on the skirt emphasizes the A-line shape. **5** Casual oversized sweaterdress in grey angora with dropped shoulder line, long sleeves and cowl-neck collar. **6** Fine-gauge, mini-length sweaterdress with a soft, high-rolled polo neckline. Elongated sleeves have integral fingerless gloves. **7** Typical sweater minidress translated in a bold, wide horizontal stripe, which has been carefully matched across the armhole and sleeve head. **8** An archetypal boyfriend sweaterdress. The deep and wide V-neck falls off the shoulder.

Soft grey mini-length sweaterdress with contrast horizontal **chevron stripes** in blue chenille and gold Lurex yarns. The long sleeves have been set into the armhole and **gathered at the wrist** to create a blouson effect. The boatneck is finished with a narrow rib, but the hemline has been left as a simple cast-on edge.

Bold **intarsia-patterned** sweaterdress in heavy-gauge yarn. Diagonal shapes feature heavily in tribal-influenced geometric patterns. **Bright colours** give a stark contrast to a mirror-image design. The pattern has been designed to match the body and sleeves, and the drop-shoulder line is disguised within the pattern.

Sleeveless, horizontal **striped** minidress with a high turtleneck. The heavy-gauge knit has been **felted** to create a dense, soft feel. The blue-and-grey stripe changes to grey and black at the bodice and again at the shoulder to give focus to the top of the garment.

Alternative neckline and sleeves: split turtleneck with raglan short sleeves

< Lively hand-knitted sweaterdress with a **homespun craft aesthetic**, mixing varying weights and compositions of yarns and colours to create an individual, slightly **ad-hoc piece**.

KNIT DRESS

Fine-gauge silk-jersey sweaterdress with contrast colour-blocked panel inserts. The focus is on the asymmetrical hemline created by a shorter front-panel insert, creating a **layered look**. Contrasting rust-coloured inserts at front panel mimic a cardigan placket and create another layer at the front hemline. The heavy-gauge **ribbed turtleneck** collar extends to a circular yoke, adding to the layering story.

T-shirt

Named after the shape of the garment's outline, and universally considered to be a casual item with references to sportswear, the T-shirt dress can also sit in a relaxed evening-wear setting and be an ideal blank canvas for costume jewelry or embellishment. It is always made in a jersey fabric in varying weights and compositions, though can be either circular knitted or panelled with side seams. The fit can be oversized – sometimes belted to alter the silhouette – or cut in a more body-conscious manner. Dress lengths vary from mini to maxi, and sleeves from cap to cuff length. Jersey-ribbed trims are common on the neckline, but can be added to the sleeves and the hem.

With its foundations in circular-knit hosiery manufacturing, the T-shirt dress evolved from the new streamlined silhouette of the 1920s. Based on the chemise, the T-shirt dress reflected the new athleticism and informal dressing of the age. With advancements in engineering, the speed of mass-produced fine-gauge knitting techniques and cut-and-sew finishing the T-shirt dress emerged as part of an ensemble or twinset.

Progressing through the decades, the dress was a feature of the beatnik subculture of the 1950s, and was heralded, then subverted, in the 1970s when punk established itself as an important fashion statement, and again in the 1980s when its blank canvas became a vehicle for political slogans and statements (such as in the work of Katharine Hamnett), as well as advertising and branding.

The silhouette of this T-shirt dress gives the impression of **two styles colliding**. For example, one slim-fitted, set-in sleeve contrasts with the drop-shoulder, wider T-shirt sleeve on the other side. The neckline is a combination of a V and a scooped, rounded neck, and is offset by the asymmetrical drape of the skirt.

Traditional tubular knit jersey body-conscious dress with cap sleeves, taking direct reference from the **basic white staple** jersey T-shirt. The basic dress is an ideal **blank canvas** for substantial styling statements.

KEY CHARACTERISTICS

- ☑ **Elongated T-shirt**
- ☑ **Casual, with references to sportswear**
- ☑ **Jersey fabric**

1 Silk-jersey dress with cowl neck and asymmetric draped leg-of-mutton sleeve. Leather neck strapping contrasts with the drape of the fabric, creating a strong focal point. **2** Oversized, foil-printed mini jersey dress. An exaggerated long sleeve, dropped shoulder and deep scoop V emphasize the relaxed feel. **3** A sarong-inspired silhouette playing with cultural references within its asymmetric style lines of wrap and drape. **4** A young and sporty T-shirt dress with a dropped waist and gathered frill skirt. The rib-trimmed round neck and set-in short sleeves are a direct translation of the basic T-shirt shape. **5** An asymmetric grown-on overlay, which ties at one shoulder, covers a deconstructed mini vest dress. Gathered fabric at waist level creates volume and drape. **6** Oversized dress with low- and wide-cut V-neck with exaggerated drop shoulder and elbow-length kimono sleeves. **7** Mélange jersey fit-and-flare T-shirt dress – an ideal backdrop for graphic logos or slogan prints. **8** Liquid-jersey dress with a grown-on dropped shoulder line and a wide, round neckline. The oversized fit accentuates the natural drape in the fabric.

> Magyar-style, long-sleeved silk-jersey dress with boatneck and dropped waistline. The **nautical influences** continue with the bib-fronted, multibutton fastening. The hemline extends and doubles back to create an envelope-shaped draped front, forming an overskirt effect.

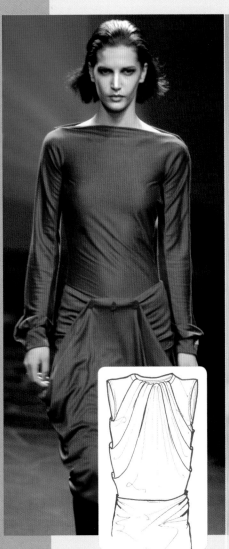

Alternative bodice and armhole: sleeveless bodice with a round neck and draped fabric from the neckline, around the sides, to the centre-back seam

Asymmetrical T-shape, with a **twisted knot** at the neckline to give drape to the front of the dress. The dropped shoulder line forms a capped sleeve to continue the relaxed, **oversized silhouette**.

KNIT DRESS

Oversized, light grey mélange-jersey dress, finishing below the knee. **The zipped-front funnel** neckline and drawstring waist and hem are punctuated by a complementary pink trim. The elbow-length rolled sleeves re-establish the relaxed, **sporty feel** of this garment.

The interesting combination of diagonal and vertical stripes is designed to give the impression that part of the garment is cut on the bias. This is achieved through **punch-card patterning** and partial knitting to create **directional striping**. Excess fabric is achieved by increasing then gathering the surplus to create drape at the front waist.

The underlying **sports vibe** of the black-and-orange knee-length, V-neck T-shirt styling is juxtaposed with **printed scrolls and cherubs**. The use of tone within the print gives the impression of a raised surface.

Tank

The tank is a sleeveless sweaterdress or jersey vest, and an extension in length of the tank top. Derived from the vest, the tank is normally a spring/summer item and is worn as an individual garment, though it can be layered over another garment with sleeves and worked as a pinafore dress.

Vivienne Westwood reshaped the T-shirt to create a tank dress, and the punk scene explored the adaption of garments by deconstruction through cutting, fraying and utilizing the rolled raw edges of the jersey. Further exploration of the tank shape was made popular in the 1980s by Madonna, who layered tank over tank with deep armholes over exposed underwear or swimwear. The garment shape has since been refined and developed from sportswear references, using jersey fabrics that take on performance features that originated in sportswear or dance wear, such as Airtex and spandex. The armholes are cut for design styling, such as racer, and, along with the neckline, finished with ribbed detail or facings, sometimes with invisible or integrated bra support.

This loosely fitted tank dress with a deep, round neckline has a **sporty aesthetic**. The use of **heavy black trim** creates a deep V at the neck and slims the silhouette, creating the impression of a sundress. Deep pockets are set into the side panel at hip level, continuing the relaxed feel.

Body-conscious, mid-thigh tank-inspired dress. The **geometric pattern** is achieved by reversing and tucking **double-faced bandages** down the centre to create a three-dimensional, two-tone effect. Jacquard bandages complete the neckline, hem and side seams.

KEY CHARACTERISTICS

☑ **Elongated vest**

☑ **Sleeveless**

☑ **Loose fitting or body conscious**

☑ **Can be layered over other garments**

1 The simple, oversized vest shape in foil-printed jersey is influenced by the 1920s flapper. The low-cut neckline and hemline have been laser cut. 2 This understated simple tank style, in fine, black linen knit, has a lightweight, semitransparent appearance that skims the body. 3 Separately knitted bandages with houndstooth patterns are linked together with individually sewn hardware

pieces. 4 Bandages in different colours are attached together to create an oversized geometric pattern. The neckline and shoulder straps are made from narrow bandages and hardware pieces. 5 Lace-knit halter-neck dress with a fitted empire-line bodice, which has been adorned with a floral corsage. Fringing gives a variety of surface interest. 6 Individually knitted

bandages are woven through hardware pieces, resulting in an all-over chainmail effect. 7 A drawstring cord at the waist gives shape to this loose dress and allows the bodice to blouson over the skirt. The cutaway shoulders create a vest effect. 8 Basketwoven knitted bandages in different colours create a one-of-a-kind piece with an intricate geometric pattern.

> Hand-knitted, heavy-gauge tank worn layered over a vest. The **ribbed hem** is knitted on smaller needles to create a tighter edge; however, the stitches get bigger towards the top to create a much looser, open fabric. Strips of woven fabric and heavy-slub yarn are used to create a **handmade**, artisan aesthetic.

Heavy-weight jersey mini-length tank dress with a scooped neckline. Two patched pockets with long, **multicoloured fringes** inset into the seams decorate the hemline of the front of the dress.

1 The crisp fabric belt contrasts with the languid drape of the wide silk jersey hemline. **2** Versatile ankle-length tank dress in contrast-colour, medium-weight jersey with side pockets. Lighter-weight jersey is gathered and inset into the zigzag bodice then layered. **3** Lightweight jersey tank dress cut on the bias and set into a high yoke with inset V panel at centre front.

The embellishment cascades to the hem.
4 Tank dress with dropped waist and knitted bodice attached to a pleated silk skirt. The dress is extended and duplicated, then folded back, creating a multiple effect. **5** Knitted tank dress that grows into a mirrored duplicate. The second dress is left open at the side seams and worn over the first dress, folding back on itself at the hemline.

6 Grey angora-mix tank dress with scooped neckline, deep armholes and single breast pocket.
7 A patchwork of multicoloured, textured scraps of knitting are stitched together in a random jigsaw of shapes to create a mini-length tank dress.
8 Nautical-inspired V-neck tank with horizontal stripes of crochet lace. The alternate patterns and widths are trimmed with stripes of knitted rib.

Polo

The oversized shift in heavy jersey knit with a **centre-front zip** opening is belted to fit the waist. The polo collar, shoulder yoke panels and pocket flaps are trimmed with contrasting fabric.

The **ribbed collar** and short rib-edged sleeves define this as a polo dress. The contrast-print, solid-colour panels give a **body-conscious effect**.

The polo dress originated from the machine-knitted Isis tennis shirt, which was first produced by British manufacturer John Smedley as early as the 1920s. Originally fully fashioned, like its shirt equivalent, the polo dress was defined by the three-buttoned placket, knitted-in one-piece opening at the front, attached to a shirt neck. The traditional short sleeve is finished with a ribbed cuff with optional set-in sleeve or alternative saddle shoulder. The style was later worn for the sport polo, hence the name. The Lacoste polo shirt became a trademark synonymous with the preppy look and validated with a place in mainstream fashion in the late 1970s and early 1980s by labels such as Perry Ellis and Ralph Lauren. The polo styling has been adopted by brands that represent understated classic styling and embrace the preppy look, such as Tommy Hilfiger, J. Crew and Jack Wills.

The fabrics used reflect sportswear styling, such as Airtex mesh jersey or knitted argyle patterned, ribbed or cabled, often sporting a branded embroidered logo. Other styling options include an inset or patch breast-pocket detail with ribbed trim. Sometimes pockets can be inset into the side seams of the dress. The polo dress is rarely worn below knee length, because the style represents a sportswear aesthetic.

KEY CHARACTERISTICS

- ☑ Elongated polo shirt
- ☑ Buttoned placket, knitted in one piece, opening at the front, attached to shirt neck
- ☑ Sportswear styling and aesthetic

1 Asymmetrical double-tiered, circular-cut frilled hem with graduating depth that complements the diagonal cut. Exposed zip tape at centre-front neck and a stand collar mimic the traditional polo shirt. **2** Contrast colours help to establish the sportswear feel. Despite the lack of a front placket opening, the ribbed collar is unmistakably polo inspired. **3** A subverted polo shirt with three-button placket and shirt neck with exaggerated proportions. The embellished fur gives it a whimsical twist. **4** Printed lightweight-jersey polo dress with short capped sleeves and a flared skirt. The green rib collar and deep dropped waistband contrast with the print. **5** Ribbed-jersey bodice with collar, four-buttoned placket and long sleeves, taking inspiration from the polo dress but creating a more feminine and formal version. **6** Bound with a contrast taping, the bib front extends to the curved hemline, crossing over the back at the hips to form the skirt of the dress. **7** Soft mercerized-cotton, polo-inspired vest cut from large rectangles with ribbed collar, bound armholes and hem. **8** Soft, feminine take on the polo dress, tapered to flare to the hemline.

Body conscious/tube/sheath

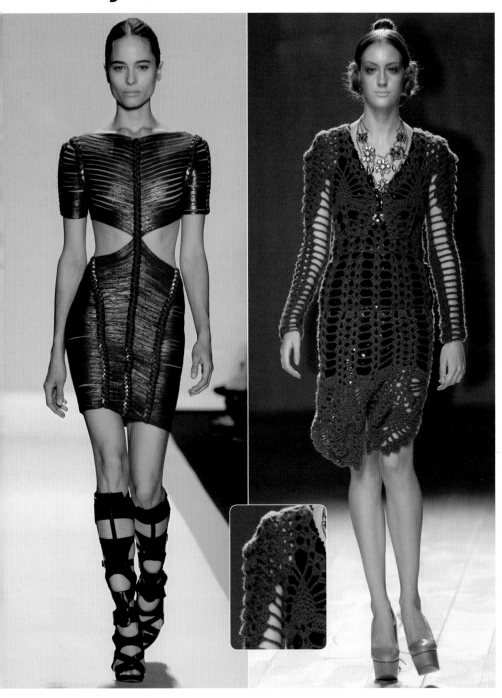

The body-conscious trend was fuelled in the 1980s by a culture promoting the ideal body – a body that demanded appreciation in figure-hugging designs. Norma Kamali brought body-conscious garments out of the domain of dance- and sportswear and into mainstream fashion. Azzedine Alaïa was influential in introducing stretch and tubular-knitted garments into mainstream fashion, with a focus on clothes that enhanced the wearer's shape, creating curves in all the right places through the use of advanced knitted textiles, clever seaming and perfect fit. Another popular technique, embraced by designers such as Pam Hogg, used colour-blocked panels instead of seams. Hervé Léger showed his impressive 'bandage' dress in 1989, a sleek dress that looked like it had been made from elasticated bandages wrapped around the body. British designer Julien Macdonald skimmed the body with gossamer knitted, complex, weblike lace structures and, more recently, knitwear designer Mark Fast has taken the crown as king of knitted body-conscious fashion with his figure-enhancing statement pieces.

The body-conscious, and particularly sheath, styles are at their most dramatic when worn full length for evening wear. The body-conscious style can be practical and comfortable for day wear, working equally as well around the knee- or mini-length. When translated in jersey fabric, body-conscious seaming and colour blocking can adopt a younger, sportier vibe. Sleeve lengths can vary from long and skinny to capped, sleeveless and strapped. Necklines maintain the inherent simplicity of the shape, with scooped, horseshoe and round necks being the most common.

Metallic-foiled bandages are braided together using the **macramé** technique. Each bandage is then secured by hand to a stretch-mesh base. The result is a body-conscious, one-of-a-kind couture dress.

Open-lace and laddering effects create design detailing and integrate the shaping. With a deep V-neck and set-in armhole, the knit-stitch detailing on the sleeve head gives the effect of a **leg-of-mutton sleeve**. The stitch structure creates a scalloped effect at the hem and neckline.

KEY CHARACTERISTICS

- ☑ Enhance body shape with advanced knitted construction
- ☑ Clever seaming and use of innovative technology for perfect fit
- ☑ New fibres and threads with inherent stretch qualities

1 Knitted bandages are linked together to create this form-fitting style. Hardware pieces woven into the body of the dress add embellishment. 2 The drape of the cowl extends to waist level, with the drape continuing into the skirt, creating a soft, fluid silhouette. 3 Knitted-jersey tunic dress with contrast colour blocking to create graphic impact. The turtleneck and capped sleeve trimmed in red, and the white yoke panel, create accents. 4 Vertically running bandages are inserted into the hip and thigh area to create an exaggerated hourglass shape. The surface of each bandage is flocked, adding a luxurious dimension. 5 Bandages in variegated widths are combined with hand-woven inserts that wrap over one shoulder and run down the side seam. 6 Nude-colour rhinestone-embellished fabric stretches over the body to form a strapless dress. Ruching at the sides creates movement and a twist at the bust adds interest. 7 Bandage panels are blocked with metallic liquid-jersey and sheer stretch-mesh panels in this form-fitting dress. 8 Individual bandages are woven through hardware pieces at the side and rib cage.

> Strapless dress with built-in bust support. Individually knitted bandages are linked together to follow and highlight the curves of the **female form**. The waist and centre-front skirt detail is made from multiple narrow bandages held together with **hardware pieces**.

High-twist rayon yarn is knitted into individual bandages that are linked together to create this **form-fitting** dress that sculpts and enhances the body shape. The **tonal leather harness** worn on top defines the waistline and highlights the silhouette.

Separately knitted and foiled bandages are **wrapped, linked and woven** together to create this unique body-contouring dress. The **metallic finish** of the bandages adds definition and dimension to each detail.

Individual bandages are linked together to create this form-fitting dress. Contrasting bandages with a **three-dimensional rubberized print** are attached on top, highlighting the silhouette and accentuating the curves.

Constructed from signature Hervé Léger bandages, this form-fitting dress has **corsetry inspired** style lines that restrain and contour the body. Open-mesh, laddered **macramé panels** embellished with metal beads are inserted at the hip and shoulder.

1 The halter neckline of the sheath dress is gathered by shoestring straps that tie at the back.
2 The column shape is broken up by a diagonal seam with a draped frill from shoulder to waist, accentuated by contrast inverted colouring.
3 A simple column-shaped dress that is broken up by a revealing, deep slash to the hip. 4 Figure-clinging sheath dress with a high neckline and elongated sleeves. A diamond-shaped cutout makes the dress backless and breaks up the solid column silhouette. 5 Multicoloured crochet circles create an artisan look. The simple tubular shape is an ideal vehicle for such a complex pattern. 6 The curved split of the dress gives a petal effect at the hemline. Fitted at the bodice to accentuate the contours of the body, the strapless effect reveals the cleavage, while a yoke attached at the underarm suggests a separate shrug. 7 A black sheath dress broken up by geometric colour blocking at the hip and neck. The split to above the knee allows for ease of movement. 8 This multistrapped knit dress has a dramatic cutaway at the waist that is balanced visually by the feathered bottom-half of the skirt.

KNIT DRESS

Use of full-fashioning creates contrasting horizontal and vertical striping that fit and complement the curves of the body. The column effect is accentuated with an **elongated silhouette**, from high neck to ankle length.

Alternative technique and bodice: colour blocking has been translated into rib texture with cutaway armholes and spaghetti straps

The illusion of multiple garments is created with the use of **varying gauges, yarns and colours**, with rib, cable and stocking stitches, and the use of full-fashioning. The colour blocking helps to accentuate the body contours with waist and bodice definition.

An ankle-length sheath dress in **bronze Lurex**. The demure high, round neckline and elbow-length sleeves are contradicted by the **clingy, reflective fabric** that reveals every curve of the body.

Separately knitted bandages in variegated widths and different shades of **grey ombré** are combined with hand-woven inserts inspired by the **lacing** on athletic footwear.

Panels in **varying colours and weights** contrast matt and shine. The jersey skirt in a heavier weight suggests **overalls** with a narrow bib front that is incorporated into the crew neck.

Alternative neckline: V-neckline with narrow double straps merging into a wrestler back

Double-faced bandages are folded and woven through elastic cording down the side seam and at the centre front of the dress. The result is a soft **geometric pattern** in a flattering, body-contouring silhouette.

Silver **sequin-embellished** knitted-mesh minidress with three-quarter-length sleeves and exaggerated shoulders. Fullness at the sleeve head helps to accentuate the **squared shoulders**.

< Fine-gauge **spandex-mix** jersey knitted dress with intarsia and printed mirror-image pattern. Typical **T-shirt silhouette** with a crew neck and short sleeves, the dress can be worn as a micro mini or teamed with separates.

KNIT DRESS

COATDRESS

Taking inspiration from outerwear, the coatdress is an essential consideration in many collections. The tailored dress style, traditionally translated in suiting or heavier-weight fabric, makes it a wardrobe staple and an ideal style for career dressing.

Button-front coatdress with 1920s flapper and 1960s Yves St Laurent influences, evident in the dropped waistline, buckled belt, bracelet-length sleeves and over-proportioned decorative revers collar.

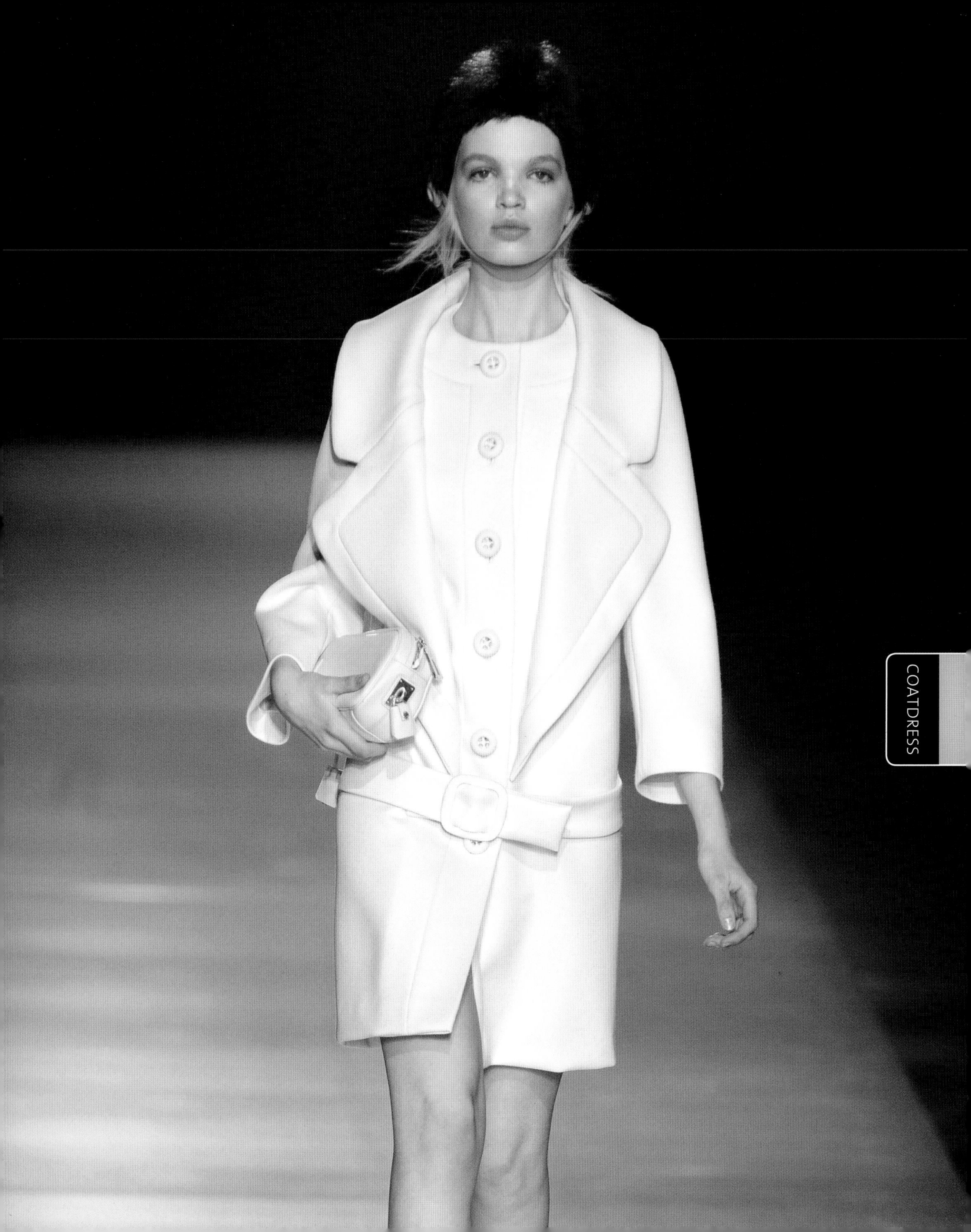

In context

From Armani's autumn 1983 ready-to-wear collection, the coatdress has obvious outerwear characteristics. The broad, padded shoulders with long set-in sleeves create a strong masculine silhouette typical of the power dressing of the 1980s. The heavy vertical stripe woven fabric gives weight to the pared-down rectangular form, and the patch pockets at hip level on each side of the front panel reinforces the coat styling.

The coatdress design references outerwear-garment details and often borrows stylistic accents from the classic trench coat and tailored suiting styles. Coatdresses can be double- or single-breasted, with leather or tie belts to add definition. The coatdress incorporates fastenings such as large button, toggle and zip closures that further reflect the outerwear style. It includes large patch, jet and welt pockets.

Today, the coatdress will usually have a front fastening, although in the 1960s the centre-back zip fastening was a popular alternative, offered in contrasting black and white and pastel-coloured cottons and wool. Designs were mainly collarless or included a Peter Pan collar with faux-front button fastening. Trims played an important part of the coatdress design, with embellished and contrast-colour binding on necklines, collars and pockets.

The popularity of the coatdress style continued into the 1970s, when it became the uniform for the strong, independent working woman. The style evolved through the decades, mirroring the silhouette of the time. In the 1980s, it became boxier in shape and less tailored, with oversized shoulder pads to accentuate the square silhouette of the time, typified by Donna Karan and Armani. The dress often had rolled-up sleeves with contrast fabric lining and was rarely worn cinched in at the waist. It was often teamed with leggings and ski pants. Rei Kawakubo subverted this less-formal approach in her 1983 collection, which included oversized coatdresses cut large and square with no definitive shape or silhouette. During the 1990s, the coatdress style was at the forefront of fashion and echoed more of a frock-coat style, with a fit-and-flare silhouette. Often sleeveless, with exaggerated wing collars, the coatdress became an ideal garment for spring/summer when translated in lighter-weight and sheer fabrics.

Today, with less distinction of silhouette and more choice in design than ever before, the coatdress emerges in a variety of styles and silhouettes.

Double-breasted coatdress in wool tweed by Dior in 1955. The oversized grown-on revers collar opens wide, touching the armhole. The side placket opening is buttoned from below the bust finishing at the hip, creating a figure-hugging silhouette to calf length. This creates a sheath style with a nipped waist accentuated by padded shoulders and full gathered sleeves.

COATDRESS

Design considerations

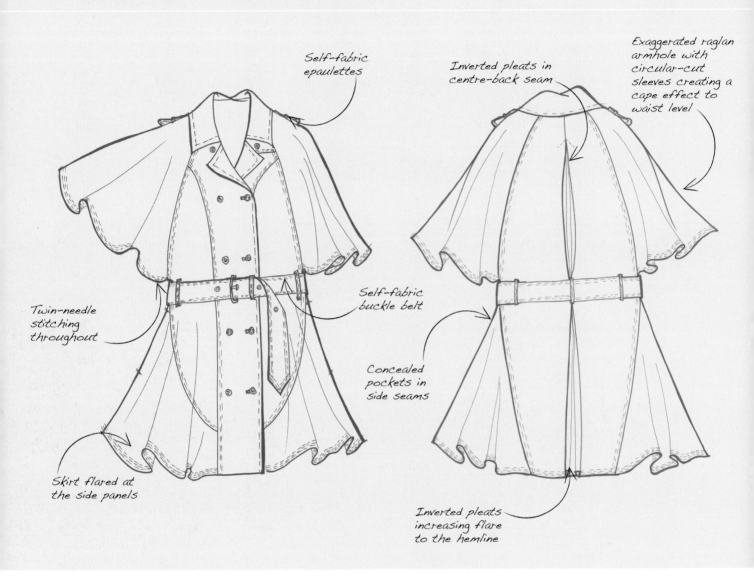

Self-fabric epaulettes

Inverted pleats in centre-back seam

Exaggerated raglan armhole with circular-cut sleeves creating a cape effect to waist level

Twin-needle stitching throughout

Self-fabric buckle belt

Concealed pockets in side seams

Skirt flared at the side panels

Inverted pleats increasing flare to the hemline

Silhouette Taking direction from outerwear and tailored garments, the coatdress silhouette is wide-ranging. From cocoon shapes inspired by generously cut winter wool coats (that is a rounded, soft form with little body definition), to semifitted silhouettes echoing the fit and structure of tailored jackets.

Shaping The coatdress can be loosely styled, semifitted or fitted, with style lines that create the desired silhouette as well as reflect the shaping on coats and tailored garments. The shape must utilize the characteristics of outerwear in order to accomplish the coatdress style.

Hemlines If designed to be worn alone, the coatdress usually falls around the knee, either slightly above or below, with a deep felled hem replicating the substantial finishings of the coat. Often designed as part of an outfit, the coatdress can be maxi length with a fluid, wider hem width.

Fabric Although traditionally manufactured in heavier-weight fabrics, such as wools and suiting, and fully lined for the autumn/winter season – to reflect its outerwear origins – the coatdress style can also be translated in lighter-weight fabrics, such as linen, georgette and organdie, making it a perfect garment for spring/summer and special occasions.

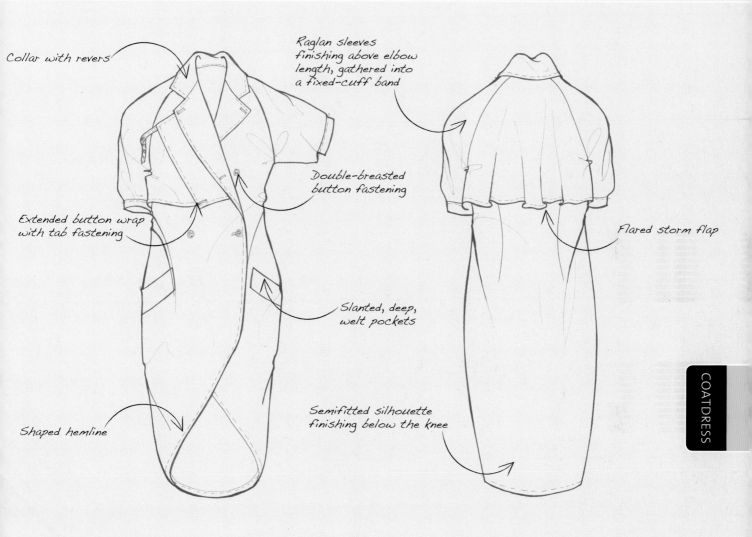

Collar with revers

Raglan sleeves finishing above elbow length, gathered into a fixed-cuff band

Double-breasted button fastening

Extended button wrap with tab fastening

Flared storm flap

Slanted, deep, welt pockets

Shaped hemline

Semifitted silhouette finishing below the knee

COATDRESS

Fastenings Can be either front- or back-neck fastened with large button or zip closures, depending on the design. Front-fastened coatdresses can be wrap, single- or double-breasted with tied or fixed belts, concealed button or zip plackets or toggles with rouleau loops.

Necklines and collars Usually round or V-neck, though if designed with a collar, the collar and fastening type will dictate the neckline shape, width and drop. Styles can include tuxedo-inspired revers, wing, mandarin or Eton collars.

Sleeves The nature of the silhouette will inform the type of armhole and sleeve. Typically, a generously cut coatdress will have wide rounded shoulders and raglan, magyar or dolman sleeves. A more fitted silhouette usually dictates narrower shoulders and skinnier sleeves, often a two-piece set-in sleeve.

Pockets Pockets are an important consideration in the design of the coat, a consideration that is also reflected in the design of the coatdress. As well as adding interest to the style, they also need to be functional and well positioned. Pockets can be welt, jet, oversized patch or concealed in side seams, reflecting tailoring details.

Tailored

Traditionally a semiformal garment resembling a dress, the tailored coatdress utilizes many stylistic features of the tailored jacket and coat. Tailoring is synonymous with craftsmanship, resolute quality and attention to detail, which the tailored coatdress aims to reflect in its design. The dress is front-fastened, button-through, and can be single- or double-breasted with collar and revers and two-piece sleeves.

Conventionally an autumn/winter garment in suiting fabric and fully lined, the tailored coatdress is now commonly translated in lighter-weight fabrics and can be worn as a dress or coat. Ranging from sleeveless to short-sleeved and long-sleeved, the tailored coatdress can be fitted and body conscious or maxi length and flared, reminiscent of the frock-coat style. Bodice seams and style lines reflect those found on tailored jackets and often include a centre-back vent for ease of movement. In contrast to the wrap coatdress style, the tailored coatdress relies on balance or symmetry. This is achieved by including identical design details placed either side of the centre front, such as pockets, tabs or stitching. The pockets on the tailored coatdress are often angled and can be jet with pocket flaps or welt. Repetition is also an important design consideration and happens when a particular feature or trim is repeated throughout the garment to create a well-balanced design.

These attributes all make the tailored coatdress an ideal garment for career dressing.

KEY CHARACTERISTICS

☑ Stylistic features of tailored jacket and coat

☑ Front fastened, button through, single or double breasted, with collar and revers and two-piece sleeves

☑ Balance and symmetry

Tailored coatdress with a wrap that crosses centre front with a **curved detail** at bodice front, reinforced by a curve at the front hem opening.

Alternative fastening and collar: straight cut, displaced button wrap with asymmetric collar

The leather bodice is cut and fastened edge to edge with a collarless neckline. The bodice is fitted and formed, defining the bust and creating a **structured** look. This is contrasted by the soft fake-fur skirt, which creates **softness and volume**.

1 A deep collarless V opening is wrapped at the waist, revealing a contrast band of black. Fastenings are hidden, maintaining an architectural, minimal structure. **2** Trapeze-style coatdress with a high V-neck. Colour-blocked side panels and sleeves create an optical illusion. **3** Tuxedo-style coatdress with an asymmetrical wrap fastened on the left. The placket and collar revers change in scale and shape. The placket opening ends at the hip but visually continues. **4** Double-breasted sharp tailored coatdress with a four-button fastening and four decoy buttons, giving a military effect. The caped shoulders form a short draped sleeve. **5** This four-button, knee-length, double-breasted sleeveless coatdress has a wide shawl collar and deep pockets with flaps. **6** Oversized trench coatdress. Silk softly blousons into the belted waist and cuffs. **7** A slim, fitted trench coatdress with traditional details, such as the tie belt through belt tabs and vertical side-slash pockets with stand. **8** Single-breasted and buttoned up the front to the neck, with a high funnel collar, this fitted dress has contrast panelling in cotton sateen, giving a bibbed tuxedo effect.

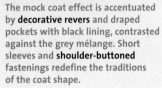

The mock coat effect is accentuated by **decorative revers** and draped pockets with black lining, contrasted against the grey mélange. Short sleeves and **shoulder-buttoned** fastenings redefine the traditions of the coat shape.

Heavy wool coatdress fitted to the waist and flared to below the knee hemline. The **diagonal darts** to the waistband create shaping and open out as boxed pleats, giving volume to the skirt. A concealed-button placket within the facing at centre front perpetuates the **uncomplicated** silhouette.

Alternative neckline: V-shaped neckline with grown-on back neck

Graphic monochromatic dress with contrast **single breast welt pocket** that continues in a sweeping curlicue to form a double-breasted, concealed-button opening. The high break point of the neckline juxtaposes with the **deep hem opening**, providing visual contrast.

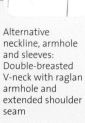

COATDRESS

< The deep, wrap-over stand collar with button-strap fastening, deep raglan armhole, epaulettes at the shoulder and buttoned cuffs give a **military feel**.

Wool coatdress with military references. It has a curved edge and a **distinctive buttoned flap** stitched into the side seam. Wide three-quarter-length sleeves are trimmed with buttoned flaps at the cuffs.

Alternative neckline, armhole and sleeves: Double-breasted V-neck with raglan armhole and extended shoulder seam

> A column silhouette is created with the positioning **vertical darts** that create definition of the bodice, then open to create pleats at each side of the back and front panels. The deep round neckline has an elongated **funnel neck**. The deep silver leather belt breaks up the column and defines the waist.

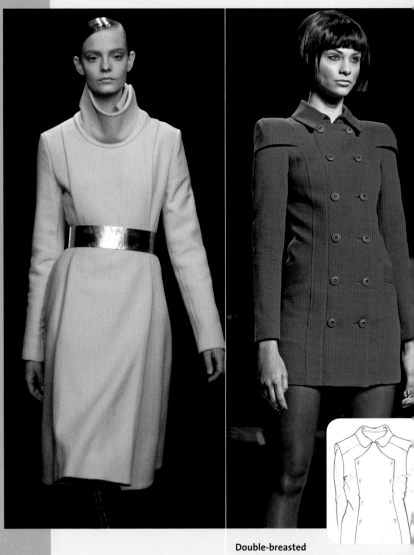

Double-breasted coatdress with shirt neck-stand collar. **Military influences** are expressed by self-fabric epaulettes. Vertical seaming, left and right of front panels, reinforces the straight-column silhouette.

Alternative shoulder detail: the double fabric front and back yoke is left unattach at the sleeve head, allowing the set-in sleeve to be inserted into the recess

With strong references to coat styling, this dress suggests a front opening with a **deep box pleat** running down the centre front. Pleats again define the shoulder, running from front to back, and continue in a vertical line outlining the **side panels**. Set-in sleeves complete the elongated column effect and centre-back fastenings allow the streamlined front to remain uncluttered.

Understated simple coatdress with no evidence of trim or embellishment. A **concealed-button front** is disguised in the placket facing with centre-front opening.

Alternative sleeves and neckline: short sleeves with a round neckline

Colourful, kaleidoscope-inspired florals decorate this otherwise simple straight coatdress. The plain black collar and **deep placket** break the pattern at centre front. Straight, long, set-in sleeves contribute to the **simple silhouette**. The dress has a sense of cultural reference, defined by the ornate pattern.

Housecoat

With its origins in the 1940s and '50s, and sometimes referred to as a duster coat, the housecoat was worn to protect the day's outfit while performing the household chores. Varying in style, though usually knee length or longer to conceal any undergarments, the housecoat developed during the 1950s into a more elegant and sophisticated garment for entertaining at home.

Originally in lightweight fabric and sometimes quilted for warmth, the housecoat had a loose and easy cut with little waist definition to allow for ease of movement. Often designed with a front and back yoke, the housecoat of the 1940s hung from the shoulders with soft gathering at the yoke seams. Front fastened with buttons or zip and with a round neck and collar, the 1940s housecoat was either long- or short-sleeved.

Over time, the housecoat silhouette evolved to reflect Dior's New Look. The waist was defined and sometimes accentuated with a tie belt, the bodice was fitted, and the skirts long and full. Styles were single- and double-breasted with more variety of collars, such as revers and shawl. Sleeves were often dolman with turn-back cuffs and could be short, long or three-quarter length. With its roots as a functional, practical garment, all housecoats had pockets, usually in the form of patch pockets, though during the 1950s the pocket designs were more varied and elaborate.

The floor-length housecoat with long sleeves has a **monastical** appearance. The high stand-up collar dips to a V-neck opening, and strategic darts help to create the stand. Fitted to the waist seam, the dress has a slight **A-line shaping** to skim the floor. The cut edges of the felted fabric are left unfinished.

The rectangular shapes, straight front placket, and tie belt demonstrate a nod to the **kimono**. The contrast of matt and shine fabrics forms the main surface interest.

Alternative belt detail: belt loops have been integrated into the main body of the design

KEY CHARACTERISTICS

- ☑ Front fastened with buttons or zip
- ☑ Diverse necklines and collars
- ☑ Pockets and pinafore references

1 Oversized geometric shapes form a loose dress. The deep V-neck meets a centre-front seam that runs to a low waistband. The skirt has a centre-front seam with a turn-back mock opening.
2 A deep funnel-neck collar falls softly to create an unstructured effect, framing the neckline. **3** Deep V-neck jersey dress with a wide self-fabric belt tied at the waist with references to the bathrobe.

Sleeves are fitted to the elbow, where a bell-shaped lower sleeve attaches. **4** Bold, geometric-printed taffeta trapeze dress. Wide elbow-length sleeves have a deep turned-back cuff. The zipped front opens to a revers collar. **5** Maxi-length, shirt-style housecoat with placket front opening buttoned to thigh. The striped fabric is cut directionally to contrast and define the different

panels. **6** Wrap housecoatdress with deep shawl collar. Cuffs are edged with narrow satin ribbon, which is also used to tie the waist. **7** Contrast panels of sheer and solid patterned chiffon are left to hang loosely from the waistline. The overlay on the right-hand bodice is looped and anchored to create a three-dimensional effect. **8** Bold-floral A-line housecoat-style dress inspired by 1950s vintage.

Wrap

The wrap coatdress has a front closure created by wrapping one side of the garment over the other and securing with a self-fabric tie or separate leather belt. The easygoing lines of the wrap create an informal balance or asymmetry to the design. The wrap closure invites the eye to travel without interruption over the entire garment. This loose-fitting, casual shape shows similarities to the menswear polo coat or camel's hair coat popularized in the 1920s, worn by polo players after their games. This gentle silhouette was modified with a dropped waistline on a shift shape for womenswear in the 1920s. Eventually, the polo-coat influence was surpassed by the emergence of the trench coat. The current wrap coatdress takes direction from both these design classics.

The traditional trench coat is a windbreaker and raincoat, with its origins in military use. Styling details, such as raglan sleeves, epaulettes and deep patch pockets with flaps, are common qualities of the wrap coatdress, particularly popular during the 1980s and the power-dressing 1990s. Although masculine in its foundation, the wrap front closure accentuates the female body and forms a flattering V-neckline, personifying the silhouette of the 1950s. At this time, the wrap coatdress was very feminine in its translation, often in taffeta, with dolman sleeves and a very full skirt, indicating little acknowledgment of its mannish heritage.

Silk gazar fabric holds its shape to achieve a strong silhouette within this dramatic coatdress. The **extended draped collar** breaks at the waist, exposing a plunging neckline. The wrap front is shaped and curved at the hemline, reinforcing the **rounded shapes**.

The **curved wrap front** is attached at the side seams. Short, puff, set-in sleeves are trimmed with a single button cuff. The **contrast colour blocking** emphasizes the collar cuff and pocket details and defines the front placket opening.

KEY CHARACTERISTICS

☑ **Front, wrap closing**

☑ **Menswear polo-coat and trench-coat influences**

☑ **Double-breasted and tie-front fastenings**

1 A round neck and softly curved shoulders of magyar sleeves create the cocoon shapes of this wrap dress. **2** Two-tone matt-and-shine woven fabrics give a contemporary edge to a traditional shape. **3** The wrap on this coatdress is deceptive, seemingly crossing in opposite directions at the bodice and the skirt. The lack of symmetry is accentuated by the shawl collar on the right and the single pocket at the left hip. **4** With kaftan references, this wrap-front dress has dropped shoulders, wide kimono sleeves, a simple round neckline and a deep sash at the waistline. **5** Coatdress with a diagonal wrap styling in quilt-effect satin. **6** Sleeveless silk coatdress with a stand collar that extends at the neck opening to form a tie. **7** The print is engineered to take into consideration the asymmetry of the garment's cut while maintaining the symmetry of the print at centre front. The A-line of the skirt is echoed in the V-neckline and emphasized by the placement of the border print. **8** Stone linen wrap coatdress with contrasting grey silk sleeves, grown-on revers collar and shoulder yoke.

Cape

Based on a sleeveless outerwear garment, the cape coatdress takes inspiration from ponchos, cloaks, capes and opera coats. Frequently used as a fashion statement, the cape shape reflects the origins of the cape as a rainwear garment, or its function to protect the fine fabrics of evening-wear garments that may be crushed by more traditional coats with set-in sleeves.

The cape is derived from a simple garment, the cloak being the longer version. Based on a circular shape, ranging from a half circle to a full circle, though rarely translated in this simple form, the cape shape nowadays requires fit and tailoring around the shoulder. The sleeveless, circular cape shape can be used to inform the entire coatdress silhouette, cut long, like a cloak, with openings in the front panels to allow easy movement of the arms without the garment's riding up. This shape can be belted at the front to define the waist and keep the fabric close to the body while hanging loose, voluminous and away from the body at the back, creating a striking side view. The shorter-length shape can often add interest to the shoulder area in the form of a tier inserted into the neckline over a fitted dress, to contrast the fullness of the circular cape. The exaggerated collar, shawl and traditional cape styles can be traced from Paul Poiret to Rei Kawakubo for Commes des Garçon.

Fitted mini-length dress with a **multicoloured basketweave** pattern. The sleeve head is set into the shoulder at the top, leaving the underarm as sleeveless. The sleeves fall over the bare arms, increasing in volume to the cuff to achieve a **cape effect**. The round neckline and patch pockets complete the look.

The asymmetrical cape detail across the **left shoulder** is attached at the waistband at front and back, and the coat style is further emphasized by the use of epaulettes.

Alternative neckline and sleeves: round neckline with button front fastening and short, flared sleeves

KEY CHARACTERISTICS

☑ Derived from ponchos, cloaks, capes and opera coats

☑ Based on a circular shape

☑ Openings in the front panels to allow easy movement of arms

1 Oversized sleeves wrap across the body to mimic a cape. The saddle shoulder leads to a dropped sleeve that has a vent opening at underarm for practicality. **2** The storm cape with buttoned epaulettes is attached to a collar that buttons at the neck and fastens with buttons to the bodice. **3** Rectangular and structured, the envelope effect is created by a pleat with a deep return that folds back vertically from the extended square shoulder line, giving the cape effect. **4** The exaggerated trapeze shape and wide, bell-shaped, three-quarter-length sleeves give the impression of a cape. **5** Heavily embellished dress with exaggerated shoulders and slash V front that forms the focal point of the design. **6** Fitted wool dress that gently flares to the knee. The oversized bell-shaped collar turns back, falling below armhole level to form a cape. **7** Fluted gathers are cut from a circle and gathered into a flat bib-front bodice; they extend over the armhole and shoulder, giving a cape effect. **8** Sleeves integrated into a voluminous floor-length cape. The round neck and circular armhole, cut from the cape, continue the curved lines.

CULTURAL INFLUENCES

The wealth of the world's cultural heritage has been a source of inspiration for designers throughout the ages, providing references for ideas that inform silhouette, pattern, detail, colour and textiles.

A substantial quantity of fabric is softly gathered at the waistline, cinched with a feature metal-buckle belt. The sleeve and bodice are integrated, cut from one piece and draped diagonally across the body into the skirt. The contrasting skintight jersey body on the left side creates a plunging V neckline to the waist.

In context

Laura Ashley captured the romantic 1970s ideals of pastoralism most often seen as British country or American prairie aesthetic. Particularly important were the ditsy floral prints, puff sleeves and sweet ruffles that decorate this dress of 1974. The dress is girlish, suggesting an innocence or absence of the cares of the world.

Throughout history, historical and cultural costume and textiles have been cross-fertilized as design references. The conquests and subsequent spoils of war have meant that exotic and valuable merchandise has been transported across the world and adopted by various civilizations. International trading throughout continents, promoting cultural exchanges, has also resulted in the cross-fertilization of ideas. With the migration of pioneers looking for new lands to create a better life, traditions and skills have transferred overseas and mingled with other cultures, inseminating knowledge, ideas, values and philosophies, and embracing new ways of looking.

The human desire to collect and interpret has led to the establishment of museums, exhibiting rich and varied collections that allowed ordinary people, without the means to travel, to view interesting relics and works of art from foreign lands.

Immigration has always been a catalyst for cultural exchange, and the melting pot of ethnicity, particularly within larger cities, has provided a rich and exciting mix of multicultural inspiration. With budget travel making the world accessible to many, and the Internet giving access to a wealth of information, international cultural influences pervade our lives.

Designers have always taken advantage of the treasure trove of resources available. Kenzo, Anna Sui and Betsey Johnson, among others, focus not only on the cultural heritage of fashion and textiles, but more widely investigate art, decorative arts, architecture and historical and popular culture. Process and techniques have also crossed nations, resulting in changes in influence on fashion houses. Design directors, crossing continents, shape changes in direction of labels such as Missoni, Chanel, Givenchy, Saint Laurent and Balenciaga.

The languid beauty of Greek sculpture influenced Madame Grès, who created stunningly modern gowns. Throughout the 1930s and 1940s Madame Grès used incredible amounts of fabric to create these pleated dresses, constructing them by hand. The inset, horizontally pleated panels create the visual effect of a small waist, while the vertical pleats elongate the figure.

Design considerations

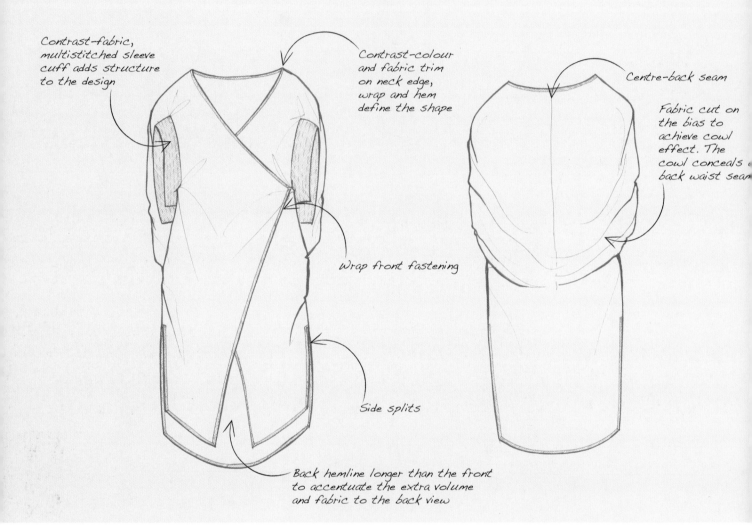

Contrast-fabric, multistitched sleeve cuff adds structure to the design

Contrast-colour and fabric trim on neck edge, wrap and hem define the shape

Wrap front fastening

Side splits

Back hemline longer than the front to accentuate the extra volume and fabric to the back view

Centre-back seam

Fabric cut on the bias to achieve cowl effect. The cowl conceals back waist seam

Silhouette The silhouette is dictated by the point of reference and can be oversized and voluminous, enveloping the body and disguising its contours, or long, lean and sheath-like. From loosely fitting, comfortable to wear and one-size-fits-all, through to semifitted or body defining, the silhouette is dictated by the cultural theme.

Length Short and sassy, long and languid – the variations of length reflect the cultural inspiration. Layering is a common trend, and asymmetrical hemlines can blur the definition of length and silhouette.

Fabrics The cultural origins of the style can be translated through richly ornate textiles: fine chiffon and sunray-pleated silks; jerseys appropriate for draping and gathering; cotton lawns, fine wools, silk habotai, terry voile, seersucker, cheesecloth, calico, linen, slubs and sanded silks; woven silk brocades, jacquards, ginghams, ikats, lace and embroidered lengths, floral and geometric prints, dip-dyeing, batik and shibori, broderie anglaise, distressed rayon, and other manmade fabrics, and many alternative fabrics that suit the particular theme.

Embellishment Lace, braiding, smocking, embroidery, beading, faggoting, pin tucks, rouleaus, shirring, frogging, quilting, appliqué and patchwork are among the numerous options available.

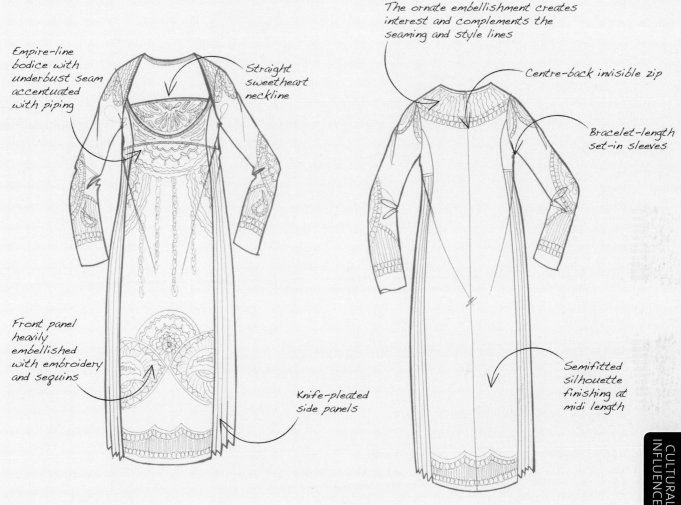

The ornate embellishment creates interest and complements the seaming and style lines

Empire-line bodice with underbust seam accentuated with piping

Straight sweetheart neckline

Centre-back invisible zip

Bracelet-length set-in sleeves

Front panel heavily embellished with embroidery and sequins

Knife-pleated side panels

Semifitted silhouette finishing at midi length

CULTURAL INFLUENCES

Necklines The design of the neckline is a strong feature because it often shows a seductive flash of cleavage or a flaunt of shoulder with a slash neck. The neckline can be a V, round and scooped, boatneck or shaped into a decorative front yoke. Cultural references can inform neckline styling, collars and yokes, creating a focal point and design statement.

Sleeves Sleeves can make a dramatic statement and define a look and theme. The sleeve may be integrated into the body if the garment is a large rectangular shape, like a kaftan. Drop shoulders are commonly used to mimic kimono sleeves, or for a Westernized version of the kaftan. More elaborate statement sleeves can be set in with gathered sleeve heads and cuffs. Spaghetti straps and capped or short puffed sleeves can provide a softer, more feminine aesthetic, particularly evident in boho and prairie styles.

Boho

The word *bohemian* describes a multicultural, gypsy traveller with artistic and romantic tendencies and exemplifies a nomadic and spirited lifestyle unconstrained by the rules of society. Boho chic reflects this spirit, and looks to the hippies of the 1970s for inspiration. The style mismatches an eclectic mix of ethnic sources, as if the wearer has travelled around the world and picked up decorative textiles and authentic garments along the way and put them back together in a melting pot of styles, patterns and colours.

Soft, unstructured cutting and draping, mixing fabric qualities, and not being afraid to mix scales of print and fabric textures are characteristics of this style. Decorative embellishments that take advantage of handicraft techniques can be added; as can braids and ribbons, ties and leather thongs and trims, fleece and fur. Gathers, dirndls, pleats and tiered layers may be used to add volume and create a feminine aesthetic. Tie-dye and batik, discharge- and dip-dyeing, and overdyeing prints with shibori techniques can all add to the ethnic quality.

Loosely fitted silhouettes with an emphasis on layering implement a variety of lengths from mini, midi to maxi. Hemlines can be asymmetrical, using handkerchief shapes, or layered with petticoats. Dresses may be sleeveless or feature big, billowing sleeve shapes with gathered sleeve heads and cuffs.

This **geometric, Aztec-inspired** sundress has a deep printed border at the hem that complements the embroidered front bodice bib. The scalloped hem of the bib is reflected in the design of the **embroidery**, and is mirrored either side of the centre-front button placket that ends just above the top-hip level.

This printed sundress has a high round neck that complements the cutaway armholes, reflecting a **sportswear cut**. The **voluminous skirt** is panelled to achieve more flare.

Alternative neckline: deep V neckline with drawstring under-bust tie

KEY CHARACTERISTICS

- ☑ **Eclectic mix of ethnic sources, prints and textures**
- ☑ **Loosely fitted silhouette**
- ☑ **Decorative embellishments that take advantage of handicraft techniques**

1 This mini shift shape has a crochet neck trim that continues down to create a detailed centre front. The skirt has deep embroidered side panels and a wide lace border at the hem. 2 The full-length skirt is gathered into the empire line to achieve volume. The horizontal bands give structure and interest to the skirt. 3 Simple A-line shaped silk dress with ornate embellishment on the chest and sheer sleeves. 4 The contrasting floral prints on the yoke, the long sleeves and the shirt-dress panels evoke a folksy boho look. 5 The use of multiple complementary prints in one design emphasizes the garment details and features. 6 This Navaho-inspired dress is mini length, with a wide and scooped neckline, a deep feather border at the hem and a heavily embroidered and appliquéd front-placement design. 7 High-waisted, peasant-style midi dress in black calico cotton. Brightly coloured embroidered florals decorate the bodice and are scattered across the skirt. 8 A loosely fitted, georgette dress with a self-fabric drawstring neckline and waist. Frills at the cuffs and hemline reflect the gathered waist.

> This velvet dress and jacket give the impression of **patchwork** construction. The silhouette, proportions, rope binding and tassels reference the 1960s and 1970s counter-culture's fascination with **alternative** craft and sources of fashion.

This cotton dress has a **wide scooped neckline**, the curve of which is reflected in the shape of the sleeves and fullness of the skirt. The folkloric-inspired **floral appliqué**, placed around the skirt border and waistline, defines the silhouette.

Alternative neckline and sleeves: square neckline with flared, short sleeves

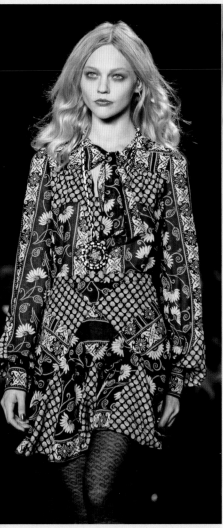

This garment has been designed to complement the **chiffon allover-print pattern** while accentuating the garment's style lines and silhouette. The bias-cut skirt and godet inserts exploit the characteristics of the lightweight chiffon fabric. The full, **bell-shaped long sleeves** gathered into a traditional cuff and oversized, self-fabric bow give a vintage appeal.

Traditional **scarf designs** have been reworked in a contemporary way to create this modern **patchwork** print. The print's colourway and the relaxed, draped silhouette achieve a boho aesthetic.

A **contemporary interpretation** of folklore-inspired lace that has been translated into a **simple kaftan shape** to maximize the fabric's design. The lace design is used instead of style lines to define the body and give proportion to the style.

Prairie

Prairie styling originates from images of the American Midwest, with design references to the idealized sentimentality and wholesome values of the pioneers of the new frontiers. Calamity Jane meets The Waltons meets Little House on the Prairie and Anne of Green Gables.

Textiles feature Navajo Indian geometric patterns, ikats, cowgirl ginghams, broderie anglaise, embroidery, lace trims, pin tucks, patchwork, chequered prints, denim and suede-leather fringes. Silhouettes include calf- or full-length gathered skirts, high-waisted or waisted, sometimes tiered or worn over lace petticoats, as well as poncho-style kaftan shapes with fringes. Dresses vary from smocks, knitted, Fair Isle sweaterdresses, dungaree dresses and full-length riding-coat dresses to oversized shirt dresses. Trims derive from fringed Indian-inspired yokes, hemlines and sleeves, to handcrafted folk art, Indian beadwork, saddlery hardware and leather strapping. Looks can be accessorized with cowgirl boots, leather belts and saddlebags.

The prairie style is the trademark look of American designer Ralph Lauren. Natural kei is also a trend that evolved in Japan in the 1970s, reflecting period and pastoral life. Laura Ashley popularized the prairie look in the 1970s and 1980s, with tiered cotton printed dresses. The trend can be seen in Marc Jacobs' spring/summer 2009 collection; Rodarte's rustic, full-length coats with patchwork and wheat prints for autumn/winter 2011; and Isabel Marant's autumn/winter 2011 collection.

This dress has a simple slashed neckline with grown-on capped sleeves in a busy allover print. The relaxed, **loosely fitted bodice**, full maxi-length gathered skirt and **ethnic-inspired woven waistband** detail add a feminine and sophisticated hippie feel to this style.

The **oversized cut** creates a relaxed, easy-to-wear garment. The raglan sleeves are voluminous and the wide, **elasticated neckline** could be worn on or off the shoulder. A striped belt defines the waistline and breaks up the bold print, while the tucks on the skirt generate additional volume.

KEY CHARACTERISTICS

- ☑ Sentimentalized American Midwest aesthetic
- ☑ Broderie anglaise, gingham and denim
- ☑ Embroidery, lace, pin tucks and hardware trims
- ☑ Layers and petticoats

1 The dress consists of two layers, with the overlayer tucked and secured at the centre-front hip level, creating a bustle effect on the back view. **2** Shirt-style dress with a gathered waist and dirndl skirt with frilled hem. The front bodice has pin-tucked and frilled panels that epitomize the prairie style. **3** Floor-length dress with full multilayered chiffon skirt and gathered frill hem.

4 The full, ankle-length skirt and long sleeves gathered into deep cuffs accentuate the beautiful drape of the fabric. The shirring detail on the shoulders, cuffs and waistline create and balance the subtle drapery. **5** Semifitted sundress with a fitted bodice and A-line skirt. The large bertha-style collar, curved front yoke and puff sleeves feature self-fabric frills. **6** The large waist tie

dominates this silhouette. The wide, round neckline has an inverted V-shaped cutout. The short raglan cap sleeves create a 1950s feel. **7** A traditional semifitted shirt bodice and short dirndl skirt, with a border detail that emphasizes the fullness of the skirt. **8** The border detail emphasizes the neckline, dropped waist and skirt border and gives a contemporary peasant feel.

Grecian

With its heritage in Greek classical dress – and taking inspiration from wet drapery evident in Greek sculpture, where the fabric appears to cling to the body – the Grecian style reveals and disguises the contours of the figure, allowing scope for the designer to enhance and conceal different parts of the female form. To achieve the fluid classical forms of the Grecian aesthetic, fabric is draped on the body rather than cut flat, to create sumptuous, flowing folds and pleats and body-revealing drape. This technique was pioneered in the 1930s by Madame Grès, with her skilful securing of vertical pleats on jersey gowns. Precursors to Madame Grès include Mariano Fortuny, Raymond Duncan and Madeleine Vionnet, all passionate advocates of classical dress. Fortuny was well versed in Greek art and costume, with an appreciation of a wide variety of cultures and ethnic dress. These combined influences inspired his rich colour palettes and beautiful textiles, and initiated the groundbreaking pleated silk Delphos dresses, reminiscent of fluted Greek columns, are still worn today. The Pleats Please brand, launched by Issey Miyake in the 1990s, took the essence of Fortuny's easy-to-wear and comfortable aesthetic and translated it into machine-washable, lightweight polyester pleats.

The Grecian influence on fashion can transpire in a variety of ways, from fluid, draped asymmetric dresses and floor-length tunics to narrow-pleated sheath-like columns. Many contemporary designers reference this classical mode of dress and acknowledge the timeless beauty encapsulated in this aesthetic.

Sunray seaming and diagonal panels accentuate the deep V. Long, **batwing sleeves** complete the look.

Alternative neckline: straight, slashed neckline with shaped waistband

Sarong-style wrap-over, **strapless**, long, tent-shaped dress. Although simple in appearance, the dress is built onto a structured foundation, giving hidden support.

KEY CHARACTERISTICS

☑ **Inspiration from wet drapery of Greek sculpture**

☑ **Reveals and disguises the contours of the figure**

☑ **Fabric draped rather than cut in flowing folds and pleats**

1 Dramatic floor-length red evening dress. The drape across the left shoulder is mirrored with an overskirt that drapes at the left hip. 2 Circular bias cutting, shirring and asymmetrical draping create a look of classical Greek styling. 3 Geometric, rectangular shapes are shirred and gathered to create soft draping. Asymmetric draping blocks one shoulder while revealing the other. 4 Over a simple minidress foundation, tonal-coloured fabrics are draped from leather straps to create an asymmetric design. 5 Mixing Grecian and sari styling, the single long sleeve and contrasting bare arm give irregularity to this cocktail dress. 6 A bodice gives fit and shape to the bustline and creates a foundation from which to overlay the chiffon draping, which continues over the sleeves and the shoulder line, then wraps and knots at the waist. Fine gathered pleating creates volume and layering to the floor-length skirt. 7 A structured high-round neckpiece is the focal point of this design and contrasts well with the sumptuous fabric of the dress. 8 Ombré-printed layers of solid and transparent fabrics give a soft, unstructured appearance to a sarong-style evening dress.

1 Short, silk satin, sleeveless skater-style dress. The contrast black V-neck insert is matched by black binding set into raglan shaping. **2** Loose-fitting, silk satin asymmetric-hem dress. The skirt is draped to create a long cowl effect on the right side. **3** Translucent organza forms a statuesque floor-length dress. Gold foiling gives the visual effect of a strapless bodice and shimmers beautifully. **4** The box shape of this dress is accentuated by the square of the slash neckline. **5** An elegant, asymmetric, single-shouldered jersey column dress. The sleeve and body are cut in one, with the wide sleeves maximizing the drape. **6** Concertina pleats are fixed to the waistband, giving definition to the body. The sleeveless armholes have been cut wide, continuing the squareness of the pattern pieces. **7** Fabric is softly draped across one shoulder, forming a wide single sleeve. The embellished border emphasizes the asymmetric neckline and adds interest to the expanse of chiffon. **8** A contrast-colour, deep border drapes from the left shoulder, around the hem and up into the back view, creating folds and a cowl effect at the side hem.

9 Silk dress with wide, plunging V neckline that leads to a curve-shaped waist seam. The flared skirt has sunray-pleated side panels enhancing the volume. **10** The bodice is cut and constructed to appear twisted at the centre front. The circular-cut, sunray-pleated skirt is reminiscent of classical columns. **11** Multilayered chiffon strapless dress with varying-length tiered hem. **12** The diagonal of the fabric forms the neckline of this one-shouldered dress. A simple strap on the alternate side prevents the dress from slipping. **13** Toga, kimono, sari and kaftan references are all evident within this maxi dress. **14** Simple, oversized rectangular shapes form a tabard style with very little shaping. Additional fabric cut into the front panel of the dress forms the drape at the slash neckline. **15** The continuity of a length of fabric knotted and draped around the body is suggested here. In fact, clever draping builds an innovative silhouette. **16** Sheer chiffon has been draped from the shoulders and secured at the waistline by a structured, contrast-colour belt. Straps define the plunging square neckline.

A washed-silk dress that is tucked and draped from the left shoulder and over the bustline to create an empire-line effect. The excess fabric from the drape is left open and fluid to accentuate the Grecian style. Fullness is added throughout the skirt, leading to an **asymmetric hemline** that finishes just below the knee at the shortest side. The clever **print placement** accentuates the shape of the dress.

A floor-length, chiffon evening dress with **thigh-high front split** in the skirt and unusual **twisted self-fabric straps**, which act as a bold finish for the neck edge as well as informing the double-strap detail. The expanse of colour and voluminous skirt, with multiple chiffon layers, create a dramatic effect.

This Lurex jersey **halter-neck** dress has a plunging, generously draped cowl neckline to the waist. The bodice blousons over the **dropped waistline** and into a draped skirt, with tucks engineered into the side seams, creating a cowl effect to the skirt and concealing pockets in the side seams.

Alternative sleeves: extended shoulder with gathered seams creating draped cap sleeves

This fluid, empire-line, floor-length dress has a generous amount of fabric gathered into the shoulder seams, forming the **batwing sleeves** and creating a deep V neckline. The bodice is softly gathered into an **underbust seam**, leading to a dramatic expanse of fabric for the skirt.

< Asymmetric, V-neckline dress with extended shoulder seams and **deep armhole openings** that complement the loose and draped design. The **off-centred V-neck** shape reflects the draped and tucked left-side detailing.

CULTURAL INFLUENCES

Silk satin, one-shouldered, floor-length dress with **train**. The bias-cut fabric enables the dress to skim the contours of the body with **minimal darting**. The dramatic dress length and ostrich-feather shawl add glamour.

Alternative neckline and sleeves: V neckline with extended shoulder line and asymmetric overlayer sash to side seam

Flared, bias-cut, floor-length evening dress with a **crossover front bodice** extended to create the grown-on, self-fabric wide straps. The bias-cut fabric contours the body to the lower hip, in contrast to the acutely **flared skirt** that reflects the diagonal strap detail.

This dramatic evening dress has a wide, plunging V neckline created from **fringing** layered over the bust cups and secured into metal clips at the underbust level to the waist, where it is left to hang over the skirt to achieve more movement when walking. The fringing is also tiered over the hip. The underskirt is floor length with a train and has two **thigh-high splits** either side of the centre front.

1 The chiffon skirt is made up of several layers of fabric, creating a billowing silhouette. The bodice has a twisted, self-fabric neck edge that continues into the shoulder straps. **2** A butterfly-effect sleeve on the left side contrasts with the sleeveless right side. The drape across the bodice is gathered into a sequined motif on the right side of the waist. Drapery continues down the right side of the skirt. **3** Silk habotai maxi dress with deep V neckline. A sequined and embroidered waistband reflects the shape of the neckline. **4** Fine sunray pleats in an abstract floral print, with gathers at the boatneck and knot-gathered waistband that add structure and drape to simple rectangular shapes. **5** Sleeveless mini-length dress with fringing tiered over the foundation garment. **6** Asymmetric wrap-over dress with an intricately draped skirt that complements the ombré fabric treatment. **7** A fitted bodice with a fringing overlay that forms a double-strap detail. The mini-length skirt is tiered with the fringing left loose. **8** Wrap-front dress with batwing sleeves. The loose-fitting bodice blousons over the belted waistline and into a draped skirt with a twisted hemline.

Kaftan

Originating in the East, the kaftan has been adapted and worn as a long, loose dress, usually belted, with long, wide sleeves, sometimes integrated into the main garment. Persian, Moroccan and African in origin, the kaftan is often colourful and heavily embellished. It is no surprise, therefore, that hippies of the late 1960s and early 1970s adopted the ethnic kaftan as part of their fashion statement.

Although the shape is designed not to hug the curves of the body, the kaftan is a sensual garment, often showing a flash of cleavage or shoulder, while soft and floaty fabrics drape and billow. Some body shaping can be achieved by fitting a sash across the front of the body and into side vents, and around the body inside the tented back of the dress, tied at the front or back. Any embellishment would generally focus on the neckline, yoke, edge of sleeves, hemline or sash. This is a good shape to dress with costume jewelry, so keeping embellishment to a minimum may be a consideration. The cultural origins of the style can be translated through richly ornate textiles, bold print treatment and strong colours.

Talitha Getty and Diana Vreeland are famous kaftan aficionados, and Emilio Pucci, Roberto Cavalli and Dior have included the kaftan in their collections. Kaftans are often used in summer collections because the loose-fitting, wide sleeves offer a cool solution in hot weather, and it is ideal as a beach cover-up. The body-enveloping proportions also make the kaftan perfect maternity wear.

Tape-embroidered **cutwork lace** detailing forms the main focus of this mini-length kaftan style. The lace is translated in a colour that is darker and slightly contrasting to the main fabric, complementing the dropped-waist elasticated band to create a somewhat **sporty aesthetic**.

Applied to a delicate chiffon base, the **sequined, ethnic-inspired embroidery** defines the V neckline, framing the face and leading the eye to an elaborate motif on the torso. The **vertical design** helps to elongate the silhouette, offsetting the generous width of the cut.

KEY CHARACTERISTICS

- ☑ Long, loose dress with long, wide sleeves
- ☑ Soft, floaty fabrics allow the dress to drape and billow
- ☑ Colourful and decorative
- ☑ Heavily embellished around neckline, yoke, cuff and hemline

1 The wide, round neckline has a centre-front seam, left open over the bust area and fastened at the neck edge. The body and sleeves are cut in one piece. 2 Maxi-length chiffon dress, cut full and circular. The fabric is drawn in at the waistline with a contrast-colour patterned waistband. 3 The boatneck and kimono-style sleeves of this simple kaftan allow the dramatic print to be viewed uninterrupted and remain the focal point. 4 The graphic colour blocking of this minidress is an ideal backdrop for the soft silhouette. The straight lines formed by the slash neck are reflected in the panelling, and create a contrast to the draped sleeves. 5 This oversized placement print is engineered to work with the garment shape and is carefully positioned in relation to the body. 6 The plunging, slashed-neck opening of this long-sleeved dress has a self-fabric trim on either side to add interest to the overall simple aesthetic. 7 A simple kaftan shape that uses print to suggest yoke and front-bodice panelling. 8 The draping from the neck creates rounded shapes that contrast with the handkerchief points at the hemline.

This contrasting **colour-blocked** kaftan-style dress is cut generously to maximize impact and create a fluid, **billowing effect**. The placement of the diagonal panelling has been considered to work perfectly with the neckline and sleeve shape, as well as to incorporate the volume of fabric needed to achieve the silhouette.

Vertical colour blocking with **Mondrian influence** reinforces the geometric shapes of the kaftan styling of this day dress. The dropped shoulder line and wide armholes, deep placket opening and round collarless neckline are all trademarks of the **traditional kaftan** shape.

Alternative colour blocking: V-shaped colour blocking

This maxi-length column dress has a Greek-mythological mosaic-inspired **placement print** with fresco border that defines the **boatneck**, shape and hem. The relaxed, easy-fit silhouette is complemented with loose kimono-style sleeves and draped side pockets.

1 A subtle asymmetric design with a soft V neckline and draped right-hand side that creates a grown-on armhole with a deep opening. 2 Fullness is achieved through the softly gathered fabric controlled within a structured self-fabric band that forms the neck edge of this kaftan. 3 Square-neck kaftan with rectangular-shaped sleeves set into a square, low armhole. 4 Silk chiffon maxi dress that completely swathes the body in fabric. The neckline is a grown-on funnel, cut close to the neck to contrast with the very full, flared skirt. 5 Voluminous, floor-length kaftan with a clever use of colour blocking to define the square neckline and displaced side seams. The back panel has been brought forwards to create a cocoon effect. 6 Round-neck dress with plunging slash-front opening. The deep, patterned hip band defines the body shape and adds interest to the solid-block colour. 7 Colour blocking creates a strong, graphic design that contrasts with the flowing fabric. Generous side splits reinforce the garment's fluidity. 8 The pleating forms a concertina effect, particularly at the hemline, which rises and dips with the movement of the body.

Kimono

The traditional kimono is made from a bolt of cloth 12 metres (13 yards) long and consists of rectangular pieces of cloth that form a T without darts or shaping. The sleeves are also geometric and square, with an underarm opening. The kimono has a placket that runs up the front opening around the neck and back down the other side, which sometimes falls short of the full length of the garment. The kimono is often lined with beautiful fabrics. The traditional garment is worn as a wrap with an obi belt as a kind of sash. Western versions are usually belted with a tie.

A traditional Japanese costume, the customary kimono is still worn today by the geisha and for special occasions. It is an indication of wealth and status, and elaborate, woven, hand-painted fabrics are still being produced using ancient methods. The kimono shape has been embraced within Western dress and, like the kaftan, is a comfortable and easy shape to wear, accommodating a variety of body shapes. Elements of the kimono, such as the sleeves, are often applied to a dress with no front opening.

Designers often take elements of the kimono as inspiration, not necessarily copying it literally. Emilio Pucci, Dries Van Noten, Haider Ackermann, Hermès, Fausto Puglisi, Lanvin, Aquilano.Rimondi, Bill Gaytten for John Galliano, Mugler and Uniqueness have translated the kimono into dresses using volume and proportion as the key, while Prada and Etro have included elements of Japanese kimono styling in dresses for Spring 2013.

Cut from **rectangles** on the bias, the bold colour-blocked stripes resembling a nautical flag emphasize the diagonal running across the body and falling in a **handkerchief hemline**. Kimono sleeves are integrated into the dress and the rectangular pieces emphasize the kimono aesthetic.

Oversized mini-length shift dress with **dropped shoulders**. The wide, bound, deep V neckline suggests a kimono placket, which is echoed in the border at the hem. The bold, **monochrome digital print**, with contrasting appliqué floral motifs, suggests kimono patterns.

KEY CHARACTERISTICS

- ☑ Rectangular pieces of cloth, without darts or shaping, forming a T
- ☑ Geometric, square sleeves
- ☑ Worn as a wrap, sometimes with an obi belt
- ☑ Luxurious, elaborate fabrics

1 Wrap kimono-inspired minidress embellished with elaborately embroidered motifs in a traditional oriental style. 2 The velvet skirt is attached to a brocaded silk bandeau that cuts straight across the bustline. The kimono sleeves in ombré chiffon fall to the fingertips. 3 The wide slash neck and kimono sleeves emphasize the simple rectangular cut. The placement of the wide black stripe within the brightly coloured, abstract-geometric print visually suggests a high waistline. 4 The geometry of the kimono sleeves contrasts with the long, fitted dress. The uneven hemline dips towards the back and reveals a flash of lining. 5 Exaggerated, bold scarf print, engineered so that the corner is curved to form the hemline. Kimono sleeve on the right and sleeveless on the left. 6 The square neckline, kimono sleeves and dropped shoulder line are counterbalanced by the soft drape of the fluid skirt. 7 Square lines are softened by bias cutting, allowing for drape at the neckline and at the deep armholes. 8 Authentic kimono references inform the shape of the wrap dress. Embroidery on the cuffs and at the back of the dress maintain the geisha influence.

> The kimono is deconstructed and subverted in this dress. Combining **rectangles and circles**, and mixing the strapping of the kimono with bias-cut rounded shapes, forms a draped skirt onto a straight hemline. **Matt and shine** fabrics help to define the cut. The diagonal bodice reveals one shoulder.

The combination of contrasting **geometric prints** in soft silk satin provides interest to an otherwise simple silhouette. With a slash neck and kimono sleeves, the dress is cut from **one piece of fabric**, taking design references from both the kimono and kaftan.

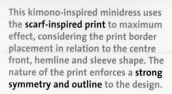

This kimono-inspired minidress uses the **scarf-inspired print** to maximum effect, considering the print border placement in relation to the centre front, hemline and sleeve shape. The nature of the print enforces a **strong symmetry and outline** to the design.

The body and sleeves of the dress are cut as one piece. Crisp organza helps to keep the sharpness of the kimono sleeves, which form a cap style. The skin-tone colour and transparency of the fabric gives the impression of a **second skin**. A vertical **panel of studs** is strategically placed down the centre-front and back panels to provide some concealment to an otherwise transparent dress.

This garment is constructed to seem like two scarves are joined together. The **large bold print** dominates the centre of the front and back panels, and the borders of the scarf trace the hemline, slash neckline, shoulder and perimeter of the armhole. The edges are finished with a **rolled hem**, keeping to the traditions of the scarf.

1 Wide kimono-inspired sleeves extend from the neckline and form the neck shape. The wide, open neckline frames the face. 2 Kimono references can be traced in the stand-collar neckline and the bold floral print with a contrast geometric flower at the front-yoke panel. 3 Asymmetrically cut panels combine print with colour blocking. The wrapped placket around the neck and the wide sleeves contribute to the kimono-inspired aesthetic. 4 Charleston-inspired, dropped-waist shift dress finishing just above the knee. The tiered fringing wraps around the dress from hip level to hem. 5 The unstitched underarm seam of the sleeve mimics the kimono. The contrast colour and the overlapping bodice give the impression of two separate garments. 6 The simple shift shape and high, round neckline are in contrast to the full circular-cut, kimono-inspired sleeve. 7 Asymmetric wrapping and layering juxtaposing varying lengths creates an abstract garment with underlying kimono features. 8 The shaping of the dress can be attributed to Ottoman and Eastern European references, but the kimono sleeves suggest a diverse mix of multicultural inspiration.

Floor-length, silk jersey dress with **plunging V neckline** to waist level. The bodice and elbow-length, kimono-inspired sleeves are cut in one piece, maximizing the inherent drape in the fabric. The **deep waistband** defines the shape and separates the slender, gradually flared skirt. A thigh-high centre-front split reflects the low neckline.

Loosely fitting, wrap-front, floor-length dress with main body and sleeves cut in one piece and secured at the waistline to achieve definition at the waist. This **uncomplicated shape** is an ideal vehicle for **bold prints**.

The bold, **Japanese-inspired** floral placement print immediately evokes the kimono. The references are continued in the shape of the wrap bodice, with the V neckline and **high waist** suggesting the obi.

Chinoiserie

Derived from the French word for *China*, this style of dress is inspired by Asian art, design and crafts. The obsession with orientalism in the 1920s manifested in the decadent work of Paul Poiret. The typical cheongsam dress features a mandarin collar with a diagonal front opening to the underarm. The fitted dress has a side split, revealing the leg, and can be knee-to ankle length. Exotic woven silks, embroideries of florals and dragons, prints inspired by hand-painted birds and bamboo, or blue and white porcelain-inspired patterns, are all trademarks of chinoiserie.

In 2004, Tom Ford embraced chinoiserie in his collection for Yves Saint Laurent, introducing the pagoda shoulder and referring back to the YSL imagery for the launch of the perfume Opium in 1977. Rodarte's autumn/winter 2010/11 and Louis Vuitton's spring/summer 2011 collections demonstrate a chinoiserie influence. Paul Smith's autumn/winter 2011 and Givenchy's spring/summer 2011 collections are also good examples of how the theme has informed shape and fabrication.

Designers hoping to attract favour with the ever-growing Chinese market by reworking Chinese cultural references and marketing these back to a Chinese customer may be in for a shock. Modern Chinese women would rather buy Western luxury brands than recycled versions of their own cultural heritage. This does not detract, however, from the continued Western obsession with the mysticism, exoticism and romanticism of the orient, and therefore chinoiserie will persist.

The high neckline of the **mandarin collar** and frog fastenings contribute to the oriental aesthetic of this floor-length coatdress. Long fitted sleeves are set into a decorative yoke shaped and curved like a **Chinese pagoda**. Embroidered fans, florals, fruit and butterflies decorate the dress.

Body-conscious dress fitted to the knee with an abstract **textured print** in a cotton sateen fabric. The dress has a round neckline and straight capped sleeves forming epaulettes at the shoulder, with kimono references.

KEY CHARACTERISTICS

☑ Inspired by Asian art, design and crafts

☑ Mandarin collar with diagonal front opening to the underarm

☑ Exotic, luxurious fabrics and prints

1 Dramatic pinafore dress with capped sleeves worn over matching oriental floral-print blouse. **2** Vertical and horizontal border print that frames images of fans and dragons. The short shift dress has a dropped shoulder and kimono sleeve to elbow length. **3** Full-length empire-line dress with long sleeves. Enlarged printed jewelry decorates the dress to give a trompe l'oeil effect.

4 The turtleneck and mini length of this dress balance the detailed, textural fabric treatment. **5** This dress has a silhouette that resembles a Chinese cheongsam. Metallic gold-on-gold brocade creates a feeling of opulence. The wrap opening of the skirt is curved in a tulip shape, giving the appearance of a sarong. **6** Pagoda references are evident in the shaped front bodice and panelled

skirt. The contrast print of the sleeves, yoke and high neckline reinforces the oriental references. **7** The trailing, graduated embroidery from shoulder to hip level balances the A-line shift shape and leads the eye to a flirty, fringed skirt. **8** Chiffon maxi dress with a panelled fishtail hem. The sheer fabric creates a nearly nude aesthetic, enabling the trailing embroidery design to take precedence.

> A simple, sleeveless shift shape with a soft V neck and dropped waistline. The dramatic, **contrast-colour** trailing embroidery has been engineered to complement the dress shape, and the **ostrich-feather skirt** gives a lighthearted and flirtatious feel to the design.

This pretty chiffon dress has been heavily **embroidered and embellished** with bold peonies that contrast with the delicate characteristics of the fabric. The garment design takes inspiration from **romantic petticoats**, with horizontal, ruched trim and scalloped, dropped waistline.

This maxi-length dress is **tiered** down its entire length, incorporating and concealing the shape needed to achieve a **perfect fit**. The embroidered floral pattern wraps around the body, complementing the design. The feather neckpiece balances the overall silhouette.

The contrasting black-and-white print placement has been engineered to work with the garment design for maximum impact. The **sweetheart neckline** frames the face, and the bias cutting enables the fabric to follow the contours of the body without interrupting the **print design**.

A bold floral print, enlarged in size to huge proportions, is an ideal choice for this simple chiffon bias-cut dress. The delicate **rouleau straps** and sheer, floaty fabric contrast with the **daring print**.

A contemporary version of a traditional **toile de Jouy pattern**. This bias-cut, maxi-length column dress has a deep **cowl neckline** that softly merges into the bodice. The bias cutting enables the dress to skim the body contours.

A chiffon wrap-over maxi-length dress with kimono style references. The full, long sleeves are gathered into cuffs, allowing the fabric to **billow** over. The neckline is finished with a wide solid border to create shape and contrast between the **sheer and matt** detail in the design. The chinoiserie-style print works well with the kimono-inspired design.

This **simple foundation** – bias cut to hug the body with delicate rouleau straps in silk chiffon – is an ideal canvas for the elaborate allover embellishment. The bold, bright embroidery and appliqué **pops** on the black background and is allowed to shine on this effortless shape.

A dramatic devoré-printed, bias-cut dress that skims the contours of the body but also maintains a fluid and flirty hemline. The **matt and sheer** characteristics of the fabric add to the **drama of the design**.

< Chinoiserie-inspired **brocade** sleeveless minidress with boatneck. The **semifitted shape** is strong and simple, making it the perfect vehicle for such an ornate fabric. The embroidered body stocking is an ideal accessory.

CULTURAL INFLUENCES

SPECIAL OCCASION

Special-occasion wear encapsulates all that is exhilarating and spectacular in the world of fashion. From the stuff of fairy tales and storybooks, romance and nostalgia, to elegance and sophistication, the dress is worn to impress.

This highly constructed yet fluid gown recalls the looks created for Hollywood bombshells of the 1950s. A cowl hung from the neck mirrors the triple tucks at the knee to create the classic mermaid-shaped dress. The diagonal swath of fabric emphasizes the smallness of the waist and voluptuous hips.

In context

This look, created by the House of Dior in 1960, would go on to typify the 1960s cocktail dress. The slip dress in gold brocade has a simple yet elegant thin, bowed sash slightly below the waist. It is paired with a matching evening cape, pillbox hat and elbow-length gloves. Similar dresses would be photographed on style icons, such as Audrey Hepburn and Jackie Kennedy, cementing this iconic look.

After World War II, the return of 'the season' re-established the importance of appropriate attire. Debutantes – young women from aristocratic backgrounds – were introduced into society in order to meet suitable husbands. The season consisted of a round of extravagant social events that took place throughout the summer months, which demanded fitting attire and were a good source of business for the couture fashion houses and private dressmakers of the time. The traditional evening wear attire was rapidly seen as outdated by young debutantes, who no longer wanted to dress like their mothers. As a consequence, by the late 1950s, couturiers found it increasingly difficult to attract a young clientele and established new ready-to-wear boutiques that guaranteed a high standard of finish, close to couture, but which only required minimal fit sessions.

The charity ball gradually replaced the private ball. Accessible by purchasing a ticket, the charity ball by the late 1970s attracted a more diverse patron. Actors, musicians and writers mixed with the aristocracy and helped pave the way for a new generation of designers, such as Ossie Clark and Zandra Rhodes, who imparted a more natural and fluid way of dressing for these formal occasions.

By the 1990s, fuelled by a growing celebrity culture, there was a new context for these formal dresses in the form of the red carpet. These glamorous dresses continue to make appearances at entertainment-industry award ceremonies, such as the Oscars, in the form of red-carpet dresses by designers such as Elie Saab, Versace and Valentino.

Special-occasion dresses are typically worn for only a few hours, and comfort is not always a priority. Women want a fantasy and an experience that can transport them to that special event like a charity function, fund-raising ball or wedding. Even the act of dressing, such as lacing the corset and complicated buttons, becomes a ritual.

Jacques Fath was an influential French designer who attracted a young, international client. This dress epitomizes the cocktail dresses of the 1950s, with the idealization of extreme beauty and the pursuit of ultimate perfection through precision cutting and proportion. The nipped-in waistline, tight bodice and full skirt accentuate the female form, while the slashed neck elongates the shoulder line, leading the eye to the exaggerated balloon sleeves.

SPECIAL OCCASION

Design considerations

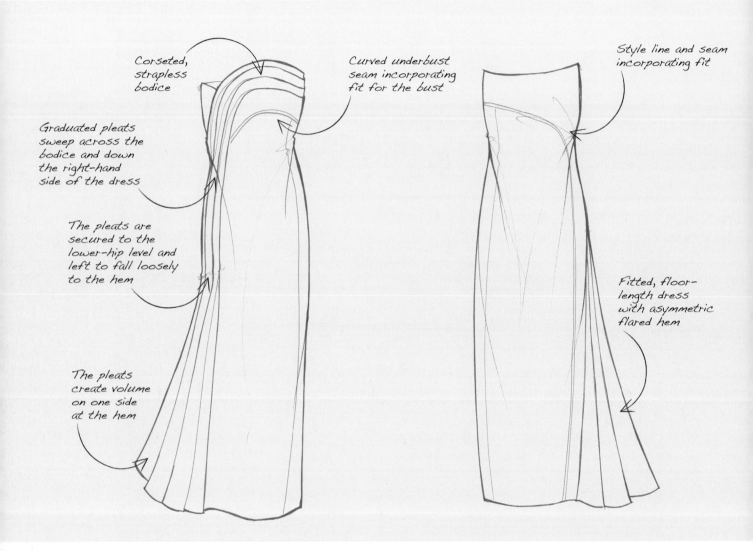

Corseted, strapless bodice

Curved underbust seam incorporating fit for the bust

Style line and seam incorporating fit

Graduated pleats sweep across the bodice and down the right-hand side of the dress

The pleats are secured to the lower-hip level and left to fall loosely to the hem

The pleats create volume on one side at the hem

Fitted, floor-length dress with asymmetric flared hem

Silhouette Special-occasion dresses are often slim fitting, either skimming the contours of the body for evening wear, or more structured and waist-defining for day wear. Foundation garments are commonly used to help create the desired silhouette, particularly popular in bridal wear and ball gowns.

Length Dress lengths will fluctuate depending on the event, and range from mini for cocktail and prom dresses, to floor length and trailing for bridal wear and ball gowns. Usually dresses worn for special occasions in the daytime, such as weddings and funerals, finish around knee length to achieve a smart, polished look.

Sleeves Depending on the occasion and climate, special-occasion dresses can be strapless, sleeveless, short-sleeved, three-quarter or long-sleeved. Any possible permutation of sleeve and armhole design can be utilized, as long as it is appropriate to the event and works in the fabric chosen.

Necklines and collars Necklines can vary from the demure to the seductive. When designing ball gowns and bridal wear, the emphasis is on exposing the décolletage. Taking inspiration from historical and cultural garments offers the designer endless styling choices where drama and extravagance is the prime consideration. Dresses worn to christenings, weddings and funerals adopt a more restrained choice of neckline.

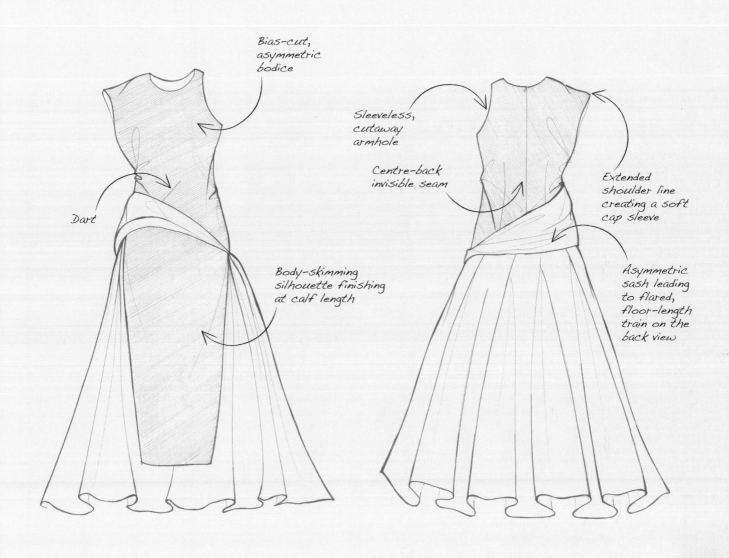

Bias-cut, asymmetric bodice

Sleeveless, cutaway armhole

Centre-back invisible seam

Dart

Body-skimming silhouette finishing at calf length

Extended shoulder line creating a soft cap sleeve

Asymmetric sash leading to flared, floor-length train on the back view

Fastenings Fastenings intended not to interrupt the flow of the design may take the form of invisible zips concealed in the seams or, in contrast, be part of the decoration, such as rouleau loops and covered buttons. Lacing and eyelets are a decorative feature, but can also help define the waist, creating the desired shape.

Details Fine detailing, such as pin tucks and shirring, are all commonly used on special-occasion dresses to add decorative interest to the silhouette, while also creating shaping and fit. Frills, flounces, ruffles, lace trims and inserts can soften and feminize the look. On ball gowns and wedding dresses, design interest or detailing may be a feature on the back, the angle at which these dresses are often viewed. Dress seams and hems must reflect the quality of the fabric and should be French-seamed if lightweight and sheer, with fine-rolled hems.

Fabric The infrequent use of a special-occasion dress can inform the fabric selection. Often delicate and needing special laundry care, the fabrics can be heavily embellished. The fabric choice is instrumental in the development of the garment design, and its weight, drape and handle should be considered. Copious amounts of luxurious fabrics, such as silk habotai, taffeta and chiffon are often used to create bridal wear, ball gowns and cocktail dresses, with more structured, medium- to heavyweight fabrics used for christenings and funerals.

SPECIAL OCCASION

Formal

The formal special-occasion dress encompasses an extensive variety of styles that reflect the traditions, protocols and etiquette of each individual event. Worn for occasions such as christenings, weddings and funerals, the formal special-occasion dress can vary from body conscious to oversized and billowing, structured to draped and fluid, and just above knee length to maxi length, though very rarely mini length. For weddings the formal dress is often in a lined lightweight woven fabric, such as georgette or chiffon, and can be brightly coloured with floral or bold geometric prints. The silhouette can be semifitted in a structured woven fabric or more voluminous in a soft woven fabric. In contrast, the formal dress for funerals is traditionally black and tailored, and accessorized with jackets and hats to cover the shoulders, arms and head.

Fabrics often reflect men's tailoring, with suiting fabrics commonly used, and silhouettes are usually semifitted, with lengths finishing around knee level. A similar style of formal dress is worn for christenings and weddings. The colour palette is cheerful, and silhouettes are often body conscious or semifitted in medium- to heavier-weight woven fabrics, depending on the season.

The influence of the **Chinese cheongsam** is suggested in the mandarin collar and capped sleeves of this elegant dress. The yolk panel is curved to front and side seam points. The soft matt skin-blushed silk falls to just below the knee, creating a relaxed, **lingerie feel**.

Grecian-style dress with dirndl **elasticated front panel** giving fit-and-flare shaping and a definition to the waist. The soft folds gather above the bustline to form a **boatneck** with a contrast shoulder-strap detail that echoes the Hellenist features.

KEY CHARACTERISTICS

- ☑ **Fabrics can reflect men's tailoring**
- ☑ **Fitted or semifitted silhouette**
- ☑ **Feminine, fluid drape, gathers and pleats**
- ☑ **Matt and shine fabrics**

1 Staggered asymmetrical features of the off-the-shoulder dress draw the eye to bare shoulders. The body-conscious silhouette is slashed at the front side. **2** Deep V-necked, sleeveless, tabard-style pinafore over cream silk underpetticoat. **3** The black strapping and panels against the floral print suggest a window frame looking onto a garden. Vertical panels elongate the body, giving a column silhouette with shaping integrated into the panels. **4** A 1950s-inspired fit-and-flare belt-waisted dress. The scooped round neck reflects the simplicity of the cut. **5** Deconstructed details, such as exposed seams, unfinished edges and a broken side zip, give a modern twist and question the correctness of formal wear. **6** Clean parallel lines, at the centre pleat-pocket vents, waistband and yoke, cut through the proportions of the dress. Contrast fabric gives the effect of a T-shirt under a pinafore. **7** The wrap-over at the front of this asymmetric dress gives way to a lower length on the left-hand side. The sloping neckline runs parallel to the hemline. **8** Slash-neck dress with a fitted bodice and wrap circular skirt. The metallic woven fabric creates a low lustre.

The graphic print and **laser-cut** pattern creates the illusion of a **three-dimensional fabric**, while the modern silhouette with clean lines complements the nature of the print. The subtly curved skirt and solid-colour border, shoulder and waist cleverly soften the design.

High-lustre silk satin, empire-line dress with **fur high-muff neck collar**. The soft, full skirt falls below the knee and is gathered below the bust to a **darted, fitted bodice**. Long set-in sleeves are fitted to below the elbow, where a full gathered bell shape spills over the tight cuff.

Colour-blocked panels give an asymmetrical, Mondrian-inspired look to the **loose-fitting shift dress**. A simple round neck and kimono dropped-shoulder sleeves emphasize the **geometric shapes**. The positioning of colour panels emphasizes the waist in order to give the illusion of shaping.

1 Vertical stripes are offset by the narrow horizontal waistband and softened by the side splits in the hemline. 2 A conservative knee-length dress with elbow-length sleeves and over bodice. Long gloves and boots ensure no flesh is revealed, while the colour gives a vibrant twist. 3 Midi-length dress with sheer chiffon sleeves and front yoke. Shoulders and side panels are solid colour and offset by a contrasting, graduated-stripe front panel that blends into a sheer striped skirt.

4 Hexagonal shapes are pieced together with faggoting embroidery to form the sleeves, neck and hemline. A printed version of the pattern is used as an underlayer. 5 Embroidered minidress with demure neckline. Black cuffs and a half-belt add to the formal aesthetic. 6 Raglan-sleeved dress with a solid-black lining and a sheer overlayer, embellished with a corded stand collar leading to a centre-front panel with a deep waist-defining band. 7 Simple silhouette with a modern aesthetic, a concealed-button placket, and horizontal half-belt that contrasts with vertical stripes. 8 The severe aesthetic of this high-necked dress is balanced by the circular-cut peplum at the waist.

Body conscious

The special-occasion interpretation of the body-conscious style is often based on today's ideas of classical dress, with the fabric draped rather than cut to fit the shape of the body.

In the 1920s, this free-flowing approach was a reaction against the style lines of the period, as epitomized by Fortuny's fine-silk pleated Delphos column dresses and the bias-cut clinging dresses of Madeleine Vionnet. In the 1930s, Hollywood became a strong inspiration for this look, where dresses were bias cut to create a slinky, body-defining silhouette. Flattering a slim figure, the bias-cut fabric subtly reveals the body underneath, which is accentuated with every move. Madame Grès's gowns of the 1930s pioneered this style and were notable for their innovative seaming and pleating, which created body-conscious drapes. In contrast to this organic approach, during the 1950s Madame Grès developed a technique that married her love of fluid classical shapes with the fashion for an extreme structured body, as popularized by Dior's New Look. Her pleated jersey gowns at this time incorporated a skilful securing of the carefully manipulated jersey onto a boned corset.

Evolving through the decades, the body-conscious dress was suited to the dance floors of the 1970s. Pioneering American designers, such as Halston and Geoffrey Beene, reworked a new aesthetic for fluid jersey and fasten-free dresses that were perfect for dancing.

The **tonal stripes** help to define the bandage effect of the panelling on this dress. The combination of vertical, horizontal and diagonal seams helps to create a slimming effect to the body-conscious silhouette. Architectural influences include **Grecian references** and column effect.

This silk jersey dress naturally clings to the body, defining its contours. The high, round neckline, square shoulders, long, fitted sleeves and maxi length create a **slinky column effect**. The gathered shoulders and elasticated **blouson waist** maximize the inherent drape in the fine-gauge jersey.

KEY CHARACTERISTICS

- ☑ Slinky, body-defining silhouette
- ☑ Innovative seaming and pleating
- ☑ Often structured with integrated foundation garments to enhance the body contours

1 Stretch-knitted fabric underlayer with horizontal bands of self fabric wrapped around the body, forming a diagonal shoulder strap. Corded bands create a vertical stripe at the left-front side.
2 This organdie dress gives the illusion of a body-conscious design with a contrast colour print delineating the shape of the body. **3** Lurex fitted dress with a high lustre that accentuates the

body-conscious shape. Darts from armhole to hip define the slimline silhouette. **4** Metallic-effect silk satin helps to define the contours of the body. Darted and seamed for maximum fit, the folded tucks above the bustline are mirrored in the turn-back sleeves. **5** Trapunto stitching follows the body contours, giving subtle surface decoration. **6** The curved yoke seam above the bust flattens

and streamlines. Snakeskin foil-effect panel gives an optically slimming effect. **7** Armadillo layering and body panelling give a sculpted look. Contour-defining directional seaming and flesh colour suggests a 1950s corset influence. **8** A sweetheart-shaped bodice is accentuated by a keyhole cutout at the midriff, as well as above the curved bodice, to give a strapless look.

Tea dress

Although traditionally English, the tea dress has become a universal staple, worn to charity events, weddings and other special occasions. The tea dress started life as a garment made solely for informal entertaining within the home, but over time has been adapted to be a more formal occasional garment.

After the turn of the twentieth century, the formal tea dress was no longer worn with corsets and became more liberating and individual, the start of a slightly more relaxed style of women's clothing. Tea dresses have taken inspiration from the Orient and Asian clothing, with the kimono and chinoiserie a primary source for design. The main characteristic of the tea dress is its soft, feminine silhouette with a semifitted bodice and flared hemline, accentuating the waist. The tea dress has survived every runway trend, with its longevity as a style rooted in its timeless vintage elegance. Bright colours and delicate prints highlight the girly, flowing silhouette. Lighter-weight fabrics create a comfortable dress that is easy to wear and transcends different occasions. Collars and necklines can vary, from scoop necks to V, Peter Pan to sweetheart. In addition to the classic cut, ending at the calf, variations in length can be below knee and maxi length.

The tea dress can be adapted for evening wear with sleeveless styling – though more traditionally it has puff sleeves – but sleeves are generally cut short, or occasionally three-quarter length. Depending on the occasion, the tea dress can be translated in finer, more luxurious fabrics and accessorized with corsages, gloves and hats to complete the look.

Fitted to the waist and flared to below the knee, this is a **typical 1950s style** but with a twist. The second of a double-layered bodice is drawn from the armholes to the waistband, where it is pulled together with the skirt and draped and gathered to give a **waterfall effect**, raising the hem at the left-hand side.

Buttoned down the front and falling **demurely** just below the knee. The suggestion of a halter neckline is created by a raglan-cut yoke at the front.

Alternative neckline and sleeves: deep V-neckline with batwing, three-quarter-length sleeves

KEY CHARACTERISTICS

☑ **Semifitted bodice and flared hemline, accentuating waist**

☑ **Lighter-weight fabrics**

☑ **Classic cut, ending at calf**

☑ **Vintage elegance**

1 · 2 · 3 · 4 · 5 · 6 · 7 · 8

1 This sumptuous silk-velvet drop-waisted dress has a simple vest-shaped bodice, softly gathered flared skirt, and self-fabric waterfall-frill trims. **2** The sleeveless raglan-shaped armhole gives a halter-neck appearance. A tie-feature stand collar is attached to a V-neckline. **3** Reminiscent of a 1930s cocktail dress, the full transparent skirt and sleeve details are contrasted with the waist

cummerbund and deep V-neck. **4** Fitted, elegant little black dress with a sweetheart neckline and wide shoulder straps decorated with self-fabric roses. **5** A fitted bodice and dirndl below-the-knee skirt give a 1950s feel. Contrast-fabric solid-colour collar, turn-back cuffs, and waistband complement the busy floral. **6** A simple, petticoat-style dress with rows of horizontal tucks detailing

the hipline. The lace detailing edging the V-neck and on the straps reinforces the lingerie references. **7** This 1960s-inspired silver sheath dress is at once youthful, with banded shoulder straps, and classic, with a traditional rose floral. **8** The A-line dress is loosely waisted with a self-fabric tie that is left to hang loose, echoing the grown-on fluted cap sleeves and longer-length back panels.

> Floral-print dress with contrasting chiffon beaded **underlayer**. The bust suppression has been incorporated into the soft gathers at the neck edge, which are reflected in the elasticated waist. The skirt is cut longer at the left side with more flare at the hem, maximizing the drape of the **bias-cut** fabric.

Pretty, floral, drop-waisted dress with a **handkerchief hemline** over a black net underskirt. The large cabbage-rose print on the skirt is combined with an Art Deco-inspired print on the bodice. Deep contrast tucks with a metallic floral clasp trim the waist. **Silver petals** scatter across the neckline, covering one shoulder.

A modern interpretation of a tea dress style, translated in **bold graduated stripes**. The stripes are used to accentuate the shape, with a vertical-striped fitted bodice that disguises the bust and waist suppression. In contrast, the skirt print has been engineered to work with the **circular shape** and is finely gathered into the waist seam. A prominent, contrasting belt and matching striped scarf complete the look.

A classic sleeveless **shift style** with quirky, oversized costume-jewelry print. Beading embellishment on selected areas of the print, creating a brooch effect, brings **humour** to the design.

Alternative neckline and bodice: boatneck with V-shape bodice panels incorporating fit

Digitally printed fit-and-flare dress with symmetrical panels and inserts that bring a formality to the abstract imagery of the print. The **V-strap** neck detail reflects the shape of the panelling, ensuring a coherent design. The flared, **fluid hemline**, cut shorter at the front, is in keeping with the nature of the print.

This refined fit-and-flare silhouette is an ideal backdrop for the lightly **quilted**, intricately patterned fabric. The **organdie overlayer** has been extended over the sleeve hem and skirt hem to create a sheer border detail.

Sleeveless, ornately embroidered maxi dress with **fringed hem** detailing. The main body of fabric has been fringed at various heights, ranging from the lower hip to mid-thigh, to highlight the fact that it is not an attached trim but **integral to the garment**.

A-line slash-neck minidress with a wide self-fabric **bow belt** that softly defines the waistline. The shell-pink colour characterizes this style, creating a young and fresh appeal.

1

2

3

4

5

6

7

8

1 Bias-cut, body-skimming, scooped-neck dress with double-layer, fluted short sleeves and complementary flared, full hem. The bust suppression and skirt flare have been incorporated into the diagonal style lines. **2** Cap-sleeved, fit-and-flare dress with deep square neckline. The dress is bias cut with a wrap-front skirt that scoops up at the front. **3** Deep V-neck sleeveless flapper-style dress with bias-cut bodice. **4** This simple tubular silhouette disguises the body's contours and is an ideal template for the flirty, asymmetric fringing that creates surface interest and movement.
5 A softly shirred neckline creates a loose-fitting bodice, complemented with short, tiered puff sleeves. Tiers continue at hip level, cut circular and gathered onto the skirt. **6** This calf-length, deep V-necked lace dress is transparent and worn over a spaghetti-strapped solid black petticoat dress. **7** This slash-neck floral dress is draped to emphasize the soft and delicate fabric. **8** Cheongsam-influenced fitted dress. The demure stand collar, extended shoulder line and body-defining silhouette are ideal for such a bold print.

> Soft, **layered** printed georgette is gathered into the waistband of this pretty tea dress, which opens at the front to expose a contrasting petticoat. The **strapless effect** of the bodice is finished by a transparent panel at the shoulder.

A pretty floral, vintage-style dress with **long gathered sleeves** and a Peter Pan collar. A deep waistband is shaped under the bustline, where the gathered yoke gives shaping. The feminine print is **scaled down** for hemline border, waistband, sleeves and collar. With a hemline above the knee, the dress is feminine and flirty – a typical example of the tea dress.

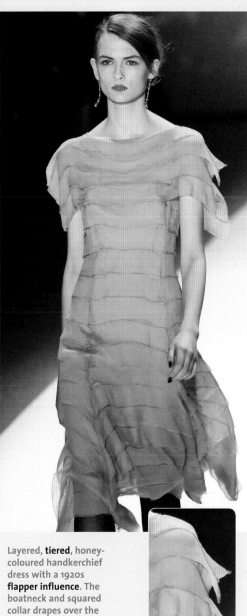

This short-sleeved raglan tea dress has a **boho aesthetic**. The look is highlighted by the skilful use of the border print, which plays on the proportion of colour and placement of the floral and defines the style, complementing the draped fluidity of the silhouette. Deliberate creasing of the fabric enhances these elements, blurring the edges of the **border print** as well as accentuating the design.

Layered, **tiered**, honey-coloured handkerchief dress with a 1920s **flapper influence**. The boatneck and squared collar drapes over the armhole, imitating a capped sleeve.

Three-quarter-sleeved chiffon minidress with deep V-neckline that is accentuated by a self-fabric placket, leading into the **full circular skirt**. The placket, waist seam and sleeve cuff are highlighted by a solid-colour **piping** insert that helps to accentuate the style details.

1 Boatneck, sleeveless dress with tiered, gathered skirt in various widths. The waist is defined by a belt. 2 Ombré-dyed pleated georgette, layered and fluted to give soft draping with Grecian overtones. 3 Multilayered dress constructed with contrasting fabrics to add depth. The cutaway layers and curved front hems, left to hang long on the back view, accentuate the drape of the fabrics.

4 Off-the-shoulder dress supported by fine spaghetti straps. The fitted bodice has a slashed neckline that is extended over the upper arms to fashion small sleeves. 5 A deep waistband is the main focus of this design, separating the dolman-sleeved bodice with plunging V-neckline and the gathered miniskirt. 6 V-neck dress with extended shoulders creating a cap-sleeve effect. Appliqué in

a contrasting colour on the neckline and front bodice leads into a delicate gathered chiffon skirt. 7 The cultural and historical influences are evident in the styling, fabrics and silhouette of this dress. The triangular inset, revealed by the deep V-neckline, is tipped by a pretty lace border. 8 Scoop-neck, sleeveless dress with fitted bodice and double-fabric tiered circular skirt.

Sleeveless fitted bodice with **demure** round neckline that creates an ideal balance for the asymmetric **origami-inspired** fold-detail skirt. The uncomplicated bodice, solid-colour fabric and simple silhouette make an ideal backdrop for the complex pattern-cut skirt.

Bias-cut wrap-over dress with a 1920s feel. The **high shine** of the fabric accentuates its inherent drape, and the uneven **handkerchief hem** maximizes the movement created when walking. The matt neck edge and skirt border define the shape.

A high-waisted, gathered, baby-doll dress with a bib front yoke. The **folkloric influences** are apparent in the skirt's floral lace print in black on a white ground. The **bib front** has contrasting braided patterning, white on black, edged with a gathered black-and-white frill. The opposite black-frill underskirt emphasizes the black-and-white contrasting theme. A brocade waistband completes the look.

SPECIAL OCCASION

Petticoat

The special-occasion petticoat dress is a more deluxe version of the sundress petticoat style. It is regularly translated in luxurious layers of translucent fabrics such as lace, silk and chiffon, often with a high-shine or low-lustre finish to the fabric. The general feel of this style can be light and slinky, taking inspiration from lingerie, slips and nightwear to inform fabric choices, silhouettes, detailing and pattern shaping. The petticoat style is an ideal choice for evening wear and red-carpet dressing.

Bias cutting, pioneered in the 1920s and '30s by Madeleine Vionnet, is a popular feature of this style, skimming the body's contours and accentuating its lines and curves, while enabling the fabric to drape softly to the hemline. Details are consistently delicate, such as fine spaghetti or ribbon straps, keyhole openings with rouleau fastenings, pin tucks, fine pleats, fragile frills, lace inserts, ribbon trimmings and embroidery. Dress lengths can vary from very short, echoing the voluminous negligee, to floor length, and trailing. Necklines are open, exposing the chest and décolletage, with bare arms and shoulders often accentuated with scalloped edges and lace trim. The petticoat dress can often adopt two distinct looks, depending on its historical inspiration, such as a more elaborate translation with frills and flounces reminiscent of nineteenth-century dress and, in contrast, the more seductive and elegant body-conscious styles evocative of 1930s glamour.

This baby-doll-style dress has a printed-chiffon **tiered miniskirt** that is circular cut and gathered into the waist seam to achieve a full, flounced skirt. The delicate straps and neckline have been trimmed with a **circular frill**, with an additional frill left loose to fall over the upper arms. A satin ribbon fastens the bodice.

The **draped-cowl** neckline of the lace bodice contrasts with the transparent **chiffon layers** of the handkerchief-cut skirt with an asymmetrical hemline. The skirt of the dress has a ballet-inspired aesthetic, offering an alternative to the petticoat dress.

KEY CHARACTERISTICS

- ☑ Luxurious layers of translucent fabrics
- ☑ Inspiration from lingerie and nightwear
- ☑ Light, slinky, delicate, feminine
- ☑ Open neckline, bare arms and shoulders

1 Panelled lace over a nude-colour underlayer suggests transparency. Puffed sleeves are edged with layers of lace; the same lace accentuates the V panelling that points to the waistline. **2** Full-length petticoat dress, bias cut from peach silk gives a nearly nude aesthetic. **3** Layering of contrasting fabrics give a range of tonal variations. The top layer of organza is scooped high above the bustline, revealing an underbra foundation. **4** Panelled transparent organza dress with flared hemline. A blue underskirt ensures a modicum of decorum, while the midriff is revealed. A lemon spandex, bra-styled underbodice balances the flash of colour. **5** Self-fabric bands have been appliquéd onto the torso of this sheer chiffon dress to create a diagonal, crossover design. **6** Horizontal bands of lace wrap around the body and over one shoulder for a barely-there look. **7** This maxi-length chiffon dress is bias cut, with a deep V-neckline that is echoed in the style lines. Full butterfly sleeves complement a flared hemline. **8** Bias-cut chiffon dress with a neckline plunging to the waist and a gathered bodice created by a drawstring neckline.

> Bias-cut, **simple**, unadulterated, white petticoat dress. The soft body-skimming silhouette is young and fresh, with **spaghetti straps** that require the absence of undergarments.

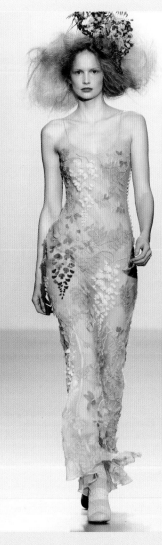

This sheer, spaghetti-strap maxi-length dress has all-over wisteria **embroidery** that enhances the feminine and delicate feel of the design.

An airy, **multilayered** chiffon dress with a delicately frilled neckline is offset by the structured contrast-fabric jacket. The strong shoulders and waistband of the jacket are in direct contrast to the ethereal feel of the chiffon. The **cutaway front skirt** with long back train accentuates the volume and fluidity of the fabric.

This simple tubular vest shape has added interest with the shaped and sheer **contrast yoke**, which includes three-dimensional floral embellishments. The scalloped **dropped-waist seam** reflects the shaped yoke and complements the handkerchief hemline.

Alternative bodice: wrap front with side tie fastening and spaghetti straps

Wide, scooped-neck chiffon dress with a cutaway skirt front and trailing back view. The **sheer**, delicate nature of the fabric is emphasized by the tonal silk flower embellishments that add **texture** to the design, graduating from the neckline to the hips.

SPECIAL OCCASION

Cocktail/prom

Usually thought of as featuring frothy skirts in tulle or organza, with glistening embellishment and strapless, fitted bodices, the cocktail or prom dress remains an important component of a woman's wardrobe. Meant for mingling at a cocktail party or for young women at formal school dances, the cocktail or prom dress is a lot less formal than the ball gown. Often designed shorter in length than the ball gown, falling just above or below the knee, or sometimes at calf length, the dress is meant to make the wearer feel glamorously attired yet relaxed and informal.

Created by Coco Chanel in the 1920s, the little black dress was an indispensable item of clothing for the cocktail hours, with dropped waistline and knee-length flounced skirt. The boyish shift silhouette created a blank canvas for trims and embellishment, while black was the acknowledged colour for formal and semiformal occasions. During the 1950s, when cocktail parties were at the height of their popularity, designers such as Christian Dior, with his New Look, explored extreme puffball or bubble shapes – revisited in 1987 by Christian Lacroix's signature 'pouf' silhouette – and re-established the cocktail dress as a timeless item of clothing. Contemporary cocktail and prom dresses have a multitude of design variations, from origami-inspired architectural dresses in structured woven fabric to slinky, sequined, silk-jersey alternatives.

Grey, geometric, constructed **squares and rectangles** inform the cut of this dress, from the square bib neckline and cutout armholes through to the square-cut seamed panel with inserted rectangles at the waist. The **split-front** straight skirt of the ankle-length dress completes the architectural forms.

Sleeveless, halter-neck slip dress. The drop-waisted bodice is fitted and heavily embellished with **sequins** to the seam just above hip level. The skirt is panelled and flares from the hip to knee length. The white-net **underskirt** gives added volume at the hemline and helps to define the flapper style.

KEY CHARACTERISTICS

- ☑ Fitted bodice and full, gathered skirt, often with underskirts
- ☑ Short length – either just above or below the knee
- ☑ Slinky, seductive and luxurious fabrics such as tulle or organza

1 Black-and-white tiered-effect dress with lace inserts and edging sewn to the dropped waistline and gathered to the hemline. **2** The bodice creates a blouson effect as it meets the waistband, and the skirt is gathered to the waistband. **3** Typical little black dress. The sweetheart-shaped neckline is accentuated as a small stand-up collar trims the neckline at shoulder level. **4** Ripstop fabric is taken out of a sportswear context to provide volume in the gathered skirt. The sheen accentuates the gathers and folds. **5** Unstructured slip-style shift dress in metallic foiled print to knee length. The simple sack-like shape is held up by braces. **6** Simple styling is the perfect canvas for the dense fringing of this mini shift dress. A high waistband stretches under the bustline, giving some definition. **7** The fitted bodice is transparent and the bra-shaped bodice of the underlayer defines the bustline. The skirt is cut wider at the waist than at the hemline and gathered to form a tulip-shaped skirt. **8** Fitted to the waist with a full skirt to calf. The bodice is drawn to the centre and gathered into a fake knot, which ties under the bust.

> This dress is constructed from separate bodice and skirt tubular panels, which have been **folded** to create fit and shaping and fixed into the waistband seam. The **bodice** stands away from the body at bustline. The contrast, sleeveless round-necked underbodice is cut separately and is also fixed at the waistband.

Alternative bodice detail: self-fabric structured bow accentuating waist

Contrasting fabrics and colour blocking define the pattern pieces within the dress. The V-neck sleeveless bodice has **lingerie references**, with black constructed panelling to mimic bra shaping. The fitted bodice dips to a V shape at the dropped waistline. **Accordion pleating** in metallic silver and a contrast-pleated panel in gold and skin-tone give an elongated column effect.

The round-neck, sleeveless **shift dress** features strategic diagonal and horizontal seaming that incorporates excess fabrics grown into the centre-front skirt panel, and diagonal to side seams that pleat and fold to form **three-dimensional structures**.

This bold, graphic-printed floor-length chiffon dress has a contradictory relaxed aesthetic, with a loosely fitted **wrap-front bodice** and low waistline. The bodice slightly blousons over the waistband, leading to a **full, gathered skirt**, which softens the geometric style of the print.

A simple, jersey vest-shaped dress that is an ideal canvas for embroidery and sequin **embellishment**. The dropped waistline and fringed, beaded hem is inspired by the **Charleston era**. The asymmetric waistband complements and informs the design of the embellishment, while also creating an informal balance.

1 Embroidered, sheer dress with halter neckline inserted into a narrow stand around the neck. A corseted, strapless foundation bodice gives structure and modesty. 2 Multilayered tulle dress with a ruched centre-front bodice that creates an inverted V-shaped waistline, complementing the generous godet skirt. 3 Metallic fit-and-flare dress with contrasting matt gathered and frilled hemline. Contrast-fabric neckband and side panels define the shape of the neckline and bodice and balance the high-shine fabric. 4 The bodice is tipped with a wide stripe that reflects the solid-colour band of the empire line. The skirt and fitted hemline create a puffball effect. 5 A deep V-neckline is edged by a continuous band placket. A deep waistband accentuates the waist. Long set-in sleeves and a peplum overskirt complete the look. 6 A classic 1950s-inspired cocktail dress with an open neckline, grown-on cap sleeves, wide waistband and full skirt. 7 A deep V-neckline directs the eye to a flared, circular-cut peplum and straight knee-length skirt. 8 Quintessential strapless cocktail dress with faux bow-effect bodice detail.

A pretty, layered, shift-style minidress with a 1970s retro **hippie influence**. The crochet cotton-lace underpetticoat has a scalloped hemline that mirrors the scallop of the **transparent overlayer**. The chiffon dress is embroidered and trimmed with tiny beads. A trim mocks a dropped waistband. The halter neck dangles to hemline after tying at the neck, and is trimmed with beads and feathers, emphasizing the hippie look.

Petticoat-style evening dress with a **fitted lace bodice**, shoulder straps and integrated bra cups. The two layers consist of solid white lining and a net overlayer decorated with lace floral friezes and tipped at the knee-length hemline with a scalloped lace edging. The bodice is more densely **embellished** with lace and beading.

Transparent **organza** shift dress, gathered at the waist by a self-fabric tie, drawn through a casing, to give a **ruched effect**. Long set-in sleeves are slightly gathered at the deep cuff. The funnel-neck collar stands high to cover the neck. French seams join the garment pieces and a back placket with covered buttons continues the **covered look**. The silver-foiled brocade print decorates the yoke, collar and sleeve heads. The garment is worn over a small underslip for modesty.

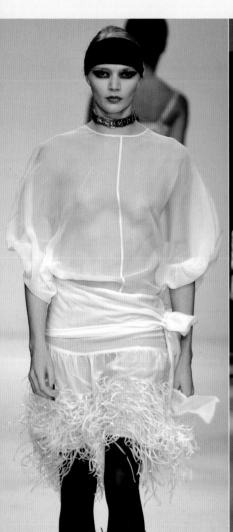

No side or shoulder seams, and integrated dolman sleeves gathered at the elbow, subvert conventional cutting. The **seaming** of the transparent fabric cuts the bodice at centre front and back. A blouson effect is created as the bodice is attached to the deep dropped waistband. The skirt is softly gathered from the hip and attached to the waistband, and the hemline is decorated with fringes that diffuse the boundaries. A self-fabric **cummerbund** ties at the side.

Shaping in the bodice is achieved by pleating and gathering into the seams, and **knotting** at the bustline creates a curved silhouette. Circular cutting creates a **puffball** shape, where the voluminous overlayer is seamed to a tighter underskirt in the same fabric

Alternative neckline: ruched, one-shoulder strap

Border-printed chiffon dress with **plunging V-neckline**, solid-colour contrast border and dropped waistband. The fine chiffon skirt is gathered into the waist seam to achieve a full, **maxi-length skirt**, maximizing the print design.

1 Textural minidress with a fitted silhouette and short set-in sleeves. 2 Off-the-shoulder dress with fitted bodice and cutout V-neck detail. The multilayered tulle skirt epitomizes this traditional cocktail style. 3 Boatneck sleeveless minidress with tiered fringing completely covering the shift shape. 4 Extreme plunging V-neckline to the waistband creates a sexy feel to this otherwise strong and graphic silhouette. The notched shoulder straps complement the square-shaped skirt sides. 5 Long-sleeved jersey body-stocking foundation with self-colour, high-shine rayon fringing overlay that creates a flirty feel, generating movement when walking. 6 Round-neck sleeveless dress with semifitted bodice and full gathered miniskirt. Self-fabric petals give a textural, three-dimensional effect. 7 High-contrast black-and-white embroidery, beads and fringes in horizontal bands decorate this pretty shell-pink dress fitted to the waist and gently flaring to just above the knee. 8 Asymmetric, taffeta structured minidress with a strapless foundation. The wide double-fabric sash adds depth to the design, creating an oversized-bow effect.

1 Capped-sleeve, V-neck, semifitted dress with self-colour mini frill embellishment on the bodice front. 2 With a fitted bodice and tiered, multilayered tulle skirt, the delicate matt fabric is contrasted with embellished shoulder straps. 3 Slash-neck, long-sleeved minidress. The intricately patterned bodice contrasts with the ostrich-feather stole-effect skirt, creating empire-line proportions. 4 Origami-inspired symmetrical tucks and folds give this sleeveless minidress a three-dimensional effect. 5 The metallic-woven fabric provides a high-lustre sheen. The shoulder yoke and flared sleeves suggest epaulettes and, with the circular neckline, give a regal feel to the slimline silhouette. 6 Strapless sundress with a fitted bodice with integrated bra foundation and shaped bustline. A full skirt is gathered into a high waistband. Gathered, layered petticoats increase the volume. 7 Gold sequins on a black ground, the luxurious fabric highlights the diagonal, fluid drape, which crosses the body. 8 Elastane knitted bodice, which accentuates the bustline. Knitted strapping trimmed with metallic hardware defines the waist, centre-front and side-bodice panels.

9 | 10 | 11 | 12

13 | 14 | 15 | 16

9 Metallic fabric, spaghetti-strap dress with slip-styling influences informing the bra cup and waistline seaming. 10 Full knee-length skirt and wide set-in sleeves are finished with a circular bias-cut frill. The round neckline has a centre-front placket to the waist seam, with a single-button fastening at neckline. 11 The elaborately sequined lace fabric is the main focus of this design, with its simple slashed neck, elbow-length set-in sleeves and full skirt. 12 Silk-velvet dress with a shapeless tubular bodice leading to a V-shaped dropped-waist seam and full circular-cut skirt. 13 A structured and strapless foundation is completely covered in tiers of ostrich feather. Delicate, sheer neck yoke and sleeves are covered with a floral embroidery design. 14 Sunray-pleated metallic minidress with crossover bra cups and halter-neck straps. 15 Intricate, laser-cut pattern applied to an organdie base to create a structured front panel. The organdie skirt has large tucks in the waist seam to create fullness at the sides. 16 Single-sleeved asymmetric dress with generous folds on the right side seam, which create diagonal drapes across the skirt.

Ball gown

With its heritage in couture dressmaking and bespoke tailoring, the modern-day ball gown assimilates traditional techniques of dressmaking, such as draping, fitting and spiralling, to create monumental works of contemporary glamour.

Ball gowns are worn to red-carpet events and charity balls, and imply a grandness and sense of occasion like no other garment, dramatizing the female form and showing off skilful craftsmanship. Traditionally supported by complicated foundation garments and often including bust pads, grosgrain waist tapes and tulle underskirts, the ball gown is a vehicle to show rich embellishments and ornate fabrics.

Rejecting the complex seaming and overt structure of traditional ball gowns, in the late 1950s/early 1960s, Hubert de Givenchy, under his brilliant mentor and friend, Cristóbal Balenciaga, set about redefining the customary cut of women's garments through the minimizing of seaming to create fit. Givenchy's minimalist endeavour, though simple on the surface, was innovative in its cut and construction, and was offset by feminizing his designs with embellishment and ornamentation, creating perfectly balanced aesthetic marvels.

With the emergence of charity balls and the rise of interest in celebrity, the traditional ball gown has evolved to reflect the changes in society, though it still remains at the core of a designer's vision, communicating the essence of his or her collection. Nowadays, the red-carpet dress is the most important platform for many designers' work, and the loyalty of a fashionable and famous client can sustain a designer's popularity.

This floor-length ball gown has an **asymmetric design** with a bodice single-shouldered on the right side, balanced by a diagonal sash on the left. The front skirt is wrapped with a shorter panel to knee length inserted underneath, creating a split to the hem. The skirt **fishtails** at the back.

This **simple, strapless floor-length** sheath dress has a slight fishtail. The blank canvas of the architectural **column silhouette** is broken by an embroidered knotted string, from bodice to calf, seemingly tied to an appliquéd pebble motif.

KEY CHARACTERISTICS

☑ Full-length

☑ Grand sense of occasion

☑ Rich embellishments and ornate fabrics

1 Chiffon floor-length dress with a wide neckline and fitted bodice. The fit-and-flare skirt incorporates solid-colour godets that increase the hem's circumference. 2 Fitted strapless bodice with baroque-inspired embroidery that contrasts with the tiered and chaotic floor-length skirt. 3 A figure-hugging silhouette with a fishtail to floor length, this ball gown is topped with a crisp white shirt-neck detail at the bust. Layers of gathered net give volume to the hemline.
4 A stretch, body-conscious foundation with demure turtle neckline and short sleeves contrasts with voluminous, chiffon floor-length godets.
5 Floor-length ditsy-print dress with a dirndl elasticated bodice. 6 A swathe of ombré pleated chiffon is fixed at the right shoulder and left to fall over the strapless foundation garment. 7 Fitted strapless dress that flares below the knee. The front panel below the waistband seam is slightly gathered to give a flattering shape to the stomach and hips. The wrap across one shoulder falls at the back of the dress to meet the long train behind.
8 The square-shouldered, metallic-leather bodice juxtaposes the sheer chiffon, voluminous skirt.

> This sleek, contemporary ball gown has a **sporty aesthetic**, with a slashed neckline and cutaway wrestler-form armholes. The shaped armholes reflect the **body-conscious** waist-defined torso, which gradually leads to the full skirt with thigh-high split and train.

This bold abstract print is engineered to complement the garment design. The **graduated colour** of the bodice contrasts the more dynamic use of colour at the **hemline**, emphasizing the hem's generous cut and swing.

A strapless **corseted bodice** creates a strong base for this maxi-length column dress with flared, panelled overskirt. The **overskirt** leaves the front view exposed to reveal the gold sequined motif.

Alternative bodice detail: turn-back cuff along neckline

The subtly graduated colour of this contemporary ball gown gives a young, fresh appeal. The high neckline and **cutaway armholes** have a sporty feel and contrast nicely with the **heavily tucked** floor-length skirt.

Grecian-inspired one-shouldered chiffon dress with draped crossover front bodice. The skirt is double layered and cut circular to achieve a **generous hem**.

1 Circular-cut floor-length skirt and circular, asymmetrically frilled neckline. The bodice is wrapped and gathered into the neck edge with a side panel. **2** This strapless dress uses contrasting colour inserts and folds to achieve an asymmetric sunburst effect that incorporates the shaping of the bodice and flare of the skirt. **3** Folklore-inspired lace bodice with scalloped lace straps and a gathered, voluminous taffeta skirt. **4** Marble-effect print reflects the flowing shapes of the chiffon-layered dress. Grecian toga styling is seen in the deep V and large armholes with dropped shoulder line. **5** Silk habotai has been swathed around a structured, strapless foundation to create an asymmetrical draped neckline and multilayered, wrapped floor-length skirt.

6 Low V-neck sleeveless dress with exaggerated dropped waistline and tiered skirt, reminiscent of traditional flamenco costumes. **7** Wide, V-neck dress with full circular-cut skirt gathered into the waistband, maximizing the fluidity and drape of the fabric. **8** Voluminous, lightweight silk skirt. The bodice is cut generously in order to create a soft fullness above the separate tied waistband.

The proportions of this single-shouldered dress create a strong silhouette. The diagonally draped fabric incorporates the bust and waist suppression enhances the **asymmetric bodice**. The diagonal waist seam mirrors the shoulder design and is offset by the **gathered, tiered** floor-length skirt.

Extreme fishtail silhouette with a long-line fitted bodice and defined bra cups. The fishtail skirt is achieved through multiple godets and is in stark contrast to the **body-conscious bodice**. The garment is softened by a sheer overlayer draped from the shoulders.

This strapless corseted bodice with full floor-length panelled skirt is a classic ball gown design. The **sweetheart neckline** reflects the shaped waist, with the self-fabric frills on the neck edge accentuating the overall shape. The **generously cut skirt** maximizes the impact of the busy allover print and allows for a modern interpretation of this design.

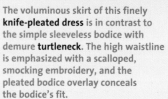

This simple floor-length, long-sleeved dress makes a good blank canvas for the pretty floral print with beaded accents. The **translucent fabric** exposes a hint of bare arms and chest, and is layered over a white slip dress. The round neckline and set-in sleeves give **maximum cover**, making the dress ideal for a more formal occasion, where showing too much flesh is inappropriate.

This dress evokes red-carpet glamour, with nearly nude body-conscious bodice and **long sleeves** covering the shoulders and arms but revealing and hinting at transparency at the bustline. Structure is achieved with a foundation built into the dress, giving a basis for the **draping** at the front of the skirt.

The voluminous skirt of this finely **knife-pleated dress** is in contrast to the simple sleeveless bodice with demure **turtleneck**. The high waistline is emphasized with a scalloped, smocking embroidery, and the pleated bodice overlay conceals the bodice's fit.

1 2 3 4

5 6 7 8

1 The floor-length lace hemline is raised at the front to reveal the calf. The high-necked sleeveless bodice is fitted to the waist. 2 The draped bodice contrasts with the box pleating of the skirt. The brocade fabric allows for both a soft drape and a sharp, defined pleat. 3 The simple cap sleeves, round neckline, and floor-length body-defining silhouette shows the allover metallic-sequined fabric to its full potential. 4 The deep scoop neck of this long-sleeved, bias-cut dress draws attention to the bustline. The body is emphasized by starburst shaping in transparent insert panels. 5 Strapless long-line bodice with metallic-lace overlay that contrasts with the multilayered tucked tulle skirt. A horizontally striped organdie full skirt defines the silhouette. 6 A strappy flapper-style dress, slashed from hemline to hip with fringes that reveal a flash of leg. 7 The juxtaposition of masculine and feminine, with tuxedo-styling references and soft gathered lace, are evident in this dress. 8 The body-conscious sheath shape, with high halter neckline and long billowing train, is achieved by the fine crystal pleating of the metallic fabric.

1 A strapless bodice is used as a foundation for this intricately tucked and draped dress. The symmetry of the draping and engineering of the colour placement brings a formality to the design. 2 The expansive A-line skirt acts as a canvas for the textural three-dimensional rosettes that cover the skirt's surface. 3 Sunray-pleated, floor-length chiffon dress. The high halter neck with extra-long self-fabric tie fastening is left to hang to the hemline. 4 The loosely fitted bodice blousons over the skirt and leads to a gathered full skirt. The uneven hem with cutaway front view accentuates the skirt's volume. 5 Floor-length, fitted, fishtail ball gown. The grown-on, draped, asymmetric, strapless bodice balances the skirt's train. 6 Body-conscious column dress accentuated by horizontal silver and white stripes. The tubular bodice is broken up by Y-shaped shoulder straps. 7 Delicately embroidered and appliquéd chiffon sleeveless dress layered over a simple, solid lining. The scalloped edges are left to blur the outline of the armholes and neckline. 8 A sheer sleeveless bodice is offset by black floral appliqué and a monochrome, feathered straight skirt.

9 The fitted bodice in black transparent chiffon contrasts with the white satin of the full skirt, cut from circular panels. **10** Striped fabric has been manipulated into pleated frills to create a tiered skirt that contrasts perfectly with the simple strapless bodice. **11** The ornate embroidery of this strapless corseted bodice leads the eye down to a heavily embellished border that gives structure to the hemline while accentuating the fullness of the skirt. **12** An off-the-shoulder corseted bodice has been extended over the upper arms to emphasize the exaggerated A-line floor-length skirt. **13** A circular cut gives a waterfall drape at the front skirt, extending to a longer train at the side of the dress. The extended front bodice stands away from the body. **14** Square shoulder and a body-conscious silhouette, flaring from hips to hemline, give a contemporary take on 1940s-inspired glamour. **15** A sleeveless tulle floor-length dress with nude jersey lining. A concentration of embellishment on the left shoulder is balanced by a half-belt on the opposite side. **16** The high-stand neckline, cutaway armholes and body-skimming bodice all create a strong, dramatic silhouette.

Wedding

Designers use the wedding dress as a vehicle to showcase their talents and epitomize their vision for that season's collection. Always the statement piece on the runway, the wedding dress often reflects the current trends and is adapted to work across a variety of silhouettes, lengths and styles.

The traditional white dress was established as a status symbol by the late eighteenth century, because it would only be worn once. The white dress now symbolizes purity and chastity. Romance and nostalgia were the main inspiration for design throughout the Victorian and Edwardian eras, and they continued to inspire through to the 1950s, when bridal dresses became more demure and sophisticated, echoing evening wear styles. In the early 1960s, wedding dresses became more clean-cut, with no frills and minimal seaming. Often the waistline was seamless and the straight or bell sleeves cut in one piece with the dress or seamed straight, like a kaftan. The simple dresses were often accessorized with elaborate headdresses. As the decade progressed, a feeling of nostalgia and romance returned, with lace, appliqué and embroidery making a comeback. This romanticism continued well into the 1970s, restrained at first, then blossoming into a retro revival in the 1980s, with bridal designs referencing historical and romantic influences.

The contemporary wedding dress is a melting pot of design, absorbing historical and cultural references and depicting current fashion trends. With civil weddings and less formal ceremonies becoming more popular, bridal wear has become more relaxed.

Edwardian meets the 1960s in this wedding dress. The demure Peter Pan collar and long **puff sleeves** are offset by the cream antique-effect lace strapless bodice and **A-line miniskirt**. The uniformity of the striped chiffon yoke and sleeves complements the intricately detailed lace fabric.

An elegant dress created with soft lines on the bodice leading to a sinuous, flowing, **full skirt**. The sheer chiffon overlayer obscures the sharp edge of the **strapless bodice**, and the dropped shoulder seams create a graceful silhouette.

KEY CHARACTERISTICS

- ☑ White statement dress
- ☑ Focus on back and front views
- ☑ Duchess satin, tulle, lace and brocade

1 Bias-cut silk-velvet dress. The asymmetrical style lines are reinforced by the diagonal neckline and single sleeve emphasized by the elaborate bow-tie shoulder. 2 The column silhouette is created by this long, silk-spandex-mix jersey dress that skims the floor and hugs the contours of the body. 3 1950s-inspired dress in duchess satin. A fitted, darted bodice is embellished by fine beading.

The waist is enhanced by a self-fabric sash tied in a large bow. 4 Floor-length wedding dress influenced by baby-doll lingerie, with empire-line, fitted lace bodice and shoulder straps. 5 Knitted dress in fine-gauge silk and elastane yarn. The illusion of a dropped waist is created through the change of knit structure. An oversized keyhole neck detail continues into a slash neckline.

6 A pin-tucked bib bodice resembles a Victorian nightgown, but the primness is counterbalanced by a short hemline. 7 Slip dress with integrated strapless bodice and fitted mini-length skirt and an overlayer of lace. A deep satin bow with floral corsage emphasizes the dropped waistline. 8 A strapless bodice foundation with a lace halter-neck overlayer and tiered bell-shaped skirt.

> Body-conscious strapless dress with built-in corset to give structure and emphasis to the **fitted waist**. The **side seams** are brought forward, giving the illusion of a slimmer silhouette. The scoop-front, tiered fishtail skirt features layers of circular-cut frills that contrast with the restrained bodice.

Edwardian-inspired floor-length wedding dress with substantial **scalloped lace train**. The dress is waisted with a godet-panelled skirt that gives flare from the hip. The scalloped hemline is echoed in the demure cape-like **stole overlayer** that is inserted into the boatneck.

This satin-backed crepe **body-conscious** wedding dress has an elegant and sophisticated appeal. The cummerbund **asymmetric sash** and multiple rouleau loops and covered buttons on the sleeve add design interest to this overall simple silhouette.

Contrasting matt and shine **floral brocade** in a traditionally styled dress. The fitted bodice has a dropped-waist seam, though a sash defines the waistline. The plunging V-neckline reveals a solid-colour underbodice. The shoulder seams have been grown on to form the stand neckline. The volume in the skirt is created using **net petticoats**.

Empire-line dress with a deep waistband and **pleated bodice** overlay that stands proud from the strapless foundation. This is reflected in the **gathered peplum**, contrasting with the elongated floor-length fishtail skirt. The bustle-effect train complements the bodice detail, creating interest at the back view.

Housecoat-style wedding dress in silk-satin fabric. The bust suppression has been manipulated and gathered into a curved yoke at the shoulders, creating drape at the **front wrap opening** and drawing the eye to the ornate buckle. The sweeping A-line floor-length skirt is split to the thigh, echoing the V of the neckline.

This **shirtwaisted dress** has a 1950s influence. Common to the period, it has a self-fabric-covered **belt and buckle**. The strapless bodice foundation has a short-sleeved, shirt-style overbodice made of self-colour lace. The neckline, shoulder and upper arms are covered to give a demure appearance.

Strapless wedding dress with a relaxed, unstructured draped bodice and skirt. The **deconstructed hemline** reflects the casual aesthetic, giving the impression of a wrapped toga style. The underskirt is layered and uneven with ethereal **Grecian qualities**. Disguised within this relaxed exterior is a structured foundation.

1 Flamenco-influenced dress with asymmetric, tiered fishtail hemline. A self-fabric band that extends over the right shoulder trims the neck edge. 2 Duchess satin dress with a boatneck and inverted V-shaped notch that mirrors the curve of the waistband, which extends into the back train. 3 Strapless corseted bodice with a circular, sunray-pleated, multilayered floor-length skirt. A delicate pleated peplum frill has voluminous pleated ties that sweep to the floor. 4 Heavy duchess satin gives volume to the long A-line silhouette. Design interest is achieved through the diagonal gathered panel. 5 The decorative waistband is the focus of this dress, with the bust and waist tucks, and angled pockets, all pointing towards the centre front. 6 Fishtail silhouette with corseted bodice emphasizing the hourglass figure. A lace-appliqué overgarment becomes the focus, suggesting a yoke. 7 The bodice is darted to the waistline with an extended fitted hip, which flares to the knee. Voluminous layers of net fall to the floor. 8 Slip-inspired dress that follows the contours of the body. The high waistline is defined by a tie belt and corsage.

> Tailored, round-neck, collarless coatdress with a formal aesthetic. The curved yoke extends to full-length magyar sleeves with a seam that extends from shoulder to cuff. The concealed-button **front placket** extends from neck to hem, adding to the **minimal look**. Patch pockets at hip level give a simple decorative and functional addition.

A contemporary version of a wedding dress translated in **jersey fabric**, giving a sporty vibe. This is echoed in the racer-style armholes and oversized **funnel neckline**. The contrasting woven welt at the hem reflects relaxed sweatshirt styling.

Slash-neck wedding dress with combined centre-front panel and grown-on cap sleeves that are designed to restrict movement. The V-shaped bodice lines lead to a defined waistline then open out to the inverted, **multipleated panel** at the centre-front skirt. The side seams of the skirt are displaced to match the bodice style lines and create more volume at the back view.

Gossamer-light silk performs well to achieve the **envelope shapes** created by geometric deconstructed cutting. The asymmetric style lines on the bodice complement the **draped skirt**, with integrated pockets set into the cowls at the sides, avoiding the need for seams.

Tiered gathered layers are strategically stitched to create an asymmetrical skirt that curves up the right-hand side seam and falls as layers on the opposite side. The **unfinished edges** of the fabric suggest fringes, with a play on direction in order to define the bodice.

1 Traditional ball-gown styling with horizontal deep tucks that add structure to the wide crinoline-style skirt. 2 This dress wraps the body, creating an envelope shape and requiring minimal seaming. Layers of tulle petticoat emerge from the hemline. 3 This bias-cut dress has a cowl neckline that falls to create a handkerchief shape with a beaded fringed trim. Accessorized with a cap sleeve and beaded silver vest. 4 Mini-length dress with a deep-sliced centre-front V. The semifitted bodice contrasts with the fullness of the unpressed box-pleated skirt. 5 Duchess-satin-silk fit-and-flare dress with a Peter Pan collar, capped set-in sleeves and ballerina-length skirt. Decorative vertical tucks create the only decorative element. 6 Crepe dress with cowl neck exaggerated at the back giving a deep backless view. 7 Silk-satin, bias-cut dress with set-in leg-of-mutton sleeves. The bodice seam is shaped as an inverted V under the bustline and decorated with beaded embroidery. 8 A drop-waist bodice is cut straight across the bustline. A halter-neck strap is attached to transparent raglan sleeves. Tucks run vertically down the front of the bodice.

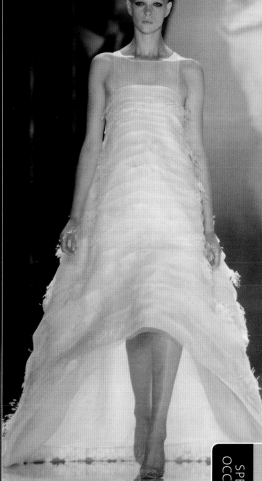

Traditional prom style with **sweetheart-shape neckline** and a strapless and corseted bodice. The waistband has a **chocolate-box bow** that cinches the waistline. The midi-length A-line skirt has a tulle overlayer heavily embellished with lace, appliqué and beading.

Dress featuring two layers. The top chiffon layer has a **shirt neck** and button-placket opening ending just below the bust. This is fitted to the waist, then extends to a peplum at the front, dipping at the back to **form a train** at the ground. The fitted lace underdress has a shaped bra cup then clings to the body and flares from the knee to the floor-length hemline.

An **exaggerated A-line** silhouette continues from the strapless bodice neckline to the hemline. Layers of **chiffon tiers** cover the entire surface area of the design, offset by the sheer single-layer neck yoke. The hem is cut away at the front, emphasizing the long train on the back view.

INNOVATIVE

This category includes dresses that question conventions and push the boundaries in terms of fabric, cut, form and construction. These are examples of visionary dresses that pave the way for future mainstream fashion.

Subverts the intrinsic qualities of lace with the juxtaposition of a hard black overlay of laser-cut black leather appliqué. A dress that is both fragile and feminine in coral pink, is contaminated and infected in a surreal and sinister manner. The nearly nude underlayer, with a foundation of boning, allows the black filigree to seemingly tattoo and engrave the body.

In context

The 1960s were greatly influenced by the burgeoning space programmes of the United States and Russia, as well as a reassessment of youth, sexuality and gender morality. Courrèges was known for his clean, modern aesthetic and great craftsmanship. The innovation of this dress is as much about the groundbreaking cutouts as the inventive precision the cutouts required to execute.

Utilizing advances in science, engineering and technology shaping the future, fashion designers are at the forefront of ground-breaking invention.

Collaborations between textiles, science, fashion and technology allow for pioneering research and cutting-edge developments. Wearable technology – incorporating sensors, circuit boards and power sources in textiles or garments – creates an interface between the dress and the computer. Light-emitting textiles and robotic articulation allow the transformation of the dress, no longer an inanimate object that purely interacts with the wearer.

The fashion laboratory can be evidenced in the 1920s, when Elsa Schiaparelli collaborated with industry, using innovative fabrics, borrowing scientific images and embracing surrealism to design the modernist dress. Influenced by space travel and science fiction in the 1960s, Pierre Cardin experimented with vacuum-formed and moulded textiles, André Courrèges explored bonded jerseys and synthetic fabrics, while Paco Rabanne developed metal chain-mail dresses. Contemporary designers such as Walter Van Beirendonck, Rei Kawakubo for Comme des Garçons, Martin Margiela and Hussein Chalayan challenge the perceptions of the body, and design fashion beyond the constraints of the fashion establishment. Japanese designers Junya Watanabe, Yohji Yamamoto and Issey Miyake master and dissect traditional craft methods, pushing the boundaries of fashion and textile design.

INNOVATIVE

Using innovative fabrics and styling in the late 1960s, Pierre Cardin was ahead of his time. Here, vacuum-formed and moulded plastic and coated fabrics create textured surfaces and a minimal, architectural aesthetic. Revolutionary at the time, Cardin has set an example for the fashion designer's aspiration for new trends and innovation.

Design considerations

Fascinated by materials and structure with an alchemist approach to fashion, Iris Van Herpen creates garments defined by innovation and craftsmanship. Inspired by architectural forms and natural organisms, she collaborates with artists, architects and researchers to produce garments composed of materials such as copper, resin, silicone lace, UV-cured polymer, acrylic and leather, combining the technology of 3D printing and hand-assembled craftmanship.

Understanding of fundamentals
Innovative dresses require new ways of looking by the designer in order to express creative ideas beyond the consideration of normal or mainstream. Understanding the fundamental traditions of fashion and textile craft and basic principles of techniques allow for rules to be broken and boundaries to be pushed.

Industry collaboration Collaboration is paramount in order to cross the individual specialist areas between textiles, technology, art, architecture, medicine and science.

User considerations Consideration of user needs and environmental concerns can take precedence over seasonal trends, offering greater credibility and longevity with sustainable consequences.

Fabrics Added value can be achieved with the choice of high-tech fabrics and finishings for original appearance, handle and high performance. For example, fabrics that appear light and delicate yet are durable and hard wearing, or breathable and waterproof, combine functionality with aesthetic without simply conforming to a fashion- or trend-led agenda.

Hussein Chalayan is known for his highly conceptual and thought-provoking work, which is at once beautiful to look at as well as technically advanced. A central theme to his work is the passage or perceptions of time and place. By a series of battery-operated pulleys, the dress transforms the silhouette from one era to another. Inherent in the presentation is the acknowledgment of our reliance on past style ideals, despite our technological sophistication.

Pattern cutting New ways of pattern cutting can be explored to minimize waste, allowing for a more ethical and considered approach. Digitally printed fabrics can be engineered to fit the pattern pieces, enhance the cut and reduce the need for style lines in order to create design interest. Reducing the need for style lines, darts and seaming, reductive pattern cutting strips away unnecessary detail but still maintains a strong silhouette and perfect fit.

The pared-down aesthetic hides a very complex and advanced form of cutting. An abstracted silhouette can be achieved through the use of subtraction pattern cutting pioneered by Julian Roberts.

The business end Innovative garments are not necessarily designed to be commercial – they often represent ideas in their purest form, which are then adapted and refined into a more marketable item. If or when garments are for ready sale,

they may require different marketing strategies. Point-of-sale labelling may require additional information that explains the fabric content or care requirements. New symbols may need to be created in order to describe new functions and end-of-life disposal. The traditional runway show may no longer be appropriate, and the seasonal fashion calendar may not be applicable.

INNOVATIVE

Pattern cutting

The shape of the dress has been cut to suggest the **wrapping of a garment** around the waist. Integrated into the seams, the **mock sleeves** wrap and tie at the centre front, with deep side pockets disguised within the garment. The end result is a soft, relaxed aesthetic.

Laser-cut leather gives a lace effect to the skirt. The softness and transparency is contrasted with the harder-edged, sculptural shapes at the neckline and bodice. The wide shoulder line and peplum effect help to disguise yet accentuate the waist, to enhance the **hourglass figure**.

Subverting shape and form through creative pattern cutting can redefine the relationship between the dress and the body, and the expectations of beauty and aesthetic. Notions of antifashion, or garments that defy trend and the established fashion hierarchy, can liberate the designer to challenge expectations and conventions.

Borrowing from sportswear requirements, cutting for movement can add a new dimension to traditional pattern cutting, increasing the functionality of the design and, in turn, improving quality of life. The design and construction of sculptural forms, much affiliated to architecture and engineering, are more likely to result in unconventional outcomes.

Japanese fashion design in the 1980s paved the way for a new approach, with designers such as Rei Kawakubo for Comme des Garçons, Issey Miyake, Yohji Yamamoto and Junya Watanabe mixing science and art with fashion and using techno fabrics and inventive construction. Deconstructivist designers, such as Hussein Chalayan, Martin Margiela and Ann Demeulemeester all take an intellectual approach to the design of the dress and push the boundaries of pattern cutting, starting with recognizable shapes and subverting them to disobey the principles of traditional cutting. Distorted proportions and body-defying shapes can blur gender and disregard function. This radical approach requires a cutting-edge approach to production and marketing, finding new ways to communicate and target the customer. Translated into a more accessible and commercial product, innovative cutting can be less overstated while still maintaining its originality.

KEY CHARACTERISTICS

☑ Subverting traditional pattern-cutting techniques

☑ Distorting proportions

☑ Consideration for user needs

1 Cocoon-like shape with rounded forms curves forwards at the shoulder line, creating a cape effect. **2** Mélange wool in a constrained garment builds architectural forms with the precision of origami. Sleeves are open underarm to expose the undergarment, allowing articulated movement. **3** A side panel curves into a cape sleeve emphasized by contrast lining. The opposite shoulder is cut asymmetrically to a yoke. **4** Abstracted shapes show feminine curves, influenced by modern art, sculpture and architecture. Minimal materials and enveloping forms, inspired by Balenciaga and Cardin. **5** Bold techno-cotton dress with origami folds and 1980s power-dressing influence. A nipped-in waist and front split reveal the feminine form. **6** Abstraction of space reveals the body, hinting at feminine curves. Fabric drapes blur the boundaries. **7** Asymmetrical shape with a casual, oversized silhouette and emphasis on the shoulder. Abstract shapes create a canvas for colour blocking. **8** Soft curves have been used to inform a strong structured shape. The padded seam and integrated curved zips are functional and create design interest.

> Aquatic theme with fantasy **mermaid** references: fish-scale layers of **silver foil** on pleated shells cascade to a fishtail at the hemline. The fabric grows into a fitted metallic bodice that forms a deep halter neck.

Defying conventions and **questioning functionality and wearability**, this conceptual dress explores the boundaries between fashion and art. The drop-waist pleated dress has multiple personalities, with **conjoined triplicate dresses** attached to the back.

The pattern pieces of the dress have been **folded** like the stages of an origami puzzle in a luminous, Lurex, **brocade fabric**. The skirt, bodice and collar are all integral components of this complex pleated structure.

Mixing circles and rounded curves with straight lines and diagonals, this dress consists of sculptural shape**s** and forms. The neckline stands high away from the neck, creating a straight line at the shoulder, forming a **rectangular silhouette** that contrasts with the skirt, which narrows to the hemline, creating diagonal lines edged with **circular ruffles**.

Unmistakable **shirt references** are exaggerated and subverted to create dynamic **sculptural forms** that challenge the preconceptions of fashion. Using layers of multiple shapes to reinforce the pattern pieces and details of the shirt, the showpiece creates a strong, bold statement that evokes the concept behind the collection and presents the climax to the grand finale.

INNOVATIVE

Fabrics

Is the future of the dress as simple as a spray of fibres directed at the body from an aerosol can? Scientific research, developed by Manel Torres in the form of the Fabrican, has made this a possibility.

Textile technology is moving at a fast pace, and innovations and new ideas are moving out of the laboratory and onto the catwalk. State-of-the-art textiles are often key to the development of original dresses, and sourcing interesting fabrics can be a challenge.

High-performance fabrics adapted from the military, space travel and extreme sportswear can be translated into wearable fashion. Advanced synthetics, interesting mixed fibres, and ingenious fabric treatments offer the designer greater choice in terms of performance, handle and visual aesthetic. Fabrics treated for crease resistance, water or stain repellency or fire retardation offer added performance value. The customer's well-being can also be considered, such as when using fabrics with bacteria-fighting properties, wicking characteristics to allow breathability, reflective qualities for high visibility or cloth that hardens on impact for physical protection. Sculptural shapes can be created using heat-set and moulded textiles that interact and shift with the body. Bonding and layering and new fibre combinations and surface treatments create hybrid textiles. Mixed-media techniques, combining digital print with digital embroidery or laser-cutting, welding, bonding, polychromatic printing and heat-setting, are only the tip of the iceberg in terms of potential embellishment and fabric manipulation.

A combination of digital print with embellishment creates a surreal interpretation of **interior scenes**, focusing on windows, lampshades, pelmets, tassels and chandeliers. Digital printing allows for a photo-realistic approach and, together with three-dimensional pattern cutting, creates a **trompe l'oeil effect**.

Leather cage dress using **latticework construction**. The body-conscious silhouette with funnel neckline encases the form in a conceptual dress combining art, fashion and architecture. It is zipped into place to **reveal and protect**, and questions notions of wearability.

KEY CHARACTERISTICS

☑ **High-performance fabrics and fabric-surface treatments**

☑ **Use of new technologies and construction methods**

☑ **Consideration of user needs**

1 Pinafore-style dress with ribbed hem and yoke mimicking knit but created by heat-moulded techniques. Embellished with embroidery and appliquéd print for maximum pattern and texture.
2 Metal-chain fringes are set into the seams and draped over a wool-jersey dress to give a Gothic-inspired look. 3 The dress is a commentary on the objectification of women. The plastic is moulded to portray breasts and hips with layers of horsehair, similar to the ponytail reminiscent of a prize-winning horse. 4 Neoprene-effect leather, moulded in chevrons for a constricted body-conscious look. Directional striping defines and softens the rounded shoulder panels. 5 The digital photo-realism within the print complements the structure of the pattern-cut shapes. 6 Latex rubber with laser-cut edges and circles that reveal layers underneath. Seams have been heat sealed. 7 Concertina effect created by heat-forming pleats and rounded shell-like curves. Allows the fabric to move with the body.
8 A vest bodice in high-gloss rubber and a full skirt pleated into the waistband. Accessorized with heavy leather bra and wide belt.

> Jewel-encrusted and heavily embellished **organic shapes** that resemble elaborate butterflies. A strong net foundation is the base for **laser-cut** multicoloured leather shapes, layered to form strata and manipulated and curled to create complex, three-dimensional forms.

Manipulated, soft-fabric horizontal and vertical strips are attached to create a **wide open mesh** that reveals the body but can be worn over contrasting layers. The deep cowl-neck collar folds over to create a drape at the neckline.

Sprayable, nonwoven fabric, patented by Fabrican, creates an instant dress directly from an aerosol can onto the body. Cross-linking fibres form a fabric, liberating designers to create new and unique garments **without the need for seams** and lending the ability to incorporate fragrances and active substances.

In homage to the House of Rabanne's founder, the dress is made of **pearls and chain links** constructed to create a stripe pattern. The body is at once exposed and protected.

Silk layered on white organza and cut and frayed between vertical rows of stitching to create a subverted pinstripe, in keeping with the **exaggerated shirt styling**.

Glossary

Angora Fleece from the Angora rabbit spun to create a soft yarn for knitting or weaving. Also describes the Angora goat, whose fleece is used for mohair.

Aran Originating from the Aran Islands off the coast of Ireland, a style of knitted patterns in natural yarn combining cables and decorative raised stitches and twists.

Argyle pattern Diamond-shaped pattern that originated in Scotland. Two or more colours are used to knit jumoers often adopted by golfers and used in sock patterns.

Art deco Originating in Paris in the 1920s, an artistic style featuring streamlined shapes and geometric patterns inspired by aerodynamic machines and sunburst motifs.

Astrakhan Lambskin from the astrakhan region of Russia. Also used to describe woven fabric designed to imitate the lambskin effect.

Baby-doll Very short minidress similar to a young girl's dress. Also describes a flimsy, short and sheer nightdress often worn over matching panties.

Bateau neck See *boatneck*.

Batwing sleeve See *dolman sleeve*.

Bellows pocket Type of patch pockets with expanding sides, commonly used on a Norfolk jacket.

Bell sleeve Sleeve that fits closely to the armhole and to mid-upper arm then flares widely to the wrist.

Bias The diagonal line that runs across the grain of the fabric at a 45-degree angle to the warp and weft. Cutting on the bias allows stretch in a garment.

Bishop sleeve Sleeve made from light fabric, widening from the shoulder and gathered into a cuff at the wrist.

Blanket stitch Decorative embroidered stitch originally used to edge blankets.

Blouson Short, loose-fitting men's jacket with gathered sleeves and cuffs. The term also describes the same gathered effect in a dress, for example, when a loose bodice is gathered into a waist seam.

Boatneck Shallow, curved neckline almost extending from shoulder to shoulder.

Bolero Inspired by traditional Spanish men's jackets, a short, cropped, open jacket, often worn over a dress.

Bombazine Twill fabric with a silk warp and a worsted weft, dyed black. Traditionally used for mourning garments.

Boning Originally strips of whalebone, and later covered flexible steel or plastic, inserted into stitched channels of fabric in garments, such as bodices or corsets, to help create shape, form and fit.

Bouclé Looped or rough-textured yarn, knitted or woven to create a fabric with a knobbly surface.

Box pleat Pleat created by two folds facing outwards and towards each other, then pressed flat.

Braid Strands of thread corded and woven together to create a ribbon effect. Used to decorate the surface or create an edging to a fabric.

Brocade Luxury woven fabrics, often using silk or metal threads, with an extra weft added to create a raised surface pattern.

Broderie anglaise Whitework embroidery creating decorative patterns – usually floral – combining pierced holes with satin stitch.

Bustle Padded shape worn under the dress at the back or sides to create volume underneath and support the outer skirt. Can be a metal frame or padded fabric forms.

Cable knit Knitted technique to create a vertical braided effect. Stitches are crossed over adjacent stitches, alternating over and under using plain and purl to define the cables.

Calico Lightweight woven cotton or linen with a semitransparent open weave.

Cheesecloth Thin, loosely woven cotton cloth originated from India. Also known as calico.

Chenille Velvety cord with a tufted surface, made from silk or synthetic yarn, used to create a soft woven or knitted fabric of the same name.

Cheongsam Close-fitting Chinese women's dress with mandarin collar and side splits. Often fastened at the neck with frogging.

Chiffon Sheer, delicate, woven fabric using twisted silk or synthetic yarns for a grainy surface.

Chintz Glazed cotton printed with bright patterns – often floral. Originally imported from India.

Corduroy Cotton fabric with soft pile of parallel ridges in various widths to create variations, such as needlecord, jumbo cord or elephant cord.

Corset Undergarment composed of a boned bodice covering bust to hips that is drawn and laced, or fastened with hooks and eyes, to create a defined and narrow waistline.

Cotton Fibres from the seed capsules of the cotton plant are spun and woven into fabric. First used in the Americas and Asia.

Couched work Decorative embroidery technique. Thicker threads are laid down on the face of the fabric then secured with stitches from finer contrasting threads, worked in and out of the fabric over the surface thread.

Couture Creation of high fashion, custom made-to-measure garments. French word for 'sewing'.

Cowl neck Large, deep, softly draped collar giving a feminine aesthetic.

Cravat Originating in Croatia, a patterned necktie with a pleated section to go around the neck, leaving a wider section to fold and drape at the front.

Crepe Thin, gauze-like woven fabric. The threads are first twisted to give greater elasticity. Crepe de chine and crepe georgette are typical fabrics.

Crew neck A round, close-fitting neckline.

Crinoline Large caged frame to create an underskirt or petticoat.

Crochet Using a hooked needle to pick up yarn or thread to make loops in decorative formats creating an openwork lace fabric as an alternative to knitting.

Cummerbund Wide satin sash worn around the waist.

Cutwork Holes cut in fabric creating decorative motifs and patterns that are edged and filled with embroidery and appliqué.

Damask Satin-weave fabric in cotton silk or linen thread in monochromatic colours to create decorative patterns. The contrast of the face and reverse of the satin weave is alternated, creating the pattern on both sides.

Dart A stitched fold on the inside of a garment to create shape and fit.

Décolletage A low-cut neckline on a woman's dress.

Deconstruct To challenge traditional concepts in fashion, for example leaving raw edges unfinished, distorting shapes or using unorthodox fabrics.

Denim Cotton twill fabric made from one coloured thread and one white thread. Used to make jeans and hardwearing work wear.

Devoré Decorative technique often seen in velvet fabrics. Areas of pile are burned away to leave a transparent pattern.

Dinner jacket Men's jacket for formal evening wear, often with satin- or silk-faced lapels.

Dirndl Traditional Austrian dress with lace-up bodice and full gathered skirt and apron.

Dolman sleeve Sleeves cut as part of the bodice panels, deep at the armhole then tapering towards the cuff.

Double-breasted Garment with front opening panels that overlap and fasten with two vertical rows of parallel buttons.

Double-faced A term used for fabric that has a finish on both sides, allowing the fabric to be reversible.

Drawn-thread work Warp and weft fabrics are removed, and the remaining laddered threads are pulled together and decoratively stitched to form a pattern.

Drill Linen or cotton woven twill used for its hardwearing qualities.

Drop waist A waistband on a dress that falls lower than the natural waistline.

Duchess satin A heavy and luxurious silk satin with a lustrous sheen.

Dyes Natural or synthetic pigments used to colour fabrics.

Embroidery Decorative stitching applied as ornamentation to fabric using self-coloured or contrast-coloured threads, such as silk, linen, cotton, and rayon.

Empire line High-waisted bodice and long, slimline skirt originating from nineteenth-century dress.

Epaulettes Originated from military uniform, detachable flaps or ornamental shoulder decoration.

Ethnic dress Traditional clothing from different cultures adapted for Western dress.

Eton collar Large, stiff, starched detachable collar derived from the uniform at Eton, the British public school.

Eyelet Hole made in fabric for a ribbon or lace to pass through, often reinforced by stitching or strengthened by metal rings.

Facing Attaching a strip of fabric, for example, at the neckline of a garment, where a duplicate shape is cut then stitched around the neckline and turned back to line and enclose the raw edges, in order to give a neat finish.

Faggoting The decorative joining of two fabrics by a series of embroidered patterns leaving a small gap in between the stitching. This can also describe the decorative embroidery between drawn-thread work where threads are removed across the warp and the weft then tied in bundles.

Fair Isle Technique originating from the Scottish island of the same name. Several coloured yarns are knitted in turn to create a repetitive horizontal series of motifs or patterns.

Felt Fabric made from woollen fleece bonded together by heat, moisture and friction. Felting can also be achieved by boiling and friction after weaving or knitting the fabric.

Flannel Woollen fabric with a plain or twill weave and a slight nap on both sides.

Fly front A fold of cloth on trouser or skirt opening that covers a row of buttons or a zip.

French seam A seam used to join transparent fabrics where the seam will be seen from the outside of the garment. The raw edges are sewn right sides together then folded back and enclosed within the second seam.

Frock Term for an informal gown or child's dress, used as an alternative for the term 'dress'.

Frogging A decorative braiding formed to create a closure and fastening, often on the opening of a coat. The frog button created by the braid passes under the braided loop.

Gabardine A wool or cotton worsted twill with diagonal ribbing. Invented by Thomas Burberry to make the famous Burberry raincoat.

Gathering A series of running stitches at the top edge of the fabric that is bunched together in order to decrease the width. Often set into a seam creating fullness at the other edge.

Georgette A lightweight sheer fabric of silk or synthetic fibres woven with a crepe texture.

Gigot See *leg-of-mutton sleeve*.

Gingham Plain-weave cotton fabric with different-coloured warp and weft threads that create a check pattern.

Godet Triangular panel inserted into the seams of panels in a skirt to create a fluted, flared shape at the hemline.

Gores Panels of a skirt tapering from the hips out towards fullness at the hem, giving a close fit at the hip and a flared hemline.

Grain The direction of a fabric that affects how a garment will hang. The warp is the vertical, lengthwise or straight grain. The weft is the horizontal, crosswise or cross grain. The diagonal is the bias, which gives stretch. The selvedge runs along the vertical edge of the fabric.

Grosgrain Heavy silk fabric or ribbon with a ribbed surface.

Gusset A piece of fabric, usually triangular in shape, inserted into a seam to give additional width in order to improve the fit.

Habotai silk A lightweight silk originating in Japan.

Halter neck A sleeveless bodice with straps that extend and tie around the back of the neck.

Herringbone A twill weave where a zigzag pattern is formed in the diagonal.

Houndstooth A type of check pattern with broken-edged squares or rectangles creating a four-pointed shape created as a twill weave.

Ikat Originating in Indonesia, the term describes the tie dying of yarn or thread that is then woven to create a blurred pattern.

Intarsia Technique used in knitting. A number of different-coloured yarns are knitted to achieve patterns across a garment. Usually used to create bold areas of colour where a single, non-repeating image is required.

Interfacing A bonded fabric used to strengthen or stiffen, giving structure to the outer fabric. Can be stitched between the lining and fabric or bonded.

Inverted pleat The reverse of a box pleat, with the folds turning inwards pointing together with the fullness behind.

Jabot A ruffle or frill at the neckline extending down as a waterfall effect.

Jacquard A fabric with a pattern woven into it, such as a damask or brocade, or knitted, such as Fair Isle. The pattern is achieved through holes punched in cards.

Jersey Knitted stretch fabric in different gauges from lightweight to heavyweight.

Kick pleat An inverted pleat at the hemline of a tight skirt, with the folds pointing inwards to give ease of movement.

Knife pleat Pleats that face one direction around a garment.

Lace Decorative fabric woven or knitted to form patterns of open web-like structures creating contrasting areas of density and openness resulting in a delicate, transparent cloth.

Lamé Fabric woven with metallic threads, often gold or silver.

Lapels The turned back folds at the front of a jacket or shirt. The lapels can also be attached to the collar.

Lawn Linen or cotton with a fine weave giving a semitransparent appearance.

Leg-of-mutton sleeve A set-in sleeve gathered to the armhole and full to the elbow, then fitted from elbow to wrist. Also known as a gigot.

Liberty print Originally hand-printed floral or paisley patterns on silk, but more recently cotton or tana lawn, created by Liberty of London.

Linen A strong fibre taken from the stem of the flax plant and woven into a fine-, medium- or heavyweight fabric, or spun and used as yarn for knitting.

Lingerie Underwear usually made from fine fabrics, such as silk. Can be decorated with lace of frills.

Lining The inside layer of a garment that adds finish, hiding elements, such as seams and raw edges. The lining gives comfort and can be used to add extra warmth or to give added benefits, such as breathability.

Lurex Trade name for a synthetic fibre yarn coated with aluminium or metallic fabrics to create lustre and sparkle.

Lycra Trade name for spandex.

Magyar sleeve Used to describe a sleeve cut from the same pattern piece as the front panel, with Hungarian origins. The sleeve can be designed to be worn at varying lengths.

Mandarin collar A stand collar with a centre-front opening, Chinese in origin.

Maxi skirt Skirt worn to ankle or floor length. The term was devised in the 1960s to differentiate between the midi and the mini.

Merino Wool spun from the fleece of the Merino sheep and woven or knitted to form a very good-quality cloth with a soft hand.

Micro mini Very short version of the mini-length skirt, worn pelmet length above the thigh.

Midi skirt Term used to describe a skirt to calf length, differentiating between the mini and the maxi length.

Miniskirt Short skirt worn above the knee to thigh level, popularized in the 1960s by British designer Mary Quant.

Mitre The corners of a join where the seam is stitched on the diagonal to the point.

Mohair The hair of the Angora goat, sheared, carded and spun then woven or knitted to create a fabric with a long or short fluffy pile.

Moiré Fabric with a watermark appearance created by a wavy pattern made by wetting and heating the fabric before running through heavy ribbed rollers.

Moleskin Cotton with a tight weave and short, soft pile giving a suede-like appearance and hand.

Nappa leather Fine, high-grade, supple leather suitable for garments that require a soft hand. Used for gloves.

Negligee Dressing gown of transparent or lightweight fabric with a glamorous aesthetic.

Nehru collar High, round-neck stand collar with a split centre front worn by the Indian leader Jawaharlal Nehru. Adopted by the hippie movement and popularized by the Beatles.

New Look The silhouette created by Dior in 1947, showing full skirts with wide hemlines from nipped-in waistlines. The look was the antidote to post-war austerity.

New Romantic Street style adopted by the youth of the late 1970s to mid-1980s. Inspired by eighteenth-century dress and created at home, adopting frills, laces, theatrical makeup and unisex dressing. The style, integral to music and the club scene, soon became embraced by mainstream fashion.

Notch Markings on a pattern to define the point where one pattern piece matches the other. Shown as a triangle shape on the pattern and cut out of the fabric.

Nylon Trade name for synthetic fabrics with a wide range of weights, properties and hands for a wide range of garments, particularly stockings traditionally known as nylons.

Ombré Fabric or thread dyed to give a graduated tonal effect. Often dip dyed.

Organdie Fine cotton or synthetic light gauze finished to give a crisp hand.

Organza Woven fabric using silk, cotton, rayon or polyester to create a light, transparent fabric with a crisp hand.

Orientalism Interpretation of Asian and Middle Eastern styling in fabrics and garment shapes, adopted by Western fashion.

Paisley pattern Decorative pattern adapted from the Indian teardrop motif, taking its name from the

Scottish village where imitation Kashmiri scarves and shawls were woven, popularizing the pattern. Liberty of London adopted the pattern in their prints, reviving its popularity.

Panné velvet Velvet with a high-lustre surface created by the directional pressing of the pile in order to achieve a soft hand.

Passementerie Term often used to describe ornamental furnishing trims, braids and tassels, but can also apply to fashion trimming. Often silk, gold or silver threads, the decoration is luxurious and sumptuous.

Patch pocket A cut-out, shaped fabric applied to the surface of the garment to form a pocket. The sides and opening can be stitched for reinforcement or decoration.

Patchwork Small pieces of fabric sewn together in a jigsaw pattern to form a fabric and create a decorative effect. The pattern can be complex and intricate with geometric combinations, or with patches connected in random formations. Often using small-scale prints, the colour and tonal values are key to the creation of repetitive, modular, interconnecting shapes.

Patent leather Coated leather with a lacquered finish to give a high-gloss sheen.

Pencil skirt Tight-fitting skirt to the knee or calf length, often with a split or pleat at the centre-back for ease of movement.

Peplum Short overskirt sewn at the waistband of a garment to give a short overlayer or edging to a garment and a flounce at the hip. The peplum can be gathered into the seam, or cut circular or panelled and sewn in straight but flaring to the hem.

Peter Pan collar Traditionally seen in women's or children's clothing, a collar with rounded edges usually applied without a stand and turned down to give a soft effect.

Petticoat Undergarment worn as a foundation beneath a dress or skirt. It can function as layers or tiers to give volume to the skirt, or as a full garment from shoulder to hem to provide modesty under a transparent or lace fabric. The petticoat can be reinforced with a frame to give additional volume.

Picot Ornamental decoration created by braids, ribbons or lace with a small loop of twisted threads forming a pattern at the edge.

Pile Extra yarn added to the surface of the woven fabric and cut to form a raised surface, such as corduroy or velvet. The nap of the fabric must be cut directionally, otherwise the pile will create a different sheen when stitched parallel.

Pin tucks Parallel lines of stitched tiny pleats for decorative effect, for example, vertically down the yoke of a bodice or vertically around the hemline of a skirt.

Piping A decorative edging or seam created by the insertion of a cord covered by a strip of fabric. The fabric will need to be bias cut if the piping is intended to fit around a curve.

Piqué Woven cotton fabric with a raised surface design, such as a honeycomb, chequered or diamond pattern.

Placket The opening at the neckline of a garment that allows the garment to be taken on or off with ease. The placket is often fastened with buttonholes, though alternative fastenings, such as snap poppers can be used.

Plaid Woven twill cloth in a chequerboard with stripe pattern in vertical and horizontal crossing formations giving endless variations in colour and size. Traditionally worn in Scotland as tartan.

Pleat Folded fabric in parallel lines to give a concertina effect, with varying combinations of formats, such as box pleat or inverted box pleat. The fabric can be heat treated for permanent pleating, or pressed and repressed after laundering. The pleat is generally fixed at one end to hold firm, with the other end flaring out, or fixed at both ends to create areas of control or for decoration. Sometimes soft pleats can be used for gathering and drape.

Polyester Synthetic fibres made into threads and woven or knitted to form fabrics that have easy-care properties that can be crease resistant or fast drying. The fabric can also be heat set to form permanent pleats or folds.

Pom-pom A decorative ball made from yarn wound repeatedly and tied, then cut. The pom-pom can also be made from fabric or feathers clumped together.

Poncho Woollen cape made from a rectangular piece of cloth with a central hole for the head, worn with the corners at centre front and back.

Poplin Traditionally a woven fabric with a silk warp and a cotton weft with fine crosswise ribs, creating a strong fabric. The fabric is now made from a combination of manmade fibres, sometimes mixed with cotton.

Power dressing Defined by the strong masculine silhouette of the 1980s, with wide padded shoulders mixed with feminine flirty nipped-in waistlines, peplums, gathers and pussy-cat bows. Short pencil skirts and high heels help to create a powerful, business aesthetic.

Preppy style American student-inspired casual dressing with chinos and blazers, Fair Isles and pleated skirts, creating an aspirational, sporty, affluent feel.

Princess line The bodice and skirt are cut in one piece with darts at the waist and gores in the skirt to give fit and flare. The waist is defined, and the hemline has volume.

Psychedelic Brightly coloured swirling patterns, sometimes with optical illusions. Also describes the hippie style of the 1960s and 1970s.

Puffed sleeves Short sleeves gathered at the sleeve head into the armhole and gathered at the lower edge to create a puff shape.

Punk style Street style created in the 1970s that subverted the conventions of fashion and society to establish a new wave of culture, invented by the disenfranchised youth. Heavily influenced by the music scene, fashion was home grown and involved distressing, ripping and embellishing with safety pins and provocative slogans to create anti-establishment, anti-fashion statements.

PVC Stands for polyvinyl chloride, which forms a plasticized fabric or a coated surface that creates a waterproof, high-gloss surface.

Quilting Layers of fabric consisting of an upper fabric and lining sandwiching a batting, with lines or patterns of stitching through top to bottom. The padded effect creates surface decoration and can be used to reinforce areas of the garment or to create insulation.

Raglan sleeve Running diagonally from underarm to neck edge, the sleeve avoids the need for shoulder seams.

Ra-ra skirt Worn by cheerleaders and popularized in the 1980s, a short frilled or gathered tiered skirt.

Rayon A silk-like fabric made from cellulose fibres from plant extracts, ideal for lingerie-inspired dresses.

Retro Used to describe designs inspired by and referencing the fashion styles of previous decades.

Revers Describes the turned-back side of the reverse of the garment and, in particular, to describe the lapel of the collar.

Rhinestone A cut stone applied as a decoration to add glitz and sparkle.

Ribbing Knitted pattern, alternating sequences of plain and purl, mostly in vertical lines, used to create a stretch fabric often utilized as hems, cuffs, collars and plackets, or simply to give contrasting areas of definition within the garment.

Roll collar A collar that rolls without the use of a sharp crease or fold.

Rolled hem A very narrow hem, ideal for fine and delicate fabrics, used on scarves and lingerie and perfect for bias and circular hemlines. The fabric edge is folded or rolled several times and has a very discreet stitch, picking up minimal fabric, disguised within the rolls. This is usually hand rendered as a couture technique.

Rouleaux Strips of bias-cut fabric stitched and turned inside out to create spaghetti tape or ribbons that can be used as straps or loops for button fastenings or edgings.

Ruching Strips of fabric gathered in the centre and attached to the garment to create a decorative frilly embellishment. The term can also describe the technique of gathering the edges of fabric, for example, at a neck edge.

Ruff A pleated collar, often detachable and can be layered and concertinaed. Made from linen or lace, the collar is starched to give shape and structure.

Ruffles Gathered frills or flounces, often running around the edges of cuffs and collars or down the front of a bodice or yoke.

Running stitch The thread is sewn in and out of the fabric creating a simple stitch that is often straight but can be used to form decorative patterns.

Sari Traditional Indian garment formed by a length of fabric wrapped around and pleated at the waist, then crossed and draped over the shoulder. Worn over a choli, which is a short fitted bodice.

Sarong Traditional Indonesian garment worn around the waist and wrapped or tied. Can also be worn underarm above the bustline. An ideal shape for beachwear.

Sash Deep belt around the waist or worn diagonally across one shoulder to opposite hip. Often self-fabric or ribbon, the sash can be tied or pinned.

Sateen Satin-weave cotton fabric with a lustre on the surface of the fabric.

Satin Fabric with a smooth shine on the surface and a dullness on the underside. This is created by warp threads crossing over a number of weft threads at a time, or vice versa.

Scoop neck A round neck cut low, and sometimes wide, revealing varying degrees of décolletage.

Seersucker Fabric with a puckered surface created by different tensions in the warp before weaving the fabric. Using cotton or synthetics, this is an ideal fabric for the sundress.

Selvedge The edge of the fabric either side of the warp when woven. The finished edge is created when the warp threads are looped back into the fabric during the weaving process and stops the fabric from fraying or ravelling.

Sequins Cut discs of plastic or metal in various shapes and sizes with a hole to allow for stitching onto fabric. The discs can be finished to create lustre and iridescence and be beaten to give texture.

Shantung silk Heavy slub silk with less-refined fibres to give a more uneven, textured surface.

Shawl collar A collar that travels around the neck increasing in width around the neck edge then tapering to the start of the V shaping at centre front. The collar is turned or rolled back.

Shirring Parallel rows of tiny stitches gathered to pull in the fabric and create areas of constriction. Sometimes shirring elastic is used to create stretch.

Shot silk Woven with different colours in the warp and weft to give an iridescent sheen and a two-tone effect.

Silk Made from the fibres of the cocoons of the silkworm. The fine, lustrous fibres are spun and woven to create a luxury fabric.

Slash pocket A pocket with a slit opening with no covering flap, which can be set horizontally, vertically or angled for variation in design.

Sleeve head The top part of the sleeve that is set or gathered into the armhole. The shape can vary considerably depending on the style of sleeve.

Slip A lightweight petticoat worn under dresses, sometimes acting as a layer under transparent fabrics. Can be adopted as a flimsy sundress or for special occasion dresses.

Smock Originally worn by farm labourers, the smock is a loose-fitting garment made from linen with a smocked yoke, often white on white. The style is adopted for children's wear or for women's informal dress, ideal for maternity wear and great for larger sizes.

Smocking Decorative embroidered technique used to control and shape through a series of parallel stitches evenly gathered to form pleats, which are stitched on top to form patterns. The original gathers are pulled out once the embroidery is complete.

Spaghetti straps Very thin straps ideal for sundresses and special occasion dresses. The straps can be fixed or tied, or tightened through a clasp.

Spandex Synthetic fibre with stretch qualities that can be combined with other fibres, such as wool or denim, to give elasticity. Used in fabric for lingerie, swimwear and sportswear to give a body-contouring effect.

Stand-and-fall collar A two-part collar with the stand rising from the round neckline and attaching to the fall – the outer visible layer that folds over.

Stand collar A collar that stands upright from the neckline opening. Variations in style include the Nehru collar.

Starch Treatment to stiffen fabric, either as a spray or washed with the fabric. Usually a plant extract although can also be chemical based. The starch can also be a coating inherent in the manufacture of the cloth, but is usually added after or during the laundry process.

Stole Worn around the shoulders like a wrap or shawl. Often using luxury fabrics for special-occasion wear.

Stone washing The distressing and aging of fabric, such as denim or silk using a technique of tumble drying in vats with stones or pebbles.

Street style Originating on the street and created by young people in order to identify their version of popular culture. Adopted by designers and repackaged to recreate a more commercial version.

Suede The nap side of tanned leather, treated to give a soft textured appearance and hand.

Sweetheart neckline Copying the heart shape, this is a curved V-neckline that gives a decorative feature to the top of the bodice.

Tabard A loose-fitting, open-sided garment worn over a dress or separates, sometimes as a protective layer.

Taffeta A silk or synthetic fabric with a heavy body, a glossy lustre, and a crisp rustle, ideal for evening wear and special-occasion wear.

Tail The long back of a man's dress coat or morning coat, or the longer hemline of a shirt designed to be tucked into trousers. The tail can be a design feature that elongates a garment, sometimes squared or curved with split side vents.

Tank top A sleeveless pullover with a crew or V-neck, knitted and worn over another garment layer. More commonly, a short garment worn with skirt and trousers, the tank can be elongated to form a dress.

Tatting The creation of a lace-like fabric or decorative border using a shuttle to make a formation of loops in a variety of patterns.

Tie dyeing Traditional African or Asian technique of dyeing after tying or knotting threads around the fabric in order to prevent the dye from absorbing, leaving the base fabric undyed in places.

Tiers Layers of gathered ruffles or flounces that overlap, often forming the skirt or petticoat of the garment.

Toga A Roman garment consisting of a semicircular piece of cloth draped and wrapped around the body and attached to form a garment.

Toggle Often worn on a duffle coat, a toggle is a cylindrical- or cone-shaped fastening traditionally made from horn or tortoiseshell and attached to a garment and fastened by a corded loop.

Train The back of the garment that falls to the floor and trails behind, originating from ceremonial costumes but adopted for evening wear and wedding dresses.

Trench coat Waterproof cotton or wool raincoat originally worn by military personnel with a caped shoulder, epaulettes and belt, worn double- or single-breasted.

Tuck A folded section of fabric stitched in a straight line to create shaping or a decorative effect. Tucks are often stitched as a series running parallel.

Index

Tulip skirt With a petal-like quality, the tulip shape wraps around the body with a curve towards the hemline, giving a rounded silhouette.

Tulle Silk or synthetic net fabric used for petticoats or veils and common in evening wear. Generally a soft handle, the fabric can be starched for a stiff, more structured effect.

Tunic A short dress traditionally worn over trousers.

Turtleneck High, round-neck, close-fitting collar that turns back on itself.

Tuxedo Men's dinner jacket often with contrast satin- or silk-faced lapels, sometimes with a shawl collar. Worn for formal or evening occasions.

Tweed Woven, woollen cloth originating in Scotland in a plain or twill format, sometimes with a checked, dogtooth, herringbone or alternative pattern in a variety of subtle to dynamic colourations.

Twill Woven fabric with a weave format where the weft crosses over and under one or more warp threads in a stepped formation to create a diagonal rib-like pattern.

Utility clothing Style of clothing that economized fabrics and manufacturing in response to a shortage of raw materials and rationing following World War II.

Variegated Often space-dyed threads are used to create a multicoloured fabric with a patchy, inconsistent appearance, but sometimes dyeing the finished fabric can achieve the results.

Velvet Cotton, silk or synthetics are used to create a fabric with a dense pile and a soft hand. The extra loops are creating in the weaving process then cut at the same length to give a visible lustre and a luxurious feel. The nap is distinctive so the garment pieces need to be cut in the same direction on the fabric.

Vent Designed to give ease of movement, this vertical slit at the back or sides of a garment usually runs from the hem but can also be placed at the front.

Vest A sleeveless undergarment pulled over the head that has been adopted to describe an outerwear garment. Varying in lengths, the vest can been worn next to the body or layered over another garment.

Vintage clothing Clothes from a previous era with a nostalgic value, reused and reworn, and often mixed between decades and with modern-day garments to create a more contemporary aesthetic.

Viscose Made from cellulose plant fibres to mimic silk. Can also be described as rayon.

Voile Lightweight sheer fabric with a crisp finished surface. Traditionally made from cotton but can also be made from silk or manmade fibres.

Volant Used to trim or decorate, a flounce or frill with a wavy edge normally cut from a circle.

Waistband The band that circles the waist at the top of separates, such as a skirt, but can also be used to define the waistline of a dress.

Waist seam The seam that attaches the skirt to bodice around the waist of a dress.

Warp Threads that run vertically on the loom, parallel to the selvedge edge, to create the basis for the interweaving of the weft.

Weave Describes the interweaving of the weft running horizontally between the vertical threads of the warp on the loom to form the cloth. Different woven structures and patterns are created by varying the number of over- and-under combinations.

Weft Threads that run horizontally, interlaced between the vertical threads on the warp of the loom to create a woven cloth.

Welt A strengthened or raised border on a garment. Also used to describe a pocket.

Whitework Embroidery using white thread on a white fabric background to create a subtle yet decorative effect. The term can also be used to describe broderie anglaise.

Wing collar Usually found on a formal men's dress shirt, a stand collar with the two end points creased and bent backwards.

Wool Farmed from an animal, such as sheep, goat or alpaca, the fleece is carded and spun, then knitted, woven or felted to create fabric.

Yarn Thread made from natural or manmade fibres that have been spun or twisted. Used to create a knitted or woven fabric.

Yoke Pattern piece of a garment at neck, shoulder panel, or sometimes around the waist of a skirt, often fitted and attached to the lower parts of the garment.

Credits

Andrey, Degtyaryov, Shutterstock, pp.119tcr, 187tl, 195tcr, 195bl

Aronov, Sam, Shutterstock, pp.17bl, 47r, 49tcl, 65tcl, 101bcl, 132tr, 143tl

Atletic, Zvonimir, Shutterstock, pp.17tr, 33bcl/bcr, 43tr, 46tr, 56l/r, 58c, 64r, 80bl, 90l, 117bcr, 129tl/tcl, 135tl, 152bcl, 188br, 199bl, 200l/r, 201r, 205tl, 219br, 223bl, 226r, 230tcr, 241c, 247bl, 257tcr

aWear, pp.103tr, 107bcl, 119tr

Bae, Yeori, pp.22tl, 67tl, 202bcr/br

Berardi, Antonio, pp.19c, 21c, 91tr, 107bl/br, 118l, 119tl, 163bcl, 165r, 235l/r, 243bcl, 244tl, 247br, 264tr

Bloom, Shutterstock, p.102tcr

Bong, Selphie, p.203c

Borodina, Tatyana, Shutterstock, pp.48c, 247bcl, 249r

Catwalker, Shutterstock, pp.17bcr, 42r, 43tcl/tcr/bl/bcl, 45c, 50bl, 53bcr, 55l, 103tcr, 111bcr, 129bcl, 132l, 136c, 137l, 141c, 163tcr, 168l, 192l, 247bcl, 254tcr, 255br, 256l/r, 257tl/tr/bcr/br, 258l/r, 259l/c, 260l/c/r, 261tcl/tr/bl/bcl/br, 263l, 264tl/tcl/bcl, 265l

Corbis, pp.12, 13, 38, 39, 73, 124, 125, 158, 159, 121

Cousland, Neale, Shutterstock, p.105r

CyberEak, Shutterstock, pp.66, 91tl, 238l, 244tr

DIMITRI, pp.17tcl, 17br, 19l, 76, 77tcl, 79l, 110l, 113c, 115bl, 152tl, 163bcr, 185tcl, 189tcr, 190c, 191l, 193tl, 195tcl, 197bcl, 220r, 239c, 243tl,tcr/bl

DIMITRI, Oliver Rauh Photography, http://oliverrauhphotography. blogspot.de, pp.171tr, 185tr, 203l,

Dotshock, Shutterstock, p.187bcl

Efecreata Photography, Shutterstock, pp.61bl, 202tl, 264br

Fabrican, www.fabricanltd.com, Gene Kiegel, p.279l

Fahri, Nicole, pp.17bcl, 33tl, 62l

Ferry Indrawang, Shutterstock, p.121bl

Fowler, Holly, p.205tcr

Getty Images, pp.96, 97

Gitlits, Alexander, Shutterstock, pp.43bcr, 45r, 50br, 54tl, 67bl, 77tr, 102tcl/tcr, 111tr, 115tl, 117tcr, 119bl, 188bcl, 223br, 230bl

Glass, Abigail, pp.103br, 248r, 249c, 250bcr

Gromovataya, Shutterstock, p.53tcl

James, Edward, pp.11, 16r, 20r, 21r, 22tcl/tcr/tr/bl/bcl, 23l/c/r, 24l/r, 25tl/tcr, 26r, 27tcl/tcr/r/bcr, 29tcl/bcl, 31l/c/r, 32l/r, 33tcl/bl/br, 35bl/bcl/bcr, 37, 49bl, 50tcr, 53tcr, 57tl/tcl/tr/bcr, 69tr/bcr/br, 71, 83r, 84l, 85tl/tcr, 87tcr/tr/bcr/br, 88l/r, 91tcr, 92l/r, 93l/c/r, 95, 101bl, 102bcr, 105l, 108r, 109tcr/tr/bl/bcl/bcr/br, 114l, 115tcl/tr/bcr/br, 117tcl, 119br, 121cl/tcr, 128l, 131c, 132bcl/br, 141r, 142l, 144r, 145tl/tcl/tcr/tr/bl/bcl/bcr, 146l, 147tr/tcr/tcl/bcl/bcr, 152bl/br, 153l/c, 157, 165l, 171tcr/bl/bcl/bcr, 173tl/tcl/tcr/bl/br, 175, 181tcr, 182r, 183c/r, 184r, 185tl/bcr/br, 195bcr/br, 197tcl/tcr/br, 198r, 199tl, 202tcl/tcr, 203r, 205bcl, 211, 221tcl/tr, 223tcr/bcr, 224r, 232l, 233bl/bcr, 240tl, 243bcr, 244bl/bcr, 245bcr, 267, 272l/r, 273tl–r/bl/bcl/bcr, 274–5, 276l/r, 277tl/tcl/tr/bl–r, 278l/r, 279r

K2 images, Shutterstock, pp.100l, 181tl, 185bcl

Kallmeyer, Daniella, pp. 26l, 28r, 115tcr

Kojoku, Shutterstock, pp.44l, 61tcr, 81r, 103bl, 108tc, 131r, 132tl, 169tcl/tr, 170r, 227bl, 241tr, 257bl

Mark III Photonics, Shutterstock, pp.51br, 69tcl, 77bcl/bcr, 80tcl/bcl, 85bl/bcl, 91bcl, 101tcr, 103bcl, 107tcr, 121br, 129tcr, 130r, 131l, 132tcl, 136r, 162l, 163tr, 167c, 230tl, 236l, 247tcr, 253bcr, 263c

Mikhaylova, Natalia, Shutterstock, p.65bcl

Miro Vrlik Photography, Shutterstock, pp.18, 102bl, 134l, 149br, 151c, 199bcr, 219tcr, 229c

Nomia Selects, pp.21l, 34l, 143tcl

Oparin, Anton, www.FashionStock. com, pp.19r, 22bcr/r, 25tcl/tr/bl/cl/cr/r, 27tl/bl/bcl/r, 29tl/tcr/tr/bl/bcr/br, 33tr, 42l, 43tl/br, 46tcr/bcr/br, 52l, 53tr, 55r, 57bcl, 60tl, 63r, 64tl, 65tr/bcr, 67tcr/bcl, 77tl, 85tr, 89r, 91tcl/bcr, 109tl, 114c/r, 116l, 117tl/tr/bl/br, 121tl, 128r, 129tr/br, 133l/r, 135tcl/tcr/tr/bl/bcl/br, 138l, 139tl/tcl/bl/bcl/bcr/br, 140l, 141l, 143bcr, 145br, 147tr/bl/br, 148tcl, 149tcr, 167r, 169tcr, 171tcl, 172r, 173bcr, 181tcl/tl/bcr, 185tcr/bl, 187tcl/tcr/tr, 188tr, 189tcl, 193tcr/bcl, 197tr, 198tcl, 199tr/bcl/br, 202bl, 216r, 217bl/br, 220tl/tcr, 222r, 223tcl/tr/bcr, 227tcr/bcl, 230tcl, 232r, 233tl, 236r, 237l/bl, 239r, 240tcl/br, 241r, 242l, 244tcl, 245bcl, 253tr, 262l, 264bcr, 277tcr, 279c

Oparin, Anton, Shutterstock, pp.16l, 28l, 45l, 47l/c, 51bcl, 52r, 53br, 54tcl, 56c, 59r, 61tcl/br, 66c, 69tcl/bcl, 77br, 80tl, 81l/c, 82c/r, 85br, 87bl, 91bl/br, 101tr, 102c, 103tl/bcr, 104r, 105c, 106c, 111tcl/tr/bl, 121tcr, 129bl, 138tcr, 140r, 143bl, 149bcl, 152tcl/tcr/bcr, 155l, 162r, 163tl, 169bcl, 173tr, 194l, 195tr, 196r, 197bcr, 198l, 204l, 216l, 217tcl/bcl, 219l/bcr, 221bl, 225l/c, 226l, 227bcr/br, 230tr/bcl, 231l, 233tcl/br/bcl, 234l, 237tcl/bcl, 246r, 247tl, 250tcl/tcr/br, 251c, 253bcl, 254tl/tcl/br, 255tl, 257tcl, 265r

Palomino, Elisa, pp.102tcl, 112bl, 202tr, 205bcr/br, 206l/r, 207l/c/r, 208–9, 216c, 223tl, 227tl/tr, 231c, 234r, 235c, 245bl, 263r

Photofriday, Shutterstock, pp.80tcr, 101tl, 102tl, 148r, 189bl, 190l, 202bcl, 250tl, 253tcl

Pyo, Rejina, p.197bl

Radin, Lev, Shutterstock, pp.17tl/tcr, 30r, 33tcr, 34r, 35tl/tcl/tcr/tr, 46tl/tcl/bl/bcl, 48l/r, 49tl/tcr/tr/bcl/bcr, 50tl, 51tl/tcl/tcr, 53tl/bcl, 54tcr/tr/bl/br, 58l, 61tr/bcl, 63c, 64l, 65br, 68r, 69bl, 77tcr/bl, 78l, 79r, 82l, 84r, 86l, 87tl/tcl/bcl, 89l, 90r, 100r, 101bcr/br, 102bcl/br, 106l/r, 107tl/tcl/tr/bcr, 108l, 111tcr, 113r, 116r, 118r, 119tcl/bcl, 121bcl, 132tcr, 133c, 138r, 139tcr,

143tcr/tr/bcl, 146r, 149tl, 150r, 152tr, 154c, 163tcl/br, 164l, 166r, 172l, 180l/r, 181bl/bcl/br, 182l, 183l, 184l, 186l, 187bl/bcr/br, 188tl/tcl/tcr/bl/bcr, 189tl/br, 190r, 191r, 193tcl/tr/br, 194r, 195tr/bcl, 196c, 197tl, 198tcr, 201l, 204r, 205tcl/bl, 217tl/tcr/tr/bcr, 218l/c, 291tr/bl, 220l, 221bcl, 222l, 225r, 228l/r, 229l, 230bcr, 231l, 233tcr, 237tr/bcr/bl, 238l/r, 240tcr/bcr, 242c/r, 243tr, 244tcr/bcl/br, 245tl–tr, 246l, 247bcr, 248l, 249l, 250bcl, 251l/r, 252l/c/r, 253tl/tcr/br, 254tr/bl/bcl/bcr, 255tcr/tr/bl/bcl, 258r, 261bcr, 264tcr, 265c

Rex Features, pp.176, 177, 213, 268–9, 270–1, 273br

Roland, Stephanie, p.170l

Sermek, Gordana, Shutterstock, pp.54bcl, 65bl, 81bcr, 101tcl, 111br, 117bcl, 123, 189bcr, 243tcl/br, 261tl

Sha, Nata, Shutterstock, pp.35br, 44r, 49br, 50tcl/tr/bl/bcr, 51bl/bcr, 53bl, 54bcr, 60l/r, 61bcr, 65tcr, 66r, 67bcr, 68l, 69tl, 78r, 79c, 80bl, 82l, 85tcl/bcr, 86r, 89c, 104l, 110r, 111bcl, 112r, 120l/r, 121bcr, 132bl/bcr, 134r, 142r, 143br, 148l, 149tr/bcr, 151l/r, 153r, 154l/r, p.163bl, 164c, 166l, 167l, 169tl/bl/br, 173bcl, 186r, 189tr/bcl, 192c/r, 193bl/bcr, 196l, 218r, 219tcl/bcl, 221bcr, 224l, 227tcl, 230br, 233tr, 237tcr, 240bl/bcl, 241l, 253bl, 255bcr, 257bcl

Smith, Gina, Shutterstock, pp.113l, 264bl

Tan, Jordan, Shutterstock, pp.76r, 245br

UAL, pp.135bcr, 164r, 169bcr

Vortexdigital, Shutterstock, p.129tcr

Wachararwish, p.221br

Wilson, Rob, Shutterstock, p.262r

All other photographs and illustrations are the copyright of Quarto Publishing plc. While every effort has been made to credit contributors, Quarto would like to apologize should there have been any errors or omissions – and would be pleased to make the appropriate correction for future editions of the book.

Collins

GCSE Maths
2 tier-higher
for AQA B

BRIAN SPEED

KEITH GORDON

KEVIN EVANS

William Collins' dream of knowledge for all began with the publication of his first book in 1819. A self-educated mill worker, he not only enriched millions of lives, but also founded a flourishing publishing house. Today, staying true to this spirit, Collins books are packed with inspiration, innovation and a practical expertise. They place you at the centre of a world of possibility and give you exactly what you need to explore it.

Collins. Do more.

Published by Collins
An imprint of HarperCollins*Publishers*
77–85 Fulham Palace Road
Hammersmith
London
W6 8JB

Browse the complete Collins catalogue at
www.collinseducation.com

© HarperCollins*Publishers* Limited 2006

10 9 8 7 6 5 4 3
ISBN-13 978-0-00-721573-7
ISBN-10 0-00-721573-8

British Library Cataloguing in Publication Data. A Catalogue record for this publication is available from the British Library

Commissioned by Marie Taylor, Vicky Butt and Michael Cotter

Project managed by Penny Fowler

Edited by Marian Bond and Paul Sterner

Answer checker: Amanda Whyte

Indexer: Michael Forder

Internal design by JPD

Cover design by JPD

Cover illustration by Andy Parker, JPD

Page make-up and indexing by Gray Publishing

Page make-up of Really Useful Maths! spreads by EMC Design

Illustrations by Gray Publishing, EMC Design, Peters and Zabransky, Peter Cornwell, Bob Lea (Artists Partners), Martin Sanders (Beehive Illustration) and Laszlo Veres (Beehive Illustration.

Production by Natasha Buckland

Printed and bound by Printing Express, Hong Kong

Acknowledgements

With special thanks to Lynn and Greg Byrd

The Publishers gratefully acknowledge the following for permission to reproduce copyright material. Whilst every effort has been made to trace the copyright holders, in cases where this has been unsuccessful or if any have inadvertently been overlooked, the Publishers will be pleased to make the necessary arrangements at the first opportunity.

AQA material is reproduced by permission of the Assessment and Qualifications Alliance. Please note that all questions used dated before 2003 are NOT from the live examinations for the current specification. New specifications for GCSE were introduced in 2003.

Grade bar photos © 2006 JupiterImages Corporation

© 2006 JupiterImages Corporation, p43, p113, p135, p173, p201, p219, p231, p243, p265, p303, p325, p363, p381, p391, p405, p433, p457, p499, p521, p537, p583, p595

© PCL / Alamy, p71

© Mr Woolman, p154

© Dave Roberts / Istock, p345

© Zinchik / Istock, p469

© SuperStock / Alamy, p228

© Hans F. Meier / Istock, p567

CONTENTS

Welcome to Collins GCSE Maths, the easiest way to learn and succeed in Mathematics. This textbook uses a stimulating approach that really appeals to students. Here are some of the key features of the textbook, to explain why.

Each chapter of the textbook begins with an **Overview**. The Overview lists the Sections you will encounter in the chapter, the key ideas you will learn, and shows how these ideas relate to, and build upon, each other. The Overview also highlights what you should already know, and if you're not sure, there is a short Quick Check activity to test yourself and recap.

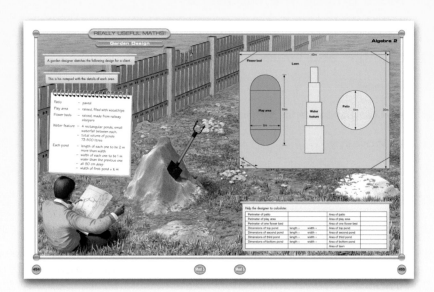

Maths can be useful to us every day of our lives, so look out for these **Really Useful Maths!** pages. These double page spreads use big, bright illustrations to depict real-life situations, and present a short series of real-world problems for you to practice your latest mathematical skills on.

Each **Section** begins first by explaining what mathematical ideas you are aiming to learn, and then lists the key words you will meet and use. The ideas are clearly explained, and this is followed by several examples showing how they can be applied to real problems. Then it's your turn to work through the exercises and improve your skills. Notice the different coloured panels along the outside of the exercise pages. These show the equivalent exam grade of the questions you are working on, so you can always tell how well you are doing.

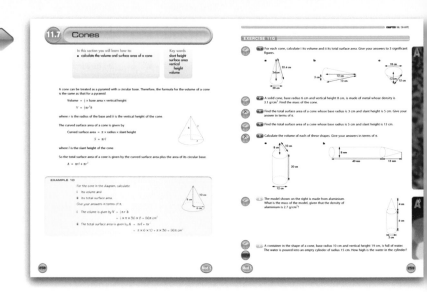

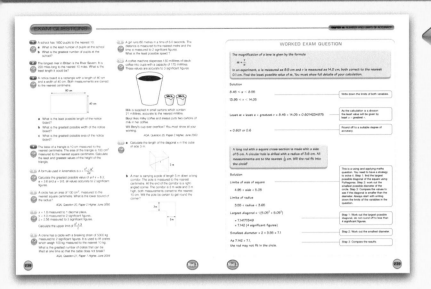

Every chapter in this textbook contains lots of **Exam Questions**. These provide ideal preparation for your examinations. Each exam question section also concludes with a fully worked example. Compare this with your own work, and pay special attention to the examiner's comments, which will ensure you understand how to score maximum marks.

Throughout the textbook you will find **Activities** – highlighted in the green panels – designed to challenge your thinking and improve your understanding.

Review the **Grade Yourself** pages at the very end of the chapter. This will show what exam grade you are currently working at. Doublecheck **What you should now know** to confirm that you have the knowledge you need to progress.

Working through these sections in the right way should mean you achieve your very best in GCSE Maths. Remember though, if you get stuck, answers to all the questions are at the back of the book (except the exam question answers which your teacher has).

We do hope you enjoy using Collins GCSE Maths, and wish you every good luck in your studies!

Brian Speed, Keith Gordon, Kevin Evans

ICONS

 Indicates Module 1: Data Handling

 Indicates Module 3: Number

 Indicates Module 5: Algebra and Space, Shape and Measures

 You may use your calculator for this question

 You should not use your calculator for this question

 Indicates a Using and Applying Mathematics question

 Indicates a Proof question

The new Specification B assumes that students taking Modules 1 and 3 have some basic understanding of other assessment objectives.

For example in Module 1 (Data Handling) and Module 3 (Number) you should know:

● that letters can represent unknown quantities
● how to substitute numbers into simple algebraic expressions

Also in Module 1 (Data Handling) you should know:

● how to cancel fractions to their simplest form
● that percentage means 'out of a hundred'
● the meaning of a simple ratio

Also in Module 3 (Number) you should know:

● how to combine like terms and manipulate simple algebraic expressions
● how to solve simple equations

This means that there will be a new style of question. These are flagged with the icon . These questions already appear in Specification A.

Statistics 1

This chapter will show you ...

- how to calculate and use the mode, median, mean and range from frequency tables of discrete data
- how to decide which is the best average for different types of data
- how to recognise the modal class and calculate an estimate of the mean from frequency tables of grouped data
- how to draw frequency polygons and histograms
- how to calculate and use a moving average
- how to design questions for questionnaires and surveys

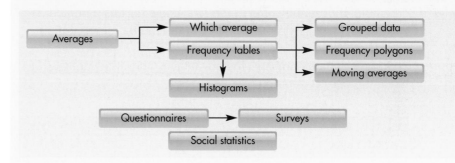

What you should already know

- How to work out the mean, mode, median and range of small sets of discrete data
- How to extract information from tables and diagrams

Quick check

1 The marks for 15 students in a maths test are

2, 3, 4, 5, 5, 6, 6, 6, 7, 7, 7, 7, 7, 8, 10

a What is the modal mark?

b What is the median mark?

c What is the range of the marks?

d What is the mean mark?

In this section you will learn how to:
- use averages
- solve more complex problems using averages
- identify the advantages and disadvantages of each type of average and learn which one to use in different situations

Key words

mean
measure of
  location
median
mode

Average is a term we often use when describing or comparing sets of data. The average is also known as a **measure of location**. For example, we refer to the average rainfall in Britain, the average score of a batsman, an average weekly wage, the average mark in an examination. In each of these examples, we are representing the whole set of many values by just one single, typical value, which we call the average.

The idea of an average is extremely useful, because it enables us to compare one set of data with another set by comparing just two values – their averages.

There are several ways of expressing an average, but the most commonly used averages are the **mode**, the **median** and the **mean**.

An average must be truly representative of a set of data. So, when you have to find an average, it is crucial to choose the *correct type of average* for this particular set of data. If you use the wrong average, your results will be distorted and give misleading information.

This table, which compares the advantages and disadvantages of each type of average, will help you to make the correct decision.

	Mode	Median	Mean
Advantages	Very easy to find Not affected by extreme values Can be used for non-numerical data	Easy to find for ungrouped data Not affected by extreme values	Easy to find Uses all the values The total for a given number of values can be calculated from it
Disadvantages	Doesn't use all the values May not exist	Doesn't use all the values Often not understood	Extreme values can distort it Has to be calculated
Used for	Non-numerical data For finding the most likely value	Data with extreme values	Data whose values are spread in a balanced way

EXAMPLE 1

The ages of 20 people attending a conference are

23, 25, 26, 28, 28, 34, 34, 34, 37, 45, 47, 48, 52, 53, 56, 63, 67, 70, 73, 77

a Find **i** the mode, **ii** the median, **iii** the mean of the data.

b Which average best represents the age of the people at the conference.

a **i** The mode is 34, **ii** the median is 46, **iii** the mean is 920 ÷ 20 = 46

b The mean is distorted because of the few very old people at the conference. The median is also distorted by the larger values, so in this case the mode would be the most representative average.

EXERCISE 1A

1 Shopkeepers always want to keep the most popular items in stock. Which average do you think is often known as the shopkeeper's average?

2 A list contains seven even numbers. The largest number is 24. The smallest number is half the largest. The mode is 14 and the median is 16. Two of the numbers add up to 42. What are the seven numbers?

3 The marks of 25 students in an English examination are as follows.

55, 63, 24, 47, 60, 45, 50, 89, 39, 47, 38, 42, 69, 73, 38, 47, 53, 64, 58, 71, 41, 48, 68, 64, 75

Find the median.

4 Decide which average you would use for each of the following. Give a reason for your answer.

a The average mark in an examination.

b The average pocket money for a group of 16-year-old students.

c The average shoe size for all the girls in Year 10.

d The average height for all the artistes on tour with a circus.

e The average hair colour for pupils in your school.

f The average weight of all newborn babies in a hospital's maternity ward.

5 A pack of matches consisted of 12 boxes. The contents of each box are as follows.

34   31   29   35   33   30   31   28   29   35   32   31

On the box it states that the average contents is 32 matches. Is this correct?

6 This table shows the annual salaries for a firm's employees.

Chairman	£43 000
Managing director	£37 000
Floor manager	£25 000
Skilled worker 1	£24 000
Skilled worker 2	£24 000
Machinist	£18 000
Computer engineer	£18 000
Secretary	£18 000
Office junior	£7 000

a What is **i** the modal salary, **ii** the median salary, and **iii** the mean salary?

b The management has suggested a pay rise for all of 6%. The shopfloor workers want a pay rise for all of £1500. What difference to the mean salary would each suggestion make?

7 Mr Brennan, a caring maths teacher, told each pupil their individual test mark and only gave the test statistics to the whole class. He gave the class the modal mark, the median mark and the mean mark.

a Which average would tell a pupil whether he/she were in the top half or the bottom half of the class?

b Which average tells the pupils nothing really?

c Which average allows a pupil really to gauge how well he/she has done compared with everyone else?

8 A list of 9 numbers has a mean of 7.6. What number must be added to the list to give a new mean of 8?

9 A dance group of 17 teenagers had a mean weight of 44.5 kg. To enter a competition there needs to be 18 people in the group with an average weight of 44.4 kg or less. What is the maximum weight that the eighteenth person could be?

10 The mean age of a group of eight walkers is 42. Joanne joins the group and the mean age changes to 40. How old is Joanne?

1.2 Frequency tables

In this section you will learn how to:
- calculate the mode and median from a frequency table
- calculate the mean from a frequency table

Key word
frequency table

When a lot of information has been gathered, it is often convenient to put it together in a **frequency table**. From this table, you can then find the values of the mode, median, mean and range of the data.

EXAMPLE 2

A survey was done on the number of people in each car leaving the Meadowhall Shopping Centre, in Sheffield. The results are summarised in the table.

Calculate **a** the mode, **b** the median, **c** the mean number of people in a car.

Number of people in each car	1	2	3	4	5	6
Frequency	45	198	121	76	52	13

a The modal number of people in a car is easy to spot. It is the number with the largest frequency (198). Hence, the modal number of people in a car is 2.

b The median number of people in a car is found by working out where the middle of the set of numbers is located. First, add up frequencies to get the total number of cars surveyed, which comes to 505. Next, calculate the middle position

$$(505 + 1) \div 2 = 253$$

You now need to add the frequencies across the table to find which group contains the 253rd item. The 243rd item is the end of the group with 2 in a car. Therefore, the 253rd item must be in the group with 3 in a car. Hence, the median number of people in a car is 3.

c The mean number of people in a car is found by calculating the total number of people, and then dividing this total by the number of cars surveyed.

Number in car	Frequency	Number in these cars
1	45	$1 \times 45 = 45$
2	198	$2 \times 198 = 396$
3	121	$3 \times 121 = 363$
4	76	$4 \times 76 = 304$
5	52	$5 \times 52 = 260$
6	13	$6 \times 13 = 78$
Totals	505	1446

Hence, the mean number of people in a car is $1446 \div 505 = 2.9$ (2 significant figures).

Using your calculator

The previous example can also be done by using the statistical mode which is available on some calculators. However, not all calculators are the same, so you will have to either read your instruction manual or experiment with the statistical keys on your calculator.

You may find one labelled

DATA or M+ or Σ+ or $\bar{x}$ where $\bar{x}$ is printed in blue.

Try the following key strokes.

EXERCISE 1B

1 Find **i** the mode, **ii** the median and **iii** the mean from each frequency table below.

a A survey of the shoe sizes of all the Y10 boys in a school gave these results.

Shoe size	4	5	6	7	8	9	10
Number of pupils	12	30	34	35	23	8	3

b This is a record of the number of babies born each week over one year in a small maternity unit.

Number of babies	0	1	2	3	4	5	6	7	8	9	10	11	12	13	14
Frequency	1	1	1	2	2	2	3	5	9	8	6	4	5	2	1

2 A survey of the number of children in each family of a school's intake gave these results.

Number of children	1	2	3	4	5
Frequency	214	328	97	26	3

a Assuming each child at the school is shown in the data, how many children are at the school?

b Calculate the mean number of children in a family.

c How many families have this mean number of children?

d How many families would consider themselves average from this survey?

3 A dentist kept records of how many teeth he extracted from his patients.

In 1970 he extracted 598 teeth from 271 patients.

In 1980 he extracted 332 teeth from 196 patients.

In 1990 he extracted 374 teeth from 288 patients.

a Calculate the average number of teeth taken from each patient in each year.

b Explain why you think the average number of teeth extracted falls each year.

4 The teachers in a school were asked to indicate the average number of hours they spent each day marking. The table summarises their replies.

Number of hours spent marking	1	2	3	4	5	6
Number of teachers	10	13	12	8	6	1

a How many teachers are at the school?

b What is the modal number of hours spent marking?

c What is the mean number of hours spent marking?

5 Two friends often played golf together. They recorded their scores for each hole over five games to determine who was more consistent and who was the better player. The results are summarised in the table.

No. of shots to hole ball	1	2	3	4	5	6	7	8	9
Roger	0	0	0	14	37	27	12	0	0
Brian	5	12	15	18	14	8	8	8	2

a What is the modal score for each player?

b What is the range of scores for each player?

c What is the median score for each player?

d What is the mean score for each player?

e Which player is the more consistent and explain why?

f Who would you say is the better player and state why?

6 The number of league goals scored by a football team over a season is given in the table.

Number of goals scored	0	1	2	3	4	5	6	7
Number of matches	3	8	10	11	4	2	1	1

a How many games were played that season?

b What is the range of goals scored?

c What is the modal number of goals scored?

d What is the median number of goals scored?

e What is the mean number of goals scored?

f Which average do you think the team's supporters would say is the average number of goals scored by the team that season?

g If the team also scored 20 goals in ten cup matches that season, what was the mean number of goals the team scored throughout the whole season?

7 The table shows the number of telephones per household for a housing estate.

Number of telephones	Numbers of houses
0	2
1	14
2	17
3	6
4	a

a What is the total number of houses ?

b Show clearly that the total number of telephones is $66 + 4a$.

c The mean number of telephones per house is 2. What is the value of a?

Grouped data

In this section you will learn how to:
- identify the modal group
- calculate and estimate the mean from a grouped table

Key words

continuous data
discrete data
estimated mean
groups
modal group

Sometimes the information we are given is grouped in some way, as in the table in Example 3, which shows the range of weekly pocket money given to Y10 students in a particular class.

EXAMPLE 3

From the data in the table

a write down the **modal group**

b calculate an estimate of the mean weekly pocket money.

Pocket money, p, (£)	$0 < p \leqslant 1$	$1 < p \leqslant 2$	$2 < p \leqslant 3$	$3 < p \leqslant 4$	$4 < p \leqslant 5$
No. of students	2	5	5	9	15

a The modal group is still easy to pick out, since it is simply the one with the largest frequency. Here the modal group is £4 to £5.

b The mean can only be estimated, since you do not have all the information. To estimate the mean, you simply assume that each person in each group has the midway amount, then you can proceed to build up the table as before.

Note how you find the midway value. The two end values are added together and then divided by two.

Pocket money, p, (£)	Frequency (f)	Midway (m)	$f \times m$
$0 < p \leqslant 1$	2	0.50	1.00
$1 < p \leqslant 2$	5	1.50	7.50
$2 < p \leqslant 3$	5	2.50	12.50
$3 < p \leqslant 4$	9	3.50	31.50
$4 < p \leqslant 5$	15	4.50	67.50
Totals	36		120

The **estimated mean** will be £120 ÷ 36 = £3.33 (rounded off).

Note the notation used for the groups.

$0 < p \leqslant 1$ means any amount above 0p up to and including £1.

$1 < p \leqslant 2$ means any amount above £1 up to and including £2.

If you had written 0.01 – 1.00, 1.01 – 2.00, etc. for the **groups**, then the midway values would have been 0.505, 1.505, etc. Although technically correct, this makes the calculation of the mean harder and does not have a significant effect on the final answer, which is an estimate anyway.

This issue only arises because money is **discrete data**, which is data that consists of separate numbers, such as goals scored, marks in a test, number of children and shoe sizes. Normally grouped tables use **continuous data** which is data which can have an infinite number of different values, such as height, weight, time, area and capacity. It is always rounded-off information.

Whatever the type of data, remember to find the midway value by adding the two end values of the group and dividing by 2.

EXERCISE 1C

1 For each table of values, find the following.

    i   the modal group   **ii** an estimate for the mean

a

x	$0 < x \leqslant 10$	$10 < x \leqslant 20$	$20 < x \leqslant 30$	$30 < x \leqslant 40$	$40 < x \leqslant 50$
Frequency	4	6	11	17	9

b

y	$0 < y \leqslant 100$	$100 < y \leqslant 200$	$200 < y \leqslant 300$	$300 < y \leqslant 400$	$400 < y \leqslant 500$	$500 < y \leqslant 600$
Frequency	95	56	32	21	9	3

c

z	$0 < z \leqslant 5$	$5 < z \leqslant 10$	$10 < z \leqslant 15$	$15 < z \leqslant 20$
Frequency	16	27	19	13

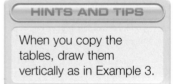

HINTS AND TIPS

When you copy the tables, draw them vertically as in Example 3.

c

Weeks	1–3	4–6	7–9	10–12	13–15
Frequency	5	8	14	10	7

2 Jason brought 100 pebbles back from the beach and weighed them all to the nearest gram. His results are summarised in this table.

Weight, w (grams)	$40 < w \leqslant 60$	$60 < w \leqslant 80$	$80 < w \leqslant 100$	$100 < w \leqslant 120$	$120 < w \leqslant 140$	$140 < w \leqslant 160$
Frequency	5	9	22	27	26	11

Find the following.

    a the modal weight of the pebbles

    b an estimate of the total weight of all the pebbles

    c an estimate of the mean weight of the pebbles

3 One hundred light bulbs were tested by their manufacturer to see whether the average life span of the manufacturer's bulbs was over 200 hours. The table summarises the results.

Life span, h (hours)	$150 < h \leqslant 175$	$175 < h \leqslant 200$	$200 < h \leqslant 225$	$225 < h \leqslant 250$	$250 < h \leqslant 275$
Frequency	24	45	18	10	3

a What is the modal length of time a bulb lasts?

b What percentage of bulbs last longer than 200 hours?

c Estimate the mean life span of the light bulbs.

d Do you think the test shows that the average life span is over 200 hours? Fully explain your answer.

4 The table shows the distances run by an athlete who is training for a marathon.

Distance, d, miles	$0 < d \leqslant 5$	$5 < d \leqslant 10$	$10 < d \leqslant 15$	$15 < d \leqslant 20$	$20 < d \leqslant 25$
Frequency	3	8	13	5	2

a It is recommended that an athlete's daily average mileage should be at least one third of the distance of the race being trained for. A marathon is 26.2 miles. Is this athlete doing enough training?

b The athlete records the times of some runs and calculates that her average pace for all runs is $6\frac{1}{2}$ minutes to a mile. Explain why she is wrong to expect a finishing time of $26.2 \times 6\frac{1}{2}$ minutes $\approx$ 170 minutes for the marathon.

c The athlete claims that the difference between her shortest and longest run is 21 miles. Could this be correct? Explain your answer.

5 The owners of a boutique did a survey to find the average age of people using the boutique. The table summarises the results.

Age (years)	14–18	19–20	21–26	27–35	36–50
Frequency	26	24	19	16	11

What do you think is the average age of the people using the boutique?

6 Three supermarkets each claimed to have the lowest average price increase over the year. The table summarises their average price increases.

Price increase (p)	1–5	6–10	11–15	16–20	21–25	26–30	31–35
Soundbuy	4	10	14	23	19	8	2
Springfields	5	11	12	19	25	9	6
Setco	3	8	15	31	21	7	3

Using their average price increases, make a comparison of the supermarkets and write a report on which supermarket, in your opinion, has the lowest price increases over the year. Don't forget to justify your answers.

In this section you will learn how to:
- draw frequency polygons for discrete and continuous data
- draw histograms for continuous data with equal intervals

Key words

continuous data
discrete data
frequency polygon
histogram

Frequency polygons

To help people understand it, statistical information is often presented in pictorial or diagrammatic form. For example, you should have seen pie charts, bar charts and stem-and-leaf diagrams. Another method of showing data is by **frequency polygons**.

Frequency polygons can be used to represent both ungrouped data and grouped data, as shown in Example 4 and Example 5 respectively. They are useful to show the shapes of distributions, and can be used to compare distributions.

EXAMPLE 4

No. of children	0	1	2	3	4	5
Frequency	12	23	36	28	16	11

This is the frequency polygon for the *ungrouped* data in the table.

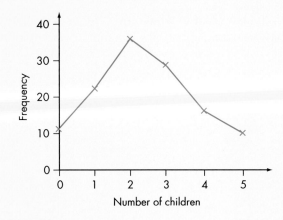

- You simply plot the coordinates from each ordered pair in the table.
- You complete the polygon by joining up the plotted points with straight lines.

EXAMPLE 5

Weight, w (kilograms)	$0 < w \leq 5$	$5 < w \leq 10$	$10 < w \leq 15$	$15 < w \leq 20$	$20 < w \leq 25$	$25 < w \leq 30$
Frequency	4	13	25	32	17	9

This is the frequency polygon for the *grouped data* in the table.

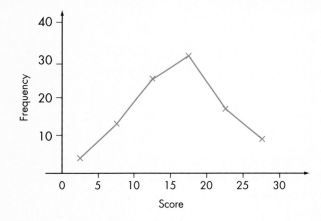

- You use the midway value of each group, just as in estimating the mean.
- You plot the ordered pairs of midway values with frequency, namely,

  (2.5, 4), (7.5, 13), (12.5, 25), (17.5, 32), (22.5, 17), (27.5, 9)

- You do not know what happens above and below the groups in the table, so do not draw lines before (2.5, 4) or after (27.5, 9). The diagram shows the shape of the distribution.

Bar charts and histograms

You should already be familiar with the bar chart in which the vertical axis represents frequency, and the horizontal axis represents the type of data. (Sometimes it is more convenient to have the axes the other way.)

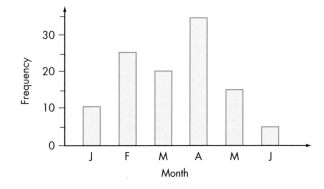

A **histogram** looks similar to a bar chart, but there are four fundamental differences.

- There are no gaps between the bars.

- The horizontal axis has a continuous scale since it represents **continuous** data, such as time, weight or length.

- The area of each bar represents the class or group frequency of the bar.

- The vertical axis is labelled "Frequency density", where

$$\text{Frequency density} = \frac{\text{Frequency of class interval}}{\text{Width of class interval}}$$

When the data is not continuous, a simple bar chart is used. For example, you would use a bar chart to represent the runs scored in a test match or the goals scored by a hockey team.

Look at the histogram below, which has been drawn from this table of times taken by people to walk to work.

Time, t (min)	$0 < t \leqslant 4$	$4 < t \leqslant 8$	$8 < t \leqslant 12$	$12 < t \leqslant 16$
Frequency	8	12	10	7
Frequency density	2	3	2.5	1.75

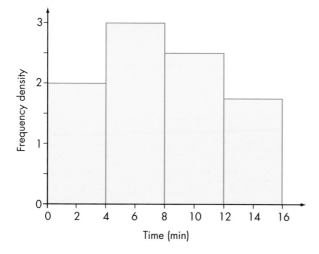

Notice that each histogram bar starts at the *least possible* time and finishes at the *greatest possible* time for its group.

Using your calculator

Histograms can also be drawn on graphics calculators or by using computer software packages. If you have access to either of these, try to use them.

EXERCISE 1D

1. The table shows how many students were absent from one particular class throughout the year.

Students absent	1	2	3	4	5
Frequency	48	32	12	3	1

   a Draw a frequency polygon to illustrate the data.

   b Calculate the mean number of absences each lesson.

2. The table shows the number of goals scored by a hockey team in one season.

Goals	1	2	3	4	5
Frequency	3	9	7	5	2

   a Draw the frequency polygon for this data.

   b Calculate the mean number of goals scored per game in the season.

3. The frequency polygon shows the amount of money spent in a corner shop by the first 40 customers on one day.

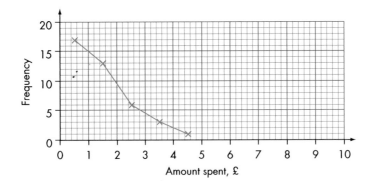

   a i Use the frequency polygon to complete the table for the amounts spent by the first 40 customers

Amount spent, m, £	$0 < m \leq 1$	$1 < m \leq 2$	$2 < m \leq 3$	$3 < m \leq 4$	$4 < m \leq 5$
Frequency					

   ii Work out the mean amount of money spent by these 40 customers.

   b Mid morning the shopkeeper records the amount spent by another 40 customers. The table below shows the data.

Amount spent, m, £	$0 < m \leq 2$	$2 < m \leq 4$	$4 < m \leq 6$	$6 < m \leq 8$	$8 < m \leq 10$
Frequency	3	5	18	10	4

   i On a copy of the graph above, draw the frequency polygon to show this data?

   ii Calculate the mean amount spent by the 40 mid-morning customers..

   c Comment on the differences between the frequency polygons and the average amounts spent by the different sets of customers.

4 The table shows the range of heights of the girls in Y11 at a London school.

Height, h (cm)	$120 < h \leqslant 130$	$130 < h \leqslant 140$	$140 < h \leqslant 150$	$150 < h \leqslant 160$	$160 < h \leqslant 170$
Frequency	15	37	25	13	5

    a Draw a frequency polygon for this data.   **b** Draw a histogram for this data

    c Estimate the mean height of the girls.

5 A doctor was concerned at the length of time her patients had to wait to see her when they came to the morning surgery. The survey she did gave her these results.

Time, m (minutes)	$0 < m \leqslant 10$	$10 < m \leqslant 20$	$20 < m \leqslant 30$	$30 < m \leqslant 40$	$40 < m \leqslant 50$	$50 < m \leqslant 60$
Monday	5	8	17	9	7	4
Tuesday	9	8	16	3	2	1
Wednesday	7	6	18	2	1	1

    a Draw a frequency polygon for each day on the same pair of axes.

    b What is the average amount of time spent waiting each day?

    c Why might the average time for each day be different?

1.5 Histograms with bars of unequal width

In this section you will learn how to:
- draw and read histograms where the bars are of unequal width
- find the median, quartiles and interquartile range from a histogram

Key words
class interval
interquartile
   range
lower quartile
median
upper
   quartile

Sometimes the data in a frequency distribution are grouped into classes whose intervals are different. In this case, the resulting histogram has bars of unequal width.

The key fact that you should always remember is that the *area* of a bar in a histogram represents the class *frequency* of the bar. So, in the case of an unequal-width histogram, the height to draw each bar is found by dividing its class frequency by its class interval width (bar width), which is the difference between the lower and upper bounds for each interval. Conversely, given a histogram, any of its class frequencies can be found by multiplying the height of the corresponding bar by its width.

It is for this reason that the scale on the vertical axes of histograms is nearly always labelled "Frequency density", where

$$\text{Frequency density} = \frac{\text{Frequency of class interval}}{\text{Width of class interval}}$$

EXAMPLE 6

The heights of a group of girls were measured. The results were classified as shown in the table.

Height, h (cm)	$151 \leqslant h < 153$	$153 \leqslant h < 154$	$154 \leqslant h < 155$	$155 \leqslant h < 159$	$159 \leqslant h < 160$
Frequency	64	43	47	96	12

It is convenient to write the table vertically and add two columns, class width and frequency density.

The class width is found by subtracting the lower class boundary from the upper class boundary. The frequency density is found by dividing the frequency by the class width.

Height, h (cm)	Frequency	Class width	Frequency density
$151 \leqslant h < 153$	64	2	32
$153 \leqslant h < 154$	43	1	43
$154 \leqslant h < 155$	47	1	47
$155 \leqslant h < 159$	96	4	24
$159 \leqslant h < 160$	12	1	12

The histogram can now be drawn. The horizontal scale should be marked off as normal from a value below the lowest value in the table to a value above the largest value in the table. In this case, mark the scale from 150 cm to 160 cm. The vertical scale is always frequency density and is marked up to at least the largest frequency density in the table. In this case, 50 is a sensible value.

Each bar is drawn between the lower **class interval** and the upper class interval horizontally, and up to the frequency density vertically.

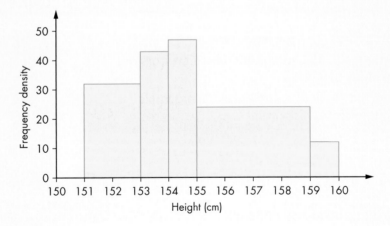

EXAMPLE 7

This histogram shows the distribution of heights of daffodils in a greenhouse.

a Complete a frequency table for the heights of the daffodils, and show the cumulative frequency.

b Find the **median** height.

c Find the **interquartile range** of the heights.

d Estimate the mean of the distribution.

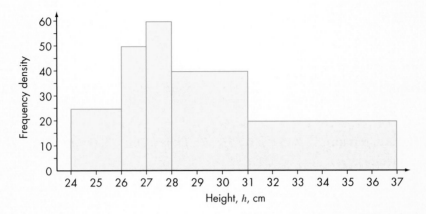

a The frequency table will have groups of $24 \leqslant h < 26$, $26 \leqslant h < 27$, etc. These are read from the height axis. The frequencies will be found by multiplying the width of each bar by the frequency density. Remember that the value on the vertical axis is not the frequency.

Height, h (cm)	$24 \leqslant h < 26$	$26 \leqslant h < 27$	$27 \leqslant h < 28$	$28 \leqslant h < 31$	$31 \leqslant h < 37$
Frequency	50	50	60	120	120
Cumulative frequency	50	100	160	280	400

b There are 400 values so the median will be the 200th value. Counting up the frequencies from the beginning we get the third row of the table above.

The median occurs in the $28 \leqslant h < 31$ group. There are 160 values before this group and 120 in it. To get to the 200th value we need to go 40 more values into this group. 40 out of 120 is one-third. One third of the way through this group is the value 29 cm. Hence the median is 29 cm.

c The interquartile range is the difference between the **upper quartile** and the **lower quartile**, the quarter and three-quarter values respectively. In this case, the lower quartile is the 100th value (found by dividing 400, the total number of values, by 4) and the upper quartile is the 300th value. So, in the same way that you found the median, you can find the lower (100th value) and upper (300th value) quartiles. The 100th value is at 27 cm and the 300th value is at 32 cm. The interquartile range is 32 cm − 27 cm = 5 cm.

d To estimate the mean, use the table to get the midway values of the groups and multiply these by the frequencies. The sum of these divided by 400 will give the estimated mean. So, the mean is

$(25 \times 50 + 26.5 \times 50 + 27.5 \times 60 + 29.5 \times 120 + 34 \times 120) \div 400$
$= 11\,845 \div 400 = 29.6$ cm (3 significant figures)

EXERCISE 1E

1 Draw histograms for these grouped frequency distributions.

a

Temperature, t (°C)	$8 \leq t < 10$	$10 \leq t < 12$	$12 \leq t < 15$	$15 \leq t < 17$	$17 \leq t < 20$	$20 \leq t < 24$
Frequency	5	13	18	4	3	6

b

Wage, w (£1000)	$6 \leq w < 10$	$10 \leq w < 12$	$12 \leq w < 16$	$16 \leq w < 24$
Frequency	16	54	60	24

c

Age, a (nearest year)	$11 \leq a < 14$	$14 \leq a < 16$	$16 \leq a < 17$	$17 \leq a < 20$
Frequency	51	36	12	20

d

Pressure, p (mm)	$745 \leq p < 755$	$755 \leq p < 760$	$760 \leq p < 765$	$765 \leq p < 775$
Frequency	4	6	14	10

e

Time, t (min)	$0 \leq t < 8$	$8 \leq t < 12$	$12 \leq t < 16$	$16 \leq t < 20$
Frequency	72	84	54	36

2 The following information was gathered about the weekly pocket money given to 14 year olds.

Pocket money, p (£)	$0 \leq p < 2$	$2 \leq p < 4$	$4 \leq p < 5$	$5 \leq p < 8$	$8 \leq p < 10$
Girls	8	15	22	12	4
Boys	6	11	25	15	6

a Represent the information about the boys on a histogram.

b Represent both sets of data with a frequency polygon, using the same pair of axes.

c What is the mean amount of pocket money given to each sex? Comment on your answer.

3 The sales of the Star newspaper over 65 years are recorded in this table.

Years	1930–50	1951–70	1971–80	1981–90	1991–95	1995–2000
Copies	62 000	68 000	71 000	75 000	63 000	52 000

Illustrate this information on a histogram. Take the class boundaries as 1930, 1950, 1970, 1980, 1990, 1995, 2000.

4 The London trains were always late, so one month a survey was undertaken to find how many trains were late, and by how many minutes (to the nearest minute). The results are illustrated by this histogram.

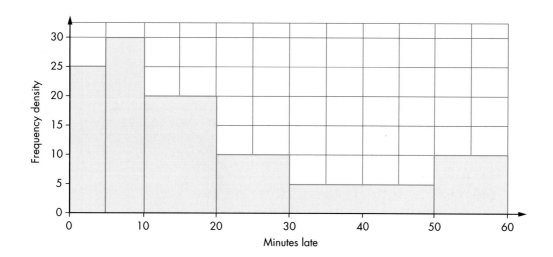

a How many trains were in the survey?

b How many trains were delayed for longer than 15 minutes?

5 For each of the frequency distributions illustrated in the histograms

i write down the grouped frequency table,

ii state the modal group,

iii estimate the median,

iv find the lower and upper quartiles and the interquartile range,

v estimate the mean of the distribution.

a

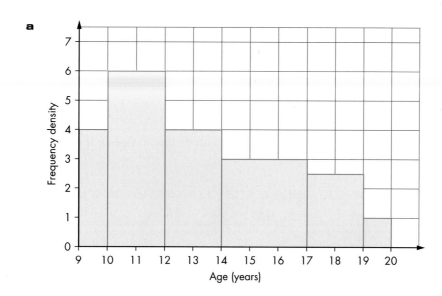

b

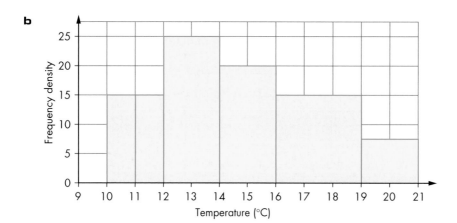

c

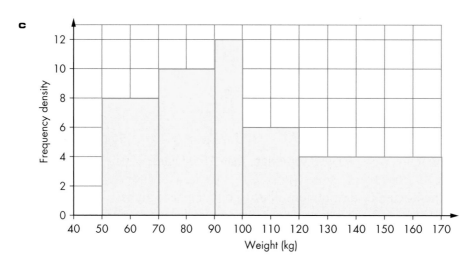

6 All the patients in a hospital were asked how long it was since they last saw a doctor. The results are shown in the table.

Hours, h	$0 \leqslant h < 2$	$2 \leqslant h < 4$	$4 \leqslant h < 6$	$6 \leqslant h < 10$	$10 \leqslant h < 16$	$16 \leqslant h < 24$
Frequency	8	12	20	30	20	10

a Find the median time since a patient last saw a doctor.

b Estimate the mean time since a patient last saw a doctor.

c Find the interquartile range of the times.

7 One summer, Albert monitored the weight of the tomatoes grown on each of his plants. His results are summarised in this table.

Weight, w (kg)	$6 \leqslant w < 10$	$10 \leqslant w < 12$	$12 \leqslant w < 16$	$16 \leqslant w < 20$	$20 \leqslant w < 25$
Frequency	8	15	28	16	10

a Draw a histogram for this distribution.

b Estimate the median weight of tomatoes the plants produced.

c Estimate the mean weight of tomatoes the plants produced.

d How many plants produced more than 15 kg?

8 A survey was carried out to find the speeds of cars passing a particular point on the M1. The histogram illustrates the results of the survey.

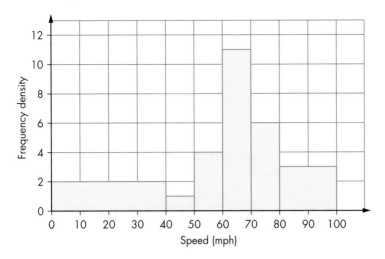

a Copy and complete this table.

Speed, v (mph)	$0 < v \leqslant 40$	$40 < v \leqslant 50$	$50 < v \leqslant 60$	$60 < v \leqslant 70$	$70 < v \leqslant 80$	$80 < v \leqslant 100$
Frequency		10	40	110		

b Find the number of cars included in the survey.

c Work out an estimate of the median speed of the cars on this part of the M1.

d Work out an estimate of the mean speed of the cars on this part of the M1.

1.6 Moving averages

In this section you will learn how to:	Key words
● calculate a moving average and use it to predict future trends	moving average seasonal trend trend line

A **moving average** gives a clear indication of the trend of a set of data. It smoothes out, for example, **seasonal trends** such as monthly variations or daily differences.

EXAMPLE 8

A van rental firm has a record of how many vans were hired in each month of a year. This data is shown in the table. Using a four-point moving average, predict the number of vans the firm will rent out during the following January.

Months	Jan	Feb	Mar	Apr	May	Jun	Jul	Aug	Sep	Oct	Nov	Dec
Vans	9	22	37	14	18	24	42	17	20	27	48	20

First, plot the raw data. The resulting line graph shows a normal variation of business for the hire firm, but does not reveal the general trend of business. Is the firm's business improving, declining or remaining the same?

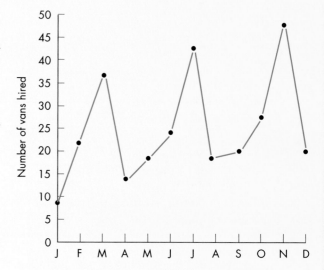

You can show the general trend by first calculating the mean for each four-month span, month on month. This is the four-point moving average.

Mean for Jan, Feb, Mar and April
$(9 + 22 + 37 + 14) \div 4 = 20.5$

Mean for Feb, Mar, Apr and May
$(22 + 37 + 14 + 18) \div 4 = 22.75$

Mean for Mar, Apr, May and Jun $(37 + 14 + 18 + 24) \div 4 = 23.25$

And so on, giving 24.5, 25.25, 25.75, 26.5, 28, 28.75 as the remaining averages.

Then plot, on the first graph, each mean value at the midpoint of the corresponding four-month span. This produces a much smoother graph, which, in this case, shows a slight upward trend. In other words, business is improving.

Draw a line of best fit (the **trend line**) through the data and read off the predicted value of the next four-point moving average. This is about 30.

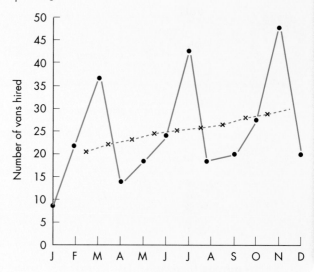

Let the value for the next January be x, then $(27 + 48 + 20 + x) \div 4 = 30$

$\Rightarrow 95 + x = 120$

$\Rightarrow \qquad x = 25$

So we can predict that the firm will rent out 25 vans the following January.

In Example 8, we used an interval of four months to construct a moving average but there is nothing special about this interval. It could well have been five or six months, except that you would then have needed data for more months to give sufficient mean values to show a trend. The number of months, weeks or even years used for moving averages depends on the likely variations of the data. You would not expect to use less than three or more than 12 items of data at a time.

EXERCISE 1F

1 The table shows the daily sales of milk at a local corner shop for a month.

Sun	Mon	Tue	Wed	Thu	Fri	Sat
12	8	6	9	4	11	15
11	7	7	6	3	15	14
14	9	7	7	5	12	15
11	12	8	7	4	14	19

Make a table showing the moving average using a seven-day span, and draw a graph to show the trend of milk sales over the month.

2 The table shows the amounts collected for a charity by the students at Pope Pius School in the ten weeks leading up to Christmas.

Week	1	2	3	4	5	6	7	8	9	10
Amount (£)	42	45	44	47	33	40	45	51	42	45

a Plot a line graph of the amounts collected and a four-week moving average.

b Comment on the trend shown.

3 The table shows the quarterly electricity bill over a four-year period.

	2002	2003	2004	2005
First quarter	£123.39	£119.95	£127.39	£132.59
Second quarter	£108.56	£113.16	£117.76	£119.76
Third quarter	£87.98	£77.98	£102.58	£114.08
Fourth quarter	£112.47	£127.07	£126.27	£130.87

a Plot the line graph of the electricity bills shown in the table, and on the same axes plot a four-quarter moving average.

b Comment on the price of electricity over the four years.

c Use the trend line of the moving averages to predict the bill for the first quarter of 2006.

4 The table shows the telephone bills for a family over four years.

	2002	2003	2004	2005
First quarter	£82	£87	£98	£88
Second quarter	£87	£88	£95	£91
Third quarter	£67	£72	£87	£78
Fourth quarter	£84	£81	£97	£87

a Plot a line graph showing the amounts paid each month.

b Plot a four-quarter moving average.

c Comment on the trend shown and give a possible reason for it.

d Use the trend line of the moving averages to predict the bill for the first quarter of 2006.

5 A factory making computer components has the following sales figures (in hundreds) for electric fans.

	Jan	Feb	Mar	Apr	May	Jun	Jul	Aug	Sep	Oct	Nov	Dec
2004	12	13	12	14	13	3	15	12	14	13	14	12
2005	13	14	12	14	13	14	13	13	15	15	15	14

a Plot a line graph of the sales, and a three-month moving average.

b Comment on the trend in the sales.

c Use the trend line of the moving averages to predict the number of electric fan sales in January 2006.

6 The table shows the total sales of video recorders and DVD players from 1999 to 2005 from an electrical store in the USA.

	1999	2000	2001	2002	2003	2004	2005
Video (thousands)	3.4	3.8	3.9	3.2	2.8	2.5	2.3
DVD (thousands)	0.2	0.8	0.9	1.5	1.9	2.8	3.7

a Plot a line graph showing the sales for each product over these years.

b On the same diagram, plot the three-year moving average of each product.

c Comment on the trends seen in the sales of video recorders and DVDs.

d Use the trend line of the moving averages to predict the number of video recorders and DVD players sold in 2006.

1.7 Surveys

In this section you will learn how to:

- conduct surveys
- ask good questions in order to collect reliable and valid data

Key words

data collection
   sheet
hypothesis
leading
   question
survey

A **survey** is an organised way of asking a lot of people a few, well-constructed questions, or of making a lot of observations in an experiment, in order to reach a conclusion about something.

Surveys are used to test out people's opinions or to test a **hypothesis**.

Simple data collection sheet

If you just need to collect some data to analyse, you will have to design a simple **data collection sheet**. This section will show you how to design a clear, easy-to-fill-in data collection sheet.

For example, if you want to find out Y10 students' preferences for the end-of-term trip from four options you could ask:

Where do you want to go for the Y10 trip at the end of term – Blackpool, Alton Towers, The Great Western Show or London?

You would put this question, on the same day, to a lot of Y10 students, and enter their answers straight onto a data collection sheet, as below.

Place	Tally	Frequency
Blackpool	⊬⊬⊬ ⊬⊬⊬ ⊬⊬⊬ ⊬⊬⊬ III	23
Alton Towers	⊬⊬⊬ ⊬⊬⊬ ⊬⊬⊬ ⊬⊬⊬ ⊬⊬⊬ ⊬⊬⊬ ⊬⊬⊬ ⊬⊬⊬ ⊬⊬⊬ I	46
The Great Western Show	⊬⊬⊬ ⊬⊬⊬ IIII	14
London	⊬⊬⊬ ⊬⊬⊬ ⊬⊬⊬ ⊬⊬⊬ II	22

Notice how plenty of space is available for the tally marks, and how the tallies are gated in groups of five to make counting easier when the survey is complete.

This is a good, simple data collection sheet because:

● only one question (*Where do you want to go?*) has to be asked

● all the four possible venues are listed

● the answer from each interviewee can be easily and quickly tallied, then on to the next interviewee.

Notice, too, that since the question listed specific places, they must appear on the data collection sheet. You would lose many marks in an examination if you just asked the open question: *Where do you want to go?*

Data sometimes needs to be collected to obtain responses for two different categories. The data collection sheet is then in the form of a two-way table.

EXAMPLE 9

The head of a school carries out a survey to find out how much time students in different year groups spend on their homework during a particular week. He asks a sample of 60 students and fills in a two-way table with headings as follows.

	0–5 hours	0–10 hours	10–20 hours	More than 20 hours
Year 7				

This is not a good table as the headings overlap. A student who does 10 hours work a week could tick either of two columns. Response sections should not overlap, so that there is only one possible place to put a tick.

A better table would be:

	0 up to 5 hours	More than 5 and up to 10 hours	More than 10 and up to 15 hours	More than 15 hours
Year 7	IIII II	IIII		
Year 8	IIII	IIII II		
Year 9	III	IIII II	II	
Year 10	III	IIII	III	I
Year 11	II	IIII	IIII	II

This gives a clearer picture of the amount of homework done in each year group.

Using your computer

Once the data has been collected for your survey, it can be put into a computer database. This allows the data to be stored and amended or updated at a later date if necessary.

From the database, suitable statistical diagrams can easily be drawn using software, and averages calculated. The results can then be published in, for example, the school magazine.

EXERCISE 1G

1 "People like the supermarket to open on Sundays."

a To see whether this statement is true, design a data collection sheet which will allow you to capture data while standing outside a supermarket.

b Does it matter on which day you collect data outside the supermarket?

2 The school tuck shop wants to know which types of chocolate it should get in to sell – plain, milk, fruit and nut, wholenut or white chocolate.

a Design a data collection sheet which you could use to ask pupils in your school which of these chocolate types are their favourite.

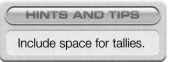

HINTS AND TIPS

Include space for tallies.

b Invent the first 30 entries on the chart.

3 When you throw two dice together, what number are you most likely to get?

    a Design a data collection sheet on which you can record the data from an experiment in which two dice are thrown together and note the sum of the two numbers shown on the dice.

    b Carry out this experiment for at least 100 throws.

    c Which sums are most likely to occur?

    d Illustrate your results on a frequency polygon.

4 Who uses the buses the most in the mornings? Is it pensioners, mums, schoolchildren, the unemployed or some other group? Design a data collection sheet to be used in a survey of bus passengers.

5 Design two-way tables to show

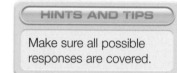

HINTS AND TIPS

Make sure all possible responses are covered.

    a how students in different year groups travel to school in the morning

    b the type of programme which different age groups prefer to watch on TV

    c the favourite sport of boys and girls

    d how much time students in different year groups spend on the computer in the evening.

Invent about 40 entries for each one.

Questionnaires

This section will show you how to put together a clear, easy-to-use questionnaire.

When you are putting together a questionnaire, you must think very carefully about the sorts of question you are going to ask. Here are five rules that you should *always* follow.

- Never ask a **leading question** designed to get a particular response.

- Never ask a personal, irrelevant question.

- Keep each question as simple as possible.

- Include questions that will get a response from whomever is asked.

- Make sure the responses do not overlap and keep the number of choices to a reasonable number (six at the most).

The following questions are badly constructed and should *never* appear in any questionnaire.

What is your age? This is personal. Many people will not want to answer. It is always better to give a range of ages.

☐ Under 15 ☐ 16–20 ☐ 21–30 ☐ 31–40 ☐ Over 40

Slaughtering animals for food is cruel to the poor defenceless animals. Don't you agree? This is a **leading question**, designed to get a "yes" response. It is better to ask an impersonal question.

Are you a vegetarian? ☐ Yes ☐ No

Do you go to discos when abroad? This can be answered only by people who have been abroad. It is better to ask a starter question, with a follow-up question.

Have you been abroad for a holiday? ☐ Yes ☐ No

If yes, did you go to a disco whilst you were away? ☐ Yes ☐ No

When you first get up in a morning and decide to have some sort of breakfast that might be made by somebody else, do you feel obliged to eat it all or not? This is a too-complicated question. It is better to ask a series of shorter questions.

What time do you get up for school? ☐ Before 7 ☐ Between 7 and 8 ☐ After 8

Do you have breakfast every day? ☐ Yes ☐ No

If No, on how many school days do you have breakfast? ☐ 0 ☐ 1 ☐ 2 ☐ 3 ☐ 4 ☐ 5

A questionnaire is usually put together to test a hypothesis or a statement. For example, a questionnaire might be constructed to test this statement.

People buy cheaper milk from the supermarket as they don't mind not getting it on their doorstep. They'd rather go out to buy it.

A questionnaire designed to test whether this statement is true or not should include these questions:

Do you have milk delivered to your doorstep?

Do you buy cheaper milk from the supermarket?

Would you buy your milk only from the supermarket?

Once these questions have been answered, the responses can be looked at to see whether the majority of people hold views that agree with the statement.

EXERCISE 1H

1 These are questions from a questionnaire on healthy eating.

a

Fast food is bad for you. Don't you agree?

☐ Strongly agree ☐ Agree ☐ Don't know

Give two criticisms of the question.

b

Do you eat fast food? ☐ Yes ☐ No

If yes, how many times on average do you eat fast food a week?

☐ Once or less ☐ 2 or 3 times ☐ 4 or 5 times ☐ More than 5 times

Give two reasons why these are good questions.

2 This is a question from a survey on pocket money.

How much pocket money do you get each week?

☐ £0–£2 ☐ £0–£5 ☐ £5–£10 ☐ £10 or more

a Give a reason why this is not a good question.

b Rewrite the question to make it good question.

3 Design a questionnaire to test this statement.

People under 16 do not know what is meant by all the jargon used in the business news on TV, but the over-twenties do.

4 Design a questionnaire to test this statement.

The under-twenties feel quite at ease with computers, while the over-forties would rather not bother with them. The 20–40s are all able to use computers effectively.

5 Design a questionnaire to test this hypothesis.

The older you get, the less sleep you need.

6 A head teacher wants to find out if her pupils think they have too much, too little or just the right amount of homework. She also wants to know the parents' views about homework.

Design a questionnaire that could be used to find the data that the head teacher needs to look at.

In this section you will learn about:
- learn about social statistics
- be introduced to some of the more common social statistics in daily use

Key words

margin of error
national census
polls
Retail Price Index
social statistics
time series

Many situations occur in daily life where statistical techniques are used to produce data. The results of surveys appear in newspapers every day. There are many on-line **polls** and phone-ins to vote in reality TV shows, for example.

Results for these polls are usually given as a percentage with a **margin of error**, which is a measure of how accurate the information is.

Here are some common social statistics in daily use.

General Index of Retail Prices

This is also know as the **Retail Price Index** (RPI). It measures how much the daily cost of living increases (or decreases). One year is chosen as the base year and given an index number, usually 100. The costs of subsequent years are compared to this and given a number proportional to the base year, say 103, etc.

Note the numbers do not represent actual values but just compare current prices to the base year.

Time series

Like the RPI, a **time series** measures changes in a quantity over time. Unlike the RPI the actual values of the quantity are used. This might measure how the exchange rate between the pound and the dollar changes over time.

National Census

A **national census** is a survey of all people and households in a country. Data about age, gender, religion, employment status, etc. is collected to enable governments to plan where to allocate resources in the future. In Britain, a national census is taken every 10 years. The last census was in 2001.

EXERCISE 1I

1 In 2000, the cost of a litre of petrol was 68p. Using 2000 as a base year, the price index of petrol for the next 5 years is shown in this table.

Year	2000	2001	2002	2003	2004	2005
Index	100	103	108	109	112	120
Price	78p					

Work out the price of petrol in each subsequent year. Give your answers to 1 decimal place.

2 The graph shows the exchange rate for the dollar against the pound for each month in 2005.

a What was the exchange rate in January?

b Between which two months did the exchange rate fall the most ?

c Explain why you could not use the graph to predict the exchange rate in January 2006.

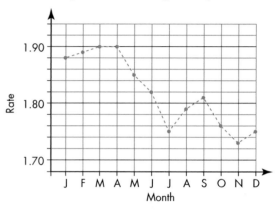

Exchange rate of the dollar against the pound, 2005

3 The following is taken from the UK government statistics website.

> In mid-2004 the UK was home to 59.8 million people, of which 50.1 million lived in England. The average age was 38.6 years, an increase on 1971 when it was 34.1 years. In mid-2004 approximately one in five people in the UK were aged under 16 and one in six people were aged 65 or over.

Use this extract to answer these questions.

a How many of the population of the UK *do not* live in England?

b By how much has the average age increased since 1971?

c Approximately how many of the population are under 16?

d Approximately how many of the population are over 65?

4 The General Index of Retail Prices started in January 1987 when it was given a base number of 100. In January 2006 the index number was 194.1.

If the "standard weekly shopping basket" cost £38.50 in January 1987, how much would it be in January 2006?

5 This time series shows car production in Britain from November 2004 to November 2005.

a Why was there a sharp drop in production in July?

b The average production over the first three months shown was 172 thousand cars.

i Work out an approximate number for the average production over the last three months shown.

ii The base month for the index is January 2000 when the index was 100. What was the approximate production in January 2000?

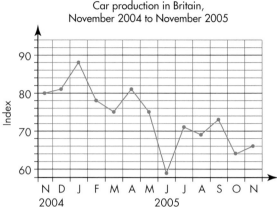

Car production in Britain, November 2004 to November 2005

1.9 Sampling

In this section you will learn how to:
- understand different methods of sampling
- collect unbiased reliable data

Key words
population
random
sample
stratified
unbiased

Statisticians often have to carry out surveys to collect information and test hypotheses about the **population** of a wide variety of things. (In statistics, population does not only mean a group of people, it also means a group of objects or events.)

It is seldom possible to survey a whole population, mainly because such a survey would cost too much and take a long time. Also there are populations for which it would be physically impossible to survey every member. For example, if you wanted to find the average length of eels in the North Sea, it would be impossible to find and measure every eel. So a statistician chooses a small part of the population to survey and assumes that the results for this **sample** are representative of the whole population.

Therefore, to ensure the accuracy of a survey, two questions have to be considered.

- Will the sample be representative of the whole population and thereby eliminate bias?

- How large should the sample be to give results which are valid for the whole population?

You will use many of these ideas in your Handling Data coursework.

Sampling methods

There are two main types of sample: **random** and **stratified**.

In a random sample, every member of the population has an equal chance of being chosen. For example, it may be the first 100 people met in a survey, or 100 names picked from a hat, or 100 names taken at random from the electoral register or a telephone directory.

In a stratified sample, the population is first divided into categories and the number of members in each category determined. The sample is then made up of members from these categories in the same proportions as they are in the population. The required sample in each category is chosen by random sampling.

EXAMPLE 10

A school's pupil numbers are given in the table. The head teacher wants to take a stratified sample of 100 pupils for a survey.

a Calculate the number of boys and girls in each year that should be interviewed.

b Explain how the pupils could then be chosen to give a random sample.

School year	Boys	Girls	Total
7	52	68	120
8	46	51	97
9	62	59	121
10	47	61	108
11	39	55	94
Total number in school			540

a To get the correct number in each category, say, boys in year 7, the calculation is done as follows.

$$\frac{52}{540} \times 100 = 9.6 \text{ (1 decimal place)}$$

After all calculations are done, you should get the values in this table.

School Year	Boys	Girls
7	9.6	12.6
8	8.5	9.4
9	11.5	10.9
10	8.7	11.3
11	7.2	10.2

Obviously you cannot have a decimal point of a pupil, so round off all values and make sure that the total is 100. This gives the final table.

School year	Boys	Girls	Total
7	10	13	23
8	8	9	17
9	12	11	23
10	9	11	20
11	7	10	17

b Within each category, choose pupils to survey at random. For example, all the year 7 girls could have their names put into a hat and 13 names drawn out or they could be listed alphabetically and a random number generator used to pick out 13 names from 68.

Sample size

Before the sampling of a population can begin, it is necessary to determine how much data needs to be collected to ensure that the sample is representative of the population. This is called the sample size.

Two factors determine sample size:

- the desired precision with which the sample represents the population

- the amount of money available to meet the cost of collecting the sample data.

The greater the precision desired, the larger the sample size needs to be. But the larger the sample size, the higher the cost will be. Therefore, the benefit of achieving high accuracy in a sample will always have to be set against the cost of achieving it.

There are statistical procedures for determining the most suitable sample size, but these are beyond the scope of the GCSE syllabus.

The next example addresses some of the problems associated with obtaining an **unbiased** sample.

EXAMPLE 11

You are going to conduct a survey among an audience of 30 000 people at a rock concert. How would you choose the sample?

1 You would not want to question all of them, so you might settle for a sample size of 2%, which is 600 people.

2 Assuming that there will be as many men at the concert as women, you would need the sample to contain the same proportion of each, namely, 300 men and 300 women.

3 Assuming that about 20% of the audience will be aged under 20, you would also need the sample to contain 120 people aged under 20 (20% of 600) and 480 people aged 20 and over (600 − 120 or 80% of 600).

4 You would also need to select people from different parts of the auditorium in equal proportions so as to get a balanced view. Say this breaks down into three equal groups of people, taken respectively from the front, the back and the middle of the auditorium. So, you would further need the sample to consist of 200 people at the front, 200 at the back and 200 in the middle.

5 If you now assume that one researcher can survey 40 concert-goers, you would arrive at this sampling strategy

600 ÷ 40 = 15 researchers to conduct the survey

15 ÷ 3 = 5 researchers in each part of the auditorium

Each researcher would need to question four men aged under 20, 16 men aged 20 and over, four women aged under 20 and 16 women aged 20 and over.

EXERCISE 1J

1 Comment on the reliability of the following ways of finding a sample.

  a Find out about smoking by asking 50 people in a non-smoking part of a restaurant.

  b Find out how many homes have video recorders by asking 100 people outside a video hire shop.

  c Find the most popular make of car by counting 100 cars in a city car park.

  d Find a year representative on a school's council by picking a name out of a hat.

  e Decide whether the potatoes have cooked properly by testing one with a fork.

2 Comment on the way the following samples have been taken. For those that are not satisfactory, suggest a better way to find a more reliable sample.

  a Joseph had a discussion with his dad about pocket money. To get some information, he asked 15 of his friends how much pocket money they each received.

  b Douglas wanted to find out what proportion of his school went abroad for holidays, so he asked the first 20 people he came across in the school yard.

  c A teacher wanted to know which lesson his pupils enjoyed most. So he asked them all.

  d It has been suggested that more females go to church than males. So Ruth did a survey in her church that Sunday and counted the number of females there.

  e A group of local people asked for a crossing on a busy road. The council conducted a survey by asking a randomly selected 100 people in the neighbourhood.

3 For a school project you have been asked to do a presentation of the social activities of the pupils in your school. You decide to interview a sample of pupils. Explain how you will choose the pupils you wish to interview if you want your results to be

  a reliable,   **b** unbiased,   **c** representative,   **d** random.

4 A fast-food pizza chain attempted to estimate the number of people who eat pizzas in a certain town. One evening they telephoned 50 people living in the town and asked: "Have you eaten a pizza in the last month?" Eleven people said "Yes". The pizza chain stated that 22% of the town's population eat pizzas. Give three criticisms of this method of estimation.

5 **a** Adam is writing a questionnaire for a survey about the Meadowhall shopping centre in Sheffield. He is told that fewer local people visit Meadowhall than people from further away. He is also told that the local people spend less money per visit. Write two questions which would help him to test these ideas. Each question should include at least three options for a response. People are asked to choose one of these options.

  b For another survey, Adam investigates how much is spent at the chocolate machines by students at his school. The number of students in each year group is shown in the table. Explain, with calculations, how Adam should obtain a stratified random sample of 100 students for his survey.

Year group	7	8	9	10	11
Numbers of students	143	132	156	131	108

6 Claire made a survey of pupils in her school. She wanted to find out their opinions on the eating facilities in the school. The size of each year group in the school is shown in the table.

Year group	Boys	Girls	Total
8	96	78	174
9	84	86	170
10	84	91	175
11	82	85	167
6th form	83	117	200
			886

Claire took a sample of 90 pupils.

a Explain why she should not have sampled equal numbers of boys and girls in the sixth form.

b Calculate the number of pupils she should have sampled in the sixth form.

Using the Internet

Through the Internet you have access to a vast amount of data on many topics, which you can use to carry out statistical investigations. This data will enable you to draw statistical diagrams, answer a variety of questions and test all manner of hypotheses.

Here are some examples of hypotheses you can test.

Football teams are most likely to win when they are playing at home.

Boys do better than girls at GCSE mathematics.

The number 3 gets drawn more often than the number 49 in the National Lottery.

The literacy rate in a country is linked to that country's average income.

People in the north of England have larger families than people who live in the south.

The following websites are a useful source of data for some of the above.

www.statistics.gov.uk

www.lufc.co.uk

www.national-lottery.co.uk

www.cia.gov/cia/publications/factbook/

1 The number of matches in 20 matchboxes is shown in the table.

No. of matches (*m*)	Frequency
42	2
43	5
44	11
45	1
46	1

Calculate the mean number of matches in the 20 boxes.

2 50 people were asked how long they had to wait for a bus. The table shows the results.

a Which class interval contains the median time?

Time taken, *t* (min)	Frequency
$0 < t \leqslant 5$	16
$5 < t \leqslant 10$	21
$10 < t \leqslant 15$	10
$15 < t \leqslant 20$	3

b Draw a frequency diagram to represent the data.

AQA, Question 8, Paper 1 Higher, May 2005

3 In year 9 there are 30 students who study both French and Spanish. Their National Curriculum levels in these subjects are shown in the two-way table.

				Level in Spanish			
		1	2	3	4	5	6
Level in French	1	0	0	0	0	0	0
	2	1	0	0	0	0	0
	3	2	1	1	0	0	0
	4	0	3	4	1	0	0
	5	0	1	2	3	2	0
	6	0	0	3	3	2	1

a What is the modal level for French?

b What is the median level for French?
Show clearly how you obtained your answer.

c What is the mean level for Spanish?
Show clearly how you obtained your answer.

d The teacher claims that the students are better at French than at Spanish. How can you tell from the table that this is true?

AQA, Question 3, Paper 2 Higher, November 2004

4 The table shows the times taken for a train journey for 20 days.

Time taken, *t* (min)	Frequency
$18 < t \leqslant 20$	4
$20 < t \leqslant 22$	6
$22 < t \leqslant 24$	5
$24 < t \leqslant 26$	3
$26 < t \leqslant 28$	2

Calculate an estimate of the mean journey time

5 Susan completes a journey in two stages.
In stage 1 of her journey, she drives at an average speed of 80 km/h and takes 1 hour 45 minutes.

a How far does Susan travel in stage 1 of her journey?

b Altogether, Susan drives 190 km and takes a total time of 2 hours 15 minutes. What is her average speed, in km/h, in stage 2 of her journey?

AQA, Question 4, Paper 1 Higher, November 2003

6 Jack and Jill are doing a survey on fast food.

a This is one of Jack's questions.

> Burgers are bad for you and make you fat.
> Yes ☐   No ☐

Give two reasons why this is not a good question.

b This is one of Jill's questions.

> How many times, on average, do you visit a fast food outlet in a week
> Never ☐   1 or 2 times ☐
> 3 or 4 times ☐   More than 4 times ☐

Give two reasons why this is good question.

7 The PE department pins up a bar chart showing the number of goals the school football team scored in each match over the season.

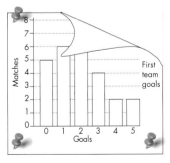

Unfortunately one of the pins has fallen out and covered part of the chart.

a The number of matches when 2 goals were scored was *n*. Write down an expression, in terms of *n*, for the total number of matches.

b Show that the total number of goals scored was $36 + 2n$.

c The mean number of goals scored over the season was 1.92. Work out the value of *n*.

8 The table shows the cost of the gas at the end of every three months and some four-point moving averages.

The graph shows the actual cost of the gas and some of the moving averages.

Year	2002				2003				2004			
Quarter	1st	2nd	3rd	4th	1st	2nd	3rd	4th	1st	2nd	3rd	4th
Cost (£)	86	90	93	99	94	94	97	103	94	98	101	
Four-point moving average		92	94	95	96	97	97	98	99			

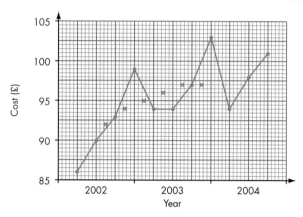

Key: • Actual cost
      ✕ Moving average

a Copy the graph and plot the last two four-point moving averages.

b Use the trend of the moving averages to predict the cost of the gas at the end of the 4th quarter of 2004.

Question 8, Paper 2 Higher, June 2005

9 The table shows the heights of 100 adults.

Height, h (cm)	Frequency
$155 < h \leq 160$	14
$160 < h \leq 165$	26
$165 < h \leq 170$	36
$170 < h \leq 175$	p
$175 < h \leq 180$	q

An estimate of the mean height of the adults is calculated as 166.5 cm. Calculate the values of p and q.

10 The masses of 50 marrows are measured.

Mass, m, (grams)	Frequency
$500 < m \leq 600$	4
$600 < m \leq 800$	8
$800 < m \leq 850$	11
$850 < m \leq 1000$	12
$1000 < m \leq 1250$	15

a Draw a histogram to show this information

b Use, your histogram, or otherwise, to estimate the median mass of the marrows.

11 The histogram shows the test scores of 320 children in a school.

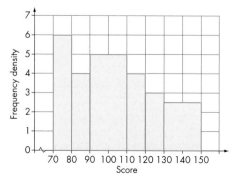

a Find the median score.

b Find the interquartile range of the scores.

AQA, Question 17, Paper 2 Higher, June 2005

12 **a** This histogram shows the test scores of 100 female students.

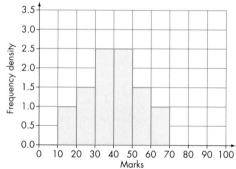

i What is the median score?

ii What is the interquartile range?

b This histogram is incomplete. It shows some of the test scores for 100 male students. The median test score for males is the same as for females. The upper quartile for the males is 50.

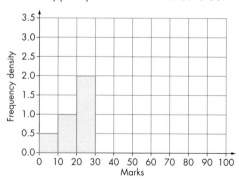

i What is the lower quartile for the male students?

ii Complete a possible histogram.

AQA, Question 24, Paper 2 Higher, November 2004

WORKED EXAM QUESTION

The distances travelled by 100 cars using 10 litres of petrol is shown in the histogram and table.

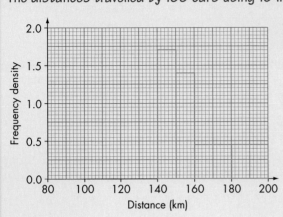

a Complete the histogram and the table.

b Estimate the number of cars that travel between 155 km and 185 km using 10 litres of petrol.

Distance (km)	80–110	110–130	130–140	140–150	150–160	160–200
Frequency	9	22	20			

Solution

a Set up the table with columns for class width and frequency density and fill in the given information, reading frequency densities from the graph (be careful with scales).

Now fill in the rest of the information using f.d. = $\dfrac{\text{frequency}}{\text{class width}}$ and

frequency = f.d. × class width.

These values are shown in red.

Complete the graph.

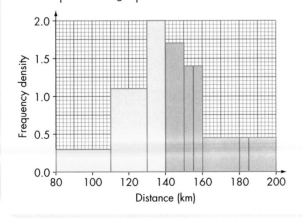

Distance (km)	Frequency	Class width	Frequency density
80–110	9	30	0.3
110–130	22	20	1.1
130–140	20	10	2
140–150	17	10	1.7
150–160	14	10	1.4
160–200	18	40	0.45

b Draw lines at 155 and 185. The number of cars is represented by the area between these lines. In the 150–160 bar the area is $\frac{1}{2}$ of the total. In the 160–200 bar the area is $\frac{5}{8}$ of the total.

Number of cars = $\frac{1}{2} \times 14 + \frac{5}{8} \times 18 = 18.25 \approx 18$ cars

Mr Davies is a dairy farmer. Every month he records the thousands of litres of milk produced by his cows.

For his business plan he compares the amount of milk he produces in 2004 with 2005.

Monthly milk production in thousands of litres		
Month	2004	2005
Jan	51	62
Feb	53	65
Mar	55	62
Apr	56	67
May	64	72
Jun	72	83
Jul	70	81
Aug	75	86
Sep	64	75
Oct	64	73
Nov	62	70
Dec	58	68

Mr Davies calculates three-month moving averages for 2004 and 2005. He plots line graphs showing the moving averages for these two years.

Help him to complete the moving averages table, and the line graphs. Comment on the trends shown.

3-month moving average for milk production in thousands of litres												
	Jan	Feb	Mar	Apr	May	Jun	Jul	Aug	Sep	Oct	Nov	Dec
2004		53	54.7									
2005	61.7	63										

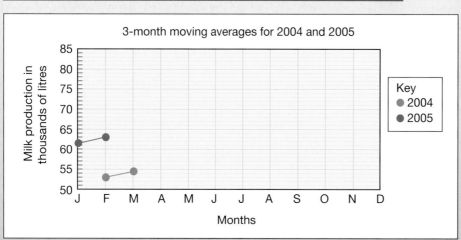

3-month moving averages for 2004 and 2005

Key
● 2004
● 2005

For his business plan Mr Davies compares the amount of milk he produces in 2005, with the graphs showing the hours of sunshine and amount of rain that year.

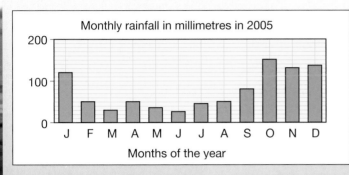

Monthly rainfall in millimetres in 2005

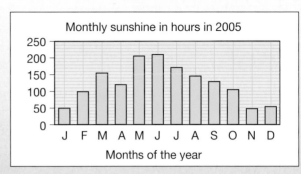

Monthly sunshine in hours in 2005

Draw two scatter graphs; one showing his monthly milk production and monthly rainfall, the other showing his monthly milk production and the monthly sunshine.

Comment on the correlation shown by these graphs.

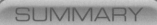

GRADE YOURSELF

D Able to find the mean from a frequency table of discrete data

D Able to draw a frequency polygon for discrete data

C Able to find an estimate of the mean from a grouped table of continuous data

C Able to draw a frequency polygon for continuous data

C Able to design questionnaires and surveys

B Able to use a moving average to predict future values

A Able to draw histograms from frequency tables with unequal class intervals

A Able to calculate the numbers to be surveyed for a stratified sample

A* Able to find the median, quartiles and the interquartile range from a histogram

What you should know now

- Which average to use in different situations
- How to find the modal class and an estimated mean for continuous data
- How to draw frequency polygons and histograms for discrete and continuous data
- How to design questionnaires and surveys

Statistics 2

1 Line graphs

2 Stem-and-leaf diagrams

3 Scatter diagrams

4 Cumulative frequency diagrams

5 Box plots

6 Measures of dispersion

This chapter will show you ...

- how to interpret and draw line graphs and stem-and-leaf diagrams
- how to draw scatter diagrams and lines of best fit
- how to interpret scatter diagrams and the different types of correlation
- how to draw and interpret cumulative frequency diagrams
- how to draw and interpret box plots
- how to calculate the standard deviation of a set of data

Visual overview

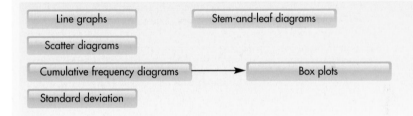

What you should already know

- How to plot coordinate points
- How to read information from charts and tables
- How to calculate the mean of a set of data from a frequency table
- How to recognise a positive or negative gradient (Chapter 23)

Quick check

1 The table shows the number of children in 10 classes in a primary school.

Calculate the mean number of children in each class.

Number of children	27	28	29	30	31
Frequency	1	2	4	2	1

In this section you will learn how to:
● draw a line graph to show trends in data

Key words
line graphs
trends

Line graphs are usually used in statistics to show how data changes over a period of time. One use is to indicate **trends**: for example, line graphs can be used to show whether the Earth's temperature is increasing as the concentration of carbon dioxide builds up in the atmosphere, or whether a firm's profit margin is falling year on year.

Line graphs are best drawn on graph paper.

EXAMPLE 1

This line graph shows the profit made each year by a company over a five-year period.

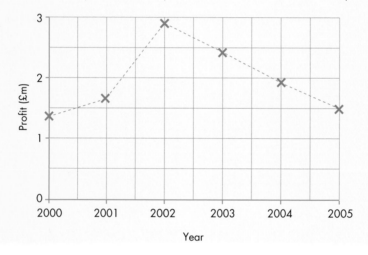

For this graph, the values between the plotted points have no meaning because the profit of the company would have been calculated at the end of every year. In cases like this, the lines are often dashed. Although the trend appears to be that profits have fallen after 2002, it would not be sensible to try to predict what will happen after 2005.

EXERCISE 2A

1 The table shows the estimated number of tourists world wide.

Year	1970	1975	1980	1985	1990	1995	2000	2005
No. of tourists (millions)	60	100	150	220	280	290	320	340

a Draw a line graph for the data.

b From your graph estimate the number of tourists in 2002.

c In which five-year period did world tourism increase the most?

d Explain the trend in world tourism. What reasons can you give to explain this trend?

2 The table shows the maximum and minimum daily temperatures for London over a week.

Day	Sunday	Monday	Tuesday	Wednesday	Thursday	Friday	Saturday
Maximum (°C)	12	14	16	15	16	14	10
Minimum (°C)	4	5	7	8	7	4	3

a Draw line graphs on the *same axes* to show the maximum and minimum temperatures.

b Find the smallest and greatest difference between the maximum and minimum temperatures.

2.2 Stem-and-leaf diagrams

In this section you will learn how to:
- draw and read information from an ordered stem-and-leaf diagram

Key words
discrete data
ordered
raw data
unordered

Raw data

If you are recording the ages of the first 20 people who line up at a bus stop in the morning, the **raw data** might look like this.

23, 13, 34, 44, 26, 12, 41, 31, 20, 18, 19, 31, 48, 32, 45, 14, 12, 27, 31, 19

This data is **unordered** and is difficult to read and analyse. When the data is **ordered**, it looks like this.

12, 12, 13, 14, 18, 19, 19, 20, 23, 26, 27, 31, 31, 31, 32, 34, 41, 44, 45, 48

This is easier to read and analyse.

Another method for displaying **discrete data** such as this, is a stem-and-leaf diagram. The tens values will be the "stem" and the units values will be the "leaves".

Key: 1 | 2 represents 12

```
1 | 2   2   3   4   8   9   9
2 | 0   3   6   7
3 | 1   1   1   2   4
4 | 1   4   5   8
```

This is called an ordered stem-and-leaf diagram and gives a better idea of how the data is distributed.

A stem-and-leaf diagram should always have a key.

EXAMPLE 2

Put the following data into an ordered stem-and-leaf diagram.

45, 62, 58, 58, 61, 49, 61, 47, 52, 58, 48, 56, 65, 46, 54

a What is the modal value?

b What is the median value?

c What is the range of the values?

First decide on the stem and leaf.

In this case, the tens digit will be the stem and the units digit will be the leaf.

Key: 4 | 5 represents 45

```
4 | 5  6  7  8  9
5 | 2  4  6  8  8  8
6 | 1  1  2  5
```

a The modal value is the most common, which is 58.

b There are 15 values, so the median will be the (15 + 1) ÷ 2th value, or 8th value. Counting from either the top or the bottom, the median is 56.

c The range is the difference between the largest and the smallest value, which is 65 − 45 = 20.

EXERCISE 2B

1 The heights of 15 tulips are measured.

43 cm, 39 cm, 41 cm, 29 cm, 36 cm,

34 cm, 43 cm, 48 cm, 38 cm, 35 cm,

41 cm, 38 cm, 43 cm, 28 cm, 48 cm

a Show the results in an ordered stem-and-leaf diagram, using this key.

Key: 4 | 3 represents 43 cm

b What is the modal height?

c What is the median height?

d What is the range of the heights?

2 A student records the number of text messages she receives each day for two weeks.

12, 18, 21, 9, 17, 23, 8, 2, 20, 13, 17, 22, 9, 9

a Show the results in an ordered stem-and-leaf diagram, using this key.

Key: 1 | 2 represents 12 messages

b What was the modal number of text messages received in a day?

c What was the median number of text messages received in a day?

In this section you will learn how to:
- draw, interpret and use scatter diagrams

Key words
line of best fit
negative
    correlation
no correlation
positive
    correlation
scatter
    diagram
variable

A **scatter diagram** (also called a scattergraph or scattergram) is a method of comparing two **variables** by plotting on a graph their corresponding values (usually taken from a table). In other words, the variables are treated just like a set of (x, y) coordinates.

In the scatter diagram below, the marks scored by pupils in an English test are plotted against the marks they scored in a mathematics test. This graph shows positive **correlation**. This means that the pupils who got high marks in the mathematics test also tended to get high marks in the English test.

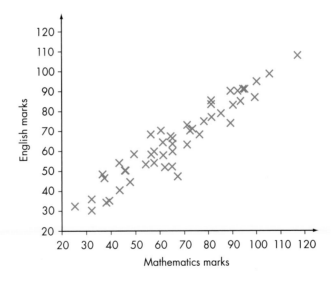

Correlation

This section will explain the different types of correlation.

Here are three statements that may or may not be true.

The taller people are, the wider their arm span is likely to be.

The older a car is, the lower its value will be.

The distance you live from your place of work will affect how much you earn.

These relationships could be tested by collecting data and plotting the data on a scatter diagram.

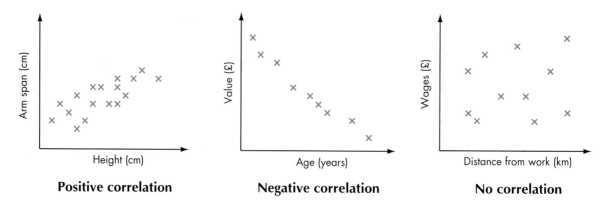

Positive correlation   **Negative correlation**   **No correlation**

For example, the first statement may give a scatter diagram like the first diagram above. This diagram has positive correlation because as one quantity increases so does the other. From such a scatter diagram we could say that the taller someone is, the wider the arm span.

Testing the second statement may give a scatter diagram like the second one. This diagram has **negative correlation** because as one quantity increases, the other quantity decreases. From such a scatter diagram we could say that as a car gets older, its value decreases.

Testing the third statement may give a scatter diagram like the third one. This scatter diagram has **no correlation**. There is no relationship between the distance a person lives from his or her work and how much the person earns.

EXAMPLE 3

The graphs show the relationship between the temperature and the amount of ice cream sold, and that between the age of people and the amount of ice cream they eat.

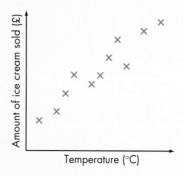 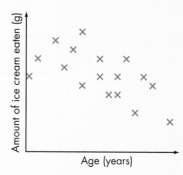

a Comment on the correlation of each graph.

b What does each graph tell you?

The first graph has positive correlation and tells us that as the temperature increases, the amount of ice cream sold increases.

The second graph has negative correlation and tells us that as people get older, they eat less ice cream.

Line of best fit

This section will explain how to draw and use a line of best fit.

The **line of best fit** is a straight line that goes between all the points on a scatter diagram, passing as close as possible to all of them. You should try to have the same number of points on both sides of the line. Because you are drawing this line by eye, examiners make a generous allowance around the correct answer. The line of best fit for the scatter diagram on page 47 is shown below.

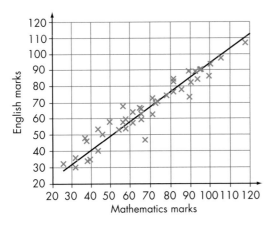
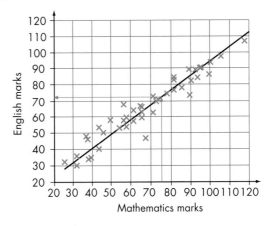

The line of best fit can be used to answer the following type of question: A girl took the mathematics test and scored 75 marks, but was ill for the English test. How many marks was she likely to have scored?

The answer is found by drawing a line up from 75 on the mathematics axis to the line of best fit and then drawing a line across to the English axis. This gives 73, which is the mark she is likely to have scored in the English test.

EXERCISE 2C

1 Describe the correlation of each of these four graphs and write in words what each graph tells you.

a

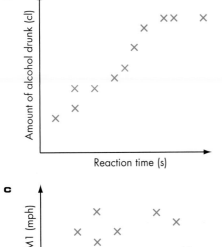

Reaction time (s)

b

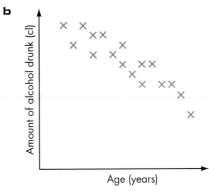

Age (years)

c

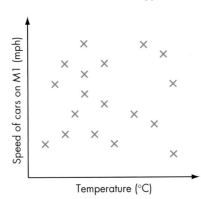

Temperature (°C)

d

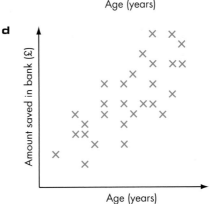

Age (years)

2 The table shows the results of a science experiment in which a ball is rolled along a desk top. The speed of the ball is measured at various points.

Distance from start (cm)	10	20	30	40	50	60	70	80
Speed (cm/s)	18	16	13	10	7	5	3	0

a Plot the data on a scatter diagram.

b Draw the line of best fit.

c If the ball's speed had been measured at 5 cm from the start, what is it likely to have been?

d How far from the start was the ball when its speed was 12 cm/s?

> **HINTS AND TIPS**
>
> Usually in exams axes are given and most, if not all, of the points are plotted.

3 The table shows the marks for ten pupils in their mathematics and geography examinations.

Pupil	Anna	Beryl	Cath	Dema	Ethel	Fatima	Greta	Hannah	Imogen	Joan
Maths	57	65	34	87	42	35	59	61	25	35
Geog	45	61	30	78	41	36	35	57	23	34

a Plot the data on a scatter diagram. Take the *x*-axis for the mathematics scores and mark it from 20 to 100. Take the *y*-axis for the geography scores and mark it from 20 to 100.

b Draw the line of best fit.

c One of the pupils was ill when she took the geography examination. Which pupil was it most likely to be?

d If another pupil, Kate, was absent for the geography examination but scored 75 in mathematics, what mark would you expect her to have got in geography?

e If another pupil, Lynne, was absent for the mathematics examination but scored 65 in geography, what mark would you expect her to have got in mathematics?

4 The heights, in centimetres, of twenty mothers and their 15-year-old daughters were measured. These are the results.

Mother	153	162	147	183	174	169	152	164	186	178
Daughter	145	155	142	167	167	151	145	152	163	168
Mother	175	173	158	168	181	173	166	162	180	156
Daughter	172	167	160	154	170	164	156	150	160	152

a Plot these results on a scatter diagram. Take the *x*-axis for the mothers' heights from 140 to 200. Take the *y*-axis for the daughters' heights from 140 to 200.

b Is it true that the tall mothers have tall daughters?

5 A form teacher carried out a survey of his class. He asked pupils to say how many hours per week they spent playing sport and how many hours per week they spent watching TV. This table shows the results of the survey.

Pupil	1	2	3	4	5	6	7	8	9	10
Hours playing sport	12	3	5	15	11	0	9	7	6	12
Hours watching TV	18	26	24	16	19	27	12	13	17	14

Pupil	11	12	13	14	15	16	17	18	19	20
Hours playing sport	12	10	7	6	7	3	1	2	0	12
Hours watching TV	22	16	18	22	12	28	18	20	25	13

a Plot these results on a scatter diagram. Take the *x*-axis as the number of hours playing sport and mark it from 0 to 20. Take the *y*-axis as the number of hours watching TV and mark it from 0 to 30.

b If you knew that another pupil from the form watched 8 hours of TV a week, would you be able to predict how long she or he spent playing sport? Explain why.

2.4 # Cumulative frequency diagrams

In this section you will learn how to:

- find a measure of dispersion (the interquartile range) and a measure of location (the median) using a graph

Key words

cumulative frequency diagram
dispersion
interquartile range
lower quartile
median
upper quartile

The **interquartile range** is a measure of the **dispersion** of a set of data. The advantage of the interquartile range is that it eliminates extreme values, and bases the measure of spread on the middle 50% of the data. This section will show how to find the interquartile range, and the median, of a set of data by drawing a **cumulative frequency diagram**.

Look back at the marks of the 50 pupils in the mathematics test (see page 47). These can be put into a grouped table, as shown on the next page. Note that it includes a column for the cumulative frequency, which is found by adding each frequency to the sum of all preceding frequencies.

Mark	Number of pupils	Cumulative frequency
21 to 30	1	1
31 to 40	6	7
41 to 50	6	13
51 to 60	8	21
61 to 70	8	29
71 to 80	6	35
81 to 90	7	42
91 to 100	6	48
101 to 110	1	49
111 to 120	1	50

This data can then be used to plot a graph of the top value of each group against its cumulative frequency. The points to be plotted are (30, 1), (40, 7), (50, 13), (60, 21), etc., which will give the graph shown below. Note that the cumulative frequency is *always* the vertical (y) axis.

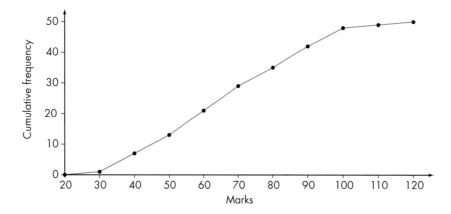

Also note that the scales on both axes are labelled at each graduation mark, in the usual way. Do not label the scales as shown here – it is wrong.

21–30	31–40	41–50

The plotted points can be joined in two different ways:

- by straight lines, to give a cumulative frequency polygon

- by a freehand curve, to give a cumulative frequency curve or ogive.

They are both called cumulative frequency diagrams.

In an examination you are most likely to be asked to draw a cumulative frequency diagram, and the type (polygon or curve) is up to you. Both will give similar results. The cumulative frequency diagram can be used in several ways, as you will now see.

The median

The **median** is the middle item of data once all the items have been put in order of size, from lowest to highest. So, if you have n items of data plotted as a cumulative frequency diagram, the median can be found from the middle value of the cumulative frequency, that is the $\frac{n}{2}$th value.

But remember, if you want to find the median from a simple list of discrete data, you *must* use the $(\frac{n+1}{2})$th value. The reason for the difference is that the cumulative frequency diagram treats the data as continuous, even when using data such as examination marks which are discrete. The reason you can use the $\frac{n}{2}$th value when working with cumulative frequency diagrams is that you are only looking for an estimate of the median.

There are 50 values in the table on page 52. The middle value will be the 25th value. Draw a horizontal line from the 25th value to meet the graph then go down to the horizontal axis. This will give an estimate of the median. In this example, the median is about 65 marks.

The interquartile range

By dividing the cumulative frequency into four parts, we obtain quartiles and the interquartile range.

The **lower quartile** is the item one quarter of the way up the cumulative frequency axis and is found by looking at the $\frac{n}{4}$th value.

The **upper quartile** is the item three-quarters of the way up the cumulative frequency axis and is found by looking at the $\frac{3n}{4}$th value.

The **interquartile range** is the difference between the lower and upper quartiles.

These are illustrated on the graph below.

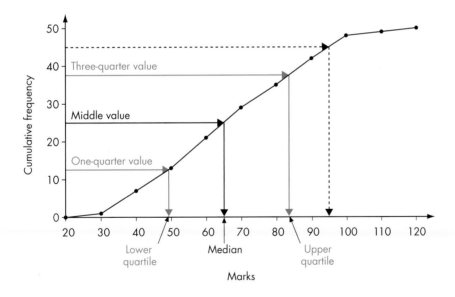

The quarter and three-quarter values out of 50 values are the 12.5th value and the 37.5th value. Draw lines across to the cumulative frequency curve from these values and down to the horizontal axis. These give the lower and upper quartiles. In this example, the lower quartile is 49 marks, the upper quartile is 83 marks, and the interquartile range is 83 − 49 = 34 marks.

Note that problems like these are often followed up with an extra question such as: The Head of Mathematics decides to give a special award to the top 10% of pupils. What would the cut-off mark be?

The top 10% would be the top 5 pupils (10% of 50 is 5). Draw a line across from the 45th pupil to the graph and down to the horizontal axis. This gives a cut-off mark of 95.

EXAMPLE 4

The table below shows the marks of 100 pupils in a mathematics SAT.

a Draw a cumulative frequency curve.

b Use your graph to find the median and the interquartile range.

c Pupils who score less than 44 do not get a SAT level awarded. How many pupils will not get a SAT level?

Mark	Number of pupils	Cumulative frequency
$21 \leqslant x \leqslant 30$	3	3
$31 \leqslant x \leqslant 40$	9	12
$41 \leqslant x \leqslant 50$	12	24
$51 \leqslant x \leqslant 60$	15	39
$61 \leqslant x \leqslant 70$	22	61
$71 \leqslant x \leqslant 80$	16	77
$81 \leqslant x \leqslant 90$	10	87
$91 \leqslant x \leqslant 100$	8	95
$101 \leqslant x \leqslant 110$	3	98
$111 \leqslant x \leqslant 120$	2	100

The groups are given in a different way to those in the table on page 424. You will meet several ways of giving groups (for example, 21–30, $20 < x \leqslant 30$, $21 < x < 30$) but the important thing to remember is to plot the top point of each group against the corresponding cumulative frequency.

a and **b** Draw the graph and put on the lines for the median (50th value), lower and upper quartiles (25th and 75th values).

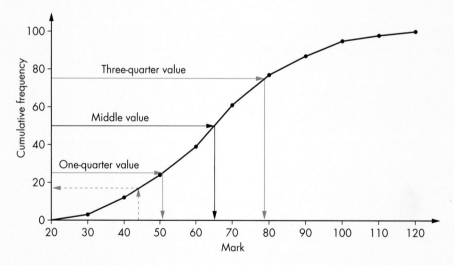

The required answers are read from the graph.

Median = 65 marks
Lower quartile = 51 marks
Upper quartile = 79 marks
Interquartile range = 79 − 51 = 28 marks

c At 44 on the mark axis draw a perpendicular line to intersect the graph, and at the point of intersection draw a horizontal line across to the cumulative frequency axis, as shown.
Number of pupils without a SAT level = 18

Note, an alternative way in which the table in Example 4 could have been set out is shown below. This arrangement has the advantage that the points to be plotted are taken straight from the last two columns. You have to decide which method you prefer. In examination papers, the columns of tables are sometimes given without headings, so you will need to be familiar with all the different ways in which the data can be set out.

Mark	Number of pupils	Less than	Cumulative frequency
$21 \leqslant x \leqslant 30$	3	30	3
$31 \leqslant x \leqslant 40$	9	40	12
$41 \leqslant x \leqslant 50$	12	50	24
$51 \leqslant x \leqslant 60$	15	60	39
$61 \leqslant x \leqslant 70$	22	70	61
$71 \leqslant x \leqslant 80$	16	80	77
$81 \leqslant x \leqslant 90$	10	90	87
$91 \leqslant x \leqslant 100$	8	100	95
$101 \leqslant x \leqslant 110$	3	110	98
$111 \leqslant x \leqslant 120$	2	120	100

EXERCISE 2D

1 A class of 30 children was asked to estimate one minute. The teacher recorded the times the pupils actually said. The table on the right shows the results.

a Copy the table and complete a cumulative frequency column.

b Draw a cumulative frequency diagram.

c Use your diagram to estimate the median time and the interquartile range.

Time (seconds)	Number of pupils
$20 < x \leqslant 30$	1
$30 < x \leqslant 40$	3
$40 < x \leqslant 50$	6
$50 < x \leqslant 60$	12
$60 < x \leqslant 70$	3
$70 < x \leqslant 80$	3
$80 < x \leqslant 90$	2

2 A group of 50 pensioners was given the same task as the children in question 1. The results are shown in the table on the right.

a Copy the table and complete a cumulative frequency column.

b Draw a cumulative frequency diagram.

c Use your diagram to estimate the median time and the interquartile range.

d Which group, the children or the pensioners, would you say was better at estimating time? Give a reason for your answer.

Time (seconds)	Number of pensioners
$10 < x \leqslant 20$	1
$20 < x \leqslant 30$	2
$30 < x \leqslant 40$	2
$40 < x \leqslant 50$	9
$50 < x \leqslant 60$	17
$60 < x \leqslant 70$	13
$70 < x \leqslant 80$	3
$80 < x \leqslant 90$	2
$90 < x \leqslant 100$	1

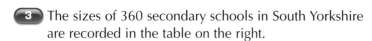

3 The sizes of 360 secondary schools in South Yorkshire are recorded in the table on the right.

a Copy the table and complete a cumulative frequency column.

b Draw a cumulative frequency diagram.

c Use your diagram to estimate the median size of the schools and the interquartile range.

d Schools with less than 350 pupils are threatened with closure. About how many schools are threatened with closure?

Number of pupils	Number of schools
100–199	12
200–299	18
300–399	33
400–499	50
500–599	63
600–699	74
700–799	64
800–899	35
900–999	11

4 The temperature at a seaside resort was recorded over a period of 50 days. The temperature was recorded to the nearest degree. The table on the right shows the results.

a Copy the table and complete a cumulative frequency column.

b Draw a cumulative frequency diagram. Note that as the temperature is to the nearest degree the top values of the groups are 7.5°C, 10.5°C, 13.5°C, 16.5°C, etc.

c Use your diagram to estimate the median temperature and the interquartile range.

Temperature (°C)	Number of days
5–7	2
8–10	3
11–13	5
14–16	6
17–19	6
20–22	9
23–25	8
26–28	6
29–31	5

5 At the school charity fête, a game consists of throwing three darts and recording the total score. The results of the first 80 people to throw are recorded in the table on the right.

a Draw a cumulative frequency diagram to show the data.

b Use your diagram to estimate the median score and the interquartile range.

c People who score over 90 get a prize. About what percentage of the people get a prize?

Total score	Number of players
$1 \leqslant x \leqslant 20$	9
$21 \leqslant x \leqslant 40$	13
$41 \leqslant x \leqslant 60$	23
$61 \leqslant x \leqslant 80$	15
$81 \leqslant x \leqslant 100$	11
$101 \leqslant x \leqslant 120$	7
$121 \leqslant x \leqslant 140$	2

6 One hundred pupils in a primary school were asked to say how much pocket money they each get in a week. The results are in the table on the right.

a Copy the table and complete a cumulative frequency column.

b Draw a cumulative frequency diagram.

c Use your diagram to estimate the median amount of pocket money and the interquartile range.

Amount of pocket money (p)	No. of pupils
51–100	6
101–150	10
151–200	20
201–250	28
251–300	18
301–350	11
351–400	5
401–450	2

Key words
box plot
highest value
lower quartile
lowest value
median
upper quartile

Another way of displaying data for comparison is by means of a box-and-whisker plot (or just **box plot**). This requires five pieces of data. These are the **lowest value**, the **lower quartile** (Q_1), the **median** (Q_2), the **upper quartile** (Q_3) and the **highest value**. They are drawn in the following way.

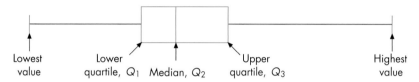

These data are always placed against a scale so that their values are accurately plotted.

The following diagrams show how the cumulative frequency curve, the frequency curve and the box plot are connected for three common types of distribution.

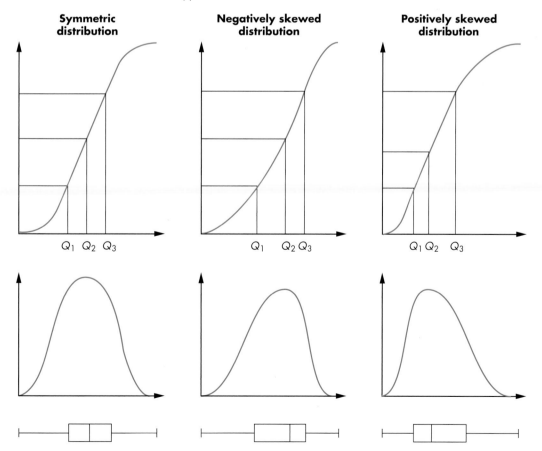

EXAMPLE 5

The box plot for the girls' marks in last year's SATs is shown on the grid below.

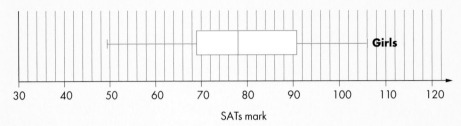

The boys' results for the same SATs are: lowest mark 39; lower quartile 65; median 78; upper quartile 87; highest mark 112.

a On the same grid, plot the box plot for the boys' marks.

b Comment on the differences between the two distributions of marks.

a The data for boys and girls is plotted on the grid below.

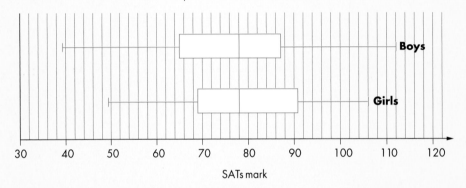

b The girls and boys have the same median mark but both the lower and upper quartiles for the girls are higher than those for the boys, and the girls' range is slightly smaller than the boys'. This suggests that the girls did better than the boys overall, even though a boy got the highest mark.

EXERCISE 2E

1 The box plot shows the times taken for a group of pensioners to do a set of ten long-division calculations.

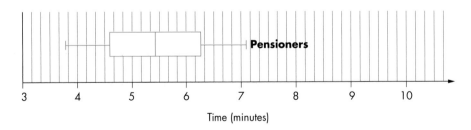

The same set of calculations was given to some students in Year 11. Their results are: shortest time 3 minutes 20 seconds; lower quartile 6 minutes 10 seconds; median 7 minutes; upper quartile 7 minutes 50 seconds; longest time 9 minutes 40 seconds.

a Copy the diagram and draw a box plot for the students' times.

b Comment on the differences between the two distributions.

Mod 1

2 The box plot shows the sizes of secondary schools in Dorset.

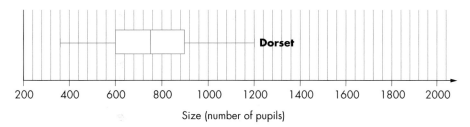

The data for schools in Rotherham is: smallest 280 pupils: lower quartile 1100 pupils; median 1400 pupils; upper quartile 1600 pupils; largest 1820 pupils.

a Copy the diagram and draw a box plot for the sizes of schools in Rotherham.

b Comment on the diferences between the two distributions.

3 The box plots for the noon temperature at two resorts, recorded over a year, are shown on the grid below.

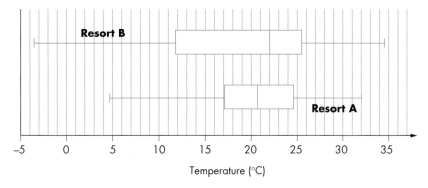

a Comment on the differences in the two distributions.

b Mary wants to go on holiday in July. Which resort would you recommend and why?

4 The following table shows some data on the annual salary for 100 men and 100 women.

	Lowest salary	Lower quartile	Median salary	Upper quartile	Highest salary
Men	£6500	£16 000	£20 000	£22 000	£44 500
Women	£7000	£14 000	£16 000	£21 500	£33 500

a Draw box plots to compare both sets of data.

b Comment on the differences between the distributions.

5 The table shows the monthly salaries of 100 families.

a Draw a cumulative frequency diagram to show the data.

b Estimate the median monthly salary and the interquartile range.

c The lowest monthly salary was £1480 and the highest was £1740.

    i Draw a box plot to show the distribution of salaries.

    ii Is the distribution symmetric, negatively skewed or positively skewed?

Monthly salary (£)	No. of families
1451–1500	8
1501–1550	14
1551–1600	25
1601–1650	35
1651–1700	14
1701–1750	4

A

6 Indicate whether the following sets of data are likely to be symmetric, negatively skewed or positively skewed.

a heights of adult males

b annual salaries of adult males

c shoe sizes of adult males

d weights of babies born in Britain

e speeds of cars on a motorway in the middle of the night

f speeds of cars on a motorway in the rush hour

g shopping bills in a supermarket the week before Christmas

h number of letters in the words in a teenage magazine

i time taken for students to get to school in the morning

j time taken for students to run one mile

2.6 Measures of dispersion

In this section you will learn how to:
- calculate standard deviation for a set of data

Key words
dispersion
measure of
  spread
standard
  deviation

Note: This section is no longer in the specification and will not be examined in either the modular or the end-of-course examination papers. However, you may find it to be useful for the data handling task needed for coursework.

Another method commonly used to compare data is the measure of **dispersion**, also called the **measure of spread**.

You have already met two measures of dispersion:

- range, which is calculated by subtracting the smallest value in the set of data from the largest

- interquartile range, which is the difference between the upper and lower quartiles.

The range is not a good measure of dispersion, as it does not eliminate extreme values. The interquartile range is a better measure, as it takes the central half of the data. The only drawback is that it is centred about the median which may not be the best measure of location.

A much better measure of dispersion centred about the mean is the **standard deviation**.

There are two tabular methods for calculating standard deviation, but it is easier and quicker to use a calculator.

Separate values (ungrouped data)

First put your calculator into statistics mode by pressing one of the following keys.

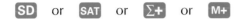

SD or SAT will usually appear on the display. (On a graphics calculator, the operation mode key is different but the method is similar.)

Enter each number followed by

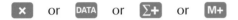

The mean, $\bar{x}$, and the standard deviation, σ, are found by pressing $\boxed{\bar{x}}$ or $\boxed{\sigma n}$ or $\boxed{\sigma x}$. But you may have to use $\boxed{\text{INV}}$ or $\boxed{\text{2ndF}}$ first.

Some calculators have a $\boxed{\sigma_{n-1}}$ key. Be careful *not* to use it.

Your calculator will also have $\boxed{\Sigma x}$, $\boxed{\Sigma x^2}$ and $\boxed{n}$ keys.

After each calculation remember to clear your data. On most calculators this is done by pressing $\boxed{\text{SAC}}$ or $\boxed{\text{CA}}$.

EXAMPLE 6

Find the mean and the standard deviation for 3, 8, 5 and 7.

First key

Then press $\boxed{\bar{x}}$. (You may first have to use $\boxed{\text{INV}}$ or $\boxed{\text{2ndF}}$.) You should get 5.75.

Finally, press $\boxed{\sigma n}$. You should get 1.92 (2 decimal places).

EXAMPLE 7

Calculate the mean and the standard deviation of the heights of the people in group A.

Group A

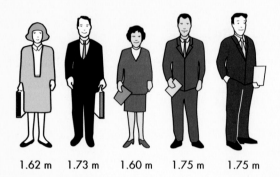

1.62 m   1.73 m   1.60 m   1.75 m   1.75 m

Check that you get $\bar{x} = 1.69$ m and $\sigma = 0.0660$ m (3 significant figures).

EXAMPLE 8

Calculate the mean and the standard deviation of the heights of the people in group B.

Group B

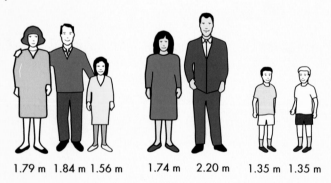

1.79 m   1.84 m   1.56 m   1.74 m   2.20 m   1.35 m   1.35 m

Check that you get $\bar{x} = 1.69$ m and $\sigma = 0.28$ m (2 decimal places).

Use of standard deviation

Using standard deviation, we can compare, for example, the two groups A and B.

Although both groups have the same mean height, we can see that group B has a much greater variation in the heights of its members than group A. Hence, the heights of the members of group B deviate much more from the mean, while the members of group A are all very similar in height.

EXERCISE 2F ✓

Use your calculator to work out the answers to these.

1 Find the mean and the standard deviation of the following sets of data.

  a 2, 5, 6, 8, 9

  b 7, 9, 11, 13, 18

  c 102, 105, 108, 110, 115

  d 201, 202, 203, 204, 205

  e 68.6, 72.3, 75.6, 78.1

  f −2, −1, −1, 0, 2, 4, 5

  g 71, 72, 78, 80, 85

  h 29.3, 31.8, 33.9, 34.9, 40.0, 40.1

2 Five numbers, 4, 5, 7, 8 and x, have a mean of 6.

  a What is the value of x?

  b What is the standard deviation of the numbers?

3 **a** Calculate the mean and the standard deviation of 4, 7, 8, 9, 12.

  b Calculate the mean and standard deviation of 14, 17, 18, 19, 22.

  c Using your answers to parts a and b, write down the mean and the standard deviation of 24, 27, 28, 29, 32.

4 The captain of the netball team needs to pick a player for an important match. She has to choose between Paula and Rose. She has a list of the number of points they have scored in their last few matches.

   Paula 7, 8, 6, 8, 7, 12, 6, 10

   Rose 2, 4, 4, 4, 6, 8, 10, 10, 16, 16

  a Calculate the mean and the standard deviation for Paula.

  b Calculate the mean and standard deviation for Rose.

  c Who would you pick and why?

Mean and standard deviation from a frequency table of data

Large sets of data often contain repeated values. For example, these are the marks of 20 pupils in a mathematics test.

   4, 5, 6, 5, 5, 4, 4, 7, 8, 10, 7, 4, 7, 8, 5, 6, 6, 5, 9, 6

Normally, they would be put in a frequency table like that shown on the right.

Follow through the next example, noting especially the *strict order* in which the input must be keyed. For example, each item of the data *always precedes* its frequency.

x	f
4	4
5	5
6	4
7	3
8	2
9	1
10	1
Total	20

Mod 1

EXAMPLE 9

Find the mean and the standard deviation for the frequency table on the right.

x	f
4	2
5	3
6	4
7	1

Enter as

4 ✕ 2 DATA 5 ✕ 3 DATA 6 ✕ 4

DATA 7 ✕ 1 DATA

Then $\bar{x}$ = 5.4   and σn = 0.92 (2 decimal places)

Note: Always clear your calculator of old data before starting a new calculation, by pressing SAC or CA

Some later models have a different way of inputting data from a frequency table.

They use a comma or a colon to separate the data from each frequency. These will appear in the display of the calculator. For example, you might see

4:2   M+   5:3   M+   6:4   M+   7:1   M+

EXERCISE 2G

Use your calculator to work out the answers to these.

1 The times (to the nearest minute) of the first 20 phone calls made from an office one morning are

2, 5, 5, 7, 3, 4, 5, 6, 7, 8, 2, 12, 2, 5, 2, 5, 7, 9, 10, 2

Put these times into a frequency table and calculate the mean and the standard deviation of the call times.

2 Calculate the mean and the standard deviation of the data in these tables.

a

x	f
0	2
1	4
2	6
3	5
4	3

b

x	f
22	4
23	6
24	7
25	6
26	4
27	3

c

x	f
100	2
101	4
102	6
103	5
104	3

d

x	f
6.7	12
7.3	41
7.8	66
8.1	43
8.5	27

e

x	f
2.2	8
3.2	13
4.2	16
5.2	3

f

x	f
0.07	12
0.09	17
0.14	25
0.17	36
0.26	17
0.27	13

3 a A dice is thrown 120 times. The results are shown in the table.

Score	1	2	3	4	5	6
Frequency	21	20	19	20	19	21

   i Calculate the mean and the standard deviation of the scores from the dice.

   ii Square the standard deviation.

b Two dice are thrown 180 times. The results are shown in the table.

Score	2	3	4	5	6	7	8	9	10	11	12
Frequency	5	11	15	20	25	31	24	19	16	9	5

   i Calculate the mean and the standard deviation of the scores from the two dice.

   ii Square the standard deviation.

c What is the approximate relationship between the answers to parts **a** and **b**?

d If three dice are thrown, estimate the mean and the standard deviation of the total scores from all three dice.

4 a Calculate the mean and the standard deviation of the data in this table.

Mark, x	121	126	131	136	141	146
Frequency, f	2	3	5	6	5	4

b 121 is subtracted from each of the values in the table above and the result is divided by 5. This gives the table below.

Mark, x	0	1	2	3	4	5
Frequency, f	2	3	5	6	5	4

Calculate the mean and the standard deviation for this table.

   i Multiply the mean by 5 and add 121.

   ii Multiply the standard deviation by 5.

c What connects your answers to parts **b i** and **b ii** and your answers to part **a**?

d What advantage does the second table have over the first?

1 The table shows the times taken for a certain train journey on 20 different occasions.

Time taken, t (min)	Frequency
$18 < t \leqslant 20$	4
$20 < t \leqslant 22$	6
$22 < t \leqslant 24$	5
$24 < t \leqslant 26$	3
$26 < t \leqslant 28$	2

Calculate an estimate of the mean journey time.

2 Brian and George played 40 games of golf. The cumulative frequency diagram shows information about Brian's scores. The box plot shows information about George's scores.

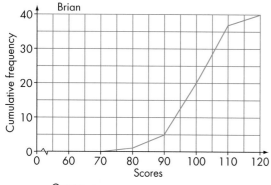

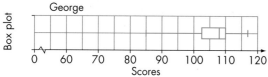

a Showing your method clearly, find
  i Brian's median score
  ii Brian's interquartile range.

b Use the cumulative frequency diagram and the box plot to answer the following.
  i Which player is the more consistent in his scoring?
  ii The winner of a game of golf is the player who has the lowest score. Who do you think is the better player? Give a reason for your choice.

AQA, Question 12, Paper 2 Higher, November 2003

3 56 boys and 52 girls took an English test. The box plots show the distributions of their marks.

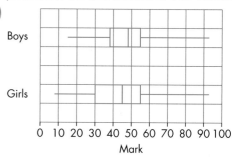

Give *two* differences between the boys' marks and the girls' marks.

AQA, Question 6, Paper 1 Higher, November 2004

4 The length of time, in minutes, of 40 telephone calls was recorded. A cumulative frequency diagram of this data is shown on the grid below.

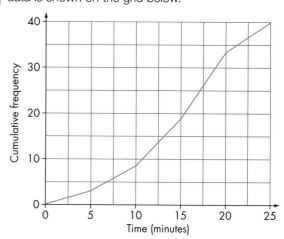

Use the diagram to find the limits between which the middle 50% of the times lie.

AQA, Question 12, Paper 2 Higher, June 2003

WORKED EXAM QUESTION

Derek makes men's and women's shirts. He needs to know the range of collar sizes so he measures 100 men's necks.
The results are shown in the table.

a Draw a cumulative frequency diagram to show this information
b Use the diagram to find
  i the median
  ii the interquartile range
c The box plot shows the neck sizes of 100 women.

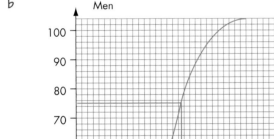

Neck size, cm

Comment on the differences in the distribution of neck sizes for men and women.

Neck size, n (cm)	Frequency
$12 < n \leqslant 13$	5
$13 < n \leqslant 14$	16
$14 < n \leqslant 15$	28
$15 < n \leqslant 16$	37
$16 < n \leqslant 17$	10
$17 < n \leqslant 18$	4

Solution

a Cumulative Frequencies: 5, 21, 49, 86, 96, 100

First work out the cumulative frequencies. The easiest way to do this is with another column on the table.

b

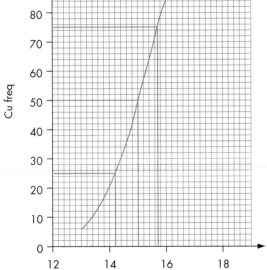

Plot the points (13, 5), (14, 21), etc.
i.e the top value of each group against the cumulative frequency.

Draw lines from 50 (median), 25 (lower quartile) and 75 (upper quartile) from the vertical axis across to the graph and down to the horizontal axis. Subtract lower quartile from upper quartile for the inter-quartile range.

Median = 15 cm
IQR = 15.7 − 14.2 = 1.5 cm

c The men have a higher median (about 1.5 cm higher) and the women have a larger interquartile range
(About 2.5 cm compared to 1.5 cm)

Comment on the differences between
The medians and the interquartile ranges.
Use numerical values to show you know how to read the box plot.

Michael Jones is a journalist. He writes articles for a monthly magazine.

He is asked to write a report on the changes in the population of the UK over the 25 years from 1976 to 2001.

Michael does some research, and finds the following figures for 1976 and 2001.

He calculates the percentage change for each age group to the nearest percent. Help him to complete the table.

Age distribution in the UK (numbers in millions)			
Age (a) in years	1976	2001	% change
$0 \le a < 15$	12.9	11.1	−14%
$15 \le a < 25$	8.1	7.2	
$25 \le a < 35$	7.9	8.4	
$35 \le a < 45$	6.4	8.8	
$45 \le a < 55$	9.8	7.8	
$55 \le a < 65$	3.1	6.2	
$65 \le a < 75$	5.1	4.9	
$75 \le a < 85$	2.3	3.3	
$85 \le a < 105$	0.5	1.1	

He also decides to find an estimate of the mean in 1976 and 2001.

He uses this table to help. Complete the calculations for him.

Midpoint of ages	1976 frequency (millions)	midpoint x frequency	2001 frequency (millions)	midpoint x frequency
7.5	12.9	96.75	11.1	83.25
20	8.1		7.2	
	7.9		8.4	
	6.4		8.8	
	9.8		7.8	
	3.1		6.2	
	5.1		4.9	
	2.3		3.3	
	0.5		1.1	
Totals				
Mean age				

Finally he wants to find the median ages and interquartile ranges (IQR).

Complete the cumulative frequencies below, then draw cumulative frequency graphs and use them to find the median and IQR for both years.

Cumulative frequencies for age distributions (in millions)									
	< 15	< 25	< 35	< 45	< 55	< 65	< 75	< 85	<105
1976	12.9	21	28.9						
2001	11.1	18.3							

Michael summarises the statistical data in a table. He rounds every answer to the nearest whole number of years.

Complete the table for him.

	1976	2001
mean		
median		
upper quartile		
lower quartile		
IQR		

Mod 1

He writes the following article. Write down the words that should go in the spaces.

Are we living longer?

Michael Jones reports on the change in the population of the UK from 1976 to 2001.

The total population for the UK in 1976 was approximately 56.1 million, which increased to 58.8 million in 2001. This means that over 25 years, the population has grown by _____ million people. During this time period, the largest percentage increase occurred in the age group _____ with a staggering _____% increase.

However the largest percentage decrease of _____% occurred in the age group _____. The reasons for this could possibly be due to rationing and a shortage of men in the decade following the second world war.

The mean age of the population has increased from _____ years old to _____ years old (both values are given to the nearest whole year).

This increase of _____ years appears to reinforce the claim made by politicians that as medical science advances and our standard of living and diet improve, it means that we are living longer.

The median age for the two years shows a slightly larger increase than the mean, going from _____ years up to _____ years. The lower and upper quartiles also increase by _____years, thus showing a shift upwards by _____ years of the central 50% of the population.

So, does this show a healthier, happier Britain?

Well, it certainly appears that we are on average living longer. The mean and median both show the average age increasing. But, will the trend continue? Certainly our standard of living has improved, and the treatment of illnesses is improving at a rapid rate, but what about our eating habits? These too are changing.

Fast food + less exercise = obesity. Is this the maths equation that will reverse the trend in the age of the population?

Read next months article, **We are what we eat – true or false?** which looks more closely at the UK's expanding waistlines.

Do you think this article is well written? Is it misleading in any way? Can you write a better article for him?

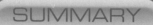

GRADE YOURSELF

D Able to draw an ordered stem-and-leaf diagram

D Able to draw a line of best fit on a scatter diagram

C Recognise the different types of correlation

C Able to interpret a line of best fit

B Able to draw a cumulative frequency diagram

B Able to find medians and quartiles from cumulative frequency diagrams

B Able to draw and interpret box plots

What you should know now

- How to read information from statistical diagrams including stem-and-leaf diagrams

- How to plot scatter diagrams, recognise correlation, draw lines of best fit and use them to predict values

- How to construct a cumulative frequency diagram

- How to draw and interpret box plots

Probability

This chapter will show you ...

● how to work out the probability of events, either using theoretical models or experimental models

● how to predict outcomes using theoretical models and compare experimental and theoretical data

● how to calculate probabilities for combined events

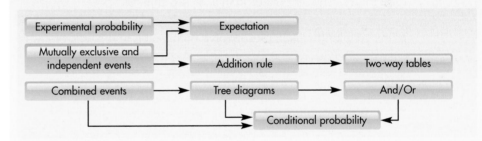

What you should already know

● That the probability scale goes from 0 to 1

● How to use the probability scale and to assess the likelihood of events depending on their position on the scale

● How to cancel, add and subtract fractions (Chapter 5)

Quick check

1 Draw a probability scale and put an arrow to show approximately the probability of each of the following events happening.

a The next TV programme you watch will have been made in Britain.

b A person in your class will have been born in April.

c It will snow in July in Spain.

d In the next Olympic Games, a man will run the 100 m race in less than 20 seconds.

e During this week, you will drink some water or pop.

Terminology

The topic of probability has its own special terminology, which will be explained as it arises. For example, a **trial** is one go at performing something, such as throwing a dice or tossing a coin. So, if we throw a dice 10 times, we perform 10 trials.

Two other probability terms are **event** and **outcome**. An event is anything whose probability we want to measure. An outcome is any way in which an event can happen.

Another probability term is **at random**. This means "without looking" or "not knowing what the outcome is in advance".

Note: "Dice" is used in this book in preference to "die" for the singular form of the noun, as well as for the plural. This is in keeping with growing common usage, including in examination papers.

Probability facts

The probability of a *certain* event is 1 and the probability of an *impossible* event is 0.

Probability is never greater than 1 or less than 0.

Many probability examples involve coins, dice and packs of cards. Here is a reminder of their outcomes.

- A coin has two outcomes: head or tail.

- An ordinary six-sided dice has six outcomes: 1, 2, 3, 4, 5, 6.

- A pack of cards consists of 52 cards divided into four suits: Hearts (red), Spades (black), Diamonds (red), and Clubs (black). Each suit consists of 13 cards bearing the following values: 2, 3, 4, 5, 6, 7, 8, 9, 10, Jack, Queen, King and Ace. The Jack, Queen and King are called "picture cards". (The Ace is sometimes also called a picture card.) So the total number of outcomes is 52.

Probability is defined as

$$P(\text{event}) = \frac{\text{Number of ways the event can happen}}{\text{Total number of all possible outcomes}}$$

This definition always leads to a fraction which should be cancelled down to its simplest form. Make sure that you know how to cancel down fractions with or without a calculator. It is acceptable to give a probability as a decimal or a percentage but a fraction is better.

This definition can be used to work out the probability of events, as the following example shows.

EXAMPLE 1

A card is drawn from a pack of cards. What is the probability that it is one of the following?

a a red card   **b** a Spade   **c** a seven

d a picture card   **e** a number less than 5   **f** a red King

a There are 26 red cards, so P(red card) = $\frac{26}{52} = \frac{1}{2}$

b There are 13 Spades, so P(Spade) = $\frac{13}{52} = \frac{1}{4}$

c There are four sevens, so P(seven) = $\frac{4}{52} = \frac{1}{13}$

d There are 12 picture cards, so P(picture card) = $\frac{12}{52} = \frac{3}{13}$

e If you count the value of an Ace as 1, there are 16 cards with a value less than 5.
So, P(number less than 5) = $\frac{16}{52} = \frac{4}{13}$

f There are 2 red Kings, so P(red King) = $\frac{2}{52} = \frac{1}{26}$

3.1 Experimental probability

In this section you will learn how to:
- calculate experimental probabilities and relative frequencies
- estimate probabilities from experiments
- use different methods to estimate probabilities

Key words
experimental probability
relative frequency
trials

The value of number of heads ÷ number of tosses is called an **experimental probability**. As the number of **trials** or experiments increases, the value of the experimental probability gets closer to the true or theoretical probability.

Experimental probability is also known as the **relative frequency** of an event. The relative frequency of an event is an estimate for the theoretical probability. It is given by

$$\text{Relative frequency of an event} = \frac{\text{Frequency of the event}}{\text{Total number of trials}}$$

EXAMPLE 2

The frequency table shows the speeds of 160 vehicles which pass a radar speed check on a dual carriageway.

Speed (mph)	20–29	30–39	40–49	50–59	60–69	70+
Frequency	14	23	28	35	52	8

a What is the experimental probability that a vehicle is travelling faster than 70 mph?

b If 500 vehicles pass the speed check, estimate how many will be travelling faster than 70 mph.

a The experimental probability is the relative frequency, which is $\frac{8}{160} = \frac{1}{20}$

b The number of vehicles travelling faster than 70 mph will be $\frac{1}{20}$ of 500.

That is, 500 ÷ 20 = 25 vehicles

Finding probabilities

There are three ways in which the probability of an event can be found.

- If we can work out the theoretical probability of an event – for example, drawing a King from a pack of cards – this is called using equally likely outcomes.

- Some events, such as buying a certain brand of dog food, cannot be calculated using equally likely outcomes. To find the probability of such an event, we can perform an experiment or conduct a survey. This is called collecting experimental data. The more data we collect, the better the estimate is.

- The probability of some events, such as an earthquake occurring in Japan, cannot be found by either of the above methods. One of the things we can do is to look at data collected over a long period of time and make an estimate (sometimes called a best guess) at the chance of the event happening. This is called looking at historical data.

EXAMPLE 3

Which method (A, B or C) would you use to estimate the probabilities of the events a to e?

    A: Use equally likely outcomes

    B: Conduct a survey/collect data

    C: Look at historical data

a Someone in your class will go abroad for a holiday this year.

b You will win the National Lottery.

c Your bus home will be late.

d It will snow on Christmas Day.

e You will pick a red seven from a pack of cards.

a   You would have to ask all the members of your class what they intended to do for their holidays this year. You would therefore conduct a survey, method B.

b   The odds on winning are about 14 million to 1. This is an equally likely outcome, method A.

c   If you catch the bus every day, you can collect data over several weeks. This would be method C.

d   If you check whether it snowed on Christmas Day for the last few years you would be able to make a good estimate of the probability. This would be method C.

e   There are two red sevens out of 52 cards, so the probability of picking one can be calculated: P(red seven) = $\frac{2}{52}$ = $\frac{1}{26}$

This is method A.

EXERCISE 3A

1 Naseer throws a dice and records the number of sixes that he gets after various numbers of throws. The table shows his results.

Number of throws	10	50	100	200	500	1000	2000
Number of sixes	2	4	10	21	74	163	329

a   Calculate the experimental probability of a six at each stage that Naseer recorded his results.

b   How many ways can a dice land?

c   How many of these ways give a six?

d   What is the theoretical probability of throwing a six with a dice?

e   If Naseer threw the dice a total of 6000 times, how many sixes would you expect him to get?

2 Marie made a five-sided spinner, like the one shown in the diagram. She used it to play a board game with her friend Sarah. The girls thought that the spinner wasn't very fair as it seemed to land on some numbers more than others. They spun the spinner 200 times and recorded the results. The results are shown in the table.

Side spinner lands on	1	2	3	4	5
Number of times	19	27	32	53	69

a   Work out the experimental probability of each number.

b   How many times would you expect each number to occur if the spinner is fair?

c   Do you think that the spinner is fair? Give a reason for your answer.

3 Sarah thought she could make a much more accurate spinner. After she had made it, she tested it and recorded how many times she scored a 5. Her results are shown in the table.

Number of spins	10	50	100	500
Number of fives	3	12	32	107

a Sarah made a mistake in recording the number of fives. Which number in the second row above is wrong? Give a reason for your answer.

b These are the full results for 500 spins.

Side spinner lands on	1	2	3	4	5
Number of times	96	112	87	98	107

Do you think the spinner is fair? Give a reason for your answer.

4 A sampling bottle contains 20 balls. The balls are either black or white. (A sampling bottle is a sealed bottle with a clear plastic tube at one end into which one of the balls can be tipped.) Kenny conducts an experiment to see how many black balls are in the bottle. He takes various numbers of samples and records how many of them showed a black ball. The results are shown in the table.

Number of samples	Number of black balls	Experimental probability
10	2	
100	25	
200	76	
500	210	
1000	385	
5000	1987	

a Copy the table and calculate the experimental probability of getting a black ball at each stage.

b Using this information, how many black balls do you think are in the bottle?

5 Another sampling bottle contains red, white and blue balls. It is known that there are 20 balls in the bottle altogether. Carrie performs an experiment to see how many of each colour are in the bottle. She starts off putting down a tally each time a colour shows in the clear plastic tube.

Red	White	Blue
IIII IIII IIII IIII II	IIII IIII IIII III	IIII IIII II

Unfortunately, she forgets to count how many times she performs the experiment, so every now and again she counts up the tallies and records them in a table (see below).

Red	White	Blue	Total
22	18	12	52
48	31	16	95
65	37	24	126
107	61	32	200
152	93	62	307
206	128	84	418

The relative frequency of the red balls is calculated by dividing the frequency of red by the total number of trials, so at each stage these are

0.423   0.505   0.516   0.535   0.495   0.493

These answers are rounded off to three significant figures.

a Calculate the relative frequencies of the white balls at each stage to three significant figures.

b Calculate the relative frequencies of the blue balls at each stage to three significant figures.

c Round off the final relative frequencies for Carrie's 418 trials to one decimal place.

d What is the total of the answers in part **c**?

e How many balls of each colour do you think are in the bottle? Explain your answer.

 6 Using card and a cocktail stick, make a six-sided spinner, as shown below.

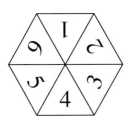 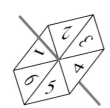

When you have made the spinner, spin it 120 times and record your results in a table like the one below.

Number	Tally	Total
1	JHT II	
2	IIII	

a Which number occurred the most?

b How many times would you expect to get each number?

c Is your spinner fair?

d Explain your answer to part **c**.

 7 Use a set of number cards from 1 to 10 (or make your own set) and work with a partner. Take it in turns to choose a card and keep a record each time of what card you get. Shuffle the cards each time and repeat the experiment 60 times. Put your results in a copy of this table.

Score	1	2	3	4	5	6	7	8	9	10
Total										

a How many times would you expect to get each number?

b Do you think you and your partner conducted this experiment fairly?

c Explain your answer to part **b**.

8 A four-sided dice has faces numbered 1, 2, 3 and 4. The score is the face on which it lands. Five pupils throw the dice to see if it is biased. They each throw it a different number of times. Their results are shown in the table.

Pupil	Total number of throws	Score			
		1	2	3	4
Alfred	20	7	6	3	4
Brian	50	19	16	8	7
Caryl	250	102	76	42	30
Deema	80	25	25	12	18
Emma	150	61	46	26	17

a Which pupil will have the most reliable set of results? Why?

b Add up all the score columns and work out the relative frequency of each score. Give your answers to two decimal places.

c Is the dice biased? Explain your answer.

9 Which of these methods would you use to estimate or state the probability of each of the events **a** to **h**?

Method A: Equally likely outcomes

Method B: Survey or experiment

Method C: Look at historical data

a How people will vote in the next election.

b A drawing pin dropped on a desk will land point up.

c A Premiership football team will win the FA Cup.

d You will win a school raffle.

e The next car to drive down the road will be red.

f You will throw a "double six" with two dice.

g Someone in your class likes classical music.

h A person picked at random from your school will be a vegetarian.

10 To test if a home-made four-sided spinner was fair, it was spun and the results recorded.
The results are shown as a percentage of throws.
The percentages are given to the nearest whole number.

Score	1	2	3	4
Percentage	16%	22%	38%	24%

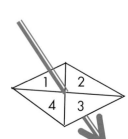

a Explain why this information on its own is not sufficient to tell how may times the spinner was spun.

b You are told that it landed on the number 1 a total of 81 times.

   i   Estimate how many times the spinner was spun in the trial.

   ii Is the spinner fair? Give a reason for your answer.

3.2 Mutually exclusive and exhaustive events

In this section you will learn how to:

● recognise mutually exclusive, complementary and exhaustive events

Key words
complementary
exhaustive
mutually
    exclusive

If a bag contains three black, two yellow and five white balls and only one ball is allowed to be taken at random from the bag, then by the basic definition of probability

$$P(\text{black ball}) = \frac{3}{10}$$

$$P(\text{yellow ball}) = \frac{2}{10} = \frac{1}{5}$$

$$P(\text{white ball}) = \frac{5}{10} = \frac{1}{2}$$

We can also say that the probability of choosing a black ball or a yellow ball is $= \frac{5}{10} = \frac{1}{2}$

The events "picking a yellow ball" and "picking a black ball" can never happen at the same time when only one ball is taken out: that is, a ball can be either black or yellow. Such events are called **mutually exclusive**. Other examples of mutually exclusive events are tossing a head or a tail with a coin, drawing a King or an Ace from a pack of cards and throwing an even or an odd number with a dice.

An example of events that are not mutually exclusive would be drawing a red card and a King from a pack of cards. There are two red Kings, so these events could be true at the same time.

EXAMPLE 4

An ordinary dice is thrown.

a What is the probability of throwing

　i an even number?　　ii an odd number?

b What is the total of the answers to part **a**?

c Is it possible to get a score on a dice that is both odd and even?

a i $P(\text{even}) = \dfrac{1}{2}$　　ii $P(\text{odd}) = \dfrac{1}{2}$　　b $\dfrac{1}{2} + \dfrac{1}{2} = 1$　　c No

Events such as those in Example 4 are mutually exclusive because they can never happen at the same time. Because there are no other possibilities, they are also called **exhaustive** events. The probabilities of exhaustive events add up to 1.

EXAMPLE 5

A bag contains only black and white balls. The probability of picking at random a black ball from the bag is $\dfrac{7}{10}$.

a What is the probability of picking a white ball from the bag?

b Can you say how many black and white balls are in the bag?

a As the event "picking a white ball" and the event "picking a black ball" are mutually exclusive and exhaustive then

$$P(\text{white}) = 1 - P(\text{black}) = 1 - \frac{7}{10} = \frac{3}{10}$$

b You cannot say precisely what the number of balls is although you can say that there could be seven black and three white, fourteen black and six white, or any combination of black and white balls in the ratio $7 : 3$.

Complementary event

If there is an event A, the **complementary** event of A is

　　Event A *not* happening

Any event is mutually exclusive and exhaustive to its complementary event. That is,

　　P(event A not happening) = 1 – P(event A happening)

which can be stated as

　　P(event) + P(complementary event) = 1

For example, the probability of getting a King from a pack of cards is $\dfrac{4}{52} = \dfrac{1}{13}$, so the probability of *not* getting a King is

$$1 - \frac{1}{13} = \frac{12}{13}$$

EXERCISE 3B

1 Say whether these pairs of events are mutually exclusive or not.

  a tossing a head with a coin/tossing a tail with a coin

  b throwing a number less than 3 with a dice/throwing a number greater than 3 with a dice

  c drawing a Spade from a pack of cards/drawing an Ace from a pack of cards

  d drawing a Spade from a pack of cards/drawing a red card from a pack of cards

  e if two people are to be chosen from three girls and two boys: choosing two girls/choosing two boys

  f drawing a red card from a pack of cards/drawing a black card from a pack of cards

2 Which of the pairs of mutually exclusive events in question **1** are also exhaustive?

3 Each morning I run to work or get a lift. The probability that I run to work is $\frac{2}{5}$.
What is the probability that I get a lift?

4 A letter is to be chosen at random from this set of letter-cards.

  a What is the probability the letter is

  i an S? **ii** a T? **iii** a vowel?

  b Which of these pairs of events are mutually exclusive?

  i picking an S / picking a T **ii** picking an S / picking a vowel

  iii picking an S / picking another consonant **iv** picking a vowel / picking a consonant

  c Which pair of mutually exclusive events in part **b** is also exhaustive?

5 Two people are to be chosen for a job from this set of five people.

  a List all of the possible pairs (there are 10 altogether).

  b What is the probability that the pair of people chosen will

  i both be female? **ii** both be male?

  iii both have the same initial? **iv** have different initials?

Jane   Dave   Anne   Jack   John

  c Which of these pairs of events are mutually exclusive?

  i picking two women/picking two men

  ii picking two people of the same sex/picking two people of opposite sex

  iii picking two people with the same initial/picking two men

  iv picking two people with the same initial/picking two women

  d Which pair of mutually exclusive events in part **c** is also exhaustive?

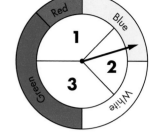

6 A spinner consists of an outer ring of coloured sectors and an inner circle of numbered sectors, as shown.

a The probability of getting 2 is $\frac{1}{4}$. The probabilities of getting 1 or 3 are equal. What is the probability of getting 3?

b The probability of getting blue is $\frac{1}{4}$. The probability of getting white $\frac{1}{4}$. The probability of getting green is $\frac{3}{8}$. What is the probability of getting red?

c Which of these pairs of events are mutually exclusive?

   i getting 3/getting 2   **ii** getting 3/getting green

   iii getting 3/getting blue   **iv** getting blue/getting red

d Explain why it is not possible to get a colour that is mutually exclusive to the event "getting an odd number".

7 At morning break, Pauline has a choice of coffee, tea or hot chocolate.
If P(she chooses coffee) = a and P(she chooses hot chocolate) = 0.2, what is P(she chooses tea)?

8 Assemblies at school are always taken by the head, the deputy head or the senior teacher. If the head takes the assembly, the probability that she goes over time is $\frac{1}{2}$. If the deputy takes the assembly, the probability that he goes over time is $\frac{1}{4}$. Explain why it is not necessarily true to say that the probability that the senior teacher goes over time is $\frac{1}{4}$.

9 A hotelier conducted a survey of guests staying at her hotel. The table shows some of the results of her survey.

Type of guest	Probability
Man	0.7
Woman	0.3
American man	0.2
American woman	0.05
Vegetarian	0.3
Married	0.6

a A guest was chosen at random. From the table, work out these probabilities.

   i the guest was American

   ii the guest was single

   iii the guest was not a vegetarian

b Explain why it is not possible to work out from the table the probability of a guest being a married vegetarian.

c From the table, give two examples of pairs of types of guest that would form a pair of mutually exclusive events.

d From the table, give one example of a pair of types of guest that would form a pair of exhaustive events.

Expectation

In this section you will learn how to:

- predict the likely number of successful events given the number of trials and the probability of any one event

When we know the probability of an event, we can predict how many times we would expect that event to happen in a certain number of trials.

Note that this is what we *expect*. It is not what is going to happen. If what we expected always happened, life would be very dull and boring and the National Lottery would be a waste of time.

EXAMPLE 6

A bag contains 20 balls, nine of which are black, six white and five yellow. A ball is drawn at random from the bag, its colour noted and then it is put back in the bag. This is repeated 500 times.

a How many times would you expect a black ball to be drawn?

b How many times would you expect a yellow ball to be drawn?

c How many times would you expect a black or a yellow ball to be drawn?

a $P(\text{black ball}) = \frac{9}{20}$

Expected number of black balls = $\frac{9}{20} \times 500 = 225$

b $P(\text{yellow ball}) = \frac{5}{20} = \frac{1}{4}$

Expected number of yellow balls = $\frac{1}{4} \times 500 = 125$

c Expected number of black or yellow balls = 225 + 125 = 350

EXAMPLE 7

Four in 10 cars sold in Britain are made by Japanese companies.

a What is the probability that the next car to drive down your road will be Japanese?

b If there are 2000 cars in a multistorey car park, how many of them would you expect to be Japanese?

a $P(\text{Japanese car}) = \frac{4}{10} = \frac{2}{5} = 0.4$

b Expected number of Japanese cars in 2000 cars = 0.4 × 2000 = 800 cars

EXERCISE 3C

 1 I throw an ordinary dice 150 times. How many times can I expect to get a score of 6?

 2 I toss a coin 2000 times. How many times can I expect to get a head?

 3 I draw a card from a pack of cards and replace it. I do this 520 times. How many times would I expect to get these?

    a a black card   **b** a King

    c a Heart   **d** the King of Hearts

 4 The ball in a roulette wheel can land in 37 spaces which are the numbers between 0 and 36 inclusive. I always bet on the same number, 13. If I play all evening and there is a total of 185 spins of the wheel in that time, how many times could I expect to win?

 5 In a bag there are 30 balls, 15 of which are red, 5 yellow, 5 green, and 5 blue. A ball is taken out at random and then replaced. This is repeated 300 times. How many times would I expect to get these outcomes?

    a a red ball   **b** a yellow or blue ball

    c a ball that is not blue   **d** a pink ball

 6 The same experiment described in question **5** is carried out 1000 times. Approximately how many times would you expect to get **a** a green ball, **b** a ball that is not blue?

 7 The table shows the probability of drawing a coloured ball at random from a bag containing only red, blue, green and white balls.

    a The probability of choosing white is twice the probability of choosing green. What are the values of a and b?

    b 1000 balls are taken at random from the bag and replaced. Estimate the number of red balls that would be chosen.

Colour	Probability
Red	0.3
Blue	0.1
Green	a
White	b

 8 Josie said: "When I throw a dice, I expect to get a score of 3.5."

"Impossible," said Paul, "you can't score 3.5 with a dice."

"Do this and I'll prove it," said Josie.

    a An ordinary dice is thrown 60 times. Fill in the table for the expected number of times each score will occur.

Score						
Expected occurrences						

    b Now work out the average score that is expected over 60 throws.

    c There is an easy way to get an answer of 3.5 for the expected average score. Can you see what it is?

 9 I have 20 tickets for a raffle and I know that the probability of my winning the prize is 0.05. How many tickets were sold altogether in the raffle?

Two-way tables

In this section you will learn how to:
- read a two-way table and use them to work out probabilities and interpret data

Key word

two-way tables

A **two-way table** is a table that links together two variables. For example, the following table shows how many boys and girls are in a form and whether they are left- or right-handed.

	Boys	Girls
Left-handed	2	4
Right-handed	10	13

This table shows the colour and make of cars in the school car park.

	Red	Blue	White
Ford	2	4	1
Vauxhall	0	1	2
Toyota	3	3	4
Peugeot	2	0	3

One variable is written in the rows of the table and the other variable is written in the columns of the table.

EXAMPLE 8

Using the first two-way table above, answer these questions.

a If a pupil is selected at random from the form what is the probability that the pupil is a left-handed boy?

b It is known that a pupil selected at random is a girl. What is the probability that she is right-handed?

a $\dfrac{2}{29}$

b $\dfrac{13}{17}$

EXAMPLE 9

Using the second two-way table above, answer these questions.

a What percentage of the cars in the car park are red?

b What percentage of the white cars are Vauxhalls?

a 28%. Seven out of 25 is the same as 28 out of 100.

b 20%. Two out of 10 is 20%.

EXERCISE 3D

1 The two-way table shows the age and sex of a sample of 50 pupils in a school.

		Age (years)				
	11	**12**	**13**	**14**	**15**	**16**
Number of boys	4	3	6	2	5	4
Number of girls	2	5	3	6	4	6

a How many pupils are aged 13 years or less?

b What percentage of the pupils in the table are 16?

c A pupil from the table is selected at random. What is the probability that the pupil will be 14 years of age. Give your answer as a fraction in its lowest form.

d There are 1000 pupils in the school. Use the table to estimate how many boys are in the school altogether.

2 The two-way table shows the number of adults and the number of cars in 50 houses in one street.

		Number of adults			
		1	**2**	**3**	**4**
Number of cars	**0**	2	1	0	0
	1	3	13	3	1
	2	0	10	6	4
	3	0	1	4	2

a How many houses have exactly two adults and two cars?

b How many houses altogether have three cars?

c What percentage of the houses have three cars?

d What percentage of the houses with just one car have three adults living in the house?

3 Jane has two four-sided spinners. One has the numbers 1 to 4 and the other has the numbers 5 to 8.

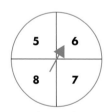

Spinner A   Spinner B

Both spinners are spun together.

The two-way table (on the next page) shows all the ways the two spinners can land.

Some of the total scores are filled in.

		Score on spinner A			
		1	2	3	4
Score on spinner B	5	6	7		
	6	7			
	7				
	8				

a Complete the table to show all the possible total scores.

b How many of the total scores are 9?

c When the two spinners are spun together what is the probability that the total score will be

i 9?

ii 8?

iii a prime number?

4 The table shows information about the number of items in Flossy's music collection.

		Type of music		
		Pop	Folk	Classical
Format	**Tape**	16	5	2
	CD	51	9	13
	Mini disc	9	2	0

a How many pop tapes does Flossy have?

b How many items of folk music does Flossy have?

c How many CDs does Flossy have?

d If a CD is chosen at random from all the CDs, what is the probability that it will be a pop CD?

5 Zoe throws a fair coin and rolls a fair dice.

If the coin shows a head she records the score on the dice.

If the coin shows tails she doubles the number on the dice.

a Complete the two-way table to show Zoe's possible scores.

		Number on dice					
		1	2	3	4	5	6
Coin	**Head**	1	2				
	Tail	2	4				

b How many of the scores are square numbers?

c What is the probability of getting a score that is a square number?

6 A gardener plants some sunflower seeds in a greenhouse and plants some in the garden. After they have fully grown, he measures the diameter of the sunflower heads. The table shows his results.

	Greenhouse	Garden
Mean diameter	16.8 cm	14.5 cm
Range of diameter	3.2 cm	1.8 cm

a The gardener who wants to enter competitions says "the sunflowers from the greenhouse are better".

Using the data in the table, give a reason to justify this statement.

b The gardener's wife, who does flower arranging says "the sunflowers from the garden are better".

Using the data in the table, give a reason to justify this statement.

7 The two-way table shows the wages for the men and women in a factory.

Wage, w, (£) per week	Men	Women
£100 < w ≤ £150	3	4
£150 < w ≤ £200	7	5
£200 < w ≤ £250	23	12
£250 < w ≤ £300	48	27
£300 < w ≤ £350	32	11
More than £350	7	1

a What percentage of the men earn between £250 and £300 per week?

b What percentage of the women earn between £250 and £300 per week?

c Is it possible to work out the mean wage of the men and women? Explain your answer.

3.5 Addition rule for events

In this section you will learn how to:
- work out the probability of two events such as P(event A) or P(event B)

Key word
either

We have used the addition rule already but it has not yet been formally defined.

When two events are mutually exclusive, we can work out the probability of **either** of them occurring by adding up the separate probabilities.

Mod 1

EXAMPLE 10

A bag contains twelve red balls, eight green balls, five blue balls and fifteen black balls. A ball is drawn at random. What is the probability of it being each of these?

   a red   **b** black   **c** red or black

   d not green   **e** neither green nor blue

a $P(\text{red}) = \dfrac{12}{40} = \dfrac{3}{10}$ **b** $P(\text{black}) = \dfrac{15}{40} = \dfrac{3}{8}$

c $P(\text{red or black}) = P(\text{red}) + P(\text{black}) = \dfrac{3}{10} + \dfrac{3}{8} = \dfrac{27}{40}$

d $P(\text{not green}) = \dfrac{32}{40} = \dfrac{4}{5}$

e $P(\text{neither green nor blue}) = P(\text{red or black}) = \dfrac{27}{40}$

The last part of Example 10 is another illustration of how confusing probability can be. You might think

$$P(\text{neither green nor blue}) = P(\text{not green}) + P(\text{not blue}) = \frac{32}{40} + \frac{35}{40} = \frac{67}{40}$$

This cannot be correct, as the answer is greater than 1. In fact, the events "not green" and "not blue" are not mutually exclusive, as there are lots of balls that are true for both events.

EXERCISE 3E

1 A bag contains 4 red and 6 blue balls. A ball is taken from the bag at random. What is the probability that it is red? Give your answer as a fraction in its simplest form.

2 Iqbal throws an ordinary dice. What is the probability that he throws these scores?

   a 2   **b** 5   **c** 2 or 5

3 Jennifer draws a card from a pack of cards. What is the probability that she draws these?

   a a Heart   **b** a Club   **c** a Heart or a Club

4 A letter is chosen at random from the letters on these cards. What is the probability of choosing each of these?

   a a B   **b** a vowel   **c** a B or a vowel

5 A bag contains 10 white balls, 12 black balls and 8 red balls. A ball is drawn at random from the bag. What is the probability of each of these outcomes?

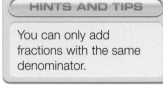
a white

b black

c black or white

d not red

e not red or black

6 At the School Fayre the tombola stall gives out a prize if you draw from the drum a numbered ticket that ends in 0 or 5. There are 300 tickets in the drum altogether and the probability of getting a winning ticket is 0.4.

a What is the probability of getting a losing ticket?

b How many winning tickets are there in the drum?

7 John needs his calculator for his mathematics lesson. It is either in his pocket, bag or locker. The probability it is in his pocket is 0.35; the probability it is in his bag is 0.45. What is the probability that

a he will have the calculator for the lesson?

b it is in his locker?

8 A spinner has numbers and colours on it, as shown in the diagram. Their probabilities are given in the tables.

When the spinner is spun what is the probability of each of the following?

a red or green

b 2 or 3

c 3 or green

d 2 or green

e **i** Explain why the answer to P(1 or red) is not 0.9.

   ii What is the answer to P(1 or red)?

Red	0.5
Green	0.25
Blue	0.25

1	0.4
2	0.35
3	0.25

9 Debbie has 20 unlabelled pirate CDs, 12 of which are rock, 5 are pop and 3 are classical. She picks a CD at random. What is the probability of these outcomes?

a rock or pop

b pop or classical

c not pop

10 The probability that it rains on Monday is 0.5. The probability that it rains on Tuesday is 0.5 and the probability that it rains on Wednesday is 0.5. Kelly argues that it is certain to rain on Monday, Tuesday or Wednesday because 0.5 + 0.5 + 0.5 = 1.5, which is bigger than 1 so that it is a certain event. Explain why she is wrong.

Mod 1

Combined events

In this section you will learn how to:
● work out the probability of two events occurring at the same time

Key words
probability
space
diagram
sample space
diagram

There are many situations where two events occur together. Some examples are given below. Note that in each case all the possible outcomes of the events are shown in diagrams. These are called **probability space diagrams** or **sample space diagrams**.

Throwing two dice

Imagine that two dice, one red and one blue, are thrown. The red dice can land with any one of six scores: 1, 2, 3, 4, 5 or 6. The blue dice can also land with any one of six scores. This gives a total of 36 possible combinations. These are shown in the left-hand diagram, where each combination is given as (2, 3), etc. The first number is the score on the blue dice and the second number is the score on the red dice.

The combination (2, 3) gives a total score of 5. The total scores for all the combinations are shown in the right-hand diagram.

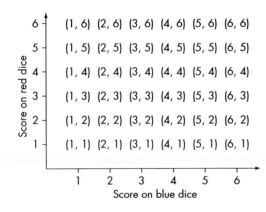

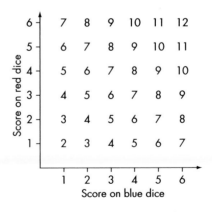

From the diagram on the right, we can see that there are two ways to get a score of 3. This gives a probability of

$$P(3) = \frac{2}{36} = \frac{1}{18}$$

From the diagram on the left, we can see that there are six ways to get a "double". This gives a probability of

$$P(double) = \frac{6}{36} = \frac{1}{6}$$

Throwing coins

Throwing one coin

There are two equally likely outcomes, head or tail

Throwing two coins together

There are four equally likely outcomes

$P(2 \text{ heads}) = \dfrac{1}{4}$

$P(\text{head and tail}) = 2 \text{ ways out of } 4 = \dfrac{2}{4} = \dfrac{1}{2}$

Dice and coins

Throwing a dice and a coin

	1	2	3	4	5	6
H	(1, H)	(2, H)	(3, H)	(4, H)	(5, H)	(6, H)
T	(1, T)	(2, T)	(3, T)	(4, T)	(5, T)	(6, T)

Outcome on coin — Score on dice

$P (\text{head and an even number}) = 3 \text{ ways out of } 12 = \dfrac{3}{12} = \dfrac{1}{4}$

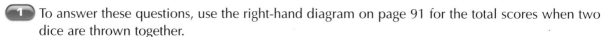

EXERCISE 3F

1 To answer these questions, use the right-hand diagram on page 91 for the total scores when two dice are thrown together.

    a What is the most likely score?

    b Which two scores are least likely?

    c Write down the probabilities of all scores from 2 to 12.

    d What is the probability of each of these scores?

        i bigger than 10   **ii** between 3 and 7   **iii** even

        iv a square number   **v** a prime number   **vi** a triangular number

2 Using the left-hand diagram on page 91 that shows, as coordinates, the outcomes when two dice are thrown together, what is the probability of each of these?

    a the score is an even "double"

    b at least one of the dice shows 2

    c the score on one dice is twice the score on the other dice

    d at least one of the dice shows a multiple of 3

Mod 1

3 Using the left-hand diagram on page 91 that shows, as coordinates, the outcomes when two dice are thrown together, what is the probability of each of these?

    a both dice show a 6

    b at least one of the dice shows a six

    c exactly one dice shows a six

4 The diagram shows the score for the event "the difference between the scores when two dice are thrown". Copy and complete the diagram.

For the event described above, what is the probability of a difference of each of these?

    a 1   **b** 0   **c** 4

    d 6   **e** an odd number

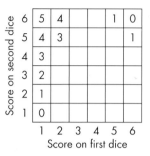

5 When two coins are thrown together, what is the probability of each of these outcomes?

    a 2 heads   **b** a head and a tail

    c at least 1 tail   **d** no tails

Use the diagram of the outcomes when two coins are thrown together, on page 92.

6 Two five-sided spinners are spun together and the total score of the faces that they land on is worked out. Copy and complete this probability space diagram.

    a What is the most likely score?

    b When two five-sided spinners are spun together, what is the probability of each of these?

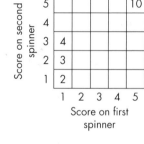

        i the total score is 5   **ii** the total score is an even number

        iii the score is a "double"   **iv** the score is less than 7

7 When three coins are tossed together, what is the probability of each of these outcomes?

    a three heads   **b** two heads and one tail

    c at least one tail   **d** no tails

8 When one coin is tossed there are two outcomes. When two coins are tossed, there are four outcomes. When three coins are tossed, there are eight outcomes.

    a How many outcomes will there be when four coins are tossed?

    b How many outcomes will there be when five coins are tossed?

    c How many outcomes will there be when ten coins are tossed?

    d How many outcomes will there be when n coins are tossed?

9 When a dice and a coin are thrown together, what is the probability of each of the following outcomes?

a You get a head on the coin and a 6 on the dice.

b You get a tail on the coin and an even number on the dice.

c You get a head on the coin and a square number on the dice.

Use the diagram on page 92 that shows the outcomes when a dice and a coin are thrown together.

3.7 Tree diagrams

In this section you will learn how to:

● use sample space diagrams and tree diagrams to work out the probability of combined events

Key words
combined events
space diagram
tree diagram

Imagine we have to draw two cards from this pack of six cards, but we must replace the first card before we select the second card.

One way we could show all the outcomes of this experiment is to construct a **probability space diagram**. For example, this could be an array set in a pair of axes, like those used for the two dice (see page 91), or a pictogram, like those used for the coins, or simply a list of all the outcomes. By showing all the outcomes of our experiment as an array, we obtain the diagram below.

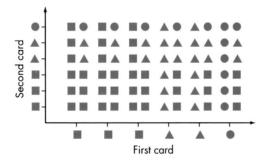

From the diagram, we can see immediately that the probability of picking, say, two squares is 9 out of 36 pairs of cards. So,

$$P(2 \text{ squares}) = \frac{9}{36} = \frac{1}{4}$$

EXAMPLE 11

Using the probability space diagram on page 94, what is the probability of getting each of these outcomes?

a a square and a triangle (in any order)

b two circles

c two shapes the same

a There are 12 combinations which give a square and a triangle together. There are six when a square is chosen first and six when a triangle is chosen first. So,

$$P(\text{square and triangle, in any order}) = \frac{12}{36} = \frac{1}{3}$$

b There is only one combination which gives two circles. So,

$$P(\text{two circles}) = \frac{1}{36}$$

c There are nine combinations of two squares together, four combinations of two triangles together, and one combination of two circles together. These give a total of 14 combinations with two shapes the same. So,

$$P(\text{two shapes the same}) = \frac{14}{36} = \frac{7}{18}$$

An alternative method to tackling problems involving **combined events** is to use a **tree diagram**.

When we pick the first card, there are three possible outcomes: a square, a triangle or a circle. For a single event,

$$P(\text{square}) = \frac{1}{2} \qquad P(\text{triangle}) = \frac{1}{3} \qquad P(\text{circle}) = \frac{1}{6}$$

We can show this by depicting each event as a branch and writing its probability on the branch.

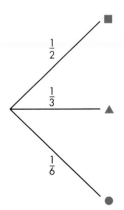

The diagram can then be extended to take into account a second choice. Because the first card has been replaced, we can still pick a square, a triangle or a circle. This is true no matter what is chosen the first time. We can demonstrate this by adding three more branches to the "squares" branch in the diagram.

Here is the complete tree diagram.

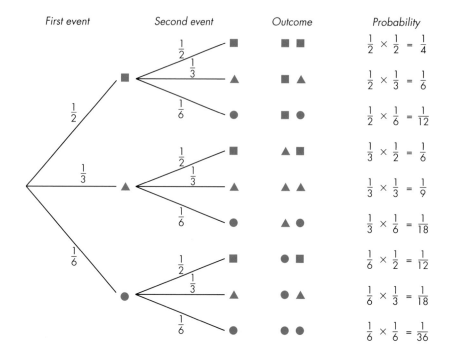

The probability of any outcome is calculated by multiplying together the probabilities on its branches. For instance,

P(two squares) = $\frac{1}{2} \times \frac{1}{2} = \frac{1}{4}$

P(triangle followed by circle) = $\frac{1}{3} \times \frac{1}{6} = \frac{1}{18}$

EXAMPLE 12

Using the tree diagram above, what is the probability of obtaining each of the following?

a two triangles

b a circle followed by a triangle

c a square and a triangle, in any order

d two circles

e two shapes the same

a P(two triangles) = $\frac{1}{9}$

b P(circle followed by triangle) = $\frac{1}{18}$

c There are two places in the outcome column which have a square and a triangle. These are the second and fourth rows. The probability of each is $\frac{1}{6}$. Their combined probability is given by the addition rule.

P(square and triangle, in any order) = $\frac{1}{6} + \frac{1}{6} = \frac{1}{3}$

d $P(\text{two circles}) = \dfrac{1}{36}$

e There are three places in the outcome column which have two shapes the same. These are the first, fifth and last rows. The probabilities are respectively $\frac{1}{4}, \frac{1}{9}$ and $\frac{1}{36}$. Their combined probability is given by the addition rule.

$$P(\text{two shapes the same}) = \frac{1}{4} + \frac{1}{9} + \frac{1}{36} = \frac{7}{18}$$

Note that the answers to parts **c**, **d** and **e** are the same as the answers obtained in Example 11.

EXERCISE 3G

1 A coin is tossed twice. Copy and complete the tree diagram below to show all the outcomes.

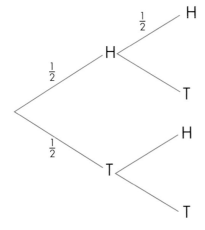

First event   Second event   Outcome   Probability

$\frac{1}{2}$ H   (H, H) $\frac{1}{2} \times \frac{1}{2} = \frac{1}{4}$

Use your tree diagram to work out the probability of each of these outcomes.

a getting two heads

b getting a head and a tail

c getting at least one tail

2 A card is drawn from a pack of cards. It is replaced, the pack is shuffled and another card is drawn.

a What is the probability that either card was an Ace?

b What is the probability that either card was not an Ace?

c Draw a tree diagram to show the outcomes of two cards being drawn as described. Use the tree diagram to work out the probability of each of these.

    i both cards will be Aces

    ii at least one of the cards will be an Ace

3 On my way to work, I drive through two sets of road works with traffic lights which only show green or red. I know that the probability of the first set being green is $\frac{1}{3}$ and the probability of the second set being green is $\frac{1}{2}$.

a What is the probability that the first set of lights will be red?

b What is the probability that the second set of lights will be red?

c Copy and complete the tree diagram below, showing the possible outcomes when passing through both sets of lights.

First event	Second event	Outcome	Probability

G — $\frac{1}{2}$ — G   (G, G) $\frac{1}{3} \times \frac{1}{2} = \frac{1}{6}$

$\frac{1}{3}$ — G

R

R — G

R

d Using the tree diagram, what is the probability of each of the following outcomes?

i I do not get held up at either set of lights

ii I get held up at exactly one set of lights

iii I get held up at least once

e Over a school term I make 90 journeys to work. On how many days can I expect to get two green lights?

4 Six out of every 10 cars in Britain are foreign made.

a What is the probability that any car will be British made?

b Two cars can be seen approaching in the distance. Draw a tree diagram to work out the probability of each of these outcomes.

i both cars will be British made

ii one car will be British and the other car will be foreign made

5 Three coins are tossed. Complete the tree diagram below and use it to answer the questions.

First event   Second event   Third event   Outcome   Probability

$$H \qquad (H, H, H) \quad \tfrac{1}{2} \times \tfrac{1}{2} \times \tfrac{1}{2} = \tfrac{1}{8}$$

If a coin is tossed three times, what is the probability that you get each of these outcomes?

a three heads

b two heads and a tail

c at least one tail

6 Thomas has to take a three-part language examination paper. The first part is speaking. He has a 0.4 chance of passing this part. The second is listening. He has a 0.5 chance of passing this part. The third part is writing. He has a 0.7 chance of passing this part. Draw a tree diagram covering three events where the first event is passing or failing the speaking part of the examination, the second event is passing or failing the listening part, and the third event is passing or failing the writing part.

a If he passes all three parts, his father will give him £20. What is the probability that he gets the money?

b If he passes two parts only, he can resit the other part. What is the chance he will have to resit?

c If he fails all three parts, he will be thrown off the course. What is the chance he is thrown off the course?

7 In a group of ten girls, six like the pop group Smudge and four like the pop group Mirage. Two girls are to be chosen for a pop quiz.

a What is the probability that the first girl chosen will be a Smudge fan?

b Draw a tree diagram to show the outcomes of choosing two girls and which pop groups they like. (Remember, once a girl has been chosen the first time she cannot be chosen again.)

c Use your tree diagram to work out the probability of each of these.

   i both girls chosen will like Smudge

   ii both girls chosen will like the same group

   iii both girls chosen will like different groups

8 Look at all the tree diagrams that have been drawn so far.

a What do the probabilities across any set of branches (outlined in the diagram below) always add up to?

b What do the final probabilities (outlined in the diagram below) always add up to?

c You should now be able to fill in all of the missing values in the diagram.

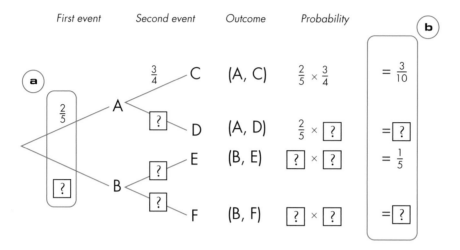

3.8 Independent events

In this section you will learn how to:
- use the connectors "and" and "or" to find the probability of combined events

Key words
and
independent events
or

If the outcome of event A does not effect the outcome of event B, then events A and B are called **independent events**. Most of the combined events we have looked at so far have been independent events.

It is possible to work out problems on combined events without using tree diagrams. The method explained in Example 13 is basically the same as that of a tree diagram but uses the words **and** and **or**.

EXAMPLE 13

The chance that Ashley hits a target with an arrow is $\frac{1}{4}$. He has two shots at the target. What is the probability of each of these?

a He hits the target both times.

b He hits the target once only.

c He hits the target at least once.

a P(hits both times) = P(first shot hits **and** second shot hits) = $\frac{1}{4} \times \frac{1}{4} = \frac{1}{16}$

b P(hits the target once only) = P (first hits **and** second misses **or** first misses **and**

second hits) = $\left(\frac{1}{4} \times \frac{3}{4}\right) + \left(\frac{3}{4} \times \frac{1}{4}\right) = \frac{3}{8}$

c P(hits at least once) = P(both hit **or** one hits) = $\frac{1}{16} + \frac{3}{8} = \frac{7}{16}$

Note the connections between the word "and" and the operation "times", and the word "or" and the operation "add".

EXERCISE 3H

1 Alf tosses a coin twice. The coin is biased so it has a probability of $\frac{2}{3}$ of landing on a head. What is the probability that he gets

    a two heads?   **b** a head and a tail (in any order)?

2 Bernice draws a card from a pack of cards, replaces it, shuffles the pack and then draws another card. What is the probability that the cards are

    a both Aces?   **b** an Ace and a King (in any order)?

3 A dice is thrown twice. What is the probability that both scores are

    a even?   **b** one even and one odd (in any order)?

4 I throw a dice three times. What is the probability of getting three sixes?

5 A bag contains 15 white beads and 10 black beads. I take out a bead at random, replace it and take out another bead. What is the probability of each of these?

    a both beads are black

    b one bead is black and the other white (in any order)

6 The probability that I am late for work on Monday is 0.4. The probability that I am late on Tuesday is 0.2. What is the probability of each of the following outcomes?

    a I am late for work on Monday and Tuesday.

    b I am late for work on Monday and on time on Tuesday.

    c I am on time on both Monday and Tuesday.

7 Ronda has to take a three-part language examination paper. The first part is speaking. She has a 0.7 chance of passing this part. The second part is listening. She has a 0.6 chance of passing this part. The third part is writing. She has a 0.8 chance of passing this part.

a If she passes all three parts, her father will give her £20. What is the probability that she gets the money?

b If she passes two parts only, she can resit the other part. What is the chance she will have to resit?

c If she fails all three parts, she will be thrown off the course. What is the chance she is thrown off the course?

"At least" problems

In examination questions concerning combined events, it is common to ask for the probability of at least one of the events occurring. There are two ways to solve such problems.

- All possibilities can be written out, which takes a long time.

- Use P(at least one) = 1 − P(none)

The second option is much easier to work out and there is less chance of making a mistake.

EXAMPLE 14

A bag contains seven red and three black balls. A ball is taken out and replaced. This is repeated three times. What is the probability of getting each of these?

a no red balls

b at least one red ball

a P(no reds) = P(black, black, black) = $\frac{7}{10} \times \frac{7}{10} \times \frac{7}{10}$ = 0.343

b P(at least one red) = 1 − P(no reds) = 1 − 0.343 = 0.657

Note that the answer to part **b** is 1 minus the answer to part **a**. Examination questions often build up answers in this manner.

EXERCISE 3I

1 A dice is thrown three times.

a What is the probability of not getting a 2?

b What is the probability of at least one 2?

2 Four coins are thrown. What is the probability of

a 4 tails?

b at least 1 head?

Mod 1

3 Adam, Bashir and Clem take a mathematics test. The probability that Adam passes is 0.6, the probability that Bashir passes is 0.9, and the probability that Clem passes is 0.7. What is the probability of each of these outcomes?

   a all three pass

   b Bashir and Adam pass but Clem does not

   c all three fail

   d at least one passes

4 A bag contains 4 red and 6 blue balls. A ball is taken out and replaced. Another ball is taken out. What is the probability of each of these?

   a both balls are red   **b** both balls are blue   **c** at least one is red

5 a A dice is thrown three times. What is the probability of

     i 3 sixes?   **ii** no sixes?   **iii** at least one six?

   b A dice is thrown four times. What is the probability of

     i 4 sixes?   **ii** no sixes?   **iii** at least one six?

   c A dice is thrown five times. What is the probability of

     i 5 sixes?   **ii** no sixes?   **iii** at least one six?

   d A dice is thrown n times. What is the probability of

     i n sixes?   **ii** no sixes?   **iii** at least one six?

6 The probability that the school canteen serves chips on any day is $\frac{2}{3}$. In a week of five days, what is the probability of each of these?

   a chips are served every day

   b chips are not served on any day

   c chips are served on at least one day

7 The probability that Steve is late for work is $\frac{5}{6}$. The probability that Nigel is late for work is $\frac{9}{10}$. The probability that Gary is late for work is $\frac{1}{2}$. What is the probability that on a particular day

   a all three are late?   **b** none of them are late?   **c** at least one is late?

More advanced use of *and* and *or*

We have already seen how certain probability problems can be solved either by tree diagrams or by the use of the *and/or* method. Both methods are basically the same but the *and/or* method works better in the case of three events following one another or in situations where the number of outcomes of one event is greater than two. This is simply because the tree diagram would get too large and involved.

EXAMPLE 15

Three cards are to be drawn from a pack of cards. Each card is to be replaced before the next one is drawn. What is the probability of drawing each of these combinations?

a three Kings

b exactly two Kings and one other card

c no Kings

d at least one King

Let K be the event "Drawing a King". Let N be the event "Not drawing a King". Then you obtain

a $P(KKK) = \frac{1}{13} \times \frac{1}{13} \times \frac{1}{13} = \frac{1}{2197}$

b $P(\text{exactly two Kings}) = P(KKN) \text{ or } P(KNK) \text{ or } P(NKK)$

$$= \left(\frac{1}{13} \times \frac{1}{13} \times \frac{12}{13}\right) + \left(\frac{1}{13} \times \frac{12}{13} \times \frac{1}{13}\right) + \left(\frac{12}{13} \times \frac{1}{13} \times \frac{1}{13}\right) = \frac{36}{2197}$$

c $P(\text{no Kings}) = P(NNN) = \frac{12}{13} \times \frac{12}{13} \times \frac{12}{13} = \frac{1728}{2197}$

d $P(\text{at least one King}) = 1 - P(\text{no Kings}) = 1 - \frac{1728}{2197} = \frac{469}{2197}$

Note that in part **b** the notation stands for the probability that the first card is a King, the second is a King and the third is not a King; or the first is a King, the second is not a King and the third is a King; or the first is not a King, the second is a King and the third is a King.

Note also that the probability of each component of part **b** is exactly the same. So we could have done the calculation as

$$3 \times \frac{1}{13} \times \frac{1}{13} \times \frac{12}{13} = \frac{36}{2197}$$

Patterns of this kind often occur in probability.

EXERCISE 3J

1 A bag contains three black balls and seven red balls. A ball is taken out and replaced. This is repeated twice. What is the probability of each of these outcomes?

a all three are black

b exactly two are black

c exactly one is black

d none are black

2 A dice is thrown four times. What is the probability of each of these?

a four sixes are thrown

b no sixes are thrown

c exactly one six is thrown

3 On my way to work I pass three sets of traffic lights. The probability that the first is green is $\frac{1}{2}$. The probability that the second is green is $\frac{1}{3}$. The probability that the third is green is $\frac{2}{3}$. What is the probability of each of these?

a all three are green

b exactly two are green

c exactly one is green

d none are green

e at least one is green

4 Alf is late for school with a probability of 0.9. Bert is late with a probability of 0.7. Chas is late with a probability of 0.6. On any particular day what is the probability of each of these?

 a exactly one of them being late   **b** exactly two of them being late

5 Daisy takes four A-levels. The probability that she will pass English is 0.7. The probability that she will pass history is 0.6. The probability she will pass geography is 0.8. The probability that she will pass general studies is 0.9. What is the probability of each of these?

 a she passes all four subjects

 b she passes exactly three subjects

 c she passes at least three subjects

6 The driving test is in two parts, a written test and a practical test. It is known that 90% of people who take the written test pass, and 60% of people who take the practical test pass. A person who passes the written test does not have to take it again. A person who fails the practical test does have to take it again.

 a What is the probability that someone passes the written test?

 b What is the probability that someone passes the practical test?

 c What is the probability that someone passes both tests?

 d What is the probability that someone passes the written test but takes two attempts to pass the practical test?

7 Six out of ten cars in Britain are made by foreign manufacturers. Three cars can be seen approaching in the distance.

 a What is the probability that the first one is foreign?

 b The first car is going so fast that its make could not be made out. What is the probability that the second car is foreign?

 c What is the probability that exactly two of the three cars are foreign?

 d Explain why, if the first car is foreign, the probability of the second car being foreign is still 6 out of 10.

8 Each day Mr Smith runs home. He has a choice of three routes: the road, the fields or the canal path. The road route is 4 miles, the fields route is 6 miles and the canal route is 5 miles. In a three-day period, what is the probability that Mr Smith runs a total distance of

 a exactly 17 miles   **b** exactly 13 miles

 c exactly 15 miles   **d** over 17 miles?

9 A rock climber attempts a difficult route. There are three hard moves at points A, B and C in the climb. The climber has a probability of 0.6, 0.3 and 0.7 respectively of completing each of these moves. What is the probability that the climber

 a completes the climb   **b** fails at move A

 c fails at move B   **d** fails at move C

Conditional probability

In this section you will learn how to:
- work out the probability of combined events when the probabilities change after each event

Key word
conditional probability

The term **conditional probability** is used to describe the situation when the probability of an event is dependent on the outcome of another event. For instance, if a card is taken from a pack and not returned, then the probabilities for the next card drawn will be altered. The following example illustrates this situation.

EXAMPLE 16

A bag contains nine balls, of which five are white and four are black.

A ball is taken out and not replaced. Another is then taken out. If the first ball removed is black, what is the probability of each of these outcomes?

a the second ball will be black

b both balls will be black

When a black ball is removed, there are five white balls and three black balls left, reducing the total to eight.

Hence, when the second ball is taken out,

a P(second ball black) = $\frac{3}{8}$

b P(both balls black) = $\frac{4}{9} \times \frac{3}{8} = \frac{1}{6}$

EXERCISE 3K

1 I put six CDs in my multi-player and put it on random play. Each CD has 10 tracks. Once a track is played, it is not played again.

a What is the chance that track 5 on CD 6 is the first one played?

b What is the maximum number of tracks that could be played before a track from CD 6 is played?

2 There are five white and one brown eggs in an egg box. Kate decides to make a two-egg omelette. She takes each egg from the box without looking at its colour.

a What is the probability that the first egg taken is brown?

b If the first egg taken is brown, what is the probability that the second egg taken will be brown?

c What is the probability that Kate gets an omelette made from each of these combinations?

i two white eggs   **ii** one white and one brown egg   **iii** two brown eggs

3 A box contains 10 red and 15 yellow balls. One is taken out and not replaced. Another is taken out.

a If the first ball taken out is red, what is the probability that the second ball is

i red?   **ii** yellow?

b If the first ball taken out is yellow, what is the probability that the second ball is

i red?   **ii** yellow?

4 A fruit bowl contains six Granny Smith apples and eight Golden Delicious apples. Kevin takes two apples at random.

a If the first apple is a Granny Smith, what is the probability that the second is

i a Granny Smith?   **ii** a Golden Delicious?

b What is the probability that

i both are Granny Smiths?   **ii** both are Golden Delicious?

5 Ann has a bargain box of tins. They are unlabelled but she knows that six tins contain soup and four contain peaches.

a She opens two tins. What is the probability that

i they are both soup?   **ii** they are both peaches?

b What is the probability that she has to open two tins before she gets a tin of peaches?

c What is the probability that she has to open three tins before she gets a tin of peaches?

d What is the probability that she will get a tin of soup if she opens five tins?

6 One in three cars on British roads is made in Britain. A car comes down the road. It is a British-made car. John says that the probability of the next car being British made is one in two because a British-made car has just gone past. Explain why he is wrong.

7 A bag contains three black balls and seven red balls. A ball is taken out and not replaced. This is repeated twice. What is the probability of each of these outcomes?

    a all three are black   **b** exactly two are black

    c exactly one is black   **d** none are black

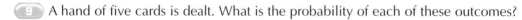

8 One my way to work, I pass two sets of traffic lights. The probability that the first is green is $\frac{1}{3}$. If the first is green, the probability that the second is green is $\frac{1}{3}$. If the first is red, the probability that the second is green is $\frac{2}{3}$. What is the probability of each of these?

    a both are green   **b** none are green

    c exactly one is green   **d** at least one is green

9 A hand of five cards is dealt. What is the probability of each of these outcomes?

    a all five are Spades

    b all five are the same suit

    c they are four Aces and any other card

    d they are four of a kind and any other card

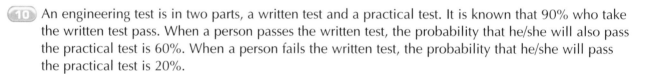

10 An engineering test is in two parts, a written test and a practical test. It is known that 90% who take the written test pass. When a person passes the written test, the probability that he/she will also pass the practical test is 60%. When a person fails the written test, the probability that he/she will pass the practical test is 20%.

    a What is the probability that someone passes both tests?

    b What is the probability that someone passes one test?

    c What is the probability that someone fails both tests?

    d What is the combined probability of the answers to parts **a**, **b** and **c**?

11 Each day Mr Smith runs home from work. He has a choice of three routes. The road, the fields or the canal path. On Monday, each route has an equal probability of being chosen. The route chosen on any day will not be picked the next day and so each of the other two routes has an equal probability of being chosen.

    a Write down all the possible combinations so that Mr Smith runs home via the canal path on Wednesday (there are four of them).

    b Calculate the probability that Mr Smith runs home via the canal path on Wednesday.

    c Calculate the probability that Mr Smith runs home via the canal path on Tuesday.

    d Using your results from parts **b** and **c**, write down the probability that Mr Smith runs home via the canal path on Thursday.

    e Explain the answers to parts **b**, **c** and **d**.

1 The probabilities of whether a student, picked at random from a school, is vegetarian or not are shown in this table.

	Boys	Girls
Vegetarian	0.08	0.2
Non-vegetarian	0.4	0.32

a What is the probability that a student chosen at random from the school is vegetarian?

b There are 320 girls in the school who are vegetarian. How many students are there in the school altogether?

AQA, Question 3, Paper 2 Higher, November 2003

 2 a Jonathan has a bag containing 10 balls. The balls are red, green or blue. He takes a ball at random from the bag and notes its colour. He then replaces the ball in the bag and repeats the experiment 500 times.

The results are

Red	Green	Blue
235	168	97

i What is the relative frequency of picking a red ball?

ii How many of each coloured ball are in the bag?

b Matthew takes a ball at random from another bag and replaces it. He does this 10 times and gets 6 reds and 4 greens. He claims that there are no blue balls in the bag.

Explain why he could be wrong.

3 A hen lays either white or brown eggs. The probability of a hen laying a brown egg is x.

 a What is the probability that the hen lays a white egg?

b The probability of the hen laying a white egg is *three* times the probability of the hen laying a brown egg. Calculate the value of x.

4 White and blue counters are in a bag in the ratio 2:5.

 a If there are 4 white counters, how many blue counters are there in the bag?

b If there are 20 blue counters in the bag, how many white counters are there?

c If there are 70 counters in the bag altogether, how many of each colour are there in the bag?

5 Arthur has a box of 10 unlabelled CDs. The CDs are pop, classical or dance. The table shows the probability of each type of music if a CD is taken out at random.

Type of music	Probability
Pop	0.6
Classical	0.1
Dance	

a What is the probability that a CD chosen at random is a dance CD?

b How many classical CDs are in the box?

c Arthur picks a CD at random and puts it in a 2-disc CD player. He then picks another CD at random and puts it in the player. Complete the tree diagram

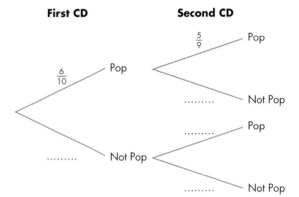

d What is the probability that neither of the CDs is pop?

 6 At the end of a training programme, students have to pass an exam to gain a certificate. The probability of passing the exam at the first attempt is 0.75.
Those who fail are allowed to re-sit.
The probability of passing the re-sit is 0.6.
No further attempts are allowed.

a i Complete the tree diagram.

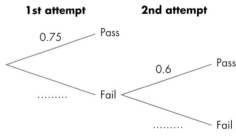

ii What is the probability that a student fails to gain a certificate?

b Three students take the exam.
What is the probability that all of them gain a certificate?

AQA, Question 20, Paper 1 Higher, June 2005

7 A bag contains 8 balls. 5 are black and 3 are white.

A ball is taken out of the bag at random and *not* replaced. Another ball is taken out of the bag at random. What is the probability that both of the balls are the same colour?

AQA, Question 23, Paper 2 Higher, November 2003

8 A drinks machine uses cartridges to supply the drink. Billy has a job lot of eight cartridges which have lost their labels. He knows he has three teas and five coffees. He makes three drinks with the cartridges.

a What is the probability he gets three teas?

b What is the probability he gets exactly two coffees?

c What is the probability that he gets at least one coffee?

d Billy makes the three drinks and leaves the room. Betty comes in, tastes one of the drinks. She finds it is tea. What is the probability that the other two drinks are also tea?

WORKED EXAM QUESTION

Harry is a pensioner. The probability that Harry goes into town on a Tuesday is $\frac{2}{5}$. The probability that Harry goes into town on a Tuesday and visits the library is $\frac{3}{20}$.

a One Tuesday Harry is in town. Calculate the probability that he visits the library.

b Calculate the probability that Harry goes into town on a Tuesday and does not visit the library.

SEG/Mod Math, Question 7, Paper 15, November 1999

Solution

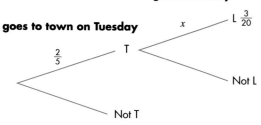

goes to library

goes to town on Tuesday

$\frac{2}{5}$ — T

x — L $\frac{3}{20}$

Not L

Not T

> Draw the part of the probability tree that you know about.

a P(Harry goes to town on Tuesday) $\times x$ = $\frac{3}{20}$

$$\frac{2}{5} \times x = \frac{3}{20}$$

P(Harry visits the library when in town on Tuesday) = $\frac{3}{20} \div \frac{2}{5}$

$$= \frac{3}{20} \times \frac{5}{2} = \frac{3}{8}$$

> Set up an equation.

> Substitute in the probabilities and solve the equation. Remember to turn the fraction upside down and multiply by it when you divide.

b P(Harry does not visit the library) = $1 - \frac{3}{8} = \frac{5}{8}$

P(Harry goes into town and does not visit the library) = $\frac{2}{5} \times \frac{5}{8} = \frac{1}{4}$

> First work out the probability of the complementary event then use the 'and' rule for combined events.

GRADE YOURSELF

D Able to calculate the probability of an event happening when you know the probability that the event does not happen and that the total probability of all possible outcomes is 1

D Able to predict the expected number of successes from a given number of trials if you know the probability of one success

C Able to calculate relative frequency from experimental evidence and compare this with the theoretical probability

B Able to draw a tree diagram to work out the probability of combined events

A Able to use *and/or* or a tree diagram to work out probabilities of specific outcomes of combined events

A* Able to work out the probabilities of combined events when the probability of each event changes depending on the outcome of the previous event

What you should know now

- How to calculate theoretical probabilities from different situations

Number

This chapter will show you ...

● how to calculate with integers and decimals

● how to round off numbers to a given number of significant figures

● how to find prime factors, least common multiples (LCM) and highest common factors (HCF)

What you should already know

● How to add, subtract, multiply and divide with integers

● What multiples, factors, square numbers and prime numbers are

● The BODMAS rule and how to substitute values into simple algebraic expressions

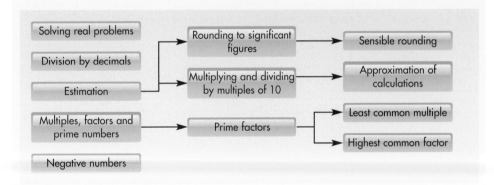

Solving real problems

Division by decimals

Estimation

Multiples, factors and prime numbers

Negative numbers

Rounding to significant figures → Sensible rounding

Multiplying and dividing by multiples of 10 → Approximation of calculations

Prime factors → Least common multiple

Prime factors → Highest common factor

Quick check

1 Work out the following.

  a 23×167 **b** $984 \div 24$ **c** $(16 + 9)^2$

2 Write down the following.

  a a multiple of 7   **b** a prime number between 10 and 20

  c a square number under 80   **d** the factors of 9

3 Work out the following.

  a $2 + 3 \times 5$ **b** $(2 + 3) \times 5$ **c** $2 + 3^2 - 6$

4.1 Solving real problems

This section will give you practice in using arithmetic to:

● solve more complex problems

Key words
long division
long
   multiplication
strategy

In your GCSE examination, you will be given *real* problems that you have to *read carefully, think about* and then plan a **strategy** without using a calculator. These will involve arithmetical skills such as **long multiplication** and **long division**. There are several ways to do these, so make sure you are familiar with and confident with at least one of them. The box method for long multiplication is shown in the first example and the standard column method for long division is shown in the second example. In this type of problem it is important to show your working as you will get marks for correct methods.

EXAMPLE 1

A supermarket receives a delivery of 235 cases of tins of beans. Each case contains 24 tins.

a How many tins of beans does the supermarket receive altogether?

b 5% of the tins were damaged. These were thrown away. The supermarket knows that it sells, on average, 250 tins of beans a day. How many days will the delivery of beans last before a new consignment is needed?

a The problem is a long multiplication 235 × 24.

The box method is shown.

×	200	30	5
20	4000	600	100
4	800	120	20

$$
\begin{array}{r}
4000 \\
600 \\
100 \\
+\quad 800 \\
120 \\
20 \\
\hline
5640
\end{array}
$$

So the answer is 5640 tins.

b 10% of 5640 is 564, so 5% is 564 ÷ 2 = 282

This leaves 5640 − 282 = 5358 tins to be sold.

There are 21 lots of 250 in 5358 (you should know that 4 × 250 = 1000), so the beans will last for 21 days before another delivery is needed.

EXAMPLE 2

A party of 613 children and 59 adults are going on a day out to a theme park.

a How many coaches, each holding 53 people, will be needed?

b One adult gets into the theme park free for every 15 children. How many adults will have to pay to get in?

a We read the problem and realise that we have to do a division sum: the number of seats on a coach into the number of people. This is $(613 + 59) \div 53 = 672 \div 53$

$$
\begin{array}{r}
12 \\
53 \overline{)672} \\
530 \\
\hline
142 \\
106 \\
\hline
36
\end{array}
$$

The answer is 12 remainder 36. So, there will be 12 full coaches and one coach with 36 people on. So, they would have to book 13 coaches.

b This is also a division, $613 \div 15$. This can be done quite easily if you know the 15 times table as $4 \times 15 = 60$, so $40 \times 15 = 600$. This leaves a remainder of 13. So 40 adults get in free and $59 - 40 = 19$ adults will have to pay.

EXERCISE 4A

1 There are 48 cans of soup in a crate. A supermarket had a delivery of 125 crates of soup.

a How many cans of soup were received?

b The supermarket is having a promotion on soup. If you buy five cans you get one free. Each can costs 39p. How much will it cost to get 32 cans of soup?

2 Greystones Primary School has 12 classes, each of which has 24 pupils.

a How many pupils are there at Greystones Primary School?

b The pupil–teacher ratio is 18 to 1. That means there is one teacher for every 18 pupils. How many teachers are at the school?

3 Barnsley Football Club is organising travel for an away game. 1300 adults and 500 juniors want to go. Each coach holds 48 people and costs £320 to hire. Tickets to the match are £18 for adults and £10 for juniors.

a How many coaches will be needed?

b The club is charging adults £26 and juniors £14 for travel and a ticket. How much profit does the club make out of the trip?

4 First-class letters cost 30p to post. Second-class letters cost 21p to post. How much will it cost to send 75 first-class and 220 second-class letters?

5 Kirsty collects small models of animals. Each one costs 45p. She saves enough to buy 23 models but when she goes to the shop she finds that the price has gone up to 55p. How many can she buy now?

6 Eunice wanted to save up for a mountain bike that costs £250. She baby-sits each week for 6 hours for £2.75 an hour, and does a Saturday job that pays £27.50. She saves three-quarters of her weekly earnings. How many weeks will it take her to save enough to buy the bike?

7 The magazine *Teen Dance* comes out every month. In a newsagent the magazine costs £2.45. The annual (yearly) subscription for the magazine is £21. How much cheaper is each magazine bought on subscription?

8 Paula buys a music centre. She pays a deposit of 10% of the cash price and then 36 monthly payments of £12.50. In total she pays £495. How much was the cash price of the music centre?

1.2 Division by decimals

This section will show you how to:
- divide by decimals by changing the problem so you divide by an integer

Key words
decimal places
decimal point
integer

It is advisable to change the problem so that you divide by an **integer** rather than a decimal. This is done by multiplying both numbers by 10 or 100, etc. This will depend on the number of **decimal places** after the **decimal point**.

EXAMPLE 3

Evaluate the following.   **a** $42 \div 0.2$ **b** $19.8 \div 0.55$

a The calculation is $42 \div 0.2$ which can be rewritten as $420 \div 2$. In this case both values have been multiplied by 10 to make the divisor into a whole number. This is then a straightforward division to which the answer is 210.

Another way to view this is as a fraction problem.

$$\frac{42}{0.2} = \frac{42}{0.2} \times \frac{10}{10} = \frac{420}{2} = \frac{210}{1} = 210$$

b $19.8 \div 0.55 = 198 \div 5.5 = 1980 \div 55$

This then becomes a long division problem.

This has been solved by the method of repeated subtraction.

```
      1980
  -   1100      20 × 55
      ────
       880
  -    440       8 × 55
      ────
       440
  -    440       8 × 55
      ────
         0      36 × 55
```

EXERCISE 4B

1 Evaluate each of these.

    a $3.6 \div 0.2$ **b** $56 \div 0.4$ **c** $0.42 \div 0.3$ **d** $8.4 \div 0.7$ **e** $4.26 \div 0.2$

    f $3.45 \div 0.5$ **g** $83.7 \div 0.03$ **h** $0.968 \div 0.08$ **i** $7.56 \div 0.4$

2 Evaluate each of these.

    a $67.2 \div 0.24$ **b** $6.36 \div 0.53$ **c** $0.936 \div 5.2$ **d** $162 \div 0.36$ **e** $2.17 \div 3.5$

    f $98.8 \div 0.26$ **g** $0.468 \div 1.8$ **h** $132 \div 0.55$ **i** $0.984 \div 0.082$

3 A pile of paper is 6 cm high. Each sheet is 0.008 cm thick. How many sheets are in the pile of paper?

4 Doris buys a big bag of safety pins. The bag weighs 180 grams. Each safety pin weighs 0.6 grams. How many safety pins are in the bag?

Estimation

This section will show you how to:

- use estimation to find approximate answers to numerical calculations

Key words

approximate
estimation
significant
figures

Rounding off to significant figures

We often use significant figures when we want to **approximate** a number with quite a few digits in it.

Look at this table which shows some numbers rounded to one, two and three **significant figures** (sf).

One sf	8	50	200	90 000	0.00007	0.003	0.4
Two sf	67	4.8	0.76	45 000	730	0.0067	0.40
Three sf	312	65.9	40.3	0.0761	7.05	0.00301	0.400

The steps taken to round off a number to a particular number of significant figures are very similar to those used for rounding to so many decimal places.

- From the left, count the digits. If you are rounding to 2 sf, count 2 digits, for 3 sf count 3 digits, and so on. When the original number is less than 1.0, start counting from the first non-zero digit.

- Look at the *next* digit to the right. When the next digit is less than 5, leave the digit you counted to the same. However if the next digit is equal to or greater than 5, add 1 to the digit you counted to.

- Ignore all the other digits, but put in enough zeros to keep the number the right size (value).

For example, look at the following table which shows some numbers rounded off to one, two and three significant figures, respectively.

Number	Rounded to 1 sf	Rounded to 2 sf	Rounded to 3 sf
45 281	50 000	45 000	45 300
568.54	600	570	569
7.3782	7	7.4	7.38
8054	8000	8100	8050
99.8721	100	100	99.9
0.7002	0.7	0.70	0.700

EXERCISE 4C

1 Round off each of the following numbers to 1 significant figure.

a 46 313	**b** 57 123	**c** 30 569	**d** 94 558	**e** 85 299
f 0.5388	**g** 0.2823	**h** 0.005 84	**i** 0.047 85	**j** 0.000 876
k 9.9	**l** 89.5	**m** 90.78	**n** 199	**o** 999.99

2 Round off each of the following numbers to 2 significant figures.

a 56 147	**b** 26 813	**c** 79 611	**d** 30 578	**e** 14 009
f 1.689	**g** 4.0854	**h** 2.658	**i** 8.0089	**j** 41.564
k 0.8006	**l** 0.458	**m** 0.0658	**n** 0.9996	**o** 0.009 82

3 Round off each of the following to the number of significant figures (sf) indicated.

a 57 402 (1 sf)	**b** 5288 (2 sf)	**c** 89.67 (3 sf)
d 105.6 (2 sf)	**e** 8.69 (1 sf)	**f** 1.087 (2 sf)
g 0.261 (1 sf)	**h** 0.732 (1 sf)	**i** 0.42 (1 sf)
j 0.758 (1 sf)	**k** 0.185 (1 sf)	**l** 0.682 (1 sf)

4 What are the least and the greatest number of sweets that can be found in these jars?

a

b

c

5 What are the least and the greatest number of people that can be found in these towns?

Elsecar   population 800 (to 1 significant figure)

Hoyland   population 1200 (to 2 significant figures)

Barnsley   population 165 000 (to 3 significant figures)

Multiplying and dividing by multiples of 10

Questions often use multiplying together multiples of 10, 100, and so on. This method is used in estimation. You should have the skill to do this mentally so that you can check that your answers to calculations are about right. (Approximation of calculations is covered on page 119.)

Use a calculator to work out the following.

a $200 \times 300 =$	**b** $100 \times 40 =$	**c** $2000 \times 0.3 =$
d $0.2 \times 50 =$	**e** $0.2 \times 0.5 =$	**f** $0.3 \times 0.04 =$

Can you see a way of doing these without using a calculator or pencil and paper? Basically, the digits are multiplied together and then the number of zeros or the position of the decimal point is worked out by combining the zeros or decimal places on the original calculation.

Dividing is almost as simple. Try doing the following on your calculator.

a 400 ÷ 20 =   **b** 200 ÷ 50 =   **c** 1000 ÷ 0.2 =

d 300 ÷ 0.3 =   **e** 250 ÷ 0.05 =   **f** 30 000 ÷ 0.6 =

Once again, there is an easy way of doing these "in your head". Look at these examples.

300 × 4000 = 1 200 000   5000 ÷ 200 = 25   20 × 0.5 = 10

0.6 × 5000 = 3000   400 ÷ 0.02 = 20 000   800 ÷ 0.2 = 4000

Can you see a connection between the digits, the number of zeros and the position of the decimal point, and the way in which these calculations are worked out?

EXERCISE 4D

1 Without using a calculator, write down the answers to these.

a 200 × 300	**b** 30 × 4000	**c** 50 × 200
d 0.3 × 50	**e** 200 × 0.7	**f** 200 × 0.5
g 0.1 × 2000	**h** 0.2 × 0.14	**i** 0.3 × 0.3
j $(20)^2$	**k** $(20)^3$	**l** $(0.4)^2$
m 0.3 × 150	**n** 0.4 × 0.2	**o** 0.5 × 0.5
p 20 × 40 × 5000	**q** 20 × 20 × 900	

2 Without using a calculator, write down the answers to these.

a 2000 ÷ 400	**b** 3000 ÷ 60	**c** 5000 ÷ 200
d 300 ÷ 0.5	**e** 2100 ÷ 0.7	**f** 2000 ÷ 0.4
g 3000 ÷ 1.5	**h** 400 ÷ 0.2	**i** 2000 × 40 ÷ 200
j 200 × 20 ÷ 0.5	**k** 200 × 6000 ÷ 0.3	**l** 20 × 80 × 60 ÷ 0.03

Approximation of calculations

How do we approximate the value of a calculation? What do we actually do when we try to approximate an answer to a problem?

For example, what is the approximate answer to 35.1 × 6.58?

To approximate the answer in this and many other similar cases, we simply round off each number to 1 significant figure, then work out the calculation. So in this case, the approximation is

35.1 × 6.58 ≈ 40 × 7 = 280

Sometimes, especially when dividing, we round off a number to something more useful at 2 significant figures instead of at 1 significant figure. For example,

$57.3 \div 6.87$

Since 6.87 rounds off to 7, then round off 57.3 to 56 because 7 divides exactly into 56. Hence,

$57.3 \div 6.87 \approx 56 \div 7 = 8$

A quick approximation is always a great help in any calculation since it often stops you writing down a silly answer.

If you are using a calculator, whenever you see a calculation with a numerator and denominator *always* put brackets around the top and the bottom. This is to remind you that the numerator and denominator must be worked out separately before they are divided into each other. You can work out the numerator and denominator separately but most calculators will work out the answer straight away if brackets are used. You are expected to use a calculator *efficiently*, so doing the calculation in stages is not efficient.

EXAMPLE 4

a Find approximate answers to **i** $\dfrac{213 \times 69}{42}$ **ii** $\dfrac{78 \times 397}{0.38}$

b Use your calculator to find the correct answer. Round off to 3 significant figures.

a i Round each value to 1 significant figure. $\dfrac{200 \times 70}{40}$

Work out the numerator. $= \dfrac{14\,000}{40}$

Divide by the denominator. $= 350$

ii Round each value to 1 significant figure. $\dfrac{80 \times 400}{0.4}$

Work out the numerator. $= \dfrac{32\,000}{0.4} = \dfrac{320\,000}{4}$

Divide by the denominator. $= 80\,000$

b Use a calculator to check your approximate answers.

i $\dfrac{213 \times 69}{42} = \dfrac{(213 \times 69)}{(42)}$

So type in

| (| 2 | 1 | 3 | × | 6 | 9 |) | ÷ | (| 4 | 2 |) | = |

The display should say 349.9285714 which rounds off to 350. This agrees exactly with the estimate.

Note that we do not have to put brackets around the 42 but it is a good habit to get into.

ii $\dfrac{78 \times 397}{0.38} = \dfrac{(78 \times 397)}{(0.38)}$

So type in

| (| 7 | 8 | × | 3 | 9 | 7 |) | ÷ | (| 0 | • | 3 | 8 |) | = |

The display should say 81489.47368 which rounds off to 81 500. This agrees with the estimate.

EXERCISE 4E

1 Find approximate answers to the following.

    a 5435×7.31 **b** 5280×3.211 **c** $63.24 \times 3.514 \times 4.2$

    d $354 \div 79.8$ **e** $5974 \div 5.29$ **f** $208 \div 0.378$

2 Work out the answers to question **1** using a calculator. Round off your answers to 3 significant figures and compare them with the estimates you made.

3 By rounding off, find an approximate answer to these.

    a $\dfrac{573 \times 783}{107}$ **b** $\dfrac{783 - 572}{24}$ **c** $\dfrac{352 + 657}{999}$

    d $\dfrac{78.3 - 22.6}{2.69}$ **e** $\dfrac{3.82 \times 7.95}{9.9}$ **f** $\dfrac{11.78 \times 61.8}{39.4}$

4 Work out the answers to question **3** using a calculator. Round off your answers to 3 significant figures and compare them with the estimates you made.

5 Find the approximate monthly pay of the following people whose annual salary is given.

    a Paul £35 200   **b** Michael £25 600   **c** Jennifer £18 125   **d** Ross £8420

6 Find the approximate annual pay of the following people whose earnings are shown.

    a Kevin £270 a week   **b** Malcolm £1528 a month   **c** David £347 a week

7 A farmer bought 2713 kg of seed at a cost of £7.34 per kg. Find the approximate total cost of this seed.

8 A greengrocer sells a box of 450 oranges for £37. Approximately how much did each orange sell for?

9 It took me 6 hours 40 minutes to drive from Sheffield to Bude, a distance of 295 miles. My car uses petrol at the rate of about 32 miles per gallon. The petrol cost £3.51 per gallon.

    a Approximately how many miles did I do each hour?

    b Approximately how many gallons of petrol did I use in going from Sheffield to Bude?

    c What was the approximate cost of all the petrol I used in the journey to Bude and back again?

10 By rounding off, find an approximate answer to these.

    a $\dfrac{462 \times 79}{0.42}$ **b** $\dfrac{583 - 213}{0.21}$ **c** $\dfrac{252 + 551}{0.78}$ **d** $\dfrac{296 \times 32}{0.325}$

    e $\dfrac{297 + 712}{0.578 - 0.321}$ **f** $\dfrac{893 \times 87}{0.698 \times 0.47}$ **g** $\dfrac{38.3 + 27.5}{0.776}$ **h** $\dfrac{29.7 + 12.6}{0.26}$

    i $\dfrac{4.93 \times 3.81}{0.38 \times 0.51}$ **j** $\dfrac{12.31 \times 16.9}{0.394 \times 0.216}$

11 Work out the answers to question **10** using a calculator. Round off your answers to 3 significant figures and compare them with the estimates you made.

12 A sheet of paper is 0.012 cm thick. Approximately how many sheets will there be in a pile of paper that is 6.35 cm deep?

13 Use your calculator to work out the following. In each case:

i   write down the full calculator display of the answer

ii round your answer to three significant figures.

a $\dfrac{12.3 + 64.9}{6.9 - 4.1}$
     b $\dfrac{13.8 \times 23.9}{3.2 \times 6.1}$
     c $\dfrac{48.2 + 58.9}{3.62 \times 0.042}$

Sensible rounding

In the GCSE you will be required to round off answers to problems to a suitable degree of accuracy. Normally three significant figures is acceptable for answers. However, a big problem is caused by rounding off during calculations. When working out values, always work to either the calculator display or at least four significant figures.

Generally, you can use common sense. For example, you would not give the length of a pencil as 14.574 cm; you would round off to something like 14.6 cm. If you were asked how many tins of paint you need to buy to do a particular job, then you would give a whole number answer and not something such as 5.91 tins.

It is hard to make rules about this, as there is much disagreement even among the experts as to how you ought to do it. But, generally, when you are in any doubt as to how many significant figures to use for the final answer to a problem, round off to no more than one extra significant figure to the number used in the original data. (This particular type of rounding is used throughout this book.)

In a question where you are asked to give an answer to a sensible or appropriate degree of accuracy then use the following rule. Give the answer to the same accuracy as the numbers in the question. So, for example, if the numbers in the question are given to 2 significant figures give your answer to 2 significant figures, but remember, unless working out an approximation, do all the working to at least 4 significant figures or use the calculator display.

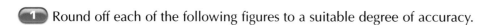

EXERCISE 4F

1 Round off each of the following figures to a suitable degree of accuracy.

a I am 1.7359 metres tall.

b It took me 5 minutes 44.83 seconds to mend the television.

c My kitten weighs 237.97 grams.

d The correct temperature at which to drink Earl Grey tea is 82.739 °C.

e There were 34 827 people at the test match yesterday.

f The distance from Wath to Sheffield is 15.528 miles.

g The area of the floor is 13.673 m^2.

Mod 3

2 Rewrite the following article, rounding off all the numbers to a suitable degree of accuracy if they need to be.

It was a hot day, the temperature was 81.699 °F and still rising. I had now walked 5.3289 km in just over 113.98 minutes. But I didn't care since I knew that the 43 275 people watching the race were cheering me on. I won by clipping 6.2 seconds off the record time. This was the 67th time it had happened since records first began in 1788. Well, next year I will only have 15 practice walks beforehand as I strive to beat the record by at least another 4.9 seconds.

3 About how many test tubes each holding 24 cm^3 of water can be filled from a 1 litre flask?

4 If I walk at an average speed of 70 metres per minute, approximately how long will it take me to walk a distance of 3 km?

5 About how many stamps at 21p each can I buy for £12?

6 I travelled a distance of 450 miles in 6.4 hours. What was my approximate average speed?

7 At Manchester United, it takes 160 minutes for 43 500 fans to get into the ground. On average, about how many fans are let into the ground every minute?

8 A 5p coin weighs 4.2 grams. Approximately how much will one million pounds worth of 5p pieces weigh?

Multiples, factors and prime numbers

4.4

This section will remind you about:
- multiples and factors
- prime numbers
- square numbers and triangular numbers
- square roots

Key words
factor
multiple
prime number
square number
triangular number

You should remember the following.

Multiples: Any number in the times table. For example, the multiples of 7 are 7, 14, 21, 28, 35, etc.

Factors: Any number that divides exactly into another number. For example, factors of 24 are 1, 2, 3, 4, 6, 8, 12, 24.

Prime numbers: Any number that only has two factors, 1 and itself. For example, 11, 17, 37 are prime numbers.

Square numbers: A number that comes from multiplying a number by itself. For example, 1, 4, 9, 16, 25, 36 … are square numbers.

Triangular numbers: Numbers that can make triangle patterns, For example, 1, 3, 6, 10, 15, 21, 28 … are triangular numbers.

Square roots: The square root of a given number is a number which, when multiplied by itself, produces the given number. For example, the square root of 9 is 3, since $3 \times 3 = 9$.

A square root is represented by the symbol $\sqrt{\ }$. For example, $\sqrt{16} = 4$.

Because $-4 \times -4 = 16$, there are always two square roots of every positive number.

So $\sqrt{16} = +4$ or -4. This can be written as $\sqrt{16} = \pm 4$, which is read as plus or minus four.

Cube roots: The cube root of a number is the number that when multiplied by itself three times gives the number. For example, the cube root of 27 is 3 and the cube root of -8 is -2.

EXERCISE 4G

1 From this box choose the numbers that fit each of these descriptions. (One number per description.)

a A multiple of 3 and a multiple of 4.

b A square number and an odd number.

c A factor of 24 and a factor of 18.

d A prime number and a factor of 39.

e An odd factor of 30 and a multiple of 3.

f A number with four factors and a multiple of 2 and 7.

g A number with five factors exactly.

h A triangular number and a factor of 20.

i An even number and a factor of 36 and a multiple of 9.

j A prime number that is one more than a square number.

k If you write the factors of this number out in order they make a number pattern in which each number is twice the one before.

l An odd triangular number that is a multiple of 7.

2 If hot-dog sausages are sold in packs of 10 and hot-dog buns are sold in packs of 8, how many of each do you have to buy to have complete hot dogs with no wasted sausages or buns?

3 Rover barks every 8 seconds and Spot barks every 12 seconds. If they both bark together, how many seconds will it be before they both bark together again?

4 A bell chimes every 6 seconds. Another bell chimes every 5 seconds. If they both chime together, how many seconds will it be before they both chime together again.

5 Copy these sums and write out the *next four* lines.

$$1 = 1$$
$$1 + 3 = 4$$
$$1 + 3 + 5 = 9$$
$$1 + 3 + 5 + 7 = 16$$

6 Write down the negative square root of each of these.

    a 4   **b** 25   **c** 49   **d** 1   **e** 81

    f 121   **g** 144   **h** 400   **i** 900   **j** 169

7 Write down the cube root of each of these.

    a 1   **b** 27   **c** 64   **d** 8   **e** 1000

    f −8   **g** −1   **h** 8000   **i** 64 000   **j** −64

8 The triangular numbers are 1, 3, 6, 10, 15, 21 …

    a Continue the sequence until the triangular number is greater than 100.

    b Add up consecutive pairs of triangular numbers starting with 1 + 3 = 4, 3 + 6 = 9, etc. What do you notice?

9 **a** $36^3 = 46\,656$. Work out $1^3, 4^3, 9^3, 16^3, 25^3$.

    b $\sqrt{46656} = 216$. Use a calculator to find the square roots of the numbers you worked out in part **a**.

    c 216 = 36 × 6. Can you find a similar connection between the answer to part b and the numbers cubed in part **a**?

    d What type of numbers are 1, 4, 9, 16, 25, 36?

10 Write down the values of these

    a $\sqrt{0.04}$ **b** $\sqrt{0.25}$ **c** $\sqrt{0.36}$ **d** $\sqrt{0.81}$

    e $\sqrt{1.44}$ **f** $\sqrt{0.64}$ **g** $\sqrt{1.21}$ **h** $\sqrt{2.25}$

11 Estimate the answers to these.

    a $\dfrac{13.7 + 21.9}{\sqrt{0.239}}$ **b** $\dfrac{29.6 \times 11.9}{\sqrt{0.038}}$ **c** $\dfrac{87.5 - 32.6}{\sqrt{0.8} - \sqrt{0.38}}$

This section will show you how to:

- write a number as a product of its prime factors
- find the least common multiple (LCM) and highest common factor (HCF) of two numbers

Key words
highest common factor (HCF)
least common multiple (LCM)
prime factor

Start with a number – say 110 – and find two numbers which, when multiplied together, give that number, for example, 2×55. Are they both prime? No. So take 55 and repeat the operation, to get 5×11. Are these prime? Yes. So:

$$110 = 2 \times 5 \times 11$$

These are the **prime factors** of 110.

This method is not very logical and needs good tables skills. There are, however, two methods that you can use to make sure you do not miss any of the prime factors.

The next two examples show you how to use the first of these methods.

EXAMPLE 5

Find the prime factors of 24.

Divide 24 by any prime number that goes into it. (2 is an obvious choice.)

Divide the answer (12) by a prime number. Repeat this process until you have a prime number as the answer.

2	24
2	12
2	6
	3

So the prime factors of 24 are $2 \times 2 \times 2 \times 3$.

A quicker and neater way to write this answer is to use index notation, expressing the answer in powers. (Powers are dealt with in Chapter 7.)

In index notation, the prime factors of 24 are $2^3 \times 3$.

EXAMPLE 6

Find the prime factors of 96.

2	96
2	48
2	24
2	12
2	6
	3

So, the prime factors of 96 are $2 \times 2 \times 2 \times 2 \times 2 \times 3 = 2^5 \times 3$.

The second method is called prime factor trees. You start by splitting the number into a multiplication sum. Then you split this, and carry on splitting until you get to prime numbers.

EXAMPLE 7

Find the prime factors of 76.

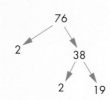

We stop splitting the factors here because 2, 2 and 19 are all prime numbers.

So, the prime factors of 76 are $2 \times 2 \times 19 = 2^2 \times 19$.

EXAMPLE 8

Find the prime factors of 420.

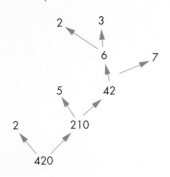

The process can be done upside down to make an upright tree.

So, the prime factors of 420 are

$$2 \times 5 \times 2 \times 3 \times 7 = 2^2 \times 3 \times 5 \times 7.$$

EXERCISE 4H

1 Copy and complete these prime factor trees.

a

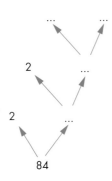

b

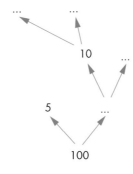

c

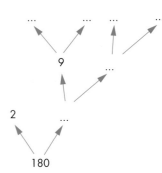

d

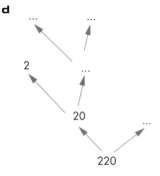

e

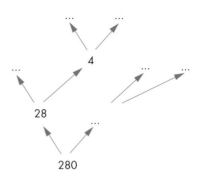

f

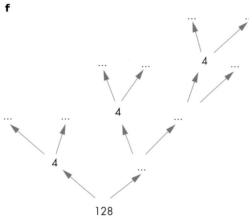

g

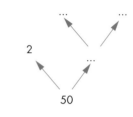

2 Using index notation, for example,

$$100 = 2 \times 2 \times 5 \times 5 = 2^2 \times 5^2$$

and $540 = 2 \times 2 \times 3 \times 3 \times 3 \times 5 = 2^2 \times 3^3 \times 5$

rewrite the answers to question **1** parts **a** to **g**.

3 Write the numbers from 1 to 50 in prime factors. Use index notation. For example,

$$1 = 1 \qquad 2 = 2 \qquad 3 = 3 \qquad 4 = 2^2 \qquad 5 = 5 \qquad 6 = 2 \times 3 \qquad \ldots$$

4 **a** What is special about the prime factors of 2, 4, 8, 16, 32, …?

b What are the next two terms in this sequence?

c What are the next three terms in the sequence 3, 9, 27, …?

d Continue the sequence 4, 16, 64, …, for three more terms.

e Write all the above sequences in index notation. For example, the first sequence is

$$2, 2^2, 2^3, 2^4, 2^5, 2^6, 2^7, \ldots$$

Least common multiple

The **least** (or lowest) **common multiple** (usually called the **LCM**) of two numbers is the smallest number that belongs in both times tables.

For example the LCM of 3 and 5 is 15, the LCM of 2 and 7 is 14 and the LCM of 6 and 9 is 18.

There are two ways of working out the LCM.

EXAMPLE 9

Find the LCM of 18 and 24.

Write out the 18 times table: 18, 36, 54, ⟨72⟩, 90, 108, … .

Write out the 24 times table: 24, 48, ⟨72⟩, 96, 120, …

You can see that 72 is the smallest (least) number in both (common) tables (multiples).

EXAMPLE 10

Find the LCM of 42 and 63.

Write 42 in prime factor form. $42 = 2 \times 3 \times 7$

Write 63 in prime factor form. $63 = 3^2 \times 7$

Write down the smallest number in prime factor form that includes all the prime factors of 42 and of 63.

You need $2 \times 3^2 \times 7$ (this includes $2 \times 3 \times 7$ and $3^2 \times 7$).

Then work it out.

$2 \times 3^2 \times 7 = 2 \times 9 \times 7 = 18 \times 7 = 126$

The LCM of 42 and 63 is 126.

Highest common factor

The **highest common factor** (usually called the **HCF**) of two numbers is the biggest number that divides exactly into both of them.

For example the HCF of 24 and 18 is 6, the HCF of 45 and 36 is 9 and the HCF of 15 and 22 is 1.

There are two ways of working out the HCF.

EXAMPLE 11

Find the HCF of 28 and 16.

Write out the factors of 28.   1, 2, ⟨4⟩, 7, 14, 28

Write out the factors of 16.   1, 2, ⟨4⟩, 8, 16

You can see that 4 is the biggest (highest) number in both (common) lists (factors).

EXAMPLE 12

Find the HCF of 48 and 120.

Write 48 in prime factor form. $48 = 2^4 \times 3$

Write 120 in prime factor form. $120 = 2^3 \times 3 \times 5$

Write down the biggest number in prime factor form that is in the prime factors of 48 and 120.

You need $2^3 \times 3$ (this is in both $2^4 \times 3$ and $2^3 \times 3 \times 5$).

Then work it out.

$2^3 \times 3 = 8 \times 3 = 24$

The HCF of 48 and 120 is 24.

EXERCISE 4I

1. Find the LCM of each of these pairs of numbers.

   a 4 and 5   **b** 7 and 8   **c** 2 and 3   **d** 4 and 7

   e 2 and 5   **f** 3 and 5   **g** 3 and 8   **h** 5 and 6

2. What connection is there between the LCM and the pairs of numbers in question **1**?

3. Find the LCM of each of these pairs of numbers.

   a 4 and 8   **b** 6 and 9   **c** 4 and 6   **d** 10 and 15

4. Does the same connection you found in question **2** still work for the numbers in question **3**? If not, can you explain why?

5. Find the LCM of each of these pairs of numbers.

   a 24 and 56   **b** 21 and 35   **c** 12 and 28   **d** 28 and 42

   e 12 and 48   **f** 18 and 27   **g** 15 and 25   **h** 16 and 36

6. Find the HCF of each of these pairs of numbers.

   a 24 and 56   **b** 21 and 35   **c** 12 and 28   **d** 28 and 42

   e 12 and 48   **f** 18 and 27   **g** 15 and 25   **h** 16 and 36

   i 42 and 27   **j** 48 and 64   **k** 25 and 35   **l** 36 and 54

7. In prime factor form $1250 = 2 \times 5^4$ and $525 = 3 \times 5^2 \times 7$.

   a Which of these are common multiples of 1250 and 525?

   i $2 \times 3 \times 5^3 \times 7$ **ii** $2^3 \times 3 \times 5^4 \times 7^2$ **iii** $2 \times 3 \times 5^4 \times 7$ **iv** $2 \times 3 \times 5 \times 7$

   b Which of these are common factors of 1250 and 525?

   i 2×3 **ii** 2×5 **iii** 5^2 **iv** $2 \times 3 \times 5 \times 7$

Negative numbers

This section will show you how to:
- multiply and divide with positive and negative numbers

Key words
positive
negative

Multiplying and dividing with negative numbers

The rules for multiplying and dividing with negative numbers are very easy.

- When the signs of the numbers are the *same*, the answer is **positive**.

- When the signs of the numbers are *different*, the answer is **negative**.

Here are some examples.

$$2 \times 4 = 8 \qquad 12 \div -3 = -4$$
$$-2 \times -3 = 6 \qquad -12 \div -3 = 4$$

Negative numbers on a calculator

You can enter a negative number into your calculator and check the result.

Enter –5 by pressing the keys **5** and **+/−** . (You may need to press **+/−** or **−** followed by **5** , depending on the type of calculator that you have.) You will see the calculator shows –5.

Now try these two calculations.

$-8 - 7 \rightarrow$ **8** **+/−** **−** **7** **=** –15

$6 - -3 \rightarrow$ **6** **−** **−** **3** **=** 9

EXERCISE 4J

1 Write down the answers to the following.

    a -3×5 **b** -2×7 **c** -4×6 **d** -2×-3 **e** -7×-2

    f $-12 \div -6$ **g** $-16 \div 8$ **h** $24 \div -3$ **i** $16 \div -4$ **j** $-6 \div -2$

    k 4×-6 **l** 5×-2 **m** 6×-3 **n** -2×-8 **o** -9×-4

2 Write down the answers to the following.

    a $-3 + -6$ **b** -2×-8 **c** $2 + -5$ **d** 8×-4 **e** $-36 \div -2$

    f -3×-6 **g** $-3 - -9$ **h** $48 \div -12$ **i** -5×-4 **j** $7 - -9$

    k $-40 \div -5$ **l** $-40 + -8$ **m** $4 - -9$ **n** $5 - 18$ **o** $72 \div -9$

D

D

3 What number do you multiply −3 by to get the following?

    a 6   **b** −90   **c** −45   **d** 81   **e** 21

4 Evaluate the following.

    a −6 + (4 − 7)   **b** −3 − (−9 − −3)   **c** 8 + (2 − 9)

5 Evaluate the following.

    a 4 × (−8 ÷ −2)   **b** −8 − (3 × −2)   **c** −1 × (8 − −4)

6 Write down six different division sums that give the answer −4.

Hierarchy of operations

You will remember BODMAS (Brackets, Order, Division, Multiplication, Addition, Subtraction) which tells you the order in which to do mathematical operations in complex calculations. Many errors are made in GCSE due to negative signs and doing calculations in the wrong order. For example -6^2 could be taken as $(-6)^2 = +36$ or $-(6^2) = -36$. It should be the second of these as the power (order) would come before the minus sign.

EXERCISE 4K

D

1 Work out each of these. Remember to work out the bracket first.

    a −2 × (−3 + 5) =   **b** 6 ÷ (−2 + 1) =   **c** (5 − 7) × −2 =

    d −5 × (−7 − 2) =   **e** −3 × (−4 ÷ 2) =   **f** −3 × (−4 + 2) =

2 Work out each of these.

    a −6 × −6 + 2 =   **b** −6 × (−6 + 2) =   **c** −6 ÷ 6 − 2 =

    d 12 ÷ (−4 + 2) =   **e** 12 ÷ −4 + 2 =   **f** 2 × (−3 + 4) =

    g $-(5)^2$ =   **h** $(-5)^2$ =   **i** $(-1 + 3)^2 - 4$ =

    j $-(1 + 3)^2 - 4$ =   **k** $-1 + 3^2 - 4$ =   **l** $-1 + (3 - 4)^2$ =

3 Copy each of these and then put in brackets where necessary to make each one true.

    a 3 × −4 + 1 = −11   **b** −6 ÷ −2 + 1 = 6   **c** −6 ÷ −2 + 1 = 4

    d 4 + −4 ÷ 4 = 3   **e** 4 + −4 ÷ 4 = 0   **f** 16 − −4 ÷ 2 = 10

4 $a = -2$, $b = 3$, $c = -5$.

    Work out the values of the following.

    a $(a + c)^2$ **b** $-(a + b)^2$ **c** $(a + b)c$ **d** $a^2 + b^2 - c^2$

1 Frank earns £12 per hour. He works for 40 hours per week. He saves $\frac{1}{5}$ of his earnings each week.

How many weeks will it take him to save £500?

2 A bathroom wall measures 2.55 metres by 2.85 metres. It is to be covered with square tiles of side 15 centimetres. Tiles are sold in boxes of 24. How many boxes are needed?

AQA, Question 6, Paper 2 Intermediate, November 2003

3 As the product of prime factors $60 = 2^2 \times 3 \times 5$

  a What number is represented by $2 \times 3^2 \times 5$?

  b Find the least common multiple (LCM) of 60 and 48?

  c Find the highest common factor (HCF) of 60 and 78?

4 **a** Write 28 as the product of its prime factors.

  b Find the least common multiple (LCM) of 28 and 42.

  AQA, Question 21, Paper 1 Intermediate, November 2004

5 Hannah, Gemma and Jo use their calculators to work out the value of

$$\frac{28.78}{4.31 \times 0.47}$$

Hannah gets 142.07, Gemma gets 14.207 and Jo gets 3.138

Use approximations to show which one of them is correct. You *must* show your working.

AQA, Question 16, Paper 1 Intermediate, November 2004

6 Use approximations to estimate the value of

$$\frac{212 \times 7.88}{0.365}$$

7 Tom, Sam and Matt are counting drum beats.

Tom hits a snare drum every 2 beats.
Sam hits a kettle drum every 5 beats.
Matt hits a bass drum every 8 beats.

Tom, Sam and Matt start by hitting their drums at the same time.

How many beats is it before Tom, Sam and Matt *next* hit their drums at the *same* time?

AQA, Question 14, Paper 1 Intermediate, June 2004

8 **a** You are given that $8x^3 = 1000$.
    Find the value of x.

  b Write 150 as the product of its prime factors.

9 **a** p and q are prime numbers such that $pq^3 = 250$
    Find the values of p and q.

  b Find the highest common factor of 250 and 80.

10 **a** a and b are prime numbers such that $(ab)^3 = 1000$
    What are the values of a and b?

  b p and q are integers such that $(pq)^3 = 216$
    Explain why it is not possible to find values of p and q.

WORKED EXAM QUESTION

Estimate the result of the calculation

$$\frac{195.71 - 53.62}{\sqrt{0.0375}}$$

Show the estimates you make.

Solution

$$\frac{200 - 50}{\sqrt{0.04}}$$

First round off each number to 1 significant figure.

$$\frac{150}{0.2}$$

Work out the numerator and do the square root in the denominator

$$\frac{150}{0.2} = \frac{1500}{2} = 750$$

Change the problem so it becomes division by an integer

GRADE YOURSELF

D Able to recognise and work out multiples, factors and primes

D Able to multiply and divide with negative numbers

D Able to estimate the values of calculations involving positive numbers bigger than one

D Able to round numbers to a given number of significant figures

C Able to estimate the values of calculations involving positive numbers between zero and one

C Able to write a number as the product of its prime factors

C Able to work out the LCM and HCF of pairs of numbers

C Able to use a calculator efficiently and know how to give answers to an appropriate degree of accuracy

B Able to work out the square roots of some decimal numbers

B Able to estimate answers involving the square roots of decimals

What you should know now

- How to solve complex real-life problems without a calculator

- How to divide by decimals of up to two decimal places

- How to estimate the values of calculations including those with decimal numbers, and use a calculator efficiently

- How to write a number in prime factor form and find LCMs and HCFs

- How to find the square roots of some decimal numbers

Fractions and percentages

This chapter will show you ...

- how to apply the four rules (addition, subtraction, multiplication and division) to fractions
- how to calculate the final value after a percentage increase or decrease
- how to calculate compound interest
- how to calculate the original value after a percentage increase or decrease

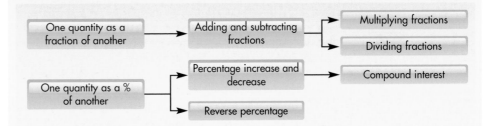

What you should already know

- How to cancel down fractions to their simplest form
- How to find equivalent fractions, decimals and percentages
- How to add and subtract fractions with the same denominator
- How to work out simple percentages, such as 10%, of quantities
- How to convert a mixed number to a top-heavy fraction and vice versa

Quick check

1 Cancel down the following fractions to their simplest form.

  a $\frac{8}{20}$ **b** $\frac{12}{32}$ **c** $\frac{15}{35}$

2 Complete this table of equivalences.

Fraction	Percentage	Decimal
$\frac{3}{4}$		
	40%	
		0.55

3 What is 10% of

  a £230   **b** £46.00   **c** £2.30

One quantity as a fraction of another

This section will show you how to:
● find one quantity as a fraction of another

Key words
cancel
fraction

An amount often needs to be given as a **fraction** of another amount.

EXAMPLE 1

Write £5 as a fraction of £20.

As a fraction this is written $\frac{5}{20}$. This **cancels** down to $\frac{1}{4}$.

EXERCISE 5A

D

1. Write the first quantity as a fraction of the second.

   a 2 cm, 6 cm   b 4 kg, 20 kg

   c £8, £20   d 5 hours, 24 hours

   e 12 days, 30 days   f 50p, £3

   g 4 days, 2 weeks   h 40 minutes, 2 hours

2. In a form of 30 pupils, 18 are boys. What fraction of the form consists of boys?

3. During March, it rained on 12 days. For what fraction of the month did it rain?

4. Linda wins £120 in a competition. She keeps some to spend and puts £50 into her bank account. What fraction of her winnings does she keep to spend?

C

5. Frank gets a pay rise from £120 a week to £135 a weak. What fraction of his original pay was his pay rise?

6. When she was born Alice had a mass of 3 kg. After a month she had a mass of 4 kg 250 g. What fraction of her original mass had she increased by?

7. After the breeding season a bat colony increased in size from 90 bats to 108 bats. What fraction had the size of the colony increased by?

8. After dieting Bart went from 80 kg to 68 kg. What fraction did his weight decrease by?

Adding and subtracting fractions

This section will show you how to:
- add and subtract fractions with different denominators

Key words

denominator
equivalent
  fraction
lowest common
  denominator

Fractions can only be added or subtracted after we have changed them to **equivalent fractions**, both having the same **denominator**.

EXAMPLE 2

Work out $\frac{5}{6} - \frac{3}{4}$

The **lowest common denominator** of 4 and 6 is 12.

The problem becomes $\frac{5}{6} - \frac{3}{4} = \frac{5}{6} \times \frac{2}{2} - \frac{3}{4} \times \frac{3}{3} = \frac{10}{12} - \frac{9}{12} = \frac{1}{12}$

EXAMPLE 3

Work out **a** $2\frac{1}{3} + 3\frac{5}{7}$ **b** $3\frac{1}{4} - 1\frac{3}{5}$

The best way to deal with addition and subtraction of mixed numbers is to deal with the whole numbers and the fractions separately.

a $2\frac{1}{3} + 3\frac{5}{7} = 2 + 3 + \frac{1}{3} + \frac{5}{7} = 5 + \frac{7}{21} + \frac{15}{21} = 5 + \frac{22}{21} = 5 + 1\frac{1}{21} = 6\frac{1}{21}$

b $3\frac{1}{4} - 1\frac{3}{5} = 3 - 1 + \frac{1}{4} - \frac{3}{5} = 2 + \frac{5}{20} - \frac{12}{20} = 2 - \frac{7}{20} = 1\frac{13}{20}$

EXERCISE 5B

1 Evaluate the following.

   a $\frac{1}{3} + \frac{1}{5}$ **b** $\frac{1}{3} + \frac{1}{4}$ **c** $\frac{1}{5} + \frac{1}{10}$ **d** $\frac{2}{3} + \frac{1}{4}$

   e $\frac{1}{5} - \frac{1}{10}$ **f** $\frac{7}{8} - \frac{3}{4}$ **g** $\frac{5}{6} - \frac{3}{4}$ **h** $\frac{5}{6} - \frac{1}{2}$

2 Evaluate the following.

   a $\frac{1}{3} + \frac{4}{9}$ **b** $\frac{1}{4} + \frac{3}{8}$ **c** $\frac{7}{8} - \frac{1}{2}$ **d** $\frac{3}{5} - \frac{8}{15}$

   e $1\frac{7}{18} + 2\frac{3}{10}$ **f** $3\frac{1}{3} + 1\frac{9}{20}$ **g** $1\frac{1}{8} - \frac{5}{9}$ **h** $1\frac{3}{16} - \frac{7}{12}$

   i $\frac{5}{6} + \frac{7}{16} + \frac{5}{8}$ **j** $\frac{7}{10} + \frac{3}{8} + \frac{5}{6}$ **k** $1\frac{1}{3} + \frac{7}{10} - \frac{4}{15}$ **l** $\frac{5}{14} + 1\frac{3}{7} - \frac{5}{12}$

D

D

3 In a class of children, three-quarters are Chinese, one-fifth are Malay and the rest are Indian. What fraction of the class are Indian?

4 In a class election, half of the pupils voted for Aminah, one-third voted for Janet and the rest voted for Peter. What fraction of the class voted for Peter?

5 A one-litre flask filled with milk is used to fill two glasses, one of capacity half a litre, and the other of capacity one-sixth of a litre. What fraction of a litre will remain in the flask?

6 Because of illness, $\frac{2}{5}$ of a school was absent one day. If the school had 650 pupils on the register, how many were absent that day?

7 Which is the biggest: half of 96, one-third of 141, two-fifths of 120, or three-quarters of 68?

8 To increase sales, a shop reduced the price of a car stereo radio by $\frac{2}{5}$. If the original price was £85, what was the new price?

9 At a burger-eating competition, Lionel ate 34 burgers in 20 minutes while Brian ate 26 burgers in 20 minutes. How long after the start of the competition would they have consumed a total of 30 burgers between them?

C

5.3 Multiplying fractions

This section will show you how to:
- multiply fractions

Key words
cancel
denominator
numerator

There are four steps to multiplying fractions.

Step 1: make any mixed numbers into top-heavy fractions.

Step 2: cancel out any common multiples on the top and bottom.

Step 3: multiply together the **numerators** to get the new numerator, and multiply the **denominators** to get the new denominator.

Step 4: if the fraction is top-heavy, make it into a mixed number.

EXAMPLE 4

Work out   **a** $\frac{4}{9} \times \frac{3}{10}$ **b** $2\frac{2}{5} \times 1\frac{7}{8}$

a 4 and 10 are both multiples of 2, and 3 and 9 are both multiples of 3. Cancel out the common multiples before multiplying.

$$\frac{{}^2\cancel{4}}{{}_3\cancel{9}} \times \frac{\cancel{3}^1}{\cancel{10}_5} = \frac{2}{15}$$

b Make the mixed numbers into top heavy fractions, then cancel if possible. Change the answer back to a mixed number.

$$2\frac{2}{5} \times 1\frac{7}{8} \qquad \frac{{}^3\cancel{12}}{{}_1\cancel{5}} \times \frac{\cancel{15}^3}{\cancel{8}_2} = \frac{9}{2} = 4\frac{1}{2}$$

EXERCISE 5C

1 Evaluate the following, leaving your answers in their simplest form.

a $\frac{1}{2} \times \frac{1}{3}$ **b** $\frac{1}{4} \times \frac{2}{5}$ **c** $\frac{3}{4} \times \frac{1}{2}$ **d** $\frac{3}{7} \times \frac{1}{2}$

e $\frac{14}{15} \times \frac{3}{8}$ **f** $\frac{8}{9} \times \frac{6}{15}$ **g** $\frac{6}{7} \times \frac{21}{30}$ **h** $\frac{9}{14} \times \frac{35}{36}$

2 Evaluate the following, leaving your answers as mixed numbers where possible.

a $1\frac{1}{4} \times \frac{1}{3}$ **b** $1\frac{2}{3} \times 1\frac{1}{4}$ **c** $2\frac{1}{2} \times 2\frac{1}{2}$ **d** $1\frac{3}{4} \times 1\frac{2}{3}$

e $3\frac{1}{4} \times 1\frac{1}{5}$ **f** $1\frac{1}{4} \times 2\frac{2}{3}$ **g** $2\frac{1}{2} \times 5$ **h** $4 \times 7\frac{1}{2}$

3 A merchant buys 28 crates, each containing three-quarters of a tonne of waste metal. What is the total weight of this order?

4 A greedy girl eats one-quarter of a cake, and then half of what is left. How much cake is left uneaten?

5 Kathleen spent three-eighths of her income on rent, and two-fifths of what was left on food. What fraction of her income was left after buying her food?

6 Which is larger, $\frac{3}{4}$ of $2\frac{1}{2}$ or $\frac{2}{5}$ of $6\frac{1}{2}$?

7 After James spent $\frac{2}{5}$ of his pocket money on magazines, and $\frac{1}{4}$ of his pocket money at a football match, he had £1.75 left. How much pocket money did he have in the beginning?

8 If £5.20 is two-thirds of three-quarters of a sum of money, what is the total amount of money?

Dividing by a fraction

This section will show you how to:
● divide by fractions

Key word
reciprocal

To divide by a fraction, we turn the fraction upside down (finding its **reciprocal**), and then multiply.

EXAMPLE 5

Work out $\quad$ **a** $\frac{5}{6} \div \frac{3}{4}$ $\qquad$ **b** $2\frac{1}{2} \div 3\frac{1}{3}$

a Rewrite as $\frac{5}{6} \times \frac{4}{3}$.

$$\frac{5}{6} \div \frac{3}{4} = \frac{5}{6} \times \frac{4^2}{3} = \frac{10}{9} = 1\frac{1}{9}$$

b First make the mixed numbers into top heavy fractions.

$$2\frac{1}{2} \div 3\frac{1}{3} = \frac{5}{2} \div \frac{10}{3} = \frac{5^1}{2} \times \frac{3}{10_2} = \frac{3}{4}$$

EXERCISE 5D

1 Evaluate the following, leaving your answers as mixed numbers where possible.

a $\frac{1}{4} \div \frac{1}{3}$ $\qquad$ **b** $\frac{2}{5} \div \frac{2}{7}$ $\qquad$ **c** $\frac{4}{5} \div \frac{3}{4}$ $\qquad$ **d** $\frac{3}{7} \div \frac{2}{5}$ $\qquad$ **e** $5 \div 1\frac{1}{4}$

f $6 \div 1\frac{1}{2}$ $\qquad$ **g** $7\frac{1}{2} \div 1\frac{1}{2}$ $\qquad$ **h** $3 \div 1\frac{3}{4}$ $\qquad$ **i** $1\frac{5}{12} \div 3\frac{3}{16}$ $\qquad$ **j** $3\frac{3}{5} \div 2\frac{1}{4}$

2 For a party, Zahar made twelve and a half litres of lemonade. His glasses could each hold five-sixteenths of a litre. How many of the glasses could he fill from the twelve and a half litres of lemonade?

3 How many strips of ribbon, each three and a half centimetres long, can I cut from a roll of ribbon that is fifty-two and a half centimetres long?

4 Joe's stride is three-quarters of a metre long. How many strides does he take to walk along a bus twelve metres long?

5 Evaluate the following, leaving your answers as mixed numbers wherever possible.

a $2\frac{2}{9} \times 2\frac{1}{10} \times \frac{16}{35}$ $\qquad$ **b** $3\frac{1}{5} \times 2\frac{1}{2} \times 4\frac{3}{4}$ $\qquad$ **c** $1\frac{1}{4} \times 1\frac{2}{7} \times 1\frac{1}{6}$ $\qquad$ **d** $\frac{18}{25} \times \frac{15}{16} \div 2\frac{2}{5}$

e $(\frac{2}{5} \times \frac{2}{5}) \times (\frac{5}{6} \times \frac{5}{6}) \times (\frac{3}{4} \times \frac{3}{4})$ $\qquad$ **f** $(\frac{4}{5} \times \frac{4}{5}) \div (1\frac{1}{4} \times 1\frac{1}{4})$

D

C

Percentage increase and decrease

This section will show you how to:
- calculate percentage increases and decreases

Key words

multiplier
percentage
decrease
percentage
increase

Increase

There are two methods for **increasing** by a **percentage**.

Method 1
Find the increase and add it to the original amount.

EXAMPLE 6

Increase £6 by 5%.

Find 5% of £6: $\frac{5}{100} \times 600p = 30p$. 5% of £6 = £0.30.

Add the £0.30 to the original amount: £6 + £0.30 = £6.30.

Method 2
Using a **multiplier**. An increase of 6% is equivalent to the original 100% plus the extra 6%. This is a total of 106% ($\frac{106}{100}$) and is equivalent to the multiplier 1.06.

EXAMPLE 7

Increase £6.80 by 5%.

A 5% increase is a multiplier of 1.05.

So £6.80 increased by 5% is £6.80 × 1.05 = £7.14

EXERCISE 5E

1 What multiplier is equivalent to a percentage increase of each of the following?

    a 10%   **b** 3%   **c** 20%   **d** 7%   **e** 12%

2 Increase each of the following by the given percentage. (Use any method you like.)

    a £60 by 4%   **b** 12 kg by 8%   **c** 450 g by 5%   **d** 545 m by 10%

    e £34 by 12%   **f** £75 by 20%   **g** 340 kg by 15%   **h** 670 cm by 23%

    i 130 g by 95%   **j** £82 by 75%   **k** 640 m by 15%   **l** £28 by 8%

3 In 2000 the population of Melchester was 1 565 000. By 2005 that had increased by 8%. What was the population of Melchester in 2005?

4 A small firm made the same pay increase for all its employees: 5%.

    a Calculate the new pay of each employee listed below. Each of their salaries before the increase is given.

        Bob, caretaker, £16 500   Jean, supervisor, £19 500
        Anne, tea lady, £17 300   Brian, manager, £25 300

    b Is the actual pay increase the same for each worker?

5 An advertisement for a breakfast cereal states that a special offer packet contains 15% more cereal for the same price than a normal 500 g packet. How much breakfast cereal is in a special offer packet?

6 At a school disco there are always about 20% more girls than boys. If at one disco there were 50 boys, how many girls were there?

7 VAT is a tax that the government adds to the price of most goods in shops. At the moment, it is 17.5% on all electrical equipment.

Calculate the price of the following electrical equipment after VAT of 17.5% has been added.

Equipment	Pre-VAT price
TV set	£245
Microwave oven	£72
CD player	£115
Personal stereo	£29.50

8 A hi-fi system was priced at £420 at the start of 2004. At the start of 2005, it was 12% more expensive. At the start of 2006, it was 15% more expensive than the price at the start of 2005. What is the price of the hi-fi at the start of 2006?

9 A quick way to work out VAT is to divide the pre-VAT price by 6. For example, the VAT on an item costing £120 is approximately £120 ÷ 6 = £20. Show that this approximate method gives the VAT correct to within £5 for pre-VAT prices up to £600.

Decrease

There are two methods for **decreasing** by a **percentage**.

Method 1
Find the decrease and take it away from the original amount.

EXAMPLE 8

Decrease £8 by 4%.

Find 4% of £8: $\dfrac{4}{100} \times 800p = 32p$. 4% of £8 = £0.32.

Take the £0.32 away from the original amount: £8 − £0.32 = £7.68.

Method 2
Using a multiplier. A 7% decrease is 7% less than the original 100%, so it represents 100% − 7% = 93% of the original. This is a multiplier of 0.93.

EXAMPLE 9

Decrease £8.60 by 5%.

A decrease of 5% is a multiplier of 0.95.

So £8.60 decreased by 5% is £8.60 × 0.95 = £8.17

EXERCISE 5F

1 What multiplier is equivalent to a percentage decrease of each of the following?

    a 8%   **b** 15%   **c** 25%   **d** 9%   **e** 12%

2 Decrease each of the following by the given percentage. (Use any method you like.)

    a £10 by 6%   **b** 25 kg by 8%   **c** 236 g by 10%

    d 350 m by 3%   **e** £5 by 2%   **f** 45 m by 12%

    g 860 m by 15%   **h** 96 g by 13%   **i** 480 cm by 25%

3 A car valued at £6500 last year is now worth 15% less. What is its value now?

4 A large factory employed 640 people. It had to streamline its workforce and lose 30% of the workers. How big is the workforce now?

5 On the last day of the Christmas term, a school expects to have an absence rate of 6%. If the school population is 750 pupils, how many pupils will the school expect to see on the last day of the Christmas term?

6 Since the start of the National Lottery a particular charity called Young Ones said it has seen a 45% decrease in the money raised from its scratch cards. If before the Lottery the charity had an annual income of £34 500 from its scratch cards, how much does it collect now?

7 Most speedometers in cars have an error of about 5% from the true reading. When my speedometer says I am driving at 70 mph,

a what is the slowest speed I could be doing,

b what is the fastest speed I could be doing?

8 You are a member of a club which allows you to claim a 12% discount off any marked price in shops. What will you pay in total for the following goods?

Sweatshirt   £19

Tracksuit   £26

9 I read an advertisement in my local newspaper last week which stated: "By lagging your roof and hot water system you will use 18% less fuel." Since I was using an average of 640 units of gas a year, I thought I would lag my roof and my hot water system. How much gas would I expect to use now?

10 A computer system was priced at £1000 at the start of 2004. At the start of 2005, it was 10% cheaper. At the start of 2006, it was 15% cheaper than the price at the start of 2005. What is the price of the computer system at the start of 2006?

11 Show that a 10% decrease followed by a 10% increase is equivalent to a 1% decrease overall.

> **HINTS AND TIPS**
>
> Choose an amount to start with.

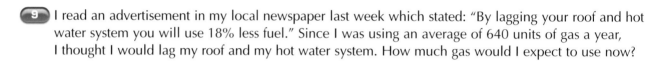

5.6 Expressing one quantity as a percentage of another

This section will show you how to:
- express one quantity as a percentage of another

Key words
percentage gain
percentage loss

Method 1

We express one quantity as a percentage of another by setting up the first quantity as a fraction of the second, making sure that the *units of each are the same*. Then, we convert that fraction to a percentage by simply multiplying it by 100%.

EXAMPLE 10

Express £6 as a percentage of £40.

Set up the fraction and multiply it by 100%. This gives:

$$\frac{6}{40} \times 100\% = 15\%$$

EXAMPLE 11

Express 75 cm as a percentage of 2.5 m.

First, change 2.5 m to 250 cm to get a common unit.

Hence, the problem becomes 75 cm as a percentage of 250 cm.

Set up the fraction and multiply it by 100%. This gives

$$\frac{75}{250} \times 100\% = 30\%$$

We can use this method to calculate **percentage gain** or **loss** in a financial transaction.

EXAMPLE 12

Bert buys a car for £1500 and sells it for £1800. What is Bert's percentage gain?

Bert's gain is £300, so his percentage gain is

$$\frac{300}{1500} \times 100\% = 20\%$$

Notice how the percentage gain is found by

$$\frac{\text{difference}}{\text{original}} \times 100\%$$

Method 2
This method uses a multiplier. Divide the increase by the original quantity and change the resulting decimal to a percentage.

EXAMPLE 13

Express 5 as a percentage of 40.

$$5 \div 40 = 0.125$$
$$0.125 = 12.5\%.$$

EXERCISE 5G

1 Express each of the following as a percentage. Give suitably rounded off figures where necessary.

a £5 of £20

b £4 of £6.60

c 241 kg of 520 kg

d 3 hours of 1 day

e 25 minutes of 1 hour

f 12 m of 20 m

g 125 g of 600 g

h 12 minutes of 2 hours

i 1 week of a year

j 1 month of 1 year

k 25 cm of 55 cm

l 105 g of 1 kg

2 John went to school with his pocket money of £2.50. He spent 80p at the tuck shop. What percentage of his pocket money had he spent?

3 In Greece, there are 3 654 000 acres of agricultural land. Olives are grown on 237 000 acres of this land. What percentage of agricultural land is used for olives?

4 During the wet year of 1981, it rained in Manchester on 123 days of the year. What percentage of days were wet?

5 Find, to one decimal place, the percentage profit on the following.

Item	Retail price (selling price)	Wholesale price (price the shop paid)
a CD player	£89.50	£60
b TV set	£345.50	£210
c Computer	£829.50	£750

6 Before Anton started to diet, he weighed 95 kg. He now weighs 78 kg. What percentage of his original weight has he lost?

7 In 2004 the Melchester County Council raised £14 870 000 in council tax. In 2005 it raised £15 970 000 in council tax. What was the percentage increase?

8 When Blackburn Rovers won the championship in 1995, they lost only four of their 42 league games. What percentage of games did they not lose?

9 In the year 1900 the value of Britain's imports were as follows.

British Commonwealth	£109 530 000
USA	£138 790 000
France	£53 620 000
Other countries	£221 140 000

a What percentage of the total imports came from each source?

b Add up the answers to part **a**. Explain your answer.

This section will show you how to:
- calculate compound interest
- solve problems involving repeated percentage change

Key words

annual rate
multiplier
principal

Compound interest is calculated where the interest earned at the end of the first year is added to the **principal** (original amount), and the new total amount then earns further interest at the same **annual rate** in the following year. (Compound interest is usually used to calculate the interest on savings accounts.) This pattern is repeated year after year while the money is in the account. Therefore, the amount in the account grows bigger by the year, as does the actual amount of interest. The best way to calculate the total interest is to use a **multiplier**.

EXAMPLE 14

A bank pays 6% compound interest per year on all amounts in a savings account. What is the final amount that Elizabeth will have in her account if she has kept £400 in her bank for three years?

The amount in the bank increases by 6% each year, so the multiplier is 1.06, and

after 1 year she will have £400 × 1.06 = £424

after 2 years she will have £424 × 1.06 = £449.44

after 3 years she will have £449.44 × 1.06 = £476.41 (rounded)

If you calculate the differences, you can see that the actual increase gets bigger and bigger.

From this example, you can see that you could have used £400 × $(1.06)^3$ to find the amount after 3 years. That is, you could have used the following formula for calculating the total amount due at any time:

total amount = P × multiplier raised to the power n = $P \times (1 + x)^n$

where P is the original amount invested, x is the rate of interest expressed as a decimal, and n is the number of years for which the money is invested.

So, in Example 14, $P = £400$, $x = 0.06$, and $n = 3$,

and the total amount = £400 × $(1.06)^3$

Using your calculator

You may have noticed that you can do the above calculation on your calculator without having to write down all the intermediate steps.

To add on the 6% each time just means multiplying by 1.06 each time. That is, you can do the calculation as

Or

[4] [0] [0] [×] [1] [•] [0] [6] [x^y] [3] [=]

Or

[4] [0] [0] [×] [1] [0] [6] [%] [x^y] [3] [=]

You need to find the method with which you are comfortable and which you understand.

The idea of compound interest does not only concern money. It can be about, for example, the growth in population, increases in salaries, or increases in body weight or height. Also the idea can involve regular reduction by a fixed percentage: for example, car depreciation, population losses and even water losses. Work through the next exercise and you will see the extent to which compound interest ideas are used.

EXERCISE 5H

1 A baby octopus increases its body weight by 5% each day for the first month of its life. In a safe ocean zoo, a baby octopus was born weighing 10 kg.

    a What was its weight after

        i 1 day?   **ii** 2 days?   **iii** 4 days?   **iv** 1 week?

    b After how many days will the octopus first weigh over 15 kg?

2 A certain type of conifer hedging increases in height by 17% each year for the first 20 years. When I bought some of this hedging, it was all about 50 cm tall. How long will it take to grow 3 m tall?

3 The manager of a small family business offered his staff an annual pay increase of 4% for every year they stayed with the firm.

    a Gareth started work at the business on a salary of £12 200. What salary will he be on after 4 years?

    b Julie started work at the business on a salary of £9350. How many years will it be until she is earning a salary of over £20 000?

4 Scientists have been studying the shores of Scotland and estimate that due to pollution the seal population of those shores will decline at the rate of 15% each year. In 2006 they counted around 3000 seals on those shores.

   a If nothing is done about pollution, how many seals will they expect to be there in

   i 2007?   **ii** 2008?   **iii** 2011?

   b How long will it take for the seal population to be less than 1000?

5 I am told that if I buy a new car its value will depreciate at the rate of 20% each year. I buy a car in 2006 priced at £8500. What would be the value of the car in

   a 2007?   **b** 2008?   **c** 2010?

6 At the peak of the drought during the summer of 1995, a reservoir in Derbyshire was losing water at the rate of 8% each day. On 1 August this reservoir held 2.1 million litres of water.

   a At this rate of losing water, how much would have been in the reservoir on the following days?

   i 2 August   **ii** 4 August   **iii** 8 August

   b The danger point is when the water drops below 1 million litres. When would this have been if things had continued as they were?

7 The population of a small country, Yebon, was only 46 000 in 1990, but it steadily increased by about 13% each year during the 1990s.

   a Calculate the population in

   i 1991   **ii** 1995   **iii** 1999.

   b If the population keeps growing at this rate, when will it be half a million?

8 How long will it take to accumulate one million pounds in the following situations?

   a An investment of £100 000 at a rate of 12% compound interest.

   b An investment of £50 000 at a rate of 16% compound interest.

 9 An oak tree is 60 cm tall. It grows at a rate of 8% per year. A conifer is 50 cm tall. It grows at a rate of 15% per year. How many years does it take before the conifer is taller than the oak?

 10 A tree increases in height by 18% per year. When it is 1 year old, it is 8 cm tall. How long will it take the tree to grow to 10 m?

 11 Show that a 10% increase followed by a 10% increase is equivalent to a 21% increase overall.

Finding the original quantity (reverse percentage)

This section will show you how to:
- calculate the original amount after you know the result of a percentage increase or decrease

Key words
multiplier
original
  amount
unitary
  method

There are situations when we know a certain percentage and wish to get back to the **original amount**. There are two methods.

Method 1
The first method is the **unitary method**.

EXAMPLE 15

The 70 men who went on strike represented only 20% of the workforce. How large was the workforce?

Since 20% represents 70 people, then

  1% will represent 70 ÷ 20 people [don't work it out]

so 100% will represent (70 ÷ 20) × 100 = 350

Hence the workforce is 350.

Method 2
Using a **multipler**.

EXAMPLE 16

The price of a refrigerator is decreased by 12% in a sale. The new price is £220. What was the original price before the reduction?

A decrease of 12% is a multiplier of 0.88.

Simply divide the new price by the multiplier to get the original price. 220 ÷ 0.88 = 250

So the original price was £250.

EXERCISE 5I

1 Find what 100% represents in these situations.

a 40% represents 320 g

b 14% represents 35 m

c 45% represents 27 cm

d 4% represents £123

e 2.5% represents £5

f 8.5% represents £34

B

2 On a gruelling army training session, only 28 youngsters survived the whole day. This represented 35% of the original group. How large was the original group?

3 VAT is a government tax added to goods and services. With VAT at 17.5%, what is the pre-VAT price of the following priced goods?

T shirt	£9.87	Tights	£1.41
Shorts	£6.11	Sweater	£12.62
Trainers	£29.14	Boots	£38.07

4 Howard spends £200 a month on food. This represents 24% of his monthly take-home pay. How much is his monthly take-home pay?

5 Tina's weekly pay is increased by 5% to £315. What was Tina's pay before the increase?

6 The number of workers in a factory fell by 5% to 228. How many workers were there originally?

7 In a sale a TV is reduced to a price of £325.50. This is a 7% reduction on the original price. What was the original price?

8 If 38% of plastic bottles in a production line are blue and the remaining 7750 plastic bottles are brown, how many plastic bottles are blue?

9 I received £3.85 back from the tax office, which represented the 17.5% VAT on a piece of equipment. How much did I pay for this equipment in the first place?

10 A man's salary was increased by 5% in one year and reduced by 5% in the next year. Is his final salary greater or less than the original one and by how many per cent?

A

11 A quick way of estimating the pre-VAT price of an item with VAT added is to divide by 6 and then multiply by 5. For example, if an item is £360 including VAT, it is approximately (360 ÷ 6) × 5 = £300 before VAT. Show that this gives an estimate to within £5 of the pre-VAT price for items costing up to £280.

1 Mrs Senior earns £320 per week.
She is awarded a pay rise of 4%.
How much does she earn each week after the pay rise?

2 Five boys run a 200 metre race.
Their times are shown in the table.

Name	Andy	Boris	Chris	Darren	Eric
Time (seconds)	25.0	23.4	26.1	22.8	24.2

a Write down the median time.

b The five boys run another 200 metre race.
They all reduce their times by 10%.

i Calculate Andy's new time.

ii Who won this race?

iii Who improved his time by the greatest amount of time?

AQA, Question 15 Foundation, Paper 1, May 2002

3 Mr Shaw's bill for new tyres is £120 plus VAT.
VAT is charged at 17.5%. What is his total bill?

4 Two shops sell CDs.

> **Pops Musical Shop**
> CDs £9.60 each
> By 2 CDs and get a third one FREE

> **Sounds Musical Shop**
> CD SALE
> 30% OFF normal price of £9.60 each

Jamie wants to buy 3 CDs. Which shop offers the better value? You must show all your working.

AQA, Question 21, Paper 2 Foundation, June 2002

5 Mr and Mrs Jones are buying a tumble dryer that normally costs £250. They save 12% in a sale.
How much do they pay for the tumble dryer?

6 Work out the value of $\frac{3}{5} - \frac{3}{8}$

7 On Monday Joe drinks $2\frac{1}{3}$ pints of milk.
On Tuesday he drinks $1\frac{3}{4}$ pints of milk.
Work out the total amount of milk that Joe drinks on Monday and Tuesday.

AQA, Question 13, Paper 1 Intermediate, June 2005

8 Linda uses $\frac{3}{5}$ of a tin of paint to paint a fence panel.
What is the *least* number of tins she needs to paint 8 fence panels?

AQA, Question 8, Paper 2 Intermediate, November 2004

9 For many years, people have tried to find an estimate for the value for π. Here are some of the estimates used.

Greek $\frac{22}{7}$ Hindu $\sqrt{10}$ Egyptian $\frac{256}{81}$ Roman $3\frac{1}{8}$

a Put these estimates in order of size, starting with the smallest. You *must* show all your working.

b The value of π on a calculator is 3.141592654
Which of the above estimates is closest to this value?

AQA, Question 8, Paper 2 Intermediate, November 2003

10 These are 150 kangaroos at a wildlife park.

a There are 66 female kangaroos.
What percentage is female?

b The number of kangaroos increases by 20% each year. Calculate the number of kangaroos in the wildlife park after 2 years.

AQA, Question 18a, Paper 1 Intermediate, November 2004

11 During 2003 the number of unemployed people in Barnsley fell from 2800 to 2576.
What was the percentage decrease?

12 a A painter has 50 litres of paint.
Each litre covers 2.5 m².
The area to be painted is 98 m².
Estimate the percentage of paint used.

13 ABCD is a rectangle with length 25 cm and width 10 cm.

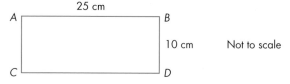

The length of the rectangle is increased by 10%.
The width of the rectangle is increased by 20%.
Find the percentage increase in the area of the rectangle.

AQA, Question 15, Paper 2 Intermediate, November 2003

14 Zoe invests £6000 in a savings account that pays 3.5% compound interest per year.
How much does she have in the account after 6 years ?

15 Work out $3\frac{3}{4} \div 4\frac{1}{2}$

16 A special savings account earns 10% per year compound interest.

 a Jill invests £2500 in the special account. How much will she have in her account after 2 years?

b James also invests in the special account. After earning interest for one year, he has £1320 in his account. How much money did James invest?

AQA, Question 22, Paper 1 Intermediate, November 2003

 17 a Miss Evans earns £240 per week. She is awarded a pay rise of 3.5%.

Mr Dale earns £220 per week. He is awarded a pay rise of 4%.

Whose weekly pay increases by the greater amount of money? You *must* show all your working.

b In 2003 the state pension was increased by 2% to £78.03 What was the state pension before this increase?

AQA, Question 12, Paper 2 Intermediate, June 2003

WORKED EXAM QUESTION

a Kelly bought a television set. After a reduction of 15% in a sale, the one she bought cost her £319.60. What was the original price of the television set?

b A plant in a greenhouse is 10 cm high. It increases its height by 15% each day. How many days does it take to double in height?

Solution

a £376.

> A 15% reduction is a multiplier of 0.85. The original price will be the new price divided by the multiplier. $319.6 \div 0.85 = 376$

b $10 \times 1.15^3 = 15.2$
$10 \times 1.15^4 = 17.5$
$10 \times 1.15^5 = 20.1$
Therefore, it takes 5 days to double in height.

> A 15% increase is a multiplier of 1.15. After n days the plant will be 10×1.15^n high. Use trial and improvement to find the value that is over 20 cm.

 Work out $\dfrac{\left(\frac{2}{3} + \frac{4}{5}\right)}{1\frac{7}{9}}$

Solution

$\dfrac{\frac{22}{15}}{1\frac{7}{9}}$

$\dfrac{22}{15} \times \dfrac{9}{16}$

$\dfrac{{}^{11}\cancel{22}}{{}^{5}\cancel{15}} \times \dfrac{\cancel{9}^{3}}{\cancel{16}^{8}} = \dfrac{33}{40}$

> First add the two fractions in the bracket by writing them with a common denominator, that is, $\frac{10}{15} + \frac{12}{15}$

> Make the mixed number into a top heavy fraction, $\frac{16}{9}$, and turn it upside down and multiply.

> Cancel out the common factors, and multiply numerators and denominators.

Mrs Woolman is a sheep farmer in Wales. When she sends her lambs to market, she keeps a record of how many lambs she sends, and the total live weight of these lambs in kilograms.

Once they have been processed, she receives an information sheet showing the total weight of the meat from the lambs in kilograms, and the total price she has been paid for this meat.

For every week that she sends lambs to the market, she calculates the mean live weight of the lambs (to the nearest kilogram).

Copy the table below and complete the *Mean live weight in kg* column for her.

Mrs Woolman is happy with the condition of her lambs if the weight of the meat as a percentage of the live weight is over 42%.

Complete the *Meat as a % of live weight* column in your table. Indicate with a tick or a cross if she is happy with the condition of those lambs. Give percentages to one decimal place.

After Mrs Woolman has been paid for the meat, she calculates the price she is paid per kilogram of meat.

Compete the final column, *Price paid per kg of meat* in your table. Give each price to the nearest penny.

Date	Number of lambs	Total live weight in kg	Mean live weight in kg	Total weight of meat in kg	Meat as % of live weight	Total price paid for meat	Price paid per kg of meat
1st April	13	468	36	211	45.1% ✓	£812.56	£3.85
15th April	8	290		134		£451.91	
22nd April	18	672		312		£1105.31	
29th April	11	398		179		£625.04	
6th May	18	657		291		£907.89	
20th May	8	309		130		£386.15	
3rd June	10	416		171		£480.46	
17th June	4	174		72		£196.54	

At the end of the season Mrs Woolman analyses the information she has calculated.

Fill in the spaces in her notebook for her.

The mean weight per lamb has increased from ____kg to ____kg. This is an increase of ____%. However the price per kg of lamb has fallen from £____ to £____, a decrease of ____%.

The only two weeks when the condition of the lambs fell below 42% were _____ and _____.

Mrs Woolman finds a line graph in a farming magazine showing the average lamb prices in England and Wales from April through to June.

Copy this graph, and complete the line showing the price per kilogram that Mrs Woolman had for her lambs.

Comment on these line graphs.

Average lamb prices, April to July

£ per kilogram of meat

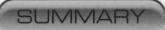

SUMMARY

GRADE YOURSELF

D Able to add, subtract, multiply and divide fractions

D Able to calculate percentage increases and decreases

C Able to calculate with mixed numbers

C Able to work out compound interest problems

B Able to do reverse percentage problems

A Able to solve complex problems involving percentage increases and decreases

What you should know now

- How to calculate with fractions
- How to do percentage problems

6

Ratios and proportion

1 Ratio

2 Speed, time and distance

3 Direct proportion problems

4 Best buys

5 Density

This chapter will show you ...

● what a ratio is
● how to divide an amount into a given ratio
● how to solve problems involving direct proportion
● how to compare prices of products
● how to calculate speed
● how to calculate density

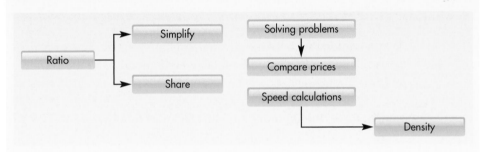

What you should already know

● Times tables up to 10×10
● How to cancel fractions
● How to find a fraction of a quantity
● How to multiply and divide, with and without a calculator

Quick check

1 Cancel down the following fractions.

a $\frac{6}{10}$ **b** $\frac{4}{20}$ **c** $\frac{4}{12}$ **d** $\frac{32}{50}$ **e** $\frac{36}{90}$ **f** $\frac{18}{24}$ **g** $\frac{16}{48}$

2 Find the following quantities.

a $\frac{2}{5}$ of £30 **b** $\frac{3}{8}$ of £88 **c** $\frac{7}{10}$ of 250 litres **d** $\frac{5}{8}$ of 24 kg

e $\frac{2}{3}$ of 60 m **f** $\frac{5}{6}$ of £42 **g** $\frac{9}{20}$ of 300 g **h** $\frac{3}{10}$ of 3.5 litres

This section will show you how to:
- simplify a ratio
- express a ratio as a fraction
- divide amounts into given ratios
- complete calculations from a given ratio and partial information

Key words
common units
fraction
ratio

A **ratio** is a way of comparing the sizes of two or more quantities.

A ratio can be expressed in a number of ways. For example, Joy is 5 years old and James is 20 years old. The ratio of their ages is Joy's age : James's age which is 5 : 20.

This simplifies to 1 : 4 (dividing both sides by 5).

A ratio can be expressed in words but it is usual to use a colon (:).

Joy's age : James's age   or   5 : 20   or   1 : 4

Common units

When working with a ratio involving different units, *always change them* to a **common unit**. A ratio can be simplified only when the units of each quantity are the *same*, because the ratio itself doesn't have any units.

For example, the ratio of 125 g to 2 kg must be changed to 125 g to 2000 g, so that we can simplify it to

	125 : 2000
Divide both sides by 25	5 : 80
Divide both sides by 5	1 : 16

Ratios as fractions

A ratio in its simplest form can be expressed as portions by changing the whole numbers in the ratio into **fractions** with the same denominator (bottom number).

EXAMPLE 1

A garden is divided into lawn and shrubs in the ratio 3 : 2.

What fraction of the garden is covered by **a** lawn, **b** shrubs?

The denominator (bottom number) of the fraction comes from *adding the numbers in the ratio* (that is, $2 + 3 = 5$).

a The lawn covers $\frac{3}{5}$ of the garden.

b The shrubs cover $\frac{2}{5}$ of the garden.

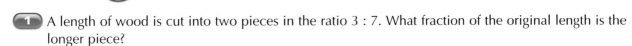

EXERCISE 6A

1 A length of wood is cut into two pieces in the ratio 3 : 7. What fraction of the original length is the longer piece?

2 Jack and Thomas find a bag of marbles which they divide between them in the ratio of their ages. Jack is 10 years old and Thomas is 15. What fraction of the marbles did Jack get?

3 Dave and Sue share a pizza in the ratio of 2 : 3. They eat it all.

    a What fraction of the pizza did Dave eat?

    b What fraction of the pizza did Sue eat?

4 A camp site allocates space to caravans and tents in the ratio 7 : 3. What fraction of the total space is given to:

    a the caravans?   **b** the tents?

5 One morning a farmer notices that her hens, Gertrude, Gladys and Henrietta, have laid eggs in the ratio 2 : 3 : 4.

    a What fraction of the eggs did Gertrude lay?

    b What fraction of the eggs did Gladys lay?

    c How many more eggs did Henrietta lay than Gertrude?

6 The recipe for a pudding is 125 g of sugar, 150 g of flour, 100 g of margarine and 175 g of fruit. What fraction of the pudding is each ingredient?

Dividing amounts into given ratios

To divide an amount into portions according to a given ratio, you first change the whole numbers in the ratio into fractions with the same common denominator. Then you multiply the amount by each fraction.

EXAMPLE 2

Divide £40 between Peter and Hitan in the ratio 2 : 3.

Changing the ratio to fractions gives:

$$\text{Peter's share} \ = \ \frac{2}{(2+3)} \ = \ \frac{2}{5}$$

$$\text{Hitan's share} \ = \ \frac{3}{(2+3)} \ = \ \frac{3}{5}$$

So, Peter receives £40 × $\frac{2}{5}$ = £16 and Hitan receives £40 × $\frac{3}{5}$ = £24.

EXAMPLE 3

Divide 63 cm in the ratio 3 : 4.

An alternative method that avoids fractions is to add the parts: 3 + 4 = 7.

Divide the original amount by the total: 63 ÷ 7 = 9.

Then multiply each portion of the original ratio by the answer: 3 × 9 = 27, 4 × 9 = 36.

So 63 cm in the ratio 3 : 4 is 27 cm : 36 cm.

Note that whichever method you use, you should always check that the final values add up to the original amount: £16 + £24 = £40 and 27 cm + 36 cm = 63 cm.

EXERCISE 6B

1 Divide the following amounts in the given ratios.

   a 400 g in the ratio 2 : 3   **b** 280 kg in the ratio 2 : 5

   c 500 in the ratio 3 : 7   **d** 1 km in the ratio 19 : 1

   e 5 hours in the ratio 7 : 5   **f** £100 in the ratio 2 : 3 : 5

   g £240 in the ratio 3 : 5 : 12   **h** 600 g in the ratio 1 : 5 : 6

2 The ratio of female to male members of Banner Cross Church is about 5 : 3. The total number of members of the church is 256.

   a How many members are female?

   b What percentage of members are male?

3 A supermarket tries to have in stock branded goods and its own goods in the ratio 2 : 5. It stocks 350 kg of breakfast cereal.

   a What percentage of the cereal stock is branded?

   b How much of the cereal stock is its own?

4 The Illinois Department of Health reported that, for the years 1981 to 1992, when it tested a total of 357 horses for rabies, the ratio of horses with rabies to those without was 1 : 16.

   a How many of these horses had rabies?

   b What percentage of the horses did not have rabies?

5 Being overweight increases the chances of an adult suffering from heart disease. The formulae below show a way to test whether an adult has an increased risk.

   W and *H* refer to waist and hip measurements.
   For women, increased risk when $W/H > 0.8$
   For men, increased risk when $W/H > 1.0$

Find whether the following people have an increased risk of heart disease or not.

    Miss Mott: waist 26 inches, hips: 35 inches

    Mrs Wright: waist 32 inches, hips: 37 inches

    Mr Brennan: waist 32 inches, hips: 34 inches

    Ms Smith: waist 31 inches, hips: 40 inches

    Mr Kaye: waist 34 inches, hips: 33 inches

 6 Rewrite the following scales as ratios, as simply as possible.

    a 1 cm to 4 km   **b** 4 cm to 5 km   **c** 2 cm to 5 km

    d 4 cm to 1 km   **e** 5 cm to 1 km   **f** 2.5 cm to 1 km

 7 A map has a scale of 1 cm to 10 km.

    a Rewrite the scale as a ratio in its simplest form.

    b How long is a lake that is 4.7 cm on the map?

    c How long will an 8 km road be on the map?

 8 A map has a scale of 2 cm to 5 km.

    a Rewrite the scale as a ratio in its simplest form.

    b How long is a path that measures 0.8 cm on the map?

    c How long should a 12 km road be on the map?

 9 You can simplify a ratio by changing it into the form $1 : n$.

For example, $5 : 7$ can be rewritten as $\dfrac{5}{5} : \dfrac{7}{5} = 1 : 1.4$

Rewrite each of the following in the form $1 : n$.

    a $5 : 8$ **b** $4 : 13$ **c** $8 : 9$

    d $25 : 36$ **e** $5 : 27$ **f** $12 : 18$

    g 5 hours : 1 day   **h** 4 hours : 1 week   **i** £4 : £5

Calculating a ratio when only part of the information is known

EXAMPLE 4

Two business partners, John and Ben, divided their total profit in the ratio $3 : 5$. John received £2100. How much did Ben get?

John's £2100 was $\frac{3}{8}$ of the total profit. (Check you know why.)

So, $\frac{1}{8}$ of the total profit = £2100 ÷ 3 = £700

Therefore, Ben's share, which was $\frac{5}{8}$ of the total, amounted to £700 × 5 = £3500.

EXERCISE 6C

1 Derek, aged 15, and Ricki, aged 10, shared, in the same ratio as their ages, all the conkers they found in the woods. Derek had 48 conkers.

   a Simplify the ratio of their ages.

   b How many conkers did Ricki have?

   c How many conkers did they find altogether?

2 Two types of crisps, Plain and Salt'n Vinegar, were bought for a school party in the ratio 5 : 3. They bought 60 packets of Salt'n Vinegar crisps.

   a How many packets of Plain crisps did they buy?

   b How many packets of crisps did they buy altogether?

3 A blend of tea is made by mixing Lapsang with Assam in the ratio 3 : 5. I have a lot of Assam tea but only 600 g of Lapsang. How much Assam do I need to make the blend with all the Lapsang?

4 The ratio of male to female spectators at ice hockey games is 4 : 5. At the Steelers' last match, 4500 men and boys watched the match. What was the total attendance at the game?

5 "Proper tea" is made by putting milk and tea together in the ratio 2 : 9. How much "proper tea" can be made by using 1 litre of milk?

6 A "good" children's book is supposed to have pictures and text in the ratio 17 : 8. In a book I have just looked at, the pictures occupy 23 pages.

   a Approximately how many pages of text should this book have to be deemed a "good" children's book?

   b What percentage of a "good" children's book will be text?

7 Three business partners, Kevin, John and Margaret, put money into a venture in the ratio 3 : 4 : 5. They shared any profits in the same ratio. Last year, Margaret made £3400 out of the profits. How much did Kevin and John make last year?

8 Gwen is making a drink from lemonade, orange and ginger in the ratio 40 : 9 : 1. If Gwen has only 4.5 litres of orange, how much of the other two ingredients does she need to make the drink?

9 When I harvested my apples I found some had been eaten by wasps, some were just rotten and some were good ones. These were in the ratio 6 : 5 : 25. Eighteen of my apples had been eaten by wasps.

   a What percentage of my apples were just rotten?

   b How many good apples did I get?

Speed, time and distance

In this section you will learn how to:
- recognise the relationship between speed, distance and time
- calculate average speed from distance and time
- calculate distance travelled from the speed and the time
- calculate the time taken on a journey from the speed and the distance

Key words

distance
speed
time

The relationship between **speed**, **time** and **distance** can be expressed in three ways:

$$Speed = \frac{Distance}{Time} \qquad Distance = Speed \times Time \qquad Time = \frac{Distance}{Speed}$$

When we refer to speed, we usually mean *average* speed, as it is unusual to maintain one exact speed for the whole of a journey.

The relationships between distance D, time T and speed S can be recalled using this diagram.

$$D = S \times T \qquad S = \frac{D}{T} \qquad T = \frac{D}{S}$$

EXAMPLE 5

Paula drove a distance of 270 miles in 5 hours. What was her average speed?

$$\text{Paula's average speed} = \frac{\text{distance she drove}}{\text{time she took}} = \frac{270 \text{ miles}}{5 \text{ hours}} = 54 \text{ miles/h}$$

EXAMPLE 6

Edith drove from Sheffield to Peebles for $3\frac{1}{2}$ hours at an average speed of 60 miles/h. How far is it from Sheffield to Peebles?

Distance = Speed × Time

So, distance from Sheffield to Peebles is given by

60 miles/h × 3.5 h = 210 miles

Note: We changed the time to a decimal number and used 3.5, **not** 3.30!

EXAMPLE 7

Sean is going to drive from Newcastle upon Tyne to Nottingham, a distance of 190 miles. He estimates that he will drive at an average speed of 50 miles/h. How long will it take him?

$$\text{Sean's time} = \frac{\text{distance he covers}}{\text{his average speed}} = \frac{190 \text{ miles}}{50 \text{ miles/h}} = 3.8 \text{ hours}$$

Change the 0.8 hour to minutes by multiplying by 60, to give 48 minutes.

So, the time for Sean's journey will be 3 hours 48 minutes.
(A sensible rounding off would give 4 hours or 3 hours 50 minutes.)

Remember: When you calculate a time and get a decimal answer, as in Example 7, *do not mistake* the decimal part for minutes. You must either:

- leave the time as a decimal number and give the unit as hours, or

- change the decimal part to minutes by multiplying it by 60 (1 hour = 60 minutes) and give the answer in hours and minutes.

EXERCISE 6D

1 A cyclist travels a distance of 90 miles in 5 hours. What is her average speed?

2 I drive to Bude in Cornwall from Sheffield in about 6 hours. The distance from Sheffield to Bude is 315 miles. What is my average speed?

3 The distance from Leeds to London is 210 miles. The train travels at an average speed of 90 mph. If I catch the 9:30 am train in London, at what time would you expect me to get to Leeds?

4 Complete the following table.

	Distance travelled	Time taken	Average speed
a	150 miles	2 hours	
b	260 miles		40 mph
c		5 hours	35 mph
d		3 hours	80 km/h
e	544 km	8 hours 30 minutes	
f		3 hours 15 minutes	100 km/h
g	215 km		50 km/h

> **HINTS AND TIPS**
>
> Remember to convert time to a decimal if you are using a calculator. For example, 8 hours 30 minutes is 8.5 hours.

5 A train travels at 50 km/h for 2 hours, then slows down to do the last 30 minutes of its journey at 40 km/h.

a What is the total distance of this journey?

b What is the average speed of the train over the whole journey?

6 Jane runs and walks to work each day. She runs the first 2 miles at a speed of 8 mph and then walks the next mile at a steady 4 mph.

   a How long does it take Jane to get to work?

   b What is her average speed?

7 Colin drives home from his son's house in 2 hours 15 minutes. He says that he drives home at an average speed of 44 mph.

   a Change the 2 hours 15 minutes to decimal time.

   b How far is it from Colin's home to his son's house?

8 The distance between Paris and Le Mans is 200 km. The express train between Paris and Le Mans travels at an average speed of 160 km/h.

   a Calculate the time taken for the journey from Paris to Le Mans, giving your answer in decimal hour notation.

   b Change your answer to part **a** to hours and minutes.

9 The distance between Sheffield and Land's End is 420 miles.

   a What is the average speed of a journey from Sheffield to Land's End if it takes 8 hours 45 minutes?

   b If I covered the distance at an average speed of 63 mph, how long would it take me?

10 Change the following speeds to metres per second.

   a 36 km/h   **b** 12 km/h   **c** 60 km/h

   d 150 km/h   **e** 75 km/h

> **HINTS AND TIPS**
>
> Remember there are 3600 seconds in an hour and 1000 metres in a kilometre.

11 Change the following speeds to kilometres per hour.

   a 25 m/s   **b** 12 m/s   **c** 4 m/s

   d 30 m/s   **e** 0.5 m/s

12 A train travels at an average speed of 18 m/s.

   a Express its average speed in km/h.

   b Find the approximate time taken to travel 500 m.

   c The train set off at 7:30 on a 40 km journey. At approximately what time will it arrive?

> **HINTS AND TIPS**
>
> To convert a decimal of an hour to minutes just multiply by 60.

Direct proportion problems

This section will show you how to:
- recognise a direct proportion problem
- solve a problem involving direct proportion

Key words
direct
    proportion
unitary
    method

Suppose you buy 12 items which each cost the *same*. The total amount you spend is 12 times the cost of one item.

That is, the total cost is said to be in **direct proportion** to the number of items bought. The cost of a single item (the unit cost) is the constant factor that links the two quantities.

Direct proportion is concerned not only with costs. Any two related quantities can be in direct proportion to each other.

Finding the single unit value first is the best way to solve all problems involving direct proportion.

This method is called the **unitary method**, because it involves referring to a single *unit* value.

Remember: Before solving a direct proportion problem, think carefully about it to make sure that you know how to find the required single unit value.

EXAMPLE 8

If eight pens cost £2.64, what is the cost of five pens?

First, we need to find the cost of one pen. This is £2.64 ÷ 8 = £0.33.

So, the cost of five pens is £0.33 × 5 = £1.65.

EXAMPLE 9

Eight loaves of bread will make packed lunches for 18 people. How many packed lunches can be made from 20 loaves?

First, we need to find how many lunches *one* loaf will make.

One loaf will make 18 ÷ 8 = 2.25 lunches.

So, 20 loaves will make 2.25 × 20 = 45 lunches.

EXERCISE 6E

1 If 30 matches weigh 45 g, what would 40 matches weigh?

2 Five bars of chocolate cost £2.90. Find the cost of 9 bars.

3 Eight men can chop down 18 trees in a day. How many trees can 20 men chop down in a day?

4 Seventy maths textbooks cost £875.

    a How much will 25 maths textbooks cost?

    b How many maths textbooks can you buy for £100?

5 A lorry uses 80 litres of diesel fuel on a trip of 280 miles.

    a How much would be used on a trip of 196 miles?

    b How far would the lorry get on a full tank of 100 litres?

6 During the winter, I find that 200 kg of coal keeps my open fire burning for 12 weeks.

    a If I want an open fire all through the winter (18 weeks), how much coal will I need to get?

    b Last year I bought 150 kg of coal. For how many weeks did I have an open fire?

7 It takes a photocopier 16 seconds to produce 12 copies. How long will it take to produce 30 copies?

6.4 Best buys

This section will show you how to:
- find the cost per unit weight
- find the weight per unit cost
- find which product is the cheaper

Key word
best buy

When you wander around a supermarket and see all the different prices for the many different-sized packets, it is rarely obvious which are the **best buys**. However, with a calculator you can easily compare value for money by finding either:

    the cost per unit weight   *or*   the weight per unit cost

To find:

- *cost per unit weight*, divide *cost by weight*

- *weight per unit cost*, divide *weight by cost*.

The next two examples show you how to do this.

EXAMPLE 10

A 300 g tin of cocoa costs £1.20.

First change £1.20 to 120p. Then divide, using a calculator, to get:

cost per unit weight　　120p ÷ 300 g = 0.4p per gram

weight per unit cost　　300 g ÷ 120p = 2.5 g per penny

EXAMPLE 11

There are two different-sized packets of Whito soap powder at a supermarket. The medium size contains 800 g and costs £1.60 and the large size contains 2.5 kg and costs £4.75. Which is the better buy?

Find the weight per unit cost for both packets.

Medium:　　　　　　　　800 g ÷ 160p = 5 g per penny

Large:　　　　　　　　2500 g ÷ 475p = 5.26 g per penny

From these we see that there is more weight per penny with the large size, which means that the large size is the better buy.

EXERCISE 6F

D

1 Compare the following pairs of product and state which is the better buy, and why.

　a Coffee: a medium jar which is 140 g for £1.10 or a large jar which is 300 g for £2.18

　b Beans: a 125 g tin at 16p or a 600 g tin at 59p

　c Flour: a 3 kg bag at 75p or a 5 kg bag at £1.20

　d Toothpaste: a large tube which is 110 ml for £1.79 or a medium tube which is 75 ml for £1.15

　e Frosties: a large box which is 750 g for £1.64 or a medium box which is 500 g for £1.10

　f Rice Krispies: a medium box which is 440 g for £1.64 or a large box which is 600 g for £2.13

　g Hair shampoo: a bottle containing 400 ml for £1.15 or a bottle containing 550 ml for £1.60

2 Julie wants to respray her car with yellow paint. In the local automart, she sees the following tins:

　small tin: 350 ml at a cost of £1.79
　medium tin: 500 ml at a cost of £2.40
　large tin: 1.5 litres at a cost of £6.70

　a Which tin is offered at the cheapest cost per litre?

　b What is the cost per litre of paint in the small tin?

3 Tisco's sells bottled water in three sizes.

　a Work out the cost per litre of the 'handy' size.

　b Which bottle is the best value for money?

Handy size 40 cl　　Family size 2 l　　Giant size 5 l
£0.38　　　　　　　£0.98　　　　　　£2.50

4 Two drivers are comparing the petrol consumption of their cars.

Ahmed says, 'I get 320 miles on a tank of 45 litres.'

Bashir says, 'I get 230 miles on a tank of 32 litres.'

Whose car is the more economical?

5 Mary and Jane are arguing about which of them is better at mathematics.

Mary scored 49 out of 80 on a test.

Jane scored 60 out of 100 on a test of the same standard.

Who is better at mathematics?

6 Paula and Kelly are comparing their running times.

Paula completed a 10-mile run in 65 minutes.

Kelly completed a 10-kilometre run in 40 minutes.

Given that 8 kilometres are equal to 5 miles, which girl has the greater average speed?

6.5 Density

This section will show you how to:	Key words
• solve problems involving density	density
	mass
	volume

Density is the mass of a substance per unit volume, usually expressed in grams per cm^3. The relationship between the three quantities is

$$Density = \frac{Mass}{Volume}$$

This is often remembered with a triangle similar to that for distance, speed and time.

$Mass = Density \times Volume$

$Density = Mass \div Volume$

$Volume = Mass \div Density$

Note: Density is defined in terms of mass, which is commonly referred to as weight, although, strictly speaking, there is a difference between them. (You may already have learnt about this in science.) In this book, the two terms are assumed to have the same meaning.

EXAMPLE 12

A piece of metal weighing 30 g has a volume of 4 cm^3. What is the density of the metal?

$$Density = \frac{Mass}{Volume} = \frac{30\ g}{4\ cm^3} = 7.5\ g/cm^3$$

EXAMPLE 13

What is the weight of a piece of rock which has a volume of 34 cm^3 and a density of 2.25 g/cm^3?

$$Weight = Volume \times Density = 34\ cm^3 \times 2.25\ g/cm^3 = 76.5\ g$$

EXERCISE 6G

1 Find the density of a piece of wood weighing 6 g and having a volume of 8 cm^3.

2 Calculate the density of a metal if 12 cm^3 of it weighs 100 g.

3 Calculate the weight of a piece of plastic, 20 cm^3 in volume, if its density is 1.6 g/cm^3.

4 Calculate the volume of a piece of wood which weighs 102 g and has a density of 0.85 g/cm^3.

5 Find the weight of a marble model, 56 cm^3 in volume, if the density of marble is 2.8 g/cm^3.

6 Calculate the volume of a liquid weighing 4 kg and having a density of 1.25 g/cm^3.

7 Find the density of the material of a pebble which weighs 34 g and has a volume of 12.5 cm^3.

8 It is estimated that the statue of Queen Victoria in Endcliffe Park, Sheffield, has a volume of about 4 m^3. The density of the material used to make the statue is 9.2 g/cm^3. What is the estimated weight of the statue?

9 I bought a 50 kg bag of coal, and estimated the total volume of coal to be about 28 000 cm^3. What is the density of coal in g/cm^3?

10 A 1 kg bag of sugar has a volume of about 625 cm^3. What is the density of sugar in g/cm^3?

1 Two towns, *A* and *B*, are connected by a motorway of length 100 miles and a dual carriageway of length 80 miles as shown.

Jack travels from *A* to *B* along the motorway at an average speed of 60 mph.
Fred travels from *A* to *B* along the dual carriageway at an average speed of 50 mph.
What is the difference in time between the two journeys? Give your answers in minutes.

AQA, Question 8, Paper 2 Intermediate, June 2005

  2 a How many 250 millilitre glasses can be filled from a 2-litre bottle of water?

b A drink is made by mixing blackcurrant juice and water in the ratio 1 : 4.
How much blackcurrant juice and how much water is needed to make 250 ml of the drink?

AQA, Question 5, Paper 1 Intermediate, May 2002

  3 Share £34 800 in the ratio 1 : 5.

 4 A short necklace has 32 gold beads and 8 black beads. A long necklace has 60 beads. Both necklaces have the same ratio of gold beads to black beads. How many black beads are on the long necklace?

AQA, Question 10, Paper 1 Intermediate, November 2004

  5 Bill and Ben buy £10 worth of lottery tickets. Ben pays £7 and Bill pays £3. They decide to share any prize in the ratio of the money they each paid.

a They win £350. How much does Bill get?

b What percentage of the £350 does Ben get?

 6 The interior angles of a triangle are in the ratio

2 : 3 : 4

Calculate the size of the smallest angle.

7 The ratio of adults to children in a pantomime audience is 3 : 16. There are 752 children in the audience. How many adults are there?

AQA, Question 15, Paper 2 Intermediate, November 2002

 8 Susan completes a journey in two stages.
In stage 1 of her journey, she drives at an average speed of 80 km/h and takes 1 hour 45 minutes.

a How far does Susan travel in stage 1 of her journey?

b Altogether, Susan drives 190 km and takes a total time of 2 hours 15 minutes. What is her average speed, in km/h, in stage 2 of her journey?

 ## WORKED EXAM QUESTION

To be on time, a train must complete a journey of 210 miles in 3 hours.

a Calculate the average speed of the train for the whole journey when it is on time.

b The train averages a speed of 56 mph over the first 98 miles of the journey. Calculate the average speed for the remainder of the journey so that the train arrives on time.

Solution

a 70 mph

> Average speed = distance ÷ time = 210 ÷ 3.
> Note that one question in the examination will ask you to state the units of your answer. This is often done with a speed question.

b 98 ÷ 56 = 1.75 which is 1 hour and 45 minutes.

> First find out how long the train took to do the first 98 miles.

(210 − 98) ÷ (3 − 1.75) = 112 ÷ 1.25 = 89.6 mph

> Now work out the distance still to be travelled (112 miles) and the time left (1 hour 15 minutes = 1.25 hours). Divide distance by time to get the average speed.

GRADE YOURSELF

D Calculate average speeds from data

D Calculate distance from speed and time

D Calculate time from speed and distance

C Solve problems using ratio in appropriate situations

B Solve problems involving density

What you should know now

- How to divide any amount into a given ratio
- The relationships between speed, time and distance
- How to do problems involving direct proportion
- How to compare the prices of products
- How to work out the density of materials

Powers, standard form and surds

1 Indices

2 Standard form

3 Reciprocals and rational numbers

4 Surds

This chapter will show you ...

- how to calculate with indices
- how to write numbers in standard form and how to calculate with standard form
- how to convert fractions to terminating and recurring decimals, and vice versa
- how to work out a reciprocal
- how to calculate with surds

Visual overview

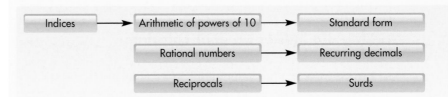

Indices → Arithmetic of powers of 10 → Standard form

Rational numbers → Recurring decimals

Reciprocals → Surds

What you should already know

- How to convert a fraction to a decimal
- How to convert a decimal to a fraction
- How to find the lowest common denominator of two fractions
- The meaning of square root and cube root

Quick check

1 Convert the following fractions to decimals.

   a $\frac{6}{10}$ **b** $\frac{11}{25}$ **c** $\frac{3}{8}$

2 Convert the following decimals to fractions.

   a 0.17   **b** 0.64   **c** 0.858

3 Work these out.   **a** $\frac{2}{3} + \frac{1}{5}$ **b** $\frac{5}{8} - \frac{2}{5}$

4 Write down the values.   **a** $\sqrt{25}$ **b** $\sqrt[3]{64}$

This section will show you how to:
- use indices (also known as powers)

Key words

index
    (pl: indices)
powers
reciprocal

The **index** is the number of times a number is multiplied by itself. For example,

$$4^6 = 4 \times 4 \times 4 \times 4 \times 4 \times 4, \ 6^4 = 6 \times 6 \times 6 \times 6, \ 7^3 = 7 \times 7 \times 7, \ 12^2 = 12 \times 12$$

Here, 4 has an index of 6, 6 has an index of 4, 7 has an index of 3 and 12 has an index of 2.

Indices (or **powers**) can also be used to simplify the writing of repetitive multiplications, For example,

$$3 \times 3 \times 3 \times 3 \times 3 \times 3 \times 3 \times 3 = 3^8, \ 13 \times 13 \times 13 \times 13 \times 13 = 13^5, \ 7 \times 7 \times 7 \times 7 = 7^4$$

A commonly used power is "2", which has the special name "squared". The only other power with a special name is "3", which is called "cubed".

The value of "7 squared" is $7^2 = 7 \times 7 = 49$ and the value of "5 cubed" is $5^3 = 5 \times 5 \times 5 = 125$.

Working out indices on your calculator

How do we work out the value of 5^7 on a calculator?

We could do the calculation as $5 \times 5 \times 5 \times 5 \times 5 \times 5 \times 5 = $. But if we tried to key this in, we would probably end up missing a "$\times 5$" or pressing a wrong key. Instead, we use the power key $\boxed{x^y}$ (or, on some calculators, $\boxed{y^x}$). So

$$5^7 = \boxed{5} \ \boxed{x^y} \ \boxed{7} \ \boxed{=} = 78\,125$$

Make sure you know where to find the power key on your calculator. It may be an INV or SHIFT function.

Two special powers

Choose any number, say 5, and use your calculator to raise it to the power 1. You will find that $5^1 = 5$. That is, a number raised to the power 1 stays the same number. This is true for *any* number, so we do not normally write down the power 1.

Choose any number, say 9, and use your calculator to raise it to the power 0. You will find that $9^0 = 1$. This is true for *any* number raised to the power 0. The answer is *always* 1.

EXERCISE 7A

 1 Write these expressions using power notation. Do not work them out yet.

    a $2 \times 2 \times 2 \times 2$ **b** $3 \times 3 \times 3 \times 3 \times 3$

    c 7×7 **d** $5 \times 5 \times 5$

    e $10 \times 10 \times 10 \times 10 \times 10 \times 10 \times 10$ **f** $6 \times 6 \times 6 \times 6$

    g 4 **h** $1 \times 1 \times 1 \times 1 \times 1 \times 1 \times 1$

    i $0.5 \times 0.5 \times 0.5 \times 0.5$ **j** $100 \times 100 \times 100$

 2 Write these power terms out in full. Do not work them out yet.

    a 3^4 **b** 9^3 **c** 6^2 **d** 10^5 **e** 2^{10}

    f 8^1 **g** 0.1^3 **h** 2.5^2 **i** 0.7^3 **j** 1000^2

 3 Using the power key on your calculator (or another method), work out the values of the power terms in question **1**.

 4 Using the power key on your calculator (or another method), work out the values of the power terms in question **2**.

 5 Without using a calculator, work out the values of these power terms.

    a 2^0 **b** 4^1 **c** 5^0 **d** 1^9 **e** 1^{235}

 6 The answers to question **5**, parts **d** and **e**, should tell you something special about powers of 1. What is it?

 7 Write the answer to question **1**, part **j** as a power of 10.

 8 Write the answer to question **2**, part **j** as a power of 10.

 9 Using your calculator, or otherwise, work out the values of these power terms.

    a $(-1)^0$ **b** $(-1)^1$ **c** $(-1)^2$ **d** $(-1)^4$ **e** $(-1)^5$

 10 Using your answers to question **9**, write down the answers to these power terms.

    a $(-1)^8$ **b** $(-1)^{11}$ **c** $(-1)^{99}$ **d** $(-1)^{80}$ **e** $(-1)^{126}$

Negative indices

A negative index is a convenient way of writing the **reciprocal** of a number or term. (That is, one divided by that number or term.) For example,

$$x^{-a} = \frac{1}{x^a}$$

Here are some other examples:

$$5^{-2} = \frac{1}{5^2} \qquad 3^{-1} = \frac{1}{3} \qquad 5x^{-2} = \frac{5}{x^2}$$

EXAMPLE 1

Rewrite the following in the form 2^n.

a 8 **b** $\frac{1}{4}$ **c** -32 **d** $-\frac{1}{64}$

a $8 = 2 \times 2 \times 2 = 2^3$ **b** $\frac{1}{4} = \frac{1}{2^2} = 2^{-2}$

c $-32 = -2^5$ **d** $-\frac{1}{64} = -\frac{1}{2^6} = -2^{-6}$

EXERCISE 7B

1 Write down each of these in fraction form.

a 5^{-3} **b** 6^{-1} **c** 10^{-5} **d** 3^{-2} **e** 8^{-2}

f 9^{-1} **g** w^{-2} **h** t^{-1} **i** x^{-m} **j** $4m^{-3}$

> **HINTS AND TIPS**
>
> If you move a power from top to bottom, or vice versa, the sign changes. Negative power means the reciprocal: it does not mean the answer is negative.

2 Write down each of these in negative index form.

a $\frac{1}{3^2}$ **b** $\frac{1}{5}$ **c** $\frac{1}{10^3}$ **d** $\frac{1}{m}$ **e** $\frac{1}{t^n}$

3 Change each of the following expressions into an index form of the type shown.

a all of the form 2^n

   i 16 **ii** $\frac{1}{2}$ **iii** $\frac{1}{16}$ **iv** -8

b all of the form 10^n

   i 1000 **ii** $\frac{1}{10}$ **iii** $\frac{1}{100}$ **iv** 1 million

c all of the form 5^n

   i 125 **ii** $\frac{1}{5}$ **iii** $\frac{1}{25}$ **iv** $\frac{1}{625}$

d all of the form 3^n

   i 9 **ii** $\frac{1}{27}$ **iii** $\frac{1}{81}$ **iv** -243

4 Rewrite each of the following expressions in fraction form.

a $5x^{-3}$ **b** $6t^{-1}$ **c** $7m^{-2}$ **d** $4q^{-4}$ **e** $10y^{-5}$

f $\frac{1}{2}x^{-3}$ **g** $\frac{1}{2}m^{-1}$ **h** $\frac{3}{4}t^{-4}$ **i** $\frac{4}{5}y^{-3}$ **j** $\frac{7}{8}x^{-5}$

5 Change each fraction to index form.

a $\dfrac{7}{x^3}$ **b** $\dfrac{10}{p}$ **c** $\dfrac{5}{t^2}$ **d** $\dfrac{8}{m^5}$ **e** $\dfrac{3}{y}$

6 Find the value of each of the following, where the letters have the given values.

a Where $x = 5$

  i x^2 **ii** x^{-3} **iii** $4x^{-1}$

b Where $t = 4$

  i t^3 **ii** t^{-2} **iii** $5t^{-4}$

c Where $m = 2$

  i m^3 **ii** m^{-5} **iii** $9m^{-1}$

d Where $w = 10$

  i w^6 **ii** w^{-3} **iii** $25w^{-2}$

Rules for multiplying and dividing numbers in index form

When we *multiply* together powers of the same number or variable, we *add* the indices. For example,

$$3^4 \times 3^5 = 3^{(4+5)} = 3^9$$

$$2^3 \times 2^4 \times 2^5 = 2^{12}$$

$$10^4 \times 10^{-2} = 10^2$$

$$10^{-3} \times 10^{-1} = 10^{-4}$$

$$a^x \times a^y = a^{(x+y)}$$

When we *divide* powers of the same number or variable, we *subtract* the indices. For example,

$$a^4 \div a^3 = a^{(4-3)} = a^1 = a$$

$$b^4 \div b^7 = b^{-3}$$

$$10^4 \div 10^{-2} = 10^6$$

$$10^{-2} \div 10^{-4} = 10^2$$

$$a^x \div a^y = a^{(x-y)}$$

When we *raise* a power term to a further power, we *multiply* the indices. For example,

$$(a^2)^3 = a^{2 \times 3} = a^6$$

$$(a^{-2})^4 = a^{-8}$$

$$(a^2)^6 = a^{12}$$

$$(a^x)^y = a^{xy}$$

Here are some examples of different kinds of power expressions.

$$2a^2 \times 3a^4 = (2 \times 3) \times (a^2 \times a^4) = 6 \times a^6 = 6a^6$$

$$4a^2b^3 \times 2ab^2 = (4 \times 2) \times (a^2 \times a) \times (b^3 \times b^2) = 8a^3b^5$$

$$12a^5 \div 3a^2 = (12 \div 3) \times (a^5 \div a^2) = 4a^3$$

$$(2a^2)^3 = (2)^3 \times (a^2)^3 = 8 \times a^6 = 8a^6$$

EXERCISE 7C

1 Write these as single powers of 5.

   a $5^2 \times 5^2$ **b** 5×5^2 **c** $5^{-2} \times 5^4$ **d** $5^6 \times 5^{-3}$ **e** $5^{-2} \times 5^{-3}$

2 Write these as single powers of 6.

   a $6^5 \div 6^2$ **b** $6^4 \div 6^4$ **c** $6^4 \div 6^{-2}$ **d** $6^{-3} \div 6^4$ **e** $6^{-3} \div 6^{-5}$

3 Simplify these and write them as single powers of a.

   a $a^2 \times a$ **b** $a^3 \times a^2$ **c** $a^4 \times a^3$

   d $a^6 \div a^2$ **e** $a^3 \div a$ **f** $a^5 \div a^4$

4 Write these as single powers of 4.

   a $(4^2)^3$ **b** $(4^3)^5$ **c** $(4^1)^6$

   d $(4^3)^{-2}$ **e** $(4^{-2})^{-3}$ **f** $(4^7)^0$

5 Simplify these expressions.

   a $2a^2 \times 3a^3$ **b** $3a^4 \times 3a^{-2}$ **c** $(2a^2)^3$

   d $-2a^2 \times 3a^2$ **e** $-4a^3 \times -2a^5$ **f** $-2a^4 \times 5a^{-7}$

> **HINTS AND TIPS**
>
> Deal with numbers and indices separately and do not confuse the rules. For example $12a^5 \div 4a^2 = (12 \div 4) \times (a^5 \div a^2)$

6 Simplify these expressions.

   a $6a^3 \div 2a^2$ **b** $12a^5 \div 3a^2$ **c** $15a^5 \div 5a$

   d $18a^{-2} \div 3a^{-1}$ **e** $24a^5 \div 6a^{-2}$ **f** $30a \div 6a^5$

7 Simplify these expressions.

   a $2a^2b^3 \times 4a^3b$ **b** $5a^2b^4 \times 2ab^{-3}$ **c** $6a^2b^3 \times 5a^{-4}b^{-5}$

   d $12a^2b^4 \div 6ab$ **e** $24a^{-3}b^4 \div 3a^2b^{-3}$

8 Simplify these expressions.

   a $\dfrac{6a^4b^3}{2ab}$ **b** $\dfrac{2a^2bc^2 \times 6abc^3}{4ab^2c}$ **c** $\dfrac{3abc \times 4a^3b^2c \times 6c^2}{9a^2bc}$

PROOF **9** Use the general rule for dividing powers of the same number, $\dfrac{a^x}{a^y} = a^{x-y}$, to prove that any number raised to the power zero is 1.

Indices of the form $\frac{1}{n}$

Consider the problem $7^x \times 7^x = 7$. This can be written as:

$$7^{(x + x)} = 7$$

$$7^{2x} = 7^1 \Rightarrow 2x = 1 \Rightarrow x = \tfrac{1}{2}$$

If we now substitute $x = \frac{1}{2}$ back into the original equation, we see that:

$$7^{\frac{1}{2}} \times 7^{\frac{1}{2}} = 7$$

This makes $7^{\frac{1}{2}}$ the same as $\sqrt{7}$.

You can similarly show that $7^{\frac{1}{3}}$ is the same as $\sqrt[3]{7}$. And that, generally,

$$x^{\frac{1}{n}} = \sqrt[n]{x} \ (n\text{th root of } x)$$

For example,

$$49^{\frac{1}{2}} = \sqrt{49} = 7 \qquad 8^{\frac{1}{3}} = \sqrt[3]{8} = 2 \qquad 10\,000^{\frac{1}{4}} = \sqrt[4]{10\,000} = 10 \qquad 36^{-\frac{1}{2}} = \frac{1}{\sqrt{36}} = \frac{1}{6}$$

EXERCISE 7D

Evaluate the following.

1. $25^{\frac{1}{2}}$
2. $100^{\frac{1}{2}}$
3. $64^{\frac{1}{2}}$
4. $81^{\frac{1}{2}}$
5. $625^{\frac{1}{2}}$

6. $27^{\frac{1}{3}}$
7. $64^{\frac{1}{3}}$
8. $1000^{\frac{1}{3}}$
9. $125^{\frac{1}{3}}$
10. $512^{\frac{1}{3}}$

11. $144^{\frac{1}{2}}$
12. $400^{\frac{1}{2}}$
13. $625^{\frac{1}{4}}$
14. $81^{\frac{1}{4}}$
15. $100\,000^{\frac{1}{5}}$

16. $729^{\frac{1}{6}}$
17. $32^{\frac{1}{5}}$
18. $1024^{\frac{1}{10}}$
19. $1296^{\frac{1}{4}}$
20. $216^{\frac{1}{3}}$

21. $16^{-\frac{1}{2}}$
22. $8^{-\frac{1}{3}}$
23. $81^{-\frac{1}{4}}$
24. $3125^{-\frac{1}{5}}$
25. $1\,000\,000^{-\frac{1}{6}}$

26. $\left(\dfrac{25}{36}\right)^{\frac{1}{2}}$
27. $\left(\dfrac{100}{36}\right)^{\frac{1}{2}}$
28. $\left(\dfrac{64}{81}\right)^{\frac{1}{2}}$
29. $\left(\dfrac{81}{25}\right)^{\frac{1}{2}}$
30. $\left(\dfrac{25}{64}\right)^{\frac{1}{2}}$

31. $\left(\dfrac{27}{125}\right)^{\frac{1}{3}}$
32. $\left(\dfrac{8}{512}\right)^{\frac{1}{3}}$
33. $\left(\dfrac{1000}{64}\right)^{\frac{1}{3}}$
34. $\left(\dfrac{64}{125}\right)^{\frac{1}{3}}$
35. $\left(\dfrac{512}{343}\right)^{\frac{1}{3}}$

 36. Use the general rule for raising a power to another power to prove that $x^{\frac{1}{n}}$ is equivalent to $\sqrt[n]{x}$

Indices of the form $\frac{a}{b}$

Here are two examples of this form.

$$t^{\frac{2}{3}} = t^{\frac{1}{3}} \times t^{\frac{1}{3}} = (\sqrt[3]{t})^2 \qquad 81^{\frac{3}{4}} = (\sqrt[4]{81})^3 = 3^3 = 27$$

EXAMPLE 2

Evaluate the following.   **a** $16^{-\frac{1}{4}}$ **b** $32^{-\frac{4}{5}}$

When dealing with negative indices do not make the mistake of thinking that the answer will be negative. Do problems like these in three steps.

Step 1: take the root of the base number given by the denominator of the fraction.

Step 2: raise the result to the power given by the numerator of the fraction.

Step 3: take the reciprocal (divide into 1) of the answer, which is what the negative power tells you to do.

a Step 1: $\sqrt[4]{16} = 2$.   Step 2: $2^1 = 2$.   Step 3: reciprocal of 2 is $\frac{1}{2}$

b Step 1: $\sqrt[5]{32} = 2$.   Step 2: $2^4 = 16$.   Step 3: reciprocal of 16 is $\frac{1}{16}$

EXERCISE 7E

1 Evaluate the following.

    a $32^{\frac{4}{5}}$ **b** $125^{\frac{2}{3}}$ **c** $1296^{\frac{3}{4}}$ **d** $243^{\frac{4}{5}}$

2 Rewrite the following in index form.

    a $\sqrt[3]{t^2}$ **b** $\sqrt[4]{m^3}$ **c** $\sqrt[5]{k^2}$ **d** $\sqrt{x^3}$

3 Evaluate the following.

    a $8^{\frac{2}{3}}$ **b** $27^{\frac{2}{3}}$ **c** $16^{\frac{3}{2}}$ **d** $625^{\frac{5}{4}}$

4 Evaluate the following.

    a $25^{-\frac{1}{2}}$ **b** $36^{-\frac{1}{2}}$ **c** $16^{-\frac{1}{4}}$ **d** $81^{-\frac{1}{4}}$

    e $16^{-\frac{1}{2}}$ **f** $8^{-\frac{1}{3}}$ **g** $32^{-\frac{1}{5}}$ **h** $27^{-\frac{1}{3}}$

5 Evaluate the following.

    a $25^{-\frac{3}{2}}$ **b** $36^{-\frac{3}{2}}$ **c** $16^{-\frac{3}{4}}$ **d** $81^{-\frac{3}{4}}$

    e $64^{-\frac{4}{3}}$ **f** $8^{-\frac{2}{3}}$ **g** $32^{-\frac{2}{5}}$ **h** $27^{-\frac{2}{3}}$

6 Evaluate the following.

    a $100^{-\frac{5}{2}}$ **b** $144^{-\frac{1}{2}}$ **c** $125^{-\frac{2}{3}}$ **d** $9^{-\frac{3}{2}}$

    e $4^{-\frac{5}{2}}$ **f** $64^{-\frac{5}{6}}$ **g** $27^{-\frac{4}{3}}$ **h** $169^{-\frac{1}{2}}$

This section will introduce you to:
- standard form and show you how to calculate with standard form

Key words

powers
standard
form

Arithmetic of powers of 10

Multiplying

You have already done some arithmetic with multiples of 10 in Chapter 4. We will now look at **powers** of 10.

How many zeros does a million have? What is a million as a power of 10? This table shows some of the pattern of the powers of 10.

Number	0.001	0.01	0.1	1	10	100	1000	10 000	100 000
Powers	10^{-3}	10^{-2}	10^{-1}	10^0	10^1	10^2	10^3	10^4	10^5

What pattern is there in the top row? What pattern is there to the powers in the bottom row?

To multiply by any power of 10, we simply move the digits according to these two rules.

- When the index is *positive*, move the digits to the *left* by the same number of places as the value of the index.

- When the index is *negative*, move the digits to the *right* by the same number of places as the value of the index.

For example,

$12.356 \times 10^2 = 1235.6$ $3.45 \times 10^1 = 34.5$

$753.4 \times 10^{-2} = 7.534$ $6789 \times 10^{-1} = 678.9$

In certain cases, we have to insert the "hidden" zeros. For example,

$75 \times 10^4 = 750\,000$ $2.04 \times 10^5 = 204\,000$

$6.78 \times 10^{-3} = 0.006\,78$ $0.897 \times 10^{-4} = 0.000\,0897$

Dividing

To divide by any power of 10, we simply move the digits according to these two rules.

- When the index is *positive*, move the digits to the *right* by the same number of places as the value of the index.

- When the index is *negative*, move the digits to the *left* by the same number of places as the value of the index.

For example,

$712.35 \div 10^2 = 7.1235$ $\qquad\qquad$ $38.45 \div 10^1 = 3.845$

$3.463 \div 10^{-2} = 346.3$ $\qquad\qquad$ $6.789 \div 10^{-1} = 67.89$

In certain cases, we have to insert the "hidden" zeros. For example,

$75 \div 10^4 = 0.0075$ $\qquad\qquad$ $2.04 \div 10^5 = 0.000\,0204$

$6.78 \div 10^{-3} = 6780$ $\qquad\qquad$ $0.08 \div 10^{-4} = 800$

When doing the next exercise, remember:

$$10\,000 = 10 \times 10 \times 10 \times 10 = 10^4$$
$$1000 = 10 \times 10 \times 10 \qquad = 10^3$$
$$100 = 10 \times 10 \qquad\quad = 10^2$$
$$10 = 10 \qquad\qquad\quad = 10^1$$

$$1 \qquad\qquad\qquad = 10^0$$
$$0.1 = 1 \div 10 \qquad = 10^{-1}$$
$$0.01 = 1 \div 100 \quad = 10^{-2}$$
$$0.001 = 1 \div 1000 = 10^{-3}$$

EXERCISE 7F

1 Write down the value of each of the following.

   a 3.1×10 **b** 3.1×100 **c** 3.1×1000 **d** $3.1 \times 10\,000$

2 Write down the value of each of the following.

   a 6.5×10 **b** 6.5×10^2 **c** 6.5×10^3 **d** 6.5×10^4

3 Write down the value of each of the following.

   a $3.1 \div 10$ **b** $3.1 \div 100$ **c** $3.1 \div 1000$ **d** $3.1 \div 10\,000$

4 Write down the value of each of the following.

   a $6.5 \div 10$ **b** $6.5 \div 10^2$ **c** $6.5 \div 10^3$ **d** $6.5 \div 10^4$

5 Evaluate the following.

   a 2.5×100 **b** 3.45×10 **c** 4.67×1000 **d** 34.6×10

   e 20.789×10 **f** 56.78×1000 **g** 2.46×10^2 **h** 0.076×10

   i 0.999×10^6 **j** 234.56×10^2 **k** 98.7654×10^3 **l** 43.23×10^6

   m $0.003\,4578 \times 10^5$ **n** 0.0006×10^7 **o** $0.005\,67 \times 10^4$ **p** 56.0045×10^4

6 Evaluate the following.

   a $2.5 \div 100$ **b** $3.45 \div 10$ **c** $4.67 \div 1000$ **d** $34.6 \div 10$

   e $20.789 \div 100$ **f** $56.78 \div 1000$ **g** $2.46 \div 10^2$ **h** $0.076 \div 10$

   i $0.999 \div 10^6$ **j** $234.56 \div 10^2$ **k** $98.7654 \div 10^3$ **l** $43.23 \div 10^6$

   m $0.003\,4578 \div 10^5$ **n** $0.0006 \div 10^7$ **o** $0.005\,67 \div 10^4$ **p** $56.0045 \div 10^4$

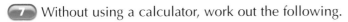

7 Without using a calculator, work out the following.

a 2.3×10^2 **b** 5.789×10^5 **c** 4.79×10^3 **d** 5.7×10^7

e 2.16×10^2 **f** 1.05×10^4 **g** 3.2×10^{-4} **h** 9.87×10^3

8 Which of these statements is true about the numbers in question **7**?

a The first part is always a number between 1 and 10.

b There is always a multiplication sign in the middle of the expression.

c There is always a power of 10 at the end.

d Calculator displays sometimes show numbers in this form.

Standard form

Standard form is also known as standard index form or SI form. On calculators, it is usually called scientific notation.

Standard form is a way of writing very large and very small numbers using powers of 10. In this form, a number is given a value between 1 and 10 multiplied by a power of 10. That is,

$a \times 10^n$ where $1 \leq a < 10$, and n is a whole number

Follow through these examples to see how numbers are written in standard form.

$$52 = \quad 5.2 \times 10 \quad = \mathbf{5.2 \times 10^1}$$

$$73 = \quad 7.3 \times 10 \quad = \mathbf{7.3 \times 10^1}$$

$$625 = \quad 6.25 \times 100 \quad = \mathbf{6.25 \times 10^2}$$ The numbers in bold are in standard form.

$$389 = \quad 3.89 \times 100 \quad = \mathbf{3.89 \times 10^2}$$

$$3147 = 3.147 \times 1000 = \mathbf{3.147 \times 10^3}$$

When writing a number in this way, two rules must always be followed.

- The first part must be a number between 1 and 10 (1 is allowed but 10 isn't).

- The second part must be a whole number (negative or positive) power of 10. Note that we would *not normally* write the power 1.

Standard form on a calculator

A number such as 123 000 000 000 is obviously difficult to key into a calculator. Instead, you enter it in standard form (assuming you are using a scientific calculator):

$$123\ 000\ 000\ 000 = 1.23 \times 10^{11}$$

The key strokes to enter this into your calculator will be

1 **·** **2** **3** **EXP** **1** **1**   (On some calculators EXP is EE.)

Your calculator display should now show

1.23 ^[11]   or   1.23   [11]

Be careful when you get an answer like this on your calculator. It needs to be written properly in standard form with × 10, not copied exactly as shown on the calculator display.

Standard form of numbers less than 1

These numbers are written in standard form. Make sure that you understand how they are formed.

a $0.4 = 4 \times 10^{-1}$

b $0.05 = 5 \times 10^{-2}$

c $0.007 = 7 \times 10^{-3}$

d $0.123 = 1.23 \times 10^{-1}$

e $0.007\,65 = 7.65 \times 10^{-3}$

f $0.9804 = 9.804 \times 10^{-1}$

g $0.0098 = 9.8 \times 10^{-3}$

h $0.000\,0078 = 7.8 \times 10^{-6}$

On a calculator you would enter 1.23×10^{-6}, for example, as

1 **·** **2** **3** **EXP** **+/−** **6**

or **1** **·** **2** **3** **EXP** **6** **+/−**

How you enter such numbers will depend on your type of calculator. Try some of the numbers **a** to **h** (above) to see what happens.

EXERCISE 7G

1 Write down the value of each of the following.

   a 3.1×0.1 **b** 3.1×0.01 **c** 3.1×0.001 **d** 3.1×0.0001

2 Write down the value of each of the following.

   a 6.5×10^{-1} **b** 6.5×10^{-2} **c** 6.5×10^{-3} **d** 6.5×10^{-4}

3 **a** What is the largest number you can enter into your calculator?

   b What is the smallest number you can enter into your calculator?

4 Work out the value of each of the following.

   a $3.1 \div 0.1$ **b** $3.1 \div 0.01$ **c** $3.1 \div 0.001$ **d** $3.1 \div 0.0001$

5 Work out the value of each of the following.

   a $6.5 \div 10^{-1}$ **b** $6.5 \div 10^{-2}$ **c** $6.5 \div 10^{-3}$ **d** $6.5 \div 10^{-4}$

6 Write these numbers out in full.

a 2.5×10^2 b 3.45×10 c 4.67×10^{-3} d 3.46×10

e 2.0789×10^{-2} f 5.678×10^3 g 2.46×10^2 h 7.6×10^3

i 8.97×10^5 j 8.65×10^{-3} k 6×10^7 l 5.67×10^{-4}

7 Write these numbers in standard form.

a 250   b 0.345   c 46 700

d 3 400 000 000   e 20 780 000 000   f 0.000 5678

g 2460   h 0.076   i 0.000 76

j 0.999   k 234.56   l 98.7654

m 0.0006   n 0.005 67   o 56.0045

In questions **8** to **10**, write the numbers given in each question in standard form.

8 One year, 27 797 runners completed the New York marathon.

9 The largest number of dominoes ever toppled by one person is 281 581, although 30 people set up and toppled 1 382 101.

10 The asteroid Phaethon comes within 12 980 000 miles of the sun, whilst the asteroid Pholus, at its furthest point, is a distance of 2997 million miles from the earth. The closest an asteroid ever came to Earth was 93 000 miles from the planet.

Calculating with standard form

Calculations involving very large or very small numbers can be done more easily using standard form. In these examples, we work out the area of a pixel on a computer screen, and how long it takes light to reach the Earth from a distant star.

EXAMPLE 3

A pixel on a computer screen is 2×10^{-2} cm long by 7×10^{-3} cm wide.

What is the area of the pixel?

The area is given by length times width:

Area $= 2 \times 10^{-2}$ cm $\times 7 \times 10^{-3}$ cm

$= (2 \times 7) \times (10^{-2} \times 10^{-3})$ cm$^2 = 14 \times 10^{-5}$ cm^2

Note that you multiply the numbers and add the powers of 10. (You should not need to use a calculator to do this calculation.) The answer is not in standard form as the first part is not between 1 and 10, so we have to change it to standard form.

Area $= 14 \times 10^{-5}$ cm$^2 = 1.4 \times 10^{-4}$ cm^2

EXAMPLE 4

The star Betelgeuse is 1.8×10^{15} miles from Earth. Light travels at 1.86×10^5 miles per second.

a How many seconds does it take light to travel from Betelgeuse to Earth? Give your answer in standard form.

b How many years does it take light to travel from Betelgeuse to Earth?

a Time = distance ÷ speed = 1.8×10^{15} miles ÷ 1.86×10^5 miles per second

$\quad = (1.8 \div 1.86) \times (10^{15} \div 10^5)$ seconds

$\quad = 0.967\ 741\ 935 \times 10^{10}$ seconds

Note that you divide the numbers and subtract the powers of 10. To change the answer to standard form, first round it off, which gives

$\quad 0.97 \times 10^{10} = 9.7 \times 10^9$ seconds

b To convert from seconds to years, you have to divide first by 3600 to get to hours, then by 24 to get to days, and finally by 365 to get to years.

$\quad 9.7 \times 10^9 \div (3600 \times 24 \times 365) = 307.6$ years

EXERCISE 7H

1 These numbers are not in standard form. Write them in standard form.

a 56.7×10^2
b 0.06×10^4
c 34.6×10^{-2}
d 0.07×10^{-2}
e 56×10
f $2 \times 3 \times 10^5$
g $2 \times 10^2 \times 35$
h 160×10^{-2}
i 23 million
j 0.0003×10^{-2}
k 25.6×10^5
l $16 \times 10^2 \times 3 \times 10^{-1}$
m $2 \times 10^4 \times 56 \times 10^{-4}$
n $18 \times 10^2 \div 3 \times 10^3$
o $56 \times 10^3 \div 2 \times 10^{-2}$

2 Work out the following. Give your answers in standard form.

a $2 \times 10^4 \times 5.4 \times 10^3$
b $1.6 \times 10^2 \times 3 \times 10^4$
c $2 \times 10^4 \times 6 \times 10^4$
d $2 \times 10^{-4} \times 5.4 \times 10^3$
e $1.6 \times 10^{-2} \times 4 \times 10^4$
f $2 \times 10^4 \times 6 \times 10^{-4}$
g $7.2 \times 10^{-3} \times 4 \times 10^2$
h $(5 \times 10^3)^2$
i $(2 \times 10^{-2})^3$

3 Work out the following. Give your answers in standard form, rounding off to an appropriate degree of accuracy where necessary.

a $2.1 \times 10^4 \times 5.4 \times 10^3$
b $1.6 \times 10^3 \times 3.8 \times 10^3$
c $2.4 \times 10^4 \times 6.6 \times 10^4$
d $7.3 \times 10^{-6} \times 5.4 \times 10^3$
e $(3.1 \times 10^4)^2$
f $(6.8 \times 10^{-4})^2$
g $5.7 \times 10 \times 3.7 \times 10$
h $1.9 \times 10^{-2} \times 1.9 \times 10^9$
i $5.9 \times 10^3 \times 2.5 \times 10^{-2}$
j $5.2 \times 10^3 \times 2.2 \times 10^2 \times 3.1 \times 10^3$
k $1.8 \times 10^2 \times 3.6 \times 10^3 \times 2.4 \times 10^{-2}$

4 Work out the following. Give your answers in standard form.

a $5.4 \times 10^4 \div 2 \times 10^3$
b $4.8 \times 10^2 \div 3 \times 10^4$
c $1.2 \times 10^4 \div 6 \times 10^4$
d $2 \times 10^{-4} \div 5 \times 10^3$
e $1.8 \times 10^4 \div 9 \times 10^{-2}$
f $\sqrt{(36 \times 10^{-4})}$
g $5.4 \times 10^{-3} \div 2.7 \times 10^2$
h $1.8 \times 10^6 \div 3.6 \times 10^3$
i $5.6 \times 10^3 \div 2.8 \times 10^2$

5 Work out the following. Give your answers in standard form, rounding off to an appropriate degree of accuracy where necessary.

a $2.7 \times 10^4 \div 5 \times 10^2$ **b** $2.3 \times 10^4 \div 8 \times 10^6$ **c** $3.2 \times 10^{-1} \div 2.8 \times 10^{-1}$

d $2.6 \times 10^{-6} \div 4.1 \times 10^3$ **e** $\sqrt{(8 \times 10^4)}$ **f** $\sqrt{(30 \times 10^{-4})}$

g $5.3 \times 10^3 \times 2.3 \times 10^2 \div 2.5 \times 10^3$ **h** $1.8 \times 10^2 \times 3.1 \times 10^3 \div 6.5 \times 10^{-2}$

6 A typical adult has about 20 000 000 000 000 red corpuscles. Each red corpuscle weighs about 0.000 000 000 1 gram. Write both of these numbers in standard form and work out the total mass of red corpuscles in a typical adult.

7 If a man puts 1 grain of rice on the first square of a chess board, 2 on the second square, 4 on the third, 8 on the fourth and so on,

a how many grains of rice will he put on the 64th square of the board?

b how many grains of rice will there be altogether?

Give your answers in standard form.

8 The surface area of the Earth is approximately 2×10^8 square miles. The surface area of the earth covered by water is approximately 1.4×10^8 square miles.

a Calculate the surface area of the Earth not covered by water. Give your answer in standard form.

b What percentage of the Earth's surface is not covered by water?

9 The moon is a sphere with a radius of 1.080×10^3 miles. The formula for working out the surface area of a sphere is

Surface area = $4\pi r^2$

Calculate the surface area of the moon.

10 Evaluate $\dfrac{E}{M}$ when $E = 1.5 \times 10^3$ and $M = 3 \times 10^{-2}$, giving your answer in standard form.

11 Work out the value of $\dfrac{3.2 \times 10^7}{1.4 \times 10^2}$ giving your answer in standard form, correct to two significant figures.

12 In 2005, British Airways carried 23 million passengers. Of these, 70% passed through Heathrow Airport. On average, each passenger carried 19.7 kg of luggage. Calculate the total weight of the luggage carried by these passengers.

13 Many people withdraw money from their banks by using hole-in-the-wall machines. Each day there are eight million withdrawals from 32 000 machines. What is the average number of withdrawals per machine?

14 The mass of Saturn is 5.686×10^{26} tonnes. The mass of the Earth is 6.04×10^{21} tonnes. How many times heavier is Saturn than the Earth? Give your answer in standard form to a suitable degree of accuracy.

Reciprocals and rational numbers

This section will explain about:

- reciprocals, and terminating and recurring decimals

Key words

rational
    number
reciprocal
recurring
    decimal
terminating
    decimal

Rational decimal numbers

A fraction, also known as a **rational number**, can be expressed as a decimal which is either a **terminating decimal** or a **recurring decimal**.

A terminating decimal contains a finite number of digits (decimal places). For example, changing $\frac{3}{16}$ into a decimal gives 0.1875 exactly.

A recurring decimal contains a digit or a block of digits that repeats. For example, changing $\frac{5}{9}$ into a decimal gives 0.5555 …, while changing $\frac{14}{27}$ into a decimal gives 0.518 518 5 … with the recurring block 518.

Recurring decimals are indicated by a dot placed over the first and last digits in the recurring block. For example, 0.5555 … becomes $0.\dot{5}$, 0.518 518 5 … becomes $0.\dot{5}1\dot{8}$, and 0.583 33 becomes $0.58\dot{3}$.

Converting decimals into fractions

Terminating decimals

When converting a terminating decimal, the numerator of the fraction is formed from the decimal, and its denominator is given by 10, 100 or 1000, depending on the number of decimal places. Because the terminating decimal ends at a specific decimal place, we know the place value at which the numerator ends. For example,

$$0.7 = \frac{7}{10}$$

$$0.045 = \frac{45}{1000} = \frac{9}{200}$$

$$2.34 = 2\frac{34}{100} = 2\frac{17}{50}$$

$$0.625 = \frac{625}{1000} = \frac{5}{8}$$

Recurring decimals

If a fraction does not give a terminating decimal, it will give a recurring decimal. You already know that $\frac{1}{3} = 0.333 … = 0.\dot{3}$. This means that the 3s go on forever and the decimal never ends. To check whether a fraction is a recurring decimal, you usually have to use a calculator to divide the numerator by the denominator. Use a calculator to check the following recurring decimals. (Note that calculators round off the last digit so it may not always be a true recurring decimal in the display.)

$$\frac{2}{11} = 0.181818\ldots = 0.\dot{1}\dot{8}$$

$$\frac{4}{15} = 0.2666\ldots = 0.2\dot{6}$$

$$\frac{8}{13} = 0.6153846153846\ldots = 0.\dot{6}1538\dot{4}$$

To convert a recurring decimal to a fraction, you have to multiply the decimal by a suitable power of 10, and then perform a subtraction. These examples demonstrate the method.

EXAMPLE 5

Convert $0.\dot{7}$ to a fraction.

Let x be the fraction. Then

$$x = 0.777\ 777\ 777\ldots \quad (1)$$

Multiply (1) by 10 $\qquad 10x = 7.777\ 777\ 777\ldots \quad (2)$

Subtract (2) − (1) $\qquad 9x = 7$

$$\Rightarrow x = \frac{7}{9}$$

EXAMPLE 6

Convert $0.\dot{5}6\dot{4}$ to a fraction.

Let x be the fraction. Then

$$x = 0.564\ 564\ 564\ldots \quad (1)$$

Multiply (1) by 1000 $\qquad 1000x = 564.564\ 564\ 564\ldots \quad (2)$

Subtract (2) − (1) $\qquad 999x = 564$

$$\Rightarrow \quad x = \frac{564}{999} = \frac{188}{333}$$

As a general rule multiply by 10 if one digit recurs, multiply by 100 if two digits recur, multiply by 1000 if three digits recur, and so on.

Reciprocals

The **reciprocal** of a number is the number divided into 1. So the reciprocal of 2 is $1 \div 2 = \frac{1}{2}$ or 0.5.

Reciprocals of fractions are quite easy to find as you just have to turn the fraction upside down.
For example, the reciprocal of $\frac{2}{3}$ is $\frac{3}{2}$.

EXERCISE 7I

1 Work out each of these fractions as a decimal. Give them as terminating decimals or recurring decimals as appropriate.

a $\frac{1}{2}$ **b** $\frac{1}{3}$ **c** $\frac{1}{4}$ **d** $\frac{1}{5}$ **e** $\frac{1}{6}$

f $\frac{1}{7}$ **g** $\frac{1}{8}$ **h** $\frac{1}{9}$ **i** $\frac{1}{10}$ **j** $\frac{1}{13}$

2 There are several patterns to be found in recurring decimals. For example,

$\frac{1}{7} = 0.142\ 857\ 142\ 857\ 142\ 857\ 142\ 857\ldots$

$\frac{2}{7} = 0.285\ 714\ 285\ 714\ 285\ 714\ 285\ 714\ldots$

$\frac{3}{7} = 0.428\ 571\ 428\ 571\ 428\ 571\ 428\ 571\ldots$

and so on.

a Write down the decimals for $\frac{4}{7}, \frac{5}{7}, \frac{6}{7}$ to 24 decimal places.

b What do you notice?

3 Work out the ninths as recurring decimals, that is $\frac{1}{9}, \frac{2}{9}, \frac{3}{9}$ and so on, up to $\frac{8}{9}$.

Describe any patterns that you notice.

4 Work out the elevenths as recurring decimals, that is $\frac{1}{11}, \frac{2}{11}, \frac{3}{11}$ and so on, up to $\frac{10}{11}$.

Describe any patterns that you notice.

5 Write each of these fractions as a decimal. Use this to write the list in order of size, smallest first.

$\frac{4}{9}$ $\frac{5}{11}$ $\frac{3}{7}$ $\frac{9}{22}$ $\frac{16}{37}$ $\frac{6}{13}$

6 Write each of the following as a fraction with a denominator of 120. Use this to put them in order of size, smallest first.

$\frac{19}{60}$ $\frac{7}{24}$ $\frac{3}{10}$ $\frac{2}{5}$ $\frac{5}{12}$

7 Convert each of these terminating decimals to a fraction.

a 0.125 **b** 0.34 **c** 0.725 **d** 0.3125

e 0.89 **f** 0.05 **g** 2.35 **h** 0.218 75

8 Use a calculator to work out the reciprocals of the following values.

a 12 **b** 16 **c** 20 **d** 25 **e** 50

9 Write down the reciprocals of the following fractions.

a $\frac{3}{4}$ **b** $\frac{5}{6}$ **c** $\frac{2}{5}$ **d** $\frac{7}{10}$

e $\frac{11}{20}$ **f** $\frac{4}{15}$

10 **a** Work out the fractions and their reciprocals from question **9** as decimals. Write them as terminating decimals or recurring decimals as appropriate.

b Is it always true that a fraction that gives a terminating decimal has a reciprocal that gives a recurring decimal?

11 Multiply together the fractions and their reciprocals from question **9**. What results do you get every time?

12 $x = 0.242\ 424\ ...$

a What is $100x$?

b By subtracting the original value from your answer to part **a**, work out the value of $99x$.

c What is x as a fraction?

13 Convert each of these recurring decimals to a fraction.

a	$0.\dot{8}$	**b**	$0.3\dot{4}$	**c**	$0.\dot{4}\dot{5}$	**d**	$0.5\dot{6}\dot{7}$
e	$0.\dot{4}$	**f**	$0.0\dot{4}$	**g**	$0.1\dot{4}$	**h**	$0.04\dot{5}$
i	$2.\dot{7}$	**j**	$7.6\dot{3}$	**k**	$3.\dot{3}$	**l**	$2.0\dot{6}$

14 **a** $\frac{1}{7}$ is a recurring decimal. $\left(\frac{1}{7}\right)^2 = \frac{1}{49}$ is also a recurring decimal.

Is it true that when you square any fraction that is a recurring decimal, you get another fraction that is also a recurring decimal? Try this with at least four numerical examples before you make a decision.

b $\frac{1}{4}$ is a terminating decimal. $\left(\frac{1}{4}\right)^2 = \frac{1}{16}$ is also a terminating decimal.

Is it true that when you square any fraction that is a terminating decimal, you get another fraction that is also a terminating decimal? Try this with at least four numerical examples before you make a decision.

c What type of fraction do you get when you multiply a fraction that gives a recurring decimal by another fraction that gives a terminating decimal? Try this with at least four numerical examples before you make a decision.

15 **a** Convert the recurring decimal $0.\dot{9}$ to a fraction.

b Prove that $0.4\dot{9}$ is equal to 0.5.

7.4 Surds

In this section you will learn how to:
- calculate and manipulate surds

Key words
rationalise
surds

It is useful at higher levels of mathematics to be able to work with **surds**, which are roots of numbers written as, for example,

$$\sqrt{2} \quad \sqrt{5} \quad \sqrt{15} \quad \sqrt{9} \quad \sqrt{3} \quad \sqrt{10}$$

Four general rules governing surds (which you can verify yourself by taking numerical examples) are:

$$\sqrt{a} \times \sqrt{b} = \sqrt{ab} \qquad\qquad C\sqrt{a} \times D\sqrt{b} = CD\sqrt{ab}$$

$$\sqrt{a} \div \sqrt{b} = \sqrt{\frac{a}{b}} \qquad\qquad C\sqrt{a} \div D\sqrt{b} = \frac{C}{D}\sqrt{\frac{a}{b}}$$

For example,

$$\sqrt{2} \times \sqrt{2} = \sqrt{4} = 2 \qquad \sqrt{2} \times \sqrt{10} = \sqrt{20} = \sqrt{(4 \times 5)} = \sqrt{4} \times \sqrt{5} = 2\sqrt{5}$$

$$\sqrt{2} \times \sqrt{3} = \sqrt{6} \qquad\qquad \sqrt{6} \times \sqrt{15} = \sqrt{90} = \sqrt{9} \times \sqrt{10} = 3\sqrt{10}$$

$$\sqrt{2} \times \sqrt{8} = \sqrt{16} = 4 \qquad\qquad 3\sqrt{5} \times 4\sqrt{3} = 12\sqrt{15}$$

EXERCISE 7J

1 Simplify each of the following. Leave your answers in surd form.

a $\sqrt{2} \times \sqrt{3}$	**b** $\sqrt{5} \times \sqrt{3}$	**c** $\sqrt{2} \times \sqrt{2}$	**d** $\sqrt{2} \times \sqrt{8}$
e $\sqrt{5} \times \sqrt{8}$	**f** $\sqrt{3} \times \sqrt{3}$	**g** $\sqrt{6} \times \sqrt{2}$	**h** $\sqrt{7} \times \sqrt{3}$
i $\sqrt{2} \times \sqrt{7}$	**j** $\sqrt{2} \times \sqrt{18}$	**k** $\sqrt{6} \times \sqrt{6}$	**l** $\sqrt{5} \times \sqrt{6}$

2 Simplify each of the following. Leave your answers in surd form.

a $\sqrt{12} \div \sqrt{3}$	**b** $\sqrt{15} \div \sqrt{3}$	**c** $\sqrt{12} \div \sqrt{2}$	**d** $\sqrt{24} \div \sqrt{8}$
e $\sqrt{40} \div \sqrt{8}$	**f** $\sqrt{3} \div \sqrt{3}$	**g** $\sqrt{6} \div \sqrt{2}$	**h** $\sqrt{21} \div \sqrt{3}$
i $\sqrt{28} \div \sqrt{7}$	**j** $\sqrt{48} \div \sqrt{8}$	**k** $\sqrt{6} \div \sqrt{6}$	**l** $\sqrt{54} \div \sqrt{6}$

3 Simplify each of the following. Leave your answers in surd form.

a $\sqrt{2} \times \sqrt{3} \times \sqrt{2}$	**b** $\sqrt{5} \times \sqrt{3} \times \sqrt{15}$	**c** $\sqrt{2} \times \sqrt{2} \times \sqrt{8}$	**d** $\sqrt{2} \times \sqrt{8} \times \sqrt{3}$
e $\sqrt{5} \times \sqrt{8} \times \sqrt{8}$	**f** $\sqrt{3} \times \sqrt{3} \times \sqrt{3}$	**g** $\sqrt{6} \times \sqrt{2} \times \sqrt{48}$	**h** $\sqrt{7} \times \sqrt{3} \times \sqrt{3}$
i $\sqrt{2} \times \sqrt{7} \times \sqrt{2}$	**j** $\sqrt{2} \times \sqrt{18} \times \sqrt{5}$	**k** $\sqrt{6} \times \sqrt{6} \times \sqrt{3}$	**l** $\sqrt{5} \times \sqrt{6} \times \sqrt{30}$

4 Simplify each of the following. Leave your answers in surd form.

a $\sqrt{2} \times \sqrt{3} \div \sqrt{2}$ **b** $\sqrt{5} \times \sqrt{3} \div \sqrt{15}$ **c** $\sqrt{32} \times \sqrt{2} \div \sqrt{8}$ **d** $\sqrt{2} \times \sqrt{8} \div \sqrt{8}$

e $\sqrt{5} \times \sqrt{8} \div \sqrt{8}$ **f** $\sqrt{3} \times \sqrt{3} \div \sqrt{3}$ **g** $\sqrt{8} \times \sqrt{12} \div \sqrt{48}$ **h** $\sqrt{7} \times \sqrt{3} \div \sqrt{3}$

i $\sqrt{2} \times \sqrt{7} \div \sqrt{2}$ **j** $\sqrt{2} \times \sqrt{18} \div \sqrt{3}$ **k** $\sqrt{6} \times \sqrt{6} \div \sqrt{3}$ **l** $\sqrt{5} \times \sqrt{6} \div \sqrt{30}$

5 Simplify each of these expressions.

a $\sqrt{a} \times \sqrt{a}$ **b** $\sqrt{a} \div \sqrt{a}$ **c** $\sqrt{a} \times \sqrt{a} \div \sqrt{a}$

6 Simplify each of the following surds into the form $a\sqrt{b}$.

a $\sqrt{18}$ **b** $\sqrt{24}$ **c** $\sqrt{12}$ **d** $\sqrt{50}$

e $\sqrt{8}$ **f** $\sqrt{27}$ **g** $\sqrt{48}$ **h** $\sqrt{75}$

i $\sqrt{45}$ **j** $\sqrt{63}$ **k** $\sqrt{32}$ **l** $\sqrt{200}$

m $\sqrt{1000}$ **n** $\sqrt{250}$ **o** $\sqrt{98}$ **p** $\sqrt{243}$

7 Simplify each of these.

a $2\sqrt{18} \times 3\sqrt{2}$ **b** $4\sqrt{24} \times 2\sqrt{5}$ **c** $3\sqrt{12} \times 3\sqrt{3}$ **d** $2\sqrt{8} \times 2\sqrt{8}$

e $2\sqrt{27} \times 4\sqrt{8}$ **f** $2\sqrt{48} \times 3\sqrt{8}$ **g** $2\sqrt{45} \times 3\sqrt{3}$ **h** $2\sqrt{63} \times 2\sqrt{7}$

i $2\sqrt{32} \times 4\sqrt{2}$ **j** $\sqrt{1000} \times \sqrt{10}$ **k** $\sqrt{250} \times \sqrt{10}$ **l** $2\sqrt{98} \times 2\sqrt{2}$

8 Simplify each of these.

a $4\sqrt{2} \times 5\sqrt{3}$ **b** $2\sqrt{5} \times 3\sqrt{3}$ **c** $4\sqrt{2} \times 3\sqrt{2}$ **d** $2\sqrt{2} \times 2\sqrt{8}$

e $2\sqrt{5} \times 3\sqrt{8}$ **f** $3\sqrt{3} \times 2\sqrt{3}$ **g** $2\sqrt{6} \times 5\sqrt{2}$ **h** $5\sqrt{7} \times 2\sqrt{3}$

i $2\sqrt{2} \times 3\sqrt{7}$ **j** $2\sqrt{2} \times 3\sqrt{18}$ **k** $2\sqrt{6} \times 2\sqrt{6}$ **l** $4\sqrt{5} \times 3\sqrt{6}$

9 Simplify each of these.

a $6\sqrt{12} \div 2\sqrt{3}$ **b** $3\sqrt{15} \div \sqrt{3}$ **c** $6\sqrt{12} \div \sqrt{2}$ **d** $4\sqrt{24} \div 2\sqrt{8}$

e $12\sqrt{40} \div 3\sqrt{8}$ **f** $5\sqrt{3} \div \sqrt{3}$ **g** $14\sqrt{6} \div 2\sqrt{2}$ **h** $4\sqrt{21} \div 2\sqrt{3}$

i $9\sqrt{28} \div 3\sqrt{7}$ **j** $12\sqrt{56} \div 6\sqrt{8}$ **k** $25\sqrt{6} \div 5\sqrt{6}$ **l** $32\sqrt{54} \div 4\sqrt{6}$

10 Simplify each of these.

a $4\sqrt{2} \times \sqrt{3} \div 2\sqrt{2}$ **b** $4\sqrt{5} \times \sqrt{3} \div \sqrt{15}$ **c** $2\sqrt{32} \times 3\sqrt{2} \div 2\sqrt{8}$

d $6\sqrt{2} \times 2\sqrt{8} \div 3\sqrt{8}$ **e** $3\sqrt{5} \times 4\sqrt{8} \div 2\sqrt{8}$ **f** $12\sqrt{3} \times 4\sqrt{3} \div 2\sqrt{3}$

g $3\sqrt{8} \times 3\sqrt{12} \div 3\sqrt{48}$ **h** $4\sqrt{7} \times 2\sqrt{3} \div 8\sqrt{3}$ **i** $15\sqrt{2} \times 2\sqrt{7} \div 3\sqrt{2}$

j $8\sqrt{2} \times 2\sqrt{18} \div 4\sqrt{3}$ **k** $5\sqrt{6} \times 5\sqrt{6} \div 5\sqrt{3}$ **l** $2\sqrt{5} \times 3\sqrt{6} \div \sqrt{30}$

11 Simplify each of these expressions.

a $a\sqrt{b} \times c\sqrt{b}$ **b** $a\sqrt{b} \div c\sqrt{b}$ **c** $a\sqrt{b} \times c\sqrt{b} \div a\sqrt{b}$

12 Find the value of a that makes each of these surds true.

a $\sqrt{5} \times \sqrt{a} = 10$

b $\sqrt{6} \times \sqrt{a} = 12$

c $\sqrt{10} \times 2\sqrt{a} = 20$

d $2\sqrt{6} \times 3\sqrt{a} = 72$

e $2\sqrt{a} \times \sqrt{a} = 6$

f $3\sqrt{a} \times 3\sqrt{a} = 54$

13 Simplify the following.

a $\left(\dfrac{\sqrt{3}}{2}\right)^2$

b $\left(\dfrac{5}{\sqrt{3}}\right)^2$

c $\left(\dfrac{\sqrt{5}}{4}\right)^2$

d $\left(\dfrac{6}{\sqrt{3}}\right)^2$

e $\left(\dfrac{\sqrt{8}}{2}\right)^2$

14 The following rules are *not* true. Try some numerical examples to show this.

a $\sqrt{(a + b)} = \sqrt{a} + \sqrt{b}$

b $\sqrt{(a - b)} = \sqrt{a} - \sqrt{b}$

Calculating with surds

The following two examples show how surds can be used in solving problems.

EXAMPLE 7

In the right-angled triangle ABC, the side BC is $\sqrt{6}$ cm and the side AC is $\sqrt{18}$ cm.

Calculate the length of AB. Leave your answer in surd form.

Using Pythagoras' theorem

$$AC^2 + BC^2 = AB^2$$
$$(\sqrt{18})^2 + (\sqrt{6})^2 = 18 + 6 = 24$$
$$\Rightarrow AB = \sqrt{24} \text{ cm}$$
$$= 2\sqrt{6} \text{ cm}$$

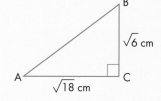

EXAMPLE 8

Calculate the area of a square with a side of $2 + \sqrt{3}$ cm. Give your answer in the form $a + b\sqrt{3}$.

Area $= (2 + \sqrt{3})^2$ cm^2

$\qquad = (2 + \sqrt{3})(2 + \sqrt{3})$ cm^2

$\qquad = 4 + 2\sqrt{3} + 2\sqrt{3} + 3$ cm^2

$\qquad = 7 + 4\sqrt{3}$ cm^2

Rationalising the denominator

It is not good mathematical practice to leave a surd on the bottom of an expression. To get rid of it, we make the denominator into a whole number, which we do by multiplying by the appropriate square root. This means that we must also multiply the top of the expression by the same root. The following example shows you what to do.

EXAMPLE 9

Rationalise the denominator of **a** $\dfrac{1}{\sqrt{3}}$ and **b** $\dfrac{2\sqrt{3}}{\sqrt{8}}$.

a Multiply the top and the bottom by $\sqrt{3}$:

$$\frac{1 \times \sqrt{3}}{\sqrt{3} \times \sqrt{3}} = \frac{\sqrt{3}}{3}$$

b Multiply the top and the bottom by $\sqrt{8}$:

$$\frac{2\sqrt{3} \times \sqrt{8}}{\sqrt{8} \times \sqrt{8}} = \frac{2\sqrt{24}}{8} = \frac{4\sqrt{6}}{8} = \frac{\sqrt{6}}{2}$$

EXERCISE 7K

1 Show that:

   a $(2 + \sqrt{3})(1 + \sqrt{3}) = 5 + 3\sqrt{3}$

   b $(1 + \sqrt{2})(2 + \sqrt{3}) = 2 + 2\sqrt{2} + \sqrt{3} + \sqrt{6}$

   c $(4 - \sqrt{3})(4 + \sqrt{3}) = 13$

2 Expand and simplify where possible.

   a $\sqrt{3}(2 - \sqrt{3})$ **b** $\sqrt{2}(3 - 4\sqrt{2})$ **c** $\sqrt{5}(2\sqrt{5} + 4)$

   d $3\sqrt{7}(4 - 2\sqrt{7})$ **e** $3\sqrt{2}(5 - 2\sqrt{8})$ **f** $\sqrt{3}(\sqrt{27} - 1)$

3 Expand and simplify where possible.

   a $(1 + \sqrt{3})(3 - \sqrt{3})$ **b** $(2 + \sqrt{5})(3 - \sqrt{5})$ **c** $(1 - \sqrt{2})(3 + 2\sqrt{2})$

   d $(3 - 2\sqrt{7})(4 + 3\sqrt{7})$ **e** $(2 - 3\sqrt{5})(2 + 3\sqrt{5})$ **f** $(\sqrt{3} + \sqrt{2})(\sqrt{3} + \sqrt{8})$

   g $(2 + \sqrt{5})^2$ **h** $(1 - \sqrt{2})^2$ **i** $(3 + \sqrt{2})^2$

4 Work out the missing lengths in each of these triangles, giving the answer in as simple a form as possible.

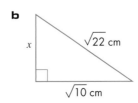
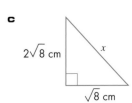

a $\sqrt{8}$ cm, x, $\sqrt{10}$ cm

b x, $\sqrt{22}$ cm, $\sqrt{10}$ cm

c $2\sqrt{8}$ cm, x, $\sqrt{8}$ cm

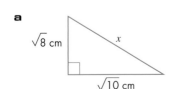

5 Calculate the area of each of these rectangles, simplifying your answers where possible.

a

$1 + \sqrt{3}$ cm

$2 - \sqrt{3}$ cm

b

$2 + \sqrt{10}$ cm

$\sqrt{5}$ cm

c

$2\sqrt{3}$ cm

$1 + \sqrt{27}$ cm

6 Rationalise the denominators of these expressions.

a $\dfrac{1}{\sqrt{3}}$

b $\dfrac{1}{\sqrt{2}}$

c $\dfrac{1}{\sqrt{5}}$

d $\dfrac{1}{2\sqrt{3}}$

e $\dfrac{3}{\sqrt{3}}$

f $\dfrac{5}{\sqrt{2}}$

g $\dfrac{3\sqrt{2}}{\sqrt{8}}$

h $\dfrac{5\sqrt{3}}{\sqrt{6}}$

i $\dfrac{\sqrt{7}}{\sqrt{3}}$

j $\dfrac{1 + \sqrt{2}}{\sqrt{2}}$

k $\dfrac{2 - \sqrt{3}}{\sqrt{3}}$

l $\dfrac{5 + 2\sqrt{3}}{\sqrt{3}}$

7 a Expand and simplify the following.

i $(2 + \sqrt{3})(2 - \sqrt{3})$

ii $(1 - \sqrt{5})(1 + \sqrt{5})$

iii $(\sqrt{3} - 1)(\sqrt{3} + 1)$

iv $(3\sqrt{2} + 1)(3\sqrt{2} - 1)$

v $(2 - 4\sqrt{3})(2 + 4\sqrt{3})$

b What happens in the answers to part **a**? Why?

c Rationalise the denominators of the following.

i $\dfrac{5}{1 - \sqrt{5}}$

ii $\dfrac{2 + \sqrt{3}}{\sqrt{3} - 1}$

1 **a** Simplify

  i $d^4 \times d^5$ **ii** $\dfrac{e^3}{e^7}$ **iii** $(3g^2h^3) \times (4gh^4)$

 b Show that the following statement is wrong.

  $6(p - 2) = 6p + 4$

2 Astronomers measure distances in the solar system in astronomical units (AU).
One AU is 150 000 000 kilometres.
The distance from the Sun to Pluto is 39.5 AU.
How many kilometres is the Sun from Pluto?
Give your answer in standard form to a sensible degree of accuracy.

  AQA, Question 9, Paper 2 Higher, June 2005

3 Here are six numbers written in standard form.

   2.6×10^5 1.75×10^6 5.84×10^0
   8.2×10^{-3} 3.5×10^{-1} 4.9×10^{-2}

 a Write down the largest number.
 b Write down the smallest number.
 c Write 4.9×10^{-2} as an ordinary number.
 d Work out $2.6 \times 10^5 \div 0.1$
  Give your answer in standard form.

  AQA, Question 5, Paper 1 Higher, June 2004

4 Simplify **a** $\dfrac{6a^2b \times 4ab^3}{8a^2b^2}$ **b** $(3x^3y^2)^4$

5 **a** $(x + p)(x - p) \equiv x^2 - 25$ is an identity.

 What is the value of p?
 b $x^2 - 25 = 0$ is an equation.
 What two values of p are solutions of the equation?

6 Find values of a and b such that

  $(2 + \sqrt{3})(4 - \sqrt{3}) = a + b\sqrt{3}$

  AQA, Question 15, Paper 2 Higher, November 2004

7 The area of this rectangle is 40 cm^2
Find the value of x. Give your answer in the form $a\sqrt{b}$ where a and b are integers

4√2 cm

x cm

8 **a** Prove that $0.\dot{7}\dot{2} = \dfrac{8}{11}$

 b Hence, or otherwise, express $0.3\dot{7}\dot{2}$ as a fraction.

9 **a i** Show that $\sqrt{32} = 4\sqrt{2}$

  ii Expand and simplify $(\sqrt{2} + \sqrt{12})^2$

 b Show clearly that this triangle is right angled

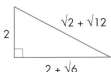

2

√2 + √12

2 + √6

10 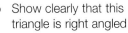 Rationalise the denominator of $\dfrac{2 + \sqrt{3}}{\sqrt{3}}$

Simplify your answer fully.

  AQA, Question 16, Paper 2 Higher, June 2004

WORKED EXAM QUESTION

a Expand and simplify as far as possible $(\sqrt{2} + 3)(\sqrt{2} - 1)$.

b Show clearly that $\dfrac{3}{\sqrt{6}} + \dfrac{\sqrt{6}}{3} = \dfrac{5}{\sqrt{6}}$

Solution

a $\sqrt{2} \times \sqrt{2} + \sqrt{2} \times -1 + 3 \times \sqrt{2} + 3 \times -1$

 $2 - \sqrt{2} + 3\sqrt{2} - 3 = -1 + 2\sqrt{2}$

> Expand the brackets to get four terms.

> Simplify the terms and collect together like terms.

b $\dfrac{3 \times 3 + \sqrt{6} \times \sqrt{6}}{\sqrt{6} \times 3}$

> Combine the fractions together with the same common denominator.

 $\dfrac{9 + 6}{\sqrt{6} \times 3} = \dfrac{15}{3\sqrt{6}} = \dfrac{5}{\sqrt{6}}$

> Simplify the terms and collect together and cancel the common multiple of 3.

A scientist is doing some research on the production and consumption of oil in the world. She looks at 10 oil producing countries and, for each country, finds the most recent figures on the country's population, and its oil production and consumption, measured in barrels per day.

With these figures she calculates for each country the oil produced per person *per year*, and the oil consumed per person *per year*, then finds the difference (all to 1 decimal place).

She then ranks the countries from 1 to 10 (highest difference to lowest difference), to see which countries are using less than they produce, and which countries are using more than they produce.

She also calculates each country's consumption as a percentage of its production (to the nearest 1%).

Help her complete the table and write a short paragraph on the results of the calculations.

USA
Population: 295 734 134
Oil production: 7.8×10^6
Oil consumption: 19.65×10^6

Venezuela
Population: 25 375 281
Oil production: 2.6×10^6
Oil consumption: 500 000

Chile
Population: 15 980 912
Oil production: 18,500
Oil consumption: 240 000

Country	Oil produced, barrels per person per year	Oil consumed, barrels per person per year	Difference (produced – consumed)	Rank order	Consumption as a % of production
Algeria	13.5	2.3	11.2	3	17%
Australia					
Chile					
Indonesia					
Japan					
Nigeria					
Saudi Arabia					
UK					
USA					
Venezuela					

Mod 3

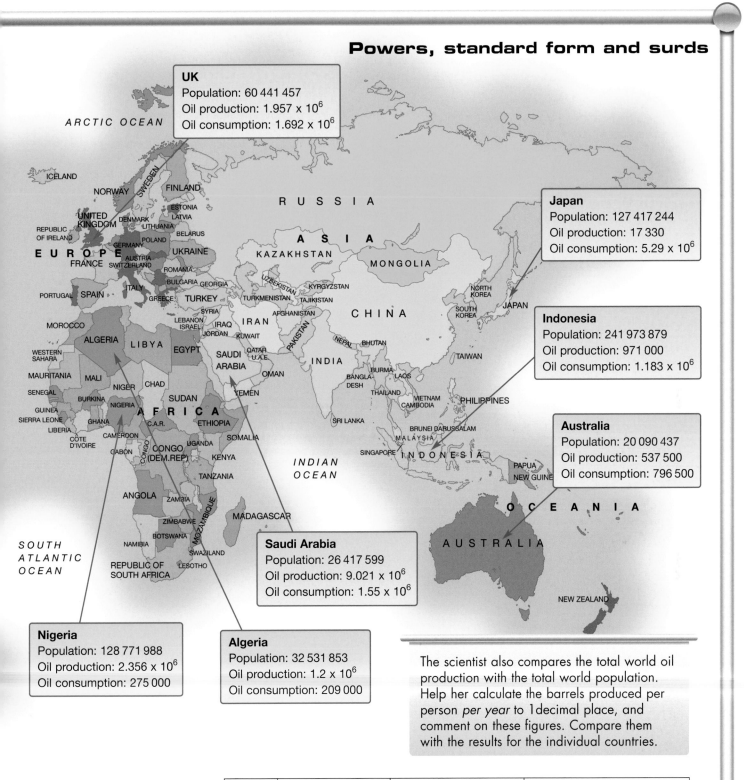

UK
Population: 60 441 457
Oil production: 1.957×10^6
Oil consumption: 1.692×10^6

Japan
Population: 127 417 244
Oil production: 17 330
Oil consumption: 5.29×10^6

Indonesia
Population: 241 973 879
Oil production: 971 000
Oil consumption: 1.183×10^6

Australia
Population: 20 090 437
Oil production: 537 500
Oil consumption: 796 500

Saudi Arabia
Population: 26 417 599
Oil production: 9.021×10^6
Oil consumption: 1.55×10^6

Nigeria
Population: 128 771 988
Oil production: 2.356×10^6
Oil consumption: 275 000

Algeria
Population: 32 531 853
Oil production: 1.2×10^6
Oil consumption: 209 000

The scientist also compares the total world oil production with the total world population. Help her calculate the barrels produced per person *per year* to 1 decimal place, and comment on these figures. Compare them with the results for the individual countries.

Year	World population	World oil production, barrels per day	World oil production, barrels per person per year
1984	4.77×10^9	5.45×10^7	4.2
1989	5.19×10^9	5.99×10^7	
1994	5.61×10^9	6.10×10^7	
1999	6.01×10^9	6.58×10^7	
2004	6.38×10^9	7.25×10^7	

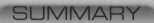

GRADE YOURSELF

D Able to write and calculate numbers written in index form

C Able to multiply and divide numbers written in index form

B Able to write numbers in standard form and use these in various problems

A Know how to use the rules of indices for negative and fractional values

A Able to convert recurring decimals to fractions

A Able to simplify surds

A* Able to manipulate expressions containing surds and rationalise denominators

A* Able to solve problems using surds

What you should know now

- How to write numbers in standard form
- How to solve problems using numbers in standard form
- How to manipulate indices, both integer (positive and negative) and fractional
- How to compare fractions by converting them to decimals
- How to convert decimals into fractions
- What surds are and how to manipulate them

More graphs and equations

1 Quadratic graphs

2 Solving equations by the method of intersection

This chapter will show you ...

- how to draw quadratic graphs
- how to use quadratic graphs to solve equations by the method of intersection

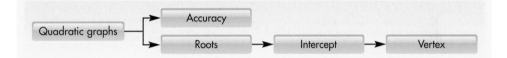

Quadratic graphs → Accuracy

Quadratic graphs → Roots → Intercept → Vertex

What you should already know

- How to plot coordinate points in all four quadrants
- How to substitute numbers into a formula (Chapter 19)

Quick check

1 Substitute

i $x = 4$

ii $x = 2$

into the following expressions:

a x^2 **b** $x^2 + 4$ **c** $x^2 - 2$ **d** $x^2 + 2x$

2 Write down the coordinates of the points A, B, C, D.

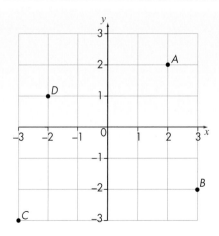

Quadratic graphs

This section will show you how to:

● draw and read values from quadratic graphs

Key words

intercept
maximum
minimum
quadratic
roots
vertex

A **quadratic** graph has a term in x^2 in its equation. All of the following are quadratic equations and each would produce a quadratic graph.

$$y = x^2 \qquad\qquad y = x^2 + 5 \qquad\qquad y = x^2 - 3x$$

$$y = x^2 + 5x + 6 \qquad\qquad y = 3x^2 - 5x + 4$$

EXAMPLE 1

Draw the graph of $y = x^2 + 5x + 6$ for $-5 \leqslant x \leqslant 3$.

Make a table, as shown below. Work out each row (x^2, $5x$, 6) separately, adding them together to obtain the values of y. Then plot the points from the table.

x	−5	−4	−3	−2	−1	0	1	2	3
x^2	25	16	9	4	1	0	1	4	9
$5x$	−25	−20	−15	−10	−5	0	5	10	15
6	6	6	6	6	6	6	6	6	6
y	6	2	0	0	2	6	12	20	30

Note that in an examination paper you may be given only the first and last rows, with some values filled in. For example,

x	−5	−4	−3	−2	−1	0	1	2	3
y	6		0		2				30

In this case, you would either construct your own table, or work out the remaining y-values with a calculator.

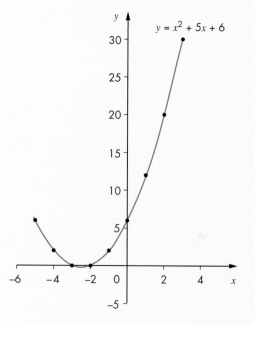

EXAMPLE 2

a Complete the table for $y = 3x^2 - 5x + 4$ for $-1 \leqslant x \leqslant 3$, then draw the graph.

x	−1	−0.5	0	0.5	1	1.5	2	2.5	3
y	12			2.25	2			10.25	16

b Use your graph to find the value of y when $x = 2.2$.

c Use your graph to find the values of x that give a y-value of 9.

a The table gives only some values. So you either set up your own table with $3x^2$, $-5x$ and $+4$, or calculate each y-value. For example, on the majority of scientific calculators, the value for -0.5 will be worked out as

Check that you get an answer of 7.25.

If you want to make sure that you are doing the correct arithmetic with your calculator, try some values for x for which you know the answer. For example, try $x = 0.5$, and see whether your answer is 2.25.

The complete table should be:

x	−1	−0.5	0	0.5	1	1.5	2	2.5	3
y	12	7.25	4	2.25	2	3.25	6	10.25	16

The graph is shown on the right.

b To find the corresponding y-value for any value of x, you start on the x-axis at that x-value, go up to the curve, across to the y-axis and read off the y-value. This procedure is marked on the graph with arrows.

Always show these arrows because even if you make a mistake and misread the scales, you may still get a mark.

When $x = 2.2$, $y = 7.5$.

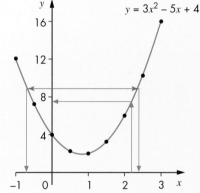

c This time start at 9 on the y-axis and read off the two x-values that correspond to a y-value of 9. Again, this procedure is marked on the graph with arrows.

When $y = 9$, $x = -0.7$ or $x = 2.4$.

Drawing accurate graphs

Note that although it is difficult to draw accurate curves, examiners work to a *tolerance of only 1 mm*.

Here are some of the more common ways in which marks are lost in an examination (see also diagrams on the following page).

- When the points are too far apart, a curve tends to "wobble".

- Drawing curves in small sections leads to "feathering".

- The place where a curve should turn smoothly is drawn "flat".

- A line is drawn through a point which, clearly, has been incorrectly plotted.

A quadratic curve drawn correctly will always give a smooth curve.

Here are some tips which will make it easier for you to draw smooth, curved lines.

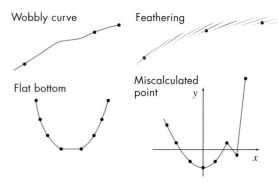

Wobbly curve   Feathering

Flat bottom   Miscalculated point

- If you are *right-handed,* turn your piece of paper or your exercise book round so that you draw from left to right. Your hand is steadier this way than trying to draw from right to left or away from your body. If you are *left-handed,* you should find drawing from right to left the more accurate way.

- Move your pencil over the points as a practice run without drawing the curve.

- Do one continuous curve and only stop at a plotted point.

- Use a *sharp* pencil and do not press too heavily, so that you may easily rub out mistakes.

Normally in an examination, grids are provided with the axes clearly marked. This is so that the examiner can place a transparent master over a graph and see immediately whether any lines are badly drawn or points are misplotted. Remember that a tolerance of 1 mm is all that you are allowed. In the exercises below, suitable ranges are suggested for the axes. You can use any type of graph paper to draw the graphs.

Also you do not need to work out all values in a table. If you use a calculator, you need only to work out the y-value. The other rows in the table are just working lines to break down the calculation.

EXERCISE 8A

1 **a** Copy and complete the table for the graph of $y = 3x^2$ for values of x from -3 to 3.

x	-3	-2	-1	0	1	2	3
y	27		3			12	

b Use your graph to find the value of y when $x = -1.5$.

c Use your graph to find the values of x that give a y-value of 10.

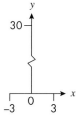

2 **a** Copy and complete the table for the graph of $y = x^2 + 2$ for values of x from -5 to 5.

x	-5	-4	-3	-2	-1	0	1	2	3	4	5
$y = x^2 + 2$	27		11					6			

b Use your graph to find the value of y when $x = -2.5$.

c Use your graph to find the values of x that give a y-value of 14.

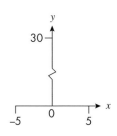

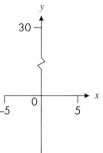

3 a Copy and complete the table for the graph of $y = x^2 - 2x - 8$ for values of x from –5 to 5.

x	–5	–4	–3	–2	–1	0	1	2	3	4	5
x^2	25		9					4			
$-2x$	10							–4			
-8	–8							–8			
y	27							–8			

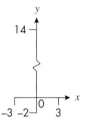

b Use your graph to find the value of y when $x = 0.5$.

c Use your graph to find the values of x that give a y-value of –3.

4 a Copy and complete the table for the graph of $y = x^2 + 2x - 1$ for values of x from –3 to 3.

x	–3	–2	–1	0	1	2	3
x^2	9				1	4	
$+2x$	–6		–2			4	
-1	–1	–1				–1	
y	2					7	

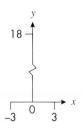

b Use your graph to find the y-value when $x = -2.5$.

c Use your graph to find the values of x that give a y-value of 1.

d On the same axes, draw the graph of $y = \dfrac{x}{2} + 2$.

e Where do the graphs $y = x^2 + 2x - 1$ and $y = \dfrac{x}{2} + 2$ cross?

5 a Copy and complete the table for the graph of $y = x^2 - x + 6$ for values of x from –3 to 3.

x	–3	–2	–1	0	1	2	3
x^2	9				1	4	
$-x$	3					–2	
$+6$	6					6	
y	18					8	

b Use your graph to find the y-value when $x = 2.5$.

c Use your graph to find the values of x that give a y-value of 8.

d Copy and complete the table to draw the graph of $y = x^2 + 5$ on the same axes.

x	–3	–2	–1	0	1	2	3
y	14		6				14

e Where do the graphs $y = x^2 - x + 6$ and $y = x^2 + 5$ cross?

6 **a** Copy and complete the table for the graph of $y = x^2 + 2x + 1$ for values of x from −3 to 3.

x	−3	−2	−1	0	1	2	3
x^2	9				1	4	
+2x	−6					4	
+1	1					1	
y	4						

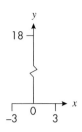

b Use your graph to find the y-value when $x = 1.7$.

c Use your graph to find the values of x that give a y-value of 2.

d On the same axes, draw the graph of $y = 2x + 2$.

e Where do the graphs $y = x^2 + 2x + 1$ and $y = 2x + 2$ cross?

7 **a** Copy and complete the table for the graph of $y = 2x^2 - 5x - 3$ for values of x from −2 to 4.

x	−2	−1.5	−1	−0.5	0	0.5	1	1.5	2	2.5	3	3.5	4
y	15	9			−3	−5				−3			9

b Where does the graph cross the x-axis?

The significant points of a quadratic graph

A quadratic graph has four points that are of interest to a mathematician. These are the points A, B, C and D on the diagram. A and B are called the **roots**, and are where the graph crosses the x-axis, C is the point where the graph crosses the y-axis (the **intercept**) and D is the **vertex**, and is the lowest or highest point of the graph.

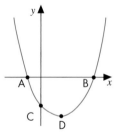
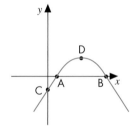

The roots

If you look at your answer to question **7** in Exercise 8A, you will see that the graph crosses the x-axis at $x = -0.5$ and $x = 3$. Since the x-axis is the line $y = 0$, the y-value at any point on the x-axis is zero. So, you have found the solution to the equation

$$0 = 2x^2 - 5x - 3 \quad \text{that is} \quad 2x^2 - 5x - 3 = 0$$

You will meet equations of this type again in Chapter 20. They are known as quadratic equations.

You will solve them either by factorisation or by using the quadratic formula. That is, you will find the values of x that make them true. Such values are called the roots of an equation. So in the case of the quadratic equation $2x^2 - 5x - 3 = 0$, its roots are −0.5 and 3.

We can check these values by substituting them into the formula:

For $x = 3.0$ $\qquad\qquad$ $2(3)^2 - 5(3) - 3 = 18 - 15 - 3 = 0$

For $x = 0.5$ $\qquad\qquad$ $2(-0.5)^2 - 5(-0.5) - 3 = 0.5 + 2.5 - 3 = 0$

We can find the roots of a quadratic equation by drawing its graph and finding where the graph crosses the x-axis.

Mod 3

EXAMPLE 3

a Draw the graph of $y = x^2 - 3x - 4$ for $-2 \leqslant x \leqslant 5$.

b Use your graph to find the roots of the equation $x^2 - 3x - 4 = 0$.

a Set up a table.

x	−2	−1	0	1	2	3	4	5
x^2	4	1	0	1	4	9	16	25
$-3x$	6	3	0	−3	−6	−9	−12	−15
-4	−4	−4	−4	−4	−4	−4	−4	−4
y	6	0	−4	−6	−6	−4	0	6

Draw the graph.

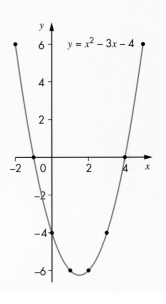

b The points where the graph crosses the x-axis are −1 and 4.

So, the roots of $x^2 - 3x - 4 = 0$ are $x = -1$ and $x = 4$.

Note that sometimes the quadratic graph may not cross the x-axis. In this case there are no roots. This will be dealt with in section 20.6.

The y-intercept

If you look at all the quadratic graphs we have drawn so far you will see a connection between the equation and the point where the graph crosses the y-axis. Very simply, the constant term of the equation $y = ax^2 + bx + c$ (that is, the value c) is where the graph crosses the y-axis. The intercept is at $(0, c)$.

The vertex

The lowest (or highest) point of a quadratic graph is called the vertex.

If it is the highest point, it is called the **maximum**.

If it is the lowest point, it is called the **minimum**.

It is difficult to find a general rule for the point, but the x-coordinate is always half-way between the roots.

The easiest way to find the y-value is to substitute the x-value into the original equation.

Another way to find the vertex is to use completing the square (see section 20.5, page 447).

EXAMPLE 4

a Write the equation $x^2 - 3x - 4 = 0$ in the form $(x - p)^2 - q = 0$

b What is the least value of the graph $y = x^2 - 3x - 4$?

a $x^2 - 3x - 4 = (x - 1\frac{1}{2})^2 - 2\frac{1}{4} - 4$

$\qquad\qquad\quad = (x - 1\frac{1}{2})^2 - 6\frac{1}{4}$

b Looking at the graph drawn in Example 3 you can see that the minimum point is at $(1\frac{1}{2}, -6\frac{1}{4})$, so the least value is $-6\frac{1}{4}$.

You should be able to see the connection between the vertex point and the equation written in completing the square form.

As a general rule when a quadratic is written in the form $(x - p)^2 + q$ then the minimum point is (p, q). Note the sign change of p.

Note: If the x^2 term is negative then the graph will be inverted and the vertex will be a maximum.

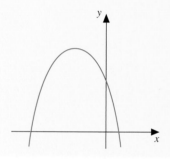

EXERCISE 8B

1 a Copy and complete the table to draw the graph of $y = x^2 - 4$ for $-4 \leqslant x \leqslant 4$.

x	−4	−3	−2	−1	0	1	2	3	4
y	12			−3				5	

b Use your graph to find the roots of $x^2 - 4 = 0$.

2 a Copy and complete the table to draw the graph of $y = x^2 - 9$ for $-4 \leqslant x \leqslant 4$.

x	−4	−3	−2	−1	0	1	2	3	4
y	7				−9			0	

b Use your graph to find the roots of $x^2 - 9 = 0$.

3 a Look at the equations of the graphs you drew in questions **1** and **2**. Is there a connection between the numbers in each equation and its roots?

b Before you draw the graphs in parts **c** and **d**, try to predict what their roots will be ($\sqrt{5} \approx 2.2$).

c Copy and complete the table to draw the graph of $y = x^2 - 1$ for $-4 \leqslant x \leqslant 4$.

x	−4	−3	−2	−1	0	1	2	3	4
y	15				−1			8	

d Copy and complete the table to draw the graph of $y = x^2 - 5$ for $-4 \leqslant x \leqslant 4$.

x	−4	−3	−2	−1	0	1	2	3	4
y	11		−1					4	

e Were your predictions correct?

4 a Copy and complete the table to draw the graph of $y = x^2 + 4x$ for $-5 \leqslant x \leqslant 2$.

x	−5	−4	−3	−2	−1	0	1	2
x^2	25			4			1	
$+4x$	−20			−8			4	
y	5			−4			5	

b Use your graph to find the roots of the equation $x^2 + 4x = 0$.

5 a Copy and complete the table to draw the graph of $y = x^2 - 6x$ for $-2 \leqslant x \leqslant 8$.

x	−2	−1	0	1	2	3	4	5	6	7	8
x^2	4			1			16				
$-6x$	12			−6			−24				
y	16			−5			−8				

b Use your graph to find the roots of the equation $x^2 - 6x = 0$.

6 a Copy and complete the table to draw the graph of $y = x^2 + 3x$ for $-5 \leqslant x \leqslant 3$.

x	−5	−4	−3	−2	−1	0	1	2	3
y	10			−2				10	

b Use your graph to find the roots of the equation $x^2 + 3x = 0$.

7 a Look at the equations of the graphs you drew in questions **4**, **5** and **6**. Is there a connection between the numbers in each equation and the roots?

b Before you draw the graphs in parts **c** and **d**, try to predict what their roots will be.

c Copy and complete the table to draw the graph of $y = x^2 - 3x$ for $-2 \leqslant x \leqslant 5$.

x	−2	−1	0	1	2	3	4	5
y	10			−2				10

d Copy and complete the table to draw the graph of $y = x^2 + 5x$ for $-6 \leqslant x \leqslant 2$.

x	−6	−5	−4	−3	−2	−1	0	1	2
y	6			−6				6	

e Were your predictions correct?

8 a Copy and complete the table to draw the graph of $y = x^2 - 4x + 4$ for $-1 \leqslant x \leqslant 5$.

x	−1	0	1	2	3	4	5
y	9				1		

b Use your graph to find the roots of the equation $x^2 - 4x + 4 = 0$.

c What happens with the roots?

9 a Copy and complete the table to draw the graph of $y = x^2 - 6x + 3$ for $-1 \leqslant x \leqslant 7$.

x	−1	0	1	2	3	4	5	6	7
y	10		−5				−2		

b Use your graph to find the roots of the equation $x^2 - 6x + 3 = 0$.

10 a Copy and complete the table to draw the graph of $y = 2x^2 + 5x - 6$ for $-5 \leqslant x \leqslant 2$.

x	−5	−4	−3	−2	−1	0	1	2
y								

b Use your graph to find the roots of the equation $2x^2 + 5x - 6 = 0$.

11 For questions **1** to **7** write down the following.

a the point of intersection of the graph with the y-axis

b the coordinates of the minimum point (vertex) of each graph

c Explain the connection between these points and the original equation.

12 a Write the equation $y = x^2 - 4x + 4$ in the form $y = (x - p)^2 + q$.

b Write down the minimum value of the equation $y = x^2 - 4x + 4$.

13 a Write the equation $y = x^2 - 6x + 3$ in the form $y = (x - p)^2 + q$.

b Write down the minimum value of the equation $y = x^2 - 6x + 3$.

14 a Write the equation $y = x^2 - 8x + 2$ in the form $y = (x - p)^2 + q$.

b Write down the minimum value of the equation $y = x^2 - 8x + 2$.

15 a Write the equation $y = -x^2 + 2x - 6$ in the form $y = -(x - p)^2 + q$.

b Write down the minimum value of the equation $y = -x^2 + 2x - 6$.

Solving equations by the method of intersection

This section will show you how to:

- solve equations by the method of intersecting graphs

Many equations can be solved by drawing two intersecting graphs on the same axes and using the x-value(s) of their point(s) of intersection. (In the GCSE examination, you are very likely to be presented with one drawn graph and asked to draw a straight line to solve a new equation.)

EXAMPLE 5

Show how each equation given below can be solved using the graph of $y = x^3 - 2x - 2$ and its intersection with another graph. In each case, give the equation of the other graph and the solution(s).

a $x^3 - 2x - 4 = 0$ **b** $x^3 - 3x - 1 = 0$

a This method will give the required graph.

Step 1: Write down the original (given) equation. $y = x^3 - 2x - 2$

Step 2: Write down the (new) equation to be solved in reverse. $0 = x^3 - 2x - 4$

Step 3: Subtract these equations. $y = + 2$

Step 4: Draw this line on the original graph to solve the new equation.

The graphs of $y = x^3 - 2x - 2$ and $y = 2$ are drawn on the same axes.

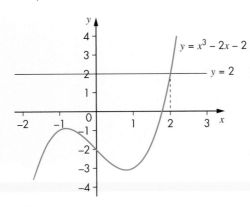

The intersection of these two graphs is the solution of $x^3 - 2x - 4 = 0$.

The solution is $x = 2$.

This works because you are drawing a straight line along with the original graph, and solving where they intersect.

At the points of intersection you can say:
  original equation = straight line

Rearranging this gives:
  (original equation) − (straight line) = 0

You have been asked to solve:
  (new equation) = 0

So (original equation) − (straight line) = (new equation)

Rearranging this again gives:
  (original equation) − (new equation) = straight line

Note: In GCSE exams the curve is always drawn already and you will only have to draw the straight line.

b Write down given graph: $\qquad\qquad\qquad\qquad\qquad$ $y = x^3 - 2x - 2$

Write down new equation: $\qquad\qquad\qquad\qquad$ $0 = x^3 - 3x - 1$

Subtract: $\qquad\qquad\qquad\qquad\qquad\qquad$ $y = \qquad + x - 1$

The graphs of $y = x^3 - 2x - 2$ and $y = x - 1$ are then drawn on the same axes.

The intersection of the two graphs is the solution of $x^3 - 3x - 1 = 0$.

The solutions are $x = -1.5, -0.3$ and 1.9.

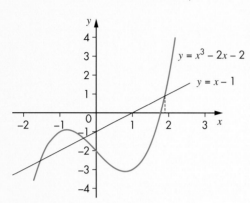

EXAMPLE 6

The graph shows the curve $y = x^2 + 3x - 2$.

By drawing a suitable straight line, solve these equations.

a $x^2 + 3x - 1 = 0$ $\qquad\qquad\qquad\qquad\qquad$ **b** $x^2 + 2x - 3 = 0$

a Given graph: $\qquad$ $y = x^2 + 3x - 2$ $\qquad\qquad$ **b** Given graph: $\qquad$ $y = x^2 + 3x - 2$

New equation: $\qquad$ $0 = x^2 + 3x - 1$ $\qquad\qquad$ New equation: $\qquad$ $0 = x^2 + 2x - 3$

Subtract: $\qquad\qquad$ $y = \qquad - 1$ $\qquad\qquad\qquad$ Subtract: $\qquad\qquad$ $y = \quad + x \; + 1$

Draw: $\qquad\qquad\quad$ $y = -1$ $\qquad\qquad\qquad\qquad$ Draw: $\qquad\qquad\quad$ $y = x + 1$

Solutions: $\qquad\quad$ $x = 0.3, -3.3$ $\qquad\qquad$ Solutions: $\qquad\quad$ $x = 1, -3$

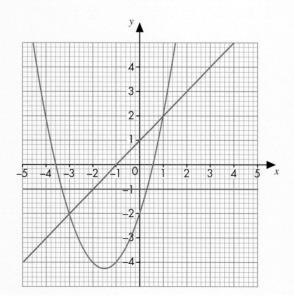

EXERCISE 8C

In questions **1** to **5**, use the graphs given here. Trace the graphs or place a ruler over them in the position of the line. Solution values only need to be given to 1 decimal place. In questions **6** to **10**, either draw the graphs yourself or use a graphics calculator to draw them.

1 Below is the graph of $y = x^2 - 3x - 6$.

    a Solve these equations.

        i $x^2 - 3x - 6 = 0$

        ii $x^2 - 3x - 6 = 4$

        iii $x^2 - 3x - 2 = 0$

    b By drawing a suitable straight line solve $2x^2 - 6x + 2 = 0$.

> **HINTS AND TIPS**
>
> Cancel by 2 first.

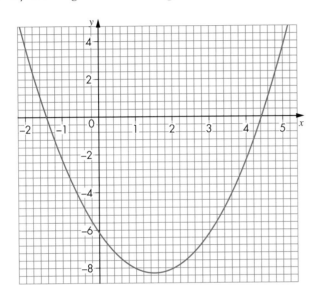

2 This is the graph of $y = x^2 + 4x - 5$.

    a Solve $x^2 + 4x - 5 = 0$.

    b By drawing suitable straight lines solve these equations.

        i $x^2 + 4x - 5 = 2$

        ii $x^2 + 4x - 4 = 0$

        iii $3x^2 + 12x + 6 = 0$

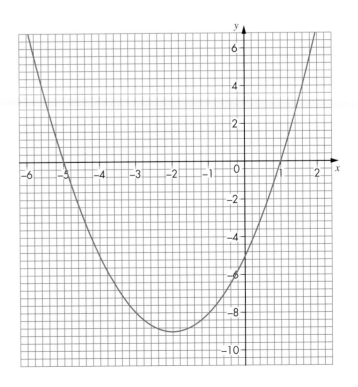

3 Below are the graphs of $y = x^2 - 5x + 3$ and $y = x + 3$.

   a Solve these equations.   **i** $x^2 - 6x = 0$ **ii** $x^2 - 5x + 3 = 0$

   b By drawing suitable straight lines solve these equations.

      i $x^2 - 5x + 3 = 2$ **ii** $x^2 - 5x - 2 = 0$

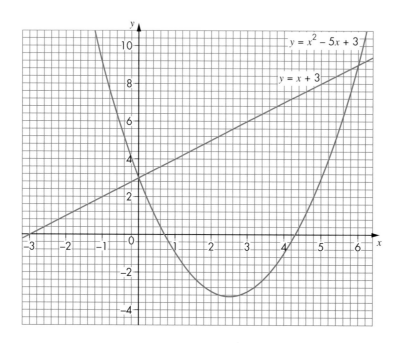

4 Below are the graphs of $y = x^2 - 2$ and $y = x + 2$.

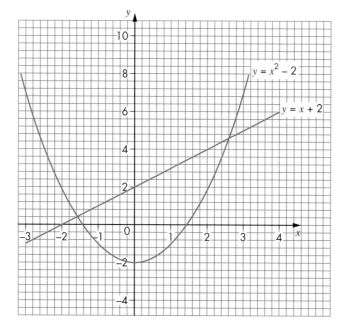

   a Solve these equations.   **i** $x^2 - x - 4 = 0$ **ii** $x^2 - 2 = 0$

   b By drawing suitable straight lines solve these equations.

      i $x^2 - 2 = 3$ **ii** $x^2 - 4 = 0$

5 Below are the graphs of $y = x^3 - 2x^2$, $y = 2x + 1$ and $y = x - 1$.

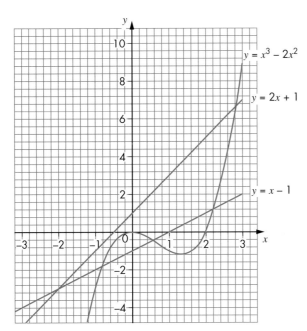

Solve these equations.

a $x^3 - 2x^2 = 0$ **b** $x^3 - 2x^2 = 3$ **c** $x^3 - 2x^2 + 1 = 0$

d $x^3 - 2x^2 - 2x - 1 = 0$ **e** $x^3 - 2x^2 - x + 1 = 0$

6 Draw the graph of $y = x^2 - 4x - 2$.

  a Solve $x^2 - 4x - 2 = 0$.

  b By drawing a suitable straight line solve $x^2 - 4x - 5 = 0$.

7 Draw the graph of $y = 2x^2 - 5$.

  a Solve $2x^2 - 5 = 0$.

  b By drawing a suitable straight line solve $2x^2 - 3 = 0$.

8 Draw the graphs of $y = x^2 - 3$ and $y = x + 2$ on the same axes. Use the graphs to solve these equations.

  a $x^2 - 5 = 0$ **b** $x^2 - x - 5 = 0$

9 Draw the graphs of $y = x^2 - 3x - 2$ and $y = 2x - 3$ on the same axes. Use the graphs to solve these equations.

  a $x^2 - 3x - 1 = 0$ **b** $x^2 - 5x + 1 = 0$

10 Draw the graphs of $y = x^3 - 2x^2 + 3x - 4$ and $y = 3x - 1$ on the same axes. Use the graphs to solve these equations.

  a $x^3 - 2x^2 + 3x - 6 = 0$ **b** $x^3 - 2x^2 - 3 = 0$

1

a Copy and complete the table of values for $y = 2x^2 - 4x - 1$.

x	−2	−1	0	1	2	3
y	15		−1		−1	5

b Draw the graph of $y = 2x^2 - 4x - 1$ for values of x from −2 to +3. Use a grid with an x-axis from −2 to 3 and a y-axis from −3 to 15.

c An approximate solution of the equation $2x^2 - 4x - 1 = 0$ is $x = 2.2$.

    i Explain how you can find this from the graph.

    ii Use your graph to write down another solution of this equation.

AQA, Question 7, Paper 1 Higher, June 2004

2

a Copy and complete the table of values for $y = (x + 3)(2 - x)$.

x	−3	−2	−1	0	1	2	3
y		4	6	6	4		

b Draw the graph of $y = (x + 3)(2 - x)$ for values of x from −3 to +3. Use a grid with an x-axis from −4 to 4 and a y-axis from −8 to 8.

c Use the graph to solve the equation $(x + 3)(2 - x) = 2$.

3

The grid below shows the graphs of

$$y = x^2 - x - 6 \quad \text{and} \quad y = x + 2.$$

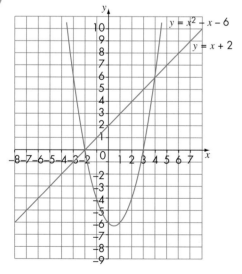

a Deduce the coordinates of the minimum point of the graph $y = x^2 - x - 12$.

b Find the quadratic equation whose solutions are the x-coordinates of the points of intersection of $y = x^2 - x - 6$ and $y = x + 2$.

AQA, Question 24, Paper 2 Higher, November 2003

4

The grid below shows the graph of $y = x^2 + 3x - 2$.

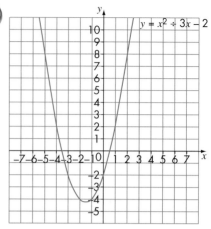

a By drawing an appropriate straight line on the graph solve this equation.

$$x^2 + 3x - 3 = 0$$

b By drawing an appropriate straight line on the graph solve this equation.

$$x^2 + 2x - 1 = 0$$

AQA, Question 22, Paper 2 Higher, June 2005

5

The grid shows graphs of the curve $y = x^2 + 2x - 2$ and three straight lines, $y = x$, $y = x - 2$ and $y = -x - 1$.

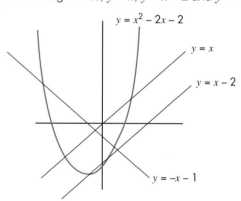

You must use the graphs to answer the following.

a Write down a pair of simultaneous linear equations that have a solution $x = \frac{1}{2}$, $y = 1\frac{1}{2}$.

b Write down and simplify a quadratic equation whose solutions are 0.3 and −3.3.

c Write down the solutions to the equation $x^2 + x - 2 = 0$.

Show how you obtained your solutions using the graphs.

WORKED EXAM QUESTION

The diagram right shows the graph of

$$y = x^3 - 12x$$

for values of x from -4 to 4.

a   Use the graph to find estimates of the three solutions of the equation

$$x^3 - 12x = 0$$

b   By drawing a suitable straight line on the grid, find estimates of the solutions of the equation

$$x^3 - 12x - 5 = 0$$

Label clearly the straight line that you have drawn.

c   By drawing a suitable straight line on the grid, find estimates of the solutions of the equation

$$x^3 - 14x + 5 = 0$$

Label clearly the straight line that you have drawn.

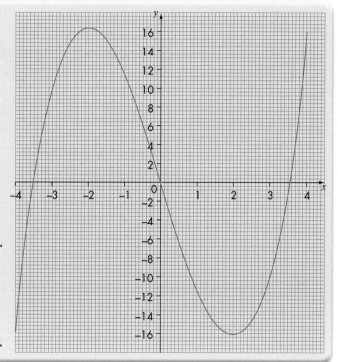

Solution

a -3.5, 0 and 3.5

> To find the values where the given graph is equal to zero read from the x-axis. These are the roots of the equation.

b -3.3, -0.5, 3.7

> To find the straight line subtract the required curve from the given curve.
>
> | | | |
> |---|---|---|
> | Given curve | y | $= x^3 - 12x$ |
> | New curve | 0 | $= x^3 - 12x - 5$ |
> | Subtract | y | $= \quad\quad + 5$ |
> | Draw | y | $= 5$ |

c -3.9, 0.4, 3.5

> To find the straight line subtract the required curve from the given curve.
>
> | | | |
> |---|---|---|
> | Given curve | y | $= x^3 - 12x$ |
> | New curve | 0 | $= x^3 - 14x + 5$ |
> | Subtract | y | $= \quad + 2x - 5$ |
> | Draw | y | $= 2x - 5$ |

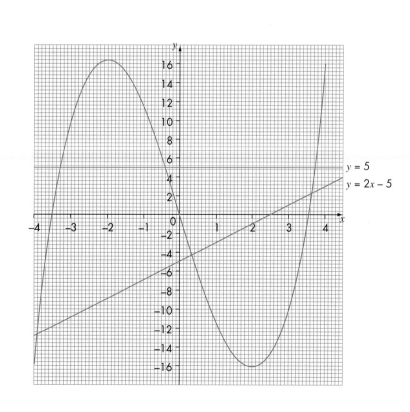

$y = 5$

$y = 2x - 5$

GRADE YOURSELF

C Able to draw quadratic graphs using a table of values

B Able to solve quadratic equations from their graphs

B Plot cubic graphs using a table of values

B Recognise the shapes of the graphs $y = x^3$ and $y = \dfrac{1}{x}$

A Able to draw a variety of graphs such as exponential graphs and reciprocal graphs using a table of values

A* Able to solve equations using the intersection of two graphs

A* Use trigonometric graphs to solve sine and cosine problems

What you should know now

- How to draw non-linear graphs
- How to solve equations by finding the intersection points of the graphs of the equations with the x-axis or other related equations

Variation

1 Direct variation

2 Inverse variation

This chapter will show you ...

- how to solve problems where two variables are connected by a relationship that varies in direct or inverse proportion

Direct proportion → Inverse proportion

What you should already know

- Squares, square roots, cubes and cube roots of integers
- How to substitute values into algebraic expressions
- How to solve simple algebraic equations

Quick check

1 Write down the value of each of the following.

  a 5^2 **b** $\sqrt{81}$ **c** 3^3 **d** $\sqrt[3]{64}$

2 Calculate the value of y if $x = 4$.

  a $y = 3x^2$ **b** $y = \dfrac{1}{\sqrt{x}}$

3 Solve the equations:

  i $2x = 4$

  ii $\dfrac{x}{4} = 7$

  iii $3x = 120$

  iv $\dfrac{x}{3} = 10$

This section will introduce you to:

- direct variation and show you how to work out the constant of proportionality

Key words

constant of
   proportionality, k
direct proportion
direct variation

The term **direct variation** has the same meaning as **direct proportion**.

There is direct variation (or direct proportion) between two variables when one variable is a simple multiple of the other. That is, their ratio is a constant.

For example:

    1 kilogram = 2.2 pounds   There is a multiplying factor of 2.2 between kilograms and pounds.

    Area of a circle = πr^2 There is a multiplying factor of π between the area of a circle and the square of its radius.

An examination question involving direct variation usually requires you first to find this multiplying factor (called the **constant of proportionality**), then to use it to solve a problem.

The symbol for variation or proportion is $\propto$.

So the statement "Pay is directly proportional to time" can be mathematically written as

    Pay $\propto$ *Time*

which implies that

    Pay $= k \times$ *Time*

where k is the constant of proportionality.

There are three steps to be followed when solving a question involving proportionality.

    Step 1: set up the proportionality equation (you may have to define variables).

    Step 2: use the given information to find the constant of proportionality.

    Step 3: substitute the constant of proportionality in the original equation and use this to find unknown values.

EXAMPLE 1

The cost of an article is directly proportional to the time spent making it. An article taking 6 hours to make costs £30. Find the following.

a the cost of an article that takes 5 hours to make

b the length of time it takes to make an article costing £40

Step 1: Let C be the cost of making an article and t the time it takes. We then have:

$$C \propto t$$

$$\Rightarrow C = kt$$

where k is the constant of proportionality.

Note that we can "replace" the proportionality sign $\propto$ with $= k$ to obtain the proportionality equation.

Step 2: Since C = £30 when t = 6 hours, then $30 = 6k$

$$\Rightarrow \frac{30}{6} = k$$

$$\Rightarrow k = 5$$

Step 3: So the formula is $C = 5t$

a When t = 5 hours $\quad C = 5 \times 5 = 25$

So the cost is £25.

b When C = £40 $\quad 40 = 5 \times t$

$$\Rightarrow \frac{40}{5} = t \Rightarrow t = 8$$

So the making time is 8 hours.

EXERCISE 9A

In each case, first find k, the constant of proportionality, and then the formula connecting the variables.

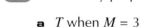 T is directly proportional to M. If $T = 20$ when $M = 4$, find the following.

a T when $M = 3$ **b** M when $T = 10$

 W is directly proportional to F. If $W = 45$ when $F = 3$, find the following.

a W when $F = 5$ **b** F when $W = 90$

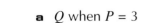 Q varies directly with P. If $Q = 100$ when $P = 2$, find the following.

a Q when $P = 3$ **b** P when $Q = 300$

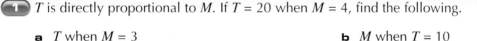 X varies directly with Y. If $X = 17.5$ when $Y = 7$, find the following.

a X when $Y = 9$ **b** Y when $X = 30$

5 The distance covered by a train is directly proportional to the time taken. The train travels 105 miles in 3 hours.

  a What distance will the train cover in 5 hours?

  b What time will it take for the train to cover 280 miles?

6 The cost of fuel delivered to your door is directly proportional to the weight received. When 250 kg is delivered, it costs £47.50.

  a How much will it cost to have 350 kg delivered?

  b How much would be delivered if the cost were £33.25?

7 The number of children who can play safely in a playground is directly proportional to the area of the playground. A playground with an area of 210 m^2 is safe for 60 children.

  a How many children can safely play in a playground of area 154 m^2?

  b A playgroup has 24 children. What is the smallest playground area in which they could safely play?

Direct proportions involving squares, cubes and square roots

The process is the same as for a linear direct variation, as the next example shows.

EXAMPLE 2

The cost of a circular badge is directly proportional to the square of its radius. The cost of a badge with a radius of 2 cm is 68p.

  a Find the cost of a badge of radius 2.4 cm.

  b Find the radius of a badge costing £1.53.

Step 1: Let C be the cost and r the radius of a badge. Then

$$C \propto r^2$$

$$\Rightarrow C = kr^2 \text{ where } k \text{ is the constant of proportionality.}$$

Step 2: $C = 68p$ when $r = 2$ cm. So

$$68 = 4k$$

$$\Rightarrow \frac{68}{4} = k \Rightarrow k = 17$$

Hence the formula is $C = 17r^2$

  a When $r = 2.4$ cm $C = 17 \times 2.4^2 p = 97.92p$

  Rounding off gives the cost as 98p.

  b When $C = 153p$ $153 = 17r^2$

$$\Rightarrow \frac{153}{17} = 9 = r^2$$

$$\Rightarrow r = \sqrt{9} = 3$$

Hence, the radius is 3 cm.

EXERCISE 9B

In each case, first find k, the constant of proportionality, and then the formula connecting the variables.

1 T is directly proportional to x^2. If $T = 36$ when $x = 3$, find the following.

   a T when $x = 5$ **b** x when $T = 400$

2 W is directly proportional to M^2. If $W = 12$ when $M = 2$, find the following.

   a W when $M = 3$ **b** M when $W = 75$

3 E varies directly with $\sqrt{C}$. If $E = 40$ when $C = 25$, find the following.

   a E when $C = 49$ **b** C when $E = 10.4$

4 X is directly proportional to $\sqrt{Y}$. If $X = 128$ when $Y = 16$, find the following.

   a X when $Y = 36$ **b** Y when $X = 48$

5 P is directly proportional to f^3. If $P = 400$ when $f = 10$, find the following.

   a P when $f = 4$ **b** f when $P = 50$

6 The cost of serving tea and biscuits varies directly with the square root of the number of people at the buffet. It costs £25 to serve tea and biscuits to 100 people.

   a How much will it cost to serve tea and biscuits to 400 people?

   b For a cost of £37.50, how many could be served tea and biscuits?

7 In an experiment, the temperature, in °C, varied directly with the square of the pressure, in atmospheres. The temperature was 20 °C when the pressure was 5 atm.

   a What will the temperature be at 2 atm?   **b** What will the pressure be at 80 °C?

8 The weight, in grams, of ball bearings varies directly with the cube of the radius measured in millimetres. A ball bearing of radius 4 mm has a weight of 115.2 g.

   a What will a ball bearing of radius 6 mm weigh?

   b A ball bearing has a weight of 48.6 g. What is its radius?

9 The energy, in J, of a particle varies directly with the square of its speed in m/s. A particle moving at 20 m/s has 50 J of energy.

   a How much energy has a particle moving at 4 m/s?

   b At what speed is a particle moving if it has 200 J of energy?

10 The cost, in £, of a trip varies directly with the square root of the number of miles travelled. The cost of a 100-mile trip is £35.

   a What is the cost of a 500-mile trip (to the nearest £1)?

   b What is the distance of a trip costing £70?

Inverse variation

This section will introduce you to:

- inverse variation and show you how to work out the constant of proportionality

Key words

constant of proportionality, k
inverse proportion

There is **inverse variation** between two variables when one variable is directly proportional to the reciprocal of the other. That is, the product of the two variables is constant. So, as one variable increases, the other decreases.

For example, the faster you travel over a given distance, the less time it takes. So there is an inverse variation between speed and time. We say speed is inversely proportional to time.

$$S \propto \frac{1}{T} \text{ and so } S = \frac{k}{T}$$

which can be written as $ST = k$.

EXAMPLE 3

M is **inversely proportional** to R. If $M = 9$ when $R = 4$, find the following.

a M when $R = 2$ b R when $M = 3$

Step 1: $M \propto \frac{1}{R} \Rightarrow M = \frac{k}{R}$ where k is the **constant of proportionality**.

Step 2: When $M = 9$ and $R = 4$, we get $9 = \frac{k}{4}$

$\Rightarrow 9 \times 4 = k \Rightarrow k = 36$

Step 3: So the formula is $M = \frac{36}{R}$

a When $R = 2$, then $M = \frac{36}{2} = 18$

b When $M = 3$, then $3 = \frac{36}{R} \Rightarrow 3R = 36 \Rightarrow R = 12$

EXERCISE 9C

In each case, first find the formula connecting the variables.

1 T is inversely proportional to m. If $T = 6$ when $m = 2$, find the following.

a T when $m = 4$ b m when $T = 4.8$

2 W is inversely proportional to x. If $W = 5$ when $x = 12$, find the following.

a W when $x = 3$ b x when $W = 10$

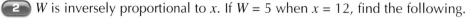

3 Q varies inversely with $(5 - t)$. If $Q = 8$ when $t = 3$, find the following.

a Q when $t = 10$ 　　　　　　　　　 b t when $Q = 16$

4 M varies inversely with t^2. If $M = 9$ when $t = 2$, find the following.

a M when $t = 3$ 　　　　　　　　　 b t when $M = 1.44$

5 W is inversely proportional to $\sqrt{T}$. If $W = 6$ when $T = 16$, find the following.

a W when $T = 25$ 　　　　　　　　　 b T when $W = 2.4$

6 The grant available to a section of society was inversely proportional to the number of people needing the grant. When 30 people needed a grant, they received £60 each.

a What would the grant have been if 120 people had needed one?

b If the grant had been £50 each, how many people would have received it?

7 While doing underwater tests in one part of an ocean, a team of scientists noticed that the temperature in °C was inversely proportional to the depth in kilometres. When the temperature was 6 °C, the scientists were at a depth of 4 km.

a What would the temperature have been at a depth of 8 km?

b To what depth would they have had to go to find the temperature at 2 °C?

8 A new engine was being tested, but it had serious problems. The distance it went, in km, without breaking down was inversely proportional to the square of its speed in m/s. When the speed was 12 m/s, the engine lasted 3 km.

a Find the distance covered before a breakdown, when the speed is 15 m/s.

b On one test, the engine broke down after 6.75 km. What was the speed?

9 In a balloon it was noticed that the pressure, in atmospheres, was inversely proportional to the square root of the height, in metres. When the balloon was at a height of 25 m, the pressure was 1.44 atm.

a What was the pressure at a height of 9 m?

b What would the height have been if the pressure was 0.72 atm?

10 The amount of waste which a firm produces, measured in tonnes per hour, is inversely proportional to the square root of the size of the filter beds, measured in m². At the moment, the firm produces 1.25 tonnes per hour of waste, with filter beds of size 0.16 m².

a The filter beds used to be only 0.01 m². How much waste did the firm produce then?

b How much waste could be produced if the filter beds were 0.75 m²?

 1 y is proportional to $\sqrt{x}$. Complete the table.

x	25		400
y	10	20	

 2 The energy, E, of an object moving horizontally is directly proportional to the speed, v, of the object. When the speed is 10 m/s the energy is 40 000 Joules.

  a Find an equation connecting E and v.

  b Find the speed of the object when the energy is 14 400 Joules.

 3 y is inversely proportional to the cube root of x. When $y = 8$, $x = \frac{1}{8}$.

  a Find an expression for y in terms of x,

  b Calculate

    i the value of y when $x = \frac{1}{125}$,

    ii the value of x when $y = 2$.

 4 The mass of a cube is directly proportional to the cube of its side. A cube with a side of 4 cm has a mass of 320 grams. Calculate the side length of a cube made of the same material with a mass of 36 450 grams

 5 y is directly proportional to the cube of x. When $y = 16$, $x = 3$. Find the value of y when $x = 6$.

 6 y is inversely proportional to the square of x. When $y = 3$, $x = 2$. Find the value of y when $x = 4$.

  AQA, Question 12, Paper 2 Higher, June 2004

 7 In an experiment measurements of t and h were taken. These are the results.

t	2	5	6
h	10	62.5	90

Which of these rules fits the results?

  a $h \propto t$

  b $h \propto t^2$

  c $h \propto t^3$

You *must* show all your working.

  AQA, Question 14, Paper 1 Higher, November 2003

 8 Two variables, x and y, are known to be proportional to each other. When $x = 10$, $y = 25$.

Find the constant of proportionality, k, if:

  a $y \propto x$

  b $y \propto x^2$

  c $y \propto \frac{1}{x}$

  d $\sqrt{y} \propto \frac{1}{x}$

 9 y is directly proportional to the cube root of x. When $x = 27$, $y = 6$.

  a Find the value of y when $x = 125$.

  b Find the value of x when $y = 3$.

 10 The surface area, A, of a solid is directly proportional to the square of the depth, d. When $d = 6$, $A = 12\pi$.

  a Find the value of A when $d = 12$. Give your answer in terms of π.

  b Find the value of d when $A = 27\pi$.

 11 The frequency, f, of sound is inversely proportional to the wavelength, w. A sound with a frequency of 36 hertz has a wavelength of 20.25 metres.

Calculate the frequency when the frequency and the wavelength have the same numerical value.

 12 y is proportional to x^3.

  a When $x = 4$, $y = 80$. Find the value of y when $x = 8$.

Also, x is inversely proportional to the square root of z.

  b When $y = 10$, $z = 16$. Find the value of z when $x = 4$.

  AQA, Question 17, Paper 2 Higher, June 2001

 13 P and Q are positive quantities. P is inversely proportional to Q^2. When $P = 160$, $Q = 20$. Find the value of P when $P = Q$.

WORKED EXAM QUESTION

y is inversely proportional to the square of x. When y is 40, $x = 5$.

a Find an equation connecting x and y.

b Find the value of y when $x = 10$.

Solution

a $\qquad y \propto \dfrac{1}{x^2}$

First set up the proportionality relationship and replace the proportionality sign with $= k$.

$\qquad y = \dfrac{k}{x^2}$

$\qquad 40 = \dfrac{k}{25}$

Substitute the given values of y and x into the proportionality equation to find the value of k.

$\Rightarrow \quad k = 40 \times 25 = 1000$

$\qquad y = \dfrac{1000}{x^2}$

Substitute the value of k to get the final equation connecting y and x.

or $\ yx^2 = 1000$

b When $x = 10$, $y = \dfrac{1000}{10^2} = \dfrac{1000}{100} = 10$

Substitute the value of x into the equation to find y.

The mass of a solid, M, is directly proportional to the cube of its height, h. When $h = 10$, $M = 4000$.

The surface area, A, of the solid is directly proportional to the square of the height, h. When $h = 10$, $A = 50$.

Find A, when $M = 32\,000$.

Solution

$M = kh^3$

$4000 = k \times 1000 \ \Rightarrow \ k = 4$

First, find the relationship between M and h using the given information.

So, $M = 4h^3$

$A = ph^2$

$50 = p \times 100 \ \Rightarrow \ p = \dfrac{1}{2}$

Next, find the relationship between A and h using the given information.

So, $A = \dfrac{1}{2} h^2$

$32\,000 = 4h^3$

$h^3 = 8000 \ \Rightarrow \ h = 20$

Find the value of h when $M = 32\,000$.

$A = \dfrac{1}{2} (20)^2 = \dfrac{400}{2} = 200$

Now find the value of A for that value of h.

Wind Power

An electricity company wants to build some offshore wind turbines (as shown below). The company is concerned about how big the turbines will look to a person standing on the shore. It asks an engineer to calculate the angle of elevation from the shore to the highest point of a turbine, when it is rotating, if the turbine was placed at different distances out to sea. Help the engineer to complete the first table below.

Distance of turbine out to sea	Angle of elevation from shore
3km	2.29°
4km	
5km	
6km	
7km	
8km	

50m

70m

The power available in the wind is measured in watts per metre squared of rotor area (W/m^2). Wind speed is measured in metres per second (m/s). The power available in the wind is proportional to the cube of its speed. A wind speed of 7 m/s can provide 210 W/m^2 of energy. Complete the table below to show the available power at different wind speeds.

Wind speed (m/s)	Available power (W/m^2)
6	
7	210
8	
9	
10	
11	
12	

The engineer investigates the different amounts of power produced by different length rotor blades at different wind speeds. He calculates the rotor area for each blade length – this is the area of the circle made by the rotors – and then works out the power produced by these blades at the different wind speeds shown. Help him to complete the table.

Remember

1 W = 1 watt
1000 W = 1 kW = 1 kilowatt
1000 kW = 1 MW = 1 megawatt

Wind speed (m/s)	Available power (W/m²)	Rotor area for 50 m blade (m²)	Power (MW)	Rotor area for 60 m blade (m²)	Power (MW)	Rotor area for 70 m blade (m²)	Power (MW)
7	210	7854	1.65				
8		7854					
9		7854					
10		7854					

Mod 3

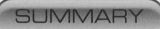

SUMMARY

GRADE YOURSELF

A Able to find formulae describing direct or inverse variation and use them to solve problems

A✳ Able to solve direct and inverse variation problems involving three variables

What you should know now

- How to recognise direct and inverse variation
- What a constant of proportionality is, and how to find it
- How to find formulae describing inverse or direct variation
- How to solve problems involving direct or inverse variation

Number and limits of accuracy

1 Limits of accuracy

2 Problems involving limits of accuracy

This chapter will show you ...

- how to find the limits of numbers rounded to certain accuracies
- how to use limits of accuracy in calculations

Limits of accuracy → Calculating with limits of accuracy

What you should already know

- How to round numbers to various degrees of accuracy

Quick check

1 Round off 6374 to

  a the nearest 10,

  b the nearest 100,

  c the nearest 1000.

2 Round off 2.389 to

  a one decimal place,

  b two decimal places.

3 Round off 47.28 to

  a one significant figure,

  b three significant figures.

Limits of accuracy

This section will show you how to:

- find the limits of accuracy of numbers that have been rounded to different degrees of accuracy

Key words

continuous data
discrete data
limits of accuracy
lower bound
rounding error
upper bound

Any recorded measurement will have been rounded off to some degree of accuracy. This defines the possible true value before rounding off took place, and hence the **limits of accuracy**. The range of values between the limits of accuracy is called the **rounding error**.

EXAMPLE 1

A stick of wood is measured as 32 cm to the nearest centimetre.

Between what limits does the actual length of the stick lie?

The lower limit is 31.5 cm as a halfway value is always rounded up.

The upper limit is 32.499999999… cm. In other words it can get as close to 32.5 cm as possible but not be 32.5 cm. However 32.5 cm is the upper limit. So we say

   31.5 cm ⩽ length of stick < 32.5 cm.

Note the use of the strict inequality for the upper limit.

EXAMPLE 2

53.7 is accurate to one decimal place. What are the limits of accuracy?

The smallest possible value is 53.65.

The largest possible value is 53.749999999… but once again we say 53.75 is the upper limit.

Hence the limits of accuracy are 53.65 ⩽ 53.7 < 53.75

EXAMPLE 3

A skip has a mass of 220 kg measured to three significant figures. What are the limits of accuracy of the mass of the skip?

The smallest possible value is 219.5 kg.

The largest possible value is 220.49999999… kg but once again we say 220.5 kg is the upper limit.

Hence the limits of accuracy are 219.5 kg ⩽ mass of skip < 220.5 kg

---

Note that the limits of accuracy are always given to one more degree of accuracy than the rounded value. For example 32 is the nearest integer and the limits are to half a unit; 53.7 is to 1 decimal place and the limits are to 2 decimal places; 220 is to 3 significant figures and the limits are to 4 significant figures.

EXAMPLE 4

A coach carrying 50 people measured to the nearest 10, is travelling at 50 mph measured to the nearest 10 mph. What are the actual limits of the number of people and the speed?

This is an example of the difference between **discrete** and **continuous data**. The number of people is discrete data as it can only take integer values, but speed is continuous data as it can take any value in a range.

The limits are 45 ≤ number of people ≤ 54, 45 mph ≤ speed < 55 mph.

Be careful as questions sometimes ask about the limits of discrete data.

EXERCISE 10A

1 Write down the limits of accuracy of the following.

  a 7 cm measured to the nearest centimetre

  b 120 grams measured to the nearest 10 grams

  c 3400 kilometres measured to the nearest 100 kilometres

  d 50 mph measured to the nearest mph

  e £6 given to the nearest £

  f 16.8 cm to the nearest tenth of a centimetre

  g 16 kg to the nearest kilogram

  h a football crowd of 14 500 given to the nearest 100

  i 55 miles given to the nearest mile

  j 55 miles given to the nearest 5 miles

2 Write down the limits of accuracy for each of the following values which are rounded to the given degree of accuracy.

  a 6 cm (1 significant figure)   **b** 17 kg (2 significant figures)   **c** 32 min (2 significant figures)

  d 238 km (3 significant figures)   **e** 7.3 m (1 decimal place)   **f** 25.8 kg (1 decimal place)

  g 3.4 h (1 decimal place)   **h** 87 g (2 significant figures)   **i** 4.23 mm (2 decimal places)

  j 2.19 kg (2 decimal places)   **k** 12.67 min (2 decimal places)   **l** 25 m (2 significant figures)

  m 40 cm (1 significant figure)   **n** 600 g (2 significant figures)   **o** 30 min (1 significant figure)

  p 1000 m (2 significant figures)   **q** 4.0 m (1 decimal place)   **r** 7.04 kg (2 decimal places)

  s 12.0 s (1 decimal place)   **t** 7.00 m (2 decimal places)

Upper and lower bounds

A journey of 26 miles measured to the nearest mile could actually be as long as 26.4999999... miles or as short as 25.5 miles. It could not be 26.5 miles, as this would round up to 27 miles. However, 26.4999999... is *virtually the same* as 26.5.

We overcome this difficulty by saying that 26.5 is the **upper bound** of the measured value and 25.5 is its **lower bound**. We can therefore write

$$25.5 \text{ miles} \leq \text{actual distance} < 26.5 \text{ miles}$$

which states that the actual distance is *greater than or equal to* 25.5 miles but *less than* 26.5 miles.

Although it is not wrong to give the upper bound as 26.49999... it is mathematically neater to give 26.5. It is wrong, however, to give the upper bound as 26.4 or 26.49. So, when stating an upper bound, always follow the accepted practice, as demonstrated here, which eliminates the difficulties that arise with recurring decimals.

A mathematical peculiarity

Let $x = 0.999\,999...$ (1)

Multiply by 10 $10x = 9.999\,999...$ (2)

Subtract (1) from (2) $9x = 9$

Divide by 9 $x = 1$

So, we have $0.\dot{9} = 1$

Hence, it is valid to give the upper bound without using recurring decimals.

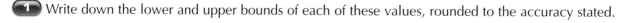

EXERCISE 10B

1 Write down the lower and upper bounds of each of these values, rounded to the accuracy stated.

    a 8 m (1 significant figure)   **b** 26 kg (2 significant figures)   **c** 25 min (2 significant figures)

    d 85 g (2 significant figures)   **e** 2.40 m (2 decimal places)   **f** 0.2 kg (1 decimal place)

    g 0.06 s (2 decimal places)   **h** 300 g (1 significant figure)   **i** 0.7 m (1 decimal place)

    j 366 d (3 significant figures)   **k** 170 weeks (2 significant figures)   **l** 210 g (2 significant figures)

2 Billy has 40 identical marbles. Each marble weighs 65 g (to the nearest gram).

    a What is the greatest possible weight of one marble?

    b What is the least possible weight of one marble?

    c What is the greatest possible weight of all the marbles?

    d What is the least possible weight of all the marbles?

In this section you will learn how to:

- Combine limits of two or more variables together to solve problems

Key words
limits of accuracy
maximum
minimum

When we calculate an area or a volume, the errors in the linear measures will be compounded and, hence, will produce a still larger error in the calculated value. There are four operations to perform on limits – addition, subtraction, multiplication and division.

To get the **maximum** value when adding two numbers given to a certain **limit of accuracy**, the maximum values of the two numbers should be added. However, to get the maximum value when two numbers are subtracted then the lower limit of the second number should be subtracted from the upper limit of the first number.

Let a and b be two numbers that lie within limits $a_{min} \leq a < a_{max}$ and $b_{min} \leq b < b_{max}$

The following table shows the combinations to give the maximum and **minimum** values for the four rules of arithmetic.

Operation	Maximum	Minimum
Addition ($a + b$)	$a_{max} + b_{max}$	$a_{min} + b_{min}$
Subtraction ($a - b$)	$a_{max} - b_{min}$	$a_{min} - b_{max}$
Multiplication ($a \times b$)	$a_{max} \times b_{max}$	$a_{min} \times b_{min}$
Division ($a \div b$)	$a_{max} \div b_{min}$	$a_{min} \div b_{max}$

Be very careful about the order when doing subtraction or division.

When solving problems involving limits, start by writing down the limits of the variables involved, as this will get you some credit in the exam, then think about which combination of limits is needed to get the required answer.

Sometimes, especially when dividing, the upper and lower limits will be given to many decimal places. Be careful where rounding these off as the rounded answer may be outside the acceptable range of the limits. If you do round answers off, give your answer to at least 3 significant figures.

EXAMPLE 5

A rectangle has sides given as 6 cm by 15 cm, to the nearest centimetre.

Calculate the limits of accuracy of the area of the rectangle.

Write down the limits: 5.5 cm ≤ width < 6.5 cm, 14.5 cm ≤ length < 15.5 cm

For maximum area, multiply maximum width by maximum length, and for minimum area, multiply minimum width by minimum length.

The upper bound of the width is 6.5 cm and of the length is 15.5 cm. Hence the upper bound of the area of the rectangle is

$$6.5 \text{ cm} \times 15.5 \text{ cm} = 100.75 \text{ cm}^2$$

The lower bound of the width is 5.5 cm and of the length is 14.5 cm. Hence the lower bound of the area of the rectangle is

$$5.5 \text{ cm} \times 14.5 \text{ cm} = 79.75 \text{ cm}^2$$

Therefore, the limits of accuracy for the area of the rectangle are

$$79.75 \text{ cm}^2 \leq \text{area} < 100.75 \text{ cm}^2$$

EXAMPLE 6

The distance from Barnsley to Sheffield is 15 miles to the nearest mile. The time Jeff took to drive between Barnsley and Sheffield was 40 minutes to the nearest 10 minutes.

Calculate the upper limit of Jeff's average speed.

Write down the limits: 14.5 miles ≤ distance < 15.5 miles, 35 mins ≤ time < 45 mins

speed = distance ÷ time

To get the maximum speed we need the maximum distance ÷ minimum time.

15.5 miles ÷ 35 mins = 0.443 (3 significant figures) miles per minute

0.443 mph × 60 = 26.6 mph

The upper limit of Jeff's average speed = 26.6 mph.

EXERCISE 10C

1 For each of these rectangles, find the limits of accuracy of the area. The measurements are shown to the level of accuracy indicated in brackets.

   a 5 cm × 9 cm (nearest cm)   **b** 4.5 cm × 8.4 cm (1 decimal place)

   c 7.8 cm × 18 cm (2 significant figures)

2 A rectangular garden has sides of 6 m and 4 m, measured to the nearest metre.

   a Write down the limits of accuracy for each length.

   b What is the maximum area of the garden?

   c What is the minimum perimeter of the garden?

3 A cinema screen is measured as 6 m by 15 m, to the nearest metre. Calculate the limits of accuracy for the area of the screen.

4 The measurements, to the nearest centimetre, of a box are given as 10 cm × 7 cm × 4 cm. Calculate the limits of accuracy for the volume of the box.

5 The area of a field is given as 350 m^2, to the nearest 10 m^2. One length is given as 16 m, to the nearest metre. Find the limits of accuracy for the other length of the field.

6 In triangle ABC, AB = 9 cm, BC = 7 cm, and ∠ABC = 37°. All the measurements are given to the nearest unit. Calculate the limits of accuracy for the area of the triangle.

7 The price of pure gold is £18.25 per gram. The density of gold is 19.3 g/cm^3. (Assume these figures are exact.) A solid gold bar in the shape of a cuboid has sides 4.6 cm, 2.2 cm and 6.6 cm. These measurements are made to the nearest 0.1 cm.

    a i What are the limits of accuracy for the volume of this gold bar?

      ii What are the upper and lower limits of the cost of this bar?

The gold bar was weighed and given a value of 1296 g, to the nearest gram.

    b What are the upper and lower limits for the cost of the bar now?.

    c Explain why the price ranges are so different.

8 A stopwatch records the time for the winner of a 100-metre race as 14.7 seconds, measured to the nearest one-tenth of a second.

    a What are the greatest and least possible times for the winner?

    b The length of the 100-metre track is correct to the nearest 1 m. What are the greatest and least possible lengths of the track?

    c What is the fastest possible average speed of the winner, with a time of 14.7 seconds in the 100-metre race?

9 A cube has a side measured as 8 cm, to the nearest millimetre. What is the greatest percentage error of the following?

    a the calculated area of one face

    b the calculated volume of the cube

10 A cube has a volume of 40 cm^3, to the nearest cm^3. Find the range of possible values of the side length of the cube.

11 A cube has a volume of 200 cm^3, to the nearest 10 cm^3. Find the limits of accuracy of the side length of the cube.

12 A model car travels 40 m, measured to one significant figure, at a speed of 2 m/s, measured to one significant figure. Between what limits does the time taken lie?

1 A school has 1850 pupils to the nearest 10.

   a What is the least number of pupils at the school

   b What is the greatest number of pupils at the school?

2 The longest river in Britain is the River Severn. It is 220 miles long to the nearest 10 miles. What is the least length it could be?

3 A notice board is a rectangle with a length of 80 cm and a width of 40 cm. Both measurements are correct to the nearest centimetre.

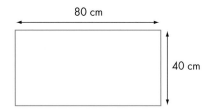

   a What is the least possible length of the notice board?

   b What is the greatest possible width of the notice board?

   c What is the greatest possible area of the notice board?

4 The base of a triangle is 10 cm measured to the nearest centimetre. The area of the triangle is 100 cm² measured to the nearest square centimetre. Calculate the least and greatest values of the height of the triangle.

5 A formula used in kinematics is $s = \dfrac{v^2 - u^2}{2a}$.

Calculate the greatest possible value of a if $v = 6.2$, $u = 3.6$ and $a = 9.8$, all values accurate to 2 significant figures.

6 A circle has an area of 100 cm², measured to the nearest square centimetre. What is the lower bound of the radius?

AQA, Question 20, Paper 2 Higher, June 2005

7 $x = 1.8$ measured to 1 decimal place,
$y = 4.0$ measured to 2 significant figures,
$z = 2.56$ measured to 3 significant figures.

Calculate the upper limit of $\dfrac{x^2 + y}{z}$.

8 A crane has a cable with a breaking strain of 5300 kg measured to 2 significant figures. It is used to lift crates which weigh 100 kg measured to the nearest 10 kg.

What is the greatest number of crates that can be lifted at one time so that the cable does not break?

AQA, Question 21, Paper 1 Higher, June 2004

9 A girl runs 60 metres in a time of 8.0 seconds. The distance is measured to the nearest metre and the time is measured to 2 significant figures. What is the least possible speed ?

10 A coffee machine dispenses 130 millilitres of black coffee into cups with a capacity of 175 millilitres. These values are accurate to 3 significant figures.

Milk is supplied in small cartons which contain 21 millilitres, accurate to the nearest millilitre.

Beryl likes milky coffee and always puts two cartons of milk in her coffee.

Will Beryl's cup ever overflow? You *must* show all your working.

AQA, Question 25, Paper 2 Higher, June 2003

11 **a** Calculate the length of the diagonal x in this cube of side 3 m.

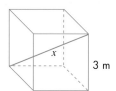

   b A man is carrying a pole of length 5 m down a long corridor. The pole is measured to the nearest centimetre. At the end of the corridor is a right-angled corner. The corridor is 3 m wide and 3 m high, both measurements correct to the nearest 10 cm. Will the pole be certain to get round the corner?

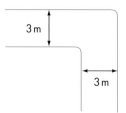

WORKED EXAM QUESTION

The magnification of a lens is given by the formula

$$m = \frac{v}{u}$$

In an experiment, u is measured as 8.5 cm and v is measured as 14.0 cm, both correct to the nearest 0.1 cm. Find the least possible value of m, You must show full details of your calculation.

Solution

$8.45 \leqslant u < 8.55$

| Write down the limits of both variables. |

$13.95 \leqslant v < 14.05$

Least m = least $u \div$ greatest $v = 8.45 \div 14.05 = 0.6014234875$

| As the calculation is a division the least value will be given by least $u \div$ greatest v. |

$= 0.601$ or 0.6

| Round off to a suitable degree of accuracy. |

A long rod with a square cross-section is made with a side of 5 cm. A circular hole is drilled with a radius of 3.6 cm. All measurements are to the nearest $\frac{1}{10}$ cm. Will the rod fit into the circle?

Solution

Limits of side of square

$4.95 <$ side < 5.05

Limits of radius

$3.55 <$ radius < 3.65

| This is a using and applying maths question. You need to have a strategy to solve it. Step 1: find the largest possible diagonal of the square using Pythagoras. Step 2: work out the smallest possible diameter of the circle. Step 3: Compare the values to see if the diagonal is smaller than the diameter. Always start with writing down the limits of the variables in the question. |

Largest diagonal $= \sqrt{(5.05^2 + 5.05^2)}$

$= 7.14177849$

$= 7.142$ (4 significant figures)

| Step 1: Work out the largest possible diagonal, do not round off to less than 4 significant figures. |

Smallest diameter $= 2 \times 3.55 = 7.1$

| Step 2: Work out the smallest diameter. |

As $7.142 > 7.1$,
the rod may not fit in the circle.

| Step 3: Compare the results. |

Mr Slater buys a new house. He decides to put laminate flooring throughout the whole ground floor.

The laminate flooring he has chosen comes in packs, which cover 2 m^2.

Each room also needs an edging strip around the perimeter of the room, excluding doorways.

The edging comes in packs, which have a total length of 12 m.

The hall and bathroom are to have beech laminate flooring, and the other rooms oak.

Mr Slater works out the upper and lower bound for each length shown on the sketch. He then calculates the maximum floor area of each room and the maximum length of edging needed for every room. Help him complete the table to find the total maximum floor area and edging he needs.

Beech effect

Room	Room Maximum floor area (m^2)	Maximum edging needed (m)
Hall		
Bathroom		
Total		

Oak effect

Room	Room Maximum floor area (m^2)	Maximum edging needed (m)
Lounge		
Sitting room		
Kitchen/diner		
Conservatory		
Total		

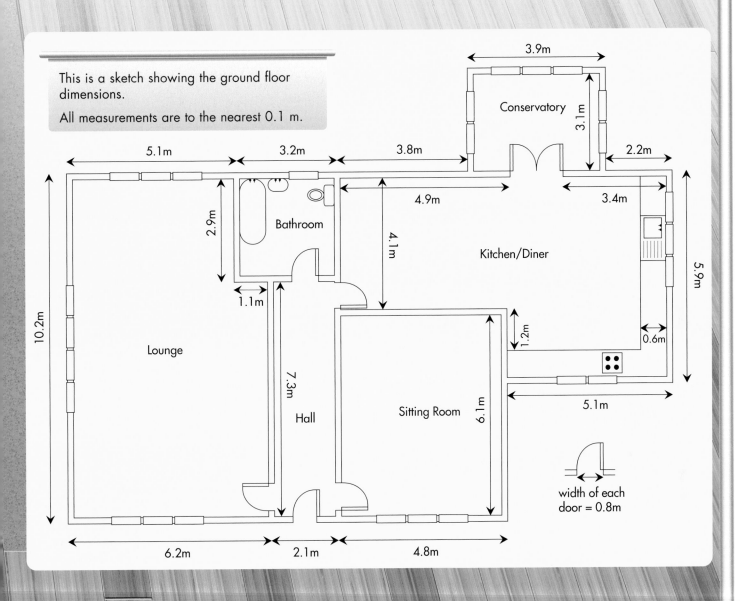

This is a sketch showing the ground floor dimensions.

All measurements are to the nearest 0.1 m.

Calculate for Mr Slater the total cost of the flooring and edging.

Oak effect

	Number of packs	Price per pack	Total cost
Beech flooring		£56.40	
Beech edging		£21.15	
Oak flooring		£61.10	
Oak edging		£25.85	
	Total:		

This total price is inclusive of VAT.

VAT is 17½%.

What is the total price, exclusive of VAT?

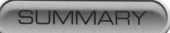

GRADE YOURSELF

B Able to find measures of accuracy for numbers given to whole number accuracies

A Able to find measures of accuracy for numbers given to decimal place or significant figure accuracies

A* Able to calculate the limits of compound measures

What you should know now

● How to find the limits of numbers given to various accuracies

● How to find the limits of compound measures by combining the appropriate limits of the variables involved

Shape

1 Circumference and area of a circle

2 Area of a trapezium

3 Sectors

4 Volume of a prism

5 Cylinders

6 Volume of a pyramid

7 Cones

8 Spheres

This chapter will show you ...

- how to calculate the length of an arc
- how to calculate the area of a sector
- how to find the area of a trapezium
- how to calculate the surface area and volume of prisms, cylinders, pyramids, cones and spheres

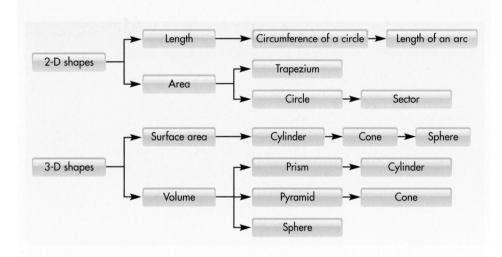

What you should already know

- The area of a rectangle is given by Area = length × width or $A = lw$
- The area of a parallelogram is given by Area = base × height or $A = bh$
- The area of a triangle is given by Area = $\frac{1}{2}$ × base × height or $A = \frac{1}{2}bh$
- The circumference of a circle is given by $C = \pi d$, where d is the diameter of the circle
- The area of a circle is given by $A = \pi r^2$, where r is the radius of the circle

continued

- The most accurate value of π that you can use is on your calculator. You should use it every time you have to work with π. Otherwise take π to be 3.142

- In problems using π, unless told otherwise, round off your answers to three significant figures

- The volume of a cuboid is given by Volume = length × width × height or $V = lwh$

- The common metric units to measure area, volume and capacity are shown in this table.

Area	Volume	Capacity
100 mm^2 = 1 cm^2	1000 mm^3 = 1 cm^3	1000 cm^3 = 1 litre
10 000 cm^2 = 1 m^2	1 000 000 cm^3 = 1 m^3	1 m^3 = 1000 litres

Quick check

1 Find the areas of the following shapes.

a

15 mm

6 mm

b

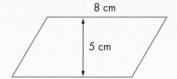

8 cm

5 cm

c

7 m

6 m

2 Find the volume of this cuboid.

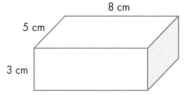

8 cm

5 cm

3 cm

If you need to revise circle calculations, you should work through Exercise 11A.

11.1 Circumference and area of a circle

In this section you will learn how to:
- calculate the circumference and area of a circle

Key words

π
area
circumference

EXAMPLE 1

Calculate the **circumference** of the circle. Give your answer to three significant figures.

$C = \pi d$

$\quad = \pi \times 5 \text{ cm}$

$\quad = 15.7 \text{ cm (to 3 significant figures)}$

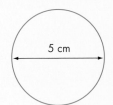

5 cm

EXAMPLE 2

Calculate the **area** of the circle. Give your answer in terms of **π**.

$A = \pi r^2$

$\quad = \pi \times 6^2 \text{ m}^2$

$\quad = 36\pi \text{ m}^2$

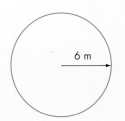

6 m

EXERCISE 11A

1 Copy and complete the following table for each circle. Give your answers to 3 significant figures.

	Radius	Diameter	Circumference	Area
a	4 cm			
b	2.6 m			
c		12 cm		
d		3.2 m		

D

2 Find the circumference of each of the following circles. Give your answers in terms of π.

  a Diameter 5 cm   **b** Radius 4 cm   **c** Radius 9 m   **d** Diameter 12 cm

3 Find the area of each of the following circles. Give your answers in terms of π.

  a Radius 5 cm   **b** Diameter 12 cm   **c** Radius 10 cm   **d** Diameter 1 m

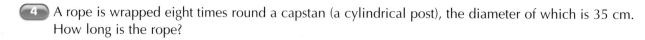

4 A rope is wrapped eight times round a capstan (a cylindrical post), the diameter of which is 35 cm. How long is the rope?

5 The roller used on a cricket pitch has a radius of 70 cm.

   a What is the circumference of the roller?

   b A cricket pitch has a length of 20 m. How many complete revolutions does the roller make when rolling the pitch?

6 The diameter of each of the following coins is as follows.

    1p: 2 cm,   2p: 2.6 cm,   5p: 1.7 cm,   10p: 2.4 cm

   Calculate the area of one face of each coin. Give your answers to 1 decimal place.

7 A circle has a circumference of 25 cm. What is its diameter?

8 What is the total perimeter of a semicircle of diameter 15 cm?

9 What is the total perimeter of a semicircle of radius 7 cm? Give your answer in terms of π.

10 Calculate the area of each of these shapes, giving your answers in terms of π.

   a
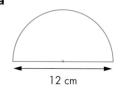
12 cm

   b

4 cm

   c
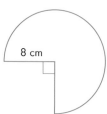
8 cm

11 Calculate the area of the shaded part of each of these diagrams, giving your answers in terms of π.

   a
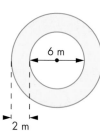
6 m
2 m

   b
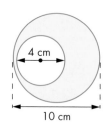
4 cm
10 cm

   c
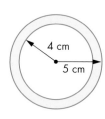
4 cm
5 cm

12 Assume that the human waist is circular.

   a What are the distances around the waists of the following people?

     Sue: waist radius of 10 cm   Dave: waist radius of 12 cm

     Julie: waist radius of 11 cm   Brian: waist radius of 13 cm

   b Compare differences between pairs of waist circumferences. What connection do they have to π?

   c What would be the difference in length between a rope stretched tightly round the Earth and another rope always held 1 m above it?

Mod 5

Area of a trapezium

In this section you will learn how to:
- find the area of a trapezium

Key word
trapezium

The area of a **trapezium** is calculated by finding the average of the lengths of its parallel sides and multiplying this by the perpendicular distance between them.

$$A = \tfrac{1}{2}(a + b)h$$

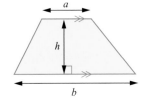

EXAMPLE 3

Find the area of the trapezium ABCD.

$$A = \tfrac{1}{2}(4 + 7) \times 3 \text{ cm}^2$$
$$= 16.5 \text{ cm}^2$$

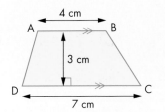

EXERCISE 11B

1. Copy and complete the following table for each trapezium.

	Parallel side 1	Parallel side 2	Vertical height	Area
a	8 cm	4 cm	5 cm	
b	10 cm	12 cm	7 cm	
c	7 cm	5 cm	4 cm	
d	5 cm	9 cm	6 cm	
e	3 m	13 m	5 m	
f	4 cm	10 cm		42 cm²
g	7 cm	8 cm		22.5 cm²
h	6 cm		5 cm	40 cm²

2. Calculate the perimeter and the area of each of these trapeziums.

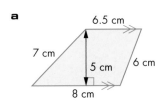

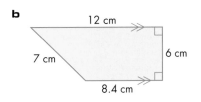

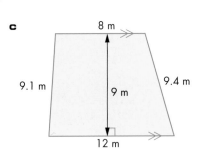

3 Calculate the area of each of these compound shapes.

a
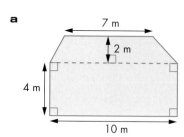

b
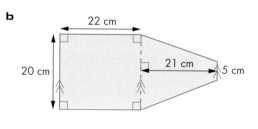

c
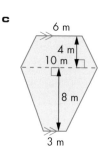

4 Calculate the area of the shaded part in each of these diagrams.

a
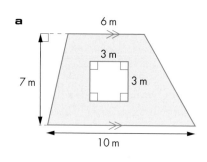

b
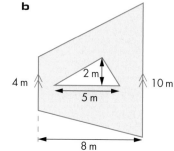

c
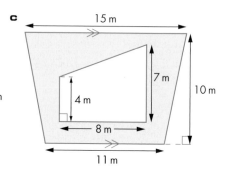

5 A trapezium has an area of 25 cm². Its vertical height is 5 cm. Write down five different possible pairs of lengths which the two parallel sides could be.

6 What percentage of this shape has been shaded?

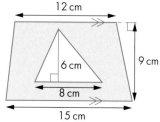

7 The shape of most of Egypt (see map) roughly approximates to a trapezium. The north coast is about 900 km long, the south boundary is about 1100 km long, and the distance from north to south is about 1100 km.

What is the approximate area of this part of Egypt?

Sections

In this section you will learn how to:
- calculate the length of an arc and the area of a sector

Key words

arc

sector

A **sector** is part of a circle, bounded by two radii of the circle and one of the **arcs** formed by the intersection of these radii with the circumference.

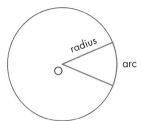

The angle subtended at the centre of the circle by the arc of a sector is known as the angle of the sector.

When a circle is divided into only two sectors, the larger one is called the major sector and the smaller one is called the minor sector.

Likewise, their arcs are called respectively the major arc and the minor arc.

Length of an arc and area of a sector

A sector is a fraction of the whole circle, the size of the fraction being determined by the size of angle of the sector. The angle is often written as θ, a Greek letter pronounced *theta*. For example, the sector shown in the diagram represents the fraction $\dfrac{\theta°}{360°}$.

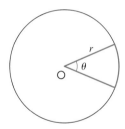

This applies to both its arc length and its area. Therefore,

$$\text{Arc length} = \frac{\theta°}{360°} \times 2\pi r \quad \text{or} \quad \frac{\theta°}{360°} \times \pi d$$

$$\text{Sector area} = \frac{\theta°}{360°} \times \pi r^2$$

EXAMPLE 4

Find the arc length and the area of the sector in the diagram.

The sector angle is 28° and the radius is 5 cm. Therefore,

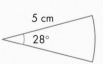

$$\text{Arc length} = \frac{28°}{360°} \times \pi \times 2 \times 5 = 2.4 \text{ cm (1 decimal place)}$$

$$\text{Sector area} = \frac{28°}{360°} \times \pi \times 5^2 = 6.1 \text{ cm}^2 \text{ (1 decimal place)}$$

EXERCISE 11C

1 For each of these sectors, calculate   **i** the arc length   **ii** the sector area

a
40°
8 cm

b
95°
5 cm

c
78°
12 cm

d
130°
7 cm

2 Calculate the arc length and the area of a sector whose arc subtends an angle of 60° at the centre of a circle with a diameter of 12 cm. Give your answer in terms of π.

3 Calculate the total perimeter of each of these sectors.   **a**

11 cm

b
22°
8.5 cm

4 Calculate the area of each of these sectors.

a
110°
7 cm

b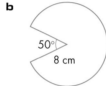
50°
8 cm

c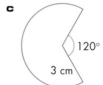
120°
3 cm

d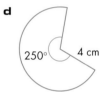
250°   4 cm

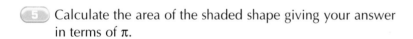

5 Calculate the area of the shaded shape giving your answer in terms of π.

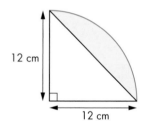
12 cm
12 cm

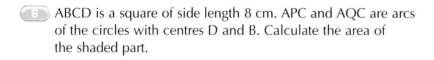

6 ABCD is a square of side length 8 cm. APC and AQC are arcs of the circles with centres D and B. Calculate the area of the shaded part.

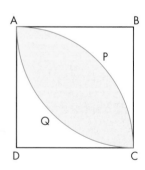
A   B
P
Q
D   C

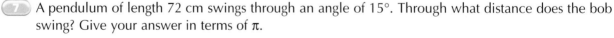

7 A pendulum of length 72 cm swings through an angle of 15°. Through what distance does the bob swing? Give your answer in terms of π.

8 Find **i** the perimeter and **ii** the area of this shape.

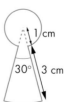
1 cm
30°   3 cm

Volume of a prism

In this section you will learn how to:
● calculate the volume of a prism

Key words
cross-section
prism

A **prism** is a 3-D shape which has the same **cross-section** running all the way through it.

Name:	Cuboid	Triangular prism	Cylinder
Cross-section:	Rectangle	Isosceles triangle	Circle

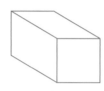

Name:	Cuboid	Hexagonal prism
Cross-section:	Square	Regular hexagon

The volume of a prism is found by multiplying the area of its cross-section by the length of the prism (or height if the prism is stood on end).

That is, Volume of prism = area of cross-section × length **or** $V = Al$

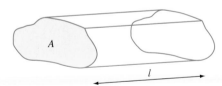

EXAMPLE 5

Find the volume of the triangular prism.

The area of the triangular cross-section = $A = \dfrac{5 \times 7}{2} = 17.5 \text{ cm}^2$

The volume is the area of its cross-section × length = Al

  $= 17.5 \times 9 = 157.5 \text{ cm}^3$

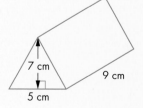

EXERCISE 11D

1 For each prism shown

   i sketch the cross-section   **ii** calculate the area of the cross-section

   iii calculate the volume.

a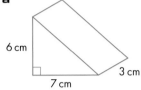

b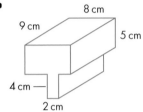

c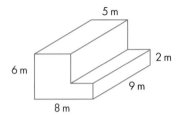

2 Calculate the volume of each of these prisms.

a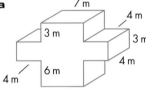

b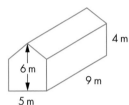

c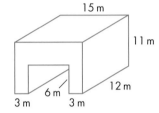

3 The uniform cross-section of a swimming pool is a trapezium with parallel sides, 1 m and 2.5 m, with a perpendicular distance of 30 m between them. The width of the pool is 10 m. How much water is in the pool when it is full? Give your answer in litres.

4 A lean-to is a prism. Calculate the volume of air inside the lean-to with the dimensions shown in the diagram. Give your answer in litres.

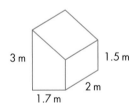

5 Each of these prisms has a regular cross-section in the shape of a right-angled triangle.

   a Find the volume of each prism.   **b** Find the total surface area of each prism.

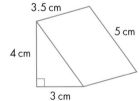
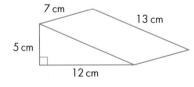

Mod 5

6 The top and bottom of the container shown here are the same size, both consisting of a rectangle, 4 cm by 9 cm, with a semicircle at each end. The depth is 3 cm. Find the volume of the container.

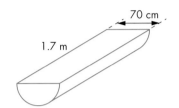

7 A tunnel is in the shape of a semicircle of radius 5 m, running for 500 m through a hill. Calculate the volume of soil removed when the tunnel was cut through the hill.

8 A horse trough is in the shape of a semicircular prism as shown. What volume of water will the trough hold when it is filled to the top? Give your answer in litres.

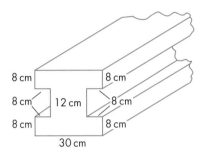

70 cm

1.7 m

9 The dimensions of the cross-section of a girder, 2 m in length, are shown on the diagram. The girder is made of iron with a density of 7.9 g/cm³. What is the mass of the girder?

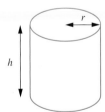

8 cm   8 cm
8 cm   12 cm   8 cm
8 cm   8 cm
        30 cm

11.5 # Cylinders

In this section you will learn how to:
- calculate the volume and surface area of a cylinder

Key words
cylinder
surface area
volume

Since a **cylinder** is an example of a prism, its **volume** is found by multiplying the area of one of its circular ends by the height.

That is, Volume = $\pi r^2 h$

where r is the radius of the cylinder and h is its height or length.

EXAMPLE 6

What is the volume of a cylinder having a radius of 5 cm and a height of 12 cm?

$$\begin{aligned} \text{Volume} &= \text{area of circular base} \times \text{height} \\ &= \pi r^2 h \\ &= \pi \times 5^2 \times 12 \text{ cm}^3 \\ &= 942 \text{ cm}^3 \text{ (3 significant figures)} \end{aligned}$$

Surface area

The total **surface area** of a cylinder is made up of the area of its curved surface plus the area of its two circular ends.

The curved surface area, when opened out, is a rectangle whose length is the circumference of the circular end.

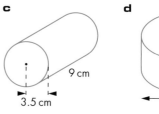

Curved surface area = circumference of end × height of cylinder

$$= 2\pi rh \quad \textbf{or} \quad \pi dh$$

Area of one end $= \pi r^2$

Therefore, total surface area $= 2\pi rh + 2\pi r^2 \quad \textbf{or} \quad \pi dh + 2\pi r^2$

EXAMPLE 7

What is the total surface area of a cylinder with a radius of 15 cm and a height of 2.5 m?

First, you must change the dimensions to a *common unit*. Use centimetres in this case.

$$
\begin{aligned}
\text{Total surface area} &= \pi dh + 2\pi r^2 \\
&= \pi \times 30 \times 250 + 2 \times \pi \times 15^2 \text{ cm}^2 \\
&= 23\,562 + 1414 \text{ cm}^2 \\
&= 24\,976 \text{ cm}^2 \\
&= 25\,000 \text{ cm}^2 \text{ (3 significant figures)}
\end{aligned}
$$

EXERCISE 11E

1 Find **i** the volume and **ii** the total surface area of each of these cylinders. Give your answers to 3 significant figures.

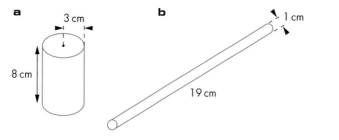

a 3 cm 8 cm

b 1 cm 19 cm

c 9 cm 3.5 cm

d 6 cm 15 cm

2 Find **i** the volume and **ii** the curved surface area of each of these cylinders. Give your answers in terms of π.

a base radius 3 cm and height 8 cm

b base diameter 8 cm and height 7 cm

c base diameter 12 cm and height 5 cm

d base radius of 10 m and length 6 m

3 The diameter of a marble, cylindrical column is 60 cm and its height is 4.2 m. The cost of making this column is quoted as £67.50 per cubic metre. What is the estimated total cost of making the column?

4 Find the mass of a solid iron cylinder 55 cm high with a base diameter of 60 cm. The density of iron is 7.9 g/cm^3.

Mod 5

5 What is the radius of a cylinder, height 8 cm, with a volume of 200π cm^3?

 6 What is the radius of a cylinder, height 12 cm, with a curved surface area of 240π cm^2?

 7 What is the height of a cylinder, diameter 12 cm, with a volume of 108π cm^3?

 8 A cylindrical container is 65 cm in diameter. Water is poured into the container until it is 1 metre deep. How much water is in the container? Give your answer in litres.

 9 A cylindrical can of soup has a diameter of 7 cm and a height of 9.5 cm. It is full of soup, which weighs 625 g. What is the density of the soup?

 10 A metal bar, 1 m long, and with a diameter of 6 cm, has a mass of 22 kg. What is the density of the metal from which the bar is made?

 11 A block of wood has a hole of radius 2.5 cm drilled out as shown on the diagram. Calculate the mass of the wood if its density is 0.95 g/cm^3.

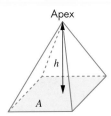

9 cm
11 cm
12 cm

11.6 Volume of a pyramid

In this section you will learn how to:
- calculate the volume of a pyramid

Key words
apex
frustum
pyramid
volume

A **pyramid** is a 3-D shape with a base from which triangular faces rise to a common vertex, called the **apex**. The base can be any polygon, but is usually a triangle, a rectangle or a square.

The **volume** of a pyramid is given by

Volume $= \frac{1}{3} \times$ base area $\times$ vertical height

$$V = \frac{1}{3}Ah$$

where A is the base area and h is the vertical height.

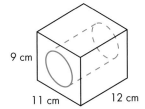

Apex
h
A

EXAMPLE 8

Calculate the volume of the pyramid on the right.

Base area $= 5 \times 4 = 20$ cm^2

Volume $= \frac{1}{3} \times 20 \times 6 = 40$ cm^3

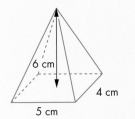

6 cm
4 cm
5 cm

EXAMPLE 9

A pyramid, with a square base of side 8 cm, has a volume of 320 cm³. What is the vertical height of the pyramid?

Let h be the vertical height of the pyramid. Then,

$$\text{Volume} = \tfrac{1}{3} \times 64 \times h = 320 \text{ cm}^3$$

$$\frac{64h}{3} = 320 \text{ cm}^3$$

$$h = \frac{960}{64} \text{ cm}$$

$$h = 15 \text{ cm}$$

EXERCISE 11F

1 Calculate the volume of each of these pyramids, all with rectangular bases.

a

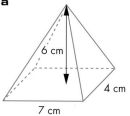

6 cm
4 cm
7 cm

b

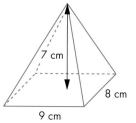

7 cm
8 cm
9 cm

c

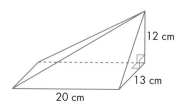

12 cm
13 cm
20 cm

d

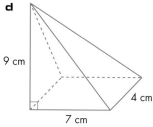

9 cm
4 cm
7 cm

e

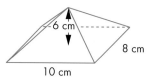

6 cm
8 cm
10 cm

2 Calculate the volume of a pyramid having a square base of side 9 cm and a vertical height of 10 cm.

3 Calculate the volume of each of these shapes.

a

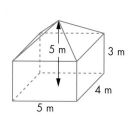

5 m
3 m
4 m
5 m

b

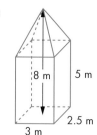

8 m
5 m
2.5 m
3 m

c

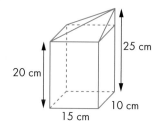

25 cm
20 cm
10 cm
15 cm

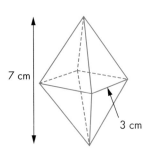

4 What is the mass of a solid pyramid having a square base of side 4 cm, a height of 3 cm and a density of 13 g/cm³?

5 A crystal is in the form of two square-based pyramids joined at their bases (see diagram). The crystal has a mass of 31.5 grams. What is its density?

7 cm

3 cm

6 Find the mass of each of these pyramids.

a

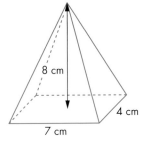

8 cm

4 cm

7 cm

Density 2.7 g/cm³

b

7 cm

6 cm

9 cm

Density 3.5 g/cm³

c

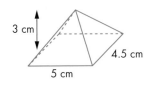

3 cm

4.5 cm

5 cm

Density 2.1 g/cm³

7 Calculate the length *x* in each of these rectangular-based pyramids.

a

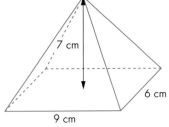

x

10 cm

12 cm

Weight 828 g
Density 2.3 g/cm³

b

5 cm

4 cm

x

Weight 180 g
Density 4.5 g/cm³

8 The pyramid in the diagram has its top 5 cm cut off as shown. The shape which is left is called a **frustum**. Calculate the volume of the frustum.

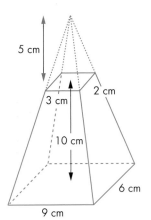

5 cm

2 cm

3 cm

10 cm

6 cm

9 cm

11.7 Cones

In this section you will learn how to:
- calculate the volume and surface area of a cone

Key words

slant height
surface area
vertical
    height
volume

A cone can be treated as a pyramid with a circular base. Therefore, the formula for the **volume** of a cone is the same as that for a pyramid.

$$\text{Volume} = \tfrac{1}{3} \times \text{base area} \times \text{vertical height}$$

$$V = \tfrac{1}{3}\pi r^2 h$$

where r is the radius of the base and h is the **vertical height** of the cone.

The curved **surface area** of a cone is given by

$$\text{Curved surface area} = \pi \times \text{radius} \times \text{slant height}$$

$$S = \pi r l$$

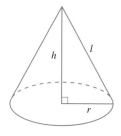

where l is the **slant height** of the cone.

So the total surface area of a cone is given by the curved surface area plus the area of its circular base.

$$A = \pi r l + \pi r^2$$

EXAMPLE 10

For the cone in the diagram, calculate

i its volume and

ii its total surface area.

Give your answers in terms of π.

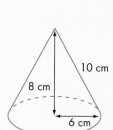

i The volume is given by $V = \tfrac{1}{3}\pi r^2 h$

$$= \tfrac{1}{3} \times \pi \times 36 \times 8 = 96\pi \text{ cm}^3$$

ii The total surface area is given by $A = \pi r l + \pi r^2$

$$= \pi \times 6 \times 10 + \pi \times 36 = 96\pi \text{ cm}^2$$

EXERCISE 11G

1 For each cone, calculate **i** its volume and **ii** its total surface area. Give your answers to 3 significant figures.

a

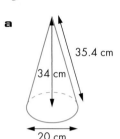

35.4 cm

34 cm

20 cm

b

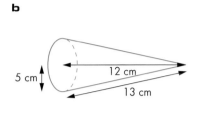

5 cm   12 cm

13 cm

c

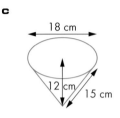

18 cm

12 cm   15 cm

2 A solid cone, base radius 6 cm and vertical height 8 cm, is made of metal whose density is 3.1 g/cm³. Find the mass of the cone.

3 Find the total surface area of a cone whose base radius is 3 cm and slant height is 5 cm. Give your answer in terms of π.

4 Find the total surface area of a cone whose base radius is 5 cm and slant height is 13 cm.

5 Calculate the volume of each of these shapes. Give your answers in terms of π.

a

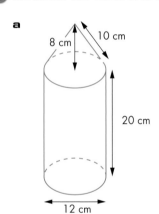

8 cm   10 cm

20 cm

12 cm

b

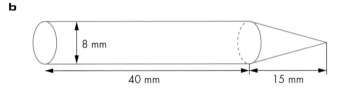

8 mm

40 mm   15 mm

6 The model shown on the right is made from aluminium. What is the mass of the model, given that the density of aluminium is 2.7 g/cm³?

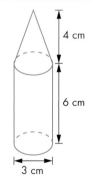

4 cm

6 cm

3 cm

7 A container in the shape of a cone, base radius 10 cm and vertical height 19 cm, is full of water. The water is poured into an empty cylinder of radius 15 cm. How high is the water in the cylinder?

Spheres

In this section you will learn how to:

● calculate the volume and surface area of a sphere

Key words

sphere
surface area
volume

The **volume** of a **sphere**, radius r, is given by

$$V = \tfrac{4}{3}\pi r^3$$

Its **surface area** is given by

$$A = 4\pi r^2$$

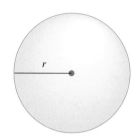

EXAMPLE 11

For a sphere of radius of 8 cm, calculate **i** its volume and **ii** its surface area.

i The volume is given by $\qquad V = \tfrac{4}{3}\pi r^3$

$$= \tfrac{4}{3} \times \pi \times 8^3 = \tfrac{2048}{3} \times \pi = 2140 \text{ cm}^3 \text{ (3 significant figures)}$$

ii The surface area is given by $\quad A = 4\pi r^2$

$$= 4 \times \pi \times 8^2 = 256 \times \pi = 804 \text{ cm}^2 \text{ (3 significant figures)}$$

EXERCISE 11H

1 Calculate the volume of each of these spheres. Give your answers in terms of π.

   a Radius 3 cm   **b** Radius 6 cm   **c** Diameter 20 cm

2 Calculate the surface area of each of these spheres. Give your answers in terms of π.

   a Radius 3 cm   **b** Radius 5 cm   **c** Diameter 14 cm

3 Calculate the volume and the surface area of a sphere with a diameter of 50 cm.

4 A sphere fits exactly into an open cubical box of side 25 cm. Calculate the following.

   a the surface area of the sphere   **b** the volume of the sphere

5 A metal sphere of radius 15 cm is melted down and recast into a solid cylinder of radius 6 cm. Calculate the height of the cylinder.

6 Lead has a density of 11.35 g/cm^3. Calculate the maximum number of shot (spherical lead pellets) of radius 1.5 mm which can be made from 1 kg of lead.

7 Calculate, correct to one decimal place, the radius of a sphere

   a whose surface area is 150 cm^2 **b** whose volume is 150 cm^3.

1 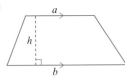 The area of the trapezium is 20 m². The parallel sides *a* and *b* are different lengths. The perpendicular height *h* is 4 m. Find a possible pair of values for *a* and *b*.

AQA, Question 4, Paper 1 Higher, June 2001

2 A semi-circular protractor has a diameter of 9 cm.

Calculate the perimeter.

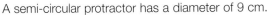
9 cm

AQA, Question 2, Paper 2 Higher, November 2003

3 OAB is a minor sector of a circle of radius 6 cm. Angle AOB = 120°

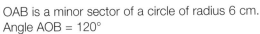

a Calculate the area of the minor sector OAB. Give your answer in terms of π.

b Calculate the perimeter of the minor sector OAB. Give your answer in terms of π.

AQA, Question 14, Paper 1 Higher, June 2001

4 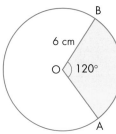 A solid cone has base radius 5 cm and slant height 12 cm. Calculate the *total* surface area of the cone. Give your answer in terms of π.

AQA, Question 19, Paper 1 Higher, May 2002

5 A cylinder of radius 7 cm and height 18 cm is half full of water. One litre of water is added. Will the water overflow? You must show all your working.

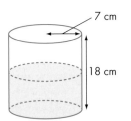
7 cm
18 cm

AQA, Question 3, Paper 2 Higher, November 2001

6 A dumbell is made from 3 cylinders of the same metal with dimensions as shown.

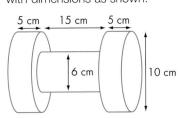
5 cm   15 cm   5 cm
6 cm   10 cm

The mass of the dumbell is 6 kilograms. What is the density of the metal?

AQA, Question 15, Paper 2 Higher, June 2002

7 A marble paperweight consists of a cuboid and a hemisphere as shown in the diagram. The hemisphere has a radius of 4 cm.

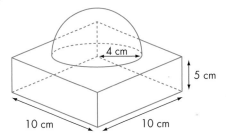
4 cm
5 cm
10 cm   10 cm

Calculate the volume of the paperweight.

AQA, Question 15, Paper 2 Higher, June 2005

WORKED EXAM QUESTION

The diagram shows a pepper pot. The pot consists of a cylinder and a hemisphere. The cylinder has a diameter of 5 cm and a height of 7 cm.

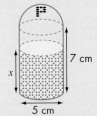
7 cm
x
5 cm

The pepper takes up half the total volume of the pot. Find the depth of pepper in the pot marked *x* in the diagram.

Solution

Volume of pepper pot

$$= \pi r^2 h + \frac{2}{3}\pi r^3$$

$$= \pi \times 2.5^2 \times 7 + \frac{2}{3} \times \pi \times 2.5^3 \text{ cm}^3$$

$$= 170.2 \text{ cm}^3$$

So volume of pepper $= 85.1 \text{ cm}^3$

Therefore,

$$\pi r^2 x = 85.1 \text{ cm}^3$$

and $x = \dfrac{85.1}{\pi \times 2.5^2} = 4.3 \text{ cm}$ (1 decimal place)

AQA, Question 17, Paper 2 Higher, June 2000

REALLY USEFUL MATHS!

Water recycling

Mr and Mrs Jones have decided to "go green". They want to install a water purifying unit and water tank in their loft to collect rain water from their roof, and use this water for the washing machine, dishwasher, shower and toilet.

Copy the table below and help them to calculate their average total daily water usage for these four items.

BATHROOM

The toilet cistern has a cross section that is a trapezium. The diagram shows the amount of water that is used in one flush of the toilet.

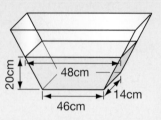

20cm · 48cm · 46cm · 14cm

[KWPTD]

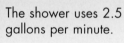

BATHROOM

The shower uses 2.5 gallons per minute.

An average shower takes 8 minutes.

Daily water usage

	litres used each: flush/shower/load	frequency used	total litres per day
Toilet		12 times a day	
Shower		2 times a day	
Washing machine		3 times a week	
Dishwasher		once every 2 days	
		TOTAL:	

262

Mod 5

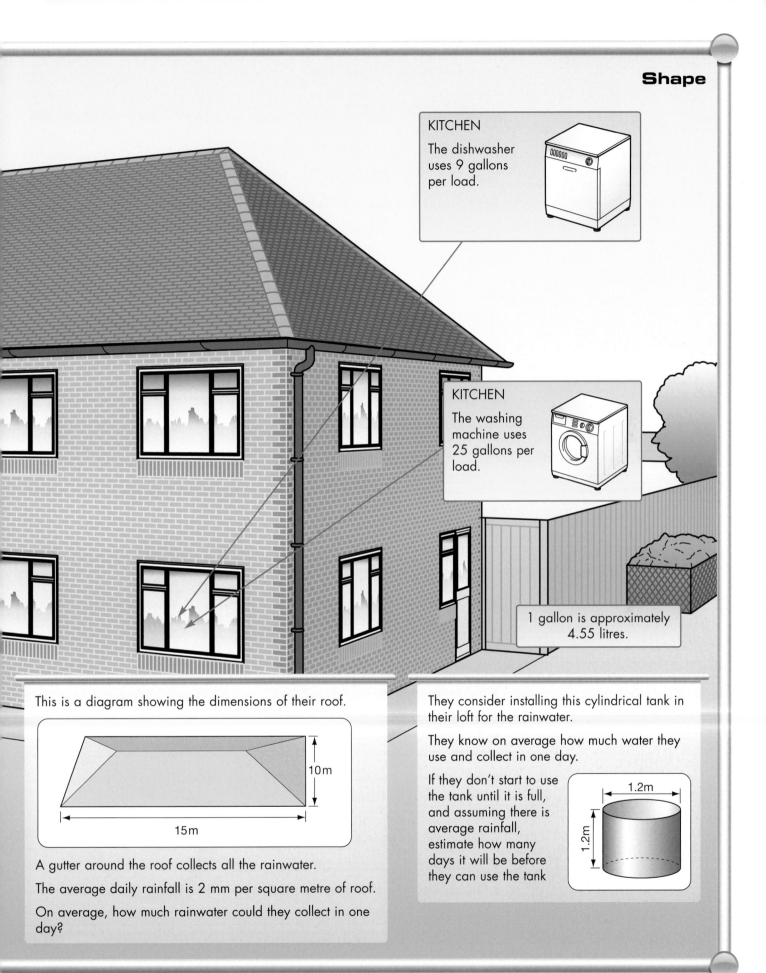

KITCHEN

The dishwasher uses 9 gallons per load.

KITCHEN

The washing machine uses 25 gallons per load.

1 gallon is approximately 4.55 litres.

This is a diagram showing the dimensions of their roof.

10m

15m

A gutter around the roof collects all the rainwater.

The average daily rainfall is 2 mm per square metre of roof.

On average, how much rainwater could they collect in one day?

They consider installing this cylindrical tank in their loft for the rainwater.

They know on average how much water they use and collect in one day.

If they don't start to use the tank until it is full, and assuming there is average rainfall, estimate how many days it will be before they can use the tank

1.2m

1.2m

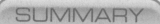

GRADE YOURSELF

D Able to calculate the circumference and area of a circle

D Able to calculate the area of a trapezium

C Able to calculate the volume of prisms and cylinders

B Able to calculate the length of an arc and the area of a sector

B Able to calculate the surface area of cylinders, cones and spheres

B Able to calculate the volume of pyramids, cones and spheres

A Able to calculate volume and surface area of compound 3-D shapes

What you should know now

- For a sector of radius r and angle θ

  Arc length = $\dfrac{\theta°}{360°} \times 2\pi r$ or $\dfrac{\theta°}{360°} \times \pi d$

  Area of a sector = $\dfrac{\theta°}{360°} \times \pi r^2$

- The area of a trapezium is given by

  $A = \frac{1}{2}(a + b)h$

  where h is the vertical height, and a and b are the lengths of the two parallel sides

- The volume of a prism is given by $V = Al$, where A is the cross-section area and l is the length of the prism

- The volume of a cylinder is given by $V = \pi r^2 h$ where r is the radius and h is the height or length of the cylinder

- The curved surface area of a cylinder is given by $S = 2\pi rh$, where r is the radius and h is the height or length of the cylinder

- The volume of a pyramid is given by $V = \frac{1}{3}Ah$, where A is the area of the base and h is the vertical height of the pyramid

- The volume of a cone is given by $V = \frac{1}{3}\pi r^2 h$ where r is the base radius and h is the vertical height of the cone

- The curved surface area of a cone is given by $S = \pi rl$, where r is the base radius and l is the slant height of the cone

- The volume of a sphere is given by $V = \frac{4}{3}\pi r^3$ where r is its radius

- The surface area of a sphere is given by $A = 4\pi r^2$ where r is its radius

Pythagoras and trigonometry

This chapter will show you ...

● how to use Pythagoras' theorem in right-angled triangles
● how to solve problems using Pythagoras' theorem
● how to use trigonometric ratios in right-angled triangles
● how to use trigonometry to solve problems

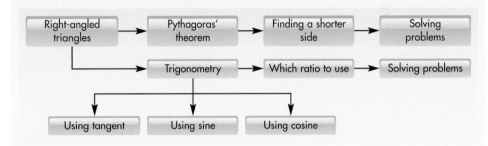

What you should already know

● how to find the square and square root of a number
● how to round numbers to a suitable degree of accuracy

Quick check

Use your calculator to evaluate the following, giving your answers to one decimal place.

1 2.3^2

2 15.7^2

3 0.78^2

4 $\sqrt{8}$

5 $\sqrt{260}$

6 $\sqrt{0.5}$

Pythagoras' theorem

In this section you will learn how to:
- calculate the length of the hypotenuse in a right-angled triangle

Key words
hypotenuse
Pythagoras' theorem

Pythagoras, who was a philosopher as well as a mathematician, was born in 580 BC, on the island of Samos in Greece. He later moved to Crotona (Italy), where he established the Pythagorean Brotherhood, which was a secret society devoted to politics, mathematics and astronomy. It is said that when he discovered his famous theorem, he was so full of joy that he showed his gratitude to the gods by sacrificing a hundred oxen.

Consider squares being drawn on each side of a right-angled triangle, with sides 3 cm, 4 cm and 5 cm.

The longest side is called the **hypotenuse** and is always opposite the right angle.

Pythagoras' theorem can then be stated as follows:

For any right-angled triangle, the area of the square drawn on the hypotenuse is equal to the sum of the areas of the squares drawn on the other two sides.

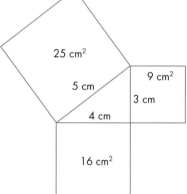

The form in which most of your parents would have learnt the theorem when they were at school – and which is still in use today – is as follows:

In any right-angled triangle, the square of the hypotenuse is equal to the sum of the squares of the other two sides.

Pythagoras' theorem is more usually written as a formula:

$$c^2 = a^2 + b^2$$

Remember that Pythagoras' theorem can only be used in right-angled triangles.

Finding the hypotenuse

EXAMPLE 1

Find the length of the hypotenuse, marked x on the diagram.

Using Pythagoras' theorem gives

$$x^2 = 8^2 + 5.2^2 \text{ cm}^2$$
$$= 64 + 27.04 \text{ cm}^2$$
$$= 91.04 \text{ cm}^2$$

So $x = \sqrt{91.04} = 9.5$ cm (1 decimal place)

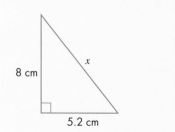

EXERCISE 12A

For each of the following triangles, calculate the length of the hypotenuse, x, giving your answers to one decimal place.

1
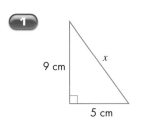
9 cm x 5 cm

2
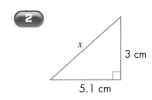
x 3 cm   5.1 cm

3
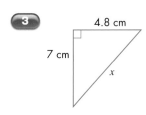
4.8 cm   7 cm x

4
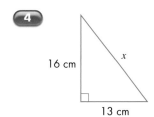
16 cm x 13 cm

5
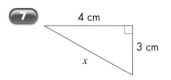
x 11 cm   15 cm

6

9 cm   15 cm x

7
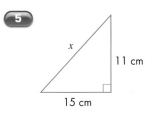
4 cm   3 cm x

8
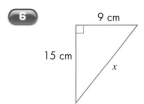
12 cm x 5 cm

9
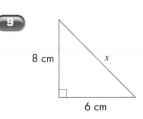
8 cm x 6 cm

The last three examples give whole number answers. Sets of whole numbers that obey Pythagoras' theorem are called Pythagorean triples. For example,

  3, 4, 5   5, 12, 13   and   6, 8, 10.

Note that 6, 8, 10 are respectively multiples of 3, 4, 5.

In this section you will learn how to:

- calculate the length of a shorter side in a right-angled triangle

Key word

Pythagoras' theorem

By rearranging the formula for **Pythagoras' theorem**, the length of one of the shorter sides can easily be calculated.

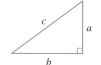

$$c^2 = a^2 + b^2$$

So, $a^2 = c^2 - b^2$ or $b^2 = c^2 - a^2$

EXAMPLE 2

Find the length x.

x is one of the shorter sides

So using Pythagoras' theorem gives

$$x^2 = 15^2 - 11^2 \text{ cm}^2$$
$$= 225 - 121 \text{ cm}^2$$
$$= 104 \text{ cm}^2$$

So $x = \sqrt{104} = 10.2$ cm (one decimal place)

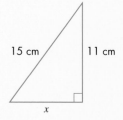

EXERCISE 12B

1 For each of the following triangles, calculate the length x, giving your answers to one decimal place.

a

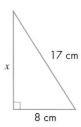

17 cm

x

8 cm

b

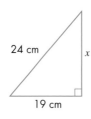

24 cm

x

19 cm

HINTS AND TIPS

In these examples you are finding a short side. The square of the other short side is subtracted from the square of the hypotenuse in every case.

c

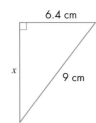

6.4 cm

x

9 cm

d

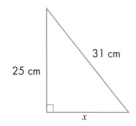

31 cm

25 cm

x

Mod 5

2 For each of the following triangles, calculate the length x, giving your answers to one decimal place.

a
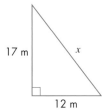
17 m x 12 m

b
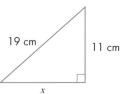
19 cm 11 cm x

c

17 m x 23 m

d
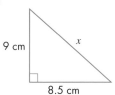
9 cm x 8.5 cm

3 For each of the following triangles, find the length marked x.

a

x 12 m 13 m

b
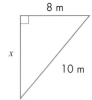
8 m x 10 m

c
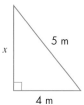
5 m x 4 m

d
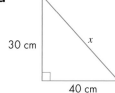
30 cm x 40 cm

12.3 Solving problems using Pythagoras' theorem

In this section you will learn how to:
- solve problems using Pythagoras' theorem

Key words
3-D
isoceles
 triangle
Pythagoras'
 theorem

Pythagoras' theorem can be used to solve certain practical problems. When a problem involves two lengths only, follow these steps.

- Draw a diagram for the problem that includes a right-angled triangle.

- Look at the diagram and decide which side has to be found: the hypotenuse or one of the shorter sides. Label the unknown side x.

- If it's the hypotenuse, then square both numbers, add the squares and take the square root of the sum.

- If it's one of the shorter sides, then square both numbers, subtract the squares and take the square root of the difference.

- Finally, round off the answer to a suitable degree of accuracy.

EXAMPLE 3

A plane leaves Manchester airport heading due east. It flies 160 km before turning due north. It then flies a further 280 km and lands. What is the distance of the return flight if the plane flies straight back to Manchester airport?

First, sketch the situation.

Using Pythagoras' theorem gives

$$x^2 = 160^2 + 280^2 \text{ km}^2$$
$$= 25\,600 + 78\,400 \text{ km}^2$$
$$= 104\,000 \text{ km}^2$$

So $x = \sqrt{104\,000} = 322$ km (3 significant figures)

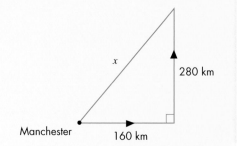

Remember the following tips when solving problems.

- Always sketch the right-angled triangle you need. Sometimes, the triangle is already drawn for you but some problems involve other lines and triangles that may confuse you. So identify which right-angled triangle you need and sketch it separately.

- Label the triangle with necessary information, such as the length of its sides, taken from the question. Label the unknown side x.

- Set out your solution as in Example 3. Avoid short cuts, since they often cause errors. You gain marks in your examination for clearly showing how you are applying Pythagoras' theorem to the problem.

- Round your answer off to a suitable degree of accuracy.

EXERCISE 12C

1 A ladder, 12 metres long, leans against a wall. The ladder reaches 10 metres up the wall. How far away from the foot of the wall is the foot of the ladder?

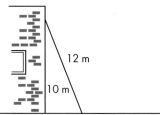

2 A model football pitch is 2 metres long and 0.5 metre wide. How long is the diagonal?

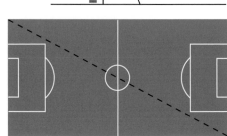

3 How long is the diagonal of a square with a side of 8 metres?

4 A ship going from a port to a lighthouse steams 15 km east and 12 km north. How far is the lighthouse from the port?

5 Some pedestrians want to get from point X on one road to point Y on another. The two roads meet at right angles.

   a If they follow the roads, how far will they walk?

   b Instead of walking along the road, they take the shortcut, XY. Find the length of the shortcut.

   c How much distance do they save?

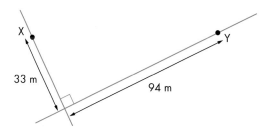

6 A mast on a sailboat is strengthened by a wire (called a stay), as shown on the diagram. The mast is 10 m tall and the stay is 11 m long. How far from the base of the mast does the stay reach?

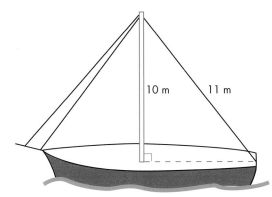

7 A ladder, 4 m long, is put up against a wall.

   a How far up the wall will it reach when the foot of the ladder is 1 m away from the wall?

   b When it reaches 3.6 m up the wall, how far is the foot of the ladder away from the wall?

8 A pole, 8 m high, is supported by metal wires, each 8.6 m long, attached to the top of the pole. How far from the foot of the pole are the wires fixed to the ground?

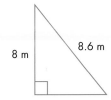

9 How long is the line that joins the two coordinates A(13, 6) and B(1, 1)?

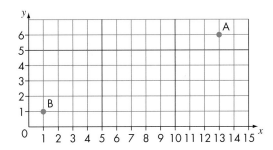

10 The regulation for safe use of ladders states that: *the foot of a 5 m ladder must be placed between 1.6 m and 2.1 m from the foot of the wall.*

    a What is the maximum height the ladder can safely reach up the wall?

    b What is the minimum height the ladder can safely reach up the wall?

11 Is the triangle with sides 7 cm, 24 cm and 25 cm, a right-angled triangle?

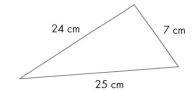

Pythagoras' theorem and isosceles triangles

This section shows you how to to use Pythagoras' theorem in isosceles triangles.

Every **isosceles triangle** has a line of symmetry that divides the triangle into two congruent right-angled triangles. So when you are faced with a problem involving an isosceles triangle, be aware that you are quite likely to have to split that triangle down the middle to create a right-angled triangle which will help you to solve the problem.

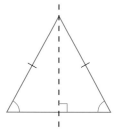

EXAMPLE 4

Calculate the area of this triangle.

It is an isosceles triangle and you need to calculate its height to find its area.

First split the triangle into two right-angled triangles to find its height.

Let the height be x.

Then, using Pythagoras' theorem,

$$x^2 = 7.5^2 - 3^2 \text{ cm}^2$$
$$= 56.25 - 9 \text{ cm}^2$$
$$= 47.25 \text{ cm}^2$$

So $x = \sqrt{47.25}$ cm

$$x = 6.87 \text{ cm}$$

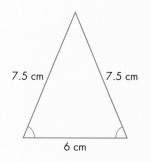

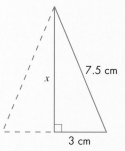

Keep the accurate figure in the calculator memory.

The area of the triangle is $\frac{1}{2} \times 6 \times 6.87$ cm^2 (from the calculator memory), which is 20.6 cm^2 (1 decimal place)

EXERCISE 12D

1 Calculate the areas of these isosceles triangles.

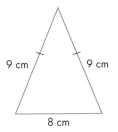

a 9 cm, 9 cm, 8 cm

b 3 cm, 2 cm

c
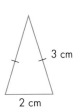
7 cm, 10 cm

2 Calculate the area of an isosceles triangle whose sides are 8 cm, 8 cm and 6 cm.

3 Calculate the area of an equilateral triangle of side 6 cm.

4 An isosceles triangle has sides of 5 cm and 6 cm.

   a Sketch the two different isosceles triangles that fit this data.

   b Which of the two triangles has the greater area?

5 **a** Sketch a regular hexagon, showing all its lines of symmetry.

   b Calculate the area of the hexagon if its side is 8 cm.

6 Calculate the area of a hexagon of side 10 cm.

7 Calculate the lengths marked x in these isosceles triangles.

a
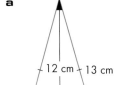
12 cm, 13 cm, x

b
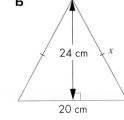
24 cm, x, 20 cm

c
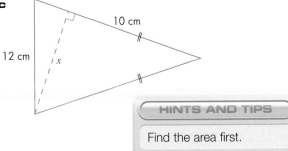
10 cm, 12 cm, x

HINTS AND TIPS

Find the area first.

Pythagoras' theorem in three dimensions

This section shows you how to solve problems in **3-D** using Pythagoras' theorem.

In your GCSE examinations, there may be questions which involve applying Pythagoras' theorem in 3-D situations. Such questions are usually accompanied by clearly labelled diagrams, which will help you to identify the lengths needed for your solutions.

You deal with these 3-D problems in exactly the same way as 2-D problems.

- Identify the right-angled triangle you need.

- Redraw this triangle and label it with the given lengths and the length to be found, usually *x* or *y*.

- From your diagram, decide whether it is the hypotenuse or one of the shorter sides which has to be found.

- Solve the problem, rounding off to a suitable degree of accuracy.

EXAMPLE 5

What is the longest piece of straight wire that can be stored in this box measuring 30 cm by 15 cm by 20 cm?

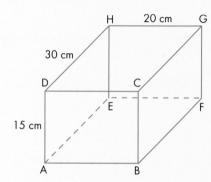

The longest distance across this box is any one of the diagonals AG, DF, CE or HB.

Let us take AG.

First, identify a right-angled triangle containing AG and draw it.

This gives a triangle AFG, which contains two lengths you do not know, AG and AF. Let AG = *x* and AF = *y*.

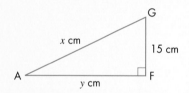

Next identify a right-angled triangle that contains the side AF and draw it.

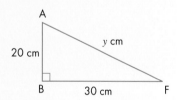

This gives a triangle ABF. You can now find AF.

By Pythagoras' theorem

$$y^2 = 30^2 + 20^2 \text{ cm}^2$$

$$y^2 = 1300 \text{ cm}^2 \text{ (there is no need to find } y\text{)}$$

Now find AG using triangle AFG.

By Pythagoras' theorem

$$x^2 = y^2 + 15^2 \text{ cm}^2$$

$$x^2 = 1300 + 225 = 1525 \text{ cm}^2$$

So *x* = 39.1 cm (1 decimal place)

So, the longest straight wire that can be stored in the box is 39.1 cm.

Note that in any cuboid with sides a, b and c, the length of a diagonal is given by

$$\sqrt{(a^2 + b^2 + c^2)}$$

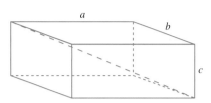

EXERCISE 12E

1 A box measures 8 cm by 12 cm by 5 cm.

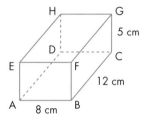

  a Calculate the lengths of the following.

  i AC   **ii** BG   **iii** BE

  b Calculate the diagonal distance BH.

2 A garage is 5 m long, 3 m wide and 3 m high. Can a 7 m long pole be stored in it?

3 Spike, a spider, is at the corner S of the wedge shown in the diagram. Fred, a fly, is at the corner F of the same wedge.

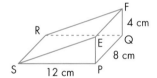

  a Calculate the two distances Spike would have to travel to get to Fred if she used the edges of the wedge.

  b Calculate the distance Spike would have to travel across the face of the wedge to get directly to Fred.

4 Fred is now at the top of a baked-beans can and Spike is directly below him on the base of the can. To catch Fred by surprise, Spike takes a diagonal route round the can. How far does Spike travel?

> **HINTS AND TIPS**
>
> Imagine the can opened out flat.

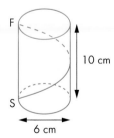

5 A corridor is 3 m wide and turns through a right angle, as in the diagram.

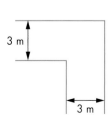

  a What is the longest pole that can be carried along the corridor horizontally?

  b If the corridor is 3 m high, what is the longest pole that can be carried along in any direction?

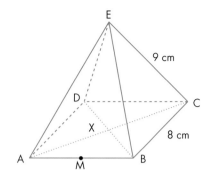

6 The diagram shows a square-based pyramid with
base length 8 cm and sloping edges 9 cm. M is the mid-point
of the side AB, X is the mid-point of the base, and E is directly
above X.

   a Calculate the length of the diagonal AC.

   b Calculate EX, the height of the pyramid.

   c Using triangle ABE, calculate the length EM.

7 The diagram shows a cuboid with sides of 40 cm, 30 cm,
and 22.5 cm. M is the mid-point of the side FG.
Calculate (or write down) these lengths, giving your answers
to three significant figures if necessary.

   a AH   **b** AG   **c** AM   **d** HM

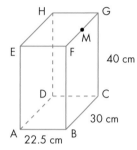

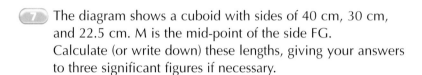

12.4   Trigonometric ratios

In this section you will learn how to:
- use the three trigonometric ratios

Key words
adjacent side
cosine
hypotenuse
opposite side
sine
tangent
trigonometry

Trigonometry is concerned with the calculation of sides and angles in triangles, and involves the use of three important ratios: **sine**, **cosine** and **tangent**. These ratios are defined in terms of the sides of a right-angled triangle and an angle. The angle is often written as θ.

In a right-angled triangle

- the side opposite the right angle is called the **hypotenuse** and is the longest side

- the side opposite the angle θ is called the **opposite side**

- the other side next to both the right angle and the angle θ is called the **adjacent side**.

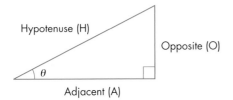

The sine, cosine and tangent ratios for θ are defined as

$$\text{sine } \theta = \frac{\text{Opposite}}{\text{Hypotenuse}} \qquad \text{cosine } \theta = \frac{\text{Adjacent}}{\text{Hypotenuse}} \qquad \text{tangent } \theta = \frac{\text{Opposite}}{\text{Adjacent}}$$

These ratios are usually abbreviated as

$$\sin \theta = \frac{O}{H} \qquad \cos \theta = \frac{A}{H} \qquad \tan \theta = \frac{O}{A}$$

These abbreviated forms are also used on calculator keys.

Memorising these formulae may be helped by a mnemonic such as

Silly **O**ld **H**itler **C**ouldn't **A**dvance **H**is **T**roops **O**ver **A**frica

in which the first letter of each word is taken in order to give

$$S = \frac{O}{H} \qquad C = \frac{A}{H} \qquad T = \frac{O}{A}$$

Using your calculator

You can use your calculator to find the sine, cosine and tangent of *any* angle.

To find the sine of an angle, press the key labelled *sin*.

To find the cosine of an angle, press the key labelled *cos*.

To find the tangent of an angle, press the key labelled *tan*.

Make sure you can find sin, cos and tan on your calculator.

Important: Make sure your calculator is working in *degrees*. Depending on the type of calculator used, you need to put it into *degree mode* before you start working on sines, cosines and tangents. This can be done either

- by using the MODE button

- or by pressing the key DRG until DEG is on display.

Try this *now* to make sure you can do it. When it is in degree mode, D or DEG appears on the calculator display.

EXAMPLE 6

Use your calculator to find the sine of 27°, written as sin 27°.

On some scientific calculators, the function is keyed in numbers first

[2] [7] [sin]

The display should read 0.453990499. (You may have more or fewer digits depending on your calculator.) This is 0.454 to three significant figures.

If you have a graphics calculator or an 'algebraic logic' (DAL) calculator, you key in the function as it reads

[sin] [2] [7]

You should get the same value as above. If you don't, then consult your calculator manual or your teacher.

EXAMPLE 7

Use your calculator to find the cosine of 56°, written as cos 56°.

cos 56° = 0.559 192 903 = 0.559 to 3 significant figures

Check that you agree with this, using as many digits as your calculator allows.

EXAMPLE 8

Use your calculator to work out 3 × cos 57°, written as 3 cos 57°.

Depending on your type of calculator, key in either

[3] [×] [5] [7] [cos] [=]   or   [3] [×] [cos] [5] [7] [=]

Check that you get an answer of 1.633 917 105 = 1.63 to 3 significant figures.

EXERCISE 12F

1 Find these values, rounding off your answers to three significant figures.

 a sin 43°   **b** sin 56°   **c** sin 67.2°   **d** sin 90°

 e sin 45°   **f** sin 20°   **g** sin 22°   **h** sin 0°

2 Find these values, rounding off your answers to three significant figures.

 a cos 43°   **b** cos 56°   **c** cos 67.2°   **d** cos 90°

 e cos 45°   **f** cos 20°   **g** cos 22°   **h** cos 0°

3 From your answers to questions **1** and **2**, what angle has the same value for sine and cosine?

4 **a** **i** What is sin 35°?   **ii** What is cos 55°?

    b **i** What is sin 12°?   **ii** What is cos 78°?

    c **i** What is cos 67°?   **ii** What is sin 23°?

    d What connects the values in parts **a**, **b** and **c**?

    e Copy and complete these sentences.

      i sin 15° is the same as cos …

      ii cos 82° is the same as sin …

      iii sin x is the same as cos …

5 Use your calculator to work out the values of

    a tan 43°   **b** tan 56°   **c** tan 67.2°   **d** tan 90°

    e tan 45°   **f** tan 20°   **g** tan 22°   **h** tan 0°

6 Use your calculator to work out the values of the following.

    a sin 73°   **b** cos 26°   **c** tan 65.2°   **d** sin 88°

    e cos 35°   **f** tan 30°   **g** sin 28°   **h** cos 5°

7 What is so different about tan compared with both sin and cos?

8 Use your calculator to work out the values of the following.

    a 5 sin 65°   **b** 6 cos 42°   **c** 6 sin 90°   **d** 5 sin 0°

9 Use your calculator to work out the values of the following.

    a 5 tan 65°   **b** 6 tan 42°   **c** 6 tan 90°   **d** 5 tan 0°

10 Use your calculator to work out the values of the following.

    a 4 sin 63°   **b** 7 tan 52°   **c** 5 tan 80°   **d** 9 cos 8°

11 Use your calculator to work out the values of the following.

    a $\dfrac{5}{\sin 63°}$ **b** $\dfrac{6}{\cos 32°}$ **c** $\dfrac{6}{\sin 90°}$ **d** $\dfrac{5}{\sin 30°}$

12 Use your calculator to work out the values of the following.

    a $\dfrac{3}{\tan 64°}$ **b** $\dfrac{7}{\tan 42°}$ **c** $\dfrac{5}{\tan 89°}$ **d** $\dfrac{6}{\tan 40°}$

13 Use your calculator to work out the values of the following.

    a 8 sin 75°   **b** $\dfrac{19}{\sin 23°}$ **c** 7 cos 71°   **d** $\dfrac{15}{\sin 81°}$

14 Use your calculator to work out the values of the following.

a 8 tan 75° **b** $\dfrac{19}{\tan 23°}$ **c** 7 tan 71° **d** $\dfrac{15}{\tan 81°}$

15 Using the following triangles calculate sin x, cos x, and tan x. Leave your answers as fractions.

a

b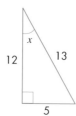

c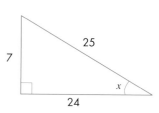

12.5 Calculating angles

In this section you will learn how to:
● use the trigonometric ratios to calculate an angle

Key word
inverse functions

The sine of 54° is 0.809 016 994 4 (to 10 decimal places).

The sine of 55° is 0.819 152 044 3 (to 10 decimal places).

What angle has a sine of 0.815?

Obviously, it is between 54° and 55°, so we could probably use a trial-and-improvement method to find it. But there is an easier way which uses the **inverse functions** on your calculator.

An inverse function can be accessed in several different ways. For example, the inverse function for sine may be any of these keys:

The inverse function printed above the sine key is usually given in either of the following ways:

$\sin^{-1}$ **sin**   or   arcsin **sin**

You will need to find out how your calculator deals with inverse functions.

When you do the inverse sine of 0.815, you should get 54.587 361 89°.

It is normal in trigonometry to round off angles to one decimal place. So, the angle with a sine of 0.815 is 54.6° (1 decimal place).

This can be written as $\sin^{-1} 0.815 = 54.6°$.

Mod 5

EXAMPLE 9

Find the angle with a cosine of 0.654.

$\cos^{-1} 0.654 = 49.156\,131\,92° = 49.2°$ (1 decimal place)

EXAMPLE 10

Find the angle with a sine of (3 ÷ 4).

How you solve this will depend on your type of calculator. So key in either

| 3 | ÷ | 4 | = | INV | sin | or | INV | sin | (| 3 | ÷ | 4 |) | = |

So $\sin^{-1} \left(\frac{3}{4}\right) = 48.590\,377\,89° = 48.6°$ (1 decimal place)

EXAMPLE 11

Find the angle with a tangent of 0.75.

$\tan^{-1} 0.75 = 36.869\,897\,65 = 36.9°$ (1 decimal place)

EXERCISE 12G

Use your calculator to find the answers to the following. Give your answers to one decimal place.

1 What angles have the following sines?

   a 0.5   **b** 0.785   **c** 0.64   **d** 0.877   **e** 0.999   **f** 0.707

2 What angles have the following cosines?

   a 0.5   **b** 0.64   **c** 0.999   **d** 0.707   **e** 0.2   **f** 0.7

3 What angles have the following tangents?

   a 0.6   **b** 0.38   **c** 0.895   **d** 1.05   **e** 2.67   **f** 4.38

4 What angles have the following sines?

   a 4 ÷ 5   **b** 2 ÷ 3   **c** 7 ÷ 10   **d** 5 ÷ 6   **e** 1 ÷ 24   **f** 5 ÷ 13

5 What angles have the following cosines?

   a 4 ÷ 5   **b** 2 ÷ 3   **c** 7 ÷ 10   **d** 5 ÷ 6   **e** 1 ÷ 24   **f** 5 ÷ 13

6 What angles have the following tangents?

   a 3 ÷ 5   **b** 7 ÷ 9   **c** 2 ÷ 7   **d** 9 ÷ 5   **e** 11 ÷ 7   **f** 6 ÷ 5

7 What happens when you try to find the angle with a sine of 1.2? What is the largest value of sine you can put into your calculator without getting an error when you ask for the inverse sine? What is the smallest?

8 a i What angle has a sine of 0.3? (Keep the answer in your calculator memory.)

ii What angle has a cosine of 0.3?

iii Add the two accurate answers of parts **i** and **ii** together.

b Will you always get the same answer to the above no matter what number you start with?

12.6 Using the sine function

In this section you will learn how to:
- find lengths of sides and angles in right-angled triangles using the sine function

Key word
sine

Remember sine $\theta = \dfrac{\text{Opposite}}{\text{Hypotenuse}}$

We can use the **sine** ratio to calculate the lengths of sides and angles in right-angled triangles.

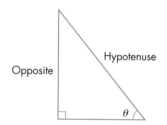

EXAMPLE 12

Find the angle θ, given that the opposite side is 7 cm and the hypotenuse is 10 cm.

Draw a diagram. (This is an essential step.)

From the information given, use sine.

$$\sin \theta = \frac{O}{H} = \frac{7}{10} = 0.7$$

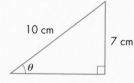

What angle has a sine of 0.7? To find out, use the inverse sine function on your calculator.

$$\sin^{-1} 0.7 = 44.4° \text{ (1 decimal place)}$$

EXAMPLE 13

Find the length of the side marked a in this triangle.

Side a is the opposite side, with 12 cm as the hypotenuse, so use sine.

$$\sin \theta = \frac{O}{H}$$

$$\sin 35° = \frac{a}{12}$$

So $a = 12 \sin 35° = 6.88$ cm (3 significant figures)

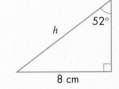

EXAMPLE 14

Find the length of the hypotenuse, h, in this triangle.

Note that although the angle is in the other corner, the opposite side is again given. So use sine.

$$\sin \theta = \frac{O}{H}$$

$$\sin 52° = \frac{8}{h}$$

So $h = \dfrac{8}{\sin 52°} = 10.2$ cm (3 significant figures)

EXERCISE 12H

1 Find the angle marked x in each of these triangles.

a

b

c
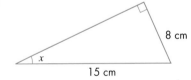

2 Find the side marked x in each of these triangles.

a
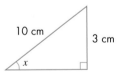

b

c
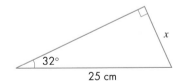

3 Find the side marked x in each of these triangles.

a
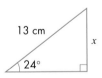

b

c
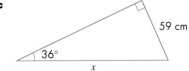

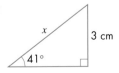

4 Find the side marked x in each of these triangles.

a

b

c

d

5 Find the value of x in each of these triangles.

a

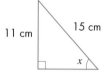

b

c

d

6 Angle θ has a sine of $\frac{3}{5}$. Calculate the missing lengths in these triangles.

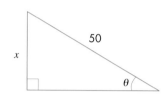

12.7 Using the cosine function

In this section you will learn how to:
- find lengths of sides and angles in right-angled triangles using the cosine function

Key word
cosine

Remember cosine $\theta = \dfrac{\text{Adjacent}}{\text{Hypotenuse}}$

We can use the **cosine** ratio to calculate the lengths of sides and angles in right-angled triangles.

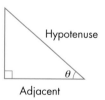

EXAMPLE 15

Find the angle θ, given that the adjacent side is 5 cm and the hypotenuse is 12 cm.

Draw a diagram. (This is an essential step.)

From the information given, use cosine.

$$\cos \theta = \frac{A}{H} = \frac{5}{12}$$

What angle has a cosine of $\frac{5}{12}$? To find out, use the inverse cosine function on your calculator.

$$\cos^{-1} = 65.4° \text{ (1 decimal place)}$$

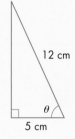

EXAMPLE 16

Find the length of the side marked a in this triangle.

Side a is the adjacent side, with 9 cm as the hypotenuse, so use cosine.

$$\cos \theta = \frac{A}{H}$$

$$\cos 47° = \frac{a}{9}$$

So $a = 9 \cos 47° = 6.14$ cm (3 significant figures)

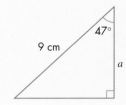

EXAMPLE 17

Find the length of the hypotenuse, h, in this triangle.

The adjacent side is given. So use cosine.

$$\cos \theta = \frac{A}{H}$$

$$\cos 40° = \frac{20}{h}$$

So $h = \dfrac{20}{\cos 40°} = 26.1$ cm (3 significant figures)

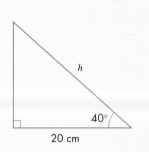

EXERCISE 12I

1 Find the angle marked x in each of these triangles.

a

8 cm
5 cm
x

b
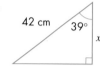
4 cm
x
1 cm

c
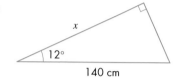
100 cm
x
160 cm

2 Find the side marked x in each of these triangles.

a

9 cm
44°
x

b
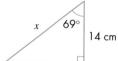
42 cm
39°
x

c
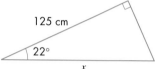
x
12°
140 cm

3 Find the side marked x in each of these triangles.

a
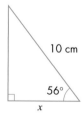
x
35°
6 cm

b
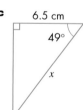
x
69°
14 cm

c
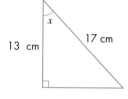
125 cm
22°
x

4 Find the side marked x in each of these triangles.

a
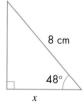
8 cm
48°
x

b

36°
x
12 cm

c

11 cm
24°
x

d

52°
14 cm
x

5 Find the value of x in each of these triangles.

a
10 cm
56°
x

b
16 cm
x
11 cm

c
6.5 cm
49°
x

d
13 cm
x
17 cm

6 Angle θ has a cosine of $\frac{5}{13}$. Calculate the missing lengths in these triangles.

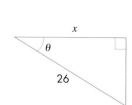
x
θ
26

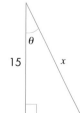
θ
15
x

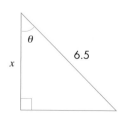
θ
6.5
x

Using the tangent function

In this section you will learn how to:
- find lengths of sides and angles in right-angled triangles using the tangent function

Key word
tangent

Remember tangent $\theta = \dfrac{\text{Opposite}}{\text{Adjacent}}$

We can use the **tangent** ratio to calculate the lengths of sides and angles in right-angled triangles.

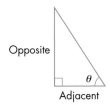

Opposite

Adjacent

EXAMPLE 18

Find the angle θ, given that the opposite side is 3 cm and the adjacent side is 4 cm.

Draw a diagram. (This is an essential step.)

From the information given, use tangent.

$$\tan \theta = \frac{O}{A} = \frac{3}{4} = 0.75$$

What angle has a tangent of 0.75? To find out, use the inverse tangent function on your calculator.

$$\tan^{-1} 0.75 = 36.9° \text{ (1 decimal place)}$$

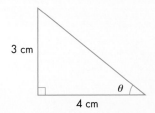

3 cm

4 cm

EXAMPLE 19

Find the length of the side marked x in this triangle.

Side x is the opposite side, with 9 cm as the adjacent side, so use tangent.

$$\tan \theta = \frac{O}{A}$$

$$\tan 62° = \frac{x}{9}$$

So $x = 9 \tan 62° = 16.9$ cm (3 significant figures)

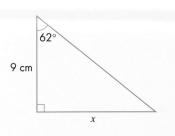

62°

9 cm

x

EXAMPLE 20

Find the length of the side marked a in this triangle.

Side a is the adjacent side and the opposite side is given.
So use tangent.

$$\tan \theta = \frac{O}{A}$$

$$\tan 35° = \frac{6}{a}$$

So $a = \dfrac{6}{\tan 35°} = 8.57$ cm (3 significant figures)

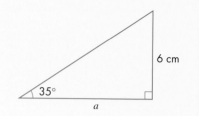

EXERCISE 12J

1 Find the angle marked x in each of these triangles.

a

6 cm
x
9 cm

b

x
20 cm
15 cm

c
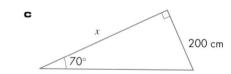
35 cm
45 cm
x

2 Find the side marked x in each of these triangles.

a

x
23°
12 cm

b
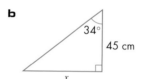
34°
45 cm
x

c
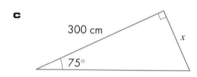
300 cm
x
75°

3 Find the side marked x in each of these triangles.

a
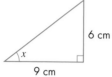
3 cm
20°
x

b
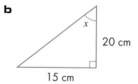
40°
x
52 cm

c
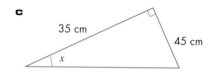
x
200 cm
70°

4 Find the side marked x in each of these triangles.

a

x
61°
5 cm

b
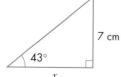
7 cm
43°
x

c

33°
11 cm
x

d

6 cm
34°
x

5 Find the value x in each of these triangles.

a

x
$63°$
7 cm

b
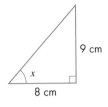
9 cm
x
8 cm

c
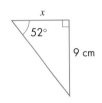
x
$52°$
9 cm

d
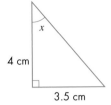
x
4 cm
3.5 cm

6 Angle θ has a tangent of $\frac{4}{3}$. Calculate the missing lengths in these triangles.

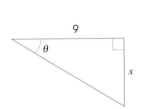
9
θ
x

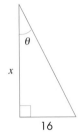
θ
x
16

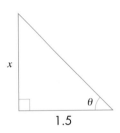
x
θ
1.5

12.9 Which ratio to use

In this section you will learn how to:
- decide which trigonometric ratio to use in a right-angled triangle

Key words
sine
cosine
tangent

The difficulty with any trigonometric problem is knowing which ratio to use to solve it.

The following examples show you how to determine which ratio you need in any given situation.

EXAMPLE 21

Find the length of the side marked x in this triangle.

Step 1 Identify what information is given and what needs to be found. Namely, x is opposite the angle and 16 cm is the hypotenuse.

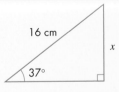
16 cm
x
$37°$

Step 2 Decide which ratio to use. Only one ratio uses opposite and hypotenuse: **sine**.

Step 3 Remember $\sin \theta = \dfrac{O}{H}$

Step 4 Put in the numbers and letters: $\sin 37° = \dfrac{x}{16}$

Step 5 Rearrange the equation and work out the answer: $x = 16 \sin 37° = 9.629\,040\,371$ cm

Step 6 Give the answer to an appropriate degree of accuracy: $x = 9.63$ cm (3 significant figures)

In reality, you do not write down every step as in Example 21. Step 1 can be done by marking the triangle. Steps 2 and 3 can be done in your head. Steps 4 to 6 are what you write down.

Remember that examiners will want to see evidence of working. Any reasonable attempt at identifying the sides and using a ratio will probably get you some method marks – but only if the fraction is the right way round.

The next examples are set out in a way that requires the *minimum* amount of working but gets *maximum* marks.

EXAMPLE 22

Find the length of the side marked x in this triangle.

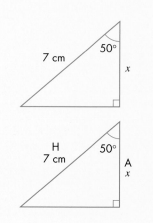

Mark on the triangle the side you know (H) and the side you want to find (A).

Recognise it is a **cosine** problem because you have A and H.

So $\cos 50° = \dfrac{x}{7}$

$x = 7 \cos 50° = 4.50$ cm (3 significant figures)

EXAMPLE 23

Find the angle marked x in this triangle.

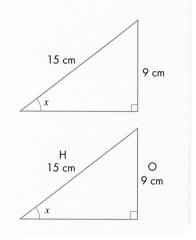

Mark on the triangle the sides you know.

Recognise it is a sine problem because you have O and H.

So $\sin x = \dfrac{9}{15} = 0.6$

$x = \sin^{-1} 0.6 = 36.9°$ (1 decimal place)

EXAMPLE 24

Find the angle marked x in this triangle.

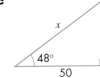

Mark on the triangle the sides you know.

Recognise it is a **tangent** problem because you have O and A.

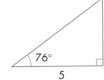

So $\tan x = \dfrac{12}{7}$

$x = \tan^{-1}\dfrac{12}{7} = 59.7°$ (1 decimal place)

EXERCISE 12K

1 Find the length marked x in each of these triangles.

a

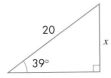

b

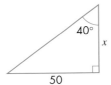

c

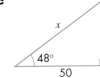

d

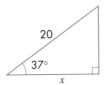

e

f

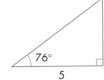

2 Find the angle marked x in each of these triangles.

a

b

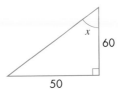

c

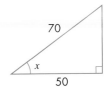

d

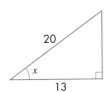

e

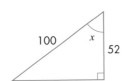

f

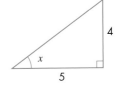

3 Find the angle or length marked *x* in each of these triangles.

a
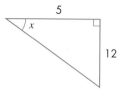

b
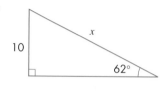

c
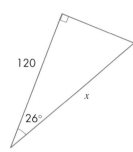

d
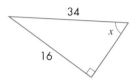

e

f
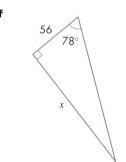

g
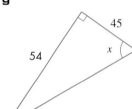

h
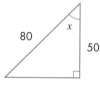

i
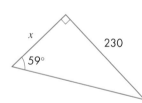

j
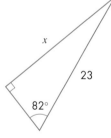

4 In a maths textbook it says:

The tangent of any angle is equal to the sine of the angle divided by the cosine of the angle.

a Show clearly that this is true for an angle of 30°.

b Prove, by using the definitions of $\sin \theta$ and $\cos \theta$, that the statement is true for this right-angled triangle.

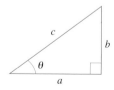

Solving problems using trigonometry

In this section you will learn how to:

- solve practical problems using trigonometry
- solve problems using an angle of elevation or an angle of depression
- solve bearing problems using trigonometry
- using trigonometry to solve problems involving isosceles triangles

Key words
angle of depression
angle of elevation
bearing
isosceles triangle
three-figure bearing
trigonometry

Most **trigonometry** problems in GCSE examination papers do not come as straightforward triangles. Usually, solving a triangle is part of solving a practical problem. You should follow these steps when solving a practical problem using trigonometry.

- Draw the triangle required.

- Put on the information given (angles and sides).

- Put on x for the unknown angle or side.

- Mark on two of O, A or H as appropriate.

- Choose which ratio to use.

- Write out the equation with the numbers in.

- Rearrange the equation if necessary, then work out the answer.

- Give your answer to a sensible degree of accuracy. Answers given to three significant figures or to the nearest degree are acceptable in exams.

EXAMPLE 25

A window cleaner has a ladder which is 7 m long. The window cleaner leans it against a wall so that the foot of the ladder is 3 m from the wall. What angle does the ladder make with the wall?

Draw the situation as a right-angled triangle.

Then mark the sides and angle.

Recognise it is a sine problem because you have O and H.

So $\sin x = \dfrac{3}{7}$

$x = \sin^{-1}\dfrac{3}{7} = 25°$ (to the nearest degree)

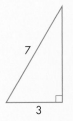

EXERCISE 12L

In these questions, give answers involving angles to the nearest degree.

1 A ladder, 6 m long, rests against a wall. The foot of the ladder is 2.5 m from the base of the wall. What angle does the ladder make with the ground?

2 The ladder in question **1** has a "safe angle" with the ground of between 60° and 70°. What are the safe limits for the distance of the foot of the ladder from the wall?

3 Another ladder, of length 10 m, is placed so that it reaches 7 m up the wall. What angle does it make with the ground?

4 Yet another ladder is placed so that it makes an angle of 76° with the ground. When the foot of the ladder is 1.7 m from the foot of the wall, how high up the wall does the ladder reach?

5 Calculate the angle that the diagonal makes with the long side of a rectangle which measures 10 cm by 6 cm.

6 This diagram shows a frame for a bookcase.

   a What angle does the diagonal strut make with the long side?

   b Use Pythagoras' theorem to calculate the length of the strut.

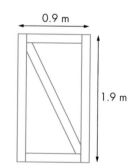

0.9 m

1.9 m

7 This diagram shows a roof truss.

   a What angle will the roof make with the horizontal?

   b Use Pythagoras' theorem to calculate the length of the sloping strut.

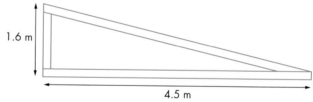

1.6 m

4.5 m

8 Alicia paces out 100 m from the base of a church. She then measures the angle to the top of the spire as 23°. How high is the church spire?

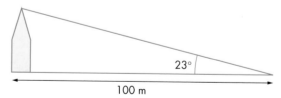

23°

100 m

9 A girl is flying a kite on a string 32 m long. The string, which is being held at 1 m above the ground, makes an angle of 39° with the horizontal. How high is the kite above the ground?

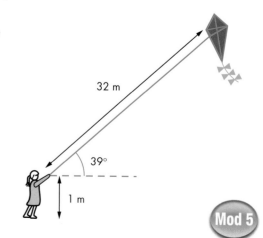

32 m

39°

1 m

10 Angle θ has a sine of $\frac{3}{5}$.

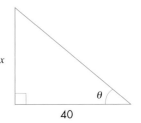

a Use Pythagoras' theorem to calculate the missing side of this triangle.

b Write down the cosine and the tangent of θ.

c Calculate the missing lengths marked x in these triangles.

i

2.5

ii

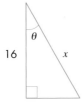

16

x

iii

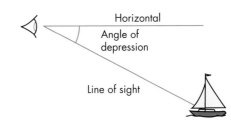

x

40

Angles of elevation and depression

When you look *up* at an aircraft in the sky, the angle through which your line of sight turns from looking straight ahead (the horizontal) is called the **angle of elevation**.

When you are standing on a high point and look *down* at a boat, the angle through which your line of sight turns from looking straight ahead (the horizontal) is called the **angle of depression**.

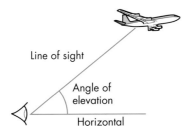

EXAMPLE 26

From the top of a vertical cliff, 100 m high, Andrew sees a boat out at sea. The angle of depression from Andrew to the boat is 42°. How far from the base of the cliff is the boat?

The diagram of the situation is shown in figure **i**.

From this, you get the triangle shown in figure **ii**.

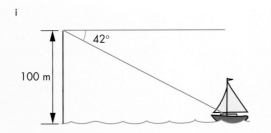

i

42°

100 m

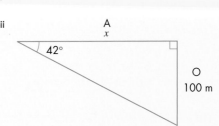

ii

A
x

42°

O
100 m

From figure **ii**, you see that this is a tangent problem.

So $\tan 42° = \dfrac{100}{x}$

$x = \dfrac{100}{\tan 42°} = 111$ m (3 significant figures)

EXERCISE 12M

In these questions, give any answers involving angles to the nearest degree.

1 Eric sees an aircraft in the sky. The aircraft is at a horizontal distance of 25 km from Eric. The angle of elevation is 22°. How high is the aircraft?

2 A passenger in an aircraft hears the pilot say that they are flying at an altitude of 4000 m and are 10 km from the airport. If the passenger can see the airport, what is the angle of depression?

3 A man standing 200 m from the base of a television transmitter looks at the top of it and notices that the angle of elevation of the top is 65°. How high is the tower?

4 From the top of a vertical cliff, 200 m high, a boat has an angle of depression of 52°. How far from the base of the cliff is the boat?

 5 From a boat, the angle of elevation of the foot of a lighthouse on the edge of a cliff is 34°.

    a If the cliff is 150 m high, how far from the base of the cliff is the boat?

    b If the lighthouse is 50 m high, what would be the angle of elevation of the top of the lighthouse from the boat?

6 A bird flies from the top of a 12 m tall tree, at an angle of depression of 34°, to catch a worm on the ground.

    a How far does the bird actually fly?   **b** How far was the worm from the base of the tree?

7 Sunil stands about 50 m away from a building. The angle of elevation from Sunil to the top of the building is about 15°. How tall is the building?

8 The top of a ski run is 100 m above the finishing line. The run is 300 m long. What is the angle of depression of the ski run?

Trigonometry and bearings

A **bearing** is the direction to one place from another. The usual way of giving a bearing is as an angle measured from north in a clockwise direction. This is how a navigational compass and a surveyor's compass measure bearings.

A bearing is always written as a three-digit number, known as a **three-figure bearing**.

The diagram shows how this works, using the main compass points as examples.

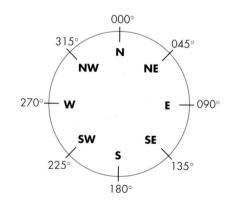

When working with bearings, follow these three rules.

- Always start from *north*.

- Always measure *clockwise*.

- Always give a bearing in degrees and as a *three-figure bearing*.

The difficulty with trigonometric problems involving bearings is dealing with those angles greater than 90° whose trigonometric ratios have negative values. To avoid this, we have to find a right-angled triangle that we can readily use. Example 27 shows you how to deal with such a situation.

EXAMPLE 27

A ship sails on a bearing of 120° for 50 km. How far east has it travelled?

The diagram of the situation is shown in figure **i**. From this, you can get the acute-angled triangle shown in figure **ii**.

From figure **ii**, you see that this is a cosine problem.

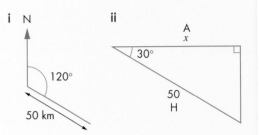

So $\cos 30° = \dfrac{x}{50}$

$x = 50 \cos 30° = 43.301 = 43.3$ km (3 significant figures)

EXERCISE 12N

1 A ship sails for 75 km on a bearing of 078°.

    a How far east has it travelled?   **b** How far north has it travelled?

2 Lopham is 17 miles from Wath on a bearing of 210°.

    a How far south of Wath is Lopham?   **b** How far east of Lopham is Wath?

3 A plane sets off from an airport and flies due east for 120 km, then turns to fly due south for 70 km before landing at Seddeth. What is the bearing of Seddeth from the airport?

4 A helicopter leaves an army base and flies 60 km on a bearing of 278°.

    a How far west has the helicopter flown?   **b** How far north has the helicopter flown?

5 A ship sails from a port on a bearing of 117° for 35 km before heading due north for 40 km and docking at Angle Bay.

    a How far south had the ship sailed before turning?

    b How far north had the ship sailed from the port to Angle Bay?

    c How far east is Angle Bay from the port?

    d What is the bearing from the port to Angle Bay?

6 Mountain A is due west of a walker. Mountain B is due north of the walker. The guidebook says that mountain B is 4.3 km from mountain A, on a bearing of 058°. How far is the walker from mountain B?

7 The diagram shows the relative distances and bearings of three ships A, B and C.

   a How far north of A is B? (Distance x on diagram.)

   b How far north of B is C? (Distance y on diagram.)

   c How far west of A is C? (Distance z on diagram.)

   d What is the bearing of A from C? (Angle $w°$ on diagram.)

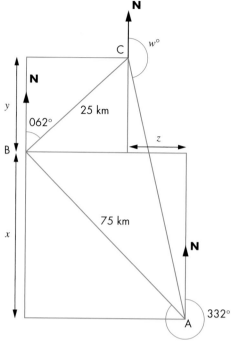

8 A ship sails from port A for 42 km on a bearing of 130° to point B. It then changes course and sails for 24 km on a bearing of 040° to point C, where it breaks down and anchors. What distance and on what bearing will a helicopter have to fly from port A to go directly to the ship at C?

Trigonometry and isosceles triangles

Isosceles triangles often feature in trigonometry problems because such a triangle can be split into two right-angled triangles that are congruent.

EXAMPLE 28

   a Find the length x in this isosceles triangle.

   b Calculate the area of the triangle.

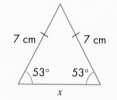

Draw a perpendicular from the apex of the triangle to its base, splitting the triangle into two congruent, right-angled triangles.

   a To find the length y, which is $\frac{1}{2}$ of x, use cosine.

     So, $\cos 53° = \dfrac{y}{7}$

     $y = 7 \cos 53° = 4.2127051$ cm

     So the length $x = 2y = 8.43$ cm (3 significant figures).

b To calculate the area of the original triangle, you first need to find its vertical height, h.

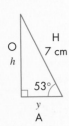

You have two choices, both of which involve the right-angled triangle of part a. We can use either Pythagoras' theorem ($h^2 + y^2 = 7^2$) or trigonometry. It is safer to use trigonometry again, since we are then still using known information.

This is a sine problem.

So, $\sin 53° = \dfrac{h}{7}$

$h = 7 \sin 53° = 5.590\,448\,6$ cm (Keep the accurate figure in the calculator.)

The area of the triangle $= \frac{1}{2} \times$ base $\times$ height. (We should use the most accurate figures we have for this calculation.)

$A = \frac{1}{2} \times 8.425\,410\,3 \times 5.590\,448\,6 = 23.6$ cm^2 (3 significant figures)

You are not expected to write down these eight-figure numbers, just to use them.

Note: If you use rounded-off values to calculate the area, the answer would be 23.5 cm^2, which is different from the one calculated using the most accurate data. So *never* use rounded-off data when you can use accurate data – unless you are just estimating.

EXERCISE 12P

In questions 1–4, find the side or angle marked x.

1

2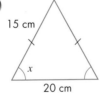

3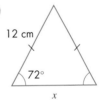

4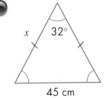

5 This diagram below shows a roof truss. How wide is the roof?

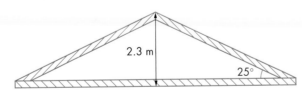

6 Calculate the area of each of these triangles.

a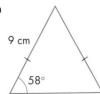

b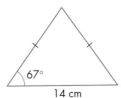

c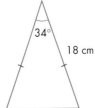

d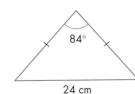

1 A rectangular field ABCD is shown.
The length of the field, AB = 160 m.
The width of the field, BC = 75 m.

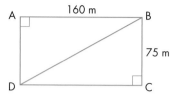

Calculate the length of the diagonal BD.

Give your answer to a suitable degree of accuracy.

AQA, Question 1, Paper 2 Higher, November 2004

2 A support for a flagpole is attached at a height of 3 m and is fixed to the ground at a distance of 1.2 m from the base.

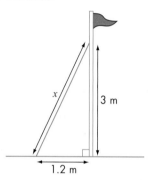

Calculate the length of the support (marked x on the diagram).

AQA, Question 1, Paper 2 Higher, June 2003

3 a The diagram shows a right-angled triangle ABC.
AB = 10 cm and AC = 15 cm

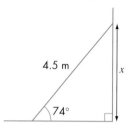

Calculate the length of BC.

b Triangle PQR is similar to triangle ABC.
angle CAB = angle RPQ
PQ = 25 cm

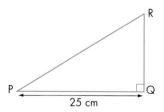

Work out the length of PR.

AQA, Question 9a, Paper 1 Higher, June 2004

4 A ladder leans against the side of a house. The ladder is 4.5 m in length.

a The ladder makes an angle of 74° with the ground. How high up the wall will it reach? (marked x in the diagram) Give your answer to an appropriate degree of accuracy.

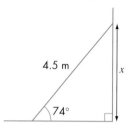

b The same ladder is now placed 0.9 m away from the side of the house. What angle does the ladder now make with the ground? (marked y in the diagram)

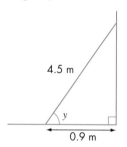

AQA, Question 10, Paper 2 Higher, June 2001

5 a ABC is a right angled triangle. AB = 10 cm, BC = 7 cm. Find the size of angle CAB (marked x in the diagram).

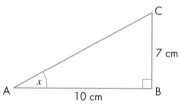

b PQR is a right-angled triangle. PQ = 12 cm, angle QPR = 48°. Find the length of PR (marked y in the diagram). Give your answer to an appropriate degree of accuracy.

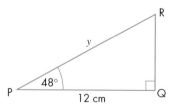

AQA, Question 3, Paper 2 Higher, November 2002

6 The diagram shows the side view of a wheelchair ramp. The ramp makes an angle of 4° with the horizontal. Calculate the length, marked x, of the ramp. Give your answer in metres to a sensible degree of accuracy.

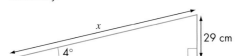

AQA, Question 5, Paper 2 Higher, November 2001

7 The diagram shows two right-angled triangles.
AD = 15 cm. CD = 6 cm.

a Given that $\cos x° = \frac{2}{3}$, calculate the length BD.

b Find the value of $\sin y°$.

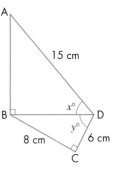

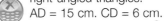

AQA, Question 9, Paper 1 Higher, November 2003

WORKED EXAM QUESTION

a ABC is a right-angled triangle. AC = 19 cm and AB = 9 cm.

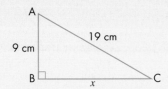

Calculate the length of BC.

b PQR is a right-angled triangle. PQ = 11 cm and QR = 24 cm.

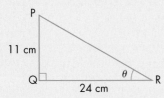

Calculate the size of angle PRQ.

c ABC and ACD are right-angled triangles. AD is parallel to BC.
AB = 12 cm, BC = 5 cm and AD = 33.8 cm.

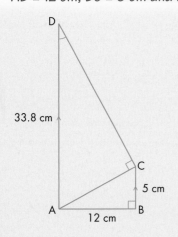

Calculate the size of angle ADC.

AQA, Question 10, Paper 2 Higher, June 2005

Solution

a Let BC = x

By Pythagoras' theorem
$$x^2 = 19^2 - 9^2 \text{ cm}^2$$
$$= 280 \text{ cm}^2$$
So $x = \sqrt{280} = 16.7$ cm (3 sf)

b Let $\angle PRQ = \theta$

So $\tan \theta = \dfrac{11}{24}$

$\theta = \tan^{-1} \dfrac{11}{24} = 24.6°$ (1 dp)

c In triangle ABC, let AC = y
By Pythagoras' theorem
$$y^2 = 5^2 + 12^2 \text{ cm}^2$$
$$= 169 \text{ cm}^2$$
$$y = \sqrt{169} = 13 \text{ cm}$$
In triangle ACD, let $\angle ADC = z$
So, $\sin z = \dfrac{13}{33.8} = 0.3846$
$z = \sin^{-1} 0.3846 = 22.6°$ (1 dp)

GRADE YOURSELF

C Able to use Pythagoras' theorem in right-angled triangles

C Able to solve problems in 2-D using Pythagoras' theorem

B Able to solve problems in 3-D using Pythagoras' theorem

B Able to use trigonometry to find lengths of sides and angles in right-angled triangles

B Able to use trigonometry to solve problems

What you should know now

- How to use Pythagoras' theorem
- How to solve problems using Pythagoras' theorem
- How to use the trigonometric ratios for sine, cosine and tangent in right-angled triangles
- How to solve problems using trigonometry
- How to solve problems using angles of elevation, angles of depression and bearings

Geometry

This chapter will show you ...

- how to find angles in triangles and quadrilaterals
- how to find interior and exterior angles in polygons
- how to find angles using circle theorems

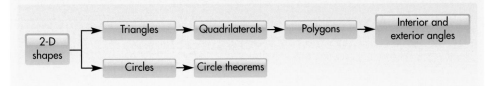

What you should already know

- Vertically opposite angles are equal. The angles labelled a and b are vertically opposite angles.

- The angles on a straight line add up to 180°, so $a + b = 180°$. This is true for any number of angles on a line. For example, $c + d + e + f = 180°$

- The sum of the angles around a point is 360°. For example, $a + b + c + d + e = 360°$

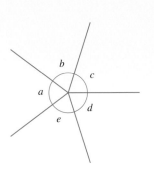

continued

- The three interior angles of a triangle add up to 180°. So, $a + b + c = 180°$

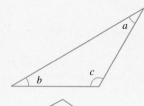

- The four interior angles of a quadrilateral add up to 360°.

  So, $a + b + c + d = 360°$

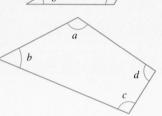

- A line which cuts parallel lines is called a transversal. The equal angles so formed are called alternate angles.

corresponding angles

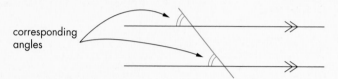

Because of their positions, the angles shown above are called corresponding angles.

Two angles positioned like a and b, which add up to 180°, are called allied angles.

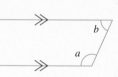

- A polygon is a 2-D shape with straight sides.
- Circle terms

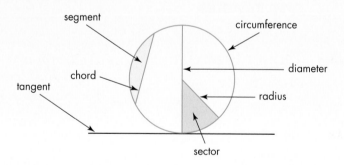

Quick check

Find the marked angles in these diagrams.

1

2

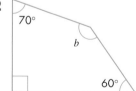

3

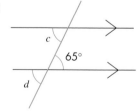

Special triangles and quadrilaterals

In this section you will learn how to:

● find angles in triangles and quadrilaterals

Key words

equilateral
   triangle
isosceles
   triangle
kite
parallelogram
rhombus
trapezium

Special triangles

An **equilateral triangle** is a triangle with all its sides equal.

Therefore, all three interior angles are 60°.

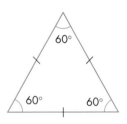

An **isosceles triangle** is a triangle with two equal sides, and therefore with two equal angles.

Notice how we mark the equal sides and equal angles.

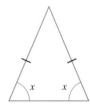

EXAMPLE 1

Find the angle marked a in the triangle.

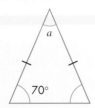

The triangle is isosceles, so both base angles are 70°.

So $a = 180° - 70° - 70° = 40°$

Special quadrilaterals

A **trapezium** has two parallel sides.

The sum of the interior angles at the ends of each non-parallel side is 180°: that is, ∠A + ∠D = 180° and ∠B + ∠C = 180°.

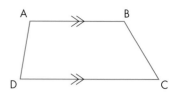

A **parallelogram** has opposite sides parallel.

Its opposite sides are equal. Its diagonals bisect each other. Its opposite angles are equal: that is, ∠A = ∠C and ∠B = ∠D.

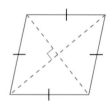

A **rhombus** is a parallelogram with all its sides equal.

Its diagonals bisect each other at right angles. Its diagonals also bisect the angles at the vertices.

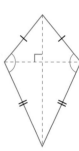

A **kite** is a quadrilateral with two pairs of equal adjacent sides.

Its longer diagonal bisects its shorter diagonal at right angles. The opposite angles between the sides of different lengths are equal.

EXAMPLE 2

Find the angles marked x and y in this parallelogram.

$x = 55°$ (opposite angles are equal) and $y = 125°$ ($x + y = 180°$)

EXERCISE 13A

D

1 Calculate the lettered angles in each triangle.

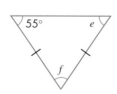

2 An isosceles triangle has an angle of 50°. Sketch the two different possible triangles that match this description, showing what each angle is.

3 Find the missing angles in these quadrilaterals.

a

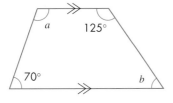

b

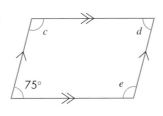

c

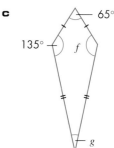

d

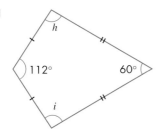

e

f

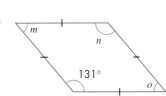

4 The three angles of an isosceles triangle are $2x$, $x - 10$ and $x - 10$. What is the actual size of each angle?

5 Calculate the lettered angles in these diagrams.

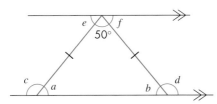

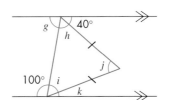

6 Calculate the values of x and y in each of these quadrilaterals.

a

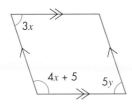

b

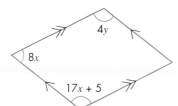

c

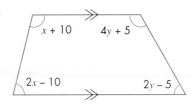

7 Find the value of x in each of these quadrilaterals and hence state the type of quadrilateral it is.

a a quadrilateral with angles $x + 10$, $x + 20$, $2x + 20$, $2x + 10$

b a quadrilateral with angles $x - 10$, $2x + 10$, $x - 10$, $2x + 10$

c a quadrilateral with angles $x - 10$, $2x$, $5x - 10$, $5x - 10$

d a quadrilateral with angles $4x + 10$, $5x - 10$, $3x + 30$, $2x + 50$

Angles in polygons

In this section you will learn how to:
- find interior angles and exterior angles in a polygon

Key words
exterior angle
heptagon
hexagon
interior angle
octagon
pentagon
polygon
regular
    polygon

A **polygon** has two kinds of angle.

- **Interior angles** are angles made by adjacent sides of the polygon and lying inside the polygon.

- **Exterior angles** are angles lying on the outside of the polygon, so that the interior angle + the exterior angle = 180°.

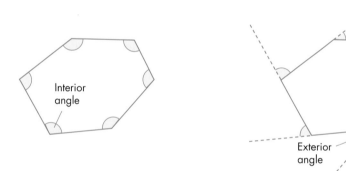

Interior
angle

Exterior
angle

The *exterior* angles of *any* polygon add up to 360°.

Interior angles

You can find the sum of the interior angles of any polygon by splitting it into triangles.

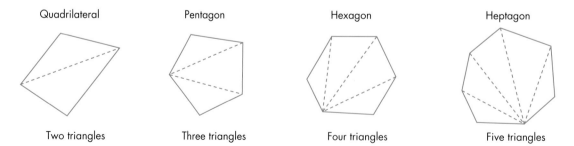

Quadrilateral	Pentagon	Hexagon	Heptagon
Two triangles	Three triangles	Four triangles	Five triangles

Since we already know that the angles in a triangle add up to 180°, the sum of the interior angles in a polygon is found by multiplying the number of triangles in the polygon by 180°, as shown in this table.

Shape	Name	Sum of interior angles
4-sided	Quadrilateral	$2 \times 180° = 360°$
5-sided	Pentagon	$3 \times 180° = 540°$
6-sided	Hexagon	$4 \times 180° = 720°$
7-sided	Heptagon	$5 \times 180° = 900°$
8-sided	Octagon	$6 \times 180° = 1080°$

As you can see from the table, for an n-sided polygon, the sum of the interior angles, S, is given by the formula

$$S = 180(n - 2)°$$

Exterior angles

As you see from the diagram, the sum of an exterior angle and its adjacent interior angle is 180°.

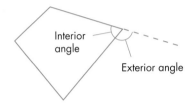

Regular polygons

A polygon is regular if all its interior angles are equal and all its sides have the same length. This means that all the exterior angles are also equal.

Here are two simple formulae for calculating the interior and the exterior angles of **regular polygons**.

The exterior angle, E, of a regular n-sided polygon is $E = \dfrac{360°}{n}$

The interior angle, I, of a regular n-sided polygon is $I = 180° - E = 180° - \dfrac{360°}{n}$

EXAMPLE 3

Find the exterior angle, x, and the interior angle, y, for this regular octagon.

$x = \dfrac{360°}{8} = 45°$ and $y = 180° - 45° = 135°$

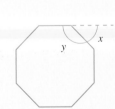

EXERCISE 13B

1 Calculate the sum of the interior angles of polygons with these numbers of sides.

    a 10 sides   **b** 15 sides   **c** 100 sides   **d** 45 sides

2 Calculate the size of the interior angle of regular polygons with these numbers of sides.

    a 12 sides   **b** 20 sides   **c** 9 sides   **d** 60 sides

3 Find the number of sides of polygons with these interior angle sums.

    a 1260°   **b** 2340°   **c** 18 000°   **d** 8640°

4 Find the number of sides of regular polygons with these exterior angles.

    a 24°   **b** 10°   **c** 15°   **d** 5°

5 Find the number of sides of regular polygons with these interior angles.

    a 150°   **b** 140°   **c** 162°   **d** 171°

6 Calculate the size of the unknown angle in each of these polygons.

    a
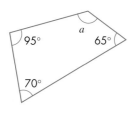

    b
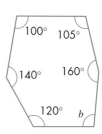

    c
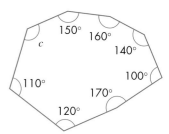

7 Find the value of x in each of these polygons.

    a
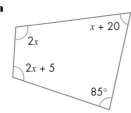

    b
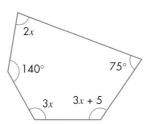

    c
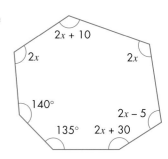

8 What is the name of the regular polygon whose interior angles are twice its exterior angles?

9 Wesley measured all the interior angles in a polygon. He added them up to make 991°, but he had missed out one angle.

    a What type of polygon did Wesley measure?

    b What is the size of the missing angle?

a In the triangle ABC, angle A is 42°, angle B is 67°.

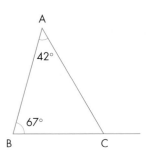

    i Calculate the value of angle C.

    ii What is the value of the exterior angle at C.

    iii What connects the exterior angle at C with the sum of
    the angles at A and B?

b Prove that any exterior angle of a triangle is equal to the sum of the
two opposite interior angles.

13.3 Circle theorems

In this section you will learn how to:
- find angles in circles

Key words

arc
circle
circumference
diameter
segment
semicircle
subtended

Here are three **circle** theorems you need to know.

- **Circle theorem 1**

The angle at the centre of a circle is twice the angle at the **circumference**
subtended by the same **arc**.

$$\angle AOB = 2 \times \angle ACB$$

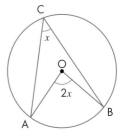

- **Circle theorem 2**

Every angle at the circumference of a **semicircle** that is subtended
by the **diameter** of the semicircle is a right angle.

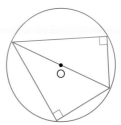

- **Circle theorem 3**

Angles at the circumference in the same **segment** of a circle are equal.

Points C_1, C_2, C_3 and C_4 on the circumference are subtended by the
same arc AB.

So $\angle AC_1B = \angle AC_2B = \angle AC_3B = \angle AC_4B$

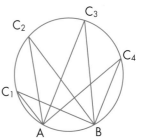

Follow through Examples 4–6 to see how these theorems are applied.

EXAMPLE 4

O is the centre of each circle. Find the angles marked *a* and *b* in each circle.

i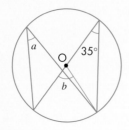

ii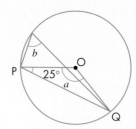

i   *a* = 35° (angles in same segment)

    b = 2 × 35° (angle at centre = twice angle at circumference)

     = 70°

ii   With OP = OQ, triangle OPQ is isosceles and the sum of the angles in this triangle = 180°

    So   *a* + (2 × 25°) = 180°

        a = 180° − (2 × 25°)

          = 130°

       b = 130° ÷ 2 (angle at centre = twice angle at circumference)

         = 65°

EXAMPLE 5

O is the centre of the circle. PQR is a straight line.

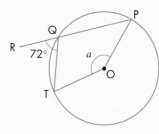

Find the angle labelled *a*.

    ∠PQT = 180° − 72° = 108° (angles on straight line)

The reflex angle ∠POT = 2 × 108° (angle at centre = twice angle at circumference)

        = 216°

   a + 216° = 360° (sum of angles around a point)

        a = 360° − 216°

        a = 144°

EXAMPLE 6

O is the centre of the circle. POQ is parallel to TR.

Find the angles labelled *a* and *b*.

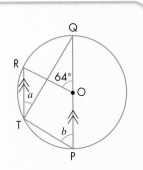

$a = 64° \div 2$ (angle at centre = twice angle at circumference)

$a = 32°$

∠TQP = *a* (alternate angles)

= 32°

∠PTQ = 90° (angle in a semicircle)

$b + 90° + 32° = 180°$ (sum of angles in △PQT)

$b = 180° - 122°$

$b = 58°$

EXERCISE 13C

1 Find the angle marked *x* in each of these circles with centre O.

a
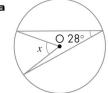

b
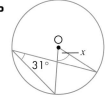

c
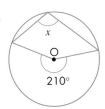

d
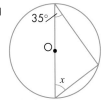

e

f
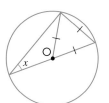

g
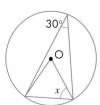

h
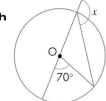

2 Find the angle marked *x* in each of these circles with centre O.

a

b

c
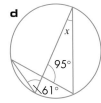

d

e
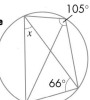

f

g

h
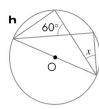

3 In the diagram, O is the centre of the circle. Find these angles.

a ∠ADB

b ∠DBA

c ∠CAD

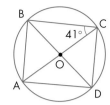

4 In the diagram, O is the centre of the circle. Find these angles.

a ∠EDF

b ∠DEG

c ∠EGF

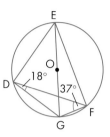

5 Find the angles marked *x* and *y* in each of these circles. O is the centre where shown.

a

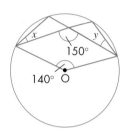

b

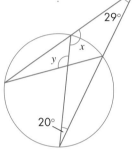

c

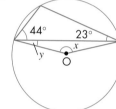

d

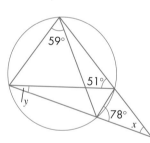

e

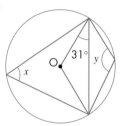

f

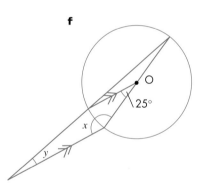

6 In the diagram, O is the centre and AD a diameter of the circle. Find *x*.

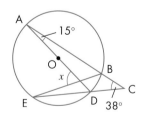

7 A, B, C and D are points on the circumference of a circle with centre O. Angle ABO is *x*° and angle CBO is *y*°.

a State the value of angle BAO.

b State the value of angle AOD

c Prove that the angle subtended by the chord AC at the centre of a circle is twice the angle subtended at the circumference.

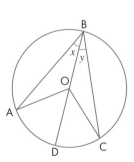

Cyclic quadrilaterals

In this section you will learn how to:

- find angles in cyclic quadrilaterals

Key word

cyclic
quadrilateral

A quadrilateral whose four vertices lie on the circumference of a circle is called a **cyclic quadrilateral**.

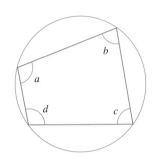

- **Circle theorem 4**

  The sum of the opposite angles of a cyclic quadrilateral is 180°.

  $a + c = 180°$ and $b + d = 180°$

EXAMPLE 7

Find the angles marked x and y in the diagram.

$x + 85° = 180°$ (angles in a cyclic quadrilateral)

So $\quad x = 95°$

$y + 108° = 180°$ (angles in a cyclic quadrilateral)

So $\quad y = 72°$

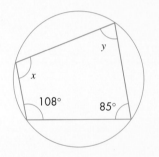

EXERCISE 13D

1 Find the sizes of the lettered angles in each of these circles.

a

85°
130°
a b

b

x c
88° x

c

d e
f 70°

d

81°
g
h 105°

e

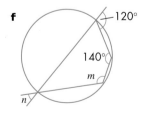

89°
l
j k

f

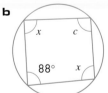

120°
140°
m
n

g

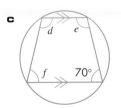

p
O 136°
q

h

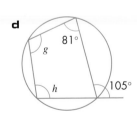

34°
x
50° y

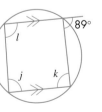

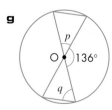

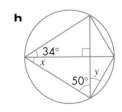

2 Find the values of *x* and *y* in each of these circles. Where shown, O marks the centre of the circle.

a
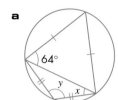

b
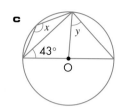

c
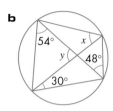

d
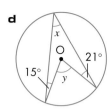

e
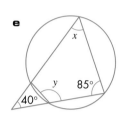

f
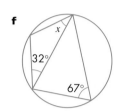

g
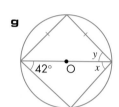

h
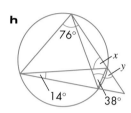

3 Find the values of *x* and *y* in each of these circles. Where shown, O marks the centre of the circle.

a
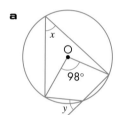

b
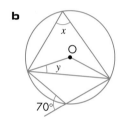

c
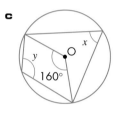

d
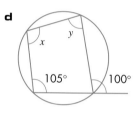

4 Find the values of *x* and *y* in each of these circles.

a
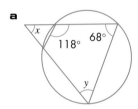

b
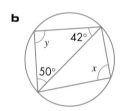

c
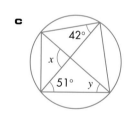

d
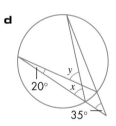

5 Find the values of *x* and *y* in each of these circles with centre O.

a
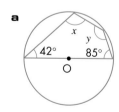

b
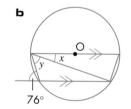

c
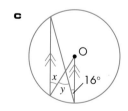

d
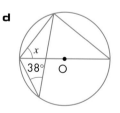

6 The cyclic quadrilateral PQRT has ∠ROQ equal to 38° where O is the centre of the circle. POT is a diameter and parallel to QR. Calculate these angles.

   a ∠ROT   **b** ∠QRT   **c** ∠QPT

7 ABCD is a cyclic quadrilateral within a circle centre O and ∠AOC is 2x°.

a Write down the value of ∠ABC.

b Write down the value of the reflex angle AOC.

c Prove that the sum of a pair of opposite angles of a cyclic quadrilateral is 180°.

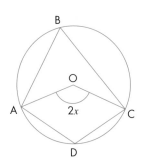

13.5 Tangents and chords

In this section you will learn how to:
- find angles in circles when tangents or chords are used

Key words
chord
point of contact
radius
tangent

A **tangent** is a straight line that touches a circle at one point only. This point is called the **point of contact**. A **chord** is a line that joins two points on the circumference.

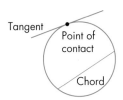

- **Circle theorem 5**

   A tangent to a circle is perpendicular to the **radius** drawn to the point of contact.

   The radius OX is perpendicular to the tangent AB.

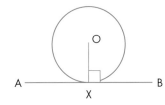

- **Circle theorem 6**

   Tangents to a circle from an external point to the points of contact are equal in length.

   AX = AY

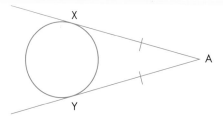

- **Circle theorem 7**

   The line joining an external point to the centre of the circle bisects the angle between the tangents.

   ∠OAX = ∠OAY

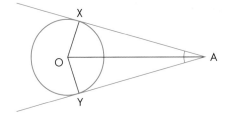

- **Circle theorem 8**

A radius bisects a chord at 90°.

If O is the centre of the circle

∠BMO = 90° and BM = CM.

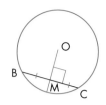

EXAMPLE 8

OA is the radius of the circle and AB is a tangent.

OA = 5 cm and AB = 12 cm.

Calculate the length OB.

∠OAB = 90° (radius is perpendicular to a tangent)

Let OB = x

By Pythagoras' theorem

$x^2 = 5^2 + 12^2$ cm^2

$x^2 = 169$ cm^2

So $x = \sqrt{169} = 13$ cm

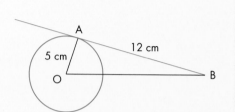

EXERCISE 13E

1 In each diagram, TP and TQ are tangents to a circle with centre O. Find each value of x.

a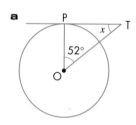

b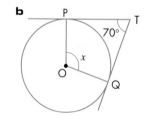

c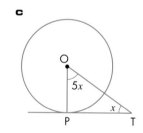

d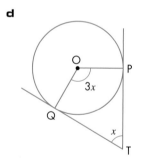

2 Each diagram shows tangents to a circle with centre O. Find each value of y.

a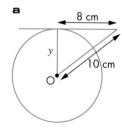

b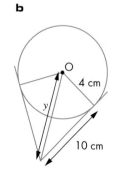

c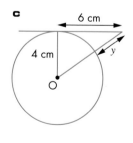

d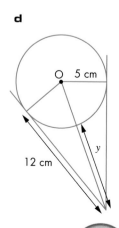

Mod 5

3 Each diagram shows a tangent to a circle with centre O. Find x and y in each case.

a

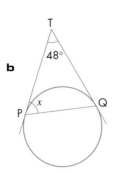
78° x
y
O

b

y
x 40°
O

c

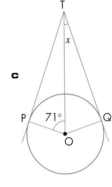
31°
O x
y

d

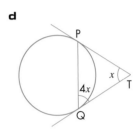
O
2x
y
x

4 In each of the diagrams, TP and TQ are tangents to the circle with centre O. Find each value of x.

a

T
28°
P x Q
O

b

T
48°
P x Q
O

c

T
x
P 71° Q
O

d

P
4x x
T
Q

5 Two circles with the same centre have radii of 7 cm and 12 cm respectively. A tangent to the inner circle cuts the outer circle at A and B. Find the length of AB.

6 AB and CB are tangents from B to the circle with centre O.
OA and OC are radii.

a Prove that angles AOB and COB are equal.

b Prove that OB bisects the angle ABC.

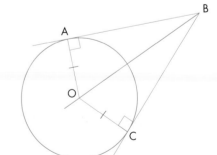
B
A
O
C

Alternate segment theorem

In this section you will learn how to:
- find angles in circles using the alternate segment theorem

Key words
alternate
   segment
chord
tangent

PTQ is the **tangent** to a circle at T. The segment containing ∠TBA is known as the **alternate segment** of ∠PTA, because it is on the other side of the **chord** AT from ∠PTA.

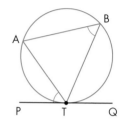

- **Circle theorem 9**

  The angle between a tangent and a chord through the point of contact is equal to the angle in the alternate segment.

      ∠PTA = ∠TBA

EXAMPLE 9

In the diagram, find **a** ∠ATS and **b** ∠TSR.

a ∠ATS = 80° (angle in alternate segment)

b ∠TSR = 70° (angle in alternate segment)

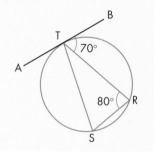

EXERCISE 13F

1 Find the size of each lettered angle.

a

b
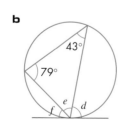

c
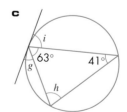

d
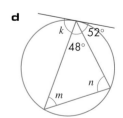

2 In each diagram, find the size of each lettered angle.

a

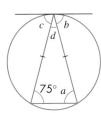

b

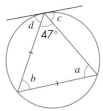

c

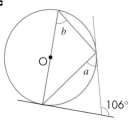

d

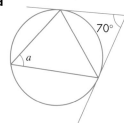

3 In each diagram, find the value of x.

a

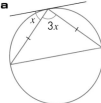

b

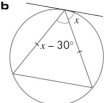

4 ATB is a tangent to each circle with centre O. Find the size of each lettered angle.

a

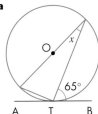

b

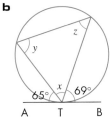

c

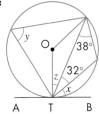

d

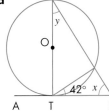

5 PT is a tangent to a circle with centre O.
AB are points on the circumference. Angle PBA is $x°$.

   a Write down the value of angle AOP.

   b Calculate the angle OPA in terms of x.

   c Prove that the angle APT is equal to the angle PBA.

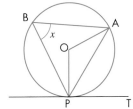

1 The diagram shows a regular octagon.

Calculate the size of the exterior angle of the regular octagon, marked y on the diagram.

AQA, Question 7, Paper 1 Intermediate, November 2004

2 The diagram shows part of a regular polygon. Each interior angle is 162°.

Calculate the number of sides of the polygon.

AQA, Question 1, Paper 1 Higher, June 2003

3 In the diagram, AOB is a diameter of the circle, centre O. TS is a tangent to the circle at C. Angle ABC = 57°.

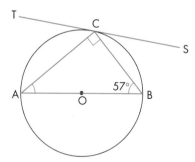

Calculate

a Angle CAB

b Angle ACS

AQA, Question 17, Paper 1 Higher, May 2002

4 A, B and C are points on the circumference of a circle with centre O. BD and CD are tangents. Angle BDC = 40°

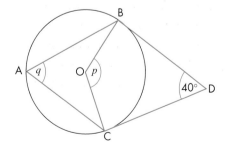

a i Work out the value of p.

ii Hence write down the value of q.

b The tangent DB is extended to T. The line AO is added to the diagram from part **a**. Angle TBA = 62°.

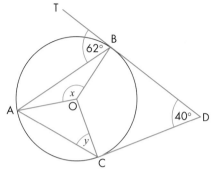

i Work out the value of x.

ii Work out the value of y.

AQA, Question 12, Paper 1 Higher, June 2005

 5 a i The diagram shows a circle with centre O.

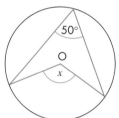

Work out the size of the angle marked x.

ii The diagram shows a different circle with centre O.

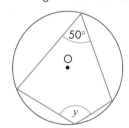

Work out the size of the angle marked y.

b The diagram shows a cyclic quadrilateral ABCD. The straight lines BA and CD are extended and meet at E.

EA = AC.
Angle ABC = $3x°$.
Angle ADC = $9x°$.
Angle DAC = $2x°$.

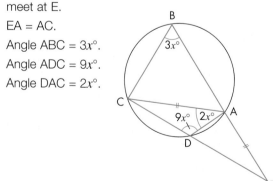

i Show that $x = 15$.

ii Calculate the size of angle EAD.

AQA, Question 15, Paper 1 Higher, November 2003

6 A, B, C are three points on a circle. ABE is a straight line and DCE is a tangent to the circle at C.
ABC is an isosceles triangle such that AB = AC.
ACE is an isosceles triangle such that AC = CE.

Find the angle BEC (marked x in the diagram).

AQA, Question 20, Paper 2 Higher, November 2002

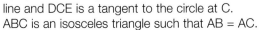

WORKED EXAM QUESTION

a

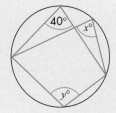

  i Write down the value of x.
  ii Calculate the value of y.

b A and C are points on the circumference of a circle centre B.
AD and CD are tangents. Angle ADB = 40°.

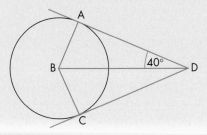

Explain why angle ABC is 100°.

c ABCD is a cyclic quadrilateral.
PAQ is a tangent to the circle at A.
BC = CD.
AD is parallel to BC.
Angle BAQ = 32°.

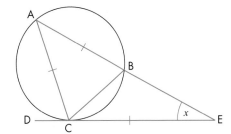

Find the size of angle BAD.
You must show all your working.

AQA, Question 14, Paper 2 Higher, November 2002

Solution

a i $x = 40°$ (angle in same segment)
    ii $y = 140°$ (opposite angles in cyclic quadrilateral = 180°)

b $\angle$BAD = 90° (radius is perpendicular to tangent)
   $\angle$ABD = 50° (angles in a triangle)
  Similarly:
  $\angle$BCD = 90° (radius is perpendicular to tangent)
  $\angle$CBD = 50° (angles in a triangle)
  So $\angle$ABC = 100°

c $\angle$ADB = 32° (alternate segment theorem)
  $\angle$DBC = 32° (alternate angles in parallel lines)
  $\angle$BDC = 32° (isosceles triangle)
  $\angle$DCB = 116° (angles in a triangle)
  So $\angle$BAD = 64° (opposite angles in cyclic quadrilateral = 180°)

GRADE YOURSELF

D Able to find angles in triangles and quadrilaterals

C Able to find interior angles and exterior angles in polygons

B Able to find angles in circles

A Able to find angles in circles using the alternate segment theorem

A* Can use circle theorems to prove geometrical results

What you should know now

- How to find angles in any triangle or in any quadrilateral
- How to calculate interior and exterior angles in polygons
- How to use circle theorems to find angles

Chapter

Transformation geometry

14

1 Congruent triangles

2 Translations

3 Reflections

4 Rotations

5 Enlargements

6 Combined transformations

This chapter will show you ...
- how to show that two triangles are congruent
- what is meant by a transformation
- how to translate, reflect, rotate and enlarge 2-D shapes

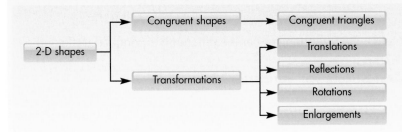

What you should already know
- How to find the lines of symmetry of a 2-D shape
- How to find the order of rotational symmetry of a 2-D shape
- How to recognise congruent shapes
- How to draw the lines with equations $y = x$ and $y = -x$, and lines with equations like $x = 2$ and $y = 3$

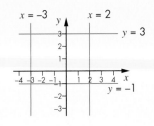

Quick check
Which of these shapes is not congruent to the others?

a 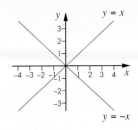 **b**   **c**   **d**

Congruent triangles

In this section you will learn how to:
- show that two triangles are congruent

Key word

congruent

Two shapes are **congruent** if they are exactly the same size and shape.

For example, these triangles are all congruent.

Notice that the triangles can be differently orientated (reflected or rotated).

Conditions for congruent triangles

Any one of the following four conditions is sufficient for two triangles to be congruent.

- **Condition 1**

All three sides of one triangle are equal to the corresponding sides of the other triangle.

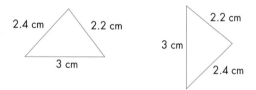

This condition is known as SSS (side, side, side).

- **Condition 2**

Two sides and the angle between them of one triangle are equal to the corresponding sides and angle of the other triangle.

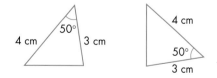

This condition is known as SAS (side, angle, side).

- **Condition 3**

Two angles and a side of one triangle are equal to the corresponding angles and side of the other triangle.

or

This condition is known as ASA (angle, side, angle) or AAS (angle, angle, side).

- **Condition 4**

Both triangles have a right angle, an equal hypotenuse and another equal side.

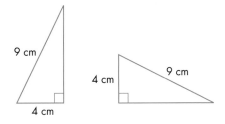

This condition is known as RHS (right angle, hypotenuse, side).

Notation

Once you have shown that triangle ABC is congruent to triangle PQR by one of the above conditions, it means that

$\angle A = \angle P$ AB = PQ

$\angle B = \angle Q$ BC = QR

$\angle C = \angle R$ AC = PR

In other words, the points ABC correspond exactly to the points PQR in that order. Triangle ABC is congruent to triangle PQR can be written as $\triangle ABC \equiv \triangle PQR$.

EXAMPLE 1

ABCD is a kite. Show that triangle ABC is congruent to triangle ADC.

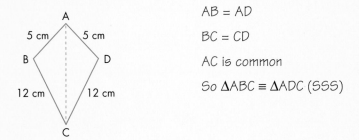

AB = AD

BC = CD

AC is common

So $\triangle ABC \equiv \triangle ADC$ (SSS)

EXERCISE 14A

1 State whether each pair of triangles in **a** to **h** is congruent. If a pair is congruent, give the condition which shows that the triangles are congruent.

a
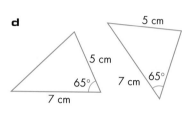

b
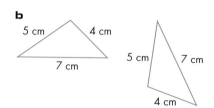

c
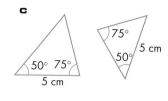

d
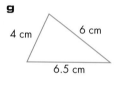

e
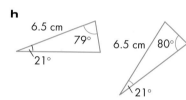

f
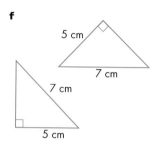

g

h

2 State whether each pair of triangles given below is congruent or not. If the triangles are congruent, give the reason and state which points correspond to which.

a ABC where AB = 8 cm, BC = 9 cm, AC = 7.4 cm
   PQR where PQ = 9 cm, QR = 7.4 cm, PR = 8 cm

b ABC where AB = 7.5 cm, AC = 8 cm, angle A = 50°
   PQR where PQ = 8 cm, QR = 75 mm, angle R = 50°

c ABC where AB = 5 cm, BC = 6 cm, angle B = 35°
   PQR where PQ = 6 cm, QR = 50 mm, angle Q = 35°

d ABC where AB = 6 cm, angle B = 35°, angle C = 115°
   PQR where PQ = 6 cm, angle Q = 115°, angle R = 35°

3 Triangle ABC is congruent to triangle PQR, ∠A = 60°, ∠B = 80° and AB = 5 cm. Find these.

i ∠P   **ii** ∠Q   **iii** ∠R   **iv** PQ

4 ABCD is congruent to PQRS, ∠A= 110°, ∠B = 55°, ∠C = 85° and RS = 4 cm. Find these.

i ∠P   **ii** ∠Q   **iii** ∠R   **iv** ∠S   **v** CD

5 Draw a rectangle EFGH. Draw in the diagonal EG. Prove that triangle EFG is congruent to triangle EHG.

6 Draw an isosceles triangle ABC where AB = AC. Draw the line from A to X, the mid-point of BC. Prove that triangle ABX is congruent to triangle ACX.

In this section you will learn how to:

● translate a 2-D shape

Key words

transformation
translation
vector

A **transformation** changes the position or the size of a shape.

There are four basic ways of changing the position and size of 2-D shapes: a translation, a reflection, a rotation or an enlargement. All of these transformations, except enlargement, keep shapes congruent.

A **translation** is the "movement" of a shape from one place to another without reflecting it or rotating it. It is sometimes called a glide, since the shape appears to glide from one place to another. Every point in the shape moves in the same direction and through the same distance.

We describe translations by using **vectors**. A vector is represented by the combination of a horizontal shift and a vertical shift.

EXAMPLE 2

Use vectors to describe the translations of the following triangles.

a A to B

b B to C

c C to D

d D to A

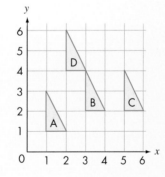

a The vector describing the translation from A to B is $\begin{pmatrix} 2 \\ 1 \end{pmatrix}$.

b The vector describing the translation from B to C is $\begin{pmatrix} 2 \\ 0 \end{pmatrix}$.

c The vector describing the translation from C to D is $\begin{pmatrix} -3 \\ 2 \end{pmatrix}$.

d The vector describing the translation from D to A is $\begin{pmatrix} -1 \\ -3 \end{pmatrix}$.

Note:

● The top number in the vector describes the horizontal movement. To the right +, to the left −.

● The bottom number in the vector describes the vertical movement. Upwards +, downwards −.

EXERCISE 14B

1 Use vectors to describe the following translations.

a i A to B	**ii** A to C	**iii** A to D	**iv** A to E	**v** A to F	**vi** A to G
b i B to A	**ii** B to C	**iii** B to D	**iv** B to E	**v** B to F	**vi** B to G
c i C to A	**ii** C to B	**iii** C to D	**iv** C to E	**v** C to F	**vi** C to G
d i D to E	**ii** E to B	**iii** F to C	**iv** G to D	**v** F to G	**vi** G to E

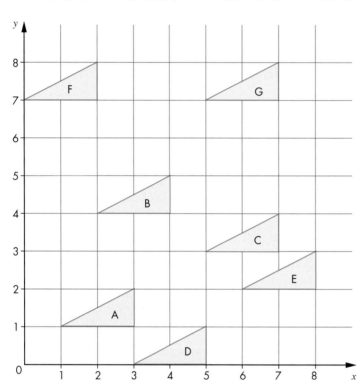

2 a Draw the triangle with coordinates A(1,1), B(2,1) and C(1,3).

   b Draw the image of ABC after a translation with vector $\begin{pmatrix} 2 \\ 3 \end{pmatrix}$. Label this triangle P.

   c Draw the image of ABC after a translation with vector $\begin{pmatrix} -1 \\ 2 \end{pmatrix}$. Label this triangle Q.

   d Draw the image of ABC after a translation with vector $\begin{pmatrix} 3 \\ -2 \end{pmatrix}$. Label this triangle R.

   e Draw the image of ABC after a translation with vector $\begin{pmatrix} -2 \\ -4 \end{pmatrix}$. Label this triangle S.

3 Using your diagram from question **2**, use vectors to describe the translation that will move

a P to Q	**b** Q to R	**c** R to S	**d** S to P
e R to P	**f** S to Q	**g** R to Q	**e** P to S

4 Take a 10 × 10 grid and the triangle A(0, 0), B(1, 0) and C(0, 1). How many different translations are there that use integer values only and will move the triangle ABC to somewhere in the grid?

Reflections

In this section you will learn how to:
- reflect a 2-D shape in a mirror line

Key words
image
mirror line
object
reflection

A **reflection** transforms a shape so that it becomes a mirror image of itself.

EXAMPLE 3

Notice the reflection of each point in the original shape, called the **object**, is perpendicular to the **mirror line**. So if you "fold" the whole diagram along the mirror line, the object will coincide with its reflection, called its **image**.

EXERCISE 14C

1. Copy the diagram below and draw the reflection of the given triangle in the following lines.

   a $x = 2$ **b** $x = -1$ **c** $x = 3$ **d** $y = 2$ **e** $y = -1$ **f** y-axis

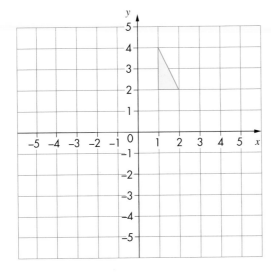

D

2 **a** Draw a pair of axes, x-axis from −5 to 5, y-axis from −5 to 5.

b Draw the triangle with coordinates A(1, 1), B(3, 1), C(4, 5).

c Reflect the triangle ABC in the x-axis. Label the image P.

d Reflect triangle P in the y-axis. Label the image Q.

e Reflect triangle Q in the x-axis. Label the image R.

f Describe the reflection that will move triangle ABC to triangle R.

3 **a** Draw a pair of axes, x-axis from −5 to +5 and y-axis from −5 to +5.

b Reflect the points A(2, 1), B(5, 0), C(−3, 3), D(3, −2) in the x-axis.

c What do you notice about the values of the coordinates of the reflected points?

d What would the coordinates of the reflected point be if the point (a, b) were reflected in the x-axis?

4 **a** Draw a pair of axes, x-axis from −5 to +5 and y-axis from −5 to +5.

b Reflect the points A(2, 1), B(0, 5), C(3, −2), D(−4, −3) in the y-axis.

c What do you notice about the values of the coordinates of the reflected points?

d What would the coordinates of the reflected point be if the point (a, b) were reflected in the y-axis?

5 Draw each of these triangles on squared paper, leaving plenty of space on the opposite side of the given mirror line. Then draw the reflection of each triangle.

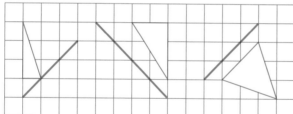

> **HINTS AND TIPS**
>
> Turn the page so that the mirror line is horizontal or vertical.

6 **a** Draw a pair of axes and the lines y = x and y = −x, as shown.

b Draw the triangle with coordinates A(2, 1), B(5, 1), C(5, 3).

c Draw the reflection of triangle ABC in the x-axis and label the image P.

d Draw the reflection of triangle P in the line y = −x and label the image Q.

e Draw the reflection of triangle Q in the y-axis and label the image R.

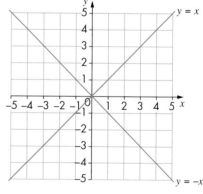

f Draw the reflection of triangle R in the line y = x and label the image S.

g Draw the reflection of triangle S in the x-axis and label the image T.

h Draw the reflection of triangle T in the line y = −x and label the image U.

i Draw the reflection of triangle U in the y-axis and label the image W.

j What single reflection will move triangle W to triangle ABC?

7 Copy the diagram and reflect the triangle in these lines.

a $y = x$

b $x = 1$

c $y = -x$

d $y = -1$

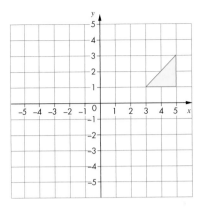

8 a Draw a pair of axes, x-axis from -5 to $+5$ and y-axis from -5 to $+5$.

b Draw the line $y = x$.

c Reflect the points A(2, 1), B(5, 0), C(–3, 2), D(–2, –4) in the line $y = x$.

d What do you notice about the values of the coordinates of the reflected points?

e What would the coordinates of the reflected point be if the point (a, b) were reflected in the line $y = x$?

9 a Draw a pair of axes, x-axis from -5 to $+5$ and y-axis from -5 to $+5$.

b Draw the line $y = -x$.

c Reflect the points A(2, 1), B(0, 5), C(3, –2), D(–4, –3) in the line $y = -x$.

d What do you notice about the values of the coordinates of the reflected points?

e What would the coordinates of the reflected point be if the point (a, b) were reflected in the line $y = -x$?

14.4 Rotations

In this section you will learn how to:

● rotate a 2-D shape about a point

Key words

angle of rotation
anticlockwise
centre of rotation
clockwise
rotation

A **rotation** transforms a shape to a new position by turning it about a fixed point called the **centre of rotation**.

EXAMPLE 4

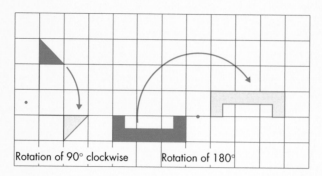

Rotation of 90° clockwise   Rotation of 180°

Note:

- The direction of turn or the **angle of rotation** is expressed as **clockwise** or **anticlockwise**.
- The position of the centre of rotation is always specified.
- The rotations 180° clockwise and 180° anticlockwise are the same.

The rotations which most often appear in examination questions are 90° and 180°.

EXERCISE 14D

1 On squared paper, draw each of these shapes and its centre of rotation, leaving plenty of space all round the shape.

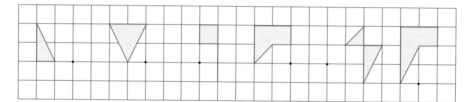

a Rotate each shape about its centre of rotation

   i first by 90° clockwise (call the image A)   **ii** then by 90° anticlockwise (call the image B).

b Describe, in each case, the rotation that would take

   i A back to its original position   **ii** A to B.

2 Copy the diagram and rotate the given triangle by the following.

a 90° clockwise about (0, 0)

b 180° about (3, 3)

c 90° anticlockwise about (0, 2)

d 180° about (−1, 0)

e 90° clockwise about (−1, −1)

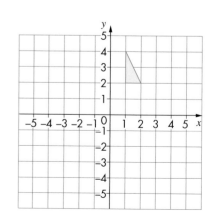

3 What other rotations are equivalent to these rotations?

a 270° clockwise   **b** 90° clockwise   **c** 60° anticlockwise   **d** 100° anticlockwise

4 **a** Draw a pair of axes where both the *x* and *y* values are from –5 to 5.

b Draw the triangle ABC, where A = (1, 2), B = (2, 4) and C = (4, 1).

c **i** Rotate triangle ABC 90° clockwise about the origin (0, 0) and label the image A', B', C', where A' is the image of A, etc.

ii Write down the coordinates of A', B', C'.

iii What connection is there between A, B, C and A', B', C'?

iv Will this connection always be so for a 90° clockwise to rotation about the origin?

5 Repeat question **4**, but rotate triangle ABC through 180°.

6 Repeat question **4**, but rotate triangle ABC 90° anticlockwise.

7 Show that a reflection in the *x*-axis followed by a reflection in the *y*-axis is equivalent to a rotation of 180° about the origin.

8 Show that a reflection in the line *y* = *x* followed by a reflection in the line *y* = –*x* is equivalent to a rotation of 180° about the origin.

9 **a** Draw a regular hexagon ABCDEF with centre O.

b Using O as the centre of rotation, describe a transformation that will result in the following movements.

i triangle AOB to triangle BOC   **ii** triangle AOB to triangle COD

iii triangle AOB to triangle DOE   **iv** triangle AOB to triangle EOF

c Describe the transformations that will move the rhombus ABCO to these positions.

i rhombus BCDO   **ii** rhombus DEFO

In this section you will learn how to:

● enlarge a 2-D shape by a scale factor

Key words
centre of
 enlargement
enlargement
scale factor

An **enlargement** changes the size of a shape to give a similar image. It always has a **centre of enlargement** and a **scale factor**. Every length of the enlarged shape will be

Original length × Scale factor

The distance of each image point on the enlargement from the centre of enlargement will be

Distance of original point from centre of enlargement × Scale factor

EXAMPLE 5

The diagram shows the enlargement of triangle ABC by scale factor 3 about the centre of enlargement X.

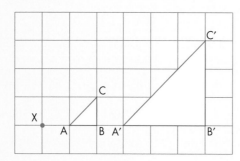

Note:

● Each length on the enlargement A'B'C' is three times the corresponding length on the original shape.

This means that the corresponding sides are in the same ratio:

AB:A'B' = AC:A'C' = BC:B'C' = 1:3

● The distance of any point on the enlargement from the centre of enlargement is three times longer than the distance from the corresponding point on the original shape to the centre of enlargement.

There are two distinct ways to enlarge a shape: the ray method and the coordinate method.

Ray method

This is the *only* way to construct an enlargement when the diagram is not on a grid.

EXAMPLE 6

Enlarge triangle ABC by scale factor 3 about the centre of enlargement X.

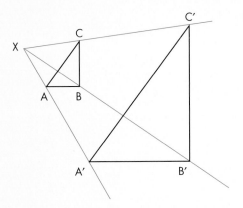

Notice that the rays have been drawn from the centre of enlargement to each vertex and beyond.

The distance from X to each vertex on triangle ABC is measured and multiplied by 3 to give the distance from X to each vertex A', B' and C' for the enlarged triangle A'B'C'.

Once each image vertex has been found, the whole enlarged shape can then be drawn.

Check the measurements and see for yourself how the calculations have been done.

Notice again that the length of each side on the enlarged triangle is three times longer than the length of the corresponding side on the original triangle.

Counting squares method

EXAMPLE 7

Enlarge the triangle ABC by scale factor 3 from the centre of enlargement (1, 2).

To find the coordinates of each image vertex, first work out the horizontal and vertical distances from each original vertex to the centre of enlargement.

Then multiply each of these distances by 3 to find the position of each image vertex.

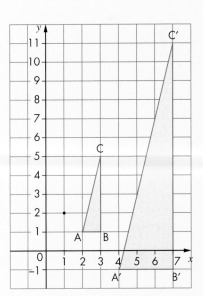

For example, to find the coordinates of C' work out the distance from the centre of enlargement (1, 2) to the point C(3, 5).

    horizontal distance = 2

    vertical distance = 3

Make these 3 times longer to give

    new horizontal distance = 6

    new vertical distance = 9

So the coordinates of C' are

    (1 + 6, 2 + 9) = (7, 11)

Notice again that the length of each side is three times longer in the enlargement.

Negative enlargement

A negative enlargement produces an image shape on the opposite side of the centre of enlargement to the original shape.

EXAMPLE 8

Triangle ABC has been enlarged by scale factor −2, with the centre of enlargement at (1, 0).

You can enlarge triangle ABC to give triangle A'B'C' by either the ray method or the coordinate method. You calculate the new lengths on the opposite side of the centre of enlargement to the original shape.

Notice how a negative scale factor also inverts the original shape.

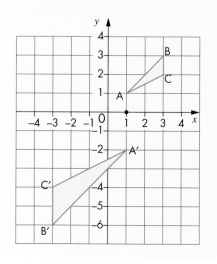

Fractional enlargement

Strange but true … you can have an enlargement in mathematics that is actually smaller than the original shape!

EXAMPLE 9

Triangle ABC has been enlarged by a scale factor of $\frac{1}{2}$ about the centre of enlargement O to give triangle A'B'C'.

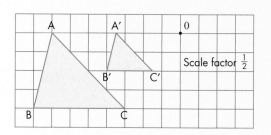

EXERCISE 14E

1 Make larger copies of each of these figures with its centre of enlargement, leaving plenty of space for the enlargement. Then enlarge it by the given scale factor, using the ray method.

Scale factor 2   Scale factor 3   Scale factor 2   Scale factor −3

2 a Draw a triangle ABC on squared paper.

b Mark four different centres of enlargement on your diagram as follows.

one above your triangle one to the left of your triangle
one below your triangle one to the right of your triangle

c Enlarge the triangle by a scale factor of 2 from each centre.

d What do you notice about each enlarged shape?

3 Enlarge each of these shapes by a scale factor of $\frac{1}{2}$ about the given centre of enlargement.

4 Copy this diagram onto squared paper.

a Enlarge the rectangle A by scale factor $\frac{1}{3}$ about the origin. Label the image B.

b Write down the ratio of the lengths of the sides of rectangle A to the lengths of the sides of rectangle B.

c Work out the ratio of the perimeter of rectangle A to the perimeter of rectangle B.

d Work out the ratio of the area of rectangle A to the area of rectangle B.

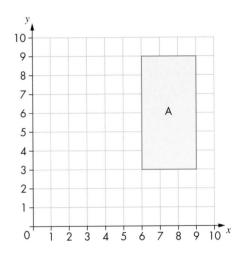

5 Copy the diagram onto squared paper.

a Enlarge A by a scale factor of 3 about a centre (4, 5).

b Enlarge B by a scale factor $\frac{1}{2}$ about a centre (−1, −3).

c Enlarge B by scale factor $-\frac{1}{2}$ about a centre (−3, −1).

d What is the centre of enlargement and scale factor which maps B onto A?

e What is the centre of enlargement and scale factor which maps A onto B?

f What is the centre of enlargement and scale factor which maps the answer to part **b** to the answer to part **c**?

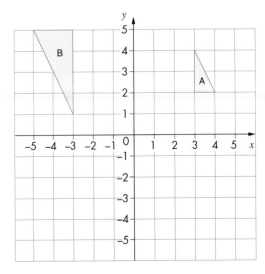

g What is the centre of enlargement and scale factor which maps the answer to part **c** to the answer to part **b**?

h What is the connection between the scale factors and the centres of enlargement in parts **d** and **e**, and in parts **f** and **g**?

Combined transformations

In this section you will learn how to:
- combine transformations

Key words
enlargement
reflection
rotation
transformation
translation

Examination questions often require you to use more than one transformation in a question. This exercise will revise the transformations you have met in this chapter.

EXERCISE 14F

1 Describe fully the transformations that will map the shaded triangle onto each of the triangles A–F.

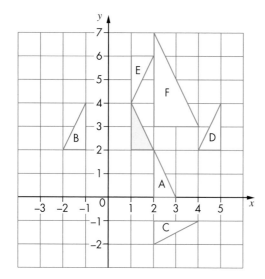

2 Describe fully the transformations that will result in the following movements.

a T_1 to T_2

b T_1 to T_6

c T_2 to T_3

d T_6 to T_2

e T_6 to T_5

f T_5 to T_4

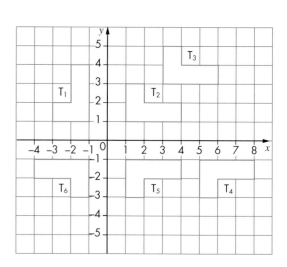

3 **a** Plot a triangle T with vertices (1,1), (2,1), (1,3).

  b Reflect triangle T in the y-axis and label the image T_b.

  c Rotate triangle T_b 90° anticlockwise about the origin and label the image T_c.

  d Reflect triangle T_c in the y-axis and label the image T_d.

  e Describe fully the transformation that will move triangle T_d back to triangle T.

4 The point P(3, 4) is reflected in the x-axis, then rotated by 90° clockwise about the origin. What are the coordinates of the image of P?

5 A point Q(5, 2) is rotated by 180°, then reflected in the x-axis.

  a What are the coordinates of the image point of Q?

  b What single transformation would have taken point Q directly to the image point?

6 Find the coordinates of the image of the point (3, 5) after a clockwise rotation of 90° about the point (1, 3).

7 Describe fully at least three different transformations that could move the square labelled S to the square labelled T.

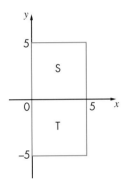

8 The point A(4, 4) has been transformed to the point A'(4, –4). Describe as many different transformations as you can that could transform point A to point A'.

9 Describe the single transformation equivalent to a reflection in the y-axis followed by a reflection in the x-axis.

1 Triangle T and triangles A, B, C, D and E are not drawn accurately.

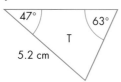

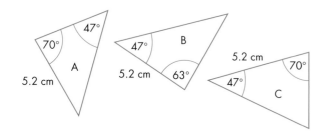

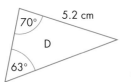

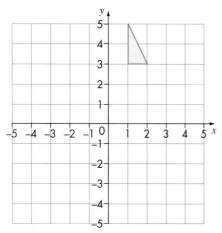

Which two of triangles A, B, C, D and E are congruent to triangle T?

AQA, Question 3, Paper 1 Higher, June 2003

2 a Copy the grid below.

 i Reflect the shaded triangle in the line $y = x$.
 Label it A.

 ii Rotate the shaded triangle 90° anticlockwise about (1, 1). Label it B.

b Describe the *single* transformation that takes triangle A to triangle B.

AQA, Question 5, Paper 2 Higher, June 2002

3 Copy the doagram below and enlarge the shaded triangle by a scale factor of 3. Use P as the centre of enlargement.

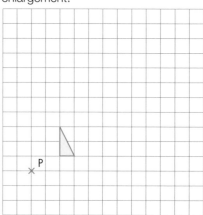

AQA, Question 12, Paper 2 Intermediate, November 2002

4 On the grid below there are two shapes, A and B.

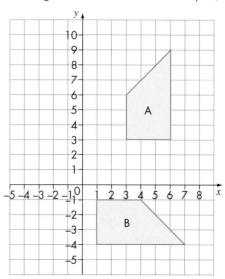

a Describe fully the *single* transformation that takes shape A to shape B.

b Copy the grid and draw the enlargement of shape A with scale factor $\frac{1}{3}$ and centre of enlargement (0, 0).

AQA, Question 9, Paper 1 Higher, November 2004

5 Triangle P is an enlargement of the shaded triangle.

 a What is the scale factor of the enlargement?

 b What is the centre of enlargement?

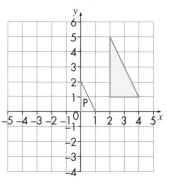

AQA, Question 9, Paper 2 Higher, June 2003

Mod 5

6 The grid shows two congruent shapes, A and B

a Describe the single transformation of shape A to shape B.

b On a copy of the grid, draw the enlargement of shape A by scale factor –2, centre of enlargement (2, 1).

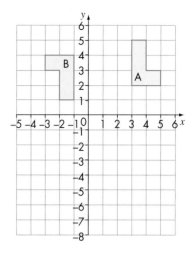

AQA, Question 3, Paper 1 Higher, November 2002

WORKED EXAM QUESTION

Triangle ABC has vertices A(6, 0), B(6, 9), C(9, 3).

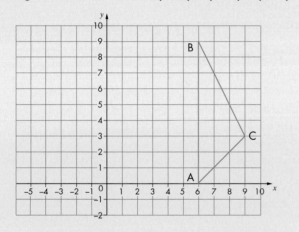

a Rotate triangle ABC through 180° about the point (2, 4). Label the image triangle R.

b Enlarge triangle ABC by scale factor $\frac{1}{3}$ from the centre of enlargement (3, 0). Label the image triangle E.

c Describe fully the single transformation which maps triangle E to triangle R.

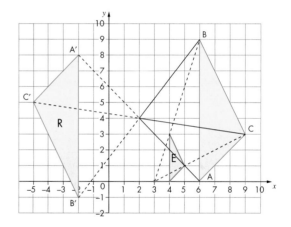

c

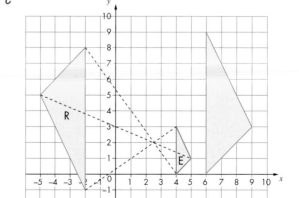

Solution

a Join each vertex to (2, 4) and rotate each line through 180°.

b Use the ray method or the counting squares method. Remember a fractional scale factor, makes the image smaller.

An enlargement of scale factor –3 about the point $(2\frac{1}{2}, 2)$. Draw in the ray lines to find the centre of enlargement.

AQA, Question 7, Paper 1 Higher, June 2001

GRADE YOURSELF

D Able to reflect a 2-D shape in a line $x = a$ or $y = b$

D Able to rotate a 2-D shape about the origin

D Able to enlarge a 2-D shape by a whole number scale factor

C Able to translate a 2-D shape by a vector

C Able to reflect a 2-D shape in the line $y = x$ or $y = -x$

C Able to rotate a 2-D shape about any point

C Able to enlarge a 2-D shape by a fractional scale factor

C Able to enlarge a 2-D shape about any point

B Know the conditions to show two triangles are congruent

B Able to enlarge a 2-D shape by a negative scale factor

A Able to prove two triangles are congruent

What you should know now

- How to translate a 2-D shape by a vector
- How to reflect a 2-D shape in any line
- How to rotate a 2-D shape about any point and through any angle
- How to enlarge a 2-D shape about any point using a positive, fractional or negative scale factor
- How to show that two triangles are congruent

Constructions

This chapter will show you ...

- how to bisect a line and an angle
- how to construct perpendiculars
- how to define a locus
- how to solve locus problems

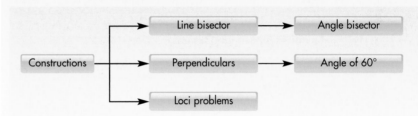

What you should already know

- How to construct triangles using a protractor and a pair of compasses
- How to use scale drawings

Quick check

Construct these triangles using a ruler, protractor and a pair of compasses.

1

4 cm 52° 6 cm

2

65° 75° 4 cm

3

5 cm 4 cm 6 cm

Bisectors

In this section you will learn how to:

- bisect a line and an angle

Key words

angle bisector
bisector
line bisector
perpendicular
   bisector

To bisect means to divide in half. So a **bisector** divides something into two equal parts.

- A **line bisector** divides a straight line into two equal lengths.

- An **angle bisector** is the straight line which divides an angle into two equal angles.

EXAMPLE 1

To construct a line bisector

It is usually more accurate to construct a line bisector than to measure its position (the midpoint of the line).

Bisect the line AB.  A ——————— B

- Open your compasses to a radius of about three quarters of the length of the line. Using A and B as centres, draw two intersecting arcs without changing the radius of your compasses.

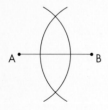

- Join the two points at which the arcs intersect to meet AB at X. This line is known as the **perpendicular bisector** of AB.

X is the midpoint of AB.

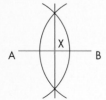

EXAMPLE 2

To construct an angle bisector

It is much more accurate to construct an angle bisector than to measure with a protractor.

Bisect ∠BAC.

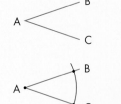

- Open your compasses to any reasonable radius. If in doubt, go for about 3 cm. With centre at A, draw an arc through both lines of the angle.

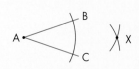

- With centres at the two points at which this arc intersects the lines, draw two more arcs so that they intersect at X. (The radius of the compasses may have to be increased to do this.)

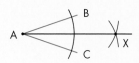

- Join AX.

  This line is the **angle bisector** of ∠BAC.

  So ∠BAX = ∠CAX.

EXERCISE 15A

In this exercise, it is important to leave in all your construction lines.

1 Draw a line 7 cm long. Bisect it using a pair of compasses and a ruler only. Check your accuracy by measuring to see if each half is 3.5 cm.

2 a Draw any triangle whose sides are between 5 cm and 10 cm.

  b On each side construct the perpendicular bisector as on the diagram. All your perpendicular bisectors should intersect at the same point.

  c Use this point as the centre of a circle that touches each vertex of the triangle. Draw this circle. This circle is known as the *circumscribed circle* of the triangle.

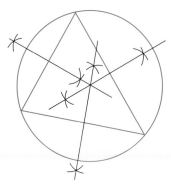

3 Repeat question **2** with a different triangle and check that you get a similar result.

4 a Draw a quadrilateral whose opposite angles add up to 180°.

  b On each side construct the perpendicular bisectors. They all should intersect at the same point.

  c Use this point as the centre of a circle that touches the quadrilateral at each vertex. Draw this circle.

5 a Draw an angle of 50°.

  b Construct the angle bisector.

  c Use a protractor to check how accurate you have been. Each angle should be 25°.

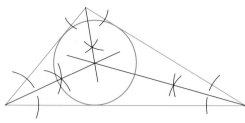

6 **a** Draw any triangle whose sides are between 5 cm and 10 cm.

b At each angle construct the angle bisector as on the diagram. All three bisectors should intersect at the same point.

c Use this point as the centre of a circle that touches each side of the triangle once. Draw this circle. This circle is known as the *inscribed circle* of the triangle.

7 Repeat question **6** with a different triangle and check that you get a similar result.

15.2 Other angle constructions

In this section you will learn how to:
- construct perpendiculars from a point
- construct an angle of 60°

Key words
construct
perpendicular

EXAMPLE 3

To construct a perpendicular from a point on a line

This construction will produce a perpendicular from a point A on a line.

- Open your compasses to about 2 or 3 cm.
  With point A as centre, draw two short arcs to intersect the line at each side of the point.

- Now extend the radius of your compasses to about 4 cm. With centres at the two points at which the arcs intersect the line, draw two arcs to intersect at X above the line.

- Join AX.

  AX is perpendicular to the line.

  Note: If you needed to construct a 90° angle at the end of a line, you would first have to extend the line.

  You could be even more accurate by also drawing two arcs underneath the line, which would give three points in line.

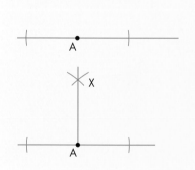

EXAMPLE 4

To construct a perpendicular from a point to a line

This construction will produce a perpendicular from a point A to a line.

- With point A as centre, draw an arc which intersects the line at two points.

- With centres at these two points of intersection, draw two arcs to intersect each other both above and below the line.

- Join the two points at which the arcs intersect. The resulting line passes through point A and is perpendicular to the line.

Examination note: When a question says *construct*, you must only use compasses – no protractor. When it says *draw*, you may use whatever you can to produce an accurate diagram. But also note, when constructing you may use your protractor to check your accuracy.

EXAMPLE 5

To construct an angle of 60°

This construction will produce an angle of 60° from a point A on a line.

- Open your compasses to about 3 cm. With point A as centre, draw an arc from above to intersect the line at point B.

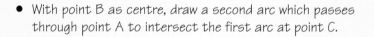

- With point B as centre, draw a second arc which passes through point A to intersect the first arc at point C.

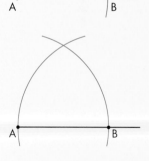

- Join AC.

    $\angle CAB = 60°$

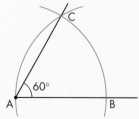

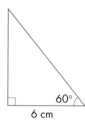

EXERCISE 15B

In this exercise, it is important to leave in all your construction lines.

1 Construct these triangles accurately without using a protractor.

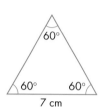

2 a Without using a protractor, construct a square of side 6 cm.

b See how accurate you have been by constructing an angle bisector on any of the right angles and seeing whether this also cuts through the opposite right angle.

3 a Construct an angle of 90°.

b Bisect this angle to construct an angle of 45°.

4 a Construct these angles.   **i** 30°   **ii** 15°   **iii** 22.5°   **iv** 75°

b Check your accuracy by measuring with a protractor. (The allowable error is ±1°.)

5 With ruler and compasses only, construct these triangles.

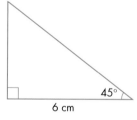 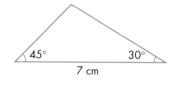 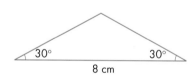

6 Construct an isosceles triangle ABC, where AB = AC = 7 cm and ∠CAB = 120°.

7 Construct a trapezium whose parallel sides are 8 cm and 6 cm, and having an angle of 60° at each end of the longer side.

8 a Construct the triangle ABC, where AB = 7 cm, ∠BAC = 60° and ∠ABC = 45°.

b Measure the lengths of AC and BC.

9 a Construct the triangle PQR, where PQ = 8 cm, ∠RPQ = 30° and ∠PQR = 45°.

b Measure the lengths of PR and RQ.

10 Construct a parallelogram which has sides of 6 cm and 8 cm and with an angle of 105°.

11 Draw a straight line and mark a point above the line. Construct the perpendicular which passes through that point to the line.

Defining a locus

In this section you will learn how to:
- draw a locus for a given rule

Key words
loci
locus

A **locus** (plural **loci**) is the movement of a point according to a given rule.

EXAMPLE 6

A point P that moves so that it is always at a distance of 5 cm from a fixed point A will have a locus that is a circle of radius 5 cm.

You can express this mathematically by saying

the locus of the point P is such that AP = 5 cm.

EXAMPLE 7

A point P that moves so that it is always the same distance from two fixed points A and B will have a locus that is the perpendicular bisector of the line joining A and B.

You can express this mathematically by saying

the locus of the point P is such that AP = BP.

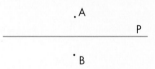

EXAMPLE 8

A point that moves so that it is always 5 cm from a line AB will have a locus that is a racetrack shape around the line.

This is difficult to express mathematically.

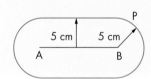

In your GCSE examination, you will usually get practical situations rather than abstract mathematical ones.

EXAMPLE 9

A point that is always 5 m from a long, straight wall will have a locus that is a line parallel to the wall and 5 m from it.

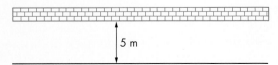

EXAMPLE 10

Imagine a grassy, flat field in which a horse is tethered to a stake by a rope that is 10 m long. What is the shape of the area that the horse can graze?

In reality, the horse may not be able to reach the full 10 m if the rope is tied round its neck but ignore fine details like that. You "model" the situation by saying that the horse can move around in a 10 m circle and graze all the grass within that circle.

In this example, the locus is the whole of the area inside the circle.

You can express this mathematically as

the locus of the point P is such that AP ⩽ 10 m.

EXERCISE 15C

1 A is a fixed point. Sketch the locus of the point P in each of these situations.

    a AP = 2 cm   **b** AP = 4 cm   **c** AP = 5 cm

2 A and B are two fixed points 5 cm apart. Sketch the locus of the point P for each of these situations.

    a AP = BP

    b AP = 4 cm and BP = 4 cm

    c P is always within 2 cm of the line AB

3 A horse is tethered in a field on a rope 4 m long. Describe or sketch the area that the horse can graze.

4 The horse is still tethered by the same rope but there is now a long, straight fence running 2 m from the stake. Sketch the area that the horse can now graze.

5 ABCD is a square of side 4 cm. In each of the following loci, the point P moves only inside the square. Sketch the locus in each case.

    a AP = BP   **b** AP < BP   **c** AP = CP

    d CP < 4 cm   **e** CP > 2 cm   **f** CP > 5 cm

6 One of the following diagrams is the locus of a point on the rim of a bicycle wheel as it moves along a flat road. Which is it?

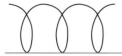 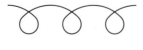  

7 Draw the locus of the centre of the wheel for the bicycle in question 6.

Mod 5

15.4 Loci problems

In this section you will learn how to:
● solve practical problems using loci

Key words
loci
scale

Most of the **loci** problems in your GCSE examination will be of a practical nature, as in the next example.

EXAMPLE 11

Imagine that a radio company wants to find a site for a transmitter. The transmitter must be the same distance from Doncaster and Leeds and within 20 miles of Sheffield.

In mathematical terms, this means they are concerned with the perpendicular bisector between Leeds and Doncaster and the area within a circle of radius 20 miles from Sheffield.

The map, drawn to a **scale** of 1 cm = 10 miles, illustrates the situation and shows that the transmitter can be built anywhere along the thick part of the blue line.

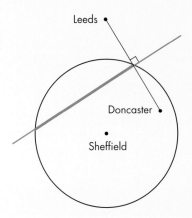

EXERCISE 15D

For questions **1** to **7**, you should start by sketching the picture given in each question on a 6 × 6 grid, each square of which is 1 cm by 1 cm. The scale for each question is given.

1 A goat is tethered by a rope, 7 m long, in a corner of a field with a fence at each side. What is the locus of the area that the goat can graze? Use a scale of 1 cm ≡ 2 m.

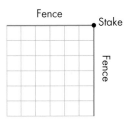

2 In a field a horse is tethered to a stake by a rope 6 m long. What is the locus of the area that the horse can graze? Use a scale of 1 cm ≡ 2 m.

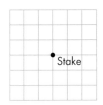

C

3 A cow is tethered to a rail at the top of a fence 6 m long. The rope is 3 m long. Sketch the area that the cow can graze. Use a scale of 1 cm ≡ 2 m.

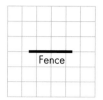

4 A horse is tethered to a stake near a corner of a fenced field, at a point 4 m from each fence. The rope is 6 m long. Sketch the area that the horse can graze. Use a scale of 1 cm ≡ 2 m.

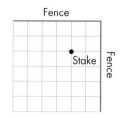

5 A horse is tethered to a corner of a shed, 2 m by 1 m. The rope is 2 m long. Sketch the area that the horse can graze. Use a scale of 1 cm ≡ 1 m.

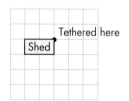

6 A goat is tethered by a 4 m rope to a stake at one corner of a pen, 4 m by 3 m. Sketch the area of the pen on which the goat cannot graze. Use a scale of 1 cm ≡ 1 m.

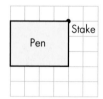

7 A puppy is tethered to a stake by a rope, 1.5 m long, on a flat lawn on which are two raised brick flower beds. The stake is situated at one corner of a bed, as shown. Sketch the area that the puppy is free to roam in. Use a scale of 1 cm ≡ 1 m.

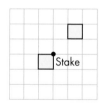

For questions **8** to **15**, you should use a copy of the map opposite. For each question, trace the map and mark on those points that are relevant to that question.

8 A radio station broadcasts from London on a frequency of 1000 kHz with a range of 300 km. Another radio station broadcasts from Glasgow on the same frequency with a range of 200 km.

a Sketch the area to which each station can broadcast.

b Will they interfere with each other?

c If the Glasgow station increases its range to 400 km, will they then interfere with each other?

9 The radar at Leeds airport has a range of 200 km. The radar at Exeter airport has a range of 200 km.

a Will a plane flying over Birmingham be detected by the Leeds radar?

b Sketch the area where a plane can be picked up by both radars at the same time.

10 A radio transmitter is to be built according to these rules.

    i   It has to be the same distance from York and Birmingham.

    ii   It must be within 350 km of Glasgow.

    iii   It must be within 250 km of London.

  a   Sketch the line that is the same distance from York and Birmingham.

  b   Sketch the area that is within 350 km of Glasgow and 250 km of London.

  c   Show clearly the possible places at which the transmitter could be built.

11 A radio transmitter centred at Birmingham is designed to give good reception in an area greater than 150 km and less than 250 km from the transmitter. Sketch the area of good reception.

12 Three radio stations pick up a distress call from a boat in the Irish Sea. The station at Glasgow can tell from the strength of the signal that the boat is within 300 km of the station. The station at York can tell that the boat is between 200 km and 300 km from York. The station at London can tell that it is less than 400 km from London. Sketch the area where the boat could be.

13 Sketch the area that is between 200 km and 300 km from Newcastle upon Tyne, and between 150 km and 250 km from Bristol.

14 An oil rig is situated in the North Sea in such a position that it is the same distance from Newcastle upon Tyne and Manchester. It is also the same distance from Sheffield and Norwich. Draw the line that shows all the points that are the same distance from Newcastle upon Tyne and Manchester. Repeat for the points that are the same distance from Sheffield and Norwich and find out where the oil rig is located.

15 Whilst looking at a map, Fred notices that his house is the same distance from Glasgow, Norwich and Exeter. Where is it?

16 Wathsea Harbour is as shown in the diagram.
A boat sets off from point A and steers so that it keeps the same distance from the sea wall and the West Pier. Another boat sets off from B and steers so that it keeps the same distance from the East Pier and the sea wall. Copy the diagram below, and on your diagram show accurately the path of each boat.

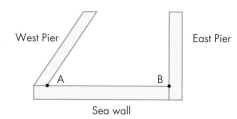

1 Make an accurate drawing of this triangle.

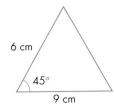

2 Construct an accurate drawing of this triangle.

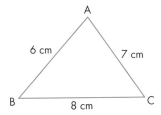

3 a Construct an accurate drawing of this triangle

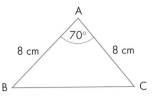

b Measure the length BC.

4 The map shows a small island with two towns A and B. Town B is north west of town A. The map is drawn to a scale of 1 square to 10 km.

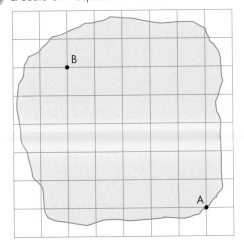

a What bearing is the direction north west?

b A mobile phone mast is to be built. It has to be within 40 km of both towns. Copy the map and shade the area in which the mast could be built.

5 a Construct an angle of 60°.

b Copy the line AB and then construct the perpendicular bisector of the points A and B.

6 In this question, you should use a ruler and compasses.

The diagram shows an equilateral triangle of side 10 cm.

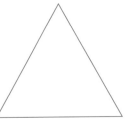

Copy the diagram and show all the points inside the triangle that are more than 5 cm from each vertex of the triangle.

You *must* show clearly all your constructions arcs.

AQA, Question 6, Paper 2 Higher, November 2004

7 This is a map of an island with two television transmitters at A and B. There is one town on the island which is shown shaded. The map is drawn to a scale of 1 cm represents 20 km. The transmitters at A and B both have a range of 40 km.

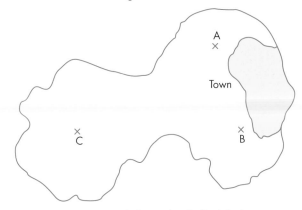

a Trace the map and show clearly that, between them, the two transmitters at A and B can send a signal to all parts of the town.

b A further transmitter is to be built at C so that the whole island can receive a signal. What minimum range should the transmitter at C have to ensure that all parts of the island can receive a signal?

AQA, Question 6, Paper 2 Higher, November 2002

8 The scale diagram below shows a plan of a room. The dimensions of the room are 9 m and 7 m.

Two plug sockets are fitted along the walls. One is at the point marked A. The other is at the point marked B. A third plug socket is to be fitted along a wall. It must be equidistant from A and B.

Using ruler and compasses, find the position of the new socket. Label it C.

Scale: 1 cm represents 1 m.

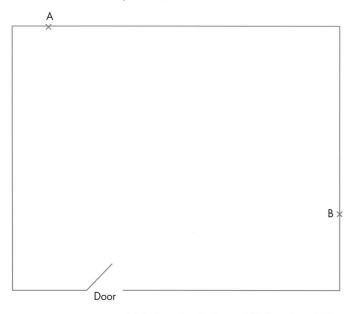

AQA, Question 5, Paper 1 Higher, June 2000

9 The diagram shows an L shape.

Copy the diagram and draw the locus of all points 2 cm from the L shape.

AQA, Question 5, Paper 1 Higher, June 2005

10 The map shows a field that is 100 m by 100 m.

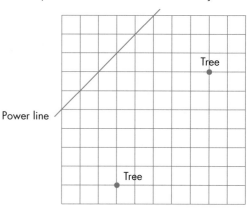

There are two large trees in the field and a power line runs across it.

a Make an accurate scale drawing of the field, using a scale of 1 cm ≡ 10 m.

b Bernice wants to fly a kite.

She cannot fly the kite within 50 m of the power line.

She cannot fly the kite within 30 m of a tree.

Show the area where she can fly the kite.

AQA, Question 5, Paper 1 Higher, November 2005

11 ABC is a triangle.
ACD is a straight line.

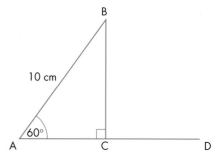

Using a ruler and compasses only, make an accurate construction of this diagram.
You *must* show clearly all your construction arcs.

AQA, Question 5, Paper 1, November 2003

Mod 5

WORKED EXAM QUESTION

The map below shows three boats, A, B and C, on a lake. Along one edge of the lake there is a straight path.

Treasure lies at the bottom of the lake.

The treasure is:

    between 150 m and 250 m from B,

    nearer to A than C,

    more than 100 m from the path.

Path

A ●

Scale: 1 cm represents 50 m

B ●

C ●

Using a ruler and compasses only, shade the region in which the treasure lies.

You must show clearly all your constructions arcs.

AQA, Question 6, Paper 1 Higher, June 2003

Solution

Draw two circles with centre at B with radii 3 cm and 5 cm.

Draw the perpendicular bisector of AC.

Draw a parallel line 2 cm from the path.

The region required is shaded on the diagram.

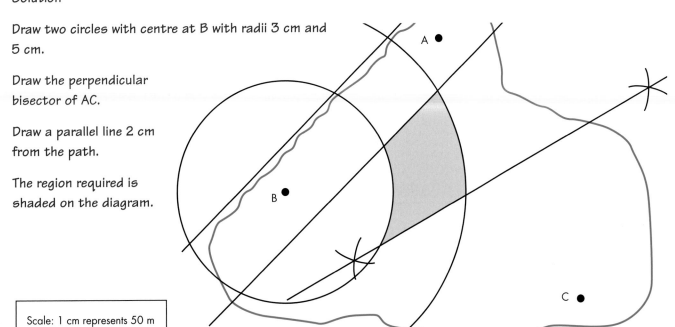

Scale: 1 cm represents 50 m

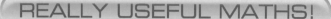

Bill the builder builds a street of 100 bungalows, 50 on each side of the street.

He builds them in blocks of 5.

The bungalows at the end of the blocks are called end-terraced, and the other bungalows are called mid-terraced.

3.2m

Key:
■ gate
■ door
■ window
— fence
□ garden shed

Here is the plan of one block of five.

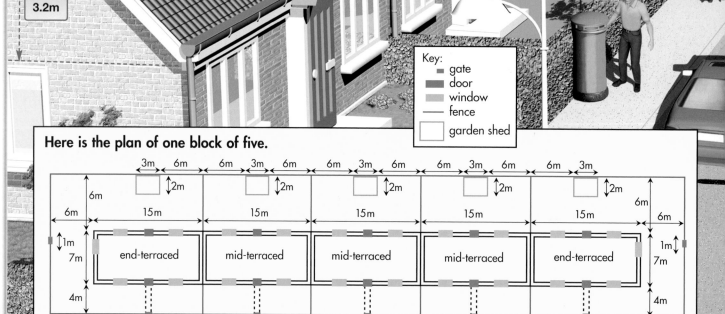

A tree is to be planted in the back garden of each mid-terraced house. The tree must be at least 2 m from the back of the house, at least 1 m from the back fence of the garden, and at least 3.5 m from each of the bottom corners of the garden. It must also be at least 1.5 m from the garden shed.

Draw an accurate scale drawing, using a scale of 1 cm ≡ 1 m, of a mid-terraced house and garden. Shade the region in which Bill can plant the tree.

Mod 5

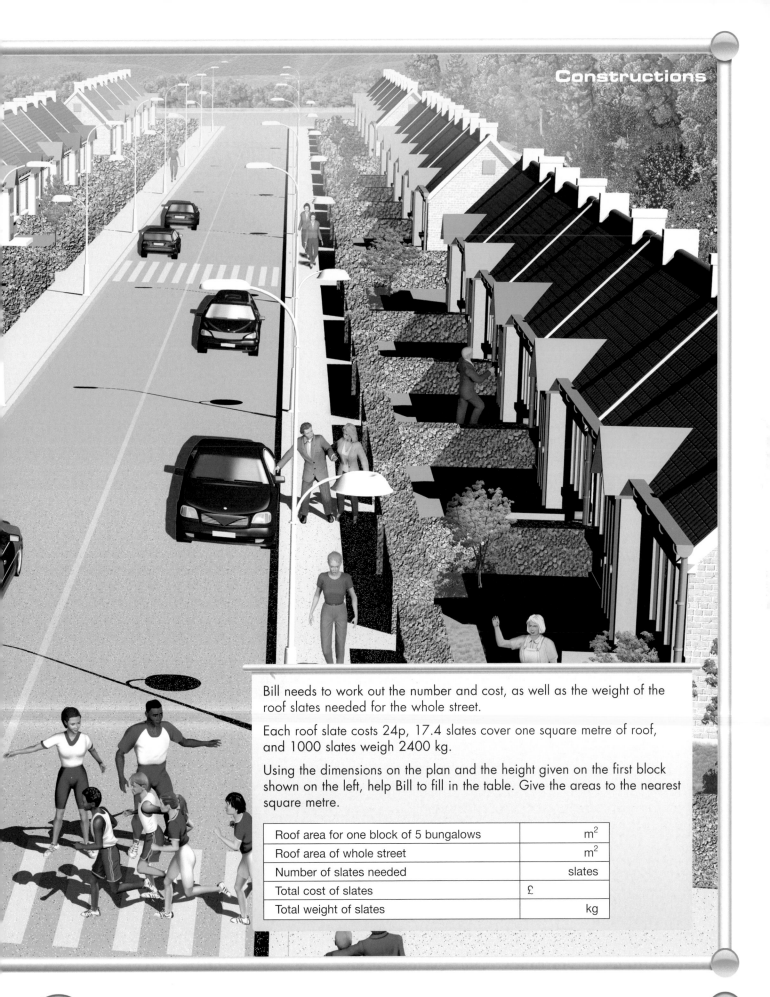

Bill needs to work out the number and cost, as well as the weight of the roof slates needed for the whole street.

Each roof slate costs 24p, 17.4 slates cover one square metre of roof, and 1000 slates weigh 2400 kg.

Using the dimensions on the plan and the height given on the first block shown on the left, help Bill to fill in the table. Give the areas to the nearest square metre.

Roof area for one block of 5 bungalows		m²
Roof area of whole street		m²
Number of slates needed		slates
Total cost of slates	£	
Total weight of slates		kg

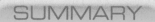

GRADE YOURSELF

C Able to construct line and angle bisectors

C Able to draw and describe the locus of a point from a given rule

C Able to solve problems using loci

B Able to construct a perpendicular from a point on a line

B Able to construct a perpendicular from a point to a line

B Able to construct an angle of 60°

What you should know now

- How to construct line and angle bisectors
- How to construct perpendiculars
- How to construct angles without a protractor
- Understand what is meant by a locus
- How to solve problems using loci

Similarity

1 Similar triangles

2 Areas and volumes of similar shapes

This chapter will show you ...

- what similar triangles are
- how to work out the scale factor between similar figures
- how to use the scale factor to work out lengths in similar figures
- how to use the scale factor to work out areas and volumes of similar shapes

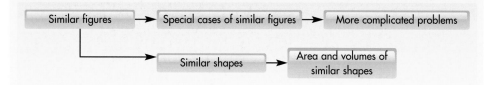

Similar figures → Special cases of similar figures → More complicated problems

Similar shapes → Area and volumes of similar shapes

What you should already know

- The meaning of congruency
- How to calculate a ratio and cancel it down
- The square and cubes of integers
- How to solve equations of the form $\frac{x}{9} = \frac{2}{3}$

Quick check

1 Which of the following triangles is congruent to this triangle.

a   b   c   d   e

2 Solve the equations.

a $\frac{x}{12} = \frac{7}{3}$ b $\frac{x}{10} = \frac{21}{15}$

In this section you will learn how to:
- show two triangles are similar
- work out the scale factor between similar triangles

Key word
similar

Triangles are **similar** if their corresponding angles are equal. Their corresponding sides are then in the same ratio.

EXAMPLE 1

The triangles ABC and PQR are similar. Find the length of the side PR.

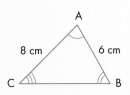 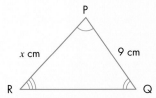

Take two pairs of corresponding sides, one pair of which must contain the unknown side. Form each pair into a fraction, so that x is on top. Since these fractions must be equal

$$\frac{PR}{AC} = \frac{PQ}{AB}$$

$$\frac{x}{8} = \frac{9}{6}$$

To find x.

$$x = \frac{9 \times 8}{6} \text{ cm} \quad \Rightarrow \quad x = \frac{72}{6} = 12 \text{ cm}$$

EXERCISE 16A

1 These diagrams are drawn to scale. What is the scale factor of the enlargement in each case?

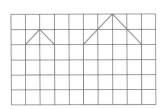 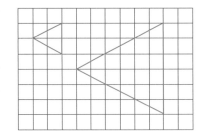

HINTS AND TIPS

If you need to revise scale of enlargement, look back at Section 14.5.

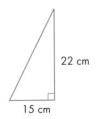

2 Are these pairs of shapes similar? If so, give the scale factor. If not, give a reason.

a
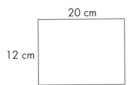
5 cm
3 cm
20 cm
12 cm

b
12 cm
5 cm
22 cm
15 cm

3 **a** Explain why these shapes are similar.

b Give the ratio of the sides.

c Which angle corresponds to angle C?

d Which side corresponds to side QP?

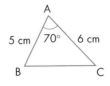
A
5 cm 70° 6 cm
B   C

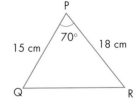
P
15 cm 70° 18 cm
Q   R

4 **a** Explain why these shapes are similar.

b Which angle corresponds to angle A?

c Which side corresponds to side AC?

B
6 cm
A   5 cm   C

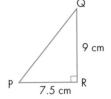
Q
9 cm
P   7.5 cm   R

5 **a** Explain why triangle ABC is similar to triangle AQR.

b Which angle corresponds to the angle at B?

c Which side of triangle AQR corresponds to side AC of triangle ABC? Your answers to question **4** may help you.

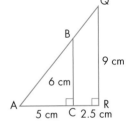
Q
B
9 cm
6 cm
A   5 cm   C   2.5 cm   R

6 In the diagrams **a** to **f**, each pair of shapes are similar but not drawn to scale. Find the lengths of the sides as requested.

a Find x.

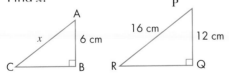
A
x   6 cm
C   B
P
16 cm   12 cm
R   Q

b Find PQ.

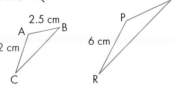
2.5 cm
A   B
2 cm
C
Q
P
6 cm
R

c Find x and y.

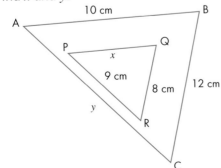
10 cm
A   B
P   Q
x
9 cm
8 cm   12 cm
y   R
C

d Find x and y.

10 cm
A   B
26 cm
x
C
12 cm
y
E   5 cm   D

e Find AB and PQ.

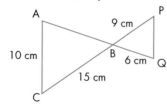

f Find QR.

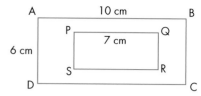

7 **a** Explain why these two triangles are similar.

b What is the ratio of their sides?

c Use Pythagoras' theorem to calculate the length of side AC of triangle ABC.

d Write down the length of the side PR of triangle PQR.

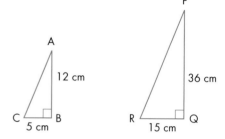

8 A model railway is made to a scale of 1 : 40. If the model bridge is 12 cm high, how high would a real railway bridge be? Give your answer in metres.

Special cases of similar triangles

EXAMPLE 2

Find the sides marked x and y in these triangles (not drawn to scale).

Triangles AED and ABC are similar. So using the corresponding sides CB, DE with AC, AD gives

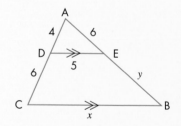

$$\frac{x}{5} = \frac{10}{4}$$

$$\Rightarrow \quad x = \frac{10 \times 5}{4} = 12.5$$

Using the corresponding sides AE, AB with AD, AC gives

$$\frac{y + 6}{6} = \frac{10}{4} \quad \Rightarrow \quad y + 6 = \frac{10 \times 6}{4} = 15$$

$$\Rightarrow \qquad y = 15 - 6 = 9$$

Mod 5

EXAMPLE 3

Ahmed wants to work out the height of a tall building. He walks 100 paces from the building and sticks a pole, 2 metres long, vertically into the ground. He then walks another 10 paces on the same line and notices that when he looks from ground level, the top of the pole and the top of the building are in line. How tall is the building?

First, draw a diagram of the situation and label it.

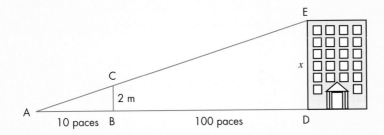

Using corresponding sides ED, CB with AD, AB gives

$$\frac{x}{2} = \frac{110}{10}$$

$$\Rightarrow \quad x = \frac{110 \times 2}{10} = 22 \text{ m}$$

Hence the building is 22 metres high.

EXERCISE 16B

1 In each of the cases below, state a pair of similar triangles and find the length marked x. Separate the similar triangles if it makes it easier for you.

a

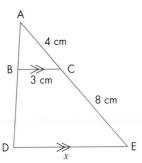

b

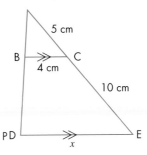

2 In the diagrams **a** to **e**, find the lengths of the sides as requested.

a Find x.

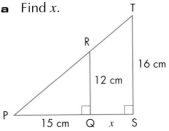

b Find CE.

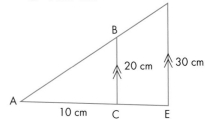

c Find x and y.

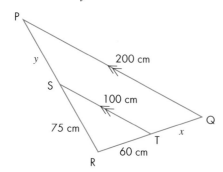

d Find x and y.

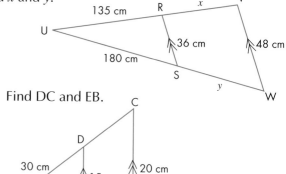

e Find DC and EB.

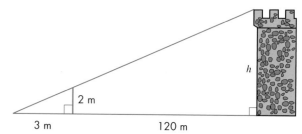

3 This diagram shows a method of working out the height of a tower.

A stick, 2 metres long, is placed vertically 120 metres from the base of a tower so that the top of the tower and the top of the stick is in line with a point on the ground 3 metres from the base of the stick. How high is the tower?

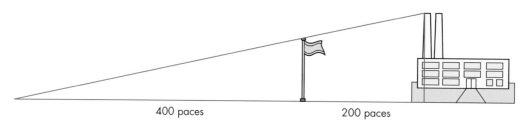

4 It is known that a factory chimney is 330 feet high. Patrick paces out distances as shown in the diagram, so that the top of the chimney and the top of the flag pole are in line with each other. How high is the flag pole?

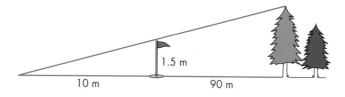

5 The shadow of a tree and the shadow of a golf flag coincide, as shown in the diagram. How high is the tree?

6 Find the height of a pole which casts a shadow of 1.5 metres when at the same time a man of height 165 cm casts a shadow of 75 cm.

7 Andrew, who is about 120 cm tall, notices that when he stands at the bottom of his garden, which is 20 metres away from his house, his dad, who is about 180 cm tall, looks as big as the house when he is about 2.5 metres away from Andrew. How high is the house?

More complicated problems

The information given in a similar triangle situation can be more complicated than anything you have so far met, and you will need to have good algebraic skills to deal with it. Example 4 is typical of the more complicated problem you may be asked to solve, so follow it through carefully.

EXAMPLE 4

Find the value of x in this triangle.

You know that triangle ABC is similar to triangle ADE.

Splitting up the triangles may help you to see what will be needed.

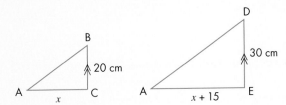

So your equation will be

$$\frac{x + 15}{x} = \frac{30}{20}$$

Cross multiplying (moving each of the two bottom terms to the opposite side and multiplying) gives

$$20x + 300 = 30x$$

$$\Rightarrow \quad 300 = 10x \quad \Rightarrow \quad x = 30 \text{ cm}$$

EXERCISE 16C

Find the lengths x or x and y in the diagrams **1** to **6**.

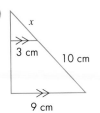

1

x

3 cm
10 cm

9 cm

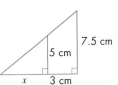

2

7.5 cm
5 cm

x 3 cm

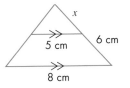

3

x

5 cm   6 cm

8 cm

4

20 cm

7.5 cm
10 cm

y

x

6 cm

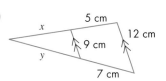

5

5 cm

x 12 cm

9 cm

y

7 cm

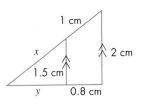

6

1 cm

x 2 cm

1.5 cm

y 0.8 cm

This section will show you how to:
- do problems involving the area and volume of similar shapes

Key words

area ratio
area scale factor
length ratio
linear scale
    factor
volume ratio
volume scale
    factor

There are relationships between the lengths, areas and volumes of similar shapes.

You saw on pages 336–338 that when a plane shape is enlarged by a given scale factor to form a new, similar shape, the corresponding lengths of the original shape and the new shape are all in the same ratio, which is equal to the scale factor. This scale factor of the lengths is called the **length ratio** or **linear scale factor**.

Two similar shapes also have an **area ratio**, which is equal to the ratio of the squares of their corresponding lengths. The area ratio, or **area scale factor**, is the square of the length ratio.

Likewise, two 3-D shapes are similar if their corresponding lengths are in the same ratio. Their **volume ratio** is equal to the ratio of the cubes of their corresponding lengths. The volume ratio, or **volume scale factor**, is the cube of the length ratio.

Generally, the relationship between similar shapes can be expressed as

Length ratio	$x : y$
Area ratio	$x^2 : y^2$
Volume ratio	$x^3 : y^3$

EXAMPLE 5

A model yacht is made to a scale of $\frac{1}{20}$ of the size of the real yacht. The area of the sail of the model is 150 cm². What is the area of the sail of the real yacht?

At first sight, it may appear that you do not have enough information to solve this problem, but it can be done as follows.

$$\text{Linear scale factor} \quad = 1 : 20$$

$$\text{Area scale factor} \quad = 1 : 400 \text{ (square of the linear scale factor)}$$

$$\text{Area of real sail} \quad = 400 \times \text{area of model sail}$$

$$= 400 \times 150 \text{ cm}^2$$

$$= 60\ 000 \text{ cm}^2 = 6 \text{ m}^2$$

EXAMPLE 6

A bottle has a base radius of 4 cm, a height of 15 cm and a capacity of 650 cm³. A similar bottle has a base radius of 3 cm.

a What is the length ratio?

b What is the volume ratio?

c What is the volume of the smaller bottle?

a The length ratio is given by the ratio of the two radii, that is 4 : 3.

b The volume ratio is therefore $4^3 : 3^3 = 64 : 27$.

c Let v be the volume of the smaller bottle. Then the volume ratio is

$$\frac{\text{Volume of smaller bottle}}{\text{Volume of larger bottle}} = \frac{v}{650} = \frac{27}{64}$$

$$\Rightarrow v = \frac{27 \times 650}{64} = 274 \text{ cm}^3 \text{ (3 significant figures)}$$

EXAMPLE 7

The cost of a paint can, height 20 cm, is £2.00 and its label has an area of 24 cm².

a If the cost is based on the amount of paint in the can, what is the cost of a similar can, 30 cm high?

b Assuming the labels are similar, what will be the area of the label on the larger can?

a The cost of the paint is proportional to the volume of the can.

Length ratio $= 20 : 30 = 2 : 3$

Volume ratio $= 2^3 : 3^3 = 8 : 27$

Let P be the cost of the larger can. Then the cost ratio is

$$\frac{\text{Cost of larger can}}{\text{Cost of smaller can}} = \frac{P}{2}$$

Therefore,

$$\frac{P}{2} = \frac{27}{8}$$

$$\Rightarrow P = \frac{27 \times 2}{8} = £6.75$$

b Area ratio $= 2^2 : 3^2 = 4 : 9$

Let A be the area of the larger label. Then the area ratio is

$$\frac{\text{Larger label area}}{\text{Smaller label area}} = \frac{A}{24}$$

Therefore,

$$\frac{A}{24} = \frac{9}{4}$$

$$\Rightarrow A = \frac{9 \times 24}{4} = 54 \text{ cm}^2$$

EXERCISE 16D

1 The length ratio between two similar solids is 2 : 5.

   a What is the area ratio between the solids?

   b What is the volume ratio between the solids?

2 The length ratio between two similar solids is 4 : 7.

   a What is the area ratio between the solids?

   b What is the volume ratio between the solids?

3 Copy and complete this table.

Linear scale factor	Linear ratio	Linear fraction	Area scale factor	Volume scale factor
2	1 : 2	$\frac{2}{1}$		
3				
$\frac{1}{4}$	4 : 1	$\frac{1}{4}$		$\frac{1}{64}$
			25	
				$\frac{1}{1000}$
	1 : 7			
	5 : 1			
			$\frac{1}{4}$	

4 Some years ago, a famous beer advertisement showed a bar attendant taking an ordinary pint glass and filling it with beer underneath the counter. When the glass reappeared, it was full of beer and its width and height were twice those of the original glass. The slogan on the advertisement was "The pint that thinks it's a quart". (A quart is 2 pints.)

   a What was the length ratio of the two glasses used in the advertisement?

   b What was the volume ratio of the two glasses?

   c The smaller glass held a pint. How much would the larger glass have held?

   d Is the advertisement fair?

5 A shape has an area of 15 cm². What is the area of a similar shape whose lengths are three times the corresponding lengths of the first shape?

6 A toy brick has a surface area of 14 cm². What would be the surface area of a similar toy brick whose lengths are?

   a twice the corresponding lengths of the first brick?

   b three times the corresponding lengths of the first brick?

7 A sheepskin rug covers 12 ft² of floor. What area would be covered by rugs with these lengths?

   a twice the corresponding lengths of the first rug

   b half the corresponding lengths of the first rug

8 A brick has a volume of 300 cm³. What would be the volume of a similar brick whose lengths are

a twice the corresponding lengths of the first brick?

b three times the corresponding lengths of the first brick?

9 Thirty cubic centimetres of clay were used to make a model sheep. What volume of clay would be needed to make a similar model sheep with these lengths?

a five times the corresponding lengths of the first model

b one half of the corresponding lengths of the first model

10 A can of paint, 6 cm high, holds a half a litre of paint. How much paint would go into a similar can which is 12 cm high?

11 It takes 1 litre of paint to fill a can of height 10 cm. How much paint does it take to fill a similar can of height 45 cm?

12 It takes 1.5 litres of paint to fill a can of height 12 cm.

a How much paint does it take to fill a similar can whose dimensions are $1\frac{1}{2}$ times the corresponding dimensions of the first can?

b Which of the information given is not needed to be able to answer part a?

13 To make a certain dress, it took 2.4 m² of material. How much material would a similar dress need if its lengths were

a 1.5 times the corresponding lengths of the first dress?

b three quarters of the corresponding lengths of the first dress?

14 A model statue is 10 cm high and has a volume of 100 cm³. The real statue is 2.4 m high. What is the volume of the real statue? Give your answer in m³.

15 A small can of paint costs 75p. What is the cost of a larger similar can whose circumference is twice that of the smaller can? Assume that the cost is based only on the volume of paint in the can.

16 A triangle has sides of 3, 4 and 5 cm. Its area is 6 cm². How long are the sides of a similar triangle that has an area of 24 cm²?

17 A ball with a radius of r cm has a volume of 10 cm³. What is the radius of a ball with a volume of 270 cm³?

18 Calculate the area of each of the shaded faces and hence calculate the volume of each of these solids. (They are not drawn to scale.)

a

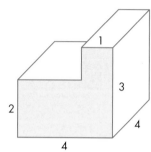

b

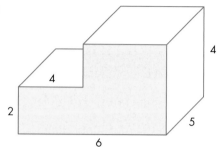

c

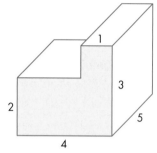

d

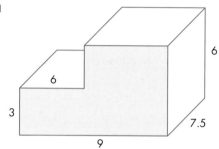

e Which two solids are similar?

Using area and volume ratios

In some problems involving similar shapes, the length ratio is not given, so we have to start with the area ratio or the volume ratio. We usually then need first to find the length ratio in order to proceed with the solution.

EXAMPLE 8

A manufacturer makes a range of clown hats that are all similar in shape. The smallest hat is 8 cm tall and uses 180 cm^2 of card. What will be the height of a hat made from 300 cm^2 of card?

The area ratio is 180 : 300

Therefore, the length ratio is $\sqrt{180} : \sqrt{300}$ (do not calculate these yet)

Let the height of the larger hat be H, then

$$\frac{H}{8} = \frac{\sqrt{300}}{\sqrt{180}} = \sqrt{\frac{300}{180}}$$

$$\Rightarrow H = 8 \times \sqrt{\frac{300}{180}} = 10.3 \text{ cm (1 decimal place)}$$

EXAMPLE 9

A supermarket stocks similar small and large cans of soup. The areas of their labels are 110 cm² and 190 cm² respectively. The weight of a small can is 450 g. What is the weight of a large can?

The area ratio is 110 : 190

Therefore, the length ratio is $\sqrt{110} : \sqrt{190}$ (do not calculate these yet)

So the volume (weight) ratio is $(\sqrt{110})^3 : (\sqrt{190})^3$.

Let the weight of a large can be W, then

$$\frac{W}{450} = \frac{(\sqrt{190})^3}{(\sqrt{110})^3} = \left(\sqrt{\frac{190}{110}}\right)^3$$

$$\Rightarrow \quad W = 450 \times \left(\sqrt{\frac{190}{110}}\right)^3 = 1020 \text{ g} \qquad \text{(3 significant figures)}$$

EXAMPLE 10

Two similar cans hold respectively 1.5 litres and 2.5 litres of paint. The area of the label on the smaller can is 85 cm². What is the area of the label on the larger can?

The volume ratio is 1.5 : 2.5

Therefore, the length ratio is $\sqrt[3]{1.5} : \sqrt[3]{2.5}$ (do not calculate these yet)

So the area ratio is $(\sqrt[3]{1.5})^2 : (\sqrt[3]{2.5})^2$

Let the area of the label on the larger can be A, then

$$\frac{A}{85} = \frac{(\sqrt[3]{2.5})^2}{(\sqrt[3]{1.5})^2} = \left(\sqrt[3]{\frac{2.5}{1.5}}\right)^2$$

$$\Rightarrow \quad A = 85 \times \left(\sqrt[3]{\frac{2.5}{1.5}}\right)^2 = 119 \text{ cm}^2 \qquad \text{(3 significant figures)}$$

EXERCISE 16E

1. A firm produces three sizes of similarly shaped labels for its products. Their areas are 150 cm², 250 cm² and 400 cm². The 250 cm² label just fits around a can of height 8 cm. Find the heights of similar cans around which the other two labels would just fit.

2. A firm makes similar gift boxes in three different sizes: small, medium and large. The areas of their lids are as follows.

    small: 30 cm²,   medium: 50 cm²,   large: 75 cm²

    The medium box is 5.5 cm high. Find the heights of the other two sizes.

3 A cone, height 8 cm, can be made from a piece of card with an area of 140 cm². What is the height of a similar cone made from a similar piece of card with an area of 200 cm²?

4 It takes 5.6 litres of paint to paint a chimney which is 3 m high. What is the tallest similar chimney that can be painted with 8 litres of paint?

5 A man takes 45 minutes to mow a lawn 25 m long. How long would it take him to mow a similar lawn only 15 m long?

6 A piece of card, 1200 cm² in area, will make a tube 13 cm long. What is the length of a similar tube made from a similar piece of card with an area of 500 cm²?

7 All television screens (of the same style) are similar. If a screen of area 220 cm² has a diagonal length of 21 cm, what will be the diagonal length of a screen of area 350 cm²?

8 Two similar statues, made from the same bronze, are placed in a school. One weighs 300 g, the other weighs 2 kg. The height of the smaller statue is 9 cm. What is the height of the larger statue?

9 A supermarket sells similar cans of pasta rings in three different sizes: small, medium and large. The sizes of the labels around the cans are as follows.

small can: 24 cm²,   medium can: 46 cm²,   large can: 78 cm²

The medium size can is 6 cm tall with a weight of 380 g. Calculate these quantities.

a the heights of the other two sizes

b the weights of the other two sizes

10 Two similar bottles are 20 cm and 14 cm high. The smaller bottle holds 850 ml. Find the capacity of the larger one.

11 A statue weighs 840 kg. A similar statue was made out of the same material but two fifths the height of the first one. What was the weight of the smaller statue?

12 A model stands on a base of area 12 cm². A smaller but similar model, made of the same material, stands on a base of area 7.5 cm². Calculate the weight of the smaller model if the larger one is 3.5 kg.

13 A solid silver statue was melted down to make 100 000 similar miniatures, each 2 cm high. How tall was the original statue?

14 Two similar models have volumes 12 m³ and 30 m³. If the surface area of one of them is 2.4 m², what are the possible surface areas of the other model?

1 Two rectangles have the dimensions shown.

12 cm

8 cm

20 cm

16 cm

Are the rectangles similar?
Explain your answer clearly.

 2 Triangle ABC is similar to triangle CDE.

Calculate the length of CD.

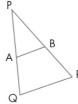

D

4.2 cm

A

E

C

2.8 cm

1.8 cm

B

3 In the triangle PQR, AB is parallel to QR. AB = 10 cm, QR = 16 cm and BR = 12 cm. Find the length PB.

P

B

A

R

Q

4 PQR and PXY are similar triangles.

Calculate the length of RY.

X

Q

15 cm

2.5 cm

P

4 cm   R   Y

5 A new AQA sign is to be erected on the Examination Board's offices in Manchester. The two As in the sign are similar in shape.

The cost of each letter A is proportional to its area. The large A costs £250 and is 250 cm high. The small A is 150 cm high. How much does the small letter cost?

NEAB, Question 18, Paper 2 Higher, June 2000

6 **a** Explain why the volume of a cube increases by a factor of 8 when the side length is doubled.

b June recently bought a small toy in the local shop.

ALIEN

Place in water and it becomes 6 times bigger!

It was originally 8 cm tall. After she placed it in water it grew to a similarly shaped alien. The height was then 14.5 cm. Is the claim on the pack justified?

AQA, Question 21, Paper 2 Higher, June 2005

WORKED EXAM QUESTION

A camping gas container is in the shape of a cylinder with a hemispherical top. The dimensions of the container are shown in the diagram.

It is decided to increase the volume of the container by 20%. The new container is mathematically similar to the old one.

Calculate the base diameter of the new container.

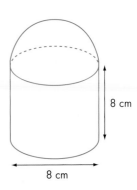

8 cm

8 cm

Solution

Old Volume : New volume = 100% : 120% = 1 : 1.2

> First find the volume scale factor.

$^3\sqrt{1} : ^3\sqrt{1.2}$ = 1 : 1.06265

> Take the cube root to get the linear scale factor.

New diameter = Old diameter × 1.06265 = 8 × 1.06265 = 8.5 cm

> Multiply the old diameter by the linear scale factor to get the new diameter.

Martin works for a light company called "Bright Ideas". He has been asked to calculate accurate measurements for a new table lamp the company are going to produce.

The three main components are the base, the stem and the shade. Below is a sketch of the side view, and an "exploded" diagram which shows the lamp in more detail.

The base and stem are made from a material which has a density of 10 g/cm³. Help Martin complete the table to find the total weight of the stem and the base.

volume of stem	cm³
weight of stem	g
volume of base	cm³
weight of base	g
total weight	g

Side view

10cm	
15cm	
30cm	
24cm	
3cm	
0.5cm	
15cm	

The lampshade is the frustum of a cone. It is to be made from a fire-proof material. Martin draws a sketch showing the dimensions he knows.

Help him to calculate the missing dimensions and then the surface area of the shade.

length of x	cm
length of L	cm
length of L	cm
surface area of small cone	cm²
surface area of large cone	cm²
surface area of lampshade	cm²

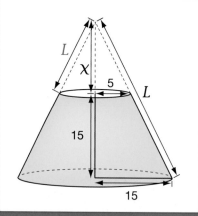

"Exploded" diagram

0.5cm

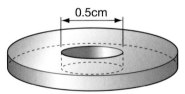
0.5cm

Martin knows a cone is made from the sector of a circle, but he needs to calculate the angle of the sector θ.

He draws this diagram of the large cone to help.

Find the angle θ for Martin.

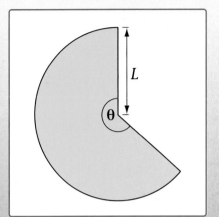

A material trim is to go around the bottom and top circles of the lampshade.

Help Martin use this diagram to calculate the total length of trim needed.

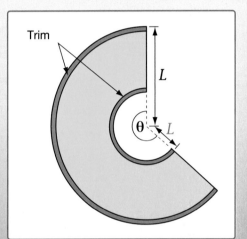

Trim

Draw an accurate scale drawing for Martin of the side view of the lamp using a scale of 3 : 1.

GRADE YOURSELF

C Know why two shapes are similar

C Able to work out unknown sides using scale factors and ratios

B Able to set up equations to find missing sides in similar triangles

A Able to solve problems using area and volume scale factors

A Able to solve practical problems using similar triangles

A* Able to solve related problems involving, for example, capacity, using area and volume scale factors

What you should know now

- How to find the ratios between two similar shapes
- How to work out unknown lengths, areas and volumes of similar 3-D shapes
- How to solve practical problems using similar shapes
- How to solve problems using area and volume ratios

Chapter 17

Dimensional analysis

1 Dimensions of length

2 Dimensions of area

3 Dimensions of volume

4 Consistent dimensions

This chapter will show you ...

- how to decide whether a formula represents a length, an area or a volume
- how to check that a formula has consistent dimensions

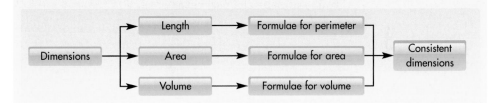

What you should already know

- The formulae for perimeters, areas and volumes of common shapes
- The common units used for length, area and volume

Quick check

Write down a formula for each of the following.

1 The perimeter of a square with side length l.

2 The circumference of a circle with diameter d.

3 The area of a triangle with base b and height h.

4 The area of a circle with radius r.

5 The volume of a cube with side length l.

6 The volume of a cylinder with radius r and height h.

In this section you will learn how to:
- find formulae for the perimeter of 2-D shapes

Key words
1-D
length
perimeter

When we have an unknown length or distance in a problem, we represent it by a single letter, followed by the unit in which it is measured. For example,

t centimetres $\qquad$ x miles $\qquad$ y kilometres

EXAMPLE 1

Find a formula the **perimeter** of each of these shapes.

a

b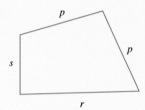

Shape **a** is a rectangle. Its perimeter is given by the formula

$P = x + y + x + y = 2x + 2y$

Shape **b** is an irregular quadrilateral. Its perimeter is given by the formula

$P = p + p + r + s = 2p + r + s$

In the example, each letter is a **length** and has the dimension or measure of length, i.e. centimetre, metre, kilometre, etc. The numbers or coefficients written before the letters are *not* lengths and therefore have *no* dimensions. So, for example, $2x$, $5y$ or $\frac{1}{2}p$ have the same dimension as x, y or p respectively.

When just lengths are involved in a formula, the formula is said to have one dimension or **1-D**, which is sometimes represented by the symbol [L].

EXERCISE 17A

Find a formula for the perimeter of each of these shapes. Each letter represents a length.

1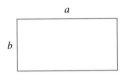

2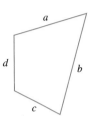

3

4

5

6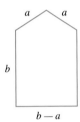

7

8

9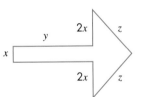

10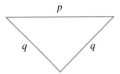

In this section you will learn how to:
● find formulae for the area of 2-D shapes

Key words
2-D
area

EXAMPLE 2

Look at these four examples of formulae for calculating area.

$A = lb$ gives the area of a rectangle
$A = x^2$ gives the area of a square
$A = 2ab + 2ac + 2bc$ gives the surface area of a cuboid
$A = \pi r^2$ gives the area of a circle

These formulae have one thing in common. They all consist of terms that are the product of two lengths. You can recognise this by counting the number of letters in each term of the formula. The first formula has two (l and b). The second has two (x and x). The third has three terms, each of two letters (a and b, a and c, b and c). The fourth also has only two letters (r and r) because π is a number (3.14159…) which has no dimension.

We can recognise formulae for **area** because they only have terms that consist of two letters – that is, two lengths multiplied together. Numbers are not defined as lengths, since they have no dimensions. These formulae therefore have two dimensions or **2-D**, which is sometimes represented by the symbol [L^2].

This confirms the units in which area is usually measured. For example,

square metres (m × m or m^2)

square centimetres (cm × cm or cm^2)

EXERCISE 17B

Find a formula for the area of each of these shapes. Each letter represents a length.

 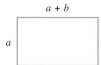   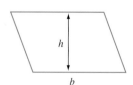

Mod 5

C

6
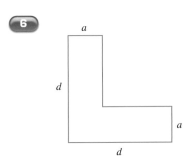
a

d

a

d

7
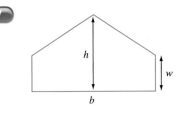
h

w

b

8
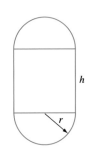
h

r

9
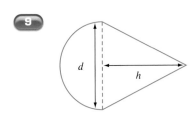
d

h

10
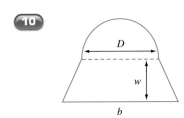
D

w

b

17.3 Dimensions of volume

In this section you will learn how to:

• find formulae for the volume of 3-D shapes

Key words
3-D
volume

EXAMPLE 3

Look at these three examples of formulae for calculating volume.

$V = lbh$ gives the volume of a cuboid
$V = x^3$ gives the volume of a cube
$V = \pi r^2 h + \frac{4}{3}\pi r^3$ gives the volume of a cylinder with hemispherical ends

Again, these formulae have one thing in common. They all consist of terms that are the product of three lengths. You can recognise this by counting the number of letters in each term of the formula. The first formula has three (*l*, *b* and *h*). The second has three (*x*, *x* and *x*). The third has two terms, each of three letters (*r*, *r* and *h*; *r*, *r* and *r*). Remember, π has no dimension.

We can recognise formulae for **volume** because they only have terms that consist of three letters – that is, three lengths multiplied together. They therefore have three dimensions or **3-D**, which is sometimes represented by the symbol [L³]. Once more, numbers are not defined as lengths, since they have no dimensions.

This confirms the units in which volume is usually measured. For example,

cubic metres (m × m × m or m³)

cubic centimetres (cm × cm × cm or cm³)

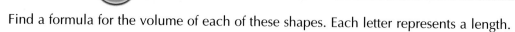

EXERCISE 17C

Find a formula for the volume of each of these shapes. Each letter represents a length.

1

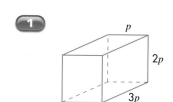

p

$2p$

$3p$

2

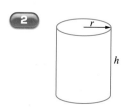

r

h

3

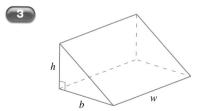

h

b

w

4

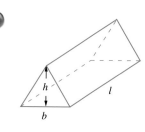

h

b

l

5

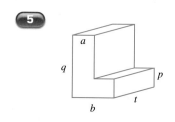

a

q

p

b

t

6

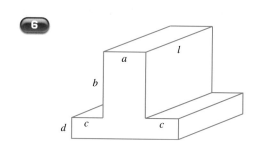

a

l

b

c

d

c

17.4 Consistent dimensions

In this section you will learn how to:

• check that the dimensions of a formula are consistent

Key words

consistency
dimension
formula

One way in which scientists and mathematicians check complicated **formulae** to see whether they are correct is to test for **consistency**. They check that every term in the formula is of the same **dimension**.

Each term in a formula must have the correct number of dimensions. It is not possible to have a formula with a mixture of terms, some of which have, for example, one dimension and some two dimensions. When terms are found to be mixed, the formula is said to be *inconsistent* and is not possible.

We are only concerned with lengths, areas and volumes, so it is easy for us to test for consistency.

EXAMPLE 4

Which of these expressions are consistent? If any are consistent, do they represent a length, an area or a volume?

a $a + bc$ **b** $\pi r^2 + ab$ **c** $r^3 + 2\pi r^2$ **d** $\dfrac{(ab^2 + a^2 b)}{2}$ **e** $\dfrac{\pi(R^2 + r^2)}{x}$

a is inconsistent because the first term has one letter (1-D), and the second has two letters (2-D). Hence, it is a mixture of length and area. So it has no physical meaning, i.e. $[L] + [L^2]$ is not possible.

b is consistent because the first term has two letters (r and r) multiplied by a dimensionless number (π), and the second term also has two letters (a and b). Hence the expression could represent an area, i.e. $[L^2] + [L^2] = [L^2]$ is consistent.

c is inconsistent because the first term is 3-D and the second term is 2-D. It is a mixture of volume and area, so it has no physical meaning, i.e. $[L^3] + [L^2]$ is not possible.

d is consistent. Each term is 3-D and hence the expression could represent a volume, i.e. $[L^3] + [L^3] = [L^3]$ is consistent.

e is consistent. There are two terms which are 2-D in the numerator and the term in the denominator is 1-D. The numerator can be cancelled to give two terms which are both 1-D. Hence the expression could represent a length, i.e. $[L^2]/[L] = [L]$ is consistent.

EXERCISE 17D

1 Each of these expressions represents a length, an area or a volume. Indicate which it is by writing L, A or V. Each letter represents a length.

a x^2 **b** $2y$ **c** πa **d** πab

e xyz **f** $3x^3$ **g** $x^2 y$ **h** $2xy$

i $4y$ **j** $3ab^2$ **k** $4xz$ **l** $5z$

m abc **n** $ab + bc$ **o** $abc + d^3$ **p** $2ab + 3bc$

q $a^2 b + ab^2$ **r** $a^2 + b^2$ **s** πa^2 **t** $\dfrac{abc}{d}$

u $\dfrac{(ab + bc)}{d}$ **v** $\dfrac{ab}{2}$ **w** $(a + b)^2$ **x** $4a^2 + 2ab$

y $3abc + 2abd + 4bcd + 2acd$ **z** $4\pi r^3 + \pi r^2 h$

2 Indicate whether each of these expressions is consistent (C) or inconsistent (I). Each letter represents a length.

a $a + b$ **b** $a^2 + b$ **c** $a^2 + b^2$ **d** $ab + c$

e $ab + c^2$ **f** $a^3 + bc$ **g** $a^3 + abc$ **h** $a^2 + abc$

i $3a^2 + bc$ **j** $4a^3 b + 2ab^2$ **k** $3abc + 2x^2 y$ **l** $3a(ab + bc)$

m $4a^2 + 3ab$ **n** $\pi a^2(a + b)$ **o** $\pi a^2 + 2r^2$ **p** $\pi r^2 h + \pi rh$

q $\pi r^2(R + r)$

r $\dfrac{(ab + bc)}{d}$

s $a(b^2 + c)$

t $\pi ab + \pi bc$

u $(a + b)(c + d)$

v $\pi(a + b)(a^2 + b^2)$

w $\pi(a^2 + b^2)$

x $\pi^2(a + b)$

y $\pi r^2 h + \pi r^3$

3 Write down whether each of these expressions is consistent (C) or inconsistent (I). When it is consistent, say whether it represents a length (L), an area (A) or a volume (V). Each letter represents a length.

a $\pi a + \pi b$

b $2\pi r^2 + h$

c $\pi r^2 h + 2\pi r^3$

d $2\pi r + h$

e $2\pi rh + 4\pi r^3$

f $\dfrac{\pi r}{6} + \pi a^2$

g $r^2 h + \pi rh^2$

h $\pi r^2(r + h)$

i $\pi r^2 h + 2r^3 + \dfrac{h^2 r}{6}$

j $2\pi r^3 + 3\pi r^2 h$

k $4\pi a + 3x$

l $3\pi r^2 a + 2\pi r$

m $\dfrac{\pi r^2 h}{3} + \dfrac{\pi r^3}{3} + x^3$

4 What power * would make each expression consistent?

a $\pi abc + a^*b$

b $\dfrac{\pi r^* h}{2} + \pi h^* + \dfrac{rh^2}{2}$

c $\pi a(b^* + ac)$

d $a^*b + ab^* + c^3$

5 Kerry has worked out a volume formula as

$$V = \dfrac{(2hD^2 + hd)}{4}$$

It is wrong. Why?

6 The diagram shows a cuboid with sides a, b and c, with a circular hole radius r drilled through it. Three of the following formulae represent

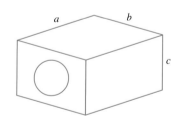

    A: the total length of all straight edges

    B: the total surface area of the six flat sides

    C: the volume.

a Match the correct formula to each of the quantities A, B and C.

    F_1: $4\pi r$ F_2: $4(a + b + c)$

    F_3: $abc - \pi r^2 a$ F_4: $2a(b + c) + 2(bc - \pi r^2)$

b Say what quantity the fourth formula represents.

1 In this question, the letters x, y and z represent lengths. State whether each expression could represent a length, an area or a volume.

a xyz

b $\pi(x + y + z)$

AQA, Question 11, Paper 1 Intermediate, Spec B, Module 5, November 2004

2 In this question, the letters x, y and z represent lengths. State whether each expression could represent a length, an area or a volume.

a $\pi x^2 y$

b $x + y + z$

c $x^2 + y^2$

AQA, Question 12, Paper 1 Intermediate, Spec B, Module 5, November 2003

3 In the formulae given below, the letters p, q and r represent lengths.

a Grant has written down this formula

$$\text{Volume} = \frac{1}{4}\pi r^4$$

Explain how you can tell that Grant has made a mistake.

b Jared has this formula

$$\text{Area} = p^2 + 2q$$

Explain how you can tell that Jared has made a mistake.

AQA, Question 5, Paper 2 Higher, Spec B, Module 5, June 2003

4 The diagram shows a hollow cylinder. It has dimensions x, y and z as marked on the diagram.

For each expression, state whether it represents a length, an area, a volume, or none of these.

a $\pi(x^2 - y^2)z$ **b** $\pi(x + y)(x - y)$ **c** $\pi xy^3 + \pi x^2 z$

AQA, Question 10, Paper 2 Higher, June 2002

5 The diagram shows an ellipse of width $2a$ cm and height $2b$ cm.

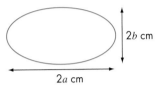

One of the following is a formula for the area of the ellipse.

Formula 1 $\pi(a + b)$

Formula 2 πab

Formula 3 $\pi a^2 b^2$

a What is the correct formula?

a Explain how you can tell that this formula is correct.

AQA, Question 4, Paper 1 Higher, June 2004

6 In the following expressions r, a and b represent lengths. For each expression state whether it represents a length, an area, a volume, or none of these.

a πab **b** $\pi r^2 a + 2\pi r$ **c** $\dfrac{\pi r a^3}{b}$

AQA, Question 11, Paper 2 Higher, June 2000

WORKED EXAM QUESTION

r, a and b are all lengths. Which of the following expressions could be a volume? Write Yes or No for each one. If the expression could not be a volume, give a reason.

$$\frac{ar}{2}(4b + \pi r) \qquad 2a^2 + \pi r^2 \qquad 4a^2 b + rb^3 \qquad 2abr + \frac{\pi a r^2}{2}$$

Solution

1 Yes, $[L^2] \times [L + L] = [L^2] \times [L] = [L^3]$

2 No, $[L^2] + [L^2]$ is an area

3 No, $[L^3] + [L^4]$ inconsistent

4 Yes, $[L^3] + [L^3] = [L^3]$

> Convert the letters in each term. If the term is a product of three letters, it can represent a volume.

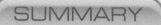

GRADE YOURSELF

D Able to work out a formula for the perimeter, area or volume of simple shapes

C Able to work out a formula for the perimeter, area or volume of complex shapes

C Able to work out whether an expression or formula is dimensionally consistent and whether it represents a length, an area or a volume

What you should know now

- How to work out a formula for the length, area or volume of a shape

- How to recognise whether a formula is 1-D, 2-D or 3-D

- How to recognise when a formula or expression is consistent

Vectors

1 Properties of vectors

2 Vectors in geometry

This chapter will show you ...

- the properties of vectors
- how to add and subtract vectors
- how to use vectors to solve geometrical problems

Visual overview

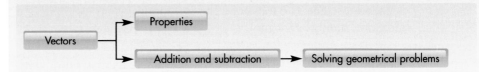

What you should already know

- Vectors are used to describe translations

Quick check

Use column vectors to describe these translations.

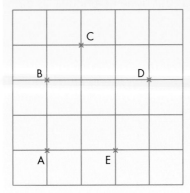

a A to C

b B to D

c C to D

d D to E

Properties of vectors

In this section you will learn how to:
● add and subtract vectors

Key words

direction
magnitude
vector

A **vector** is a quantity which has both **magnitude** and **direction**. It can be represented by a straight line which is drawn in the direction of the vector and whose length represents the magnitude of the vector. Usually, the line includes an arrowhead.

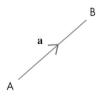

The translation or movement from A to B is represented by the vector **a**.

a is always printed in bold type, but is written as <u>a</u>.

a can also be written as $\overrightarrow{AB}$.

A quantity which is completely described by its magnitude, and has no direction associated with it, is called a scalar. The mass of a bus (10 tonnes) is an example of a scalar. Another example is a linear measure, such as 25.4 mm.

Multiplying a vector by a number (scalar) alters its magnitude (length) but not its direction. For example, the vector 2**a** is twice as long as the vector **a**, but in the same direction.

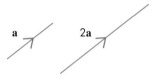

A negative vector, for example **–b**, has the same magnitude as the vector **b**, but is in the opposite direction.

Addition and subtraction of vectors

Take two non-parallel vectors **a** and **b**, then **a** + **b** is defined to be the translation of **a** followed by the translation of **b**. This can easily be seen on a vector diagram.

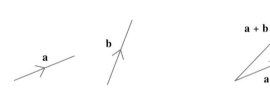

Similarly, **a** – **b** is defined to be the translation of **a** followed by the translation of –**b**.

Look at the parallelogram grid below. **a** and **b** are two independent vectors that form the basis of this grid. It is possible to define the position, with reference to O, of any point on this grid by a vector expressed in terms of **a** and **b**. Such a vector is called a position vector.

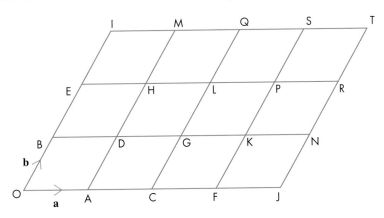

For example, the position vector of K is $\overrightarrow{OK}$ or **k** = 3**a** + **b**, the position vector of E is $\overrightarrow{OE}$ or **e** = 2**b**. The vector $\overrightarrow{HT}$ = 3**a** + **b**, the vector $\overrightarrow{PN}$ = **a** – **b**, the vector $\overrightarrow{MK}$ = 2**a** – 2**b**, and the vector $\overrightarrow{TP}$ = –**a** – **b**.

Note $\overrightarrow{OK}$ and $\overrightarrow{HT}$ are called equal vectors because they have exactly the same length and are in the same direction. $\overrightarrow{MK}$ and $\overrightarrow{PN}$ are parallel vectors but $\overrightarrow{MK}$ is twice the magnitude of $\overrightarrow{PN}$.

EXAMPLE 1

  a Using the grid above, write down the following vectors in terms of **a** and **b**.

   i $\overrightarrow{BH}$ **ii** $\overrightarrow{HP}$ **iii** $\overrightarrow{GT}$

   iv $\overrightarrow{TI}$ **v** $\overrightarrow{FH}$ **vi** $\overrightarrow{BQ}$

  b What is the relationship between the following vectors?

   i $\overrightarrow{BH}$ and $\overrightarrow{GT}$ **ii** $\overrightarrow{BQ}$ and $\overrightarrow{GT}$ **iii** $\overrightarrow{HP}$ and $\overrightarrow{TI}$

  c Show that B, H and Q lie on the same straight line.

  a **i** **a** + **b**   **ii** 2**a**   **iii** 2**a** + 2**b**   **iv** –4**a**   **v** –2**a** + 2**b**   **vi** 2**a** + 2**b**

  b **i** $\overrightarrow{BH}$ and $\overrightarrow{GT}$ are parallel and $\overrightarrow{GT}$ is twice the length of $\overrightarrow{BH}$.

   ii $\overrightarrow{BQ}$ and $\overrightarrow{GT}$ are equal.

   iii $\overrightarrow{HP}$ and $\overrightarrow{TI}$ are in opposite directions and $\overrightarrow{TI}$ is twice the length of $\overrightarrow{HP}$.

  c $\overrightarrow{BH}$ and $\overrightarrow{BQ}$ are parallel and start at the same point B. Therefore, B, H and Q must lie on the same straight line.

EXAMPLE 2

Use a vector diagram to show that   **a** + **b** = **b** + **a**

Take two independent vectors **a** and **b**

a + **b** and **b** + **a** have the same magnitude and direction and are therefore equal.

EXERCISE 18A

1 On this grid, $\overrightarrow{OA}$ is **a** and $\overrightarrow{OB}$ is **b**.

  a Name three other vectors equivalent to **a**.

  b Name three other vectors equivalent to **b**.

  c Name three vectors equivalent to –**a**.

  d Name three vectors equivalent to –**b**.

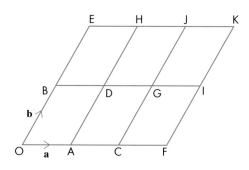

2 Using the same grid as in question **1**, give the following vectors in terms of **a** and **b**.

  a $\overrightarrow{OC}$ **b** $\overrightarrow{OE}$ **c** $\overrightarrow{OD}$ **d** $\overrightarrow{OG}$ **e** $\overrightarrow{OJ}$

  f $\overrightarrow{OH}$ **g** $\overrightarrow{AG}$ **h** $\overrightarrow{AK}$ **i** $\overrightarrow{BK}$ **j** $\overrightarrow{DI}$

  k $\overrightarrow{GJ}$ **l** $\overrightarrow{DK}$

3 **a** What do the answers to parts **2c** and **2g** tell you about the vectors $\overrightarrow{OD}$ and $\overrightarrow{AG}$?

  b On the grid in question **1**, there are three vectors equivalent to $\overrightarrow{OG}$. Name all three.

4 **a** What do the answers to parts **2c** and **2e** tell you about vectors $\overrightarrow{OD}$ and $\overrightarrow{OJ}$?

  b On the grid in question **1**, there is one other vector that is twice the size of $\overrightarrow{OD}$. Which is it?

  c On the grid in question **1**, there are three vectors that are three times the size of $\overrightarrow{OA}$. Name all three.

5 On a copy of this grid, mark on the points C to P to show the following.

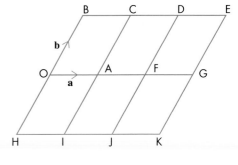

a $\overrightarrow{OC} = 2\mathbf{a} + 3\mathbf{b}$ **b** $\overrightarrow{OD} = 2\mathbf{a} + \mathbf{b}$

c $\overrightarrow{OE} = \mathbf{a} + 2\mathbf{b}$ **d** $\overrightarrow{OF} = 3\mathbf{b}$

e $\overrightarrow{OG} = 4\mathbf{a}$ **f** $\overrightarrow{OH} = 4\mathbf{a} + 2\mathbf{b}$

g $\overrightarrow{OI} = 3\mathbf{a} + 3\mathbf{b}$ **h** $\overrightarrow{OJ} = \mathbf{a} + \mathbf{b}$

i $\overrightarrow{OK} = 2\mathbf{a} + 2\mathbf{b}$ **j** $\overrightarrow{OM} = 2\mathbf{a} + \frac{3}{2}\mathbf{b}$ **k** $\overrightarrow{ON} = \frac{1}{2}\mathbf{a} + 2\mathbf{b}$ **l** $\overrightarrow{OP} = \frac{5}{2}\mathbf{a} + \frac{3}{2}\mathbf{b}$

6 **a** Look at the diagram in question **5**. What can you say about the points O, J, K and I?

b How could you tell this by looking at the vectors for parts **5g**, **5h** and **5i**?

c There is another point on the same straight line as O and D. Which is it?

d Copy and complete these statements and then mark the appropriate points on the diagram you drew for question **5**.

     i The point Q is on the straight line ODH. The vector $\overrightarrow{OQ}$ is given by

$$\overrightarrow{OQ} = \mathbf{a} + \ldots\ldots \mathbf{b}$$

     ii The point R is on the straight line ODH. The vector $\overrightarrow{OR}$ is given by

$$\overrightarrow{OR} = 3\mathbf{a} + \ldots\ldots \mathbf{b}$$

e Copy and complete the following statement.

     Any point on the line ODH has a vector $n\mathbf{a} + \ldots\ldots \mathbf{b}$, where n is any number.

7 On this grid, $\overrightarrow{OA}$ is **a** and $\overrightarrow{OB}$ is **b**.

Give the following vectors in terms of **a** and **b**.

a $\overrightarrow{OH}$ **b** $\overrightarrow{OK}$

c $\overrightarrow{OJ}$ **d** $\overrightarrow{OI}$

e $\overrightarrow{OC}$ **f** $\overrightarrow{CO}$

g $\overrightarrow{AK}$ **h** $\overrightarrow{DI}$

i $\overrightarrow{JE}$ **j** $\overrightarrow{AB}$ **k** $\overrightarrow{CK}$ **l** $\overrightarrow{DK}$

8 **a** What do the answers to parts **7e** and **7f** tell you about the vectors $\overrightarrow{OC}$ and $\overrightarrow{CO}$?

b On the grid in question **7**, there are five other vectors opposite to $\overrightarrow{OC}$. Name at least three.

9 **a** What do the answers to parts **7j** and **7k** tell you about vectors $\overrightarrow{AB}$ and $\overrightarrow{CK}$?

b On the grid in question **7**, there are two vectors that are twice the size of $\overrightarrow{AB}$ and in the opposite direction. Name both of them.

c On the grid in question **7**, there are three vectors that are three times the size of $\overrightarrow{OA}$ and in the opposite direction. Name all three.

A

10 On a copy of this grid, mark on the points C to P to show the following.

a $\overrightarrow{OC} = 2\mathbf{a} - \mathbf{b}$　　　　b $\overrightarrow{OD} = 2\mathbf{a} + \mathbf{b}$

c $\overrightarrow{OE} = \mathbf{a} - 2\mathbf{b}$　　　　d $\overrightarrow{OF} = \mathbf{b} - 2\mathbf{a}$

e $\overrightarrow{OG} = -\mathbf{a}$　　　　　f $\overrightarrow{OH} = -\mathbf{a} - 2\mathbf{b}$

g $\overrightarrow{OI} = 2\mathbf{a} - 2\mathbf{b}$　　　h $\overrightarrow{OJ} = -\mathbf{a} + \mathbf{b}$

i $\overrightarrow{OK} = -\mathbf{a} - \mathbf{b}$　　j $\overrightarrow{OM} = -\mathbf{a} - \frac{3}{2}\mathbf{b}$　　k $\overrightarrow{ON} = -\frac{1}{2}\mathbf{a} - 2\mathbf{b}$　　l $\overrightarrow{OP} = \frac{3}{2}\mathbf{a} - \frac{3}{2}\mathbf{b}$

A*

11 This grid shows the vectors $\overrightarrow{OA} = \mathbf{a}$ and $\overrightarrow{OB} = \mathbf{b}$.

a Name three vectors equivalent to $\mathbf{a} + \mathbf{b}$.

b Name three vectors equivalent to $\mathbf{a} - \mathbf{b}$.

c Name three vectors equivalent to $\mathbf{b} - \mathbf{a}$.

d Name three vectors equivalent to $-\mathbf{a} - \mathbf{b}$.

e Name three vectors equivalent to $2\mathbf{a} - \mathbf{b}$.

f Name three vectors equivalent to $2\mathbf{b} - \mathbf{a}$.

g For each of these, name one equivalent vector.

　i $3\mathbf{a} - \mathbf{b}$　　　　　　ii $2(\mathbf{a} + \mathbf{b})$　　　　　iii $3\mathbf{a} - 2\mathbf{b}$

　iv $3(\mathbf{a} - \mathbf{b})$　　　　　v $3(\mathbf{b} - \mathbf{a})$　　　　vi $3(\mathbf{a} + \mathbf{b})$

　vii $-3(\mathbf{a} + \mathbf{b})$　　　　viii $2\mathbf{a} + \mathbf{b} - 3\mathbf{a} - 2\mathbf{b}$　　ix $2(2\mathbf{a} - \mathbf{b}) - 3(\mathbf{a} - \mathbf{b})$

12 The points P, Q and R lie on a straight line. The vector $\overrightarrow{PQ}$ is $2\mathbf{a} + \mathbf{b}$, where $\mathbf{a}$ and $\mathbf{b}$ are vectors. Which of the following vectors could be the vector $\overrightarrow{PR}$ and which could not be the vector $\overrightarrow{PR}$ (two of each).

a $2\mathbf{a} + 2\mathbf{b}$　　　　b $4\mathbf{a} + 2\mathbf{b}$　　　　c $2\mathbf{a} - \mathbf{b}$　　　　d $-6\mathbf{a} - 3\mathbf{b}$

13 The points P, Q and R lie on a straight line. The vector $\overrightarrow{PQ}$ is $3\mathbf{a} - \mathbf{b}$, where $\mathbf{a}$ and $\mathbf{b}$ are vectors.

a Write down any other vector that could represent $\overrightarrow{PR}$.

b How can you tell from the vector $\overrightarrow{PS}$ that S lies on the same straight line as P, Q and R?

14 Use the diagram in question **11** to prove the following results.

a KB is parallel to IE.

b L, A and F are on a straight line.

15 Use a vector diagram to show that $\mathbf{a} + (\mathbf{b} + \mathbf{c}) = (\mathbf{a} + \mathbf{b}) + \mathbf{c}$.

18.2 Vectors in geometry

In this section you will learn how to:
- use vectors to solve geometrical problems

Key word

vector

Vectors can be used to prove many results in geometry, as the following examples show.

EXAMPLE 3

In the diagram, $\overrightarrow{OA} = \mathbf{a}$, $\overrightarrow{OB} = \mathbf{b}$, and $\overrightarrow{BC} = 1.5\mathbf{a}$. M is the midpoint of BC, N is the midpoint of AC and P is the midpoint of OB.

a Find these vectors in terms of **a** and **b**.

   i $\overrightarrow{AC}$ **ii** $\overrightarrow{OM}$ **iii** $\overrightarrow{BN}$

b Prove that $\overrightarrow{PN}$ is parallel to $\overrightarrow{OA}$.

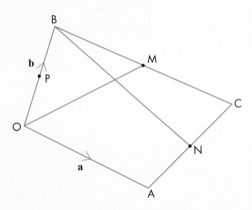

a i You have to get from A to C in terms of vectors that you know.

$$\overrightarrow{AC} = \overrightarrow{AO} + \overrightarrow{OB} + \overrightarrow{BC}$$

Now $\overrightarrow{AO} = -\overrightarrow{OA}$, so you can write

$$\overrightarrow{AC} = -\mathbf{a} + \mathbf{b} + \tfrac{3}{2}\mathbf{a}$$
$$= \tfrac{1}{2}\mathbf{a} + \mathbf{b}$$

Note that the letters "connect up" as we go from A to C, and that the negative of a vector represented by any pair of letters is formed by reversing the letters.

ii In the same way

$$\overrightarrow{OM} = \overrightarrow{OB} + \overrightarrow{BM} = \overrightarrow{OB} + \tfrac{1}{2}\overrightarrow{BC}$$
$$= \mathbf{b} + \tfrac{1}{2}(\tfrac{3}{2}\mathbf{a})$$
$$\overrightarrow{OM} = \tfrac{3}{4}\mathbf{a} + \mathbf{b}$$

iii $\overrightarrow{BN} = \overrightarrow{BC} + \overrightarrow{CN} = \overrightarrow{BC} - \frac{1}{2}\overrightarrow{AC}$

$\qquad = \frac{3}{2}\mathbf{a} - \frac{1}{2}(\frac{1}{2}\mathbf{a} + \mathbf{b})$

$\qquad = \frac{3}{2}\mathbf{a} - \frac{1}{4}\mathbf{a} - \frac{1}{2}\mathbf{b}$

$\qquad = \frac{5}{4}\mathbf{a} - \frac{1}{2}\mathbf{b}$

Note that if you did this as $\overrightarrow{BN} = \overrightarrow{BO} + \overrightarrow{OA} + \overrightarrow{AN}$, you would get the same result.

b $\overrightarrow{PN} = \overrightarrow{PO} + \overrightarrow{OA} + \overrightarrow{AN}$

$\qquad = \frac{1}{2}(-\mathbf{b}) + \mathbf{a} + \frac{1}{2}(\frac{1}{2}\mathbf{a} + \mathbf{b})$

$\qquad = -\frac{1}{2}\mathbf{b} + \mathbf{a} + \frac{1}{4}\mathbf{a} + \frac{1}{2}\mathbf{b}$

$\qquad = \frac{5}{4}\mathbf{a}$

$\overrightarrow{PN}$ is a multiple of **a** only, so must be parallel to $\overrightarrow{OA}$.

EXAMPLE 4

OACB is a parallelogram. $\overrightarrow{OA}$ is represented by the vector **a**. $\overrightarrow{OB}$ is represented by the vector **b**. P is a point $\frac{2}{3}$ the distance from O to C, and M is the midpoint of AC. Show that B, P and M lie on the same straight line.

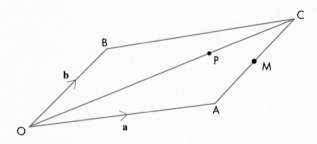

$\overrightarrow{OC} = \overrightarrow{OA} + \overrightarrow{AC} = \mathbf{a} + \mathbf{b}$

$\overrightarrow{OP} = \frac{2}{3}\overrightarrow{OC} = \frac{2}{3}\mathbf{a} + \frac{2}{3}\mathbf{b}$

$\overrightarrow{OM} = \overrightarrow{OA} + \overrightarrow{AM} = \overrightarrow{OA} + \frac{1}{2}\overrightarrow{AC} = \mathbf{a} + \frac{1}{2}\mathbf{b}$

$\overrightarrow{BP} = \overrightarrow{BO} + \overrightarrow{OP} = -\mathbf{b} + \frac{2}{3}\mathbf{a} + \frac{2}{3}\mathbf{b} = \frac{2}{3}\mathbf{a} - \frac{1}{3}\mathbf{b} = \frac{1}{3}(2\mathbf{a} - \mathbf{b})$

$\overrightarrow{BM} = \overrightarrow{BO} + \overrightarrow{OM} = -\mathbf{b} + \mathbf{a} + \frac{1}{2}\mathbf{b} = \mathbf{a} - \frac{1}{2}\mathbf{b} = \frac{1}{2}(2\mathbf{a} - \mathbf{b})$

Therefore, $\overrightarrow{BM}$ is a multiple of $\overrightarrow{BP}$ ($\overrightarrow{BM} = \frac{3}{2}\overrightarrow{BP}$).

Therefore, $\overrightarrow{BP}$ and $\overrightarrow{BM}$ are parallel and as they have a common point, B, they must lie on the same straight line.

EXERCISE 18B

1 The diagram shows the vectors $\overrightarrow{OA}$ = **a** and $\overrightarrow{OB}$ = **b**. M is the midpoint of AB.

   a **i** Work out the vector $\overrightarrow{AB}$.

      ii Work out the vector $\overrightarrow{AM}$.

      iii Explain why $\overrightarrow{OM} = \overrightarrow{OA} + \overrightarrow{AM}$.

      iv Using your answers to parts **ii** and **iii**, work out $\overrightarrow{OM}$ in terms of **a** and **b**.

   b **i** Work out the vector $\overrightarrow{BA}$.

      ii Work out the vector $\overrightarrow{BM}$.

      iii Explain why $\overrightarrow{OM} = \overrightarrow{OB} + \overrightarrow{BM}$.

      iv Using your answers to parts **ii** and **iii**, work out $\overrightarrow{OM}$ in terms of **a** and **b**.

   c Copy the diagram and show on it the vector $\overrightarrow{OC}$ which is equal to **a** + **b**.

   d Describe in geometrical terms the position of M in relation to O, A, B and C.

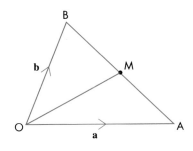

2 The diagram shows the vectors $\overrightarrow{OA}$ = **a** and $\overrightarrow{OC}$ = –**b**. N is the midpoint of AC.

   a **i** Work out the vector $\overrightarrow{AC}$.

      ii Work out the vector $\overrightarrow{AN}$.

      iii Explain why

         $\overrightarrow{ON} = \overrightarrow{OA} + \overrightarrow{AN}$.

      iv Using your answers to parts **ii** and **iii**, work out $\overrightarrow{ON}$ in terms of **a** and **b**.

   b **i** Work out the vector $\overrightarrow{CA}$.

      ii Work out the vector $\overrightarrow{CN}$.

      iii Explain why $\overrightarrow{ON} = \overrightarrow{OC} + \overrightarrow{CN}$.

      iv Using your answers to parts **ii** and **iii**, work out $\overrightarrow{ON}$ in terms of **a** and **b**.

   c Copy the diagram above and show on it the vector $\overrightarrow{OD}$ which is equal to **a** – **b**.

   d Describe in geometrical terms the position of N in relation to O, A, C and D.

3 Copy this diagram and on it draw vectors that represent

   a **a** + **b**   **b** **a** – **b**

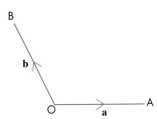

4 The diagram shows the vectors $\overrightarrow{OA} = \mathbf{a}$ and $\overrightarrow{OB} = \mathbf{b}$.

The point C divides the line AB in the ratio 1:2
(i.e. AC is $\frac{1}{3}$ the distance from A to B).

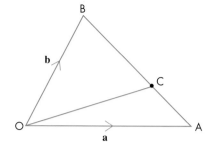

a i Work out the vector $\overrightarrow{AB}$.

ii Work out the vector $\overrightarrow{AC}$.

iii Work out the vector $\overrightarrow{OC}$ in terms of $\mathbf{a}$ and $\mathbf{b}$.

b If C now divides the line AB in the ratio 1:3 (i.e. AC is $\frac{1}{4}$ the distance from A to B), write down the vector that represents $\overrightarrow{OC}$.

5 The diagram shows the vectors $\overrightarrow{OA} = \mathbf{a}$ and $\overrightarrow{OB} = \mathbf{b}$.

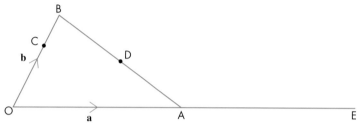

The point C divides OB in the ratio 2:1 (i.e. OC is $\frac{2}{3}$ the distance from O to B). The point E is such that $\overrightarrow{OE} = 2\overrightarrow{OA}$. D is the midpoint of AB.

a Write down (or work out) these vectors in terms of $\mathbf{a}$ and $\mathbf{b}$.

i $\overrightarrow{OC}$ **ii** $\overrightarrow{OD}$ **iii** $\overrightarrow{CO}$

b The vector $\overrightarrow{CD}$ can be written as $\overrightarrow{CD} = \overrightarrow{CO} + \overrightarrow{OD}$. Use this fact to work out $\overrightarrow{CD}$ in terms of $\mathbf{a}$ and $\mathbf{b}$.

c Write down a similar rule to that in part **b** for the vector $\overrightarrow{DE}$. Use this rule to work out $\overrightarrow{DE}$ in terms of $\mathbf{a}$ and $\mathbf{b}$.

d Explain why C, D and E lie on the same straight line.

6 ABCDEF is a regular hexagon. $\overrightarrow{AB}$ is represented by the vector $\mathbf{a}$, and $\overrightarrow{BC}$ by the vector $\mathbf{b}$.

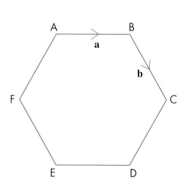

a By means of a diagram, or otherwise, explain why $\overrightarrow{CD} = \mathbf{b} - \mathbf{a}$.

b Express these vectors in terms of $\mathbf{a}$ and $\mathbf{b}$.

i $\overrightarrow{DE}$ **ii** $\overrightarrow{EF}$ **iii** $\overrightarrow{FA}$

c Work out the answer to

$$\overrightarrow{AB} + \overrightarrow{BC} + \overrightarrow{CD} + \overrightarrow{DE} + \overrightarrow{EF} + \overrightarrow{FA}$$

Explain your answer.

d Express these vectors in terms of $\mathbf{a}$ and $\mathbf{b}$.

i $\overrightarrow{AD}$ **ii** $\overrightarrow{BE}$ **iii** $\overrightarrow{CF}$ **iv** $\overrightarrow{AE}$ **v** $\overrightarrow{DF}$

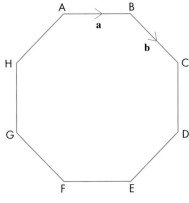

7 ABCDEFGH is a regular octagon. $\overrightarrow{AB}$ is represented by the vector **a**, and $\overrightarrow{BC}$ by the vector **b**.

 a By means of a diagram, or otherwise, explain why $\overrightarrow{CD} = \sqrt{2}\mathbf{b} - \mathbf{a}$.

 b By means of a diagram, or otherwise, explain why $\overrightarrow{DE} = \mathbf{b} - \sqrt{2}\mathbf{a}$.

 c Express the following vectors in terms of **a** and **b**.

  i $\overrightarrow{EF}$ **ii** $\overrightarrow{FG}$ **iii** $\overrightarrow{GH}$ **iv** $\overrightarrow{HA}$

  v $\overrightarrow{HC}$ **vi** $\overrightarrow{AD}$ **vii** $\overrightarrow{BE}$ **viii** $\overrightarrow{BF}$

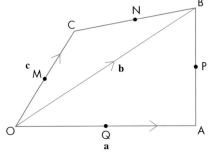

8 In the quadrilateral OABC, M, N, P and Q are the midpoints of the sides as shown. $\overrightarrow{OA}$ is represented by the vector **a**, and $\overrightarrow{OC}$ by the vector **c**. The diagonal $\overrightarrow{OB}$ is represented by the vector **b**.

 a Express these vectors in terms of **a**, **b** and **c**.

  i $\overrightarrow{AB}$ **ii** $\overrightarrow{AP}$ **iii** $\overrightarrow{OP}$

  Give your answers as simply as possible.

 b **i** Express the vector $\overrightarrow{ON}$ in terms of **b** and **c**.

  ii Hence express the vector $\overrightarrow{PN}$ in terms of **a** and **c**.

 c **i** Express the vector $\overrightarrow{QM}$ in terms of **a** and **c**.

  ii What relationship is there between $\overrightarrow{PN}$ and $\overrightarrow{QM}$?

  iii What sort of quadrilateral is PNMQ?

 d Prove that $\overrightarrow{AC} = 2\overrightarrow{QM}$.

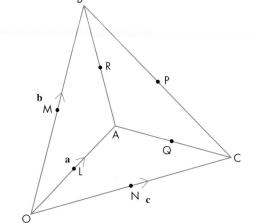

9 L, M, N, P, Q, R are the midpoints of the line segments, as shown. $\overrightarrow{OA} = \mathbf{a}$, $\overrightarrow{OB} = \mathbf{b}$, $\overrightarrow{OC} = \mathbf{c}$.

 a Express these vectors in terms of **a** and **c**.

  i $\overrightarrow{OL}$ **ii** $\overrightarrow{AC}$

  iii $\overrightarrow{OQ}$ **iv** $\overrightarrow{LQ}$

 b Express these vectors in terms of **a** and **b**.

  i $\overrightarrow{LM}$ **ii** $\overrightarrow{QP}$

 c Prove that the quadrilateral LMPQ is a parallelogram.

 d Find two other sets of four points that form parallelograms.

1 In triangle ABC, M lies on BC such that $BM = \frac{3}{4}BC$.
$\overrightarrow{AB} = \mathbf{s}$ and $\overrightarrow{AC} = \mathbf{t}$

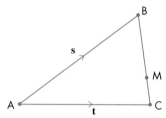

Find $\overrightarrow{AM}$ in terms of $\mathbf{s}$ and $\mathbf{t}$.

Give your answer in its simplest form.

AQA, Question 17, Paper 1 Higher, June 2005

2 In the diagram OACD, OADB and ODEB are parallelograms.
$\overrightarrow{OA} = \mathbf{a}$ and $\overrightarrow{OB} = \mathbf{b}$

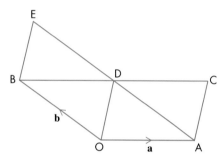

a Express, in terms of $\mathbf{a}$ and $\mathbf{b}$, the following vectors. Give your answers in their simplest form.

  i $\overrightarrow{OD}$
  ii $\overrightarrow{OC}$
  iii $\overrightarrow{AB}$

b The point F is such that OCFE is a parallelogram. Write the vector $\overrightarrow{CF}$ in terms of $\mathbf{a}$ and $\mathbf{b}$.

c What geometrical relationship is there between the points O, D and F? Justify your answer.

AQA, Question 22, Paper 2 Higher, November 2004

3 OABC is a quadrilateral.
$\overrightarrow{OA} = \mathbf{a}$, $\overrightarrow{OB} = \mathbf{b}$, $\overrightarrow{OC} = \mathbf{c}$.

The midpoints of OC, CB, BA, AO are P, Q, R and S, respectively.

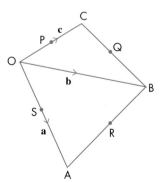

a Find these vectors in terms of $\mathbf{a}$, $\mathbf{b}$ and $\mathbf{c}$.
  i $\overrightarrow{PS}$
  ii $\overrightarrow{QB}$
  iii $\overrightarrow{BR}$

b What type of quadrilateral is PQRS? Give a reason for your answer.

AQA, Question 21, Paper 2 Higher, June 2001

4 In the diagram, $\overrightarrow{OP} = 3\mathbf{a}$, $\overrightarrow{PA} = \mathbf{a}$, $\overrightarrow{OB} = 4\mathbf{b}$ and $\overrightarrow{BR} = 2\mathbf{b}$. Q is the midpoint of AB.

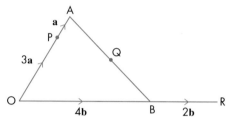

Find, in terms of $\mathbf{a}$ and $\mathbf{b}$, the following vectors.

a $\overrightarrow{AB}$

b $\overrightarrow{PQ}$

c Explain clearly why the points PQR lie on a straight line.

AQA, Question 22, Paper 2 Higher, November 2001

5

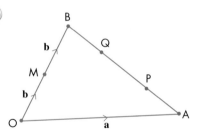

OAB is a triangle where M is the midpoint of OB. P and Q are points on AB such that $AP = PQ = QB$.
$\overrightarrow{OA} = \mathbf{a}$ and $\overrightarrow{OB} = 2\mathbf{b}$

a Find, in terms of $\mathbf{a}$ and $\mathbf{b}$, expressions for these vectors.
  i $\overrightarrow{BA}$
  ii $\overrightarrow{MQ}$
  iii $\overrightarrow{OP}$

b What can you deduce about quadrilateral OMQP? Give a reason for your answer.

AQA, Question 18, Paper 1 Higher, June 2003

6 The diagram shows quadrilateral OABC.
$\overrightarrow{OA} = \mathbf{a}$, $\overrightarrow{OC} = \mathbf{c}$ and $\overrightarrow{OB} = 2\mathbf{a} + \mathbf{c}$

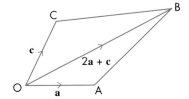

a Find expressions for these vectors in terms of **a** and **c**.
  i $\overrightarrow{AB}$
  ii $\overrightarrow{CB}$

b What kind of quadrilateral is OABC? Give a reason for your answer.

c Point P lies on AC and $AP = \frac{1}{3}AC$.
  i Find an expression for $\overrightarrow{OP}$ in terms of **a** and **c**. Write your answer in its simplest form.
  ii Describe, as fully as possible, the position of P.

AQA, Question 23, Paper 1 Higher, May 2002

7 In the triangle OAB, P is the midpoint of AB, X is the midpoint of OB, $\overrightarrow{OA} = \mathbf{a}$ and $\overrightarrow{OB} = \mathbf{b}$. Q is the point that divides OP in the ratio 2 : 1.

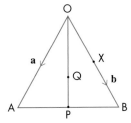

a Express these vectors in terms of **a** and **b**.
  i $\overrightarrow{AB}$ **ii** $\overrightarrow{AP}$
  iii $\overrightarrow{OP}$ **iv** $\overrightarrow{OQ}$
  v $\overrightarrow{AQ}$ **vi** $\overrightarrow{AX}$

b Deduce that $\overrightarrow{AX} = k\overrightarrow{AQ}$, where k is a scalar, and find the value of k.

WORKED EXAM QUESTION

The diagram shows triangle OAB. M is the midpoint of OA. P lies on BM and $BP = \frac{2}{3}BM$. $\overrightarrow{OA} = 2\mathbf{a}$ and $\overrightarrow{OB} = 2\mathbf{b}$

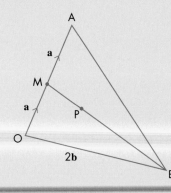

a Find expressions, in terms of **a** and **b**, for **i** $\overrightarrow{BM}$ and **ii** $\overrightarrow{OP}$. Write each answer in its simplest form.

b N is the midpoint of OB. Q lies on AN and $AQ = \frac{2}{3}AN$.
  i Find an expression for $\overrightarrow{OQ}$, in terms of **a** and **b**. Write your answer in its simplest form.
  ii What do your answers for $\overrightarrow{OP}$ and $\overrightarrow{OQ}$ tell you about the points P and Q?

AQA, Question 18, Paper 1 Higher, November 2002

Solution

a i $\overrightarrow{BM} = \mathbf{a} - 2\mathbf{b}$

> Find a route from B to M in terms of known vectors. $\overrightarrow{BM} = \overrightarrow{BO} + \overrightarrow{OM}$

ii $\overrightarrow{OP} = \overrightarrow{OB} + \frac{2}{3}\overrightarrow{BM} = 2\mathbf{b} + \frac{2}{3}\mathbf{a} - \frac{4}{3}\mathbf{b} = \frac{2}{3}\mathbf{a} + \frac{2}{3}\mathbf{b}$

> Find a route from O to P in terms of known vectors. $\overrightarrow{OP} = \overrightarrow{OB} + \overrightarrow{BP}$

b i $\overrightarrow{OQ} = \overrightarrow{OA} + \overrightarrow{AQ} = \overrightarrow{OA} + \frac{2}{3}\overrightarrow{AN}$ with $\overrightarrow{AN} = \mathbf{b} - 2\mathbf{a}$

So $\overrightarrow{OQ} = 2\mathbf{a} + \frac{2}{3}(\mathbf{b} - 2\mathbf{a}) = 2\mathbf{a} + \frac{2}{3}\mathbf{b} - \frac{4}{3}\mathbf{a} = \frac{2}{3}\mathbf{a} + \frac{2}{3}\mathbf{b}$

> Find a route from O to Q in terms of known vectors. $\overrightarrow{OQ} = \overrightarrow{OA} + \overrightarrow{AQ}$

ii $\overrightarrow{OP} = \overrightarrow{OQ}$, so P and Q are the same point

SUMMARY

GRADE YOURSELF

A Able to solve problems using addition and subtraction of vectors

A✳ Able to solve more complex geometrical problems

What you should know now

- How to add and subtract vectors
- How to apply vector methods to solve geometrical problems

Algebra 1

This chapter will show you ...

- how to manipulate basic algebraic expressions by multiplying terms together, expanding brackets and collecting like terms
- how to factorise linear expressions
- how to solve linear equations
- how to solve simultaneous equations
- how to rearrange formulae

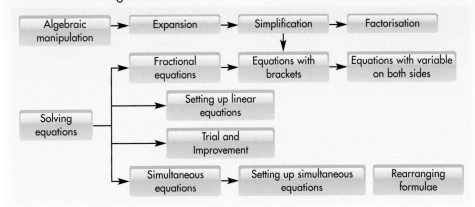

What you should already know

- The basic language of algebra
- How to collect together like terms
- How to multiply together terms such as $2m \times 3m$

Quick check

1 Expand the following.

  a $2(x + 6)$ **b** $4(x - 3)$ **c** $6(2x - 1)$

2 Simplify the following.

  a $4y + 2y - y$ **b** $3x + 2 + x - 5$ **c** $2(x + 1) - 3(x + 2)$

3 Simplify the following.

  a $3 \times 2x$ **b** $4y \times 2y$ **c** $c^2 \times 2c$

4 Solve the following equations

  a $2x + 4 = 6$ **b** $3x - 5 = 4$ **c** $\dfrac{x}{3} + 2 = 5$

  d $\dfrac{x}{2} = 4$ **e** $\dfrac{x}{3} = 8$ **f** $\dfrac{2x}{5} = 6$

Basic algebra

This section will show you how to:

- substitute into, manipulate and simplify algebraic expressions

Key words
bracket
coefficient
like terms
expand
expression
substitute
simplification
variable

Substitution

EXAMPLE 1

Find the value of $3x^2 - 5$ when　**a** $x = 3$,　**b** $x = -4$.

Whenever you **substitute** a number for a **variable** in an **expression** always put the value in a bracket before working it out. This will avoid errors in calculation, especially with negative numbers.

a When $x = 3$,　$3(3)^2 - 5 = 3 \times 9 - 5 = 27 - 5 = 22$

b When $x = -4$,　$3(-4)^2 - 5 = 3 \times 16 - 5 = 48 - 5 = 43$

EXAMPLE 2

Find the value of $L = a^2 - 8b^2$ when $a = -6$ and $b = \frac{1}{2}$.

Substitute for the letters.

$L = (-6)^2 - 8(\frac{1}{2})^2$

$L = 36 - 8 \times \frac{1}{4} = 36 - 2 = 34$

Note: if you do not use brackets and write -6^2, this could be wrongly evaluated as -36.

EXERCISE 19A

1 Find the value of $4b + 3$ when　**a** $b = 2.5$,　**b** $b = -1.5$,　**c** $b = \frac{1}{2}$.

2 Evaluate $\frac{x}{3}$ when　**a** $x = 6$,　**b** $x = 24$,　**c** $x = -30$.

3 Find the value of $\frac{12}{y}$ when　**a** $y = 2$,　**b** $y = 4$,　**c** $y = -6$.

4 Evaluate $3w - 4$ when　**a** $w = -1$,　**b** $w = -2$,　**c** $w = 3.5$.

5 Find the value of $\frac{24}{x}$ when　**a** $x = -5$,　**b** $x = \frac{1}{2}$,　**c** $x = \frac{3}{4}$.

6 Where $P = \dfrac{5w - 4y}{w + y}$, find P when

   a $w = 3$ and $y = 2$,   **b** $w = 6$ and $y = 4$,   **c** $w = 2$ and $y = 3$.

7 Where $A = b^2 + c^2$, find A when

   a $b = 2$ and $c = 3$,   **b** $b = 5$ and $c = 7$,   **c** $b = -1$ and $c = -4$.

8 Where $A = \dfrac{180(n - 2)}{n + 5}$, find A when

   a $n = 7$,   **b** $n = 3$,   **c** $n = -1$.

9 Where $Z = \dfrac{y^2 + 4}{4 + y}$, find Z when

   a $y = 4$,   **b** $y = -6$,   **c** $y = -1.5$.

Expansion

In mathematics, the term "**expand**" usually means "multiply out". For example, expressions such as $3(y + 2)$ and $4y^2(2y + 3)$ can be expanded by multiplying out.

You need to remember that there is an invisible multiplication sign between the outside number and the **bracket**. So that $3(y + 2)$ is really $3 \times (y + 2)$, and $4y^2(2y + 3)$ is really $4y^2 \times (2y + 3)$.

We expand by multiplying *everything inside* the bracket by what is outside the bracket.

So in the case of the two examples above,

$$3(y + 2) = 3 \times (y + 2) = 3 \times y + 3 \times 2 = 3y + 6$$

$$4y^2(2y + 3) = 4y^2 \times (2y + 3) = 4y^2 \times 2y + 4y^2 \times 3 = 8y^3 + 12y^2$$

Look at these next examples of expansion, which show clearly how the term outside the bracket has been multiplied with the terms inside it.

$2(m + 3) = 2m + 6$ $y(y^2 - 4x) = y^3 - 4xy$

$3(2t + 5) = 6t + 15$ $3x^2(4x + 5) = 12x^3 + 15x^2$

$m(p + 7) = mp + 7m$ $-3(2 + 3x) = -6 - 9x$

$x(x - 6) = x^2 - 6x$ $-2x(3 - 4x) = -6x + 8x^2$

$4t(t^3 + 2) = 4t^4 + 8t$ $3t(2 + 5t - p) = 6t + 15t^2 - 3pt$

Note: the signs change when a negative quantity is outside the bracket. For example,

$a(b + c) = ab + ac$ $a(b - c) = ab - ac$

$-a(b + c) = -ab - ac$ $-a(b - c) = -ab + ac$

$-(a - b) = -a + b$ $-(a + b - c) = -a - b + c$

EXERCISE 19B

Expand these expressions.

1 $2(3 + m)$ **2** $5(2 + l)$ **3** $3(4 - y)$ **4** $4(5 + 2k)$

5 $3(2 - 4f)$ **6** $2(5 - 3w)$ **7** $5(2k + 3m)$ **8** $4(3d - 2n)$

9 $t(t + 3)$ **10** $k(k - 3)$ **11** $4t(t - 1)$ **12** $2k(4 - k)$

13 $4g(2g + 5)$ **14** $5h(3h - 2)$ **15** $y(y^2 + 5)$ **16** $h(h^3 + 7)$

17 $k(k^2 - 5)$ **18** $3t(t^2 + 4)$ **19** $3d(5d^2 - d^3)$ **20** $3w(2w^2 + t)$

21 $5a(3a^2 - 2b)$ **22** $3p(4p^3 - 5m)$ **23** $4h^2(3h + 2g)$ **24** $2m^2(4m + m^2)$

Simplification

Simplification is the process whereby an expression is written down as simply as possible, any **like terms** being combined. Like terms are terms which have the same letter(s) raised to the same power and can differ only in their numerical **coefficients** (numbers in front). For example,

m, $3m$, $4m$, $-m$ and $76m$ are all like terms in m

t^2, $4t^2$, $7t^2$, $-t^2$, $-3t^2$ and $98t^2$ are all like terms in t^2

pt, $5tp$, $-2pt$, $7pt$, $-3tp$ and $103pt$ are all like terms in pt

Note also that all the terms in tp are also like terms to all the terms in pt.

In simplifying an expression, only like terms can be added or subtracted. For example,

$4m + 3m = 7m$	$3y + 4y + 3 = 7y + 3$	$4h - h = 3h$
$2t^2 + 5t^2 = 7t^2$	$2m + 6 + 3m = 5m + 6$	$7t + 8 - 2t = 5t + 8$
$3ab + 2ba = 5ab$	$5k - 2k = 3k$	$10g - 4 - 3g = 7g - 4$

Expand and simplify

When two brackets are expanded there are often like terms that can be collected together. Algebraic expressions should always be simplified as much as possible.

EXAMPLE 3

$$3(4 + m) + 2(5 + 2m) = 12 + 3m + 10 + 4m = 22 + 7m$$

EXAMPLE 4

$$3t(5t + 4) - 2t(3t - 5) = 15t^2 + 12t - 6t^2 + 10t = 9t^2 + 22t$$

EXERCISE 19C

1 Simplify these expressions.

a $4t + 3t$ **b** $3d + 2d + 4d$ **c** $5e - 2e$ **d** $3t - t$

e $2t^2 + 3t^2$ **f** $6y^2 - 2y^2$ **g** $3ab + 2ab$ **h** $7a^2d - 4a^2d$

2 Expand and simplify.

a $3(4 + t) + 2(5 + t)$ **b** $5(3 + 2k) + 3(2 + 3k)$

c $4(3 + 2f) + 2(5 - 3f)$ **d** $5(1 + 3g) + 3(3 - 4g)$

3 Expand and simplify.

a $4(3 + 2h) - 2(5 + 3h)$ **b** $5(3g + 4) - 3(2g + 5)$

c $5(5k + 2) - 2(4k - 3)$ **d** $4(4e + 3) - 2(5e - 4)$

> **HINTS AND TIPS**
>
> Be careful with minus signs. For example
> $-2(5e - 4) = -10e + 8$

4 Expand and simplify.

a $m(4 + p) + p(3 + m)$ **b** $k(3 + 2h) + h(4 + 3k)$

c $4r(3 + 4p) + 3p(8 - r)$ **d** $5k(3m + 4) - 2m(3 - 2k)$

5 Expand and simplify.

a $t(3t + 4) + 3t(3 + 2t)$ **b** $2y(3 + 4y) + y(5y - 1)$

c $4e(3e - 5) - 2e(e - 7)$ **d** $3k(2k + p) - 2k(3p - 4k)$

6 Expand and simplify.

a $4a(2b + 3c) + 3b(3a + 2c)$ **b** $3y(4w + 2t) + 2w(3y - 4t)$

c $5m(2n - 3p) - 2n(3p - 2m)$ **d** $2r(3r + r^2) - 3r^2(4 - 2r)$

19.2 # Factorisation

This section will show you how to:
- factorise an algebraic expression

Key words
common factor
factorisation

Factorisation is the opposite of expansion. It puts an expression back into the brackets it may have come from.

In factorisation, we have to look for the **common factors** in *every* term of the expression.

EXAMPLE 5

Factorise. **a** $6t + 9m$ **b** $6my + 4py$ **c** $5k^2 - 25k$ **d** $10a^2b - 15ab^2$

a First look at the numerical coefficients 6 and 9. These have a common factor of 3. Then look at the letters, t and m. These do not have any common factors as they do not appear in both terms. The expression can be thought of as $3 \times 2t + 3 \times 3m$, which gives the factorisation

$$6t + 9m = 3(2t + 3m)$$

Note: you can always check a factorisation by expanding the answer.

b First look at the numbers, these have a common factor of 2. m and p do not occur in both terms but y does, and is a common factor, so the factorisation is

$$6my + 4py = 2y(3m + 2p)$$

c 5 is a common factor of 5 and 25 and k is a common factor of k^2 and k.

$$5k^2 - 25k = 5k(k - 5)$$

d 5 is a common factor of 10 and 15, a is a common factor of a^2 and a, b is a common factor of b and b^2.

$$10a^2b - 15ab^2 = 5ab(2a - 3b)$$

Note: if you multiply out each answer, you will get the expressions you started with.

EXERCISE 19D

Factorise the following expressions.

1 $6m + 12t$ **2** $9t + 3p$ **3** $8m + 12k$

4 $4r + 8t$ **5** $mn + 3m$ **6** $5g^2 + 3g$

7 $4w - 6t$ **8** $3y^2 + 2y$ **9** $4t^2 - 3t$

10 $3m^2 - 3mp$ **11** $6p^2 + 9pt$ **12** $8pt + 6mp$

13 $8ab - 4bc$ **14** $5b^2c - 10bc$ **15** $8abc + 6bed$

16 $4a^2 + 6a + 8$

17 $6ab + 9bc + 3bd$ **18** $5t^2 + 4t + at$ **19** $6mt^2 - 3mt + 9m^2t$

20 $8ab^2 + 2ab - 4a^2b$ **21** $10pt^2 + 15pt + 5p^2t$

22 Factorise the following expressions where possible. List those which do not factorise.

a $7m - 6t$ **b** $5m + 2mp$ **c** $t^2 - 7t$

d $8pt + 5ab$ **e** $4m^2 - 6mp$ **f** $a^2 + b$

g $4a^2 - 5ab$ **h** $3ab + 4cd$ **i** $5ab - 3b^2c$

Solving linear equations

In this section you will learn how to:

- solve equations in which the variable appears as part of the numerator of a fraction
- solve equations where you have to expand brackets first
- solve equations where the variable (the letter) appears on both sides of the equals sign
- set up equations from given information, and then solve them

Key words

brackets
do the same to both sides
equation
rearrange
solution
solve

Fractional equations

EXAMPLE 6

Solve this equation.

$$\frac{x}{3} + 1 = 5$$

First subtract 1 from both sides:

$$\frac{x}{3} = 4$$

Now multiply both sides by 3:

$$x = 12$$

EXAMPLE 7

Solve this equation.

$$\frac{x-2}{5} = 3$$

First multiply both sides by 5:

$$x - 2 = 15$$

Now add 2 to both sides:

$$x = 17$$

EXAMPLE 8

Solve this equation.

$$\frac{3x}{4} - 3 = 1$$

First add 3 to both sides:

$$\frac{3x}{4} = 4$$

Now multiply both sides by 4:

$$3x = 16$$

Now divide both sides by 3:

$$x = \frac{16}{3} = 5\frac{1}{3}$$

EXERCISE 19E

Solve these equations.

1 $\dfrac{f}{5} + 2 = 8$

2 $\dfrac{w}{3} - 5 = 2$

3 $\dfrac{x}{8} + 3 = 12$

4 $\dfrac{5t}{4} + 3 = 18$

5 $\dfrac{3y}{2} - 1 = 8$

6 $\dfrac{2x}{3} + 5 = 12$

7 $\dfrac{t}{5} + 3 = 1$

8 $\dfrac{x + 3}{2} = 5$

9 $\dfrac{t - 5}{2} = 3$

10 $\dfrac{x + 10}{2} = 3$

11 $\dfrac{2x + 1}{3} = 5$

12 $\dfrac{5y - 2}{4} = 3$

13 $\dfrac{6y + 3}{9} = 1$

14 $\dfrac{2x - 3}{5} = 4$

15 $\dfrac{5t + 3}{4} = 1$

Brackets

When we have an equation which contains **brackets**, we first must multiply out the brackets and then solve the resulting equation.

EXAMPLE 9

Solve $5(x + 3) = 25$.

First multiply out the bracket to get:

$5x + 15 = 25$

Rearrange: $\qquad 5x = 25 - 15 = 10$

Divide by 5: $\qquad \dfrac{5x}{5} = \dfrac{10}{5}$

$\qquad\qquad\qquad x = 2$

EXAMPLE 10

Solve $3(2x - 7) = 15$.

Multiply out the bracket to get:

$6x - 21 = 15$

Add 21 to both sides: $\qquad 6x = 36$

Divide both sides by 6: $\qquad x = 6$

EXERCISE 19F

Solve each of the following equations. Some of the answers may be decimals or negative numbers. Remember to check that each answer works for its original equation. Use your calculator if necessary.

1 $2(x + 5) = 16$

2 $5(x - 3) = 20$

3 $3(t + 1) = 18$

4 $4(2x + 5) = 44$

5 $2(3y - 5) = 14$

6 $5(4x + 3) = 135$

7 $4(3t - 2) = 88$

8 $6(2t + 5) = 42$

9 $2(3x + 1) = 11$

10 $4(5y - 2) = 42$

11 $6(3k + 5) = 39$

12 $5(2x + 3) = 27$

13 $9(3x - 5) = 9$

14 $2(x + 5) = 6$

15 $5(x - 4) = -25$

16 $3(t + 7) = 15$

17 $2(3x + 11) = 10$

18 $4(5t + 8) = 12$

> **HINTS AND TIPS**
>
> Once the brackets have been expanded the equations become straightforward. Remember to multiply *everything* inside the bracket with what is outside.

Equations with the variable on both sides

When a letter (or variable) appears on both sides of an equation, it is best to use the "**do the same to both sides**" method of **solution**, and collect all the terms containing the letter on the left-hand side of the equation. But when there are more of the letter on the right-hand side, it is easier to turn the equation round. When an equation contains brackets, they must be multiplied out first.

EXAMPLE 11

Solve $5x + 4 = 3x + 10$.

There are more xs on the left-hand side, so leave the equation as it is.

Subtract $3x$ from both sides: $\quad 2x + 4 = 10$

Subtract 4 from both sides: $\quad 2x = 6$

Divide both sides by 2: $\quad x = 3$

EXAMPLE 12

Solve $2x + 3 = 6x - 5$.

There are more xs on the right-hand side, so turn round the equation.

$$6x - 5 = 2x + 3$$

Subtract $2x$ from both sides: $\quad 4x - 5 = 3$

Add 5 to both sides: $\quad 4x = 8$

Divide both sides by 4: $\quad x = 2$

EXAMPLE 13

Solve this equation. $\qquad$ $3(2x + 5) + x = 2(2 - x) + 2$

Multiply out both brackets: $\qquad$ $6x + 15 + x = 4 - 2x + 2$

Simplify both sides: $\qquad$ $7x + 15 = 6 - 2x$

There are more *x*s on the left-hand side, so leave the equation as it is.

Add $2x$ to both sides: $\qquad$ $9x + 15 = 6$

Subtract 15 from both sides: $\qquad$ $9x = -9$

Divide both sides by 9: $\qquad$ $x = -1$

EXERCISE 19G

Solve each of the following equations.

1 $2x + 3 = x + 5$

2 $5y + 4 = 3y + 6$

3 $4a - 3 = 3a + 4$

4 $5t + 3 = 2t + 15$

5 $7p - 5 = 3p + 3$

6 $6k + 5 = 2k + 1$

7 $4m + 1 = m + 10$

8 $8s - 1 = 6s - 5$

9 $2(d + 3) = d + 12$

10 $5(x - 2) = 3(x + 4)$

11 $3(2y + 3) = 5(2y + 1)$

12 $3(h - 6) = 2(5 - 2h)$

13 $4(3b - 1) + 6 = 5(2b + 4)$

14 $2(5c + 2) - 2c = 3(2c + 3) + 7$

> **HINTS AND TIPS**
>
> Remember the rule "change sides, change signs".
> Show all your working on this type of question.
> **Rearrange** before you simplify. If you try to rearrange and simplify at the same time you will probably get it wrong.

Setting up linear equations

Equations are used to represent situations, so that we can solve real-life problems.

EXAMPLE 14

A milkman sets off from the dairy with eight crates of milk, each containing *b* bottles. He delivers 92 bottles to a large factory and finds that he has exactly 100 bottles left on his milk float. How many bottles were in each crate?

The equation is: $\qquad$ $8b - 92 = 100$

$\qquad\qquad\qquad$ $8b = 192$ $\qquad$ (Add 92 to both sides)

$\qquad\qquad\qquad$ $b = 24$ $\qquad$ (Divide both sides by 8)

Checking the answer gives: $\quad$ $8 \times 24 - 92 = 192 - 92 = 100$

which is correct.

Mod 5

EXAMPLE 15

The rectangle shown has a perimeter of 40 cm.

Find the value of x.

The perimeter of the rectangle is:

$$3x + 1 + x + 3 + 3x + 1 + x + 3 = 40$$

This simplifies to: $\qquad 8x + 8 = 40$

Subtract 8 $\qquad\qquad 8x = 32$

Divide by 8 $\qquad\qquad x = 4$

Checking the answer gives:

$$3x + 1 = 3 \times 4 + 1 = 13$$

$$x + 3 = 4 + 3 = 7$$

$$\text{perimeter} = 13 + 7 + 13 + 7$$

$$= 40$$

which is correct.

Rectangle labelled $3x + 1$ along the top and $x + 3$ on the right side.

EXERCISE 19H

Set up an equation to represent each situation described below. Then solve the equation. Do not forget to check each answer.

1 A man buys a daily paper from Monday to Saturday for d pence. On Sunday he buys the *Observer* for £1. His weekly paper bill is £4.30.

How much is his daily paper?

2 The diagram shows a rectangle.

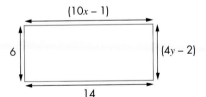

a What is the value of x?

b What is the value of y?

> **HINTS AND TIPS**
>
> Use the letter x for the variable unless you are given a letter to use. Once the equation is set up, solve it by the methods above.

3 In this rectangle, the length is 3 centimetres more than the width. The perimeter is 12 cm.

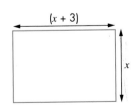

a What is the value of x?

b What is the area of the rectangle?

4 Mary has two bags of sweets, each of which contains the same number of sweets. She eats four sweets. She then finds that she has 30 sweets left. How many sweets were in each bag to start with?

5 A boy is Y years old. His father is 25 years older than he is. The sum of their ages is 31. How old is the boy?

6 Another boy is X years old. His sister is twice as old as he is. The sum of their ages is 27. How old is the boy?

7 The diagram shows a square.
Find x if the perimeter is 44 cm.

$(4x - 1)$

8 Max thought of a number. He then multiplied his number by 3. He added 4 to the answer. He then doubled that answer to get a final value of 38. What number did he start with?

19.4 Trial and improvement

In this section you will learn how to:

- estimate the answer to some equations that do not have exact solutions, using the method of trial and improvement

Key words

comment
decimal place
guess
trial and
    improvement

Certain equations cannot be solved exactly. However, a close enough solution to such an equation can be found by the **trial-and-improvement** method (sometimes wrongly called the trial-and-error method).

The idea is to keep trying different values in the equation which will take it closer and closer to its "true" solution. This step-by-step process is continued until a value is found which gives a solution that is close enough to the accuracy required.

The trial-and-improvement method is the way in which computers are programmed to solve equations.

EXAMPLE 16

Find a solution to the equation $x^3 + x = 105$, giving the solution to 1 **decimal place**.

The best way to do this is to set up a table to show working. There will be three columns: **guess** (the trial); the equation we are solving; and a **comment** whether the value of the guess is too high or too low.

Step 1 We must find the two consecutive whole numbers between which x lies. We do this by intelligent guessing.

Try $x = 5$: $125 + 5 = 130$ Too high – next trial needs to be smaller

Try $x = 4$: $64 + 4 = 68$ Too low

So we now know that a solution lies between $x = 4$ and $x = 5$.

Step 2 We must find the two consecutive one-decimal place numbers between which x lies. Try 4.5, which is halfway between 4 and 5.

This gives $91.125 + 4.5 = 95.625$ Too small

So we attempt to improve this by trying 4.6.

This gives $97.336 + 4.6 = 101.936$ Still too small

Try 4.7, which gives 108.523.   This is too high, so we know the solution is between 4.6 and 4.7.

It looks as though 4.6 is closer but there is a very important final step. Never assume that the one-decimal place number that gives the closest value to a solution is the answer.

Step 3 Now try the value that is halfway between the two one-decimal place values. In this case 4.65.

This gives 105.194 625   Too high

This means that an actual solution is between 4.60 and 4.65.

The diagram and table summarise our results.

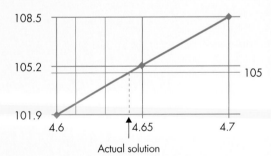

Guess	$x^3 + x$	Comment
4	68	Too low
5	130	Too high
4.5	95.625	Too low
4.6	101.936	Too low
4.7	108.523	Too high
4.65	105.194625	Too high

The approximate answer is $x = 4.6$ to 1 decimal place.

EXERCISE 19I

1 For each of the following equations, find a pair of consecutive *whole numbers*, between which a solution lies.

a $x^2 + x = 24$ **b** $x^3 + 2x = 80$ **c** $x^3 - x = 20$

2 Copy and complete the table to find an approximate solution, using trial and improvement, to this equation.

$$x^3 + 2x = 50$$

Give your answer to 1 decimal place.

Guess	$x^3 + 2x$	Comment
3	33	Too low
4	72	Too high

3 Copy and complete the table to find an approximate solution, using trial and improvement, to this equation.

$$x^3 - 3x = 40$$

Give your answer to 1 decimal place.

Guess	$x^3 - 3x$	Comment
4	52	Too high

4 Use trial and improvement to find an approximate solution to this equation.

$$2x^3 + x = 35$$

Give your answer to 1 decimal place.

You are given that the solution lies between 2 and 3.

> **HINTS AND TIPS**
>
> Set up a table to show your working.
> This makes it easier for you to show your method, and for the examiner to mark.

5 Use trial and improvement to find an exact solution to this equation.

$$4x^2 + 2x = 12$$

Do not use a calculator.

6 Find a solution to each of the following equations to 1 decimal place.

a $2x^3 + 3x = 35$ **b** $3x^3 - 4x = 52$ **c** $2x^3 + 5x = 79$

7 A rectangle has an area of 100 cm². Its length is 5 cm longer than its width.

a Show that, if x is the width then $x^2 + 5x = 100$

b Find, correct to 1 decimal place, the dimensions of the rectangle.

8 Use trial and improvement to find a solution to the equation $x^2 + x = 30$.

> I want to find a number that when you square it and add it to itself the answer is 30.

Simultaneous equations

In this section you will learn how to:
- solve simultaneous linear equations in two variables

Key words
balance
check
coefficient
eliminate
simultaneous
　equations
substitute
variable

A pair of **simultaneous equations** is exactly that – two equations (usually linear) for which we want the *same* solution, and which we therefore *solve together*. For example,

$x + y = 10$ has many solutions:

$x = 2, y = 8$ 　　 $x = 4, y = 6$ 　　 $x = 5, y = 5$ ...

and $2x + y = 14$ has many solutions:

$x = 2, y = 10$ 　　 $x = 3, y = 8$ 　　 $x = 4, y = 6$ ...

But only *one* solution, $x = 4$ and $y = 6$, satisfies *both* equations at the *same time*.

Elimination method

Here, we solve simultaneous equations by the *elimination method*. There are six steps in this method. Step 1 is to **balance** the **coefficients** of one of the **variables**. Step 2 is to **eliminate** this variable by adding or subtracting the equations. Step 3 is to solve the resulting linear equation in the other variable. Step 4 is to **substitute** the value found back into one of the previous equations. Step 5 is to solve the resulting equation. Step 6 is to **check** that the two values found satisfy the original equations.

EXAMPLE 17

Solve the equations $6x + y = 15$ and $4x + y = 11$.

The equations should be labelled so that the method can be clearly explained.

$6x + y = 15$ 　　　　　　　　 (1)

$4x + y = 11$ 　　　　　　　　 (2)

Step 1: Since the y-term in both equations has the same coefficient there is no need to balance them.

EXAMPLE 17 (contd)

Step 2: Subtract one equation from the other. (Equation (1) minus equation (2) will give positive values.)

$$(1) - (2) \qquad\qquad 2x = 4$$

Step 3: Solve this equation: $\qquad x = 2$

Step 4: Substitute $x = 2$ into one of the original equations. (Usually the one with smallest numbers involved.)

So substitute into: $\qquad\qquad 4x + y = 11$

which gives: $\qquad\qquad 8 + y = 11$

Step 5: Solve this equation: $\qquad y = 3$

Step 6: Test our solution in the original equations. So substitute $x = 2$ and $y = 3$ into $6x + y$, which gives $12 + 3 = 15$ and into $4x + y$, which gives $8 + 3 = 11$. These are correct, so we can confidently say the solution is $x = 2$ and $y = 3$.

EXAMPLE 18

Solve these equations. $\qquad 5x + y = 22 \qquad\qquad (1)$

$$2x - y = 6 \qquad\qquad (2)$$

Step 1: Both equations have the same y-coefficient but with *different* signs so there is no need to balance them.

Step 2: As the signs are different we *add* the two equations, to eliminate the y-terms.

$$(1) + (2) \qquad\qquad 7x = 28$$

Step 3: Solve this equation: $\qquad x = 4$

Step 4: Substitute $x = 4$ into one of the original equations, $5x + y = 22$,

which gives: $\qquad\qquad 20 + y = 22$

Step 5: Solve this equation: $\qquad y = 2$

Step 6: Test our solution by putting $x = 4$ and $y = 2$ into the original equations, $2x - y$, which gives $8 - 2 = 6$ and $5x + y$ which gives $20 + 2 = 22$. These are correct, so our solution is $x = 4$ and $y = 2$.

Substitution method

This is an alternative method (which is covered again on page 542). Which method you use depends very much on the coefficients of the variables and the way that the equations are written in the first place. There are five steps in the substitute method. Step 1 is to rearrange one of the equations into the form $y = \ldots$ or $x = \ldots$. Step 2 is to substitute the right hand side of this equation into the other equation in place of the variable on the left hand side. Step 3 is to expand and solve this equation. Step 4 is to substitute the value into the $y = \ldots$ or $x = \ldots$ equation. Step 5 is to check that the values work in both original equations.

EXAMPLE 19

Solve the simultaneous equations $y = 2x + 3$, $3x + 4y = 1$.

Because the first equation is in the form $y = \ldots$ it suggests that the substitution method should be used.

Equations should still be labelled to help with explaining the method

$$y = 2x + 3 \qquad\qquad (1)$$
$$3x + 4y = 1 \qquad\qquad (2)$$

Step 1: As equation (1) is in the form $y = \ldots$ there is no need to rearrange an equation.

Step 2: Substitute the right hand side of equation (1) into equation (2) for the variable y.

$$3x + 4(2x + 3) = 1$$

Step 3: Expand and solve the equation. $3x + 8x + 12 = 1$, $11x = -11$, $x = -1$

Step 4: Substitute $x = -1$ into $y = 2x + 3$: $y = -2 + 3 = 1$

Step 5: Test the values in $y = 2x + 3$ which gives $1 = -2 + 3$ and $3x + 4y = 1$, which gives $-3 + 4 = 1$. These are correct so the solution is $x = -1$ and $y = 1$.

EXERCISE 19J

In this exercise the coefficients of one of the variables in questions **1** to **9** are the same so there is no need to balance them. Subtract the equations when the identical terms have the same sign. Add the equations when the identical terms have opposite signs. In questions **10** to **12** use the substitution method.

Solve these simultaneous equations.

1 $4x + y = 17$

$\quad\; 2x + y = 9$

2 $5x + 2y = 13$

$\quad\; x + 2y = 9$

3 $2x + y = 7$

$\quad\; 5x - y = 14$

4 $3x + 2y = 11$

$\quad\; 2x - 2y = 14$

5 $3x - 4y = 17$

$\quad\; x - 4y = 3$

6 $3x + 2y = 16$

$\quad\; x - 2y = 4$

7 $x + 3y = 9$

$\quad\; x + y = 6$

8 $2x + 5y = 16$

$\quad\; 2x + 3y = 8$

9 $3x - y = 9$

$\quad\; 5x + y = 11$

10 $2x + 5y = 37$

$\quad\;\; y = 11 - 2x$

11 $4x - 3y = 7$

$\quad\;\; x = 13 - 3y$

12 $4x - y = 17$

$\quad\;\; x = 2 + y$

You were able to solve all the pairs of equations in Exercise 19J simply by adding or subtracting the equations in each pair, or just by substituting without rearranging. This does not always happen. The next examples show you what to do when there are no identical terms to begin with, or when you need to rearrange.

EXAMPLE 20

Solve these equations.

$$3x + 2y = 18 \qquad (1)$$
$$2x - y = 5 \qquad (2)$$

Step 1: Multiply equation (2) by 2. There are other ways to balance the coefficients but this is the easiest and leads to less work later. You will get used to which will be the best way to balance the coefficients.

$$2 \times (2) \qquad 4x - 2y = 10 \qquad (3)$$

Label this equation as number (3).

Be careful to multiply every term and not just the y term, it sometimes helps to write:

$$2 \times (2x - y = 5) \quad \Rightarrow \quad 4x - 2y = 10 \qquad (3)$$

Step 2: As the signs of the y-terms are opposite, add the equations.

$$(1) + (3) \qquad 7x = 28$$

Be careful to add the correct equations. This is why labelling them is useful.

Step 3: Solve this equation: $\qquad x = 4$

Step 4: Substitute $x = 4$ into any equation, say $2x - y = 5 \quad \Rightarrow \quad 8 - y = 5$

Step 5: Solve this equation: $\qquad y = 3$

Step 6: Check: (1), $3 \times 4 + 2 \times 3 = 18$ and (2), $2 \times 4 - 3 = 5$, which are correct so the solution is $x = 4$ and $y = 3$.

EXAMPLE 21

Solve the simultaneous equations $3x + y = 5$ and $5x - 2y = 12$ using the substitution method.

Looking at the equations there is only one that could be sensibly rearranged without involving fractions.

Step 1: Rearrange $\qquad 3x + y = 5$ to get $y = 5 - 3x \qquad (1)$

Step 2: Substitute $\qquad y = 5 - 3x$ into $5x - 2y = 12 \qquad (2)$

$$5x - 2(5 - 3x) = 12$$

Step 3: Expand and solve $\qquad 5x - 10 + 6x = 12 \quad \Rightarrow \quad 11x = 22 \quad \Rightarrow \quad x = 2$

Step 4: Substitute into equation (1): $y = 5 - 3 \times 2 = 5 - 6 = -1$

Step 5: Check: (1), $3 \times 2 + -1 = 5$ and (2), $5 \times 2 - 2 \times -1 = 10 + 2 = 12$, which are correct so the solution is $x = 2$ and $y = -1$.

EXERCISE 19K

Solve questions **1** to **3** by the substitution method and the rest by first changing one of the equations in each pair to obtain identical terms, and then adding or subtracting the equations to eliminate those terms.

1 $5x + 2y = 4$

$4x - y = 11$

2 $4x + 3y = 37$

$2x + y = 17$

3 $x + 3y = 7$

$2x - y = 7$

4 $2x + 3y = 19$

$6x + 2y = 22$

5 $5x - 2y = 26$

$3x - y = 15$

6 $10x - y = 3$

$3x + 2y = 17$

7 $3x + 5y = 15$

$x + 3y = 7$

8 $3x + 4y = 7$

$4x + 2y = 1$

9 $5x - 2y = 24$

$3x + y = 21$

10 $5x - 2y = 4$

$3x - 6y = 6$

11 $2x + 3y = 13$

$4x + 7y = 31$

12 $3x - 2y = 3$

$5x + 6y = 12$

There are also cases where *both* equations have to be changed to obtain identical terms. The next example shows you how this is done.

Note the substitution method is not suitable for these type of equations as you end up with fractional terms.

EXAMPLE 22

Solve these equations.

$4x + 3y = 27$ (1)

$5x - 2y = 5$ (2)

Both equations have to be changed to obtain identical terms in either *x* or *y*. However, we can see that if we make the *y*-coefficients the same, we will add the equations. This is always safer than subtraction, so this is obviously the better choice. We do this by multiplying the first equation by 2 (the *y*-coefficient of the other equation) and the second equation by 3 (the *y*-coefficient of the other equation).

Step 1:   (1) × 2 or 2 × $(4x + 3y = 27)$ $\Rightarrow$ $8x + 6y = 54$ (3)

(2) × 3 or 3 × $(5x - 2y = 5)$ $\Rightarrow$ $15x - 6y = 15$ (4)

Label the new equations (3) and (4).

Step 2: Eliminate one of the variables: (3) + (4) $23x = 69$

Step 3: Solve the equation: $x = 3$

Step 4: Substitute into equation (1): $12 + 3y = 27$

Step 5: Solve the equation: $y = 5$

Step 6: Check: (1), $4 \times 3 + 3 \times 5 = 12 + 15 = 27$, and (2), $5 \times 3 - 2 \times 5 = 15 - 10 = 5$, which are correct so the solution is $x = 3$ and $y = 5$.

EXERCISE 19L

Solve the following simultaneous equations.

1 $2x + 5y = 15$

$3x - 2y = 13$

2 $2x + 3y = 30$

$5x + 7y = 71$

3 $2x - 3y = 15$

$5x + 7y = 52$

4 $3x - 2y = 15$

$2x - 3y = 5$

5 $5x - 3y = 14$

$4x - 5y = 6$

6 $3x + 2y = 28$

$2x + 7y = 47$

7 $2x + y = 4$

$x - y = 5$

8 $5x + 2y = 11$

$3x + 4y = 8$

9 $x - 2y = 4$

$3x - y = -3$

10 $3x + 2y = 2$

$2x + 6y = 13$

11 $6x + 2y = 14$

$3x - 5y = 10$

12 $2x + 4y = 15$

$x + 5y = 21$

13 $3x - y = 5$

$x + 3y = -20$

14 $3x - 4y = 4.5$

$2x + 2y = 10$

15 $x - 5y = 15$

$3x - 7y = 17$

Solving problems by using simultaneous equations

We are now going to meet a type of problem which has to be expressed as a pair of simultaneous equations so that it can be solved. The next example shows you how to tackle such a problem.

EXAMPLE 23

On holiday last year, I was talking over breakfast to two families about how much it cost them to go to the theatre. They couldn't remember how much was charged for each adult or each child, but they could both remember what they had paid altogether.

The Advani family, consisting of Mr and Mrs Advani with their daughter Rupa, paid £23.

The Shaw family, consisting of Mrs Shaw with her two children, Len and Sue, paid £17.50.

How much would I have to pay for my wife, my four children and myself?

We make a pair of simultaneous equations from the situation as follows.

Let x be the cost of an adult ticket, and y be the cost of a child's ticket. Then

$2x + y = 23$ for the Advani family

and $x + 2y = 17.5$ for the Shaw family

We solve these equations just as we have done in the previous examples, to obtain

$x = £9.50$ and $y = £4$. I can now find my cost, which will be

$(2 \times £9.50) + (4 \times £4) = £35$.

EXERCISE 19M

Read each situation carefully, then make a pair of simultaneous equations in order to solve the problem.

1 Amul and Kim have £10.70 between them. Amul has £3.70 more than Kim. Let x be the amount Amul has and y be the amount Kim has. Set up a pair of simultaneous equations. How much does each have?

2 The two people in front of me at the Post Office were both buying stamps. One person bought 10 second-class and five first-class stamps at a total cost of £3.45. The other bought eight second-class and 10 first-class stamps at a total cost of £4.38.

   a Let x be the cost of second-class stamps and y be the cost of first-class stamps. Set up two simultaneous equations.

   b How much did I pay for 3 second-class and 4 first-class stamps?

3 At a local tea room I couldn't help noticing that at one table, where the customers had eaten six buns and had three teas, the bill came to £4.35. At another table, the customers had eaten 11 buns and had seven teas at a total cost of £8.80.

   a Let x be the cost of a bun and y be the cost of a cup of tea. Show the situation as a pair of simultaneous equations.

   b My family and I had five buns and six teas. What did it cost us?

4 Three chews and four bubblies cost 72p. Five chews and two bubblies cost 64p. What would three chews and five bubblies cost?

5 On a nut-and-bolt production line, all the nuts weighed the same and all the bolts weighed the same. An order of 50 nuts and 60 bolts weighed 10.6 kg. An order of 40 nuts and 30 bolts weighed 6.5 kg. What should an order of 60 nuts and 50 bolts weigh?

6 A taxi firm charges a fixed amount plus so much per mile. A journey of 6 miles costs £3.70. A journey of 10 miles costs £5.10. What would be the cost of a journey of 8 miles?

7 Two members of the same church went to the same shop to buy material to make Christingles. One bought 200 oranges and 220 candles at a cost of £65.60. The other bought 210 oranges and 200 candles at a cost of £63.30. They only needed 200 of each. How much should it have cost them?

8 When you book Bingham Hall for a conference, you pay a fixed booking fee plus a charge for each delegate at the conference. The total charge for a conference with 65 delegates was £192.50. The total charge for a conference with 40 delegates was £180. What will be the charge for a conference with 70 delegates?

9 My mother-in-law uses this formula to cook a turkey:

   $T = a + bW$

   where T is the cooking time (minutes), W is the weight of the turkey (kg), and a and b are constants. She says it takes 4 hours 30 minutes to cook a 12 kg turkey, and 3 hours 10 minutes to cook an 8 kg turkey. How long will it take to cook a 5 kg turkey?

Rearranging formulae

In this section you will learn how to:

- rearrange formulae using the same methods as for solving equations

Key words

expression
rearrange
subject
transpose
variable

The **subject** of a formula is the **variable** (letter) in the formula which stands on its own, usually on the left-hand side of the equals sign. For example, x is the subject of each of the following equations.

$$x = 5t + 4 \qquad x = 4(2y - 7) \qquad x = \frac{1}{t}$$

If we wish to change the existing subject to a different variable, we have to **rearrange** (**transpose**) the formula to get that variable on the left-hand side. We do this by using the same rules as for solving equations. Move the terms concerned from one side of the equals sign to the other. The main difference is that when you solve an equation each step gives a numerical value. When you rearrange a formula each step gives an algebraic **expression**.

EXAMPLE 24

Make m the subject of this formula. $\qquad\qquad T = m - 3$

Move the 3 away from the m. $\qquad\qquad T + 3 = m$

Reverse the formula. $\qquad\qquad m = T + 3$

EXAMPLE 25

From the formula $P = 4t$, express t in terms of P.

(This is another common way of asking you to make t the subject.)

Divide both sides by 4: $\qquad\qquad \dfrac{P}{4} = \dfrac{4t}{4}$

Reverse the formula: $\qquad\qquad t = \dfrac{P}{4}$

EXAMPLE 26

From the formula $C = 2m^2 + 3$, make m the subject.

Move the 3 away from the $2m^2$: $\qquad C - 3 = 2m^2$

Divide both sides by 2: $\qquad \dfrac{C - 3}{2} = \dfrac{2m^2}{2}$

Reverse the formula: $\qquad m^2 = \dfrac{C - 3}{2}$

Square root both sides: $\qquad m = \sqrt{\dfrac{C - 3}{2}}$

EXERCISE 19N

1 $T = 3k$ Make k the subject.

HINTS AND TIPS

Remember about inverse operations, and the rule "change sides, change signs".

2 $X = y - 1$ Express y in terms of X.

3 $Q = \dfrac{p}{3}$ Express p in terms of Q.

4 $A = 4r + 9$ Make r the subject.

5 $W = 3n - 1$ Make n the subject.

6 $p = m + t$ **a** Make m the subject.   **b** Make t the subject.

7 $g = \dfrac{m}{v}$ Make m the subject.

8 $t = m^2$ Make m the subject.

9 $C = 2\pi r$ Make r the subject.

10 $A = bh$ Make b the subject.

11 $P = 2l + 2w$ Make l the subject.

12 $m = p^2 + 2$ Make p the subject.

13 $v = u + at$ **a** Make a the subject.   **b** Make t the subject.

14 $A = \dfrac{1}{4}\pi d^2,$ Make d the subject.

15 $W = 3n + t$ **a** Make n the subject.   **b** Express t in terms of n and W.

16 $x = 5y - w$ **a** Make y the subject.   **b** Express w in terms of x and y.

17 $k = 2p^2$ Make p the subject.

18 $v = u^2 - t$ **a** Make t the subject.   **b** Make u the subject.

19 $k = m + n^2$ **a** Make m the subject.   **b** Make n the subject.

20 $T = 5r^2$ Make r the subject.

21 $K = 5n^2 + w$ **a** Make w the subject.   **b** Make n the subject.

1 a Multiply out $\quad 3(4x - 5)$
   b Solve $\quad 3(4x - 5) = 27$

2 Solve the equation $\quad 7x - 1 = 3(x + 2)$

3 A solution of the equation $x^3 - 8x = 110$ lies between $x = 5$ and $x = 6$. Use trial and improvement to find this solution. Give your answer to one decimal place.

4 a Expand and simplify $\quad 3(4x - 3) + 2(x + 5)$
   b Expand $\quad 2x(x^2 - 3x)$
   c Expand and simplify $\quad (x + 2)(x - 1)$

5 a Make t the subject of the formula $\quad s = 2 - 3t$
   b Solve the equation $\quad \frac{1}{3}x - 4 = \frac{1}{6}x + 2$

6 Solve the equations
   a $\quad \dfrac{17 - x}{3} = 4.5$
   b $\quad 2(y - 3) = 5 - 3y$
   c $\quad 3(2z - 1) + 4(z + 3) = 5(2z - 1) + 4(3z - 1)$

   AQA, Question 11, Paper 2 Higher, June 2005

7 Dario is using trial and improvement to find a solution to the equation

   $$x + \frac{1}{x} = 5$$

   The table shows his first trial.

x	$x + \dfrac{1}{x}$	Comment
4	4.25	Too low

   Continue the table to find a solution to the equation.
   Give your answer to 1 decimal place.

   AQA, Question 17, Paper 2 Intermediate, June 2004

8 a i Multiply out $\quad s(s^2 + 6)$
      ii Multiply out and simplify $\quad 4(x - 2) + 3(x + 2)$
      iii Multiply out and simplify $\quad (n + 3)^2$
   b Factorise completely the following expressions
      i $\quad 2a^2 + a$
      ii $\quad 8x^3y^2 - 4xy^3$

   AQA, Question 5, Paper 2 Higher, June 2004

9 a Expand and simplify
      $$4(2x - 1) + 3(x + 6)$$
   b Expand
      $$x^2(4 - 2x)$$

   AQA, Question 16, Paper 2 Intermediate, June 2003

10 Make t the subject of the formula $\quad t^2 + s = 10$

11 Make x the subject of the formula
      $$3x + 2y = 8y - 3$$
   Simplify your answer as much as possible.

   AQA, Question 8, Paper 2 Higher, June 2004

12 Solve the simultaneous equations
      $$4x + 3y = 14$$
      $$2x + y = 5$$
   You *must* show your working.
   Do *not* use trial and improvement.

   AQA, Question 23, Paper 1 Intermediate, June 2004

13 Wendy does a 25 kilometre mountain race. She ran x kilometres to the top of the mountain at a speed of 9 km/h and then y kilometres to the finish at a speed of 12 km/h. She finishes the race in 2 hours and 20 minutes.

   By setting up two simultaneous equations in x and y, find how long it took Wendy to reach the top of the mountain.

14 Consider the simultaneous equations
      $$y = x + 1$$
      $$y^2 = x + 6$$
   a Show why x is the solution of the equation
      $$x^2 + x - 5 = 0$$
   b Use trial and improvement to find a positive solution to $x^2 + x - 5 = 0$. Give your answer to 1 decimal place.

WORKED EXAM QUESTIONS

1 $4x + 3y = 6$
$3x - 2y = 13$
Solve these simultaneous equations algebraically. Show your method clearly.

$4x + 3y = 23$		(1)
$3x - 2y = 13$		(2)

Label the equations and decide on the best way to get the coefficients of one variable the same.

(1) $\times 2$	$8x + 6y = 46$		(3)
(2) $\times 3$	$9x - 6y = 39$		(4)
(3) + (4)	$17x$	$= 85$	

Making the y coefficients the same will be the most efficient way as the resulting equations will be added.

$x = 5$

Substitute into (1) $20 + 3y = 23$

$y = 1$

Solve the resulting equation and substitute into one of the original equations to find the other value.

$4 \times 5 + 3 \times 1 = 23$ ✓

$3 \times 5 - 2 \times 1 = 13$ ✓

Check that these values work in the original equations

2 Temperatures can be measured in degrees Celsius (°C), degrees Fahrenheit (°F) or degrees Kelvin (°K). The relationships between the scales of temperature are given by
$$C = \frac{5(F - 32)}{9} \text{ and}$$
$$K = C + 273$$
Express F
  i in terms of C
  ii in terms of K

i $9C = 5(F - 32)$
$9C = 5F - 160$
$5F = 9C + 160$
$F = \dfrac{9C + 160}{5}$

Multiply both sides of the first equation by 9, then expand the bracket. Add 160 to both sides and change the equation round. Divide both sides by 5. Make sure you divide all of the right-hand side by 5.

ii $C = K - 273$
$F = \dfrac{9(K - 273) + 160}{5}$
$F = \dfrac{9K - 2457 + 160}{5}$
$F = \dfrac{9K - 2297}{5}$

Make C the subject of the second equation. Substitute for C in the answer to part **i**, expand the bracket and tidy up the top line of the fraction.

Julia starts her new job at a riding stables, where she is responsible for six new horses. She measures the length and girth of each horse, and then uses the bodyweight calculator to work out its weight in kilograms. She then uses the feed chart and worming paste instructions to calculate how much feed and worming paste each horse needs.

Copy the stewardship table and help her to complete it for these six horses.

Summer
girth: 220 cm
length: 142 cm
work: medium

Sally
girth: 190 cm
length: 95 cm
work: hard

Skip
girth: 200 cm
length: 114 cm
work: hard

Simon
girth: 180 cm
length: 124 cm
work: medium

Stewardship table

Body weight of horse in (kg)	Weight of feed (in kg) at different levels of work	
	Medium work	Hard work
300	2.4	3.0
350	2.8	3.5
400	3.2	4.0
450	3.6	4.5
500	4.0	5.0
Extra feed per 50 kg	300 g	400 g

Horse	Weight in kg	Feed in kg	Worming paste in tubes
Summer			
Sally			
Skip			
Simon			
Barney			
Teddy			

Instructions for using the bodyweight calculator

Put a ruler from the girth line to the length line. Where the ruler crosses the weight line is the approximate weight of the horse. Give each horse's weight to the nearest 10 kg.

Barney
girth: 160 cm
length: 110 cm
work: medium

Teddy
girth: 190 cm
length: 140 cm
work: hard

Bodyweight Calculator

Girth (cm)	Weight (km)	Length (cm)
111.8	115.7	71.75
112	125	75
120	150	80
130	175	85
140	200	90
	225	
150	250	95
	275	
160	300	100
	325	
	350	105
170	400	110
180	450	115
	500	
190	550	120
200	600	125
	650	
210	700	130
	750	
	800	135
220	850	
	900	140
230	950	
	1000	145
240	1045.6	
246.4		150 / 150.5

Worming paste instructions

Weight of horse (w) in kg	Amount of paste
w < 150	0.25 of tube
150 ≤ w < 300	0.5 of tube
300 ≤ w < 450	0.75 of tube
continue increasing dosage of paste, 0.25 of tube for every 150 kg	

During her first day, Julia sees a group of three adults and two children pay £136.50 for a 1½ hour ride. Then another group of four adults and five children pay £241.50 to go on the same ride.

Julia is hopeless at simultaneous equations. Work out for her the cost for an adult and the cost for a child to go on this ride.

GRADE YOURSELF

D Able to expand a linear bracket

D Able to substitute numbers into expressions

D Able to factorise simple linear expresions

D Able to solve simple linear equations which include the variable inside a bracket

D Able to solve linear equations where the variable occurs in the numerator of a fraction

D Able to solve linear equations where the variable appears on both sides of the equals sign.

C Able to expand and simplify expressions

C Able to solve equations using trial and improvement

C Able to rearrange simple formulae

B Able to solve two simultaneous linear equations

B Able to rearrange more complicated formulae

A Able to set up and solve two simultaneous equations from a practical problem

What you should know now

- How to manipulate and simplify algebraic expressions, including those with linear brackets

- How to factorise linear expressions

- How to solve all types of linear equations

- How to find a solution to equations by trial and improvement

- How to set up and/or solve a pair of linear simultaneous equations

Algebra 2

This chapter will show you ...

- how to expand two linear brackets to obtain a quadratic expression
- how to factorise a quadratic expression
- how to solve quadratic equations by factorisation, the quadratic formula and completing the square

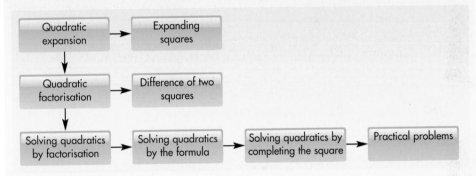

What you should already know

- The basic language of algebra
- How to collect together like terms
- How to multiply together two algebraic expressions
- How to solve simple linear equations

Quick check

1 Simplify the following.

    a $-2x - x$
    b $3x - x$
    c $-5x + 2x$

    d $2m \times 3m$
    e $3x \times -2x$
    f $-4p \times 3p$

2 Solve these equations.

    a $x + 6 = 0$
    b $2x + 1 = 0$
    c $3x - 2 = 0$

Expanding brackets

This section will show you how to:

- expand two linear brackets to obtain a quadratic expression

Key words
coefficient
linear
quadratic
   expression

Quadratic expansion

A **quadratic expression** is one in which the highest power of the variables is 2. For example,

$$y^2 \qquad 3t^2 + 5t \qquad 5m^2 + 3m + 8$$

An expression such as $(3y + 2)(4y - 5)$ can be expanded to give a quadratic expression.

This multiplying out of such pairs of brackets is usually called **quadratic expansion**.

The rule for expanding expressions such as $(t + 5)(3t - 4)$ is similar to that for expanding single brackets: multiply everything in one bracket by everything in the other bracket.

There are several methods for doing this. Examples 1 to 3 show the three main methods, "expansion", "FOIL" and "the box method".

EXAMPLE 1

In the expansion method split up the first bracket and make each of its terms multiply the second bracket. We then simplify the outcome.

Expand $(x + 3)(x + 4)$.

$$(x + 3)(x + 4) = x(x + 4) + 3(x + 4)$$
$$= x^2 + 4x + 3x + 12$$
$$= x^2 + 7x + 12$$

EXAMPLE 2

FOIL stands for First, Outer, Inner and Last. This is the order of multiplying the terms from each bracket.

Expand $(t + 5)(t - 2)$.

First terms give: $t \times t = t^2$. Outer terms give: $t \times -2 = -2t$.

Inner terms give: $5 \times t = 5t$. Last terms give: $+5 \times -2 = -10$.

$$(t + 5)(t - 2) = t^2 - 2t + 5t - 10$$
$$= t^2 + 3t - 10$$

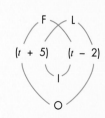

EXAMPLE 3

The box method is similar to that used to do long multiplication.

Expand $(k - 3)(k - 2)$.

$$(k - 3)(k - 2) = k^2 - 2k - 3k + 6$$
$$= k^2 - 5k + 6$$

×	k	−3
k	k^2	−3k
−2	−2k	+6

Warning: Be careful with the signs. This is the main place where marks are lost in examination questions involving the expansion of brackets.

EXERCISE 20A

Expand the following expressions.

1 $(x + 3)(x + 2)$ **2** $(t + 4)(t + 3)$ **3** $(w + 1)(w + 3)$

4 $(m + 5)(m + 1)$ **5** $(k + 3)(k + 5)$ **6** $(a + 4)(a + 1)$

7 $(x + 4)(x - 2)$ **8** $(t + 5)(t - 3)$ **9** $(w + 3)(w - 1)$

10 $(f + 2)(f - 3)$ **11** $(g + 1)(g - 4)$ **12** $(y + 4)(y - 3)$

13 $(x - 3)(x + 4)$ **14** $(p - 2)(p + 1)$ **15** $(k - 4)(k + 2)$

16 $(y - 2)(y + 5)$ **17** $(a - 1)(a + 3)$ **18** $(t - 3)(t + 4)$

> **HINTS AND TIPS**
>
> Use whichever method you prefer. There is no fixed method in GCSE examinations. Examiners give credit for all methods.

> **HINTS AND TIPS**
>
> A common error is to get minus signs wrong.
> $-2x - 3x = -5x$ and
> $-2 \times -3 = +6$

The expansions of the expressions below follow a pattern. Work out the first few and try to spot the pattern that will allow you immediately to write down the answers to the rest.

19 $(x + 3)(x - 3)$ **20** $(t + 5)(t - 5)$ **21** $(m + 4)(m - 4)$

22 $(t + 2)(t - 2)$ **23** $(y + 8)(y - 8)$ **24** $(p + 1)(p - 1)$

25 $(5 + x)(5 - x)$ **26** $(7 + g)(7 - g)$ **27** $(x - 6)(x + 6)$

All the algebraic terms in x^2 in Exercise 20A have a **coefficient** of 1 or –1. The next two examples show you what to do if you have to expand brackets containing terms in x^2 whose coefficients are not 1 or –1.

EXAMPLE 4

Expand $(2t + 3)(3t + 1)$.

$$(2t + 3)(3t + 1) = 6t^2 + 2t + 9t + 3$$
$$= 6t^2 + 11t + 3$$

×	2t	+3
3t	$6t^2$	+9t
+1	+2t	+3

EXAMPLE 5

Expand $(4x - 1)(3x - 5)$.

$(4x - 1)(3x - 5) = 4x(3x - 5) - (3x - 5)$ [**Note:** $(3x - 5)$ is the same as $1(3x - 5)$.]

$\qquad\qquad\qquad\quad = 12x^2 - 20x - 3x + 5$

$\qquad\qquad\qquad\quad = 12x^2 - 23x + 5$

EXERCISE 20B

Expand the following expressions.

1 $(2x + 3)(3x + 1)$ **2** $(3y + 2)(4y + 3)$

3 $(3t + 1)(2t + 5)$ **4** $(4t + 3)(2t - 1)$

5 $(5m + 2)(2m - 3)$ **6** $(4k + 3)(3k - 5)$

7 $(3p - 2)(2p + 5)$ **8** $(5w + 2)(2w + 3)$

9 $(2a - 3)(3a + 1)$ **10** $(4r - 3)(2r - 1)$

11 $(3g - 2)(5g - 2)$ **12** $(4d - 1)(3d + 2)$

13 $(5 + 2p)(3 + 4p)$ **14** $(2 + 3t)(1 + 2t)$ **15** $(4 + 3p)(2p + 1)$

16 $(6 + 5t)(1 - 2t)$ **17** $(4 + 3n)(3 - 2n)$ **18** $(2 + 3f)(2f - 3)$

19 $(3 - 2q)(4 + 5q)$ **20** $(1 - 3p)(3 + 2p)$ **21** $(4 - 2t)(3t + 1)$

> **HINTS AND TIPS**
>
> Always give answers in the form $\pm ax^2 \pm bx \pm c$ even if the quadratic coefficient is negative.

EXERCISE 20C

Try to spot the pattern in each of the following expressions so that you can immediately write down the expansion.

1 $(2x + 1)(2x - 1)$ **2** $(3t + 2)(3t - 2)$ **3** $(5y + 3)(5y - 3)$

4 $(4m + 3)(4m - 3)$ **5** $(2k - 3)(2k + 3)$ **6** $(4h - 1)(4h + 1)$

7 $(2 + 3x)(2 - 3x)$ **8** $(5 + 2t)(5 - 2t)$ **9** $(6 - 5y)(6 + 5y)$

10 $(a + b)(a - b)$ **11** $(3t + k)(3t - k)$ **12** $(2m - 3p)(2m + 3p)$

13 $(5k + g)(5k - g)$ **14** $(ab + cd)(ab - cd)$ **15** $(a^2 + b^2)(a^2 - b^2)$

Expanding squares

Whenever you see a **linear** bracket squared you must write the bracket down twice and then use whichever method you prefer to expand the brackets.

EXAMPLE 6

Expand $(x + 3)^2$.

$(x + 3)^2 = (x + 3)(x + 3)$

$\qquad = x(x + 3) + 3(x + 3)$

$\qquad = x^2 + 3x + 3x + 9$

$\qquad = x^2 + 6x + 9$

EXAMPLE 7

Expand $(3x - 2)^2$.

$(3x - 2)^2 = (3x - 2)(3x - 2)$

$\qquad = 9x^2 - 6x - 6x + 4$

$\qquad = 9x^2 - 12x + 4$

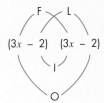

EXERCISE 20D

Expand the following squares.

HINTS AND TIPS

Remember *always* write down the bracket twice. Do not try to take any short cuts.

1 $(x + 5)^2$	**2** $(m + 4)^2$	**3** $(6 + t)^2$
4 $(3 + p)^2$	**5** $(m - 3)^2$	**6** $(t - 5)^2$
7 $(4 - m)^2$	**8** $(7 - k)^2$	

9 $(3x + 1)^2$	**10** $(4t + 3)^2$	**11** $(2 + 5y)^2$	**12** $(3 + 2m)^2$
13 $(4t - 3)^2$	**14** $(3x - 2)^2$	**15** $(2 - 5t)^2$	**16** $(6 - 5r)^2$
17 $(x + y)^2$	**18** $(m - n)^2$	**19** $(2t + y)^2$	**20** $(m - 3n)^2$
21 $(x + 2)^2 - 4$	**22** $(x - 5)^2 - 25$	**23** $(x + 6)^2 - 36$	**24** $(x - 2)^2 - 4$

This section will show you how to:

• factorise a quadratic expression into two linear brackets

Key words
brackets
coefficient
difference of
    two squares
factorisation
quadratic
    expression

Factorisation involves putting a **quadratic expression** back into its **brackets** (if possible). We start with the factorisation of quadratic expressions of the type

$$x^2 + ax + b$$

where a and b are integers.

Sometimes it is easy to put a quadratic expression back into its brackets, other times it seems hard. However, there are some simple rules that will help you to factorise.

• Each bracket will start with an x, and the signs in the quadratic expression show which signs to put after the xs.

• When the *second* sign in the expression is a *plus*, both bracket signs are the *same* as the *first* sign.

   $x^2 + ax + b = (x + ?)(x + ?)$ Since everything is positive.

   $x^2 - ax + b = (x - ?)(x - ?)$ Since $-ve \times -ve = +ve$.

• When the *second* sign is a *minus*, the bracket signs are *different*.

   $x^2 + ax - b = (x + ?)(x - ?)$ Since $+ve \times -ve = -ve$.

   $x^2 - ax - b = (x + ?)(x - ?)$

• Next, look at the *last* number, b, in the expression. When multiplied together, the two numbers in the brackets must give b.

• Finally, look at the *coefficient of x* number, a. The *sum* of the two numbers in the brackets will give a.

EXAMPLE 8

Factorise $x^2 - x - 6$.

Because of the signs we know the brackets must be $(x + ?)(x - ?)$.

Two numbers that have a product of -6 and a sum of -1 are -3 and $+2$.

So, $x^2 - x - 6 = (x + 2)(x - 3)$

EXAMPLE 9

Factorise $x^2 - 9x + 20$.

Because of the signs we know the brackets must be $(x - ?)(x - ?)$.

Two numbers that have a product of $+20$ and a sum of -9 are -4 and -5.

So, $x^2 - 9x + 20 = (x - 4)(x - 5)$

EXERCISE 20E

Factorise the following.

1 $x^2 + 5x + 6$ **2** $t^2 + 5t + 4$ **3** $m^2 + 7m + 10$ **4** $k^2 + 10k + 24$

5 $p^2 + 14p + 24$ **6** $r^2 + 9r + 18$ **7** $w^2 + 11w + 18$ **8** $x^2 + 7x + 12$

9 $a^2 + 8a + 12$ **10** $k^2 + 10k + 21$ **11** $f^2 + 22f + 21$ **12** $b^2 + 20b + 96$

13 $t^2 - 5t + 6$ **14** $d^2 - 5d + 4$ **15** $g^2 - 7g + 10$ **16** $x^2 - 15x + 36$

17 $c^2 - 18c + 32$ **18** $t^2 - 13t + 36$ **19** $y^2 - 16y + 48$ **20** $j^2 - 14j + 48$

21 $p^2 - 8p + 15$ **22** $y^2 + 5y - 6$ **23** $t^2 + 2t - 8$

24 $x^2 + 3x - 10$ **25** $m^2 - 4m - 12$ **26** $r^2 - 6r - 7$

27 $n^2 - 3n - 18$ **28** $m^2 - 7m - 44$ **29** $w^2 - 2w - 24$

30 $t^2 - t - 90$ **31** $h^2 - h - 72$ **32** $t^2 - 2t - 63$

33 $d^2 + 2d + 1$ **34** $y^2 + 20y + 100$ **35** $t^2 - 8t + 16$ **36** $m^2 - 18m + 81$

37 $x^2 - 24x + 144$ **38** $d^2 - d - 12$ **39** $t^2 - t - 20$ **40** $q^2 - q - 56$

> **HINTS AND TIPS**
>
> First decide on the signs in the brackets, then look at the numbers.

Difference of two squares

In Exercise 20C, you multiplied out, for example, $(a + b)(a - b)$ and obtained $a^2 - b^2$. This type of quadratic expression with only two terms, both of which are perfect squares separated by a minus sign, is called the **difference of two squares**. You should have found that all the expansions in Exercise 20C are the differences of two squares.

The exercise illustrates a system of factorisation that will *always* work for the difference of two squares such as these.

$$x^2 - 9 \qquad x^2 - 25 \qquad x^2 - 4 \qquad x^2 - 100$$

- Recognise the pattern of the expression as x^2 minus a square number n^2.

- Its factors are $(x + n)(x - n)$.

EXAMPLE 10

Factorise $x^2 - 36$.

- Recognise the difference of two squares x^2 and 6^2.
- So it factorises to $(x + 6)(x - 6)$.

Expanding the brackets shows that they do come from the original expression.

EXAMPLE 11

$9x^2 - 169$

- Recognise the difference of two squares $(3x)^2$ and 13^2.
- So it factorises to $(3x + 13)(3x - 13)$.

EXERCISE 20F

Each of these is the difference of two squares. Factorise them.

HINTS AND TIPS

Learn how to spot the difference of two squares as it occurs a lot in GCSE examinations.

1 $x^2 - 9$

2 $t^2 - 25$

3 $m^2 - 16$

4 $9 - x^2$

5 $49 - t^2$

6 $k^2 - 100$

7 $4 - y^2$

8 $x^2 - 64$

9 $t^2 - 81$

10 $x^2 - y^2$

11 $x^2 - 4y^2$

12 $x^2 - 9y^2$

13 $9x^2 - 1$

14 $16x^2 - 9$

15 $25x^2 - 64$

16 $4x^2 - 9y^2$

17 $9t^2 - 4w^2$

18 $16y^2 - 25x^2$

Factorising $ax^2 + bx + c$

We can adapt the method for factorising $x^2 + ax + b$ to take into account the factors of the **coefficient** of x^2.

EXAMPLE 12

Factorise $3x^2 + 8x + 4$.

- First we note that both signs are positive. So both bracket signs must be $(?x + ?)(?x + ?)$
- As 3 has only 3×1 as factors, the brackets must be $(3x + ?)(x + ?)$
- Next, we note that the factors of 4 are 4×1 and 2×2.
- We now have to find which pair of factors of 4 combine with 3×1 to give 8.

$$\begin{array}{cc|cc} ③ & 4 & ② \\ ① & 1 & ② \end{array}$$

We see that the combination 3×2 and 1×2 adds up to 8.

- So, the complete factorisation becomes $(3x + 2)(x + 2)$.

EXAMPLE 13

Factorise $6x^2 - 7x - 10$.

- First we note that both signs are negative. So both bracket signs must be $(?x + ?)(?x - ?)$
- As 6 has 6×1 and 3×2 as factors, the brackets could be $(6x \pm ?)(x \pm ?)$ or $(3x \pm ?)(2x \pm ?)$
- Next, we note that the factors of 10 are 5×2 and 1×10.
- We now have to find which pair of factors of 10 combine with the factors of 6 to give -7.

$$\begin{array}{cc|cc} 3 & ⑥ & \pm 1 & (\pm 2) \\ 2 & ① & \pm 10 & (\pm 5) \end{array}$$

We see that the combination 6×-2 and 1×5 adds up to -7.

- So, the complete factorisation becomes $(6x + 5)(x - 2)$.

Although this seems to be very complicated, it becomes quite easy with practice and experience.

EXERCISE 20G

Factorise the following expressions.

1 $2x^2 + 5x + 2$ **2** $7x^2 + 8x + 1$ **3** $4x^2 + 3x - 7$

4 $24t^2 + 19t + 2$ **5** $15t^2 + 2t - 1$ **6** $16x^2 - 8x + 1$

7 $6y^2 + 33y - 63$ **8** $4y^2 + 8y - 96$ **9** $8x^2 + 10x - 3$

10 $6t^2 + 13t + 5$ **11** $3x^2 - 16x - 12$ **12** $7x^2 - 37x + 10$

A

Solving quadratic equations by factorisation

This section will show you how to:

- solve a quadratic equation by factorisation

Key words

factors
solve

Solving the quadratic equation $x^2 + ax + b = 0$

To **solve** a quadratic equation such as $x^2 - 2x - 3 = 0$, you first have to be able to factorise it. Follow through Examples 14 to 16 below to see how this is done.

EXAMPLE 14

Solve $x^2 + 6x + 5 = 0$.

This factorises into $(x + 5)(x + 1) = 0$.

The only way this expression can ever equal 0 is if the value of one of the brackets is 0. Hence either $(x + 5) = 0$ or $(x + 1) = 0$

$\Rightarrow x + 5 = 0$ or $x + 1 = 0$

$\Rightarrow x = -5$ or $x = -1$

So the solution is $x = -5$ or $x = -1$.

EXAMPLE 15

Solve $x^2 + 3x - 10 = 0$.

This factorises into $(x + 5)(x - 2) = 0$.

Hence $x + 5 = 0$ or $x - 2 = 0$

$\Rightarrow x = -5$ or $x = 2$

So the solution is $x = -5$ or $x = 2$.

EXAMPLE 16

Solve $x^2 - 6x + 9 = 0$.

This factorises into $(x - 3)(x - 3) = 0$.

The equation has repeated roots. That is $(x - 3)^2 = 0$.

Hence, there is only one solution, $x = 3$.

EXERCISE 20H

Solve these equations.

1 $(x + 2)(x + 5) = 0$

2 $(t + 3)(t + 1) = 0$

3 $(a + 6)(a + 4) = 0$

4 $(x + 3)(x - 2) = 0$

5 $(x + 1)(x - 3) = 0$

6 $(t + 4)(t - 5) = 0$

7 $(x - 1)(x + 2) = 0$

8 $(x - 2)(x + 5) = 0$

9 $(a - 7)(a + 4) = 0$

10 $(x - 3)(x - 2) = 0$

11 $(x - 1)(x - 5) = 0$

12 $(a - 4)(a - 3) = 0$

First factorise, then solve these equations.

13 $x^2 + 5x + 4 = 0$

14 $x^2 + 11x + 18 = 0$

15 $x^2 - 6x + 8 = 0$

16 $x^2 - 8x + 15 = 0$

17 $x^2 - 3x - 10 = 0$

18 $x^2 - 2x - 15 = 0$

19 $t^2 + 4t - 12 = 0$

20 $t^2 + 3t - 18 = 0$

21 $x^2 - x - 2 = 0$

22 $x^2 + 4x + 4 = 0$

23 $m^2 + 10m + 25 = 0$

24 $t^2 - 8t + 16 = 0$

25 $t^2 + 8t + 12 = 0$

26 $k^2 - 2k - 15 = 0$

27 $a^2 - 14a + 49 = 0$

First rearrange these equations, then solve them.

28 $x^2 + 10x = -24$

29 $x^2 - 18x = -32$

30 $x^2 + 2x = 24$

31 $x^2 + 3x = 54$

32 $t^2 + 7t = 30$

33 $x^2 - 7x = 44$

34 $t^2 - t = 72$

35 $x^2 = 17x - 72$

36 $x^2 + 1 = 2x$

> **HINTS AND TIPS**
>
> You cannot solve a quadratic equation unless it is in the form $x^2 + ax + b = 0$

Solving the general quadratic equation by factorisation

The general quadratic equation is of the form $ax^2 + bx + c = 0$ where a, b and c are positive or negative whole numbers. (It is easier to make sure that a is always positive). Before any quadratic equation can be solved it must be rearranged to this form.

The method is similar to that used to solve equations of the form $x^2 + ax + b = 0$. That is, we have to find two **factors** of $ax^2 + bx + c$ whose product is 0.

EXAMPLE 17

Solve these quadratic equations. **a** $12x^2 - 28x = -15$ **b** $30x^2 - 5x - 5 = 0$

a First, rearrange the equation to the general form.

$$12x^2 - 28x + 15 = 0$$

This factorises into $(2x - 3)(6x - 5) = 0$.

The only way this product can equal 0 is if the value of one of the brackets is 0. Hence,

either $2x - 3 = 0$ or $6x - 5 = 0$

$\Rightarrow$ $2x = 3$ or $6x = 5$

$\Rightarrow$ $x = \frac{3}{2}$ or $x = \frac{5}{6}$

So the solution is $x = 1\frac{1}{2}$ or $x = \frac{5}{6}$.

Note: It is almost always the case that if a solution is a fraction which is then changed into a rounded-off decimal number, the original equation cannot be evaluated exactly using that decimal number. So it is preferable to leave the solution in its fraction form. This is called the rational form (see page 188).

b This equation is already in the general form and it will factorise to $(15x + 5)(2x - 1) = 0$ or $(3x + 1)(10x - 5) = 0$.

Look again at the equation. There is a common factor of 5 which can be factorised out to give

$$5(6x^2 - x - 1 = 0).$$

This is much easier to factorise to $5(3x + 1)(2x - 1) = 0$, which can be solved to give $x = -\frac{1}{3}$ or $x = \frac{1}{2}$.

Sometimes the values of b and c are zero. (Note that if a is zero the equation is no longer a quadratic equation but a linear equation. These were covered in Chapter 19.)

EXAMPLE 18

Solve these quadratic equations. **a** $3x^2 - 4 = 0$ **b** $4x^2 - 25 = 0$ **c** $6x^2 - x = 0$

a Rearrange to get $3x^2 = 4$.

Divide both sides by 3: $x^2 = \frac{4}{3}$

Square root both sides: $x = \pm\sqrt{\frac{4}{3}} = \pm\frac{2}{\sqrt{3}}$

Note: A square root can be positive or negative. The answer is in surd form (see Chapter 7).

b You can use the method of part **a** or you should recognise this as the difference of two squares (page 439). This can be factorised to $(2x - 5)(2x + 5) = 0$

Each bracket can be put equal to zero.

$2x - 5 = 0$ $\Rightarrow$ $x = +\frac{5}{2}$

$2x + 5 = 0$ $\Rightarrow$ $x = -\frac{5}{2}$ So the solution is $x = \pm\frac{5}{2}$.

c There is a common factor of x, so factorise as $x(6x - 1) = 0$

There is only one bracket this time but each factor can be equal to zero, so $x = 0$ or $6x - 1 = 0$

Hence $x = 0$ or $\frac{1}{6}$.

EXERCISE 20I

Give your answers either in rational form or as mixed numbers.

1 Solve the following equations.

a $3x^2 + 8x - 3 = 0$

b $6x^2 - 5x - 4 = 0$

c $5x^2 - 9x - 2 = 0$

d $4t^2 - 4t - 35 = 0$

e $18t^2 + 9t + 1 = 0$

f $3t^2 - 14t + 8 = 0$

g $6x^2 + 15x - 9 = 0$

h $12x^2 - 16x - 35 = 0$

i $15t^2 + 4t - 35 = 0$

j $28x^2 - 85x + 63 = 0$

k $24x^2 - 19x + 2 = 0$

l $16t^2 - 1 = 0$

m $4x^2 + 9x = 0$

n $25t^2 - 49 = 0$

p $9m^2 - 24m - 9 = 0$

2 Rearrange into the general form then solve the following equations.

a $x^2 - x = 42$

b $8x(x + 1) = 30$

c $(x + 1)(x - 2) = 40$

d $13x^2 = 11 - 2x$

e $(x + 1)(x - 2) = 4$

f $10x^2 - x = 2$

g $8x^2 + 6x + 3 = 2x^2 + x + 2$

h $25x^2 = 10 - 45x$

i $8x - 16 - x^2 = 0$

j $(2x + 1)(5x + 2) = (2x - 2)(x - 2)$

k $5x + 5 = 30x^2 + 15x + 5$

l $2m^2 = 50$

m $6x^2 + 30 = 5 - 3x^2 - 30x$

n $4x^2 + 4x - 49 = 4x$

p $2t^2 - t = 15$

 20.4

Solving a quadratic equation by the quadratic formula

This section will show you how to:

● solve a quadratic equation by using the quadratic formula

Key words

quadratic formula
soluble
solve

Many quadratic equations cannot be solved by factorisation because they do not have simple factors. Try to factorise, for example, $x^2 - 4x - 3 = 0$ or $3x^2 - 6x + 2 = 0$. You will find it is impossible.

One way to **solve** this type of equation is to use the **quadratic formula**. This formula can be used to solve *any* quadratic equation that is **soluble**. (Some are not, which the quadratic formula would immediately show. See section 20.6.)

The solution of the equation $ax^2 + bx + c = 0$ is given by:

$$x = \frac{-b \pm \sqrt{b^2 - 4ac}}{2a}$$

This is the quadratic formula. It is given on the formula sheet of GCSE exams but it is best to learn it.

The symbol ± states that the square root has a positive and a negative value, *both* of which must be used in solving for *x*.

EXAMPLE 19

Solve $5x^2 - 11x - 4 = 0$, correct to two decimal places.

Take the quadratic formula:

$$x = \frac{-b \pm \sqrt{b^2 - 4ac}}{2a}$$

and put $a = 5$, $b = -11$ and $c = -4$, which gives:

$$x = \frac{-(-11) \pm \sqrt{(-11)^2 - 4(5)(-4)}}{2(5)}$$

Note that the values for *a*, *b* and *c* have been put into the formula in brackets. This is to avoid mistakes in calculation. It is a very common mistake to get the sign of *b* wrong or to think that -11^2 is -121. Using brackets will help you do the calculation correctly.

$$x = \frac{11 \pm \sqrt{121 + 80}}{10} = \frac{11 \pm \sqrt{201}}{10}$$

$\Rightarrow \quad x = 2.52$ or -0.32

Note: The calculation has been done in stages. With a calculator it is possible just to work out the answer, but make sure you can use your calculator properly. If not, break the calculation down. Remember the rule "if you try to do two things at once, you will probably get one of them wrong".

Examination tip: If you are asked to solve a quadratic equation to one or two decimal places, you can be sure that it can be solved *only* by the quadratic formula.

EXERCISE 20J

Solve the following equations using the quadratic formula.
Give your answers to 2 decimal places.

HINTS AND TIPS

Use brackets when substituting and do not try to work two things out at the same time.

1. $2x^2 + x - 8 = 0$
2. $3x^2 + 5x + 1 = 0$

3. $x^2 - x - 10 = 0$
4. $5x^2 + 2x - 1 = 0$

5. $7x^2 + 12x + 2 = 0$
6. $3x^2 + 11x + 9 = 0$

7. $4x^2 + 9x + 3 = 0$
8. $6x^2 + 22x + 19 = 0$
9. $x^2 + 3x - 6 = 0$

10. $3x^2 - 7x + 1 = 0$
11. $2x^2 + 11x + 4 = 0$
12. $4x^2 + 5x - 3 = 0$

13. $4x^2 - 9x + 4 = 0$
14. $7x^2 + 3x - 2 = 0$
15. $5x^2 - 10x + 1 = 0$

20.5 Solving a quadratic equation by completing the square

This section will show you how to:

- solve a quadratic equation by completing the square

Key words

completing the square
square root
surd

Another method for solving quadratic equations is **completing the square**. This method can be used to give answers to a specified number of decimal places or to leave answers in **surd** form.

You will remember that:

$$(x + a)^2 = x^2 + 2ax + a^2$$

which gives:

$$x^2 + 2ax = (x + a)^2 - a^2$$

This is the basic principle behind completing the square.

EXAMPLE 20

Rewrite $x^2 + 4x - 7$ in the form $(x + a)^2 - b$. Hence solve the equation $x^2 + 4x - 7 = 0$, giving your answers to 2 decimal places.

We note that:

$$x^2 + 4x = (x + 2)^2 - 4$$

So, we have:

$$x^2 + 4x - 7 = (x + 2)^2 - 4 - 7 = (x + 2)^2 - 11$$

When $x^2 + 4x - 7 = 0$, we can rewrite the equations using completing the square, as $(x + 2)^2 - 11 = 0$.

Rearranging gives $(x + 2)^2 = 11$

Taking the **square root** of both sides gives

$x + 2 = \pm\sqrt{11}$

$\Rightarrow x = -2 \pm \sqrt{11}$

This answer is in surd form and could be left like this, but we are asked to evaluate it to $x = 1.32$ or -5.32 (to 2 decimal places)

EXAMPLE 21

Solve $x^2 - 6x - 1 = 0$ by completing the square. Leave your answer in the form $a \pm \sqrt{b}$.

$x^2 - 6x = (x - 3)^2 - 9$

So $x^2 - 6x - 1 = (x - 3)^2 - 9 - 1 = (x - 3)^2 - 10$

When $x^2 - 6x - 1 = 0$, then $(x - 3)^2 - 10 = 0$

$\Rightarrow (x - 3)^2 = 10$

Taking the square root of both sides gives:

$x - 3 = \pm\sqrt{10}$

$\Rightarrow x = 3 \pm\sqrt{10}$

EXERCISE 20K

1 Write an equivalent expression in the form $(x \pm a)^2 - b$.

   a $x^2 + 4x$ **b** $x^2 + 14x$ **c** $x^2 - 6x$ **d** $x^2 + 6x$

   e $x^2 - 4x$ **f** $x^2 + 3x$ **g** $x^2 - 5x$ **h** $x^2 + x$

   i $x^2 + 10x$ **j** $x^2 + 7x$ **k** $x^2 - 2x$ **l** $x^2 + 2x$

2 Write an equivalent expression in the form $(x \pm a)^2 - b$.

   Question **1** will help with **a** to **h**.

   a $x^2 + 4x - 1$ **b** $x^2 + 14x - 5$ **c** $x^2 - 6x + 3$ **d** $x^2 + 6x + 7$

   e $x^2 - 4x - 1$ **f** $x^2 + 3x + 3$ **g** $x^2 - 5x - 5$ **h** $x^2 + x - 1$

   i $x^2 + 8x - 6$ **j** $x^2 + 2x - 1$ **k** $x^2 - 2x - 7$ **l** $x^2 + 2x - 9$

3 Solve the following equations by completing the square. Leave your answers in surd form where appropriate. The answers to question **2** will help.

   a $x^2 + 4x - 1 = 0$ **b** $x^2 + 14x - 5 = 0$ **c** $x^2 - 6x + 3 = 0$

   d $x^2 + 6x + 7 = 0$ **e** $x^2 - 4x - 1 = 0$ **f** $x^2 + 3x + 3 = 0$

   g $x^2 - 5x - 5 = 0$ **h** $x^2 + x - 1 = 0$ **i** $x^2 + 8x - 6 = 0$

   j $x^2 + 2x - 1 = 0$ **k** $x^2 - 2x - 7 = 0$ **l** $x^2 + 2x - 9 = 0$

> **HINTS AND TIPS**
>
> When the coefficient of x is an odd number you will get fractional values.

4 Solve by completing the square. Give your answers to two decimal places.

   a $x^2 + 2x - 5 = 0$ **b** $x^2 - 4x - 7 = 0$ **c** $x^2 + 2x - 9 = 0$

5 Prove that the solutions to the equation $x^2 + bx + c = 0$ are

$$-\frac{b}{2} \pm \sqrt{\left(\frac{b^2}{4} - c\right)}$$

Mod 5

Problems using quadratic equations

This section will show you why:

Key word

discriminant

- some quadratic equations do not factorise and explain how to solve practical problems using quadratic equations

Quadratic equations with no solution

The quantity $(b^2 - 4ac)$ in the quadratic formula is known as the **discriminant**.

When $b^2 > 4ac$, $(b^2 - 4ac)$ is positive. This has been the case in almost all of the quadratics you have solved so far and it means there are two solutions.

When $b^2 = 4ac$, $(b^2 - 4ac)$ is zero. This has been the case in some of the quadratics you have solved so far. It means there is only one solution (the repeated root).

When $b^2 < 4ac$, $(b^2 - 4ac)$ is negative. So its square root is that of a negative number.

Such a square root cannot be found (at GCSE level) and therefore there are no solutions. You will not be asked about this in examinations but if it happens then you will have made a mistake and should check your working.

EXAMPLE 22

Find the discriminant $b^2 - 4ac$ of the equation $x^2 + 3x + 5 = 0$ and explain what the result tells you.

$b^2 - 4ac = (3)^2 - 4(1)(5) = 9 - 20 = -11$.

This means there are no solutions for x.

EXERCISE 20L

Work out the discriminant $b^2 - 4ac$ of the following equations. In each case say how many solutions the equation has.

1. $3x^2 + 2x - 4 = 0$
2. $2x^2 - 7x - 2 = 0$
3. $5x^2 - 8x + 2 = 0$
4. $3x^2 + x - 7 = 0$
5. $16x^2 - 23x + 6 = 0$
6. $x^2 - 2x - 16 = 0$
7. $5x^2 + 5x + 3 = 0$
8. $4x^2 + 3x + 2 = 0$
9. $5x^2 - x - 2 = 0$
10. $x^2 + 6x - 1 = 0$
11. $17x^2 - x + 2 = 0$
12. $x^2 + 5x - 3 = 0$

A

Using the quadratic formula without a calculator

In the non-calculator paper, you could be asked to solve a quadratic equation that does not factorise. The clue would be that you would be asked to leave your answer in root or surd form. You could use completing the square but this gets very messy if the coefficient of x^2 is not 1 and/or the coefficient of x is not an even number. In these cases the quadratic formula is easier to use.

EXAMPLE 23

Solve the equation $x^2 - 5x - 5 = 0$. Give your answer in the form $a \pm \sqrt{b}$.

Using the quadratic formula gives:

$$x = \frac{-(-5) \pm \sqrt{(-5)^2 - 4(1)(-5)}}{2(1)}$$

$$x = \frac{5 \pm \sqrt{45}}{2} = \frac{5}{2} \pm \frac{3\sqrt{5}}{2}$$

EXAMPLE 24

Solve the equation $2x^2 + 6x - 5 = 0$. Give your answer in surd form.

Using the quadratic formula gives:

$$x = \frac{-(6) \pm \sqrt{(6)^2 - 4(2)(-5)}}{2(2)}$$

$$x = \frac{-6 \pm \sqrt{76}}{4} = \frac{-6 \pm 2\sqrt{19}}{4} = \frac{-3 \pm \sqrt{19}}{2}$$

EXERCISE 20M

1. Solve the following equations by the quadratic formula.

   Give your answers in the form $a \pm \sqrt{b}$.

   a $x^2 - 2x - 4 = 0$ **b** $x^2 + 2x - 7 = 0$

   c $x^2 + 4x - 44 = 0$ **d** $x^2 + 2x - 6 = 0$

   e $x^2 - 8x + 2 = 0$ **f** $x^2 - 4x + 2 = 0$

> **HINTS AND TIPS**
>
> The form $a \pm \sqrt{b}$ and surd form are basically the same thing. You should try to simplify surds if possible.

2. Solve the following equations by the quadratic formula. Give your answers in surd form.

   a $2x^2 + 4x - 5 = 0$ **b** $2x^2 + 4x - 7 = 0$ **c** $2x^2 + 6x - 5 = 0$

   d $2x^2 - 5x - 8 = 0$ **e** $5x^2 + x - 3 = 0$ **f** $2x^2 + 3x - 3 = 0$

Problems solved by quadratic equations

You are likely to have to solve a problem which involves generating a quadratic equation and finding its solution.

EXAMPLE 25

Find the sides of the right-angled triangle shown in the diagram.

Applying the theorem of Pythagoras gives:

$$(x + 5)^2 + (x - 2)^2 = 13^2$$
$$(x^2 + 10x + 25) + (x^2 - 4x + 4) = 169$$
$$2x^2 + 6x + 29 = 169$$
$$2x^2 + 6x - 140 = 0$$

Divide by a factor of 2: $\quad x^2 + 3x - 70 = 0$

This factorises to $\quad\quad (x + 10)(x - 7) = 0$

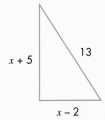

Giving $x = -10$ or 7. We reject the negative value as it would give negative lengths.

Hence the sides of the triangle are 5, 12 and 13.

Note: You may know the Pythagorean triple 5, 12, 13 and guessed the answer but you would be expected to show working. Most "real-life" problems will end up with a quadratic that factorises as the questions are complicated enough without expecting you to use the quadratic formula or completing the square.

EXAMPLE 26

Solve this equation. $\quad\quad\quad\quad\quad\quad\quad 2x - \dfrac{3}{x} = 5$

Multiply through by x to give: $\quad\quad\quad 2x^2 - 3 = 5x$

Rearrange into the general form: $\quad\quad 2x^2 - 5x - 3 = 0$

This factorises to: $\quad\quad\quad\quad\quad (2x + 1)(x - 3) = 0$

So $x = -\dfrac{1}{2}$ or $x = 3$.

EXAMPLE 27

A coach driver undertook a journey of 300 km. Her actual average speed turned out to be 10 km/h slower than expected. Therefore, she took 1 hour longer over the journey than expected. Find her actual average speed.

Let the driver's actual average speed be x km/h. So the estimated speed would have been $(x + 10)$ km/h.

Time taken $= \dfrac{\text{Distance travelled}}{\text{Speed}}$ $\quad$ At x km/h, she did the journey in $\dfrac{300}{x}$ hours.

At $(x + 10)$ km/h, she would have done the journey in $\dfrac{300}{x + 10}$ hours.

Since the journey took 1 hour longer than expected, then

time taken $= \dfrac{300}{x + 10} + 1 = \dfrac{300 + x + 10}{x + 10} = \dfrac{310 + x}{x + 10}$

So $\quad\quad = \dfrac{300}{x} = \dfrac{310 + x}{x + 10} \Rightarrow 300(x + 10) = x(310 + x) \Rightarrow 300x + 3000 = 310x + x^2$

Rearranging into the general form gives: $\quad x^2 + 10x - 3000 = 0$

This factorises into: $\quad\quad\quad\quad\quad\quad (x + 60)(x - 50) = 0 \Rightarrow x = -60$ or 50

The coach's average speed could not be -60 km/h, so it has to be 50 km/h.

EXERCISE 20N

1. The sides of a right-angled triangle are x, $(x + 2)$ and $(2x - 2)$. The hypotenuse is length $(2x - 2)$. Find the actual dimensions of the triangle.

2. The length of a rectangle is 5 m more than its width. Its area is 300 m². Find the actual dimensions of the rectangle.

3. The average weight of a group of people is 45.2 kg. A newcomer to the group weighs 51 kg, which increases the average weight by 0.2 kg. How many people are now in the group?

4. Solve the equation $x + \dfrac{3}{x} = 7$. Give your answers correct to 2 decimal places.

5. Solve the equation $2x + \dfrac{5}{x} = 11$.

6. A tennis court has an area of 224 m². If the length were decreased by 1 m and the width increased by 1 m, the area would be increased by 1 m². Find the dimensions of the court.

7. On a journey of 400 km, the driver of a train calculates that if he were to increase his average speed by 2 km/h, he would take 20 minutes less. Find his average speed.

8. The difference of the squares of two positive numbers, whose difference is 2, is 184. Find these two numbers.

9. The length of a carpet is 1 m more than its width. Its area is 9 m². Find the dimensions of the carpet to 2 decimal places.

10. The two shorter sides of a right-angled triangle differ by 2 cm. The area is 24 cm². Find the shortest side of the triangle.

11. Helen worked out that she could save 30 minutes on a 45 km journey if she travelled at an average speed which was 15 km/h faster than that at which she had planned to travel. Find the speed at which Helen had originally planned to travel.

12. Claire intended to spend £3.20 on balloons for her party. But each balloon cost her 2p more than she expected, so she had to buy 8 fewer balloons. Find the cost of each balloon.

13. The sum of a number and its reciprocal is 2.05. What are the two numbers?

14. A woman buys goods for £60x and sells them for £(600 − 6x) at a loss of x%. Find x.

15. A train has a scheduled time for its journey. If the train averages 50 km/h, it arrives 12 minutes early. If the train averages 45 km/h, it arrives 20 minutes late. Find how long the train should take for the journey.

16. A rectangular garden measures 15 m by 11 m and is surrounded by a path of uniform width whose area is 41.25 m². Find the width of the path.

1 **a** Factorise $8p - 6$ **b** Factorise $r^2 + 6r$
c Simplify $s^2 \times s^4$

2 Find, using trial and improvement, an exact solution of
$$3x^2 - 2x = 96$$

x	$3x^2 - 2x$	Comment
1	1	Too small

AQA, Spec B, Question 12, Module 5, Paper 1 Intermediate,
June 2005

3 **a** Factorise $\qquad\qquad x^5 - 4x^2$
b i Factorise $\qquad\qquad x^2 - 3x - 10$
ii Hence solve the equation $\quad x^2 - 3x - 10 = 0$

4 Multiply and simplify $(2p - 5q)(3p - q)$

AQA, Spec B, Question 15, Module 5, Paper 1 Intermediate,
November 2004

5 **a** Expand and simplify $\qquad (a + b)(a - b)$
b i Factorise $\qquad\qquad x^2 - 20x + 36$
ii Hence solve the equation $\quad x^2 - 20x + 36 = 0$

6 The perimeter of a rectangle is 25 cm.
The length of the rectangle is x cm
a Write down an expression for the width of the
rectangle in terms of x.
b The area of the rectangle is 38 cm². Show that
$2x^2 - 25x + 76 = 0$.
c Solve the equation given in part b to find the value
of x. Give your answer to 2 decimal places.

AQA, Spec B, Question 12, Module 5, Paper 2 Higher, June 2005

7 **a** Find the values of a and b such that
$$x^2 + 10x + 40 = (x + a)^2 + b$$
b Hence, or otherwise, write down the minimum
value of $x^2 + 10x + 40$

AQA, Spec B, Question 14, Module 5, Paper 1 Higher, June 2005

8 Factorise fully $\qquad 3x^2 - 12y^2$

9 **a** Factorise $\qquad 2n^2 + 5n + 3$
b Hence, or otherwise, write 253 as the product of
two prime factors.

AQA, Question 16, Paper 1 Higher, June 2004

10 Solve the equation $x^2 + 4x - 10 = 0$
Give your answers to 2 decimal places.
Your *must* show your working.

AQA, Spec B, Question 10, Module 5, Paper 2 Intermediate,
June 2003

11 **a** Find the values of a and b such that
$$x^2 + 6x - 3 = (x + a)^2 + b$$
b Hence, or otherwise, solve the equation
$$x^2 + 6x - 3 = 0$$
giving your answers in surd form.

AQA, Question 20, Paper 1 Higher, June 2004

12 **a** Factorise $\qquad x^2 - 8x + 12$
b Hence, or otherwise, solve the equation
$$(y + 1)^2 - 8(y + 1) + 12 = 0$$

AQA, Question 18a, Paper 1 Higher, June 2004

WORKED EXAM QUESTION

a You are given that
$$(2x + b)^2 + c = ax^2 - 4x - 5$$
Calculate the values a, b and c

b You are given $q = a(p + 3)^{-3}$. When $p = 7$, $q = 2$.
Find p when $q = \frac{1}{4}$.

Solution

a $4x^2 + 4bx + b^2 + c = ax^2 - 4x - 5$
$\quad 4x^2 = ax^2 \qquad \Rightarrow \qquad a = 4$
$\quad 4bx = -4x \qquad \Rightarrow \qquad b = -1$
$\quad b^2 + c = -5 \qquad \Rightarrow \qquad c = -6$

> Expand and simplify the left-hand side.

> Equate the terms in x^2, x and the constant term. Solve the resulting equations.

b $2 = a(7 + 3)^{-3} \Rightarrow \quad 2 = \dfrac{a}{1000} \Rightarrow a = 2000$

> Substitute the given values into the equation and solve to get the value of a.

$\dfrac{1}{4} = 2000(p + 3)^{-3} \qquad \dfrac{1}{4} = \dfrac{2000}{(p + 3)^3}$

$(p + 3)^3 = 8000 \quad p + 3 = 20 \quad p = 17$

> Substitute these values into the equation and solve to get p.

A garden designer sketches the following design for a client.

This is his notepad with the details of each area.

Patio	— paved
Play area	— raised, filled with woodchips
Flower beds	— raised, made from railway sleepers
Water feature	— 4 rectangular ponds, small waterfall between each. — total volume of ponds 73 800 litres
Each pond	— length of each one to be 2 m more than width — width of each one to be 1 m wider than the previous one — all 90 cm deep — width of first pond = χ m

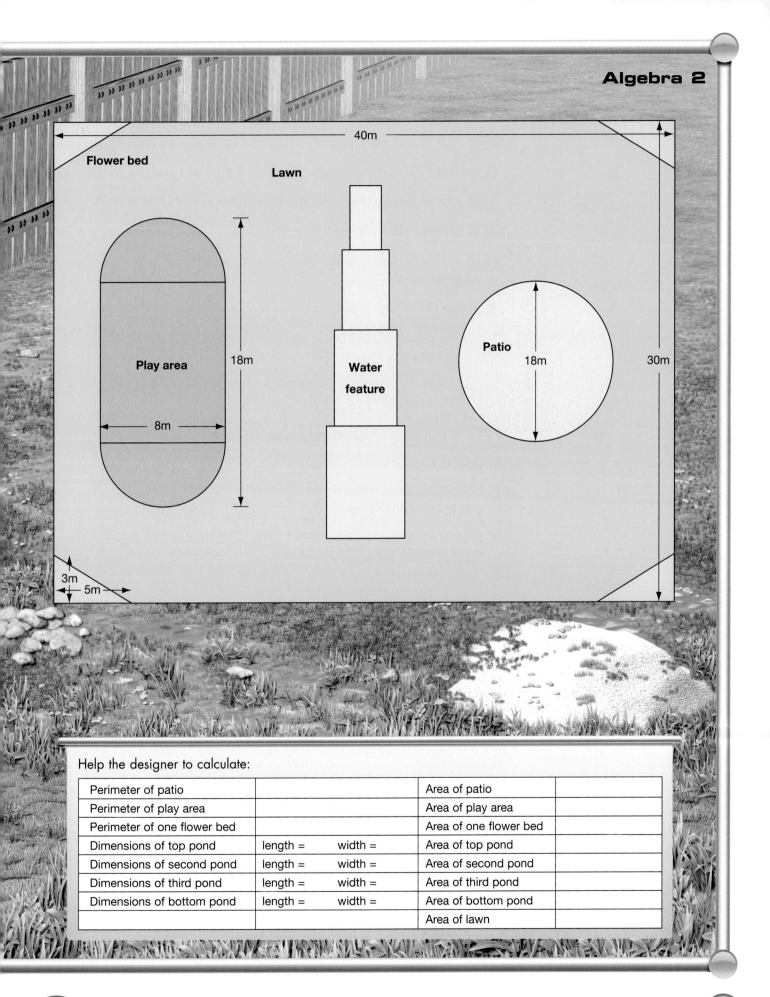

Help the designer to calculate:

Perimeter of patio		Area of patio	
Perimeter of play area		Area of play area	
Perimeter of one flower bed		Area of one flower bed	
Dimensions of top pond	length = width =	Area of top pond	
Dimensions of second pond	length = width =	Area of second pond	
Dimensions of third pond	length = width =	Area of third pond	
Dimensions of bottom pond	length = width =	Area of bottom pond	
		Area of lawn	

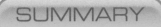

SUMMARY

GRADE YOURSELF

C Able to expand a pair of linear brackets to get a quadratic expression

B Able to factorise a quadratic expression of the form $x^2 + ax + b$

B Able to solve a quadratic equation of the form $x^2 + ax + b = 0$

A Able to factorise a quadratic expression of the form $ax^2 + bx + c$

A Able to solve a quadratic equation of the form $ax^2 + bx + c = 0$ by factorisation

A Able to solve a quadratic equation of the form $ax^2 + bx + c = 0$ by the quadratic formula

A* Able to solve a quadratic equation using completing the square

A* Able to solve real-life problems that lead to a quadratic equation

What you should know now

- How to expand linear brackets
- How to solve quadratic equations by factorisation, the quadratic formula and completing the square
- How to set up practical problems using algebra to obtain a quadratic equation which can then be solved

Real-life graphs

1 Straight-line distance–time graphs

2 Straight-line velocity–time graphs

3 Other types of graphs

This chapter will show you ...

- how to interpret distance–time and velocity–time graphs
- how to interpret other types of graph associated with real-life situations

Visual overview

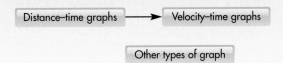

Distance–time graphs $\longrightarrow$ Velocity–time graphs

Other types of graph

What you should already know

- How to plot coordinate points
- How to read scales

Quick check

1 Give the coordinates of points A, B and C.

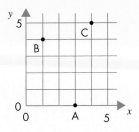

2 What are the values shown on the following scales?

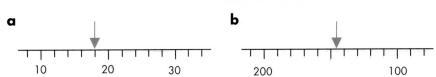

a

10   20   30

b

200   100

21.1 Straight-line distance–time graphs

This section you will learn how to:

● interpret distance–time graphs

Key words
distance
gradient
speed
time

Units of speed

Sometimes when using **distance–time** graphs, you will need to change the given units of **speed**.

EXAMPLE 1

Change 15 metres per second to kilometres per hour.

15 m/s = 15 × 60 × 60 metres per hour = 54 000 m/h

54 000 m/h = 54 000 ÷ 1000 km/h = 54 km/h

EXAMPLE 2

Change 24 kilometres per hour to metres per minute.

24 km/h = 24 × 1000 m/h = 24 000 m/h

24 000 m/h = 24 000 ÷ 60 m/min = 400 m/min

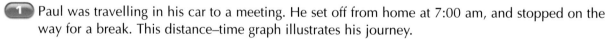

EXERCISE 21A

D

1 Paul was travelling in his car to a meeting. He set off from home at 7:00 am, and stopped on the way for a break. This distance–time graph illustrates his journey.

   a At what time did he:

     i stop for his break?

     ii set off after his break?

     iii get to his meeting place?

   b At what average speed was he travelling:

     i over the first hour?

     ii over the second hour?

     iii for the last part of his journey?

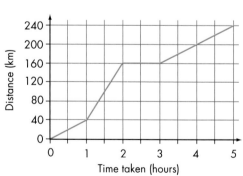

D

2 James was travelling to Cornwall on his holidays. This distance–time graph illustrates his journey.

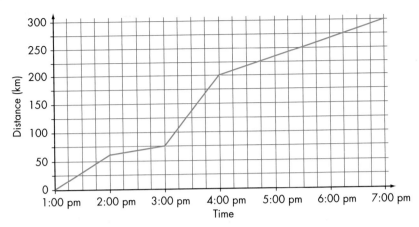

a His fastest speed was on the motorway.

   i How much motorway did he use?

   ii What was his average speed on the motorway?

b **i** When did he travel the slowest?

   ii What was his slowest average speed?

3 Richard and Paul had a 5000 m race. The distance covered is illustrated below.

a Paul ran a steady race. What is his average speed in:

   i metres per minute?

   ii km/h?

b Richard ran in spurts. What was his quickest average speed?

c Who won the race and by how much?

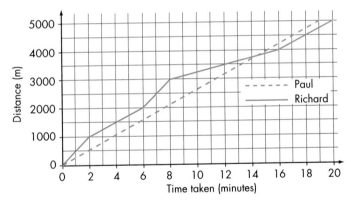

4 Three friends, Patrick, Araf and Sean, ran a 1000 metres race. The race is illustrated on the distance–time graph below.

a Describe the race of each friend.

b **i** What is the average speed of Araf in m/s?

   ii What is this speed in km/h?

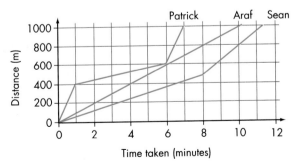

Gradient of straight-line distance–time graphs

The **gradient** of a straight line is a measure of its slope.

The gradient of this line can be found by constructing a right-angled triangle whose hypotenuse (sloping side) is on the line. Then:

$$\text{Gradient} = \frac{\text{Distance measured vertically}}{\text{Distance measured horizontally}} = \frac{6}{4} = 1.5$$

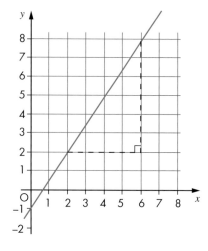

Look at the following examples of straight lines and their gradients.

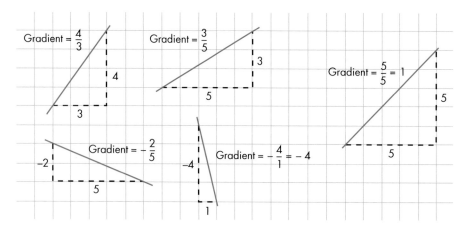

Note: Lines which slope downwards from left to right have *negative gradients*.

In the case of a straight-line graph between two quantities, its gradient is found using the *scales* on its axes, *not* the actual number of grid squares. The gradient usually represents a third quantity whose value we want to know. For example, look at the next graph.

The gradient on this distance–time graph represents average speed.

$$\text{Gradient} = \frac{500 \text{ km}}{2 \text{ h}} = 250 \text{ km/h}$$

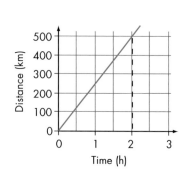

1 Calculate the gradient of each line, using the scales on the axes.

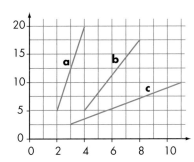

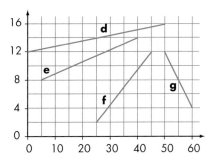

2 Calculate the average speed of the journey represented by each line in the following diagrams.

a

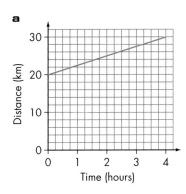

b

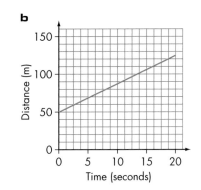

c

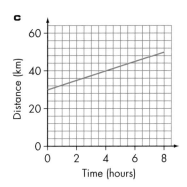

3 From each diagram below, calculate the speed between each stage of each journey.

a

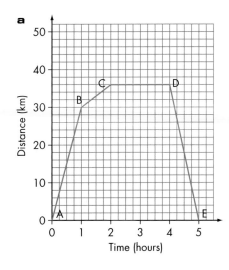

b

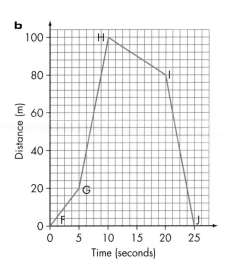

Straight-line velocity–time graphs

In this section you will learn how to:

- interpret velocity–time graphs

Velocity

In our calculations of speed, we have ignored the sign of the **gradient**. The sign of the gradient of a distance–time graph gives the *direction of travel*. Once we introduce the direction of travel into our calculations, then we must use the term **velocity** instead of speed.

Velocity at time t is the gradient of the distance–time graph at t, *including its sign*.

When the velocity of a moving object is plotted against time, the gradient of the **velocity–time** graph at any time t is equal to the **acceleration** of the object at that time.

Acceleration is rate of change of velocity, so when the gradient becomes negative, the object is slowing down. Negative acceleration is called *deceleration*.

The units of acceleration and deceleration are m/s^2 or m s^{-2}, and km/h^2 or km h^{-2}.

EXAMPLE 3

Below is the velocity–time graph of a particle over a 6-second period, drawn from measurements made during a scientific experiment. Describe what is happening at each stage of the 6 seconds.

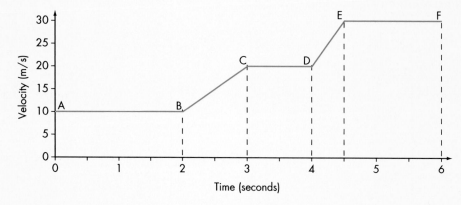

The graph shows a constant particle velocity of 10 m/s for the first 2 seconds (AB). Then the velocity increases uniformly from 10 m/s to 20 m/s over 1 second (BC). Then follows another period of constant velocity (20 m/s) over 1 second (CD), after which the velocity increases uniformly from 20 m/s to 30 m/s in 0.5 seconds (DE). During the final 1.5 seconds the velocity is constant at 30 m/s.

There are two periods of acceleration: BC and DE.

$$\text{Acceleration over BC} = \text{gradient of BC} = \frac{10 \text{ m/s}}{1 \text{ s}} = 10 \text{ m/s}^2$$

$$\text{Acceleration over DE} = \text{gradient of DE} = \frac{10 \text{ m/s}}{0.5 \text{ s}} = 20 \text{ m/s}^2$$

EXERCISE 21C

1 The diagram shows the velocity of a model car over 6 seconds.

Calculate the acceleration:

a over the first second

b after 5 seconds.

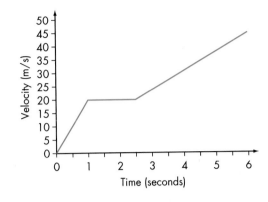

2 The diagram shows the velocity–time graph for a short tram journey between stops.

Find:

a the acceleration over the first 10 seconds

b the deceleration over the last 10 seconds.

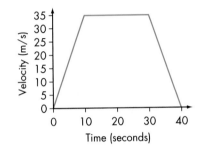

3 The diagram shows the velocity of a boat over an 18-hour period.

Calculate:

a the times at which the boat was travelling at a constant velocity

b the acceleration during each part of the journey.

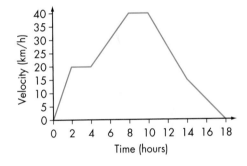

4 An aircraft flying at a constant height of 300 m dropped a load fitted to a parachute. During the times stated, the velocity of the parachute was as follows:

0–2 seconds	The load accelerated uniformly up to 20 m/s.
2–6 seconds	The parachute opened, which brought the velocity down uniformly to 2 m/s.
After 6 seconds	The load fell with a constant speed of 2 m/s.

Draw a velocity–time graph for the first 8 seconds.

5 Starting from rest (zero velocity), a particle travels as indicated below.

- Accelerates at a constant rate over 5 seconds to reach 15 m/s.
- Keeps this velocity for 10 seconds.
- Accelerates over the next 5 seconds to reach 25 m/s.
- Steadily slows down to reach rest (zero velocity) over the next 10 seconds.

a Draw the velocity–time graph.

b Calculate the acceleration over the first 5 seconds.

In this section you will learn how to:

- identify and draw some of the more unusual types of real-life graphs

Some situations can lead to unusual graphs. For example, this graph represents the cost of postage of a first-class letter against its weight.

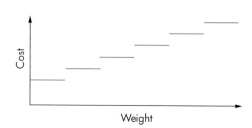

This next graph shows the change in the depth of water in a flat-bottomed flask, as it is filled from a tap delivering water at a steady rate. The graph shows that at first the depth of water increases quickly then slows down as the flask gets wider. As the flask gets narrower, the depth increases at a faster rate. Finally, when the water reaches the neck, which has a constant cross-section, the depth increases at a constant rate to the top of the neck.

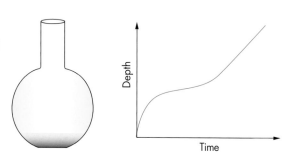

The application of graphs to describe the rate of change of depth as a container is filled with water is also covered in question **1** (Exercise 21D).

Two other examples of the use of graphs are set-out in Exercise 21D. They are the calculation of personal income tax (question **2**) and the calculation of mortgage repayments (question **3**).

Further practical applications of graphs, with special reference to finding the formulae or rules governing them, are featured on pages 511.

EXERCISE 21D

1 Draw a graph of the depth of water in each of these containers as it is filled steadily.

a
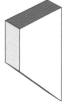

b

c

d

e

f

2 The following is a simplified model of how income tax is calculated for an individual.

The first £4000 earned is tax free. Any income over £4000 up to £30 000 is taxed at 25%. For example, a person who earns £10 000 per year would pay 25% of £6000 = £1500. Any income over £30 000 is taxed at 40%.

a Draw a graph to show the amount of tax paid by people who earn up to £40 000 per year.

(Take the horizontal axis as "Income" from £0 to £40 000. Take the vertical axis as "Tax paid" from £0 to £11 000.)

b For people who earn up to £40 000 per year, draw a graph of the percentage of income paid as tax against income.

(Take the horizontal axis as "Income" from £0 to £40 000. Take the vertical axis as "Percentage of income paid as tax" from 0% to 30%.)

 3 In a repayment mortgage, a fixed amount is paid per month for a long period (usually 15 to 25 years). At first, most of the money is used to pay off the interest and only a small amount is paid off the sum borrowed. Over time, the amount due to interest reduces and more money is used to pay off the sum borrowed. The following is a simple model for a loan of £50 000 (the capital) borrowed over 15 years at a fixed annual rate of interest of 5%. The monthly amount to be paid is £400.

a Copy and complete the following calculations to show that it takes approximately 15 years to pay off the money borrowed plus interest.

Amount owing at end of year 1	=	50 000 + 5%	=	52 500
Repayments over year 1	=	12 × 400	=	4 800
Total owed at end of year 1			=	47 700
Amount owing at end of year 2	=	47 700 + 5%	=	50 085
Repayments over year 2	=	12 × 400	=	4 800
Total owed at end of year 2			=	45 285
Amount owing at end of year 3	=	45 285 + 5%	=	………
Repayments over year 3	=	12 × 400	=	4 800
Total owed at end of year 3			=	………

and so on

b Draw a graph of "Amount owing (£)" against "Time (years)".

(Take the horizontal axis as "Time" from 0 to 15 years.
Take the vertical axis as "Amount owing" from £0 to £50 000.)

Plot the first point as (0, 50 000), The second as (1, 47 700), and so on.

1 Mr Smith leaves home at 10 am to go to the shopping mall. He walks to the station where he catches a train. He gets off at the mall. The travel graph shows his journey.

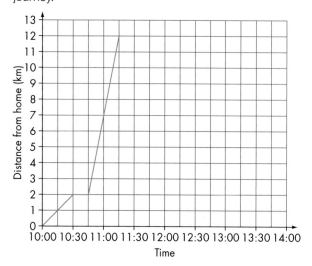

After shopping Mr Smith goes home by taxi. The taxi leaves the mall at 1 pm and arrives at his home at 1:45 pm.

a Complete the travel graph.

b Calculate the average speed of the taxi.

AQA, Question 1, Paper 2 (2-tier trial), June 2005

2 Wayne cycles from Newcastle to Ashington, a distance of 20 miles. The diagram shows the distance–time graph of his journey.

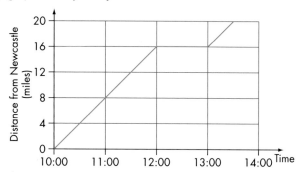

a Describe what is happening between 12:00 and 13:00.

b How far does Wayne travel in the first 2 hours of his journey?

c What is Wayne's average speed over the first 2 hours of his journey?

d Darren travels from Ashington to Newcastle by bus. He leaves Ashington at 10:00 and arrives in Newcastle at 11:00. Copy the diagram and draw a possible distance–time graph of Darren's journey on it.

AQA, Question 5, Paper 2 Intermediate, June 2003

3 A train travels from Glasgow to London in $4\frac{3}{4}$ hours. The distance travelled is 323 miles. Find the average speed of the train in miles per hour.

4 A motorbike drives from Sheffield to Plymouth. The journey is 468 kilometres in total. 372 kilometres are on motorway and 96 kilometres on normal roads. On normal roads the bike does 15 kilometres to a litre of petrol. In total the bike uses 25 litres of petrol on the journey. How many kilometres per litre does the bike do on average on motorways?

5 **a** Liquid is poured at a steady rate into the bottle shown in the diagram.

As the bottle is filled, the height, h, of the liquid in the bottle changes.

Which of the five graphs below shows this change? Give a reason for your choice.

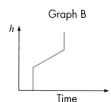

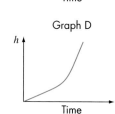

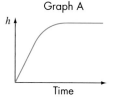

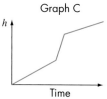

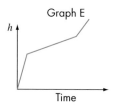

b Liquid is poured at a steady rate into another container. The graph shows how the height, h, of the liquid in this container changes. Sketch a picture of this container.

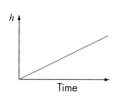

AQA, Question 5, Paper 2 Higher, November 2003

6 A swimming pool takes 6 hours to fill. For the first 2 hours the pool is filled at 80 000 litres per hour. For the next two hours the pool is filled at 100 000 litres per hour. For the last 2 hours the pool is filled at 70 000 litres per hour.

a Show this information on a graph with a horizontal axis showing time from 0 to 6 hours and a vertical axis showing litres from 0 to 800 000.

b The pool takes 10 hours to empty at a steady rate. What is the rate of flow when the pool is emptying?

AQA, Question 4, Paper 2 Higher, November 2003

 7 A cyclist sets off on a ride over the moors at 9 am. The climb up to the highest point is 25 km. It takes the cyclist 1 hour 30 minutes to do this. She rests at the highest point for 15 minutes then sets off back. She arrives home at 11:45 am.

a Show this information on a travel graph with a horizontal axis showing time from 9 am to 12 pm and a vertical axis showing distance from home from 0 to 40 km.

b Calculate the average speed of the return journey in km per hour.

AQA, Question 8, Paper 2 Higher, June 2005

WORKED EXAM QUESTION

Jane cycles from A to B and then from B to C. Details of each stage of her journey are given below.

A to B   Distance 55 km
               Average speed 22 km per hour

B to C   Time taken 1 hour 30 minutes
               Average speed 30 km per hour

Calculate Jane's average speed over the whole of her journey from A to C.

Time = Distance ÷ Speed = 55 ÷ 22 = 2.5 hours
                            = 2 hours 30 minutes

> Calculate the time taken for the journey from A to B. Remember to convert the decimal to hours and minutes.

Distance = Speed × Time = 30 × 1.5 = 45 km

> Now calculate the distance of the journey from A to B. Remember to change the time from hours and minutes to a decimal.

Average speed = Total distance ÷ Total time
                   = (55 + 45) ÷ (1.5 + 2.5) = 100 ÷ 4
                   = 25 km/h

> Now calculate the total distance and total time. Remember to change the time from hours and minutes to a decimal.

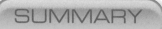

GRADE YOURSELF

D Able to draw and read information from a distance–time graph

C Able to calculate the gradient of a straight line and use this to find speed from a distance–time graph

B Able to interpret real-life graphs

A Able to interpret and draw more complex real-life graphs

What you should know now

- How to find the speed from a distance–time graph
- How to interpret real-life graphs

Trigonometry

1 Some 2-D problems

2 Some 3-D problems

3 Trigonometric ratios of angles between 90° and 360°

4 Solving any triangle

5 Sine, cosine and tangent of 30°, 45° and 60°

6 Using sine to find the area of a triangle

This chapter will show you ...

● how to use trigonometric relationships to solve more complex 2-D problems and 3-D problems

● how to use the sine and cosine rules to solve problems involving non right-angled triangles

● how to find the area of a triangle using the rule Area = $\frac{1}{2}ab$ sin C

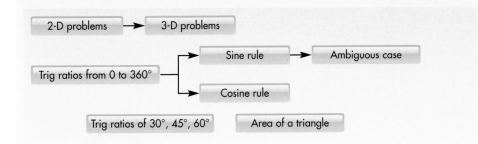

What you should already know

● How to find the sides of right-angled triangles using Pythagoras' theorem

● How to find angles and sides of right-angled triangles using sine, cosine and tangent

Quick check

1 Find the side x in this triangle.

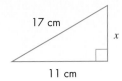

17 cm

x

11 cm

2 Find the angle x in this triangle.

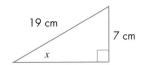

19 cm

7 cm

x

Some 2-D problems

In this section you will learn how to:
- use trigonometric ratios and Pythagoras' theorem to solve more complex two-dimensional problems

Key words
area
length
perpendicular

EXAMPLE 1

In triangle ABC, AB = 6 cm, BC = 9 cm and angle ABC = 52°. Calculate the following.

a the **length** of the **perpendicular** from A to BC

b the **area** of the triangle

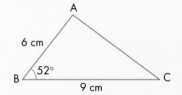

a Drop the perpendicular from A to BC to form the right-angled triangle ADB.

Let h be the length of the perpendicular AD. Then

$h = 6 \sin 52° = 4.73$ (3 significant figures)

b The area of triangle ABC is given by

Area $= \frac{1}{2} \times$ base $\times$ height

$= \frac{1}{2} \times 9 \times h = 21.3$ cm^2 (3 significant figures)

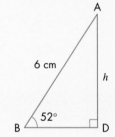

EXAMPLE 2

SR is a diameter of a circle whose radius is 25 cm. PQ is a chord at right angles to SR. X is the midpoint of PQ. The length of XR is 1 cm. Calculate the length of the arc PQ.

To find the length of the arc PQ, you need first to find the angle it subtends at the centre of the circle. (See page 311.)

So join P to the centre of the circle O to obtain the angle POX, which is equal to half the angle subtended by PQ at O.

In right-angled triangle POX

OX = OR − XR
OX = 25 − 1 = 24 cm

Therefore,

$\cos x = \dfrac{24}{25}$

$\Rightarrow \ x = \cos^{-1} 0.96 = 16.26°$

So, the angle subtended at the centre by the arc PQ is $2 \times 16.26° = 32.52°$, giving the length of the arc PQ as

$\dfrac{32.52}{360} \times 2 \times \pi \times 25 = 14.2$ cm   (3 significant figures)

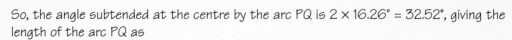

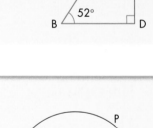

1 AC and BC are tangents to a circle of radius 7 cm.
Calculate the length of AB.

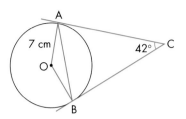

2 CD, length 20 cm, is a diameter of a circle.
AB, length 12 cm, is a chord at right angles to DC.
Calculate the angle AOB.

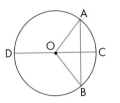

3 Calculate the length of AB.

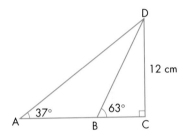

4 A building has a ledge halfway up, as shown in the diagram. Alf measures the length AB as 100 m, the angle CAB as 31° and the angle EAB as 42°. Use this information to calculate the width of the ledge CD.

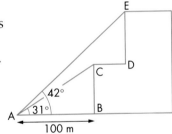

> **HINTS AND TIPS**
>
> Remember, the ledge is halfway, so ED = CB.

5 AB and CD are two equal, perpendicular chords of a circle that intersect at X. The circle is of radius 6 cm and the angle COA is 113°. Calculate these.

a the length AC

b the angle XAO

c the length XB

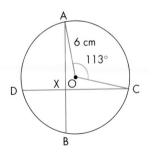

> **HINTS AND TIPS**
>
> AX = XC

6 A vertical flagpole PQ is held by a wooden framework, as shown in the diagram. The framework is in the same vertical plane. Angle SRP = 25°, SQ = 6 m and PR = 4 m. Calculate the size of the angle QRP.

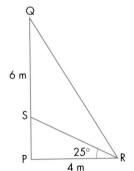

Some 3-D problems

In this section you will learn how to:

● use trigonometric ratios and Pythagoras' theorem to solve more complex three-dimensional problems

Solving a problem set in three dimensions nearly always involves identifying a right-angled triangle that contains the length or angle required. This triangle will have to contain (apart from the right angle) two known measures from which the required calculation can be made.

It is essential to extract the triangle you are going to use from its 3-D situation and redraw it as a separate, plain, right-angled triangle. (It is rarely the case that the required triangle appears as a true right-angled triangle in its 3-D representation. Even if it does, it should still be redrawn as a separate figure.)

The redrawn triangle should be annotated with the known quantities and the unknown quantity to be found.

EXAMPLE 3

A, B and C are three points at ground level. They are in the same horizontal plane. C is 50 km east of B. B is north of A. C is on a bearing of 050° from A.

An aircraft, flying in an easterly direction, passes over B and over C at the same height. When it passes over B, the angle of elevation from A is 12°. Find the angle of elevation of the aircraft from A when it is over C.

First, draw a diagram containing all the known information.

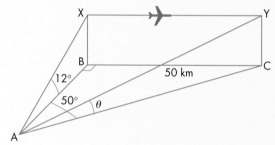

Next, use the right-angled triangle ABC to calculate AB and AC.

$$AB = \frac{50}{\tan 50°} = 41.95 \text{ km} \qquad \text{(4 significant figures)}$$

$$AC = \frac{50}{\sin 50°} = 65.27 \text{ km} \qquad \text{(4 significant figures)}$$

Then use the right-angled triangle ABX to calculate BX, and hence CY.

$$BX = 41.95 \tan 12° = 8.917 \text{ km} \quad \text{(4 significant figures)}$$

Finally, use the right-angled triangle ACY to calculate the required angle of elevation, θ.

$$\tan \theta = \frac{8.917}{65.27} = 0.1366$$

$$\Rightarrow \theta = \tan^{-1} 0.1366 = 7.8° \quad \text{(one decimal place)}$$

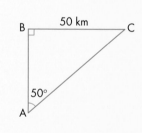

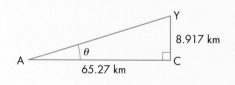

Always write down working values to at least 4 significant figures, to avoid inaccuracy in the final answer.

EXAMPLE 4

The diagram shows a cuboid 22.5 cm by 40 cm by 30 cm.
M is the midpoint of FG.

Calculate these angles.

a ABE

b ECA

c EMH

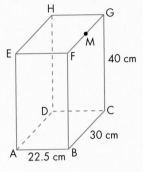

a The right-angled triangle containing the angle
required is ABE.

Solving for α gives

$$\tan \alpha = \frac{40}{22.5} = 1.7777$$

$$\Rightarrow \quad \alpha = \tan^{-1} 1.7777 = 60.6° \qquad \text{(3 significant figures)}$$

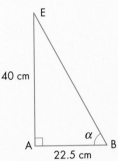

b The right-angled triangle containing the angle
required is ACE, but for which only AE is known.
Therefore, you need to find AC by applying
Pythagoras to the right-angled triangle ABC.

$$x^2 = (22.5)^2 + (30)^2 \text{ cm}^2$$

$$\Rightarrow x = 37.5 \text{ cm}$$

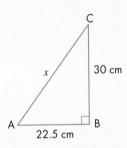

Returning to triangle ACE, you obtain

$$\tan \beta = \frac{40}{37.5} = 1.0666$$

$$\Rightarrow \quad \beta = 46.8° \qquad \text{(3 significant figures)}$$

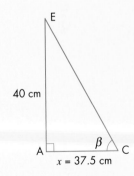

c EMH is an isosceles triangle.

Drop the perpendicular from M to N, the midpoint of HE,
to form two right-angled triangles. Angle HMN equals
angle EMN, and HN = NE = 15 cm.

Taking triangle MEN, you obtain

$$\tan \theta = \frac{15}{22.5} = 0.66666$$

$$\Rightarrow \quad \theta = \tan^{-1} 0.66666 = 33.7°$$

Therefore, angle HME is $2 \times 33.7° = 67.4°$ \qquad (3 significant figures)

EXERCISE 22B

1. The diagram shows a pyramid. The base is a horizontal rectangle ABCD, 20 cm by 15 cm. The length of each sloping edge is 24 cm. The apex, V, is over the centre of the rectangular base. Calculate these.

   a the size of the angle VAC

   b the height of the pyramid

   c the volume of the pyramid

   d the size of the angle between the face VAD and the base ABCD

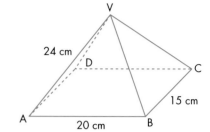

2. The diagram shows the roof of a building. The base ABCD is a horizontal rectangle 7 m by 4 m. The triangular ends are equilateral triangles. Each side of the roof is an isosceles trapezium. The length of the top of the roof, EF, is 5 m. Calculate these.

   a the length EM, where M is the midpoint of AB

   b the size of angle EBC

   c the size of the angle between the face EAB and the base ABCD

   d the surface area of the roof (excluding the base)

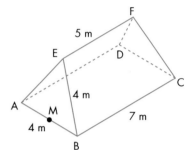

3. ABCD is a vertical rectangular plane. EDC is a horizontal triangular plane. Angle CDE = 90°, AB = 10 cm, BC = 4 cm and ED = 9 cm. Calculate these.

   a angle AED   **b** angle DEC

   c EC   **d** angle BEC

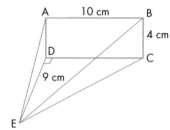

4. The diagram shows a tetrahedron. The base ABC is a horizontal equilateral triangle of side 8 cm. The vertex D is 5 cm directly above the point B. Calculate these angles.

   a DCB

   b the angle between the face ADC and the face ABC

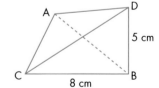

5. The diagram shows a tetrahedron, each face of which is an equilateral triangle of side 6 m. The lines AN and BM meet the sides CB and AC at a right angle. The lines AN and BM intersect at X, which is directly below the vertex, D. Calculate these.

   a the distance AX

   b the angle between the side DBC and the base ABC

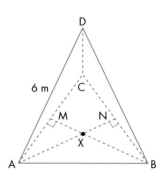

Trigonometric ratios of angles between 90° and 360°

This section will show you how to:

● find the sine, cosine and tangent of any angle from 0° to 360°

Key words

cosine
sine
tangent

ACTIVITY

a Copy and complete this table using your calculator and rounding off to three decimal places.

x	$\sin x$	x	$\sin x$	x	$\sin x$	x	$\sin x$
0°		180°		180°		360°	
15°		165°		195°		335°	
30°		150°		210°		320°	
45°		135°		225°		315°	
60°		120°		240°		300°	
75°		105°		255°		285°	
90°		90°		270°		270°	

b Comment on what you notice about the **sine** of each acute angle, and the sines of its corresponding non-acute angles.

c Draw a graph of sin x against x. Take x from 0° to 360° and sin x from –1 to 1.

d Comment on any symmetries your graph has.

You should have discovered these three facts.

● When $90° < x < 180°$, $\sin x = \sin (180° - x)$
  For example, $\sin 153° = \sin (180° - 153°) = \sin 27° = 0.454$

● When $180° < x < 270°$, $\sin x = - \sin (x - 180°)$
  For example, $\sin 214° = - \sin (214° - 180°) = - \sin 34° = - 0.559$

● When $270° < x < 360°$, $\sin x = - \sin (360° - x)$
  For example, $\sin 287° = - \sin (360° - 287°) = - \sin 73° = - 0.956$

Note:

- Each and every value of sine between –1 and 1 gives *two* angles between 0° and 360°.

- When the value of sine is positive, both angles are between 0° and 180°.

- When the value of sine is negative, both angles are between 180° and 360°.

- You can use the sine graph from 0° to 360° to check values approximately.

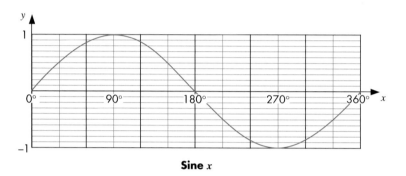

Sine *x*

EXAMPLE 5

Find the angles with a sine of 0.56.

You know that both angles are between 0° and 180°.

Using your calculator to find sin⁻¹ 0.56, you obtain 34.1°.

The other angle is, therefore,

180° − 34.1° = 145.9°

So, the angles are 34.1° and 145.9°.

EXAMPLE 6

Find the angles with a sine of −0.197.

You know that both angles are between 180° and 360°.

Using your calculator to find sin⁻¹ 0.197, you obtain 11.4°.

So the angles are

180° + 11.4° and 360° − 11.4°

which give 191.4° and 348.6°.

You can always use your calculator to check your answer to this type of problem by first keying in the angle and the appropriate trigonometric function (which would be sine in the above examples).

EXERCISE 22C

State the two angles between 0° and 360° for each of these sine values.

1 0.6 **2** 0.8 **3** 0.75 **4** –0.7

5 –0.25 **6** –0.32 **7** –0.175 **8** –0.814

9 0.471 **10** –0.097 **11** 0.553 **12** –0.5

ACTIVITY

a Copy and complete this table using your calculator and rounding off to three decimal places.

x	$\cos x$	x	$\cos x$	x	$\cos x$	x	$\cos x$
0°		180°		180°		360°	
15°		165°		195°		335°	
30°		150°		210°		320°	
45°		135°		225°		315°	
60°		120°		240°		300°	
75°		105°		255°		285°	
90°		90°		270°		270°	

b Comment on what you notice about the **cosines** of the angles.

c Draw a graph of cos x against x. Take x from 0° to 360° and cos x from –1 to 1.

d Comment on the symmetry of the graph.

You should have discovered these three facts.

- When $90° < x < 180°$, $\cos x = -\cos (180 - x)°$
  For example, $\cos 161° = -\cos (180° - 161°) = -\cos 19° = -0.946$ (3 significant figures)

- When $180° < x < 270°$, $\cos x = -\cos (x - 180°)$
  For example, $\cos 245° = -\cos (245° - 180°) = -\cos 65° = -0.423$ (3 significant figures)

- When $270° < x < 360°$, $\cos x = \cos (360° - x)$
  For example, $\cos 310° = \cos (360° - 310°) = \cos 50° = 0.643$ (3 significant figures)

Note:

- Each and every value of cosine between –1 and 1 gives *two* angles between 0° and 360°.

- When the value of cosine is positive, one angle is between 0° and 90°, and the other is between 270° and 360°.

- When the value of cosine is negative, both angles are between 90° and 270°.

- You can use the cosine graph from 0° to 360° to check values approximately.

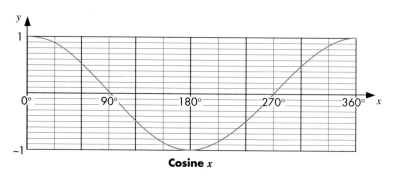

Cosine *x*

EXAMPLE 7

Find the angles with a cosine of 0.75.

One angle is between 0° and 90°, and that the other is between 270° and 360°.

Using your calculator to find $\cos^{-1} 0.75$, you obtain 41.4°.

The other angle is, therefore,

$$360° – 41.4° = 318.6°$$

So, the angles are 41.4° and 318.6°.

EXAMPLE 8

Find the angles with a cosine of –0.285.

You know that both angles are between 90° and 270°.

Using your calculator to find $\cos^{-1} 0.285$, you obtain 73.4°.

The two angles are, therefore,

$$180° – 73.4° \text{ and } 180° + 73.4°$$

which give 106.6° and 253.4°.

Here again, you can use your calculator to check your answer, by keying in cosine.

EXERCISE 22D

State the two angles between 0° and 360° for each of these cosine values.

1 0.6   **2** 0.58   **3** 0.458   **4** 0.575

5 0.185   **6** –0.8   **7** –0.25   **8** –0.175

9 –0.361   **10** –0.974   **11** 0.196   **12** 0.714

EXERCISE 22E

 1 Write down the sine of each of these angles.

   a 135°   **b** 269°   **c** 305°   **d** 133°

 2 Write down the cosine of each of these angles.

   a 129°   **b** 209°   **c** 95°   **d** 357°

 3 Write down the two possible values of x ($0° < x < 360°$) for each equation. Give your answers to one decimal place.

   a $\sin x = 0.361$ **b** $\sin x = -0.486$

   c $\cos x = 0.641$ **d** $\cos x = -0.866$

   e $\sin x = 0.874$ **f** $\cos x = 0.874$

 4 Find two angles such that the sine of each is 0.5.

 5 $\cos 41° = 0.755$. What is $\cos 139°$?

 6 Write down the value of each of the following, correct to three significant figures.

   a $\sin 50° + \cos 50°$ **b** $\cos 120° - \sin 120°$

   c $\sin 136° + \cos 223°$ **d** $\sin 175° + \cos 257°$

   e $\sin 114° - \sin 210°$ **f** $\cos 123° + \sin 177°$

 7 It is suggested that $(\sin x)^2 + (\cos x)^2 = 1$ is true for all values of x. Test out this suggestion to see if you agree.

 8 Suppose the sine key on your calculator is broken, but not the cosine key. Show how you could calculate these.

   a $\sin 25°$

   b $\sin 130°$

 9 Find a solution to each of these equations.

   a $\sin (x + 20°) = 0.5$

   b $\cos (5x) = 0.45$

 10 By any suitable method, find the solution to the equation $\sin x = (\cos x)^2$.

ACTIVITY

a Try to find tan 90°. What do you notice?

Which is the closest angle to 90° for which you can find the **tangent** on your calculator?

What is the largest value for tangent that you can get on your calculator?

b Find values of tan x where $0° < x < 360°$. Draw a graph of your results.

State some rules for finding both angles between 0° and 360° that have any given tangent.

EXAMPLE 9

Find the angles between 0° and 360° with a tangent of 0.875.

One angle is between 0° and 90°, and the other is between 180° and 270°.

Using your calculator to find $\tan^{-1} 0.875$, you obtain 41.2°.

The other angle is, therefore,

　　180° + 41.2° = 221.2°

So, the angles are 41.2° and 221.2°.

EXAMPLE 10

Find the angles between 0° and 360° with a tangent of –1.5.

We know that one angle is between 90° and 180°, and that the other is between 270° and 360°.

Using your calculator to find $\tan^{-1} 1.5$, you obtain 56.3°.

The angles are, therefore,

　　180° – 56.3° and 360° – 56.3°

which give 123.7° and 303.7°.

EXERCISE 22F

State the angles between 0° and 360° which have each of these tangent values.

1 0.258 **2** 0.785 **3** 1.19 **4** 1.875

5 2.55 **6** –0.358 **7** –0.634 **8** –0.987

9 –1.67 **10** –3.68 **11** 1.397 **12** 0.907

13 –0.355 **14** –1.153 **15** 4.15 **16** –2.05

17 –0.098 **18** 0.998 **19** 1.208 **20** –2.5

22.4 Solving any triangle

This section will show you how to:

- find the sides and angles of any triangle whether it has a right angle or not

Key words

cosine rule
included angle
sine rule

We have already established that any triangle has six elements: three sides and three angles. To solve a triangle (that is, to find any unknown angles or sides), we need to know at least three of the elements. Any combination of three elements – *except that of all three angles* – is enough to work out the rest. In a right-angled triangle, one of the known elements is, of course, the right angle.

When we need to solve a triangle which contains no right angle, we can use one or the other of two rules, depending on what is known about the triangle. These are the **sine rule** and the **cosine rule**.

The sine rule

Take a triangle ABC and draw the perpendicular from A to the opposite side BC.

From right-angled triangle ADB

$$h = c \sin B$$

From right-angled triangle ADC

$$h = b \sin C$$

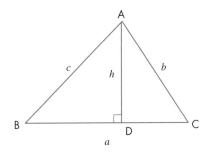

Therefore,

$$c \sin B = b \sin C$$

which can be rearranged to give

$$\frac{c}{\sin C} = \frac{b}{\sin B}$$

By drawing a perpendicular from each of the other two vertices to the opposite side (or by algebraic symmetry), we see that

$$\frac{a}{\sin A} = \frac{c}{\sin C} \quad \text{and that} \quad \frac{a}{\sin A} = \frac{b}{\sin B}$$

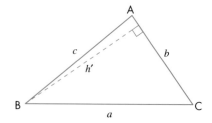

These are usually combined in the form

$$\frac{a}{\sin A} = \frac{b}{\sin B} = \frac{c}{\sin C}$$

which can be inverted to give

$$\frac{\sin A}{a} = \frac{\sin B}{b} = \frac{\sin C}{c}$$

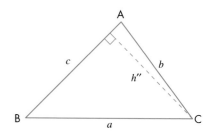

Usually, a triangle is not conveniently labelled as in these diagrams. So, when using the sine rule, it is easier to remember to proceed as follows: take each side in turn, divide it by the sine of the angle opposite, and then equate the resulting quotients.

Note:

- When you are calculating a *side*, use the rule with the *sides on top*.

- When you are calculating an *angle*, use the rule with the *sines on top*.

EXAMPLE 11

In triangle ABC, find the value of x.

Use the sine rule with sides on top, which gives

$$\frac{x}{\sin 84°} = \frac{25}{\sin 47°}$$

$$\Rightarrow \quad x = \frac{25 \sin 84°}{\sin 47°} = 34.0 \text{ cm} \quad \text{(3 significant figures)}$$

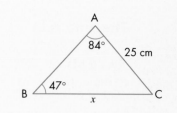

EXAMPLE 12

In the triangle ABC, find the value of the acute angle x.

Use the sine rule with sines on top, which gives

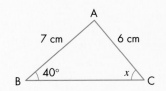

$$\frac{\sin x}{7} = \frac{\sin 40°}{6}$$

$$\Rightarrow \sin x = \frac{7 \sin 40°}{6} = 0.7499$$

$$\Rightarrow \quad x = \sin^{-1} 0.7499 = 48.6° \quad \text{(3 significant figures)}$$

The ambiguous case

EXAMPLE 13

In triangle ABC, AB = 9 cm, AC = 7 cm and angle ABC = 40°. Find the angle ACB.

As you sketch triangle ABC, note that C can have two positions, giving two different configurations.

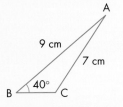 **or**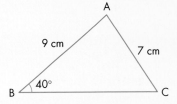

But you still proceed as in the normal sine rule situation, obtaining

$$\frac{\sin C}{9} = \frac{\sin 40°}{7}$$

$$\Rightarrow \sin C = \frac{9 \sin 40°}{7}$$

$$= 0.8264$$

Keying inverse sine on our calculator gives C = 55.7°. But there is another angle with a sine of 0.8264, given by (180° − 55.7°) = 124.3°.

These two values for C give the two different situations shown above.

When an illustration of the triangle is given, it will be clear whether the required angle is acute or obtuse. When an illustration is not given, the more likely answer is an acute angle.

Examiners will not try to catch you out with the ambiguous case. They will indicate clearly, either with the aid of a diagram or by stating it, what is required.

EXERCISE 22G

1 Find the length x in each of these triangles.

a
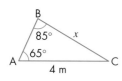

b
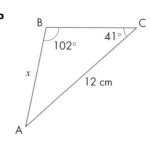

c
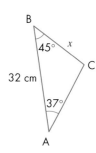

2 Find the angle x in each of these triangles.

a
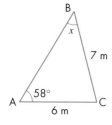

b
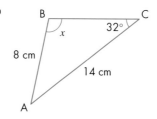

c
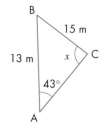

3 In triangle ABC, the angle at A is 38°, the side AB is 10 cm and the side BC is 8 cm. Find the two possible values of the angle at C.

4 In triangle ABC, the angle at A is 42°, the side AB is 16 cm and the side BC is 14 cm. Find the two possible values of the side AC.

5 To find the height of a tower standing on a small hill, Mary made some measurements (see diagram).

From a point B, the angle of elevation of C is 20°, the angle of elevation of A is 50°, and the distance BC is 25 m.

a Calculate these angles.

 i ABC

 ii BAC

b Using the sine rule and triangle ABC, calculate the height h of the tower.

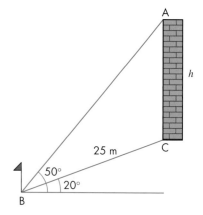

Mod 5

6 Use the information on this sketch to calculate the width, *w*, of the river.

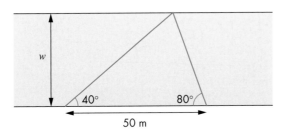

7 An old building is unsafe, so it is protected by a fence. To work out the height of the building, Annie made the measurements shown on the diagram.

  a Use the sine rule to work out the distance AB.

  b Calculate the height of the building, BD.

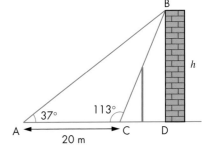

8 A weight is hung from a horizontal beam using two strings. The shorter string is 2.5 m long and makes an angle of 71° with the horizontal. The longer string makes an angle of 43° with the horizontal. What is the length of the longer string?

9 An aircraft is flying over an army base. Suddenly, two searchlights, 3 km apart, are switched on. The two beams of light meet on the aircraft at an angle of 125° vertically above the line joining the searchlights. One of the beams of light makes an angle of 31° with the horizontal. Calculate the height of the aircraft.

10 Two ships leave a port in directions that are 41° from each other. After half an hour, the ships are 11 km apart. If the speed of the slower ship is 7 km/h, what is the speed of the faster ship?

11 For any triangle ABC, prove the sine rule

$$\frac{a}{\sin A} = \frac{b}{\sin B} = \frac{c}{\sin C}$$

The cosine rule

Take the triangle, shown on the right, where D is the foot of the perpendicular to BC from A.

Using Pythagoras on triangle BDA

$$h^2 = c^2 - x^2$$

Using Pythagoras on triangle ADC

$$h^2 = b^2 - (a - x)^2$$

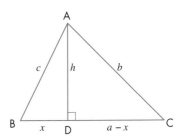

Therefore,

$$c^2 - x^2 = b^2 - (a - x)^2$$

$$c^2 - x^2 = b^2 - a^2 + 2ax - x^2$$

$$\Rightarrow \quad c^2 = b^2 - a^2 + 2ax$$

From triangle BDA, $x = c \cos B$.

Hence

$$c^2 = b^2 - a^2 + 2ac \cos B$$

Rearranging gives

$$b^2 = a^2 + c^2 - 2ac \cos B$$

By algebraic symmetry

$$a^2 = b^2 + c^2 - 2bc \cos A \quad \text{and} \quad c^2 = a^2 + b^2 - 2ab \cos C$$

This is the cosine rule, which can be best remembered by the diagram on the right, where

$$a^2 = b^2 + c^2 - 2bc \cos A$$

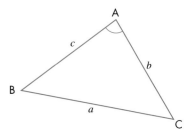

Note the symmetry of the rule and how the rule works using two adjacent sides and the angle between them.

The formula can be rearranged to find any of the three angles

$$\cos A = \frac{b^2 + c^2 - a^2}{2bc}$$

$$\cos B = \frac{a^2 + c^2 - b^2}{2ac}$$

$$\cos C = \frac{a^2 + b^2 - c^2}{2ab}$$

Note that the cosine rule $a^2 = b^2 + c^2 - 2bc \cos A$ is given in the formula sheets in the GCSE examination but the rearranged formula for the angle is not given. You are advised to learn this as trying to rearrange usually ends up with an incorrect formula.

EXAMPLE 14

Find x in this triangle.

By the cosine rule

$$x^2 = 6^2 + 10^2 - 2 \times 6 \times 10 \times \cos 80°$$

$$x^2 = 115.16$$

$$\Rightarrow x = 10.7 \qquad \text{(3 significant figures)}$$

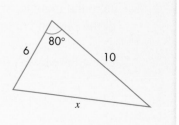

EXAMPLE 15

Find x in this triangle.

By the cosine rule

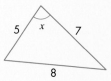

$$\cos x = \frac{5^2 + 7^2 - 8^2}{2 \times 5 \times 7} = 0.1428$$

$\Rightarrow \ x = 81.8°$ (3 significant figures)

EXAMPLE 16

A ship sails from a port on a bearing of 055° for 40 km. It then changes course to 123° for another 50 km. On what course should the ship be steered to get it straight back to the port?

Previously, you have solved this type of problem using right-angled triangles. This method could be applied here but it would involve at least six separate calculations.

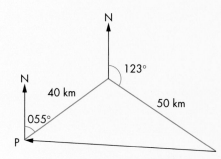

With the aid of the cosine and sine rules, however, you can reduce the solution to two separate calculations, as follows.

The course diagram gives the triangle PAB (on the right), where angle PAB is found by using alternate angles and angles on a line.
55° + (180° − 123°) = 112°

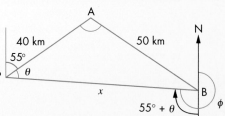

Let ϕ be the bearing to be steered, then

$$\phi = \theta + 55° + 180°$$

To find θ, you first have to obtain PB(= x), using the cosine rule.

$$x^2 = 40^2 + 50^2 - 2 \times 40 \times 50 \times \cos 112° \text{ km}^2$$

(Remember: the cosine of 112° is negative.)

$\Rightarrow x^2 = 5598.43 \text{ km}^2$

$\Rightarrow \ x = 74.82 \text{ km}$

You can now find θ from the sine rule.

$$\frac{\sin \theta}{50} = \frac{\sin 112°}{74.82}$$

$$\Rightarrow \sin \theta = \frac{50 \times \sin 112°}{74.82} = 0.6196$$

$$\Rightarrow \quad \theta = 38.3°$$

So the ship should be steered on a bearing of

$$38.3° + 55° + 180° = 273.3°$$

EXERCISE 22H

A

1 Find the length x in each of these triangles.

a
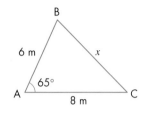

b
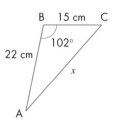

c
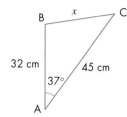

2 Find the angle x in each of these triangles.

a
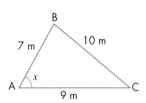

b
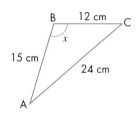

c
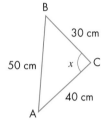

d Explain the significance of the answer to part c.

3 In triangle ABC, AB = 5 cm, BC = 6 cm and angle ABC = 55°. Find AC.

4 A triangle has two sides of length 40 cm and an angle of 110°. Work out the length of the third side of the triangle.

5 The diagram shows a trapezium ABCD. AB = 6.7 cm, AD = 7.2 cm, CB = 9.3 cm and angle DAB = 100°. Calculate these.

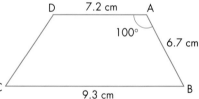

a length DB

b angle DBA

c angle DBC

d length DC

e area of the trapezium

A*

6 A quadrilateral ABCD has AD = 6 cm, DC = 9 cm, AB = 10 cm and BC = 12 cm. Angle ADC = 120°. Calculate angle ABC.

7 A triangle has two sides of length 30 cm and an angle of 50°. Unfortunately, the position of the angle is not known. Sketch the two possible triangles and use them to work out the two possible lengths of the third side of the triangle.

8 A ship sails from a port on a bearing of 050° for 50 km then turns on a bearing of 150° for 40 km. A crewman is taken ill, so the ship drops anchor. What course and distance should a rescue helicopter from the port fly to reach the ship in the shortest possible time?

The three sides of a triangle are given as $3a$, $5a$ and $7a$. Calculate the smallest angle in the triangle.

10 ABCD is a trapezium where AB is parallel to CD. AB = 4 cm, BC = 5 cm, CD = 8 cm, DA = 6 cm. A line BX is parallel to AD and cuts DC at X. Calculate these.

 a angle BCD

 b length BD

11 For any triangle ABC prove the cosine rule

$$a^2 = b^2 + c^2 - 2bc \cos A$$

Choosing the correct rule

When solving triangles, there are only four situations that can occur, each of which can be solved completely in three stages.

Two sides and the included angle

1 Use the cosine rule to find the third side.

2 Use the sine rule to find either of the other angles.

3 Use the sum of the angles in a triangle to find the third angle.

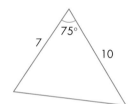

Two angles and a side

1 Use the sum of the angles in a triangle to find the third angle.

2, 3 Use the sine rule to find the other two sides.

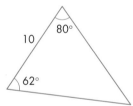

Three sides

1 Use the cosine rule to find one angle.

2 Use the sine rule to find another angle.

3 Use the sum of the angles in a triangle to find the third angle.

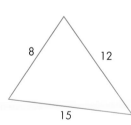

Two sides and a non-included angle

This is the ambiguous case already covered (page 483).

1 Use the sine rule to find the two possible values of the appropriate angle.

2 Use the sum of the angles in a triangle to find the two possible values of the third angle.

3 Use the sine rule to find the two possible values for the length of the third side.

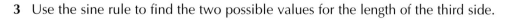

Note: Apply the sine rule wherever you can – it is always easier to use than the cosine rule. The cosine rule should never need to be used more than once.

EXERCISE 22I

1 Find the length or angle x in each of these triangles.

a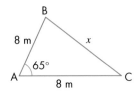

b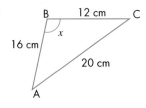

c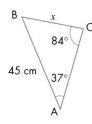

d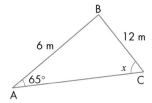

e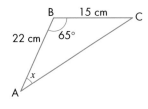

f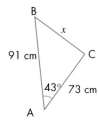

g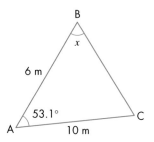

h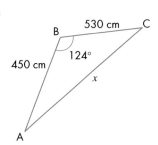

i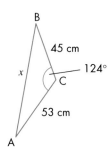

2 The hands of a clock have lengths 3 cm and 5 cm. Find the distance between the tips of the hands at 4 o'clock.

3 A spacecraft is seen hovering at a point which is in the same vertical plane as two towns, X and F. Its distances from X and F are 8.5 km and 12 km respectively. The angle of elevation of the spacecraft when observed from F is 43°. Calculate the distance between the two towns.

4 Two boats, Mary Jo and Suzie, leave port at the same time. Mary Jo sails at 10 knots on a bearing of 065°. Suzie sails on a bearing of 120° and after 1 hour Mary Jo is on a bearing of 330° from Suzie. What is Suzie's speed? (A knot is a nautical mile per hour.)

5 Two ships leave port at the same time, Darling Dave sailing at 12 knots on a bearing of 055°, and Merry Mary at 18 knots on a bearing of 280°.

  a How far apart are the two ships after 1 hour?

  b What is the bearing of Merry Mary from Darling Dave?

Sine, cosine and tangent of 30°, 45° and 60°

In this section you will learn how to:

● work out the trigonometric ratios of 30°, 45° and 60° in surd form

---

EXAMPLE 17

Using an equilateral triangle whose sides are 2 units, write down expressions for the sine, cosine and tangent of 60° and 30°.

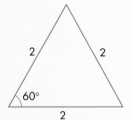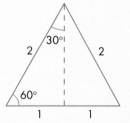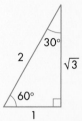

Divide the equilateral triangle into two equal right-angled triangles. Taking one of them, use Pythagoras and the definition of sine, cosine and tangent to obtain

$$\sin 60° = \frac{\sqrt{3}}{2} \qquad \cos 60° = \frac{1}{2} \qquad \tan 60° = \sqrt{3}$$

and

$$\sin 30° = \frac{1}{2} \qquad \cos 30° = \frac{\sqrt{3}}{2} \qquad \tan 30° = \frac{1}{\sqrt{3}} = \frac{\sqrt{3}}{3}$$

EXAMPLE 18

Using a right-angled isosceles triangle whose equal sides are 1 unit, find the sine, cosine and tangent of 45°.

By Pythagoras, the hypotenuse of the triangle is $\sqrt{2}$ units.

From the definition of sine, cosine and tangent, you obtain

$$\sin 45° = \frac{1}{\sqrt{2}} = \frac{\sqrt{2}}{2} \qquad \cos 45° = \frac{1}{\sqrt{2}} = \frac{\sqrt{2}}{2} \qquad \tan 45° = 1$$

EXERCISE 22J

1 The sine of angle x is $\frac{4}{5}$. Work out the cosine of angle x.

2 The cosine of angle x is $\dfrac{3}{\sqrt{15}}$. Work out the sine of angle x.

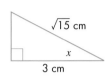

3 The two short sides of a right-angled triangle are $\sqrt{6}$ and $\sqrt{13}$. Write down the exact value of the hypotenuse of this triangle, and the exact value of the sine, cosine and tangent of the smallest angle in the triangle.

4 The tangent of angle A is $\frac{6}{11}$. Use this fact to label two sides of the triangle.

    a Calculate the third side of the triangle.

    b Write down the exact values of sin A and cos A.

5 Calculate the exact value of the area of an equilateral triangle of side 6 cm.

6 Work out the exact value of the area of a right-angled isosceles triangle whose hypotenuse is 40 cm.

22.6 Using sine to find the area of a triangle

This section will show you how to:

- work out the area of a triangle if you know two sides and the included angle

Take triangle ABC, whose vertical height is BD and whose base is AC.

Let BD = h and AC = b, then the area of the triangle is given by

$$\tfrac{1}{2} \times AC \times BD = \tfrac{1}{2}bh$$

However, in triangle BCD

$$h = BC \sin C = a \sin C$$

where BC = a.

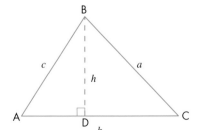

Mod 5

Substituting into $\frac{1}{2}bh$ gives

$$\tfrac{1}{2}b \times (a \sin C) = \tfrac{1}{2}ab \sin C$$

as the area of the triangle.

By taking the perpendicular from A to its opposite side BC, and the perpendicular from C to its opposite side AB, we can show that the area of the triangle is also given by

$$\tfrac{1}{2}ac \sin B \quad \text{and} \quad \tfrac{1}{2}bc \sin A$$

Note the pattern: the area is given by the product of two sides multiplied by the sine of the included angle.

EXAMPLE 19

Find the area of triangle ABC.

Area $= \tfrac{1}{2}ab \sin C$

Area $= \tfrac{1}{2} \times 5 \times 7 \times \sin 38° = 10.8 \text{ cm}^2$ (3 significant figures)

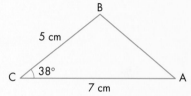

EXAMPLE 20

Find the area of triangle ABC.

You have all three sides but no angle. So first you must find an angle in order to apply the area sine rule.

Find angle C, using the cosine rule.

$$\cos C = \frac{a^2 + b^2 - c^2}{2ab}$$

$$= \frac{13^2 + 19^2 - 8^2}{2 \times 13 \times 19} = 0.9433$$

$$\Rightarrow \quad C = \cos^{-1} 0.9433 = 19.4°$$

(Keep the exact value in your calculator memory.)

Now you apply the area sine rule

$$\tfrac{1}{2}ab \sin C = \tfrac{1}{2} \times 13 \times 19 \times \sin 19.4°$$

$$= 41.0 \text{ cm}^2 \qquad \text{(3 significant figures)}$$

EXERCISE 22K

1 Find the area of each of the following triangles.

   a Triangle ABC where BC = 7 cm, AC = 8 cm and angle ACB = 59°

   b Triangle ABC where angle BAC = 86°, AC = 6.7 cm and AB = 8 cm

   c Triangle PQR where QR = 27 cm, PR = 19 cm and angle QRP = 109°

   d Triangle XYZ where XY = 231 cm, XZ = 191 cm and angle YXZ = 73°

   e Triangle LMN where LN = 63 cm, LM = 39 cm and angle NLM = 85°

2 The area of triangle ABC is 27 cm². If BC = 14 cm and angle BCA = 115°, find AC.

3 The area of triangle LMN is 113 cm², LM = 16 cm and MN = 21 cm. Angle LMN is acute. Calculate these angles.

   a LMN   **b** MNL

4 In a quadrilateral ABCD, DC = 4 cm, BD = 11 cm, angle BAD = 32°, angle ABD = 48° and angle BDC = 61°. Calculate the area of the quadrilateral.

5 A board is in the shape of a triangle with sides 60 cm, 70 cm and 80 cm. Find the area of the board.

6 Two circles, centres P and Q, have radii of 6 cm and 7 cm respectively. The circles intersect at X and Y. Given that PQ = 9 cm, find the area of triangle PXQ.

7 The points A, B and C are on the circumference of a circle, centre O and radius 7 cm. AB = 4 cm and BC = 3.5 cm. Calculate these.

   a angle AOB

   b area of quadrilateral OABC

8 Prove that for any triangle ABC

   Area = $\frac{1}{2}ab \sin C$

9 **a** ABC is a right-angled isosceles triangle with short sides of 1 cm. Write down the value of sin 45°.

   b Calculate the area of triangle PQR.

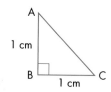

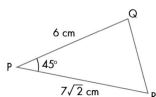

1 a ABC is a right-angled triangle.
AC = 19 cm and AB = 9 cm.

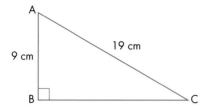

Calculate the length of BC.

b PQR is a right-angled triangle.
PQ = 11 cm and QR = 24 cm.

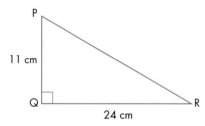

Calculate the size of angle PRQ.

c ABC and ACD are right-angled triangles.
AD is parallel to BC.
AB = 12 cm, BC = 5 cm and AD = 33.8 cm.

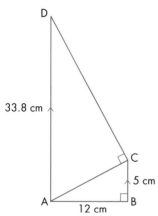

Calculate the size of angle ADC.

AQA, Question 10, Paper 2 Higher, June 2005

2 ABD and BCD are two right-angled triangles.
AB = 12 cm, CD = 8 cm, ∠BAD = 30°.

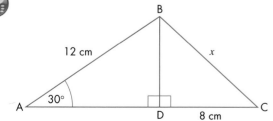

The two triangles are joined together as shown in the diagram. ADC is a straight line. Calculate the length BC, marked *x* on the diagram.

AQA, Question 7, Paper 2 Higher, June 2002

3 ABC is a right-angled triangle.
AB = 7 cm, ∠CAB = 52°.
Find the length of BC
(marked *x* in the diagram).
Give your answer to a suitable
degree of accuracy.

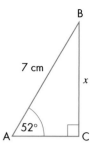

4 PQR is a triangle.
PQ = 12 cm, PR = 15cm, QR = 20 cm.

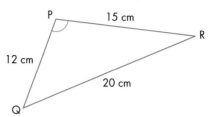

Calculate the angle QPR.

5 A ruined tower is fenced off for safety reasons. To find the height of the tower Rashid stands at a point A and measures the angle of elevation as 18°. He then walks 20 metres directly towards the base of the tower to point B where the angle of elevation is 31°.

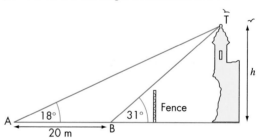

Calculate the height *h*, of the tower.

AQA, Question 17, Paper 2 Higher, November 2004

6 In triangle PQR, PQ = 13 cm, QR = 11 cm and
PR = 12 cm.

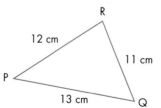

Find the area of triangle PQR.

7 Two ships, A and B, leave port at 13:00 hours.
Ship A travels at a constant speed of 18 km per hour
on a bearing of 070°. Ship B travels at a constant
speed of 25 km per hour on a bearing of 152°.

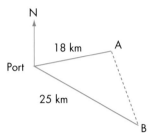

Calculate the distance between A and B at
14:00 hours.

AQA, Question 18, Paper 2 Higher, June 2003

8 ABCDEFGH is a cuboid with sides of 5 cm, 5 cm and
12 cm as shown.

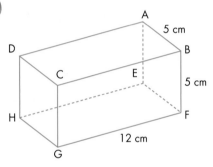

Calculate angle DFH.

AQA, Question 17, Paper 2 Higher, June 2003

9 In triangle PQR, PR = 6 cm, PQ = 10 cm and angle
PRQ = 105°.

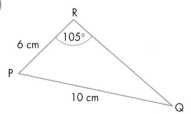

Calculate the area of triangle PQR.

10 VABCD is a right pyramid with a square base.
V is vertically above the centre of the square.
All the slant lengths are 30 cm.
The square base has a side of 20 cm.

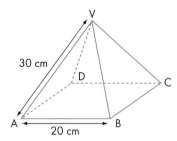

Calculate the angle between the face VAB and the
base ABCD.

11 ABCD is a quadrilateral. AB = 7 cm, AD = 6 cm and
BC = 9 cm. Angle ABC = 75° and angle ADC = 90°.

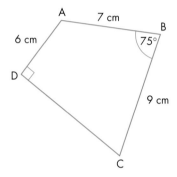

Calculate the perimeter of ABCD.

AQA, Question 21, Paper 2 Higher, June 2004

12 A rectangular based pyramid has a base of length
6 cm and width 4 cm.

The vertex of the pyramid is directly over the midpoint
of the base.

The volume of the pyramid is 200 cm³.

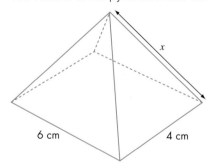

Find the length of the slant edge of the pyramid.

WORKED EXAM QUESTIONS

The diagram represents a level triangular piece of land. AB = 61 metres, AC = 76 metres, and the area of the land is 2300 m². Angle BAC is acute.

Calculate the length of BC. Give your answer to an appropriate degree of accuracy.

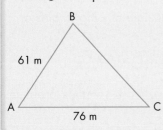

Solution

$\frac{1}{2} \times 61 \times 76 \times \sin BAC = 2300$

∴ sin BAC = 0.9922 ...

∴ Angle BAC = 82.9°

> Use Area = $\frac{1}{2}bc$ sin A to set up an equation and solve it to get angle A. You are given that A is acute so there is no problem with any ambiguity.

$BC^2 = 61^2 + 76^2 - 2 \times 61 \times 76 \times \cos 82.9 = 8343.75$

BC = 91.3 m

> Use the cosine rule to work out the side BC. If possible keep values in your calculator display but if you have to write down values then use at least 4 significant figures for trig ratios and at least 1 decimal place for angles. This will avoid any inaccuracy in the final answer.

A tetrahedron has one face which is an equilateral triangle of side 6 cm and three faces which are isosceles triangles with sides 6 cm, 9 cm and 9 cm.

Calculate the surface area of the tetrahedron.

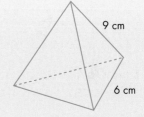

Solution

First work out the area of the base, which has angles of 60°.

Area base = $\frac{1}{2} \times 6 \times 6 \times \sin 60° = 15.59$ cm²　　　　(4 significant figures)

Next, work out the vertex angle of one side triangle using the cosine rule.

$\cos x = \dfrac{9^2 + 9^2 - 6^2}{2 \times 9 \times 9} = 0.7778$

So　　x = 38.9°　　　　(Keep the exact value in your calculator.)

Work out the area of one side face and then add all faces together.

Area side face = $\frac{1}{2} \times 9 \times 9 \times \sin 38.9° = 25.46$ cm²　　　　(4 significant figures)

Total area = 3 × 25.46 + 15.59 = 92.0 cm²　　　　(3 significant figures)

GRADE YOURSELF

(A) Able to solve more complex 2-D problems using Pythagoras' theorem and trigonometry

(A) Able to use the sine and cosine rules to calculate missing angles or sides in non right-angled triangles

(A) Able to find the area of a triangle using the formula Area = $\frac{1}{2}ab \sin C$

(A✳) Able to use the sine and cosine rules to solve more complex problems involving non right-angled triangles

(A✳) Able to solve 3-D problems using Pythagoras' theorem and trigonometric ratios

(A✳) Able to find two angles between 0° and 360° for any given value of a trigonometric ratio (positive or negative)

(A✳) Able to solve simple equations where the trigonometric ratio is the subject

What you should know now

- How to use the sine and cosine rules
- How to find the area of a triangle using Area = $\frac{1}{2}ab \sin C$

Linear graphs and equations

1 Linear graphs

2 Finding the equation of a line from its graph

3 Uses of graphs

4 Parallel and perpendicular lines

This chapter will show you ...

- how to draw and find the equations of linear graphs
- how to use graphs to find exact or approximate solutions to equations

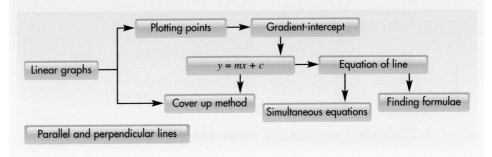

What you should already know

- How to read and plot coordinates
- How to substitute into simple algebraic functions
- How to plot a graph from a given table of values

Quick check

1 This table shows values of $y = 2x + 3$ for $-2 \leqslant x \leqslant 5$.

x	−2	−1	0	1	2	3	4	5
y	−1	1	3	5	7	9	11	

a Complete the table for $x = 5$

b Copy these axes and plot the points to draw the graph of $y = 2x + 3$.

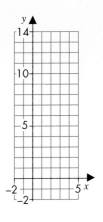

Linear graphs

In this section you will learn how to:

- draw linear graphs without using flow diagrams

Key words

axis
  (pl: axes)
coefficient
gradient-
  intercept
linear
  graphs

This chapter is concerned with drawing straight-line graphs. These graphs are usually referred to as **linear graphs**.

The minimum number of points needed to draw a linear graph is two but three or more are better because that gives at least one point to act as a check. There is no rule about how many points to plot but here are some tips.

- Use a sharp pencil and mark each point with an accurate cross.

- Get your eyes directly over the graph. If you look from the side, you will not be able to line up your ruler accurately.

Drawing graphs by finding points

This method is a bit quicker and does not need flow diagrams. However, if you prefer flow diagrams, use them. Follow through Example 1 to see how to draw a graph by finding points.

EXAMPLE 1

Draw the graph of $y = 4x - 5$ for values of x from 0 to 5. This is usually written as $0 \leqslant x \leqslant 5$.

Choose three values for x: these should be the highest and lowest x-values and one in between.

Work out the y-values by substituting the x-values into the equation.

When $x = 0$, $y = 4(0) - 5 = -5$. This gives the point $(0, -5)$.

When $x = 3$, $y = 4(3) - 5 = 7$. This gives the point $(3, 7)$.

When $x = 5$, $y = 4(5) - 5 = 15$. This gives the point $(5, 15)$.

Keep a record of your calculations in a table.

x	0	3	5
y	-5	7	15

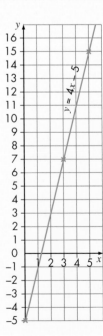

You now have to decide the extent (range) of the **axes**. You can find this out by looking at the coordinates that you have so far. The smallest x-value is 0, the largest is 5. The smallest y-value is -5, the largest is 15.

Now draw the axes, plot the points and complete the graph. It is usually a good idea to choose 0 as one of the x-values. In an examination, the range for the x-values will usually be given and the axes already drawn.

Read through these hints before drawing the linear graphs required in Exercise 23A.

- Use the highest and lowest values of x given in the range.

- Don't pick x-values that are too close together, for example, 1 and 2. Try to space them out so that you can draw a more accurate graph.

- Always label your graph with its equation. This is particularly important when you are drawing two graphs on the same set of axes.

- If you want to use a flow diagram, use one.

- Create a table of values. You will often have to complete these in your examinations.

EXERCISE 23A

1 Draw the graph of $y = 3x + 4$ for x-values from 0 to 5 $(0 \leqslant x \leqslant 5)$.

2 Draw the graph of $y = 2x - 5$ for $0 \leqslant x \leqslant 5$.

3 Draw the graph of $y = \dfrac{x}{2} - 3$ for $0 \leqslant x \leqslant 10$.

4 Draw the graph of $y = 3x + 5$ for $-3 \leqslant x \leqslant 3$.

5 Draw the graph of $y = \dfrac{x}{3} + 4$ for $-6 \leqslant x \leqslant 6$.

6 **a** On the same set of axes, draw the graphs of $y = 3x - 2$ and $y = 2x + 1$ for $0 \leqslant x \leqslant 5$.

   b At which point do the two lines intersect?

7 **a** On the same axes, draw the graphs of $y = 4x - 5$ and $y = 2x + 3$ for $0 \leqslant x \leqslant 5$.

   b At which point do the two lines intersect?

8 **a** On the same axes, draw the graphs of $y = \dfrac{x}{3} - 1$ and $y = \dfrac{x}{2} - 2$ for $0 \leqslant x \leqslant 12$.

   b At which point do the two lines intersect?

9 **a** On the same axes, draw the graphs of $y = 3x + 1$ and $y = 3x - 2$ for $0 \leqslant x \leqslant 4$.

   b Do the two lines intersect? If not, why not?

10 **a** Copy and complete the table to draw the graph of $x + y = 5$ for $0 \leqslant x \leqslant 5$.

x	0	1	2	3	4	5
y	5		3		1	

   b Now draw the graph of $x + y = 7$ for $0 \leqslant x \leqslant 7$ on the same axes.

Gradient

The slope of a line is called its gradient. The steeper the slope of the line, the larger the value of the gradient.

The gradient of the line shown here can be measured by drawing, as large as possible, a right-angled triangle which has part of the line as its hypotenuse (sloping side). The gradient is then given by:

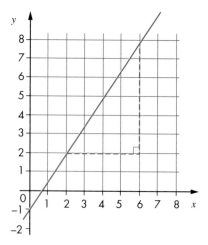

$$\text{gradient} = \frac{\text{distance measured up}}{\text{distance measured along}}$$

$$= \frac{\text{difference on } y\text{-axis}}{\text{difference on } x\text{-axis}}$$

For example, to measure the steepness of the line in the next figure, you first draw a right-angled triangle whose hypotenuse is part of this line. It does not matter where you draw the triangle but it makes the calculations much easier if you choose a sensible place. This usually means using existing grid lines, so that you avoid fractional values.

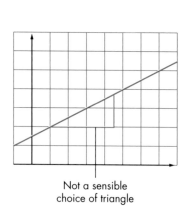

Not a sensible choice of triangle

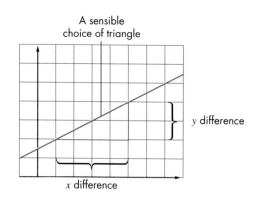

A sensible choice of triangle

y difference

x difference

After you have drawn the triangle, you measure (or count) how many squares there are on the vertical side. This is the difference between your *y*-coordinates. In the case above, this is 2.

You then measure (or count) how many squares there are on the horizontal side. This is the difference between your *x*-coordinates. In the case above, this is 4.

To work out the gradient, you do the following calculation.

$$\text{gradient} = \frac{\text{difference of the } y\text{-coordinates}}{\text{difference of the } x\text{-coordinates}} = \frac{2}{4} = \frac{1}{2} \text{ or } 0.5$$

Note that the value of the gradient is not affected by where the triangle is drawn. As we are calculating the ratio of two sides of the triangle, the gradient will always be the same wherever we draw the triangle.

Remember: When a line slopes down from left to right, the gradient is negative, so a minus sign must be placed in front of the calculated fraction.

EXAMPLE 2

Find the gradient of each of these lines.

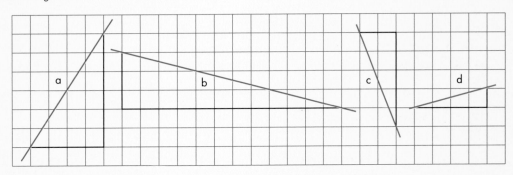

In each case, a sensible choice of triangle has already been made.

a y difference = 6, x difference = 4   Gradient = $6 \div 4 = \dfrac{3}{2} = 1.5$

b y difference = 3, x difference = 12   Line slopes down left to right,

so gradient = $-(3 \div 12) = -\dfrac{1}{4} = -0.25$

c y difference = 5, x difference = 2   Line slopes down from left to right,

so gradient = $-(5 \div 2) = -\dfrac{5}{2} = -2.5$

d y difference = 1, x difference = 4   Gradient = $1 \div 4 = \dfrac{1}{4} = 0.25$

Drawing a line with a certain gradient

To draw a line with a certain gradient, you reverse the process described above. That is, you first draw the right-angled triangle using the given gradient. For example, take a gradient of 2.

Start at a convenient point (A in the diagrams below). A gradient of 2 means for an x-step of 1 the y-step must be 2 (because 2 is the fraction $\frac{2}{1}$). So, move one square across and two squares up, and mark a dot.

Repeat this as many times as you like and draw the line. You can also move one square back and two squares down, which gives the same gradient, as the third diagram shows.

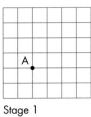

Stage 1

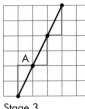

Stage 2

Stage 3

EXAMPLE 3

Draw lines with these gradients.   **a** $\frac{1}{3}$ **b** -3 **c** $-\frac{1}{4}$

a This is a fractional gradient which has a *y*-step of 1 and an *x*-step of 3. Move three squares across and one square up every time.

b This is a negative gradient, so for every one square across, move three squares down.

c This is also a negative gradient and it is a fraction. So for every four squares across, move one square down.

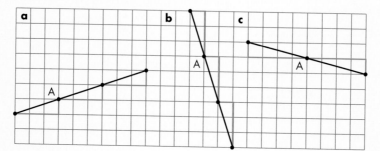

EXERCISE 23B

1 Find the gradient of each of these lines.

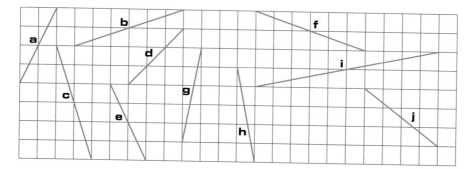

2 Draw lines with these gradients.

a 4   **b** $\frac{2}{3}$ **c** -2 **d** $-\frac{4}{5}$ **e** 6   **f** -6

3 Find the gradient of each of these lines. What is special about these lines?

a

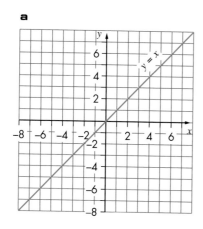

b

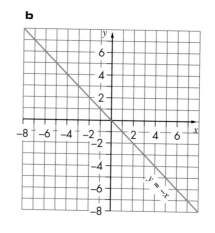

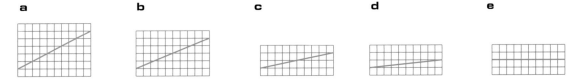

4 The line on grid **e** is horizontal. The lines on grids **a** to **d** get nearer and nearer to the horizontal.

a   b   c   d   e

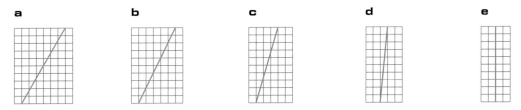

Find the gradient of each line in grids **a** to **d**. By looking at the values you obtain, what do you think the gradient of a horizontal line is?

5 The line on grid **e** is vertical. The lines on grids **a** to **d** get nearer and nearer to the vertical.

a   b   c   d   e

Find the gradient of each line in grids **a** to **d**. By looking at the values you obtain, what do you think the gradient of a vertical line is?

Gradient-intercept method for drawing graphs

The ideas that you have discovered in the last activity lead to another way of plotting lines, known as the **gradient-intercept** method.

EXAMPLE 4

Draw the graph of $y = 3x - 1$, using the gradient-intercept method.

- Because the constant term is –1, we know that the graph goes through the y-axis at –1. We mark this point with a dot or a cross (**A** on diagram **i**).

- The number in front of x (called the **coefficient** of x) gives the relationship between y and x. Because the coefficient of x is 3, this tells us that y is 3 times the x value, so the gradient of the line is 3. For an x-step of one unit, there is a y-step of three. Starting at –1 on the y-axis, we move one square across and three squares up and mark this point with a dot or a cross (**B** on diagram **i**).

Repeat this from every new point. You can also move one square back and three squares down. When enough points have been marked, join the dots (or crosses) to make the graph (diagram **ii**). Note that if the points are not in a straight line, a mistake has been made.

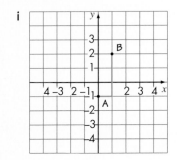

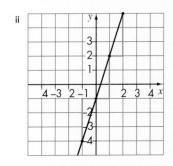

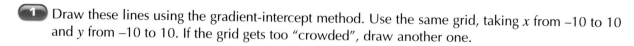

1 Draw these lines using the gradient-intercept method. Use the same grid, taking x from -10 to 10 and y from -10 to 10. If the grid gets too "crowded", draw another one.

a $y = 2x + 6$

b $y = 3x - 4$

c $y = \frac{1}{2}x + 5$

d $y = x + 7$

e $y = 4x - 3$

f $y = 2x - 7$

g $y = \frac{1}{4}x - 3$

h $y = \frac{2}{3}x + 4$

i $y = 6x - 5$

j $y = x + 8$

k $y = \frac{4}{5}x - 2$

l $y = 3x - 9$

2 **a** Using the gradient-intercept method, draw the following lines on the same grid. Use axes with ranges $-6 \leqslant x \leqslant 6$ and $-8 \leqslant y \leqslant 8$.

i $y = 3x + 1$ **ii** $y = 2x + 3$

b Where do the lines cross?

3 **a** Using the gradient-intercept method, draw the following lines on the same grid. Use axes with ranges $-14 \leqslant x \leqslant 4$ and $-2 \leqslant y \leqslant 6$.

i $y = \dfrac{x}{3} + 3$ **ii** $y = \dfrac{x}{4} + 2$

b Where do the lines cross?

4 **a** Using the gradient-intercept method draw the following lines on the same grid. Use axes with ranges $-4 \leqslant x \leqslant 6$ and $-6 \leqslant y \leqslant 8$.

i $y = x + 3$ **ii** $y = 2x$

b Where do the lines cross?

Cover-up method for drawing graphs

The x-axis has the equation $y = 0$. This means that all points on the x-axis have a y-value of 0.

The y-axis has the equation $x = 0$. This means that all points on the y-axis have an x-value of 0.

We can use these facts to draw any line that has an equation of the form:

$ax + by = c$.

EXAMPLE 5

Draw the graph of $4x + 5y = 20$.

Because the value of x is 0 on the y-axis, we can solve the equation for y:

$$4(0) + 5y = 20$$

$$5y = 20$$

$$\Rightarrow \quad y = 4$$

Hence, the line passes through the point $(0, 4)$ on the y-axis (diagram **A**).

Because the value of y is 0 on the x-axis, we can also solve the equation for x:

$$4x + 5(0) = 20$$

$$4x = 20$$

$$\Rightarrow \quad x = 5$$

Hence, the line passes through the point $(5, 0)$ on the x-axis (diagram **B**). We need only two points to draw a line. (Normally, we would like a third point but in this case we can accept two.) The graph is drawn by joining the points $(0, 4)$ and $(5, 0)$ (diagram **C**).

A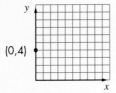

B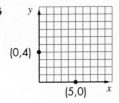

C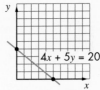

This type of equation can be drawn very easily, without much working at all, using the cover-up method.

Start with the equation	$4x + 5y = 20$
Cover up the x-term:	$\square + 5y = 20$
Solve the equation (when $x = 0$):	$y = 4$
Now cover up the y-term:	$4x + \square = 20$
Solve the equation (when $y = 0$):	$x = 5$

This gives the points $(0, 4)$ on the y-axis and $(5, 0)$ on the x-axis.

EXAMPLE 6

Draw the graph of $2x - 3y = 12$.

Start with the equation	$2x - 3y = 12$
Cover up the x-term:	$\square - 3y = 12$
Solve the equation (when $x = 0$):	$y = -4$
Now cover up the y-term:	$2x + \square = 12$
Solve the equation (when $y = 0$):	$x = 6$

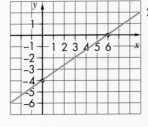

This gives the points $(0, -4)$ on the y-axis and $(6, 0)$ on the x-axis.

EXERCISE 23D

1 Draw these lines using the cover-up method. Use the same grid, taking x from –10 to 10 and y from –10 to 10. If the grid gets too "crowded", draw another.

a $3x + 2y = 6$ **b** $4x + 3y = 12$ **c** $4x - 5y = 20$

d $x + y = 10$ **e** $3x - 2y = 18$ **f** $x - y = 4$

g $5x - 2y = 15$ **h** $2x - 3y = 15$ **i** $6x + 5y = 30$

j $x + y = -5$ **k** $x + y = 3$ **l** $x - y = -4$

2 **a** Using the cover-up method, draw the following lines on the same grid. Use axes with ranges $-2 \leqslant x \leqslant 6$ and $-2 \leqslant y \leqslant 6$.

     i $2x + y = 4$ **ii** $x - 2y = 2$

    b Where do the lines cross?

3 **a** Using the cover-up method, draw the following lines on the same grid. Use axes with ranges $-2 \leqslant x \leqslant 6$ and $-3 \leqslant y \leqslant 6$.

     i $x + 2y = 6$ **ii** $2x - y = 2$

    b Where do the lines cross?

4 **a** Using the cover-up method, draw the following lines on the same grid. Use axes with ranges $-6 \leqslant x \leqslant 8$ and $-2 \leqslant y \leqslant 8$.

     i $x + y = 6$ **ii** $x - y = 2$

    b Where do the lines cross?

23.2 Finding the equation of a line from its graph

In this section you will learn how to:
- find the equation of a line using its gradient and intercept

Key words
coefficient
gradient
intercept

The equation $y = mx + c$

When a graph can be expressed in the form $y = mx + c$, the **coefficient** of x, m, is the **gradient**, and the constant term, c, is the **intercept** on the y-axis.

This means that if we know the gradient, m, of a line and its intercept, c, on the y-axis, we can write down the equation of the line immediately.

For example, if $m = 3$ and $c = -5$, the equation of the line is $y = 3x - 5$.

All linear graphs can be expressed in the form $y = mx + c$.

This gives us a method of finding the equation of any line drawn on a pair of coordinate axes.

EXAMPLE 7

Find the equation of the line shown in diagram **A**.

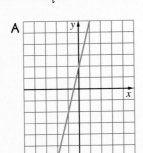 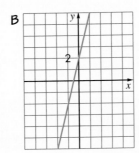 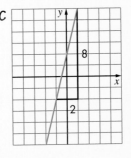

First, we find where the graph crosses the y-axis (diagram **B**).

So $c = 2$.

Next, we measure the gradient of the line (diagram **C**).

$$y\text{-step} = 8$$
$$x\text{-step} = 2$$
$$\text{gradient} = 8 \div 2 = 4$$

So $m = 4$.

Finally, we write down the equation of the line: $y = 4x + 2$.

EXERCISE 23E

1 Give the equation of each of these lines, all of which have positive gradients. (Each square represents 1 unit.)

a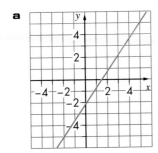

b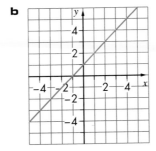

c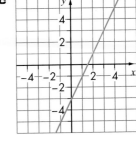

d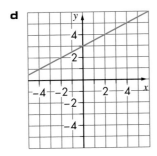

e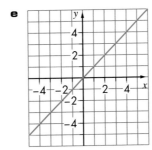

f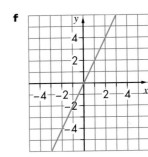

2 In each of these grids, there are two lines. (Each square represents 1 unit.)

a 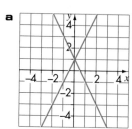   **b** 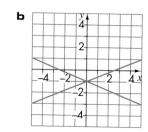   **c**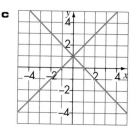

For each grid:

i find the equation of each of the lines,

ii describe any symmetries that you can see,

iii what connection is there between the gradients of each pair of lines?

3 Give the equation of each of these lines, all of which have negative gradients. (Each square represents 1 unit.)

a 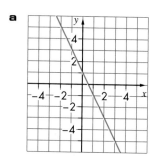   **b** 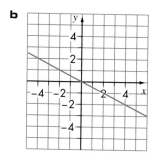   **c**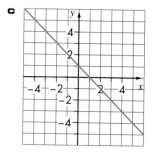

d 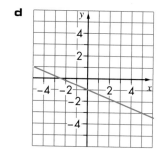   **e**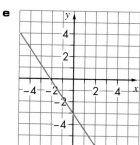

4 In each of these grids, there are three lines. One of them is $y = x$. (Each square represents one unit.)

a 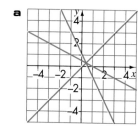   **b** 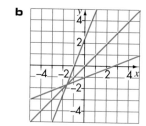   **c**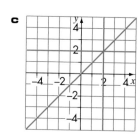

For each grid:

i find the equation of each of the other two lines,

ii describe any symmetries that you can see,

iii what connection is there between the gradients of each group of lines?

Uses of graphs

In this section you will learn how to:
- use straight-line graphs to find formulae
- solve simultaneous linear equations using graphs

Key words

formula
    (pl: formulae)
rule

On page 464, you met two uses of graphs in kinematics, and the use of graphs to represent mortgage repayment and the rate of change of depth as a container is filled with water. Two other uses of graphs which we will now consider are finding formulae and solving simultaneous equations. Solving quadratic and other equations by graphical methods was covered in Chapter 8.

Finding formulae or rules

EXAMPLE 8

A taxi fare will cost more the further you go. The graph on the right illustrates the fares in one part of England.

The taxi company charges a basic hire fee to start with of £2.00. This is shown on the graph as the point where the line cuts through the hire-charge axis (when distance travelled is 0).

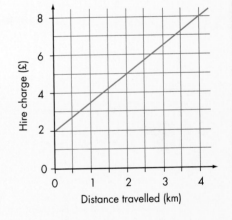

The gradient of the line is:

$$\frac{8-2}{4} = \frac{6}{4} = 1.5$$

This represents the hire charge per kilometre travelled.

So the total hire charge is made up of two parts: a basic hire charge of £2.00 and an additional charge of £1.50 per kilometre travelled. This can be put in a formula as

Hire charge = £2.00 + £1.50 per kilometre.

In this example, £2.00 is the constant term in the formula (the equation of the graph).

B

1 This graph is a conversion graph between °C and °F.

    a How many °F are equivalent to a temperature of 0 °C?

    b What is the gradient of the line?

    c From your answers to parts **a** and **b**, write down a rule which can be used to convert °C to °F.

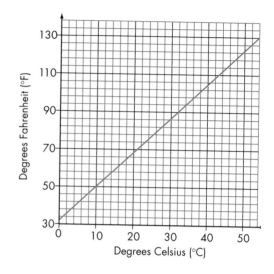

2 This graph illustrates charges for fuel.

    a What is the gradient of the line?

    b The standing charge is the basic charge before the cost per unit is added. What is the standing charge?

    c Write down the rule used to work out the total charge for different amounts of units used.

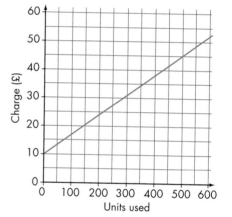

3 This graph shows the hire charge for heaters over so many days.

    a Calculate the gradient of the line.

    b What is the basic charge before the daily hire charge is added on?

    c Write down the rule used to work out the total hire charge.

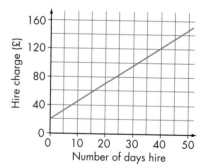

4 This graph shows the hire charge for a conference centre depending on the number of people at the conference.

    a Calculate the gradient of the line.

    b What is the basic fee for hiring the conference centre?

    c Write down the rule used to work out the total hire charge for the centre.

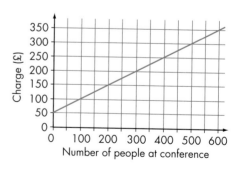

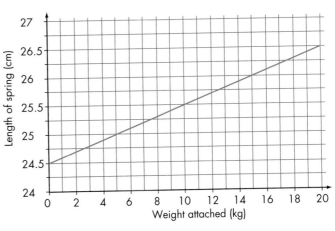

5 This graph shows the length of a spring when different weights are attached to it.

   a Calculate the gradient of the line.

   b How long is the spring when no weight is attached to it?

   c By how much does the spring extend per kilogram?

   d Write down the rule for finding the length of the spring for different weights.

Solving simultaneous equations

EXAMPLE 9

By drawing their graphs on the same grid, find the solution of these simultaneous equations.

   a $3x + y = 6$ **b** $y = 4x - 1$

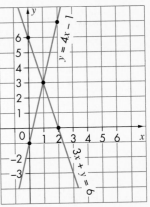

a The first graph is drawn using the cover-up method. It crosses the x-axis at $(2, 0)$ and the y-axis at $(0, 6)$.

b This graph can be drawn by finding some points or by the gradient-intercept method. If you use the gradient-intercept method, you find the graph crosses the y-axis at -1 and has a gradient of 4.

The point where the graphs intersect is $(1, 3)$. So the solution to the simultaneous equations is $x = 1$, $y = 3$.

EXERCISE 23G

By drawing their graphs, find the solution of each of these pairs of simultaneous equations.

1 $x + 4y = 8$
   $x - y = 3$

2 $y = 2x - 1$
   $3x + 2y = 12$

3 $y = 2x + 4$
   $y = x + 7$

4 $y = x$
   $x + y = 10$

5 $y = 2x + 3$
   $5x + y = 10$

6 $y = 5x + 1$
   $y = 2x + 10$

7 $y = x + 8$
   $x + y = 4$

8 $y - 3x = 9$
   $y = x - 3$

9 $y = -x$
   $y = 4x - 5$

10 $3x + 2y = 18$
   $y = 3x$

11 $y = 3x + 2$
   $y + x = 10$

12 $y = \dfrac{x}{3} + 1$
   $x + y = 11$

Parallel and perpendicular lines

This section will show you how to:

- draw linear graphs parallel or perpendicular to other lines and passing through a specific point

Key words

negative
reciprocal
parallel
perpendicular

EXAMPLE 10

In each of these grids, there are two lines.

a 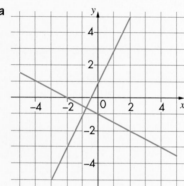   **b** 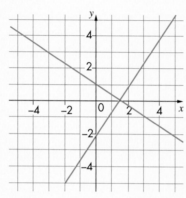   **c**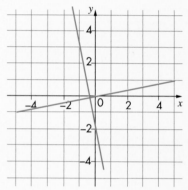

For each grid:

i find the equation of each line,

ii describe the geometrical relationship between the lines,

iii describe the numerical relationships between their gradients.

i Grid a: the lines have equations $y = 2x + 1$, $y = -\frac{1}{2}x - 1$

Grid b: the lines have equations $y = \frac{3}{2}x - 2$, $y = -\frac{2}{3}x + 1$

Grid c: the lines have equations $y = \frac{1}{5}x$, $y = -5x - 2$

ii In each case the lines are perpendicular (at right angles)

iii In each case the gradients are reciprocals of each other but with different signs.

Note: If two lines are **parallel**, then their gradients are equal.

If two lines are **perpendicular**, their gradients are **negative reciprocals** of each other.

EXAMPLE 11

Find the line that is perpendicular to the line $y = \frac{1}{2}x - 3$ and passes through $(0, 5)$.

The gradient of the new line will be the negative reciprocal of $\frac{1}{2}$ which is -2.

The point $(0, 5)$ is the intercept on the y-axis so the equation of the line is $y = -2x + 5$.

EXAMPLE 12

The point A is $(2, -1)$ and the point B is $(4, 5)$.

a Find the equation of the line parallel to AB and passing through $(2, 8)$.

b Find the equation of the line perpendicular to the midpoint of AB.

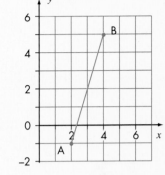

a The gradient of AB is 3, so the new equation is of the form

$$y = 3x + c.$$

The new line passes through $(2, 8)$, so $8 = 3 \times 2 + c$
$$\Rightarrow c = 2$$

Hence the line is $y = 3x + 2$.

b The midpoint of AB is $(3, 2)$.

The gradient of the perpendicular line is the negative reciprocal of 3, which is $-\frac{1}{3}$.

We could find c as in part **a** but we can also do a sketch on the grid. This will show that the perpendicular line passes through $(0, 3)$.

Hence the equation of the line is $y = -\frac{1}{3}x + 3$.

EXERCISE 23H

1 Write down the negative reciprocals of the following numbers.

a 2   b -3 c 5   d -1

e $\frac{1}{2}$ f $\frac{1}{4}$ g $-\frac{1}{3}$ h $-\frac{2}{3}$

i 1.5   j 10   k -6 l $\frac{4}{3}$

2 Write down the equation of the line perpendicular to each of the following lines and which passes through the same point on the y-axis.

a $y = 2x - 1$ b $y = -3x + 1$ c $y = x + 2$ d $y = -x + 2$

e $y = \frac{1}{2}x + 3$ f $y = \frac{1}{4}x - 3$ g $y = -\frac{1}{3}x$ h $y = -\frac{2}{3}x - 5$

3 Write down the equations of these lines.

a parallel to $y = 4x - 5$ and passes through $(0, 1)$

b parallel to $y = \frac{1}{2}x + 3$ and passes through $(0, -2)$

c parallel to $y = -x + 2$ and passes through $(0, 3)$

4 Write down the equations of these lines.

a perpendicular to $y = 3x + 2$ and passes through $(0, -1)$

b perpendicular to $y = -\frac{1}{3}x - 2$ and passes through $(0, 5)$

c perpendicular to $y = x - 5$ and passes through $(0, 1)$

5 A is the point $(1, 5)$. B is the point $(3, 3)$.

a Find the equation of the line parallel to AB and passing through $(5, 9)$.

b Find the equation of the line perpendicular to AB and passing through the midpoint of AB.

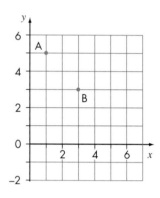

6 Find the equation of the line that passes through the midpoint of AB, where A is $(-5, -3)$ and B is $(-1, 3)$, and has a gradient of 2.

7 Find the equation of the line perpendicular to $y = 4x - 3$, passing though $(-4, 3)$.

8 A is the point $(0, 6)$, B is the point $(5, 5)$ and C is the point $(4, 0)$.

a Write down the point where the line BC intercepts the y-axis.

b Work out the equation of the line AB.

c Write down the equation of the line BC.

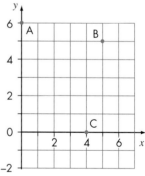

9 Find the equation of the perpendicular bisector of the points A $(1, 2)$ and B $(3, 6)$.

10 A is the point $(0, 4)$, B is the point $(4, 6)$ and C is the point $(2, 0)$.

a Find the equation of the line BC.

b Show that the point of intersection of the perpendicular bisectors of AB and AC is $(3, 3)$.

c Show algebraically that this point lies on the line BC.

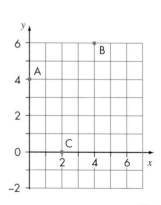

1 **a** Draw the graph of $y = 2x + 3$ for values of x from 0 to 5. Use a grid with axes covering $0 \leqslant x \leqslant 6$ and $0 \leqslant y \leqslant 14$.

  b Use your graph to solve $6.5 = 2x + 3$.

2 The diagram shows a sketch of the graph of $y = 3x + 1$.

Copy the diagram, and draw and label sketch graphs of these.

  a $y = 1$

  b $y = x + 1$

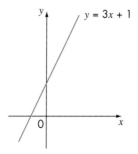

3 **a** Find the equation of the line AB.

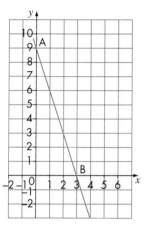

  b Give the y-coordinate of the point on the line with an x-coordinate of 6.

  c Write down the gradient of a line perpendicular to AB.

AQA, Question 7, Paper 2 Higher, November 2004

4 Here are the equations of six lines.

  i $y = 2x + 1$ **ii** $y = -\frac{1}{3}x - 3$

  iii $y = \frac{1}{3}x - 1$ **iv** $y = 2x - 2$

  v $y = 3x + 2$ **vi** $y = \frac{1}{2}x - 2$

  a Which two lines are parallel?

  b Which pairs of lines are perpendicular?

  a Which two lines intersect on the y-axis?

5 The diagram shows the points A(–1, 7), B(0, 5) and C(4, –3).

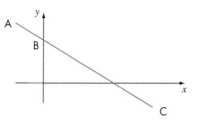

Find the equation of the straight line which passes through A, B and C.

6 Find the equation of the straight line through the point (0, 3) which is perpendicular to the line $y = \frac{3}{5}x + 5$.

7 A is the point (5, 5). B is the point (3, 1). Find the equation of the line perpendicular to AB and passing through the midpoint of AB.

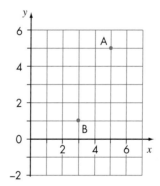

8 Find the equation of the line parallel to the line $y = 3x + 5$ passing through the point (2, 9).

9 Find the equation of the perpendicular bisector of the points A(4, 3) and B(8, 5).

10 A is the point (6, 3), B is the point (0, 5). Find algebraically, the point of intersection of the line perpendicular to AB passing through the midpoint and the line $2y + x = 4$.

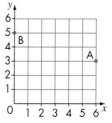

WORKED EXAM QUESTION

a Find the equation of the line shown.

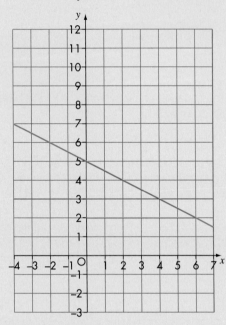

b Find the equation of the line perpendicular to the line shown and passing through $(0, -5)$.

Solution

a Intercept is at $(0, 5)$

First identify the point where the line crosses the y-axis. This is the intercept, c.

Gradient $= -\dfrac{3}{6} = -\dfrac{1}{2}$

Draw a right-angled triangle using grid lines as two sides of the triangle and part of the line as the hypotenuse. (Shown in red on diagram.)

Measure the y-step and the x-step of the triangle and divide the y-step by the x-step to get the gradient, m.

As the line slopes down from left to right the gradient is negative.

Equation of the line is $y = -\dfrac{1}{2}x + 5$

Put the two numbers into the equation $y = mx + c$ to get the equation of the line.

b Gradient is 2

Gradient of y a perpendicular line is the negative reciprocal of $-\dfrac{1}{2}$.

Intercept is $(0, -5)$

Intercept is given.

Equation is $y = 2x - 5$

Give equation in the form $y = mx + c$.

GRADE YOURSELF

D Able to draw straight lines by plotting points

C Able to draw straight lines using the gradient-intercept method

B Able to solve a pair of linear simultaneous equations from their graphs

A Able to find the equations of linear graphs parallel and perpendicular to other linear graphs, that pass through specific points

What you should know now

- How to draw linear graphs

- How to solve simultaneous linear equations by finding the intersection point of the graphs of the equations or other related equations

- How to use gradients to find equations of parallel and perpendicular graphs

Other graphs

This chapter will show you ...

- how to draw cubic, reciprocal and exponential graphs

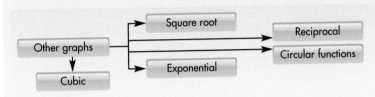

What you should already know

- How to draw linear graphs using a table of values
- How to draw a quadratic graph using a table of values

Quick check

Copy and complete the table and plot the graph of $y = x^2 + 2x - 1$.

x	−4	−3	−2	−1	0	1	2
y	7	2		−4	−1		7

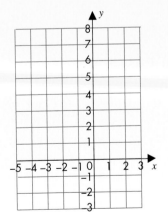

Square root and reciprocal graphs

This section will show you how to:
- recognise square root and reciprocal graphs

Key words

asymptote
reciprocal
square root

Square-root graphs

The graph of $y^2 = x$ is one you should be able to recognise and draw.

When you are working out coordinates in order to plot $y = \sqrt{x}$, remember that for every value of x (except $x = 0$) there are two **square roots**, one positive and the other negative, which give pairs of coordinates. For example,

when $x = 1$, $y = \pm 1$ giving coordinates $(1, -1)$ and $(1, 1)$

when $x = 4$, $y = \pm 2$ giving coordinates $(4, -2)$ and $(4, 2)$

In the case of $x = 0$, $y = 0$ and so there is only one coordinate: $(0, 0)$.

Using these five points, you can draw the graph.

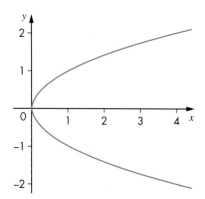

Reciprocal graphs

A **reciprocal** equation has the form $y = \dfrac{a}{x}$.

Examples of reciprocal equations are:

$$y = \frac{1}{x} \qquad y = \frac{4}{x} \qquad y = -\frac{3}{x}$$

All reciprocal graphs have a similar shape and some symmetry properties.

EXAMPLE 1

Complete the table to draw the graph of $y = \dfrac{1}{x}$ for $-4 \leqslant x \leqslant 4$.

x	−4	−3	−2	−1	1	2	3	4
y								

Values are rounded off to two decimal places, as it is unlikely that you could plot a value more accurately than this. The completed table is

x	−4	−3	−2	−1	1	2	3	4
y	−0.25	−0.33	−0.5	−1	1	0.5	0.33	0.25

The graph plotted from these values is shown in **A**. This is not much of a graph and does not show the properties of the reciprocal function. If we take x-values from −0.8 to 0.8 in steps of 0.2, we get the next table.

Note that we cannot use $x = 0$ since $\dfrac{1}{0}$ is infinity.

x	−0.8	−0.6	−0.4	−0.2	0.2	0.4	0.6	0.8
y	−1.25	−1.67	−2.5	−5	5	2.5	1.67	1.25

Plotting these points as well gives the graph in **B**.

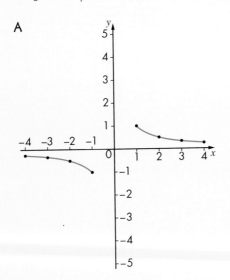

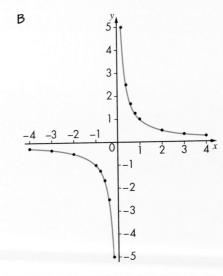

From the graph in **B**, the following properties can be seen.

- The lines $y = x$ and $y = -x$ are lines of symmetry.

- The closer x gets to zero, the nearer the graph gets to the y-axis.

- As x increases, the graph gets closer to the x-axis.

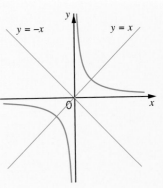

The graph never actually touches the axes, it just gets closer and closer to them. A line to which a graph gets closer but never touches or crosses is called an **asymptote**.

These properties are true for all reciprocal graphs.

1 **a** Copy and complete the table to draw the graph of $y = \dfrac{2}{x}$ for $-4 \leqslant x \leqslant 4$.

x	0.2	0.4	0.5	0.8	1	1.5	2	3	4
y	10		4	2.5			1		0.5

b Use your graph to find the following.

i the y-value when $x = 2.5$ **ii** the x-value when $y = -1.25$

2 **a** Copy and complete the table to draw the graph of $y^2 = 25x$ for $0 \leqslant x \leqslant 5$.

x	0	1	2	3	4	5
$\sqrt{x}$					2 and -2	
$y = 5\sqrt{x}$					10 and -10	

b Use your graph to find the following.

i the values of y when $x = 3.5$ **ii** the value of x when $y = 8$

3 **a** Copy and complete the table to draw the graph of $4y^2 = x$ for $0 \leqslant x \leqslant 5$.

x	0	1	2	3	4	5
$\sqrt{x}$					2 and -2	
$y = \frac{1}{2}\sqrt{x}$					1 and -1	

b Use your graph to find the following.

i the values of y when $x = 2.5$ **ii** the value of x when $y = 0.75$

4 **a** Copy and complete the table to draw the graph of $y = \dfrac{1}{x}$ for $-5 \leqslant x \leqslant 5$.

x	0.1	0.2	0.4	0.5	1	2	2.5	4	5
y	10		2.5		1				0.2

b On the same axes, draw the line $x + y = 5$.

c Use your graph to find the x-values of the points where the graphs cross.

5 **a** Copy and complete the table to draw the graph of $y = \dfrac{5}{x}$ for $-20 \leqslant x \leqslant 20$.

x	0.2	0.4	0.5	1	2	5	10	15	20
y	25		10						0.25

b On the same axes, draw the line $y = x + 10$.

c Use your graph to find the x-values of the points where the graphs cross.

Cubic graphs

This section will show you how to:

- draw and recognise cubic graphs

Key word

cubic

Cubic graphs

A **cubic** function or graph is one which contains a term in x^3. The following are examples of cubic graphs:

$$y = x^3 \qquad y = x^3 - 2x^2 - 3x - 4 \qquad y = x^3 - x^2 - 4x + 4 \qquad y = x^3 + 3x$$

The techniques used to draw them are exactly the same as those for quadratic and reciprocal graphs.

EXAMPLE 2

a Complete the table to draw the graph of $y = x^3 - x^2 - 4x + 4$ for $-3 \leqslant x \leqslant 3$.

x	-3	-2.5	-2	-1.5	-1	-0.5	0	0.5	1	1.5	2	2.5	3
y	-20.00		0.00		6.00		4.00	1.88				3.38	10.00

b By drawing a suitable line on the graph find the solution of the equation $x^3 - x^2 - 4x + 4 = 5$.

a The completed table (to 2 decimal places) is given below.

x	-3	-2.5	-2	-1.5	-1	-0.5	0	0.5	1	1.5	2	2.5	3
y	-20.00	-7.88	0.00	4.38	6.00	5.63	4.00	1.88	0.00	-0.88	0.00	3.38	10.00

The graph of the left-hand side is already drawn.

Hence, you simply need to draw the straight line $y = 5$ and find the x-coordinates of the points where it crosses

$$y = x^3 - x^2 - 4x + 4.$$

The solutions can now be read from the graph as

$$x = -1.4, -0.3 \text{ and } 2.7.$$

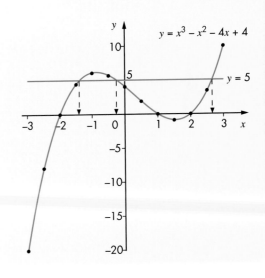

EXERCISE 24B

1 **a** Copy and complete the table to draw the graph of $y = x^3 + 3$ for $-3 \leqslant x \leqslant 3$.

x	-3	-2.5	-2	-1.5	-1	-0.5	0	0.5	1	1.5	2	2.5	3
y	-24.00	-12.63			2.00		3.00	3.13			11.00		30.00

b Use your graph to find the y-value for an x-value of 1.2.

2 a Copy and complete the table to draw the graph of $y = 2x^3$ for $-3 \leqslant x \leqslant 3$.

x	−3	−2.5	−2	−1.5	−1	−0.5	0	0.5	1	1.5	2	2.5	3
y		−31.25		−6.75			0.00	0.25			16.00		

b Use your graph to find the y-value for an x-value of 2.7.

3 a Copy and complete the table to draw the graph of $y = -x^3$ for $-3 \leqslant x \leqslant 3$.

x	−3	−2.5	−2	−1.5	−1	−0.5	0	0.5	1	1.5	2	2.5	3
y	27.00		8.00	3.38			0.00	−0.13			−8.00	−15.63	

b Use your graph to find the y-value for an x-value of −0.6.

4 a Copy and complete the table to draw the graph of $y = x^3 + 3x$ for $-3 \leqslant x \leqslant 3$.

x	−3	−2.5	−2	−1.5	−1	−0.5	0	0.5	1	1.5	2	2.5	3
y	−36.00		−14.00	−7.88			0.00	1.63				23.13	

b Use your graph to find the x-value for a y-value of 2.

5 a Copy and complete the table to draw the graph of $y = x^3 - 3x^2 - 3x$ for $-3 \leqslant x \leqslant 3$.

x	−3	−2.5	−2	−1.5	−1	−0.5	0	0.5	1	1.5	2	2.5	3
y	−45.00		−14.00	−5.63			0.00	−0.63				−10.63	

b Use your graph to find the y-value for an x-value of 1.8.

6 a Copy and complete the table to draw the graph of $y = x^3 - 2x + 5$ for $-3 \leqslant x \leqslant 3$.

x	−3	−2.5	−2	−1.5	−1	−0.5	0	0.5	1	1.5	2	2.5	3
y	−16.00		1.00	4.63			5.00	4.13				15.63	

b On the same axes, draw the graph of $y = x + 6$.

c Use your graph to find the x-values of the points where the graphs cross.

7 a Complete the table to draw the graph of $y = x^3 - 2x + 1$ for $-3 \leqslant x \leqslant 3$.

x	−3	−2.5	−2	−1.5	−1	−0.5	0	0.5	1	1.5	2	2.5	3
y	−20.00		−3.00	0.63			1.00	0.13				11.63	

b On the same axes, draw the graph of $y = x$.

c Use your graph to find the x-values of the points where the graphs cross.

8 Write down whether each of these graphs are "linear", "quadratic", "reciprocal", "cubic" or "none of these".

a
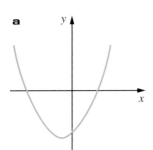

b
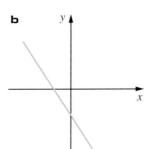

c
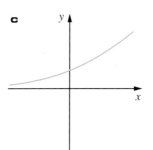

d
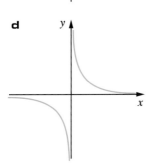

e
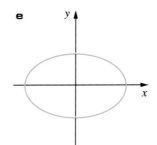

f
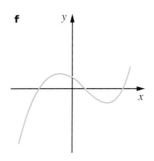

g
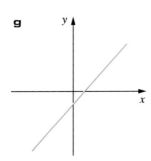

h
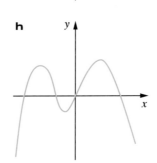

i
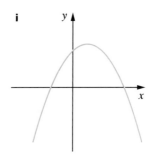

24.3 ## Exponential graphs

This section will show you how to:

● draw and recognise exponential functions

Key words
exponential
functions

Equations which have the form $y = k^x$, where k is a positive number, are called **exponential functions**.

Exponential functions share the following properties.

● When k is greater than 1, the value of y increases steeply as x increases, which you can see from the graph on the right.

● Also when k is greater than 1, as x takes on increasingly large negative values, the closer y gets to zero, and so the graph gets nearer and nearer to the negative x-axis. y never actually becomes zero and so the graph never actually touches the negative x-axis. That is, the negative x-axis is an asymptote to the graph. (See also page 523.)

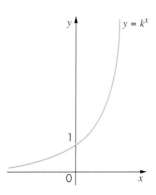

- Whatever the value of k, the graph always intercepts the y-axis at 1, because here $y = k^0$.

- The reciprocal graph, $y = k^{-x}$, is the reflection in the y-axis of the graph of $y = k^x$, as you can see from the graph (on the right).

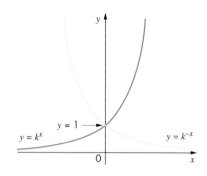

$y = k^x$ $y = 1$ $y = k^{-x}$

EXAMPLE 3

a Complete the table below for $y = 2^x$ for values of x from −5 to +5. (Values are rounded to 2 decimal places.)

x	−5	−4	−3	−2	−1	0	1	2	3	4	5
$y = 2^x$	0.03	0.06	0.13			1	2	4			32

b Plot the graph of $y = 2^x$ for $-5 \leqslant x \leqslant 5$.

c Use your graph to estimate the value of y when $x = 2.5$.

d Use your graph to estimate the value of x when $y = 0.75$.

a The values missing from the table are: 0.25, 0.5, 8 and 16.

b Part of the graph (drawn to scale) is shown opposite.

c Draw a line vertically from $x = 2.5$ until it meets the graph and then read across.
   The y-value is 5.7.

d Draw a line horizontally from $y = 0.75$, the x-value is −0.4.

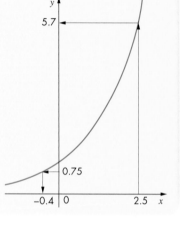

EXERCISE 24C

1 a Complete the table below for $y = 3^x$ for values of x from −4 to +3. (Values are rounded to 2 decimal places.)

x	−4	−3	−2	−1	0	1	2	3
$y = 3^x$	0.01	0.04			1	3		

b Plot the graph of $y = 3^x$ for $-4 \leqslant x \leqslant 3$. (Take the y-axis from 0 to 30.)

c Use your graph to estimate the value of y when $x = 2.5$.

d Use your graph to estimate the value of x when $y = 0.5$.

2 a Complete the table below for $y = (\frac{1}{2})^x$ for values of x from −5 to +5. (Values are rounded to 2 decimal places.)

x	−5	−4	−3	−2	−1	0	1	2	3	4	5
$y = (\frac{1}{2})^x$			8			1				0.06	0.03

b Plot the graph of $y = (\frac{1}{2})^x$ for $-5 \leqslant x \leqslant 5$. (Take the y-axis from 0 to 35.)

c Use your graph to estimate the value of y when $x = 2.5$.

d Use your graph to estimate the value of x when $y = 0.75$.

One grain of rice is placed on the first square of a chess board. Two grains of rice are placed on the second square, four grains on the third square and so on.

a Explain why $y = 2^{(n-1)}$ gives the number of grains of rice on the nth square.

b Complete the table for the number of grains of rice on the first 10 squares

Square	1	2	3	4	5	6	7	8	9	10
Grains	1	2	4							

c Use the rule to work out how many grains of rice there are on the 64th square.

d If 1000 grains of rice are worth 5p, how much is the rice on the 64th square worth?

An extremely large sheet of paper is 0.01 cm thick. It is torn in half and one piece placed on top of the other. These two pieces are then torn in half and one half is placed on top of the other half to give a pile 4 sheets thick. This process is repeated 50 times.

a Complete the table to show how many pieces there are in the pile after each tear.

Tears	1	2	3	4	5	6	7	8
Pieces	2	4						

b Write down a rule for the number of pieces after n tears.

c How many pieces will there be piled up after 50 tears?

d How thick is this pile?

The circular function graphs

This section will show you how to:

- draw and recognise sine and cosine graphs

Key words

sine

cosine

You saw the graphs of $y = \sin x$ and $y = \cos x$ in Chapter 22.

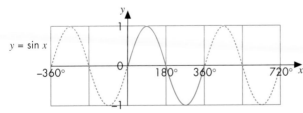

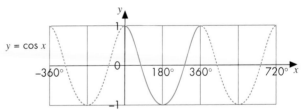

These graphs have some special properties.

- They are cyclic. This means that they repeat indefinitely in both directions.

- For every value of **sine** or **cosine** between –1 and 1 there are 2 angles between 0° and 360°, and an infinite number of angles altogether.

- The sine graph has rotational symmetry about (180°, 0) and has line symmetry between 0° and 180° about $x = 90°$, and between 180° and 360° about $x = 270°$.

- The cosine graph has line symmetry about $x = 180°$, and has rotational symmetry between 0° and 180° about (90°, 0) and between 180° and 360° about (270°, 0).

The graphs can be used to find angles with certain values of sine and cosine.

EXAMPLE 4

Given that cos 110° = −0.342, find two angles between 0° and 360° that have a cosine of +0.342.

Plot the approximate values −0.342 and 0.342 on the cosine graph and use the symmetry to work out the values.

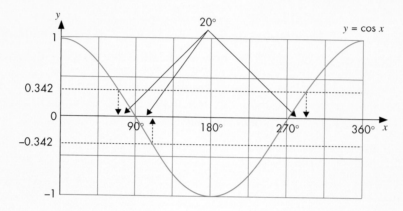

The required values are 90° − 20° = 70° and 270° + 20° = 290°.

A*

1 Given that sin 65° = 0.906, find another angle between 0° and 360° that also has a sine of 0.906.

2 Given that sin 213° = −0.545, find another angle between 0° and 360° that also has a sine of −0.545.

3 Given that cos 36° = 0.809, find another angle between 0° and 360° that also has a cosine of 0.809.

4 Given that cos 165° = −0.966, find another angle between 0° and 360° that also has a cosine of −0.966.

5 Given that sin 30° = 0.5, find two angles between 0° and 360° that have a sine of −0.5.

6 Given that cos 45° = 0.707, find two angles between 0° and 360° that have a cosine of −0.707.

7 Given that sin 26° = 0.438

   a write down an angle between 0° and 90° that has a cosine of 0.438,

   b find two angles between 0° and 360° that have a sine of −0.438,

   c find two angles between 0° and 360° that have a cosine of −0.438.

1 **a** Four graphs are sketched.

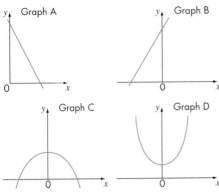

Graph A   Graph B

Graph C   Graph D

Complete the following statements.

$y = 2x + 4$ matches graph ....

$y = x^2 + 4$ matches graph ....

$y + 2x = 4$ matches graph ....

b Sketch the graph of $y = x^3$

AQA, Question 7, Paper 2 Higher, June 2005

2 **a** Complete the table of values for $y = (0.8)^x$

x	0	1	2	3	4
y	1	0.8	0.64		0.41

b Using a grid with a x-axis from 0 to 4 and a y-axis from 0 to 1 draw the graph of $y = (0.8)^x$ for values of x from 0 to 4.

c Use your graph to solve the equation $(0.8)^x = 0.76$.

3 The sketch shows the graphs of $y = \frac{1}{x}$ and $y = x$. The graphs intersect at the points A and B.

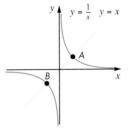

4 The graph shows a sketch of the function $y = x^3 + x^2 - 4x - 4$.

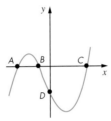

The expression $x^3 + x^2 - 4x - 4$ can be factorised to

$x^3 + x^2 - 4x - 4 = (x + 2)(x + 1)(x - 2)$

The curve crosses the x-axis at A, B and C.

The curve crosses the y-axis at D.

Write down the coordinates of the points A, B, C and D.

5 The sketch shows the graph of the function $y = 3^x$.

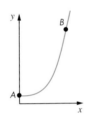

a A is the point where the curve intersects the y-axis. Write down the coordinates of A.

b Another point on the curve is B. Write down a possible coordinates of B.

WORKED EXAM QUESTION

Three graphs are sketched and four equations are given.

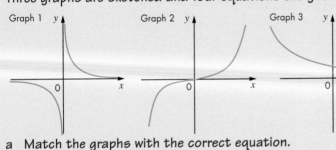

Graph 1   Graph 2   Graph 3

Equation 1: $y = x^3$

Equation 2: $y = \sin x$

Equation 3: $y = \frac{1}{x}$

Equation 4: $y = 2^{-x}$

a Match the graphs with the correct equation.

b Sketch the graph of the equation that is not used.

Solution

a Graph 1 matches equation **3**   Graph 2 matches equation **1**   Graph 3 matches equation **4**.

b

• You need to know the characteristic shape of these graphs.

• If you are aked to sketch sin x if cos x then do it for x from 0° to 360°.

GRADE YOURSELF

B Plot cubic graphs using a table of values

B Recognise the shapes of the graphs $y = x^3$ and $y = \dfrac{1}{x}$

A Able to draw a variety of graphs such as exponential graphs and reciprocal graphs using a table of values

A* Able to solve equations using the intersection of two graphs

A* Use trigonometric graphs to solve sine and cosine problems

What you should know now

- How to draw non-linear graphs
- How to solve equations by finding the intersection points of the graphs of the equations with the x-axis or other related equations

Algebra 3

This chapter will show you ...

- how to combine fractions algebraically and solve equations with algebraic fractions
- how to solve linear and non-linear simultaneous equations
- some of the common sequences of numbers
- how to express a rule for a sequence in words and algebraically
- how to transpose a formula where the subject appears twice

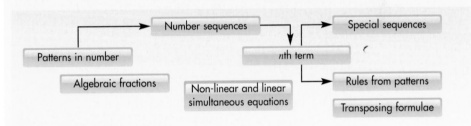

What you should already know

- How to state a rule for a simple linear sequence in words
- How to substitute numbers into an algebraic expression
- How to factorise simple linear expressions
- How to expand a pair of linear brackets to get a quadratic equation

Quick check

1 Write down the next three terms of these sequences.

   a 2, 5, 8, 11, 14, ...   **b** 1, 3, 6, 10, 15, 21, ...

   c 40, 35, 30, 25, 20, ...   **d** 1, 4, 9, 16, 25, 36, ...

2 Work out the value of the expression $3n - 2$ for

   a $n = 1$ **b** $n = 2$ **c** $n = 3$

3 Factorise

   a $2x + 6$ **b** $x^2 - x$ **c** $10x^2 + 2x$

4 Expand

   a $(x + 6)(x + 2)$ **b** $(2x + 1)(x - 3)$ **c** $(x - 2)^2$

5 Make x the subject of

   a $2y + x = 3$ **b** $x - 3y = 4$ **c** $4y - x = 3$

Algebraic fractions

In this section you will learn how to:
- simplify algebraic fractions
- solve equations containing algebraic fractions

Key words
brackets
cancel
cross-multiply
expression
factorise

The following four rules are used to work out the value of fractions.

Addition:
$$\frac{a}{b} + \frac{c}{d} = \frac{ad + bc}{bd}$$

Subtraction:
$$\frac{a}{b} - \frac{c}{d} = \frac{ad - bc}{bd}$$

Multiplication:
$$\frac{a}{b} \times \frac{c}{d} = \frac{ac}{bd}$$

Division:
$$\frac{a}{b} \div \frac{c}{d} = \frac{ad}{bc}$$

Note that a, b, c and d can be numbers, other letters or algebraic **expressions**. Remember:

- use **brackets**, if necessary

- **factorise** if you can

- **cancel** if you can.

EXAMPLE 1

Simplify
a $\dfrac{1}{x} + \dfrac{x}{2y}$
b $\dfrac{2}{b} - \dfrac{a}{2b}$

a Using the addition rule:
$$\frac{1}{x} + \frac{x}{2y} = \frac{(1)(2y) + (x)(x)}{(x)(2y)} = \frac{2y + x^2}{2xy}$$

b Using the subtraction rule:
$$\frac{2}{b} - \frac{a}{2b} = \frac{(2)(2b) - (a)(b)}{(b)(2b)} = \frac{4b - ab}{2b^2}$$
$$= \frac{\cancel{b}(4 - a)}{2b^{\cancel{2}}} = \frac{4 - a}{2b}$$

Note: There are different ways of working out fraction calculations. Part **b** could have been done by making the denominator of each fraction the same. Namely,

$$\frac{(2)2}{(2)b} - \frac{a}{2b} = \frac{4 - a}{2b}$$

EXAMPLE 2

Simplify $\quad$ **a** $\dfrac{x}{3} \times \dfrac{x+2}{x-2}$ $\qquad$ **b** $\dfrac{x}{3} \div \dfrac{2x}{7}$

a Using the multiplication rule: $\quad \dfrac{x}{3} \times \dfrac{x+2}{x-2} = \dfrac{(x)(x+2)}{(3)(x-2)} = \dfrac{x^2+2x}{3x-6}$

Remember that the line that separates the top from the bottom of an algebraic fraction acts as a bracket as well as a divide sign. Note that it is sometimes preferable to leave an algebraic fraction in a factorised form.

b Using the division rule: $\quad \dfrac{x}{3} \div \dfrac{2x}{7} = \dfrac{(\cancel{x})(7)}{(3)(2\cancel{x})} = \dfrac{7}{6}$

EXAMPLE 3

Solve this equation. $\qquad \dfrac{x+1}{3} - \dfrac{x-3}{2} = 1$

Use the rule for combining fractions, and also **cross-multiply** the denominator of the left-hand side to the right-hand side.

$$\dfrac{(2)(x+1)-(3)(x-3)}{(2)(3)} = 1$$

$$2(x+1)-3(x-3) = 6 \;(= 1 \times 2 \times 3)$$

Note the brackets. These will avoid problems with signs and help you to expand to get a linear equation.

$$2x+2-3x+9=6 \quad \Rightarrow \quad -x=-5 \quad \Rightarrow \quad x=5$$

EXAMPLE 4

Solve this equation. $\qquad \dfrac{3}{x-1} - \dfrac{2}{x+1} = 1$

Use the rule for combining fractions, and cross multiply the denominator as in Example 3. Use brackets to help with expanding and to avoid problems with minus signs.

$$3(x+1)-2(x-1) = (x-1)(x+1)$$

$$3x+3-2x+2 = x^2-1 \quad \text{(Right-hand side is the difference of two squares.)}$$

Rearrange into the general quadratic form (see Chapter 20).

$$x^2-x-6=0$$

Factorise and solve $\quad (x-3)(x+2)=0 \quad \Rightarrow \quad x=3 \text{ or } -2$

Note that when your equation is rearranged into the quadratic form it should factorise. If it doesn't, then you have almost certainly made a mistake. If the question required an answer as a decimal or a surd it would say so.

EXAMPLE 5

Simplify: $\dfrac{2x^2 + x - 3}{4x^2 - 9}$

Factorise the numerator and denominator: $\dfrac{(2x + 3)(x - 1)}{(2x + 3)(2x - 3)}$

Denominator is the difference of two squares.

Cancel any common factors: $\dfrac{\cancel{(2x + 3)}(x - 1)}{\cancel{(2x + 3)}(2x - 3)}$

If at this stage there isn't a common factor on top and bottom, you should check your factorisations.

Remaining term is the answer: $\dfrac{(x - 1)}{(2x - 3)}$

EXERCISE 25A

1 Simplify each of these.

a $\dfrac{x}{2} + \dfrac{x}{3}$
b $\dfrac{3x}{4} + \dfrac{x}{5}$
c $\dfrac{3x}{4} + \dfrac{2x}{5}$

d $\dfrac{x}{2} + \dfrac{y}{3}$
e $\dfrac{xy}{4} + \dfrac{2}{x}$
f $\dfrac{x + 1}{2} + \dfrac{x + 2}{3}$

g $\dfrac{2x - 1}{2} + \dfrac{3x - 1}{4}$
h $\dfrac{x}{5} + \dfrac{2x - 1}{3}$
i $\dfrac{x - 2}{2} + \dfrac{x + 3}{4}$

j $\dfrac{x - 4}{5} + \dfrac{2x - 3}{2}$

2 Simplify each of these.

a $\dfrac{x}{2} - \dfrac{x}{3}$
b $\dfrac{3x}{4} - \dfrac{x}{5}$
c $\dfrac{3x}{4} - \dfrac{2x}{5}$

d $\dfrac{x}{2} - \dfrac{y}{3}$
e $\dfrac{xy}{4} - \dfrac{2}{y}$
f $\dfrac{x + 1}{2} - \dfrac{x + 2}{3}$

g $\dfrac{2x + 1}{2} - \dfrac{3x + 3}{4}$
h $\dfrac{x}{5} - \dfrac{2x + 1}{3}$
i $\dfrac{x - 2}{2} - \dfrac{x - 3}{4}$

j $\dfrac{x - 4}{5} - \dfrac{2x - 3}{2}$

3 Solve the following equations.

a $\dfrac{x + 1}{2} + \dfrac{x + 2}{5} = 3$
b $\dfrac{x + 2}{4} + \dfrac{x + 1}{7} = 3$
c $\dfrac{4x + 1}{3} - \dfrac{x + 2}{4} = 2$

d $\dfrac{2x - 1}{3} + \dfrac{3x + 1}{4} = 7$
e $\dfrac{2x + 1}{2} - \dfrac{x + 1}{7} = 1$
f $\dfrac{3x + 1}{5} - \dfrac{5x - 1}{7} = 0$

4 Simplify each of these.

a $\dfrac{x}{2} \times \dfrac{x}{3}$

b $\dfrac{2x}{7} \times \dfrac{3y}{4}$

c $\dfrac{4x}{3y} \times \dfrac{2y}{x}$

d $\dfrac{4y^2}{9x} \times \dfrac{3x^2}{2y}$

e $\dfrac{x}{2} \times \dfrac{x-2}{5}$

f $\dfrac{x-3}{15} \times \dfrac{5}{2x-6}$

g $\dfrac{2x+1}{2} \times \dfrac{3x+1}{4}$

h $\dfrac{x}{5} \times \dfrac{2x+1}{3}$

i $\dfrac{x-2}{2} \times \dfrac{4}{x-3}$

j $\dfrac{x-5}{10} \times \dfrac{5}{x^2-5x}$

5 Simplify each of these.

a $\dfrac{x}{2} \div \dfrac{x}{3}$

b $\dfrac{2x}{7} \div \dfrac{4y}{14}$

c $\dfrac{4x}{3y} \div \dfrac{x}{2y}$

d $\dfrac{4y^2}{9x} \div \dfrac{2y}{3x^2}$

e $\dfrac{x}{2} \div \dfrac{x-2}{5}$

f $\dfrac{x-3}{15} \div \dfrac{5}{2x-6}$

g $\dfrac{2x+1}{2} \div \dfrac{4x+2}{4}$

h $\dfrac{x}{6} \div \dfrac{2x^2+x}{3}$

i $\dfrac{x-2}{12} \div \dfrac{4}{x-3}$

j $\dfrac{x-5}{10} \div \dfrac{x^2-5x}{5}$

6 Simplify each of these. Factorise and cancel where appropriate.

a $\dfrac{3x}{4} + \dfrac{x}{4}$

b $\dfrac{3x}{4} - \dfrac{x}{4}$

c $\dfrac{3x}{4} \times \dfrac{x}{4}$

d $\dfrac{3x}{4} \div \dfrac{x}{4}$

e $\dfrac{3x+1}{2} + \dfrac{x-2}{5}$

f $\dfrac{3x+1}{2} - \dfrac{x-2}{5}$

g $\dfrac{3x+1}{2} \times \dfrac{x-2}{5}$

h $\dfrac{x^2-9}{10} \times \dfrac{5}{x-3}$

i $\dfrac{2x+3}{5} \div \dfrac{6x+9}{10}$

j $\dfrac{2x^2}{9} - \dfrac{2y^2}{3}$

7 Show that each algebraic fraction simplifies to the given expression.

a $\dfrac{2}{x+1} + \dfrac{5}{x+2} = 3$ simplifies to $3x^2 + 2x - 3 = 0$

b $\dfrac{4}{x-2} + \dfrac{7}{x+1} = 3$ simplifies to $3x^2 - 14x + 4 = 0$

c $\dfrac{3}{4x+1} - \dfrac{4}{x+2} = 2$ simplifies to $8x^2 + 31x + 2 = 0$

d $\dfrac{2}{2x-1} - \dfrac{6}{x+1} = 11$ simplifies to $22x^2 + 21x - 19 = 0$

e $\dfrac{3}{2x-1} - \dfrac{4}{3x-1} = 1$ simplifies to $x^2 - x = 0$

  Solve the following equations.

a $\dfrac{4}{x+1} + \dfrac{5}{x+2} = 2$

b $\dfrac{18}{4x-1} - \dfrac{1}{x+1} = 1$

c $\dfrac{2x-1}{2} - \dfrac{6}{x+1} = 1$

d $\dfrac{3}{2x-1} - \dfrac{4}{3x-1} = 1$

9 Simplify the following expressions.

a $\dfrac{x^2 + 2x - 3}{2x^2 + 7x + 3}$

b $\dfrac{4x^2 - 1}{2x^2 + 5x - 3}$

c $\dfrac{6x^2 + x - 2}{9x^2 - 4}$

d $\dfrac{4x^2 + x - 3}{4x^2 - 7x + 3}$

e $\dfrac{4x^2 - 25}{8x^2 - 22x + 5}$

25.2 Linear and non-linear simultaneous equations

In this section you will learn how to:

- solve linear and non-linear simultaneous equations

Key words

linear
non-linear
substitute

You have already seen the method of substitution for solving **linear** simultaneous equations (see page 420). Example 6 is a reminder.

EXAMPLE 6

Solve these simultaneous equations.

$2x + 3y = 7$ (1)

$x - 4y = 9$ (2)

First, rearrange equation (2) to obtain:

$x = 9 + 4y$

Substitute the expression for x into equation (1), which gives:

$2(9 + 4y) + 3y = 7$

Expand and solve this equation to obtain:

$18 + 8y + 3y = 7$

$\Rightarrow \qquad 11y = -11$

$\Rightarrow \qquad y = -1$

Now substitute y into either equation (1) or (2) to find x. Using equation (1), we have

$\Rightarrow 2x - 3 = 7$

$\Rightarrow \quad x = 5$

We can use a similar method when we need to solve a pair of equations, one of which is linear and the other of which is **non-linear**. But we must *always* **substitute** from the linear into the non-linear.

EXAMPLE 7

Solve these simultaneous equations.

$$x^2 + y^2 = 5$$
$$x + y = 3$$

Call the equations (1) and (2):

$$x^2 + y^2 = 5 \; (1)$$
$$x + y = 3 \; (2)$$

Rearrange equation (2) to obtain:

$$x = 3 - y$$

Substitute this into equation (1), which gives:

$$(3 - y)^2 + y^2 = 5$$

Expand and rearrange into the general form of the quadratic equation:

$$9 - 6y + y^2 + y^2 = 5$$
$$2y^2 - 6y + 4 = 0$$

Cancel by 2:

$$y^2 - 3y + 2 = 0$$

Factorise:

$$(y - 1)(y - 2) = 0$$
$$\Rightarrow \qquad y = 1 \text{ or } 2$$

Substitute for y in equation (2):

When $y = 1$, $x = 2$; and when $y = 2$, $x = 1$.

Note you should always give answers as a pair of values in x and y.

EXERCISE 25B

 Solve these pairs of linear simultaneous equations using the substitution method.

a $2x + y = 9$
$x - 2y = 7$

b $3x - 2y = 10$
$4x + y = 17$

c $x - 2y = 10$
$2x + 3y = 13$

 Solve these pairs of simultaneous equations.

a $xy = 2$
$y = x + 1$

b $xy = -4$
$2y = x + 6$

A*

3 Solve these pairs of simultaneous equations.

a $x^2 + y^2 = 25$
$x + y = 7$

b $x^2 + y^2 = 9$
$y = x + 3$

c $x^2 + y^2 = 13$
$5y + x = 13$

4 Solve these pairs of simultaneous equations.

a $y = x^2 + 2x - 3$
$y = 2x + 1$

b $y = x^2 - 2x - 5$
$y = x - 1$

c $y = x^2 - 2x$
$y = 2x - 3$

5 Solve these pairs of simultaneous equations.

a $y = x^2 + x - 2$
$y = 5x - 6$

b $y = x^2 + 2x - 3$
$y = 4x - 4$

c What is the geometrical significance of the answers to parts **a** and **b**?

25.3 Number sequences

In this section you will learn how to:
- recognise how number sequences are built up
- find the nth term of a sequence
- recognise some special sequences

Key words
coefficient
consecutive
difference
nth term
sequence
term

A number **sequence** is an ordered set of numbers with a rule to find every number in the sequence. The rule which takes you from one number to the next could be a simple addition or multiplication, but often it is more tricky than that. So you need to look most carefully at the pattern of a sequence.

Each number in a sequence is called a **term** and is in a certain position in the sequence.

Look at these sequences and their rules.

3, 6, 12, 24, … doubling the last term each time … 48, 96, …

2, 5, 8, 11, … adding 3 to the last term each time … 14, 17, …

1, 10, 100, 1000, … multiplying the last term by 10 each time … 10 000, 100 000, …

1, 8, 15, 22, … adding 7 to the last term each time … 29, 36, …

These are all quite straightforward once you have looked for the link from one term to the next (**consecutive** terms).

Differences

For some sequences we need to look at the **differences** between consecutive terms to determine the pattern.

EXAMPLE 8

Find the next two terms of the sequence 1, 3, 6, 10, 15, ...

Looking at the differences between each pair of consecutive terms, we notice:

1　　3　　6　　10　　15
　　↑　　↑　　↑　　↑
　　2　　3　　4　　5

So, we can continue the sequence as follows:

1　　3　　6　　10　　15　　21　　28
　　↑　　↑　　↑　　↑
　　2　　3　　4　　5　 +6 　 +7

The differences usually form a number sequence of their own, so you need to find out the sequence of the differences before you can expand the original sequence.

Generalising to find the rule

When using a number sequence, we sometimes need to know, say, its 50th term, or even a later term in the sequence. To do so, we need to find the rule which produces the sequence in its general form.

Let's first look at the problem backwards. That is, we'll take a rule and see how it produces a sequence.

EXAMPLE 9

A sequence is formed by the rule $3n + 1$, where $n = 1, 2, 3, 4, 5, 6, ...$. Write down the first five terms of the sequence.

Substituting $n = 1, 2, 3, 4, 5$ in turn, we get:

$(3 \times 1 + 1), (3 \times 2 + 1), (3 \times 3 + 1), (3 \times 4 + 1), (3 \times 5 + 1), ...$

　　4　　　　7　　　　10　　　　13　　　　16

So the sequence is 4, 7, 10, 13, 16, ...

Notice that the difference between each term and the next is always 3, which is the **coefficient** of n (the number attached to n). The constant term is the difference between the first term and the coefficient (in this case, $4 - 3 = 1$).

EXAMPLE 10

The **nth term** of a sequence is $4n - 3$. Write down the first five terms of the sequence.

Substituting $n = 1, 2, 3, 4, 5$ in turn, we get

$$(4 \times 1 - 3), (4 \times 2 - 3), (4 \times 3 - 3), (4 \times 4 - 3), (4 \times 5 - 3)$$

$$1 \qquad 5 \qquad 9 \qquad 13 \qquad 17$$

So the sequence is 1, 5, 9, 13, 17, ...

Notice that the difference between each term and the next is always 4, which is the coefficient of **n**. The constant term is the difference between the first term and the coefficient ($1 - 4 = -3$).

EXERCISE 25C

1 Look carefully at each number sequence below. Find the next two numbers in the sequence and try to explain the pattern.

a 1, 1, 2, 3, 5, 8, 13, ...

b 1, 4, 9, 16, 25, 36, ...

c 3, 4, 7, 11, 18, 29, ...

2 Triangular numbers are found as follows.

1   3   6   10

Find the next four triangular numbers.

3 Hexagonal numbers are found as follows.

 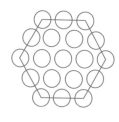 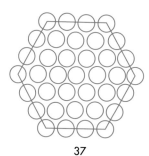

1   7   19   37

Find the next three hexagonal numbers.

4 The first two terms of the sequence of fractions $\dfrac{n-1}{n+1}$ are:

$$n = 1: \frac{1-1}{1+1} = \frac{0}{2} = 0 \qquad n = 2: \frac{2-1}{2+1} = \frac{1}{3}$$

Work out the next five terms of the sequence.

Mod 5

5 A sequence is formed by the rule $\frac{1}{2} \times n \times (n + 1)$ for $n = 1, 2, 3, 4, \ldots$

The first term is given by $n = 1$: $\frac{1}{2} \times 1 \times (1 + 1) = 1$

The second term is given by $n = 2$: $\frac{1}{2} \times 2 \times (2 + 1) = 3$

a Work out the next five terms of this sequence.

b This is a well-known sequence you have met before. What is it?

6 5! means "factorial 5", which is $5 \times 4 \times 3 \times 2 \times 1 = 120$

In the same way 7! means $7 \times 6 \times 5 \times 4 \times 3 \times 2 \times 1 = 5040$

a Calculate 2!, 3!, 4! and 6!

b If your calculator has a factorial button, check that it gives the same answers as you get for part **a**. What is the largest factorial you can work out with your calculator before you get an error?

Finding the nth term of a linear sequence

A linear sequence has the *same difference* between each term and the next.

For example:

2, 5, 8, 11, 14, ... difference of 3

The nth term of this sequence is given by $3n - 1$.

Here is another linear sequence:

5, 7, 9, 11, 13, ... difference of 2

The nth term of this sequence is given by $2n + 3$.

So, you can see that the nth term of a linear sequence is *always* of the form $An + b$, where:

- A, the coefficient of n, is the difference between each term and the next term (consecutive terms)

- b is the difference between the first term and A.

EXAMPLE 11

Find the nth term of the sequence 5, 7, 9, 11, 13, ...

The difference between consecutive terms is 2. So the first part of the nth term is $2n$.

Subtract the difference, 2, from the first term, 5, which gives $5 - 2 = 3$.

So the nth term is given by $2n + 3$.

(You can test it by substituting $n = 1, 2, 3, 4, \ldots$.)

EXAMPLE 12

Find the nth term of the sequence 3, 7, 11, 15, 19, …

The difference between consecutive terms is 4. So the first part of the nth term is $4n$.

Subtract the difference 4 from the first term 3, which gives $3 - 4 = -1$.

So the nth term is given by $4n - 1$.

EXAMPLE 13

From the sequence 5, 12, 19, 26, 33, … find the following.

    a the nth term   **b** the 50th term   **c** the first term that is greater than 1000

a The difference between consecutive terms is 7. So the first part of the nth term is $7n$.

    Subtract the difference 7 from the first term 5, which gives $5 - 7 = -2$.

    So the nth term is given by $7n - 2$.

b The 50th term is found by substituting $n = 50$ into the rule, $7n - 2$.

    So 50th term $= 7 \times 50 - 2 = 350 - 2$
                         $= 348$

c The first term that is greater than 1000 is given by

      $7n - 2 > 1000$

    $\Rightarrow$ $7n > 1000 + 2$

    $\Rightarrow$ $n > \dfrac{1002}{7}$

          $n > 143.14$

So the first term (which has to be a whole number) over 1000 is the 144th.

Special sequences

There are some number sequences that occur frequently. It is useful to know these as they are very likely to occur in examinations.

Even numbers

The even numbers are 2, 4, 6, 8, 10, 12, …..

The nth term of this sequence is $2n$

Odd numbers

The odd numbers are 1, 3, 5, 7, 9, 11, ….

The nth term of this sequence is $2n - 1$

Square numbers

The square numbers are 1, 4, 9, 16, 25, 36, ….

The nth term of this sequence is n^2

Triangular numbers

The triangular numbers are 1, 3, 6, 10, 15, 21, ...

The nth term of this sequence is $\frac{1}{2}n(n + 1)$

Powers of 2

The powers of 2 are 2, 4, 8, 16, 32, 64, ...

The nth term of this sequence is 2^n

Powers of 10

The powers of 10 are 10, 100, 1000, 10 000, 100 000, 1 000 000, ...

The nth term of this sequence is 10^n

Prime numbers

The first 20 prime numbers are 2, 3, 5, 7, 11, 13, 17, 19, 23, 29, 31, 37, 41, 43, 47, 53, 59, 61, 67, 71

A prime number is a number that only has two factors, 1 and itself.

There is no pattern to the prime numbers so they do not have an nth term.

One important fact that you should remember is that there is only one even prime number, 2.

EXERCISE 25D

1 Find the next two terms and the nth term in each of these linear sequences.

HINTS AND TIPS

Remember to look at the differences and the first term.

a 3, 5, 7, 9, 11, ...　　　　**b** 5, 9, 13, 17, 21, ...

c 8, 13, 18, 23, 28, ...　　　**d** 2, 8, 14, 20, 26, ...

e 5, 8, 11, 14, 17, ...　　　**f** 2, 9, 16, 23, 30, ...

g 1, 5, 9, 13, 17, ...　　　**h** 3, 7, 11, 15, 19, ...　　　**i** 2, 5, 8, 11, 14, ...

j 2, 12, 22, 32, ...　　　　**k** 8, 12, 16, 20, ...　　　　**l** 4, 9, 14, 19, 24, ...

2 Find the nth term and the 50th term in each of these linear sequences.

a 4, 7, 10, 13, 16, ...　　　**b** 7, 9, 11, 13, 15, ...　　　**c** 3, 8, 13, 18, 23, ...

d 1, 5, 9, 13, 17, ...　　　**e** 2, 10, 18, 26, ...　　　　**f** 5, 6, 7, 8, 9, ...

g 6, 11, 16, 21, 26, ...　　**h** 3, 11, 19, 27, 35, ...　　**i** 1, 4, 7, 10, 13, ...

j 21, 24, 27, 30, 33, ...　　**k** 12, 19, 26, 33, 40, ...　　**l** 1, 9, 17, 25, 33, ...

C

3 **a** Which term of the sequence 5, 8, 11, 14, 17, … is the first one to be greater than 100?

b Which term of the sequence 1, 8, 15, 22, 29, … is the first one to be greater than 200?

c Which term of the sequence 4, 9, 14, 19, 24, … is the closest to 500?

4 For each sequence **a** to **j**, find

i the nth term   **ii** the 100th term   **iii** the term closest to 100.

a 5, 9, 13, 17, 21, …   **b** 3, 5, 7, 9, 11, 13, …

c 4, 7, 10, 13, 16, …   **d** 8, 10, 12, 14, 16, …

e 9, 13, 17, 21, …   **f** 6, 11, 16, 21, …

g 0, 3, 6, 9, 12, …   **h** 2, 8, 14, 20, 26, …

i 7, 15, 23, 31, …   **j** 25, 27, 29, 31, …

5 A sequence of fractions is $\frac{3}{4}, \frac{5}{7}, \frac{7}{10}, \frac{9}{13}, \frac{11}{16}, \ldots$

a Find the nth term in the sequence.

b By changing each fraction to a decimal, can you see a pattern?

c What, as a decimal, will be the value of the

i 100th term?   **ii** 1000th term?

d Use your answers to part **c** to predict what the 10 000th term and the millionth term are. (Check these out on your calculator.)

6 Repeat question **5** for $\frac{3}{6}, \frac{7}{11}, \frac{11}{16}, \frac{15}{21}, \frac{19}{26}, \ldots$

7 The powers of 2 are $2^1, 2^2, 2^3, 2^4, 2^5, \ldots$

This gives the sequence 2, 4, 8, 16, 32, …

The nth term is given by 2^n.

a Continue the sequence for another five terms.

b Give the nth term of these sequences.

i 1, 3, 7, 15, 31, …

ii 3, 5, 9, 17, 33, …

iii 6, 12, 24, 48, 96, …

8 The powers of 10 are $10^1, 10^2, 10^3, 10^4, 10^5, \ldots$

This gives the sequence 10, 100, 1000, 10 000, 100 000, …

The nth term is given by 10^n.

a Describe the connection between the numbers of zeros in each term and the power of the term.

b If $10^n = 1\,000\,000$, what is the value of n?

c Give the nth term of these sequences.

   i 9, 99, 999, 9 999, 99 999, …

   ii 20, 200, 2000, 20 000, 200 000, …

9 a Pick any odd number.

Pick any other odd number.

Add the two numbers together. Is the answer odd or even?

Complete this table.

+	Odd	Even
Odd	Even	
Even		

b Pick any odd number.

Pick any other odd number.

Multiply the two numbers together. Is the answer odd or even?

Complete this table.

×	Odd	Even
Odd	Odd	
Even		

10 The square numbers are 1, 4, 9, 16, 25, …

The nth term of this sequence is n^2.

a Continue the sequence for another five terms.

b Give the nth term of these sequences.

   i 2, 5, 10, 17, 26, …

   ii 2, 8, 18, 32, 50, …

   iii 0, 3, 8, 15, 24, …

11 Write down the next two lines of this number pattern.

$$1 = 1 = 1^2$$

$$1 + 3 = 4 = 2^2$$

$$1 + 3 + 5 = 9 = 3^2$$

12 The triangular numbers are 1, 3, 6, 10, 15, 21, …

a Continue the sequence for another four terms.

b The *n*th term of this sequence is given by $\frac{1}{2}n(n + 1)$.

Use the formula to find:

i The 20th triangular number

ii the 100th triangular number

c Add consecutive terms of the triangular number sequence.

For example, 1 + 3 = 4, 3 + 6 = 9, etc.

What do you notice?

13 *p* is an odd number, *q* is an even number. State if the following are odd or even.

a $p + 1$

b $q + 1$

c $p + q$

d p^2

e $qp + 1$

f $(p + q)(p - q)$

g $q^2 + 4$

h $p^2 + q^2$

i p^3

14 *p* is a prime number, *q* is an even number.

State if the following are odd or even, or could be either odd or even.

a $p + 1$

b $p + q$

c p^2

d $qp + 1$

e $(p + q)(p - q)$

f $2p + 3q$

25.4 General rules from given patterns

In this section you will learn how to:
- find the *n*th term from practical problems

Key words
difference
pattern
rule

Many problem-solving situations that you are likely to meet involve number sequences. So you need to be able to formulate general **rules** from given number **patterns**.

EXAMPLE 14

The diagram shows a pattern of squares building up.

a How many squares will be on the base of the *n*th pattern?

b Which pattern has 99 squares in its base?

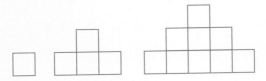

a First, we build up the following table for the patterns.

Pattern number	1	2	3	4	5
Number of squares in base	1	3	5	7	9

Looking at the **difference** between consecutive patterns, we see it is always two squares. So, we use 2*n*.

Subtract the difference 2 from the first number, which gives $1 - 2 = -1$.

So the number of squares on the base of the *n*th pattern is $2n - 1$.

b We have to find *n* when $2n - 1 = 99$:

$$2n - 1 = 99$$
$$2n = 99 + 1 = 100$$
$$n = 100 \div 2 = 50$$

The pattern with 99 squares in its base is the 50th.

EXERCISE 25E

1 A pattern of squares is built up from matchsticks as shown.

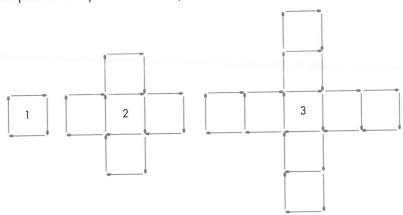

a Draw the 4th diagram.

b How many squares are in the *n*th diagram?

c How many squares are in the 25th diagram?

d With 200 squares, which is the biggest diagram that could be made?

> **HINTS AND TIPS**
>
> Write out the number sequences to help you see the patterns.

2 A pattern of triangles is built up from matchsticks.

   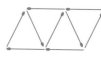

1   2   3   4

a Draw the 5th set of triangles in this pattern.

b How many matchsticks are needed for the nth set of triangles?

c How many matchsticks are needed to make the 60th set of triangles?

d If there are only 100 matchsticks, which is the largest set of triangles that could be made?

3 A conference centre had tables each of which could sit six people. When put together, the tables could seat people as shown.

 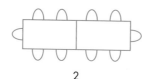 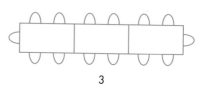

1   2   3

a How many people could be seated at four tables put together this way?

b How many people could be seated at n tables put together in this way?

c A conference had 50 people who wished to use the tables in this way. How many tables would they need?

4 Prepacked fencing units come in the shape shown on the right, made of four pieces of wood. When you put them together in stages to make a fence, you also need joining pieces, so the fence will start to build up as shown below.

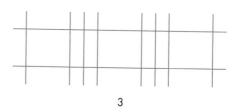

2   3

a How many pieces of wood would you have in a fence made up in:

i five stages   **ii** n stages   **iii** 45 stages?

b I made a fence out of 124 pieces of wood. How many stages did I use?

5 Regular pentagons of side length 1 cm are joined together to make a pattern as shown.

Copy this pattern and write down the perimeter of each shape.

 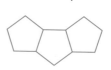 

1   2   3   4

a What is the perimeter of patterns like this made from

i six pentagons?   **ii** n pentagons?   **iii** 50 pentagons?

b What is the largest number of pentagons that can be put together like this to have a perimeter less than 1000 cm?

6 Lamp-posts are put at the end of every 100 m stretch of a motorway, as shown.

1   2   3

a How many lamp-posts are needed for

   i 900 m of this motorway?   **ii** 8 km of this motorway?

b The M99 is a motorway being built. The contractor has ordered 1598 lamp-posts. How long is this motorway?

7 A school dining hall had tables in the shape of a trapezium. Each table could seat five people, as shown on the right. When the tables were joined together as shown below, each table could not seat as many people.

 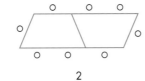 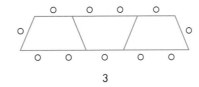

1   2   3

a In this arrangement, how many could be seated if there were:

   i four tables?   **ii** n tables?   **iii** 13 tables?

b For an outside charity event, up to 200 people had to be seated. How many tables arranged like this did they need?

8 When setting out tins to make a display of a certain height, you need to know how many tins to start with at the bottom.

a How many tins are needed on the bottom if you wish the display to be:

   i five tins high?   **ii** n tins high?   **iii** 18 tins high?

b I saw a shop assistant starting to build a display, and noticed he was starting with 20 tins on the bottom. How high was the display when it was finished?

9 a The values of 2 raised to a positive whole-number power are 2, 4, 8, 16, 32, …

What is the nth term of this sequence?

b A supermarket sells four different sized bottles of water: pocket size, 100 ml; standard size, 200 ml; family size, 400 ml; giant size, 800 ml.

   i Describe the number pattern that the contents follow.

   ii The supermarket introduces a super giant size, which is the next sized bottle in the pattern. How much does this bottle hold?

Quadratic sequences

In this section you will learn how to:
- work out the nth term of a non-linear rule

Key words
non-linear
quadratic rule
second difference

Some problem-solving situations involve number sequences which are governed by a **quadratic rule**.

You can always identify a pattern as being quadratic from its **second differences**, which are *constant*. (A second difference is the result of subtracting one difference between consecutive terms from the next difference.)

The simpler rules

These sequences will nearly always be based on n^2 alone. So you do need to recognise the pattern 1, 4, 9, 16, 25, … .

The differences between consecutive terms of this pattern are the odd numbers 3, 5, 7, 9, … . So if you find that the differences form an odd-number sequence, you know the pattern is based on n^2.

EXAMPLE 15

Find the nth term in the sequence 2, 5, 10, 17, 26, … .

The differences are the odd numbers 3, 5, 7, 9, … so we know the rule is based on n^2.

The second differences are 2, a constant.

Next, we look for a link with the square numbers. We do this by subtracting from each term the corresponding square number:

$$
\begin{array}{ccccc}
2 & 5 & 10 & 17 & 26 \\
-1 & -4 & -9 & -16 & -25 \\
\hline
1 & 1 & 1 & 1 & 1
\end{array}
$$

Clearly, the link is +1, so the nth term is $n^2 + 1$.

(You should always quickly check the generalisation by substituting $n = 1, 2, 3, 4$ to see whether it does work.)

EXAMPLE 16

Find the nth term in the sequence 1, 6, 13, 22, 33, … .

The differences are 5, 7, 9, 11, … so we know the pattern is based on n^2.

The second differences are 2, a constant.

Next, we have to find the link. We notice that the first difference is 5 not 3, which means that the series of square numbers we use starts at 4, not at 1.

It follows that to obtain 4, 9, 16, 25, … from the original sequence simply add 3 to each term of that sequence.

So to get from the square numbers to the sequence 1, 6, 13, 22, 33, … we have to use $(n + 1)^2$, since the sequence is based on 4, 9, 16, … .

The final step in finding the rule is to take away the 3, which gives the nth term as $(n + 1)^2 - 3$.

More complicated rules

EXAMPLE 17

Find the nth term in the sequence 2, 6, 12, 20, 30, …

Looking at the differences tells us that the sequence is non-linear, and is not based on n^2.

So we split each term into factors to see whether we can find a pattern which shows how the numbers have been formed. Constructing a table like the one below can help us to sort out which factors to use when we have a choice.

Term	2	6	12	20	30
Factors	1×2	2×3	3×4	4×5	5×6

We can break down the factors to obtain:

$$1 \times (1 + 1) \qquad 2 \times (2 + 1) \qquad 3 \times (3 + 1) \qquad 4 \times (4 + 1) \qquad 5 \times (5 + 1)$$

We can now see quite easily that the pattern is $n \times (n + 1)$. That is the nth term is $n(n + 1)$.

EXAMPLE 18

Find the nth term in the sequence of the triangular numbers 1, 3, 6, 10, 15, … .

Looking at the differences tells us that the sequence is non-linear and is not based on n^2.

So we split each term into factors and construct a table. (We have no problem with the choice of factors.)

Term	1	3	6	10	15
Factors	1×1	1×3	2×3	2×5	3×5

At this stage, we may not yet have spotted a pattern. So we investigate the effect of multiplying the smaller of each pair of factors by 2, and obtain an interesting pattern.

Term	1	3	6	10	15
Factors	1×1	1×3	2×3	2×5	3×5
Smaller $\times$ 2	2×1	2×3	4×3	4×5	6×5

That is:

$$1 \times 2 \qquad 2 \times 3 \qquad 3 \times 4 \qquad 4 \times 5 \qquad 5 \times 6$$

We can further break down this last set of numbers to obtain:

$$1 \times (1 + 1) \qquad 2 \times (2 + 1) \qquad 3 \times (3 + 1) \qquad 4 \times (4 + 1) \qquad 5 \times (5 + 1)$$

the pattern of which is given by $n \times (n + 1)$.

This gives terms twice the size of those in the sequence 1, 3, 6, 10, 15, … so we need to change the expression to $\frac{1}{2} \times n (n + 1)$.

So the nth term is $\frac{1}{2}n(n + 1)$.

Expressions of the form $an^2 + bn + c$

These expressions are unlikely to appear in a GCSE exam but could easily appear in an AO1 coursework task. This method will give an algebraic means of showing a sequence.

EXAMPLE 19

Find the nth term of the sequence 5, 15, 31, 53, ...

Set up a difference table.

n	1	2	3	4
nth term	5	15	31	53
1st difference		10	16	22
2nd difference			6	6

Now extend the table backwards to get the term for $n = 0$ and call the three lines of the table c, $a + b$ and $2a$.

n	0	1	2	3	4
c	1	5	15	31	53
$a + b$		4	10	16	22
$2a$			6	6	6

This gives $2a = 6 \implies a = 3$, $\quad a + b = 4 \implies b = 1$, $\quad c = 1$

Giving the nth term as: $\quad 3n^2 + n + 1$

EXAMPLE 20

Find the nth term of the sequence 3, 5, 8, 12, 17, ...

Set up a difference table.

n	0	1	2	3	4	5
c	2	3	5	8	12	17
$a + b$		1	2	3	4	5
$2a$			1	1	1	1

This gives $2a = 1 \implies a = \frac{1}{2}$, $\quad a + b = 1 \implies b = \frac{1}{2}$, $\quad c = 2$

Giving the nth term as: $\quad \frac{1}{2}n^2 + \frac{1}{2}n + 2$

EXERCISE 25F

1 For each of the sequences **a** to **e**   **i** write down the next two terms   **ii** find the *n*th term.

    a 0, 3, 8, 15, 24, …   **b** 3, 6, 11, 18, 27, …   **c** 4, 7, 12, 19, 28, …

    d −1, 2, 7, 14, 23, …   **e** 11, 14, 19, 26, …

2 For each of the sequences **a** to **e**   **i** write down the next two terms   **ii** find the *n*th term.

    a 5, 10, 17, 26, …   **b** 3, 8, 15, 24, …   **c** 9, 14, 21, 30, …

    d 10, 17, 26, 37, …   **e** 8, 15, 24, 35, …

3 Look at each of the following sequences to see whether the rule is linear, quadratic on n^2 alone or fully quadratic. Then

    i write down the *n*th term   **ii** write down the 50th term.

    a 5, 8, 13, 20, 29, …   **b** 5, 8, 11, 14, 17, …   **c** 3, 8, 15, 24, 35, …

    d 5, 12, 21, 32, 45, …   **e** 3, 6, 11, 18, 27, …   **f** 1, 6, 11, 16, 21, …

4 Find the *n*th terms of the following sequences in the form $an^2 + bn + c$.

    a 1, 4, 11, 22, 37, ….   **b** 2, 13, 30, 53, 82, ….   **c** 4, 8, 13, 19, 26, …..

25.6 Changing the subject of a formula

In this section you will learn how to:

● change the subject of a formula where the subject occurs more than once

Key words

subject
transpose

You already have met changing the **subject** of a formula in which the subject appears only once (see page 426). This is like solving an equation but using letters. You have also solved equations in which the unknown appears on both sides of the equation. This requires the unknown (usually *x*) terms to be collected on one side and the numbers to be collected on the other.

We can do something similar, to **transpose** formulae in which the subject appears more than once. The principle is the same. Collect all the subject terms on the same side and everything else on the other side. Most often, we then need to factorise the subject out of the resulting expression.

EXAMPLE 21

Make x the subject of this formula.

$$ax + b = cx + d$$

First, rearrange the formula to get all the x terms on the left-hand side and all the other terms on the right-hand side. (The rule "change sides – change signs" still applies.)

$$ax - cx = d - b$$

Factorise x out of left-hand side to get:

$$x(a - c) = d - b$$

Divide by the bracket, which gives:

$$x = \frac{d - b}{a - c}$$

EXAMPLE 22

Make p the subject of this formula.

$$5 = \frac{ap + b}{cp + d}$$

First, multiply both sides by the denominator of the algebraic fraction, which gives:

$$5(cp + d) = ap + b$$

Expand the bracket to get:

$$5cp + 5d = ap + b$$

Now continue as in Example 21:

$$5cp - ap = b - 5d$$

$$p(5c - a) = b - 5d$$

$$p = \frac{b - 5d}{5c - a}$$

EXERCISE 25G

In questions **1** to **10**, make the letter in brackets the subject of each formula.

1 $3(x + 2y) = 2(x - y)$ (x)

2 $3(x + 2y) = 2(x - y)$ (y)

3 $5 = \dfrac{a + b}{a - c}$ (a)

4 $p(a + b) = q(a - b)$ (a)

5 $p(a + b) = q(a - b)$ (b)

6 $A = 2\pi rh + \pi rk$ (r)

7 $v^2 = u^2 + av^2$ (v)

8 $s(t - r) = 2r - 3$ (r)

9 $s(t - r) = 2(r - 3)$ (r)

10 $R = \dfrac{x - 3}{x - 2}$ (x)

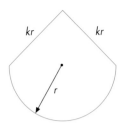

11 **a** The perimeter of the shape shown on the right is given by the formula $P = \pi r + 2kr$. Make r the subject of this formula.

b The area of the same shape is given by $A = \frac{1}{2}[\pi r^2 + r^2\sqrt{(k^2 - 1)}]$ Make r the subject of this formula.

12 When £P is invested for Y years at a simple interest rate of R, the following formula gives the amount, A, at any time:

$$A = P + \frac{PRY}{100}$$

Make P the subject of this formula.

13 When two resistors with values a and b are connected in parallel, the total resistance is given by:

$$R = \frac{ab}{a + b}$$

a Make b the subject of the formula.

b Write the formula when a is the subject.

14 **a** Make x the subject of this formula.

$$y = \frac{x + 2}{x - 2}$$

b Show that the formula $y = 1 + \dfrac{4}{x - 2}$ can be rearranged to give:

$$x = 2 + \frac{4}{y - 1}$$

c Combine the right-hand sides of each formula in part **b** into single fractions and simplify as much as possible.

d What do you notice?

15 The volume of the solid shown is given by:

$$V = \tfrac{2}{3}\pi r^3 + \pi r^2 h$$

a Explain why it is not possible to make r the subject of this formula.

b Make π the subject.

c If $h = r$, can the formula be rearranged to make r the subject? If so, rearrange it to make r the subject.

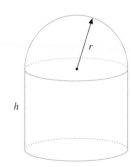

16 Make x the subject of this formula.

$$W = \tfrac{1}{2}z(x + y) + \tfrac{1}{2}y(x + z)$$

1 a Here is a sequence of numbers.

29   25   21   17   13

i Write down the next two numbers in the sequence.

ii Write down the rule for continuing the sequence.

b Another sequence of numbers begins:

2   5   14   41

The rule for continuing this sequence is:

> Multiply by 3 and subtract 1

i What is the next number in the sequence?

ii The same rule is used for a sequence that starts with the number 7. What is the second number in this sequence?

iii The same rule is also used for a sequence that starts with the number −2. What is the second number in this sequence?

2 The first 10 prime numbers are 2, 3, 5, 7, 11, 13, 17, 19, 23, 29.

P is a prime number.
Q is an odd number.
State whether each of the following is always odd, always even or could be either odd or even.

3 The nth term of a sequence is $3n - 1$.

a Write down the first and second terms of the sequence.

b Which term of the sequence is equal to 32?

c Explain why 85 is not a term in this sequence.

4 a The nth term of a sequence is $4n - 1$.

i Write down the first three terms of the sequence.

ii Is 132 a term in this sequence? Explain your answer.

b Tom builds fencing from pieces of wood as shown.

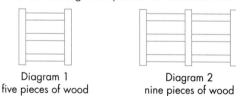

Diagram 1
five pieces of wood

Diagram 2
nine pieces of wood

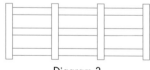

Diagram 3
13 pieces of wood

How many pieces of wood will be in diagram n?

5 a i Multiply out $s(s^2 + 6)$

ii Multiply out and simplify $4(x - 2) + 3(x + 2)$

iii Multiply out and simplify $(n + 3)^2$

b Factorise completely the following expressions

i $2a^2 + a$

ii $8x^3y^2 - 4xy^3$

AQA, Question 5, Paper 2 Higher, June 2004

6 Here is a sequence made from a pattern of dots.

1st pattern   2nd pattern   3rd pattern

a Complete the table.

Pattern	1	2	3	4	5
Number of dots	5	8	11		

b How many dots are in the 7th pattern?

c How many dots are in the nth pattern?

d Which pattern has 62 dots in it?

7 Make x the subject of this formula.

$w = x^2 + y$

AQA, Question 11, Paper 2 Higher, June 2003

8 a Solve the equation

$$\frac{x \div 1}{2} + \frac{x - 3}{4} = 2$$

You *must* show all your working.

AQA, Question 11b, Paper 2 Higher, June 2004

9 A star shape is made by cutting quadrants of a circle from a square of side $2r$.

a Show that the shaded area is given by the formula

$A = 4r^2 - \pi r^2$

b Rearrange the formula

$A = 4r^2 - \pi r^2$

to make r the subject.

AQA, Question 22, Paper 2 (2-tier trial), June 2005

10 Make x the subject of this formula.

$p(q - x) = px + q^2$

11 Make x the subject of this formula.

$$y = \frac{2x + 3}{x - 5}$$

12 A straight line has the equation $y = 2x + 1$
A curve has the equation $y^2 = 8x$
Find the point of intersection of the line and the curve.

13 Solve the equation
$$\frac{4}{2x + 1} - \frac{1}{3x - 1} = 5$$
AQA, Question 19, Paper 2 Higher, June 2005

14 Simplify fully
$$\frac{3x^2 - 5x - 2}{x^2 + x - 6}$$

15 Solve the simultaneous equations
$$y = x \div 2$$
$$y = 3x^2$$
You *must* show your working. Do *not* use trial and improvement.
AQA, Question 20, Paper 2 Higher, June 2004

16 Simplify
$$\frac{x^2 - 9}{x^2 + 3x}$$
AQA, Question 18b, Paper 2 Higher, June 2004

17 Solve the equation
$$\frac{1}{x + 2} + \frac{3x}{x - 1} = 3$$
AQA, Question 20 (modified), Paper 2 Higher, November 2003

WORKED EXAM QUESTION

Make *g* the subject of the following formula.
$$\frac{t(3 + g)}{8 - g} = 2$$

$t(3 + g) = 2(8 - g)$ ——— Cross multiply to get rid of the fraction

$3t + gt = 16 - 2g$ ——— Expand the brackets

$gt + 2g = 16 - 3t$ ——— Collect all the *g* terms on the left-hand side and other terms on the right-hand side.

$g(t + 2) = 16 - 3t$ ——— Simplify, $gt + 2g = g(t + 2)$, and divide by $(t + 2)$.

$$g = \frac{16 - 3t}{t + 2}$$

A group of friends plan an eight-day walking holiday. The profile of their first four daily walks is shown below.

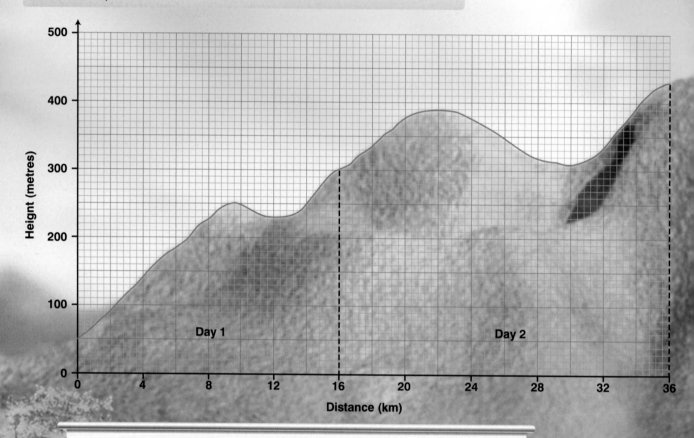

For every day they work out the horizontal distance they walk in kilometres, and the height they climb in metres.

They calculate the time each day's walk will take using the formula

$$T = 15D + \frac{H}{10}$$

where: T = time in minutes D = distance in km
H = height climbed in m

This formula assumes an average walking speed of 4km/h and an extra minute for each 10 metres climbed.

Copy this table and help them complete it. Work out the time each day's walk will take, and the time that the group expects to finish.

Day	Distance in km	Height climbed in metres	Time in minutes	Time in hours and minutes	Start time	Time allowed for breaks	Finish time
1	16	250	265	4h 25m	9:30 am	2 hours	3:55 pm
2					9.00 am	2¾ hours	
3					10:00 am	2½ hours	
4					10:30 am	2¼ hours	

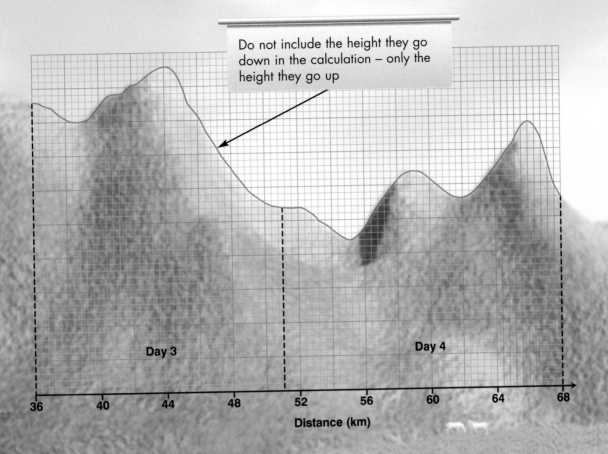

Do not include the height they go down in the calculation – only the height they go up

Day 3

Day 4

Distance (km)

36   40   44   48   52   56   60   64   68

This table shows the information for their walks from Day 5 to Day 8.

Unfortunately coffee has been spilt on the table! Help them to work out the values covered by the coffee.

Day	Distance in km	Height climbed in metres	Time in minutes	Time in hours and minutes	Start time	Time allowed for breaks	Finish time
5	18		282		10:00 am		5:12 pm
6		290	284			2 hours	5:14 pm
7		90		5h 39m	10:00 am	2¾ hours	
8	12			3h 30m	10:30 am		4:15 pm

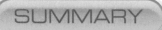

GRADE YOURSELF

D Able to substitute numbers into an *n*th term rule

D Able to understand how odd and even numbers interact in addition, subtraction and multiplication problems

C Able to give the *n*th term of a linear sequence

C Able to give the *n*th term of a sequence of powers of 2 or 10

B Able to find the *n*th term of a quadratic sequence

B Able to solve linear equations involving algebraic fractions where the subject appears as the numerator

A Able to rearrange a formula where the subject appears twice

A Able to combine algebraic fractions using the four rules of addition, subtraction, multiplication and division

A✱ Able to rearrange more complicated formulae where the subject may appear twice or as a power

A✱ Able to solve a quadratic equation obtained from algebraic fractions where the variable appears in the denominator

A✱ Able to simplify algebraic fractions by factorisation and cancellation

A✱ Able to solve a pair of simultaneous equations where one is linear and the other is non-linear

What you should know now

- Be able to manipulate algebraic fractions and solve equations resulting from the simplified fractions
- Be able to solve a pair of simultaneous equations where one is linear and one is non-linear
- Be able to recognise a linear sequence and find its *n*th term
- Be able to recognise a sequence of powers of 2 or 10
- Be able to recognise a non-linear sequence and find its *n*th term
- Be able to rearrange a formula where the subject appears twice

Inequalities and regions

1 Solving inequalities

2 Graphical inequalities

3 Problem solving

This chapter will show you ...

- how to solve a linear inequality
- how to find a region on a graph that obeys a linear inequality in two variables
- how inequalities can be used to represent and solve problems

Visual overview

| Linear inequalities | → | Inequalities in two variables | → | Problem solving |

What you should already know

- How to solve linear equations
- How to draw linear graphs

Quick check

1 Solve these equations.

a $\dfrac{2x + 5}{3} = 7$ **b** $2x - 7 = 13$

2 On a grid with x and y axes from 0 to 10, draw the graphs of these equations.

a $y = 3x + 1$ **b** $2x + 3y = 12$

Solving inequalities

This section will show you how to:
- solve a simple linear inequality

Key words

inequality
number line

Inequalities behave similarly to equations which you have already met. In the case of linear inequalities, we use the same rules to solve them as we use for linear equations. There are four inequality signs, $<$ which means "less than", $>$ which means "greater than", $\leqslant$ which means "less than or equal to" and $\geqslant$ which means "greater than or equal to".

EXAMPLE 1

Solve $2x + 3 < 14$.

This is rewritten as:

$$2x < 14 - 3$$
$$2x < 11$$

Divide both sides by 2:

$$\frac{2x}{2} < \frac{11}{2}$$
$$\Rightarrow x < 5.5$$

This means that x can take any value below 5.5 but *not* the value 5.5.

Note: The inequality sign given in the problem is the sign to give in the answer.

EXAMPLE 2

Solve $\frac{x}{2} + 4 \geqslant 13$.

Solve just like an equation but leave the inequality sign in place of the equals sign.

Subtract 4 from both sides:

$$\frac{x}{2} \geqslant 9$$

Multiply both sides by 2:

$$x \geqslant 18$$

This means that x can take any value above and including 18.

EXAMPLE 3

Solve $\dfrac{3x + 7}{2} < 14$.

This is rewritten as: $\qquad\qquad\qquad\qquad 3x + 7 < 14 \times 2$

That is: $\qquad\qquad\qquad\qquad\qquad\quad 3x + 7 < 28$

$\qquad\qquad\qquad\qquad\Rightarrow\qquad 3x < 28 - 7$

$\qquad\qquad\qquad\qquad\Rightarrow\qquad 3x < 21$

$\qquad\qquad\qquad\qquad\Rightarrow\qquad\ x < 21 \div 3$

$\qquad\qquad\qquad\qquad\Rightarrow\qquad\ x < 7$

EXAMPLE 4

Solve $1 < 3x + 4 \leqslant 13$.

Divide the inequality into two parts, and treat each part separately.

$\qquad\quad 1 < 3x + 4 \qquad\qquad\qquad\qquad 3x + 4 \leqslant 13$

$\Rightarrow 1 - 4 < 3x \qquad\qquad\qquad \Rightarrow\qquad 3x \leqslant 13 - 4$

$\Rightarrow\quad -3 < 3x \qquad\qquad\qquad \Rightarrow\qquad 3x \leqslant 9$

$\Rightarrow\quad -\dfrac{3}{3} < x \qquad\qquad\qquad \Rightarrow\qquad x \leqslant \dfrac{9}{3}$

$\Rightarrow\quad -1 < x \qquad\qquad\qquad\quad \Rightarrow\qquad x \leqslant 3$

$\qquad\qquad\qquad$ Hence, $-1 < x \leqslant 3$.

EXERCISE 26A

1 Solve the following linear inequalities.

a $x + 4 < 7$ $\qquad\qquad$ **b** $t - 3 > 5$ $\qquad\qquad$ **c** $p + 2 \geqslant 12$

d $2x - 3 < 7$ $\qquad\qquad$ **e** $4y + 5 \leqslant 17$ $\qquad\qquad$ **f** $3t - 4 > 11$

g $\dfrac{x}{2} + 4 < 7$ $\qquad\qquad$ **h** $\dfrac{y}{5} + 3 \leqslant 6$ $\qquad\qquad$ **i** $\dfrac{t}{3} - 2 \geqslant 4$

j $3(x - 2) < 15$ $\qquad\qquad$ **k** $5(2x + 1) \leqslant 35$ $\qquad\qquad$ **l** $2(4t - 3) \geqslant 34$

2 Write down the largest integer value of x that satisfies each of the following.

a $x - 3 \leqslant 5$, where x is positive

b $x + 2 < 9$, where x is positive and even

c $3x - 11 < 40$, where x is a square number

d $5x - 8 \leqslant 15$, where x is positive and odd

e $2x + 1 < 19$, where x is positive and prime

3 Write down the smallest integer value of x that satisfies each of the following.

a $x - 2 \geqslant 9$, where x is positive

b $x - 2 > 13$, where x is positive and even

c $2x - 11 \geqslant 19$, where x is a square number

4 Solve the following linear inequalities.

a $4x + 1 \geqslant 3x - 5$ **b** $5t - 3 \leqslant 2t + 5$ **c** $3y - 12 \leqslant y - 4$

d $2x + 3 \geqslant x + 1$ **e** $5w - 7 \leqslant 3w + 4$ **f** $2(4x - 1) \leqslant 3(x + 4)$

5 Solve the following linear inequalities.

a $\dfrac{x + 4}{2} \leqslant 3$ **b** $\dfrac{x - 3}{5} > 7$ **c** $\dfrac{2x + 5}{3} < 6$

d $\dfrac{4x - 3}{5} \geqslant 5$ **e** $\dfrac{3t - 2}{7} > 4$ **f** $\dfrac{5y + 3}{5} \leqslant 2$

6 Solve the following linear inequalities.

a $7 < 2x + 1 < 13$ **b** $5 < 3x - 1 < 14$ **c** $-1 < 5x + 4 \leqslant 19$

d $1 \leqslant 4x - 3 < 13$ **e** $11 \leqslant 3x + 5 < 17$ **f** $-3 \leqslant 2x - 3 \leqslant 7$

The number line

The solution to a linear inequality can be shown on the **number line** by using the following conventions.

Below are five examples.

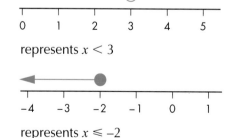

represents $x < 3$

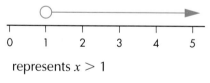

represents $x > 1$

represents $x \leqslant -2$

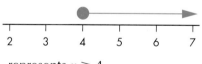

represents $x \geqslant 4$

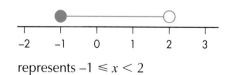

represents $-1 \leqslant x < 2$

Mod 5

EXAMPLE 5

a Write down the inequality shown by this diagram.

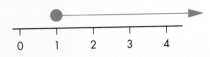

b i Solve the following inequality $2x + 3 < 11$.

ii Mark the solution on a number line.

c Write down the integers that satisfy both the inequalities in **a** and **b**.

a The inequality shown is $x \geqslant 1$.

b i $2x + 3 < 11 \implies 2x < 8 \implies x < 4$

ii

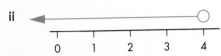

c The integers that satisfy both inequalities are 1, 2 and 3.

EXERCISE 26B

1 Write down the inequality that is represented by each diagram below.

a

b

c
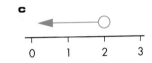

d
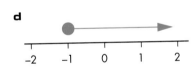

e
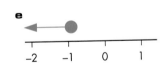

f
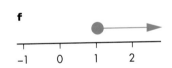

2 Draw diagrams to illustrate the following.

a $x \leqslant 3$ **b** $x > -2$ **c** $x \geqslant 0$ **d** $x < 5$

e $x \geqslant -1$ **f** $2 < x \leqslant 5$ **g** $-1 \leqslant x \leqslant 3$ **h** $-3 < x < 4$

3 Solve the following inequalities and illustrate their solutions on number lines.

a $x + 4 \geqslant 8$ **b** $x + 5 < 3$ **c** $4x - 2 \geqslant 12$ **d** $2x + 5 < 3$

e $2(4x + 3) < 18$ **f** $\dfrac{x}{2} + 3 \leqslant 2$ **g** $\dfrac{x}{5} - 2 > 8$ **h** $\dfrac{x}{3} + 5 \geqslant 3$

4 Solve the following inequalities and illustrate their solutions on number lines.

a $\dfrac{2x + 5}{3} > 3$ **b** $\dfrac{3x + 4}{2} \geqslant 11$ **c** $\dfrac{2x + 8}{3} \leqslant 2$ **d** $\dfrac{2x - 1}{3} \geqslant -3$

Inequalities involving x^2

When we have an inequality such as $x^2 < 9$, we have to think very carefully because there are two possible solutions to $x^2 = 9$. They are $x = 3$ and $x = -3$.

The solution $x = 3$ to the equation $x^2 = 9$ would suggest the condition $x < 3$ is a solution to $x^2 < 9$. Clearly, $x < 3$ does satisfy the inequality $x^2 < 9$. The condition to be obtained from the solution $x = -3$ is not $x < -3$. (Think about $(-5)^2$.) So it must be $x > -3$. That is, the inequality sign is *changed*. For convenience, $x > -3$ can be turned to give $-3 < x$.

Show this situation on a number line and the solution becomes clear.

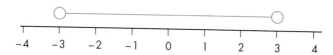

Namely, $-3 < x < 3$.

EXAMPLE 6

Solve the inequality $x^2 > 16$ and show your solution on a number line.

The solution to $x^2 > 16$ will be $x > 4$ and $x < -4$, which is represented as

Notice the difference between inequalities of the type $x^2 < a^2$ and those of the type $x^2 > a^2$.

EXERCISE 26C

Solve the following inequalities, showing their solutions on number lines.

1 $x^2 \leqslant 4$

2 $x^2 > 25$

3 $x^2 < 49$

4 $x^2 \geqslant 1$

5 $x^2 \geqslant 9$

6 $x^2 - 1 > 8$

7 $x^2 + 2 \leqslant 6$

8 $x^2 - 3 < 13$

9 $x^2 + 5 > 6$

10 $x^2 - 4 \geqslant 5$

11 $2x^2 - 1 > 7$

12 $3x^2 - 5 < 22$

13 $5x^2 + 3 \leqslant 8$

14 $2x^2 - 4 < 28$

15 $3x^2 - 9 \geqslant 66$

16 $x^2 \geqslant 100$

17 $x^2 < 2.25$

18 $x^2 \geqslant 0.25$

19 $x^2 - 5 \leqslant 76$

20 $x^2 > 0$

Graphical inequalities

This section will show you how to:

- show a graphical inequality and how to find regions that satisfy more than one graphical inequality

Key words

boundary
included
origin
region

A linear inequality can be plotted on a graph. The result is a **region** that lies on one side or the other of a straight line. You will recognise an inequality by the fact that it looks like an equation but instead of the equals sign it has an inequality sign: $<$, $>$, $\leq$, or $\geq$.

The following are examples of linear inequalities which can be represented on a graph.

$$y < 3 \qquad x > 7 \qquad -3 \leq y < 5 \qquad y \geq 2x + 3 \qquad 2x + 3y < 6 \qquad y \leq x$$

The method for graphing an inequality is to draw the **boundary** line that defines the inequality. This is found by replacing the inequality sign with an equals sign. When a strict inequality is stated ($<$ or $>$), the boundary line should be drawn as a *dashed* line to show that it is not included in the range of values. When $\leq$ or $\geq$ are used to state the inequality, the boundary line should be drawn as a *solid* line to show that the boundary is **included**.

After the boundary line has been drawn, the *required region is shaded*.

To confirm on which side of the line the region lies, choose any point that is not on the boundary line and test it in the inequality. If it satisfies the inequality, that is the side required. If it doesn't, the other side is required.

Work through the six inequalities on this page and the next, to see how the procedure is applied.

EXAMPLE 7

Show each of the following inequalities on a graph.

a $y \leq 3$ **b** $x > 7$ **c** $-3 \leq y < 5$ **d** $y \leq 2x + 3$ **e** $2x + 3y < 6$ **f** $y \leq x$

a Draw the line $y = 3$. Since the inequality is stated as $\leq$, the line is solid. Test a point that is not on the line. The **origin** is always a good choice if possible, as 0 is easy to test.

Putting 0 into the inequality gives $0 \leq 3$. The inequality is satisfied and so the region containing the origin is the side we want.

Shade it in.

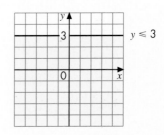

b Since the inequality is stated as >, the line is *dashed*. Draw the line $x = 7$.

Test the origin (0, 0), which gives $0 > 7$. This is not true, so we want the other side of the line from the origin.

Shade it in.

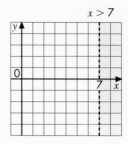

$x > 7$

c Draw the lines $y = -3$ (solid for ≤) and $y = 5$ (dashed for <).

Test a point that is not on either line, say (0, 0). Zero is between −3 and 5, so the required region lies between the lines.

Shade it in.

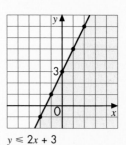

$-3 \leq y < 5$

d Draw the line $y = 2x + 3$. Since the inequality is stated as ≤, the line is solid.

Test a point that is not on the line, (0, 0). Putting these x and y-values in the inequality gives $0 \leq 2(0) + 3$, which is true. So the region that includes the origin is what we want.

Shade it in.

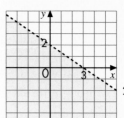

$y \leq 2x + 3$

e Draw the line $2x + 3y = 6$. Since the inequality is stated as <, the line is dashed.

Test a point that is not on the line, say (0, 0). Is it true that $2(0) + 3(0) < 6$? The answer is yes, so the origin is in the region that we want.

Shade it in.

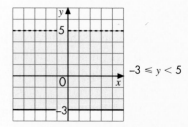

$2x + 3y < 6$

f Draw the line $y = x$. Since the inequality is stated as ≤, the line is solid.

This time the origin is on the line, so pick any other point, say (1, 3). Putting $x = 1$ and $y = 3$ in the inequality gives $3 \leq 1$. This is not true, so the point (1, 3) is not in the region we want.

Shade in the other side to (1, 3).

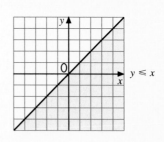

$y \leq x$

More than one inequality

When we have to show a region that satisfies more than one inequality, it is clearer to *shade* the regions *not required*, so that the *required region* is left *blank*.

EXAMPLE 8

a On the same grid, show the regions that represent the following inequalities by shading the unwanted regions.

  i $x > 2$ **ii** $y \geqslant x$ **iii** $x + y < 8$

b Are the points $(3, 4)$, $(2, 6)$ and $(3, 3)$ in the region that satisfies all three inequalities?

i 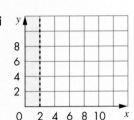   **ii** 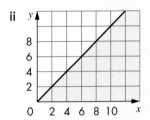   **iii**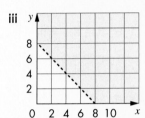

a **i** This region is shown unshaded in diagram **i**.

The boundary line is $x = 2$ (dashed).

ii This region is shown unshaded in diagram **ii**.

The boundary line is $y = x$ (solid).

iii This region is shown unshaded in diagram **iii**.

The boundary line is $x + y = 8$ (dashed). The regions have first been drawn separately so that each may be clearly seen. The diagram on the right shows all three regions on the same grid. The white triangular area defines the region that satisfies all three inequalities.

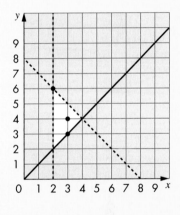

b **i** The point $(3, 4)$ is clearly within the region that satisfies all three inequalities.

ii The point $(2, 6)$ is on the boundary lines $x = 2$ and $x + y = 8$. As these are dashed lines, they are not included in the region defined by all three inequalities. So, the point $(2, 6)$ is not in this region.

iii The point $(3, 3)$ is on the boundary line $y = x$. As this is a solid line, it is included in the region defined by all three inequalities. So, the point $(3, 3)$ is included in this region.

EXERCISE 26D

1 **a** Draw the line $x = 2$ (as a solid line).

b Shade the region defined by $x \leqslant 2$.

2 **a** Draw the line $y = -3$ (as a dashed line).

b Shade the region defined by $y > -3$.

3 **a** Draw the line $x = -2$ (as a solid line).

b Draw the line $x = 1$ (as a solid line) on the same grid.

c Shade the region defined by $-2 \leqslant x \leqslant 1$.

4 **a** Draw the line $y = -1$ (as a dashed line).

b Draw the line $y = 4$ (as a solid line) on the same grid.

c Shade the region defined by $-1 < y \leqslant 4$.

5 **a** On the same grid, draw the regions defined by these inequalities.

i $-3 \leqslant x \leqslant 6$ **ii** $-4 < y \leqslant 5$

b Are the following points in the region defined by both inequalities?

i (2, 2)   **ii** (1, 5)   **iii** (−2, −4)

6 **a** Draw the line $y = 2x - 1$ (as a dashed line).

b Shade the region defined by $y < 2x - 1$.

7 **a** Draw the line $3x - 4y = 12$ (as a solid line).

b Shade the region defined by $3x - 4y \leqslant 12$.

8 **a** Draw the line $y = \frac{1}{2}x + 3$ (as a solid line).

b Shade the region defined by $y \geqslant \frac{1}{2}x + 3$.

9 Shade the region defined by $y < -3$.

10 **a** Draw the line $y = 3x - 4$ (as a solid line).

b Draw the line $x + y = 10$ (as a solid line) on the same diagram.

c Shade the diagram so that the region defined by $y \geqslant 3x - 4$ is left *unshaded*.

d Shade the diagram so that the region defined by $x + y \leqslant 10$ is left *unshaded*.

e Are the following points in the region defined by both inequalities?

i (2, 1)   **ii** (2, 2)   **iii** (2, 3)

11 **a** Draw the line $y = x$ (as a solid line).

b Draw the line $2x + 5y = 10$ (as a solid line) on the same diagram.

c Draw the line $2x + y = 6$ (as a dashed line) on the same diagram.

d Shade the diagram so that the region defined by $y \geqslant x$ is left *unshaded*.

e Shade the diagram so that the region defined by $2x + 5y \geqslant 10$ is left *unshaded*.

f Shade the diagram so that the region defined by $2x + y < 6$ is left *unshaded*.

g Are the following points in the region defined by these inequalities?

i (1, 1)   **ii** (2, 2)   **iii** (1, 3)

> **HINTS AND TIPS**
>
> In exams it is always made clear which region is to be labelled or shaded. Make sure you do as the question asks, and label or shade as required otherwise you could lose a mark.

12 **a** On the same grid, draw the regions defined by the following inequalities. (Shade the diagram so that the overlapping region is left blank.)

i $y > x - 3$ **ii** $3y + 4x \leqslant 24$ **iii** $x \geqslant 2$

b Are the following points in the region defined by all three inequalities?

i (1, 1)   **ii** (2, 2)   **iii** (3, 3)   **iv** (4, 4)

26.3 Problem solving

This section will show you:

- some of the problems that can be solved using inequalities

Inequalities can arise in the solution of certain kinds of problem. The next example illustrates such a situation.

EXAMPLE 9

James has to buy drinks for himself and four friends. He has £2.50 to spend. A can of Cola costs 60 pence and a can of Orange costs 40 pence. He buys x cans of Cola and y cans of Orange.

a Explain why   **i** $x + y \geqslant 5$ **ii** $6x + 4y \leqslant 25$

b Write down all the possible numbers of each type of drink he can buy.

a **i** James needs to buy at least five cans as there are five people. So the total number of cans of Cola and Orange must be at least five. This is expressed as $x + y \geqslant 5$.

ii x cans of Cola cost $60x$ pence, and y cans of Orange cost $40y$ pence. So

total cost = $60x + 40y$

But he has only 250 pence to spend, so total cost cannot exceed 250 pence. Hence,

$60x + 40y \leqslant 250$

This cancels through by 10 to give

$6x + 4y \leqslant 25$

b By trying different values of x and y, the following four combinations are found to satisfy the condition.

one can of Cola and four cans of Orange

two cans of Cola and three cans of Orange

five or six cans of Orange

EXERCISE 26E

1 A company sells two types of bicycle, the Chapper and the Graffiti. A Chapper costs £148 and a Graffiti cost £125.

   a How much do x Chappers cost?

   b How much do y Graffitis cost?

   c How much do x Chappers and y Graffitis cost altogether?

2 A computer firm makes two types of machine. The Z210 and the Z310. The price of the Z210 is £A and that of the Z310 is £B. How much are the following?

   a x Z210s and y Z310s

   b x Z210s and twice as many Z310s

   c 9 Z210s and $(9 + y)$ Z310s

3 If $x + y > 40$, which of the following *may* be true?

   a $x > 40$ **b** $x + y \leqslant 20$ **c** $x - y = 10$ **d** $x \leqslant 5$

4 A bookshelf holds P paperback and H hardback books. The bookshelf can hold a total of 400 books. Which of the following *may* be true?

   a $P + H < 300$ **b** $P \geqslant H$ **c** $P + H > 500$

5 A school uses two coach firms, Excel and Storm, to take pupils home from school. An Excel coach holds 40 pupils and a Storm coach holds 50 pupils. 1500 pupils need to be taken home by coach. If E Excel coaches and S Storm coaches are used, explain why:

$4E + 5S \geqslant 150$

6 A boy goes to the fair with £6.00 in his pocket. He only likes rides on the big wheel and eating hot-dogs. A big wheel ride costs £1.50 and a hot-dog costs £2.00. He has W big wheel rides and D hot-dogs. Explain why:

   a $W \leqslant 4$ **b** $D \leqslant 3$ **c** $3W + 4D \leqslant 12$

   d If he cannot eat more than two hot-dogs without being ill, write down an inequality that *must* be true.

   e Which of these combinations of big wheel rides and hot-dogs are possible if they obey all of the above conditions?

      i two big wheel rides and one hot-dog

      ii three big wheel rides and two hot-dogs

      iii two big wheel rides and two hot-dogs

      iv one big wheel ride and one hot-dog

7 Pens cost 45p each and pencils cost 25p each. Jane has £2.00 with which to buy pens and pencils. She buys x pens and y pencils.

a Write down an inequality that must be true.

b She must have at least two more pencils than pens. Write down an inequality that must be true.

8 Mushtaq has to buy some apples and some pears. He has £3.00 to spend. Apples cost 30p each and pears cost 40p each. He must buy at least two apples and at least three pears, and at least seven fruits altogether. He buys x apples and y pears.

a Explain each of these inequalities.

   i $3x + 4y \leqslant 30$ **ii** $x \geqslant 2$ **iii** $y \geqslant 3$ **iv** $x + y \geqslant 7$

b Which of these combinations satisfy all of the above inequalities?

   i three apples and three pears   **ii** four apples and five pears

   iii no apples and seven pears   **iv** three apples and five pears

9 A shop decides to stock only sofas and beds. A sofa takes up 4 m^2 of floor area and is worth £300. A bed takes up 3 m^2 of floor area and is worth £500. The shop has 48 m^2 of floor space for stock. The insurance policy will allow a total of only £6000 of stock to be in the shop at any one time. The shop stocks x sofas and y beds.

a Explain each of these inequalities.

   i $4x + 3y \leqslant 48$ **ii** $3x + 5y \leqslant 60$

b Which of these combinations satisfy both of the above inequalities?

   i ten sofas and no beds   **ii** eight sofas and six beds

   iii ten sofas and five beds   **iv** six sofas and eight beds

10 The 300 pupils in Year 7 are to go on a trip to Adern Towers theme park. The local bus company has six 40-seat coaches and five 50-seat coaches. The school hires x 40-seat coaches and y 50-seat coaches.

a Explain each of these inequalities.

   i $4x + 5y \geqslant 30$ **ii** $x \leqslant 6$ **iii** $y \leqslant 5$

b Check that each of these combinations obeys each of the inequalities above.

   i six 40-seaters and two 50-seaters

   ii two 40-seaters and five 50-seaters

   iii four 40-seaters and three 50-seaters

   iv three 40-seaters and four 50-seaters

c The cost of hiring each coach is £100 for a 40-seater and £120 for a 50-seater. Which of the combinations in part **b** would be the cheapest option?

d There is one combination that is even cheaper than the answer to part **c**. What is it?

1 **a** Solve the inequality $2x + 3 \geqslant 1$

b Write down the inequality shown by the following diagram.

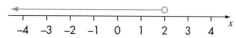

c Write down all the integers that satisfy both inequalities shown in parts **a** and **b**.

AQA, Question 19, Paper 2 Higher, June 2004

2 **a** Solve the inequality $4x + 3 < 13$

b Write down the largest integer that is a solution of $4x + 3 < 13$

3 **a** Solve the inequality $7y < 3y + 6$

b Make r the subject of the formula $p = 3 + 2r$

c Solve the equation $\frac{1}{2}x - 5 = \frac{1}{4}x + 3$

AQA, Question 2, Paper 1 Higher, June 2005

4 **a** Solve the inequality $5x - 9 \geqslant 6$

b **i** Solve the inequality $2x + 7 > 15 - 3x$

ii If x is an integer, what is the smallest possible value of x?

5 Find all the integer values of n that satisfy the inequality
$-3 \leqslant 2n + 1 < 9$

6 **a** Solve the inequality $4x - 9 < x + 3$

b Solve the inequality $x^2 < 25$

7 On a grid show the region that is defined by the three inequalities
$x \geqslant 1 \qquad y \leqslant 3 \qquad x + y \leqslant 5$
Mark the region with an R.

8 On a grid show the region that is defined by the three inequalities
$x \geqslant 0 \qquad y \leqslant 2x + 1 \qquad x + y \leqslant 4$
Mark the region with an R.

9 The region R is shown shaded below.

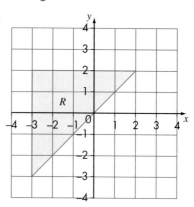

Write down three inequalities which together describe the shaded region.

AQA, Question 15, Paper 2 (2-tier trial), June 2005

10 Copy the grid below and indicate clearly on it the region defined by the three inequalities

$y \leqslant 4$

$x \geqslant -3$

$y \geqslant x + 2$

Mark the region with an R.

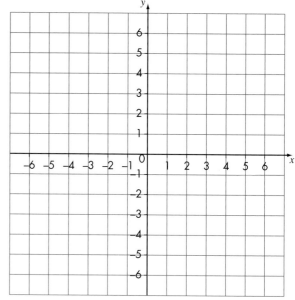

AQA, Question 11, Paper 2 Higher, November 2004

11 n is an integer that satisfies the inequality

$$\frac{121}{n^2} \geqslant 8$$

List all the possible values of n.

WORKED EXAM QUESTION

a On the number lines show the inequalities

i $-2 \leqslant n < 4$

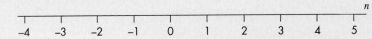

ii $n < 2$

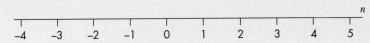

b n is an integer. Find the values of n that satisfy both inequalities in part **a**

c Solve the inequalities

i $3x + 8 > 2$

ii $3(x - 4) \leqslant \frac{1}{2}(x + 1)$

Solution

a i

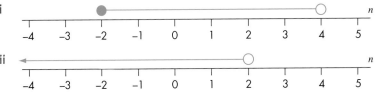

ii

> Remember that a strict inequality has an open circle to show the boundary and an inclusive inequality has a solid circle to show the boundary.

b $\{-2, -1, 0, 1\}$

> The integers that satisfy both inequalities are in the overlap of both lines.

c i $3x + 8 > 2$

$3x > -6$

$x > -2$

> As when solving an equation do the same thing to both sides. First subtract 8, then divide by 3.

ii $3(x - 4) \leqslant \frac{1}{2}(x + 1)$

$6(x - 4) \leqslant x + 1$

$6x - 24 < x + 1$

$5x < 25$

$x < 5$

> First multiply by 2 to get rid of the fraction, then expand the brackets. Then collect all the x terms on the left-hand side and the number terms on the right-hand side. Then simplify and divide by 5.

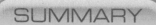

GRADE YOURSELF

C Able to solve inequalities such as $3x + 2 < 5$ and represent the solution on a number line

B Able to represent a region that satisfies a linear inequality graphically, and to solve more complex linear inequalities

B Able to represent a region that simultaneously satisfies more than one linear inequality graphically

A Able to translate a problem into inequalities

What you should know now

- How to solve simple inequalities
- How to create algebraic inequalities from verbal statements
- How to represent linear inequalities on a graph
- How to depict a region satisfying more than one linear inequality

Transformation of graphs

(1) Transformations of the graph $y = f(x)$

This chapter will show you ...

- how to transform a graph
- how to recognise the relationships between graphs and their equations

Visual overview

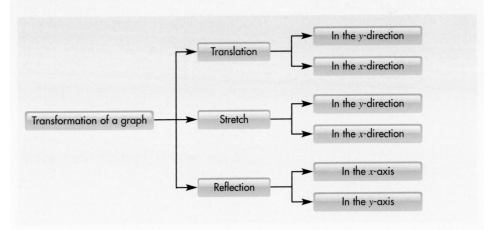

What you should already know

- How to transform a shape by a translation and a reflection
- A translation is described by a column vector
- A reflection is described by a mirror line

continued

• The graphs of $y = x^2$, $y = x^3$, $y = \dfrac{1}{x}$, $y = \sin x$, $y = \cos x$ and $y = \tan x$

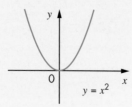
$y = x^2$

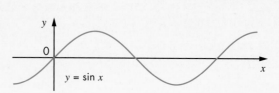
$y = \sin x$

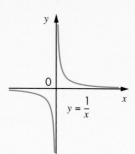
$y = x^3$

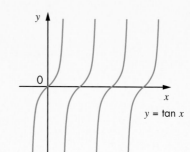
$y = \cos x$

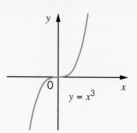
$y = \dfrac{1}{x}$

$y = \tan x$

Quick check

Starting with the shaded triangle every time, do the following transformations.

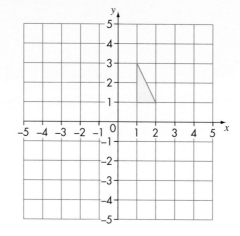

a translation

  i $\begin{pmatrix} 3 \\ 0 \end{pmatrix}$ **ii** $\begin{pmatrix} 0 \\ -2 \end{pmatrix}$

b reflection in the   **i** y-axis   **ii** x-axis

c rotation of 180° about the origin

This section will show you how to:

● transform a graph

Key words

function
reflection
scale factor
stretch
transform
translation
vector

We use the notation $f(x)$ to represent a **function** of x. A function of x is any algebraic expression in which x is the only variable. Examples of functions are: $f(x) = x + 3$, $f(x) = 5x$, $f(x) = 2x - 7$, $f(x) = x^2$, $f(x) = x^3 + 2x - 1$, $f(x) = \sin x$ and $f(x) = \frac{1}{x}$.

Below and on page 586 are six general statements or rules about **transforming** graphs.

This work is much easier to understand if you have access to a graphics calculator or a graph-drawing computer program.

The graph on the right represents any function $y = f(x)$.

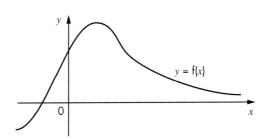

Rule 1 The graph of $y = f(x) + a$ is a **translation** of the graph of $y = f(x)$ by a **vector** $\begin{pmatrix} 0 \\ a \end{pmatrix}$.

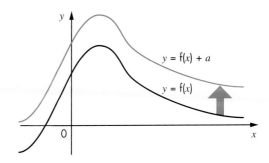

Rule 2 The graph of $y = f(x - a)$ is a translation of the graph of $y = f(x)$ by a vector $\begin{pmatrix} a \\ 0 \end{pmatrix}$.

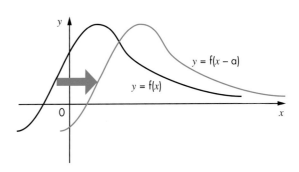

A **stretch** is an enlargement that takes place in one direction only. It is described by a **scale factor** and the direction of the stretch

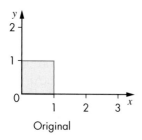

Original

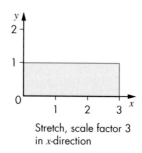

Stretch, scale factor 3
in x-direction

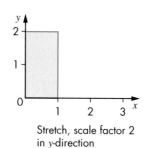

Stretch, scale factor 2
in y-direction

Rule 3 The graph of $y = kf(x)$ is a stretch of the graph $y = f(x)$ by a scale factor of k in the y-direction.

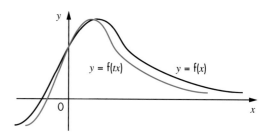

Rule 4 The graph of $y = f(tx)$ is a stretch of the graph $y = f(x)$ by a scale factor of $\dfrac{1}{t}$ in the x-direction.

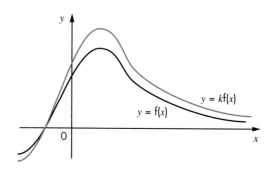

Rule 5 The graph of $y = -f(x)$ is the **reflection** of the graph $y = f(x)$ in the x-axis.

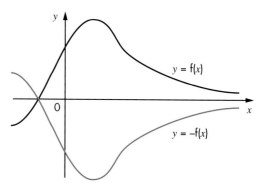

Rule 6 The graph of $y = f(-x)$ is the reflection of the graph $y = f(x)$ in the y-axis.

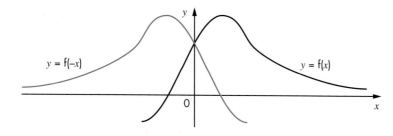

EXAMPLE 1

Sketch the following graphs.

a $y = x^2$ **b** $y = 5x^2$ **c** $y = x^2 - 5$

d $y = -x^2$ **e** $y = (x - 5)^2$ **f** $y = 2x^2 + 3$

Describe the transformation(s) that change(s) graph **a** to each of the other graphs.

Graph **a** is the basic graph to which we apply the rules to make the necessary transformations: graph **b** uses Rule 3, graph **c** uses Rule 1, graph **d** uses Rule 5, graph **e** uses Rule 2, and graph **f** uses Rules 3 and 1.

The graphs are

a

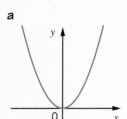

b

c

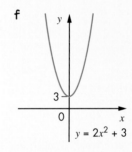

d

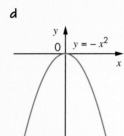

e

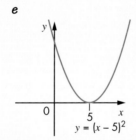

f

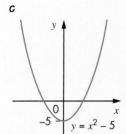

The transformations are:

    graph **b** is a stretch of scale factor 5 in the y-direction,

    graph **c** is a translation of $\begin{pmatrix} 0 \\ -5 \end{pmatrix}$,

    graph **d** is a reflection in the x-axis,

    graph **e** is a translation of $\begin{pmatrix} 5 \\ 0 \end{pmatrix}$,

    graph **f** is a stretch of scale factor 2 in the y-direction, followed by a translation of $\begin{pmatrix} 0 \\ 3 \end{pmatrix}$.

Note that two of the transformations cause problems because they seem to do the opposite of what is expected. These are:

$y = f(x + a)$ (Rule 2)

The translation is $\begin{pmatrix} -a \\ 0 \end{pmatrix}$, so the sign of the constant inside the bracket changes in the vector (see part **e** in Example 1).

$y = f(ax)$ (Rule 4)

This is not a stretch. It actually closes the graph up. Just like an enlargement (see Chapter 14) can make something smaller, a stretch can make it squeeze closer to the axes.

EXERCISE 27A

1 On the same axes sketch the following graphs.

a $y = x^2$ **b** $y = 3x^2$ **c** $y = \frac{1}{2}x^2$ **d** $y = 10x^2$

e Describe the transformation(s) that take(s) the graph in part **a** to each of the graphs in parts **b** to **d**.

2 On the same axes sketch the following graphs.

a $y = x^2$ **b** $y = x^2 + 3$ **c** $y = x^2 - 1$ **d** $y = 2x^2 + 1$

e Describe the transformation(s) that take(s) the graph in part **a** to each of the graphs in parts **b** to **d**.

3 On the same axes sketch the following graphs.

a $y = x^2$ **b** $y = (x + 3)^2$ **c** $y = (x - 1)^2$ **d** $y = 2(x - 2)^2$

e Describe the transformation(s) that take(s) the graph in part **a** to each of the graphs in parts **b** to **d**.

4 On the same axes sketch the following graphs.

a $y = x^2$ **b** $y = (x + 3)^2 - 1$ **c** $y = 4(x - 1)^2 + 3$

d Describe the transformation(s) that take(s) the graph in part **a** to each of the graphs in parts **b** and **c**.

5 On the same axes sketch the following graphs.

a $y = x^2$ **b** $y = -x^2 + 3$ **c** $y = -3x^2$ **d** $y = -2x^2 + 1$

e Describe the transformation(s) that take(s) the graph in part **a** to each of the graphs in parts **b** to **d**.

6 On the same axes sketch the following graphs.

a $y = \sin x$ **b** $y = 2\sin x$ **c** $y = \frac{1}{2}\sin x$ **d** $y = 10\sin x$

e Describe the transformation(s) that take(s) the graph in part **a** to each of the graphs in parts **b** to **d**.

7 On the same axes sketch the following graphs.

a $y = \sin x$ **b** $y = \sin 3x$ **c** $y = \sin \dfrac{x}{2}$ **d** $y = 5\sin 2x$

e Describe the transformation(s) that take(s) the graph in part **a** to each of the graphs in parts **b** to **d**.

8 On the same axes sketch the following graphs.

a $y = \sin x$ **b** $y = \sin (x + 90°)$ **c** $y = \sin (x - 45°)$ **d** $y = 2\sin (x - 90°)$

e Describe the transformation(s) that take(s) the graph in part **a** to the graphs in parts **b** to **d**.

9 On the same axes sketch the following graphs.

a $y = \sin x$ **b** $y = \sin x + 2$ **c** $y = \sin x - 3$ **d** $y = 2\sin x + 1$

e Describe the transformation(s) that take(s) the graph in part **a** to each of the graphs parts **b** to **d**.

10 On the same axes sketch the following graphs.

a $y = \sin x$ **b** $y = -\sin x$ **c** $y = \sin(-x)$ **d** $y = -\sin(-x)$

e Describe the transformation(s) that take(s) the graph in part **a** to each of the graphs in parts **b** to **d**.

11 On the same axes sketch the following graphs.

a $y = \cos x$ **b** $y = 2\cos x$ **c** $y = \cos(x - 60°)$ **d** $y = \cos x + 2$

e Describe the transformation(s) that take(s) the graph in part **a** to each of the graphs in parts **b** to **d**.

12 **a** Describe the transformations of the graph of $y = x^2$ needed to obtain these graphs.

i $y = 4x^2$ **ii** $y = 9x^2$ **iii** $y = 16x^2$

b Describe the transformations of the graph of $y = x^2$ needed to obtain these graphs.

i $y = (2x)^2$ **ii** $y = (3x)^2$ **iii** $y = (4x)^2$

c Describe two different transformations that take the graph of $y = x^2$ to the graph of $y = (ax)^2$, where a is a positive number.

13 On the right is a sketch of the function $y = f(x)$. Use this to sketch the following.

a $y = f(x) + 2$ **b** $y = 2f(x)$

c $y = f(x - 3)$ **d** $y = -f(x)$

e $y = 2f(x) + 3$ **f** $y = -f(x) - 2$

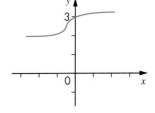

14 What is the equation of the graph obtained when the following transformations are performed on the graph of $y = x^2$?

a stretch by a factor of 5 in the y-direction

b translation of $\begin{pmatrix} 0 \\ 7 \end{pmatrix}$

c translation of $\begin{pmatrix} -3 \\ 0 \end{pmatrix}$

d translation of $\begin{pmatrix} -2 \\ -3 \end{pmatrix}$

e stretch by a factor of 3 in the y-direction followed by a translation of $\begin{pmatrix} 0 \\ 4 \end{pmatrix}$

f reflection in the x-axis, followed by a stretch, scale factor 3, in the y-direction

15 What is the equation of the graph obtained when the following transformations are performed on the graph of $y = \cos x$?

  a stretch by a factor of 6 in the y-direction

  b translation of $\begin{pmatrix} 0 \\ 3 \end{pmatrix}$

  c translation of $\begin{pmatrix} -30 \\ 0 \end{pmatrix}$

  d translation of $\begin{pmatrix} 45 \\ -2 \end{pmatrix}$

  e stretch by a factor of 3 in the y-direction followed by a translation of $\begin{pmatrix} 0 \\ -2 \end{pmatrix}$

16 **a** Sketch the graph $y = x^3$.

  b Use your sketch in part **a** to draw the graphs obtained after $y = x^3$ is transformed as follows.

    i reflection in the x-axis   **ii** translation of $\begin{pmatrix} 0 \\ -2 \end{pmatrix}$

    iii stretch by a scale factor of 3 in the y-direction   **iv** translation of $\begin{pmatrix} -2 \\ 0 \end{pmatrix}$

  c Give the equation of each of the graphs obtained in part **b**.

17 **a** Sketch the graph of $y = \dfrac{1}{x}$.

  b Use your sketch in part **a** to draw the graphs obtained after $y = \dfrac{1}{x}$ is transformed as follows.

    i translation of $\begin{pmatrix} 0 \\ 4 \end{pmatrix}$

    ii translation of $\begin{pmatrix} 4 \\ 0 \end{pmatrix}$

    iii stretch, scale factor 3 in the y-direction

    iv stretch, scale factor $\frac{1}{2}$ in the x-direction

  c Give the equation of each of the graphs obtained in part **b**.

18 The graphs below are all transformations of $y = x^2$. Two points through which each graph passes are indicated. Use this information to work out the equation of each graph.

a 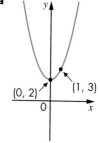   **b** 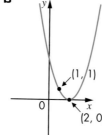   **c** 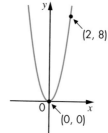   **d**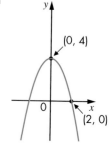

19 The graphs below are all transformations of $y = \sin x$. Two points through which each graph passes are indicated. Use this information to work out the equation of each graph.

a

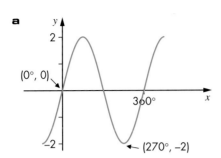

b

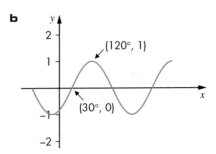

c

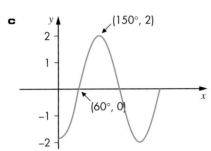

d

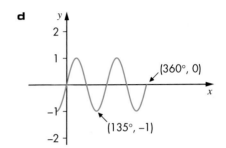

20 Below are the graphs of $y = \sin x$ and $y = \cos x$.

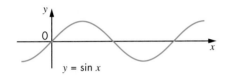

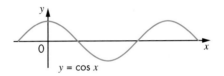

a Describe a series of transformations that would take the first graph to the second.

b Which of these is equivalent to $y = \cos x$?

   i $y = \sin (x + 90°)$ **ii** $y = -\sin (x - 90°)$ **iii** $y = 2\cos \dfrac{x}{2}$

21   **A**

B

C

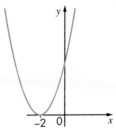

D

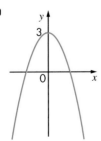

E

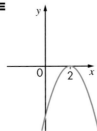

Match each of the graphs **A**, **B**, **C**, **D** and **E** to one of these equations.

   i $y = x^2$ **ii** $y = -x^2 + 3$ **iii** $y = -(x - 2)^2$ **iv** $y = (x + 2)^2$ **v** $y = x^2 + 4$

1 The diagrams, which are not drawn to scale, show the graph of $y = x^2$ and four other graphs A, B, C and D. A, B, C and D represent four different transformations of $y = x^2$.

Find the equation of each of the graphs A, B, C and D.

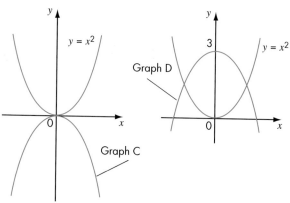

AQA, Question 18, Paper 1 Higher, November 2003

2 The sketch to the right is of the graph of $y = x^2$

Copy these axes and sketch the following graphs.

a $y = x^2 + 2$

b $y = (x - 2)^2$

c $y = \frac{1}{2}x^2$

AQA, Question 21, Paper 1 Higher, November 2004

3 A sketch of $y = f(x)$ for $0° \leqslant x \leqslant 360°$ is shown on the grid below.

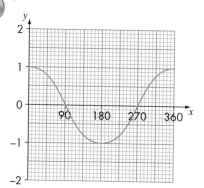

a Choose the correct equation for $y = f(x)$.

$$y = \sin x \qquad y = \cos x \qquad y = \tan x$$

b Grids **i**, **ii** and **iii** show sketches of transformations of the function $y = f(x)$. For each sketch, write down the equation of the transformed function.

i

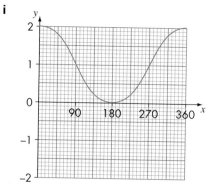

ii

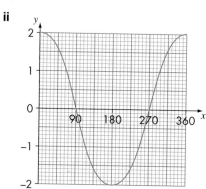

iii

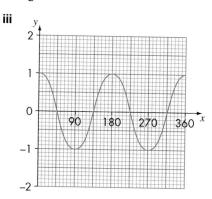

AQA, Question 15, Paper 1 Higher, June 2001

4 The graph of $y = \sin x$ for $0° \leqslant x \leqslant 360°$ is shown on the grid below. The point $P(90, 1)$ lies on the curve.

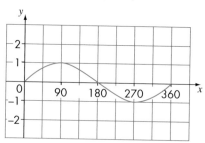

On a copy of the grid, sketch the graphs of:

a $y = \sin(x - 45)$

b $y = 2 \sin x$

AQA, Question 20, Paper 1 Higher, June 2003

WORKED EXAM QUESTION

The sketch shows the graph $y = x^3$.

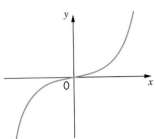

On the axes below sketch the graphs indicated.
p is a positive integer greater than 1.
(The graph $y = x^3$ is shown dotted to help you.)

a $y = x^3 - p$

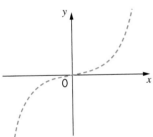

b $y = (x + p)^3$

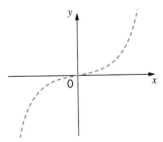

c $y = \dfrac{x^3}{p}$

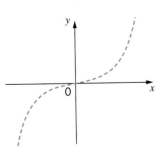

AQA, Question 22, Paper 2 Higher, November 2000

Solution

a This is a translation of $y = x^3$ by the vector $\begin{pmatrix} 0 \\ -p \end{pmatrix}$

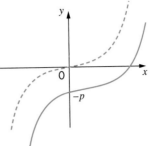

b This is a translation of $y = x^3$ by the vector $\begin{pmatrix} -p \\ 0 \end{pmatrix}$.

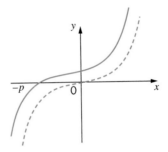

c This is a stretch of $y = x^3$ by a scale factor of $\dfrac{1}{p}$ in the y-direction.

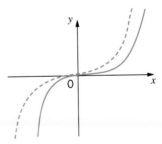

> You do not know what the actual value of p is so make sure that the translation is clear. Alternatively, make a value for p up, say 2.

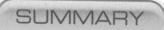
GRADE YOURSELF

A* Able to transform the graph of a given function

A* Able to identify the equation of a function from its graph, which has been formed by a transformation on a known function

What you should know now

- How to sketch the graphs of functions such as $y = f(ax)$ and $y = f(x + a)$ from the known graph of $y = f(x)$

- How to describe from their graphs the transformation of one function into another

- How to identify equations from the graphs of transformations of known graphs

Prouf

Chapter 28

1 Proving standard results

2 Algebraic proof

This chapter will show you ...

- the meaning of "a counter-example"
- the difference between a numerical demonstration and a proof
- how to prove results using rigorous and logical mathematical arguments

Visual overview

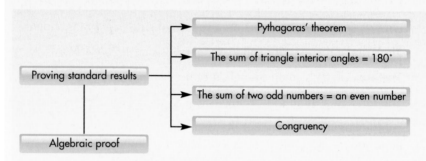

What you should already know

The mathematical results in this book, such as:

- The interior angles in a triangle add up to 180°
- The sum of any two odd numbers is always an even number
- The theorems concerning circles
- Pythagoras' theorem

Quick check

1 Give the value of the angle marked z in terms of x and y.

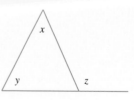

2 Write down a relationship between p, q and r.

3 Copy and complete this table.

+	even	odd
even	even	
odd		

This section will remind you of:
- the difference between a proof and a demonstration

Key words
demonstration
proof
prove
show that

Can you **prove** any of the mathematical results listed on the previous page?

The method of mathematical **proof** is to proceed in logical steps, establishing a series of mathematical statements by using facts which are already known to be true. With few exceptions, a proof will also require the use of algebraic manipulation.

In the next pages, we prove four standard results: Pythagoras' theorem, the sum of the interior angles of a triangle is 180°, the sum of any two odd numbers is always an even number, and congruency. Follow them through, making sure that you understand each step in the process.

Proof of Pythagoras' theorem

Draw a square of side c inside a square of side $(a + b)$, as shown.

The area of the exterior square is $(a + b)^2 = a^2 + 2ab + b^2$.

The area of each small triangle around the shaded square is $\frac{1}{2}ab$.

The total area of all four triangles is $4 \times \frac{1}{2}ab = 2ab$.

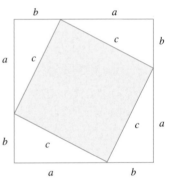

Subtracting the total area of the four triangles from the area of the large square gives the area of the shaded square:

$$a^2 + 2ab + b^2 - 2ab = a^2 + b^2$$

But the area of the shaded square is c^2, so

$$c^2 = a^2 + b^2$$

which is Pythagoras' theorem.

The sum of the interior angles of a triangle is 180°

One of your earlier activities in geometry may have been to draw a triangle, to cut off its corners and to stick them down to **show that** they make a straight line.

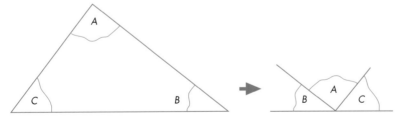

Does this prove that the interior angles make 180° or were you just lucky and picked a triangle that worked? Was the fact that everyone else in the class managed to pick a triangle that worked also a lucky coincidence?

Of course not! But this was a **demonstration**, not a proof. You would have to show that this method worked for *all* possible triangles (there is an infinite number!) to say that you have proved this result.

Your proof must establish that the result is true for *all* triangles.

Look at the following proof.

Start with triangle ABC with angles α, β and γ (figure **i**).

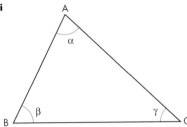 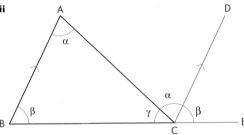

On figure **i** draw a line CD parallel to side AB and extend BC to E, to give figure **ii**.

Since AB is parallel to CD

∠ACD = ∠BAC = α (alternate angles)   ∠DCE = ∠ABC = β (corresponding angles)

BCE is a straight line, so γ + α + β = 180°. Therefore the interior angles of a triangle = 180°.

This proof assumes that alternate angles are equal and that corresponding angles are equal. Strictly speaking, we should prove these results, but we have to accept certain results as true. These are based on Euclid's axioms from which all geometric proofs are derived.

The sum of any two odd numbers is always an even number

If you try this with numbers, you can see that the result is true. For example, 3 + 5 = 8, 11 + 17 = 28. But this is not a proof. Once again, we may have been lucky and found some results that work. Until we have tried an infinite number of different pairs, we cannot be sure.

Look at the following algebraic proof.

Let n be any whole number.

Whatever whole number is represented by n, $2n$ has to be even. So, $2n + 1$ represents any odd number.

Let one odd number be $2n + 1$, and let the other odd number be $2m + 1$.

The sum of these is

$(2n + 1) + (2m + 1) = 2n + 2m + 1 + 1 = 2n + 2m + 2 = 2(n + m + 1)$, which must be even.

Congruency

There are four conditions to prove congruency. These are commonly known as SSS (three sides the same), SAS (two sides and the included angle the same), ASA (or AAS) (two angles and one side the same) and RHS (right-angled triangle, hypotenuse, and one short side the same). **Note:** AAA (three angles the same) is not a condition for congruency.

When you prove a result, you must explain or justify every statement or line. Proofs have to be rigorous and logical.

EXAMPLE 1

ABCD is a parallelogram. X is the point where the diagonals meet.

Prove that triangles AXB and CXD are congruent.

∠BAX = ∠DCX (alternate angles)

∠ABX = ∠CDX (alternate angles)

AB = CD (opposite sides in a parallelogram)

Hence ΔAXB is congruent to ΔCXD (ASA).

Note that you could have used ∠AXB = ∠CXD (vertically opposite angles) as the second line but whichever approach is used you *must* give a reason for each statement.

In some questions, a numerical example is used to give you a clue which will help you to write down an algebraic proof.

1 a Choose any odd number and any even number. Add these together. Is the result odd or even? Does this always work for any odd number and even number you choose?

b Let any odd number be represented by $2n + 1$. Let any even number be represented by $2m$, where m and n are integers. Prove that the sum of an odd number and an even number always gives an odd number.

2 Prove the following results.

a the sum of two even numbers is even

b the product of two even numbers is even

c the product of an odd number and an even number is even

d the product of two odd numbers is odd

e the sum of four consecutive numbers is always even

f half the sum of four consecutive numbers is always odd

3 a Show that the triangle ABC (figure **i**) is isosceles.

b Prove that the triangle DEF (figure **ii**) with one angle of $x°$ and an exterior angle of $90°$ $+ \dfrac{x°}{2}$ is isosceles.

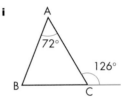

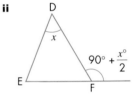

4 Prove that a triangle with an interior angle of $\dfrac{x°}{2}$ and an exterior angle of $x°$ is isosceles.

5 a Using the theorem that the angle subtended by an arc at the centre of a circle is twice the angle subtended by the same arc at the circumference, find the values of angles DAB and ACB in the circle shown in figure **i**.

b Prove that the sum of the opposite angles of a cyclic quadrilateral is 180°. (You may find figure **ii** useful.)

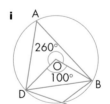

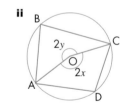

6 A Fibonacci sequence is formed by adding the previous two terms to get the next term. For example, if we start with 3 and 4, the series is

3, 4, 7, 11, 18, 29, 47, 76, 123, 199, ...

a Continue the Fibonacci sequence up to 10 terms. 1, 1, 2, ...

b Continue the Fibonacci sequence up to 10 terms. a, b, $a + b$, $a + 2b$, $2a + 3b$, ...

c Prove that the difference between the 8th term and the 5th term of any Fibonacci sequence is twice the sixth term.

7 The nth term in the sequence of triangular numbers 1, 3, 6, 10, 15, 21, 28, ... is given by

$\frac{1}{2}n(n + 1)$.

a Show that the sum of the 11th and 12th terms is a perfect square.

b Explain why the $(n + 1)$th term of the triangular number sequence is given by $\frac{1}{2}(n + 1)(n + 2)$.

c Prove that the sum of any two consecutive triangular numbers is always a square number.

8 a The triangle ABC is isosceles. BCD and AED are straight lines. Find the value of the angle CED, marked x, in figure **i**.

b Prove that angle ACB = angle CED in figure **ii**.

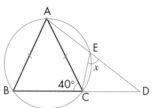
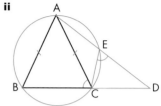

9 The diagram shows part of a 10×10 "hundred square".

a One 2×2 square is marked.

12	13	14	15
22	23	24	25
32	33	34	35
42	43	44	45

i Work out the difference between the product of the bottom-left and top-right values and the product of the top-left and bottom-right values:

$$22 \times 13 - 12 \times 23$$

ii Repeat this for any other 2×2 square of your choosing.

b Prove that this will always give an answer of 10 for any 2×2 square chosen.

c The diagram shows a calendar square (where the numbers are arranged in rows of seven).

Prove that you always get a value of 7 if you repeat the procedure in part **a i**.

1	2	3	4	5	6	7
8	9	10	11	12	13	14
15	16	17	18	19	20	21
22	23	24	25	26	27	28
29	30	31				

d Prove that in a number square that is arranged in rows of n numbers then the difference is always n if you repeat the procedure in part **a i**.

10 Prove that if you add any two-digit number from the 9 times table to the reverse of itself (that is, swap the tens digit and units digit), the result will always be 99.

28.2 Algebraic proof

In this section you will learn how to:
• give a rigorous and logical algebraic proof

Key words
area
length
width

There are three levels of "proof": **Verify** that…, **Show** that…, and **Prove** that….
• At the lowest level (verification), all you have to do is to substitute numbers into the result to show that it works.
• At the middle level, you have to show that both sides of the result are the same algebraically.
• At the highest level (proof), you have to manipulate the left-hand side of the result to become its right-hand side.

The following example demonstrates these three different procedures.

EXAMPLE 2

You are given that $n^2 + (n+1)^2 - (n+2)^2 = (n-3)(n+1)$

a Verify that this result is true.

b Show that this result is true.

c Prove that this result is true.

a Choose a number for n, say $n = 5$. Put this value into both sides of the expression, which gives:

$$5^2 + (5+1)^2 - (5+2)^2 = (5-3)(5+1)$$
$$25 + 36 - 49 = 2 \times 6$$
$$12 = 12$$

Hence, the result is true.

b Expand the LHS and the RHS of the expression to get:

$$n^2 + n^2 + 2n + 1 - (n^2 + 4n + 4) = n^2 - 2n - 3$$

Collect like terms on each side, which gives:

$$n^2 + n^2 - n^2 + 2n - 4n + 1 - 4 = n^2 - 2n - 3$$
$$n^2 - 2n - 3 = n^2 - 2n - 3$$

That is, both sides are algebraically the same.

c Expand the LHS of the expression to get: $n^2 + n^2 + 2n + 1 - (n^2 + 4n + 4)$

Collect like terms, which gives: $n^2 + n^2 - n^2 + 2n - 4n + 1 - 4 = n^2 - 2n - 3$

Factorise the collected result: $n^2 - 2n - 3 = (n-3)(n+1)$ which is the RHS of the original expression.

EXERCISE 28B

1 Speed Cabs charges 45 pence per kilometre for each journey. Evans Taxis has a fixed charge of 90p plus 30p per kilometre.

   a i Verify that Speed Cabs is cheaper for a journey of 5 km.

     ii Verify that Evans Taxis is cheaper for a journey of 7 km.

   b Show clearly why both companies charge the same for a journey of 6 km.

   c Show that if Speed Cabs charges a pence per kilometre, and Evans Taxis has a fixed charge of £b plus a charge of c pence per kilometre, both companies charge the same for a journey of $\dfrac{100b}{(a-c)}$ kilometres.

2 You are given that:

$$(a+b)^2 + (a-b)^2 = 2(a^2 + b^2)$$

   a Verify that this result is true for $a = 3$ and $b = 4$.

   b Show that the LHS is the same as the RHS.

   c Prove that the LHS can be simplified to the RHS.

3 Prove that $(a+b)^2 - (a-b)^2 = 4ab$.

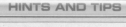

4 The rule for converting from degrees Fahrenheit to degrees Celsius is to subtract 32° and then to multiply by $\frac{5}{9}$.

Prove that the temperature that has the same value in both scales is –40°.

5 The sum of the series $1 + 2 + 3 + 4 + \ldots + (n - 2) + (n - 1) + n$ is given by $\frac{1}{2}n(n + 1)$.

a Verify that this result is true for $n = 6$.

b Write down a simplified value, in terms of n, for the sum of these two series.

$$1 + 2 + 3 + \ldots + (n - 2) + (n - 1) + n$$
and $n + (n - 1) + (n - 2) + \ldots + 3 + 2 + 1$

c Prove that the sum of the first n integers is $\frac{1}{2}n(n + 1)$.

> **HINTS AND TIPS**
>
> Add together the first terms in each series, the second terms in each series, and so on.

6 The following is a "think of a number" trick.

- Think of a number. ⟶ • Multiply it by 2.
- Add 10. ⟶ • Divide the result by 2.
- Subtract the original number.

The result is always 5.

a Verify that the trick works when you pick 7 as the original number.

b Prove why the trick *always* works.

7 You are told that "when two numbers have a difference of 2, the difference of their squares is twice the sum of the two numbers".

a Verify that this is true for 5 and 7.

b Prove that the result is true.

c Prove that when two numbers have a difference of n, the difference of their squares is n times the sum of the two numbers.

> **HINTS AND TIPS**
>
> Use a and $a + 2$ as the numbers.

8 Four consecutive numbers are 4, 5, 6 and 7.

a Verify that their product plus 1 is a perfect square.

b Complete the multiplication square and use it to show that
$$(n^2 - n - 1)^2 = n^4 - 2n^3 - n^2 + 2n + 1$$

	n^2	$-n$	-1
n^2	n^4		$-n^2$
$-n$		n^2	
-1			

c Let four consecutive numbers be $(n - 2)$, $(n - 1)$, n, $(n + 1)$. Prove that the product of four consecutive numbers plus 1 is a perfect square.

9 Here is another mathematical trick to try on a friend.

- Think of two single-digit numbers.
- Multiply one number (your choice) by 2.
- Add 5 to this answer.
- Multiply this answer by 5.
- Add the second number.
- Subtract 4.
- Ask your friend to state his or her final answer.
- Mentally subtract 21 from his or her answer.

The two digits you get are the two digits your friend first thought of.

Prove why this works.

EXERCISE 28C

You may not be able algebraically to prove all of these results. Some of them can be disproved by a counter-example. You should first try to verify each result, then attempt to prove it – or at least try to demonstrate that the result is probably true by trying lots of examples.

1 T represents any triangular number. Prove the following.

a $8T + 1$ is always a square number

b $9T + 1$ is always another triangular number

2 Lewis Carroll, who wrote *Alice in Wonderland*, was also a mathematician. In 1890, he suggested the following results.

a For any pair of numbers, x and y, if $x^2 + y^2$ is even, then $\frac{1}{2}(x^2 + y^2)$ is the sum of two squares.

b For any pair of numbers, x and y, $2(x^2 + y^2)$ is always the sum of two squares.

c Any number whose square is the sum of two squares is itself the sum of two squares.

Can you prove these statements to be true or false?

3 For all values of n, $n^2 - n + 41$ gives a prime number. True or false?

4 For any integer n, $2n$, $n^2 - 1$ and $n^2 + 1$ form three numbers that obey Pythagoras' theorem. Can you prove this?

5 Waring's theorem states that: "Any whole number can be written as the sum of not more than four square numbers."

For example, $27 = 3^2 + 3^2 + 3^2$ and $23 = 3^2 + 3^2 + 2^2 + 1^2$.

Is this always true?

6 Take a three-digit multiple of 37, for example, $7 \times 37 = 259$. Write these digits in a cycle.
Take all possible three-digit numbers from the cycle, for example, 259, 592 and 925.
Divide each of these numbers by 37 to find that

$259 = 7 \times 37$ $592 = 16 \times 37$ $925 = 25 \times 37$.

Is this true for all three-digit multiples of 37?

Is it true for a five-digit multiple of 41?

7 Prove that the sum of the squares of two consecutive integers is an odd number.

8 PQRS is a parallelogram. Prove that triangles PQS and RQS are congruent.

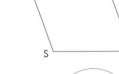

9 OB is a radius of a circle, centre O. C is the point where the perpendicular bisector of OB meets the circumference. Prove that triangle OBC is equilateral.

10 In the following grid, $\overrightarrow{OA} = \mathbf{a}$ and $\overrightarrow{OB} = \mathbf{b}$.
Prove that AB is parallel to EF.

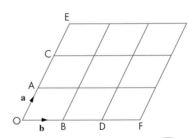

Mod 5

1 Show that the sum of any three consecutive integers is always a multiple of 3.

AQA, Question 9, Paper 2 Higher, November 2003

 2 a This is a page from Zoe's exercise book.

$2^3 - 1^3 = 7$ (prime)

$3^3 - 2^3 = 19$ (prime)

$4^3 - 3^3 = 37$ (prime)

The difference between consecutive cube numbers is always a prime number.

Give a counter example to show that Zoe is wrong. Justify your answer.

b Prove that $(n + 5)^2 - (n + 3)^2 = 4(n + 4)$

AQA, Question 16, Paper 2 Higher, June 2005

 3 In the diagram, the lines AC and BD intersect at E. AB and DC are parallel and AB = CD.

Prove that triangles ABE and CDE are congruent.

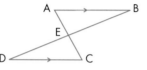

AQA, Question 15, Paper 2 Higher, June 2003

 4 Annie, Bert and Charu are investigating the number sequence

21, 40, 65, 96, 133, …

a Annie has found the following pattern.

1st term	$1 \times 2 + 3^2 + 2 \times 5 =$	21
2nd term	$2 \times 3 + 4^2 + 3 \times 6 =$	40
3rd term	$3 \times 4 + 5^2 + 4 \times 7 =$	65
4th term	$4 \times 5 + 6^2 + 5 \times 8 =$	96
5th term	$5 \times 6 + 7^2 + 6 \times 9 =$	133

Complete the nth term for Annie's pattern.

nth term $\quad n \times (n + 1) + \text{………} + \text{………} \times \text{………}$

b Bert has found this formula for the nth term

$(3n + 1)(n + 3) + 5$

Charu has found this formula for the nth term

$(2n + 3)^2 - (n + 1)^2$

Prove that these two formulae are equivalent.

AQA, Question 14, Paper 2 Higher, November 2004

WORKED EXAM QUESTION

a n is a positive integer.

  i Explain why $n(n + 1)$ must be an even number.

  ii Explain why $2n + 1$ must be an odd number.

b Expand and simplify $\quad (2n + 1)^2$

c Prove that the square of any odd number is always 1 more than a multiple of 8.

Solution

a i If n is odd, $n + 1$ is even

  If n is even, $n + 1$ is odd

  Even times odd is always even

This is a lead in to the rest of the task. An explanation in words is good enough. Keep the words to a minimum.

  ii $2n$ must be even so $2n + 1$ must be odd

An explanation in words is good enough.

b $(2n + 1)^2 = (2n + 1)(2n + 1) = 4n^2 + 2n + 2n + 1 = 4n^2 + 4n + 1$

Always write down a squared bracket twice then expand it by whichever method you prefer.

c $(2n + 1)^2 = 4n^2 + 4n + 1$

$4n^2 + 4n + 1 = 4n(n + 1) + 1$

Use the fact that $2n + 1$ is odd, and it has been "squared" in part **b**.

$4 \times n(n + 1) + 1 = 4 \times \text{even} + 1$, which must be a multiple of 8 plus 1.

The "one more than" is taken care of with the +1.

Show that the $4n^2 + 4n$ is a multiple of 8 using the result in part **a i**.

GRADE YOURSELF

B Able to verify results by substituting numbers into them

B Able to understand the proofs of simple theorems such as an exterior angle of a triangle is the sum of the two opposite interior angles

A Able to show that an algebraic statement is true, using both sides of the statement to justify your answer

A* Able to prove algebraic and geometric results with rigorous and logical mathematical arguments

What you should know now

- The meaning of the terms "verify that", "show that" and "prove"

- How to prove some standard results in mathematics, such as Pythagoras' theorem

- How to use your knowledge of proof to answer the questions throughout the book that are flagged with the proof icon

Coursework guidance

Module 2

During your GCSE course, you will need to do two coursework modules. Module 2 will cover the content from Handling Data (AO4 task). The module will be assessed and marked by your teacher or by the examination board. This module will carry 10% of the total marks for the examination. The module has three strands, with a maximum mark of 8 in each strand. The table, which follows, will give you some idea of what each strand means and what you need to do in order to obtain a particular mark in each strand.

- **Strand i**: Planning. This is about how you decide to design the problem by specifying your aims and hypotheses and planning an overall strategy.
- **Strand ii**: Collection and presentation of data. This is about the methods you use to collect the data for the problem and how you use statistical calculations, diagrams or computer software to illustrate the data.
- **Strand iii**: Interpretation. This is about how you interpret and summarise the results based on your statistical calculations and diagrams. It also involves evaluating your strategy and how you could make improvements.

Mark	Strand i: Specify and plan	Strand ii: Process and represent	Strand iii: Interpret and discuss
1–2	Collect data relevant to the problem. State your overall plan and aims.	Present your results on diagrams such as bar charts or pictograms. Use the mode and range for the data.	Make a comment on the data. Attempt to summarise any results you notice in the data.
3–4	Your plan should include a suitable hypothesis relevant to the problem. Decide how to collect your data and use an appropriate sample size.	Use relevant statistical calculations for the problem, such as mode, median, mean and range. Present your data in a variety of forms, such as stem-and-leaf diagrams, scatter graphs or pie charts, and link them with a relevant explanation.	Interpret any graphs and statistical calculations used and draw sensible conclusions, which relate to your original hypothesis.. Comment on how you could improve your work.
5–6	In a more complex problem, you should develop hypotheses that are linked and where comparisons can be made. Consider how to overcome any practical problems when choosing your sample.	Ensure that your data is relevant, and use more complex statistical calculations, such as the mean for grouped data. Use appropriate diagrams, such as cumulative frequency graphs, box plots or lines of best fit, and give clear reasons for your choice of presentation.	Summarise and correctly interpret your diagrams and statistical calculations. Make relevant comparisons and show that the nature of the sampling method used may have some significance on your results. Evaluate the effectiveness of your strategy.
7–8	In a more demanding problem, you should plan and look for practical problems that you might encounter and consider how to avoid bias, modifying your method of data collection in light of this. Use other suitable data collection techniques and refine these to enhance the problem.	You should ensure that all practical problems are dealt with, and use effectively a wide range of more advanced statistical calculations to present a convincing argument. Use a range of diagrams, such as histograms, to help you to summarise the data and show how the variables are related.	All diagrams and calculations should be correctly interpreted in order to appreciate the significance of the results. You should explain why any possible bias might affect your conclusions, and make suggestions on how you could make an improvement. Comment on any limitations in your work.

Coursework guidance (continued)

Module 4

Module 4 will cover the content from Number and Algebra and/or Shape and Space (AO1 task). The module will be assessed and marked by your teacher or by the examination board. This module will carry 10% of the total marks for the examination. The module has three strands, with a maximum mark of 8 in each strand. The table, which follows, will give you some idea of what each strand means and what you need to do in order to obtain a particular mark in each strand.

- **Strand i**: Decisions. This is about how you decide to solve a particular problem and then how you ask your own questions in order to extend the problem.
- **Strand ii**: Presentation. This is about how you present your work mathematically. It involves making tables of results, drawing graphs, using algebraic notation or using computer software.
- **Strand iii**: Reasons. This is about finding solutions to problems and drawing conclusions. You need to find patterns, rules or formulae and to explain how you obtained them.

Mark	Strand i: Making and monitoring decisions to solve problems	Strand ii: Communicating mathematically	Strand iii: Developing skills of mathematical reasoning
1	You should show that you understand the problem by giving an example.	You should explain how you intend to solve the problem by giving an example or by drawing a diagram.	You should find an easy example that fits the problem.
2	You should plan a suitable method to help solve the problem further by giving at least three examples.	You should write out your results clearly and carefully in a list or show them on diagrams.	You should look for any patterns in your results.
3	You should identify the information needed to solve the problem and check that your results are correct.	You should show your results in a clearly labelled table or by using diagrams and symbols.	You should explain the pattern, or find a rule for your results.
4	You should break down the problem into easier and more manageable stages.	You should link your tables, diagrams or graphs with a clear explanation.	You should test a different example to show that your pattern or rule works and comment on the outcome.
5	You should introduce some questions of your own in order to extend the problem to give a further solution.	You should find an algebraic formula to explain the rule and show by substitution that the formula works.	You should explain why your rule or formula works by using simple algebra, graphs or computer software.
6	You should develop the problem further by using algebra, graphs or trigonometry.	You should introduce more difficult algebra or trigonometry on at least three occasions.	You should comment constructively on your solution to show that you have fully understood the problem.
7	You should analyse a more complex problem by considering approaches which manipulate three variables.	You should show you can present an accurate and convincing mathematical solution or proof.	You should give reasons why you are considering using approaches which use three variables.
8	You should introduce new content or an area of mathematics that is unfamiliar into a more complex problem.	You should use mathematical techniques efficiently to give a complete and concise solution or proof.	You should provide an accurate proof to a more complex problem and explain the conditions under which it remains valid.

Really Useful Maths!

Chapter 1
Really Useful Maths!: Dairy farm

3-month moving average for milk production in thousands of litres												
	Jan	Feb	Mar	Apr	May	Jun	Jul	Aug	Sep	Oct	Nov	Dec
2004		53	54.7	58.3	64	68.7	72.3	69.7	67.7	63.3	61.3	69.7
2005	61.7	63	64.7	67	74	78.7	83.3	80.7	78	72.7	70.3	

Comments on line graphs: Each year, January has the lowest production. It rises steadily towards July, then decreases again towards the following January. 2005 production is about 10,000 litres more per month than 2004.

Comments on Scatter graphs: Monthly sunshine/milk production: positive correlation. Monthly rainfall/milk production: negative correlation.

Chapter 2
Really Useful Maths!: Are we living longer?

Age distribution in the UK (numbers in millions)			
Age (*a*) in years	1976	2001	% change
$0 \leqslant a < 15$	12.9	11.1	−14%
$15 \leqslant a < 25$	8.1	7.2	−11%
$25 \leqslant a < 35$	7.9	8.4	6%
$35 \leqslant a < 45$	6.4	8.8	38%
$45 \leqslant a < 55$	9.8	7.8	−20%
$55 \leqslant a < 65$	3.1	6.2	100%
$65 \leqslant a < 75$	5.1	4.9	−4%
$75 \leqslant a < 85$	2.3	3.3	43%
$85 \leqslant a < 105$	0.5	1.1	120%

Midpoint of ages	1976 frequency (millions)	Midpoint × frequency	2001 frequency (millions)	Midpoint × frequency
7.5	12.9	96.75	11.1	83.25
20	8.1	162	7.2	144
30	7.9	237	8.4	252
40	6.4	256	8.8	352
50	9.8	490	7.8	390
60	3.1	186	6.2	372
70	5.1	357	4.9	343
80	2.3	184	3.3	264
95	0.5	47.5	1.1	104.5
Totals	56.1	2016.25	58.8	2304.75
Mean age		35.94		39.20

Cumulative frequencies for age distributions (in millions)									
	<15	<25	<35	<45	<55	<65	<75	<85	<105
1976	12.9	21	28.9	35.3	45.1	48.2	53.3	55.6	56.1
2001	11.1	18.3	26.7	35.5	43.3	49.5	54.4	57.7	58.8

	1976	2001
Mean	36	39
Median	34	38
Upper quartile	52	56
Lower quartile	16	20
IQR	36	36

The missing numbers from the article are: 2.7, $85 \leqslant a < 105$, 120, 20, $45 \leqslant a < 55$, 36, 39, 3, 34, 38, 4, 4

Chapter 5
Really Useful Maths!: Sheep Farmer

Date	Number of lambs	Total live weight in kg	Mean live weight in kg	Total weight of meat in kg	Meat as % of live weight	Total price paid for meat	Price paid per kg of meat
1st April	13	468	36	211	45.1% ✓	£812.56	£3.85
15th April	8	290	36	134	46.2% ✓	£451.91	£3.37
22nd April	18	672	37	312	46.4% ✓	£1105.31	£3.54
29th April	11	398	36	179	45.0% ✓	£625.04	£3.49
6th May	18	657	37	291	44.3% ✓	£907.89	£3.12
20th May	8	309	39	130	42.1% ✓	£386.15	£2.97
3rd June	10	416	42	171	41.1% ✗	£480.46	£2.81
17th June	4	174	44	72	41.4% ✗	£196.54	£2.73

The mean weight per lamb has increased from 36 kg to 44 kg. This is an increase of 22%. However the price per kg of lamb has fallen from £3.85 to £2.73, a decrease of 29%. The only two weeks when the condition of the lambs fell below 42% were 3rd June and 17th June.

Comment: There were only 3 weeks when Mrs Woolman earned less than the average lamb price. The trend of both Mrs Woolman's prices and the average prices were decreasing from April to June.

Chapter 7
Really Useful Maths!: Oil

Country	Oil produced, barrels per person per year	Oil consumed, barrels per person per year	Difference produced − consumed	Rank order	Consumption as a % of production
Algeria	13.5	2.3	11.2	3	17%
Australia	9.8	14.5	−4.7	7	148%
Chile	0.4	5.5	−5.1	8	1297%
Indonesia	1.5	1.8	−0.3	6	122%
Japan	0.05	15.2	−15.15	10	30 525%
Nigeria	6.7	0.8	5.9	4	12%
Saudi Arabia	124.6	21.4	103.2	1	17%
UK	11.8	10.2	1.6	5	86%
USA	9.6	24.3	−14.7	9	252%
Venezuela	37.4	7.2	30.2	2	19%

Year	World population	World oil production, barrels per day	World oil production, barrels per person per day
1984	4.77×10^9	5.45×10^7	4.2
1989	5.19×10^9	5.99×10^7	4.2
1994	5.61×10^9	6.10×10^7	4.0
1999	6.01×10^9	6.58×10^7	4.0
2004	6.38×10^9	7.25×10^7	4.1

Chapter 9
Really Useful Maths!: Windpower

Distance of turbine out to sea	Angle of elevation from shore
3 km	2.29°
4 km	1.72°
5 km	1.37°
6 km	1.15°
7 km	0.98°
8 km	0.86°

Wind speed (m/s)	Available power (W/m²)
6	132.34
7	210
8	313.47
9	446.33
10	612.24
11	814.90
12	1057.96

Wind speed (m/s)	Available power (W/m²)	Rotor area for 50 m blade (m²)	Power (MW)	Rotor area for 60 m blade (m²)	Power (MW)	Rotor area for 70 m blade (m²)	Power (MW)
7	210	7854	1.65	11310	2.38	15394	3.23
8	313.47	7854	2.46	11310	3.55	15394	4.83
9	446.33	7854	3.51	11310	5.05	15394	6.87
10	612.24	7854	4.81	11310	6.92	15394	9.42

Chapter 10
Really Useful Maths!: A new floor

Oak effect Room	Maximum floor area (m²)	Maximum edging needed (m)
Lounge	61.24	32.35
Sitting room	29.8275	21.25
Kitchen/diner	45.175	27.5
Conservatory	12.4425	11.95
Total:	148.685	93.05

The area of the lounge and kitchen/diner may be calculated in several ways.
Other possible answers are:

Lounge: 61.07 m² and 61.13 m²   Kitchen/Diner: 44.9675 m²
(if this alternative answer is given, total maximum floor area for oak effect becomes
148.4775 m², the numbers of packs of flooring required is unaffected)

Similarly, the edging required for the Kitchen/Diner could be calculated as 27.35 m (if
this alternative answer is given, total maximum edging needed for oak effect becomes
92.9 m, numbers of packs required is unaffected)

Chapter 11
Really Useful Maths!: Water recycling

Daily water usage			
	Litres used each: flush/shower/load	Frequency used	Total litres per day
Toilet	13.16	12 times a day	157.92
Shower	91	2 times a day	182
Washing machine	113.75	3 times a week	48.75
Dishwasher	40.95	once every 2 days	20.475
Total:			409.145

They can collect 300 litres from the roof in 1 day.
It will take $4\frac{1}{2}$ days to fill the tank.

Chapter 15
Really Useful Maths!: The street

Roof area for one block of 5 bungalows	711 m²
Roof area of whole street	14,227 m²
Number of slates needed	247,552 slates
Total cost of slates	£59,412.48
Total weight of slates	594,124.8 kg

Chapter 16
Really Useful Maths!: Bright ideas

Volume of stem	164.9 cm³	Length of x	7.5 cm
Weight of stem	1649 g	Length of L	9 cm
Volume of base	88.3 cm³	Length of L	27 cm
Weight of base	883 g	Surface area of small cone	141 cm²
Total weight	2532 g	Surface area of large cone	1272 cm²
		Surface area of lampshade	1131 cm²

$\theta = 200°$.
Total length of trim = 125.66 cm.

Beech effect Room	Maximum floor area (m²)	Maximum edging needed (m)
Hall	15.8025	15.25
Bathroom	9.5875	11.65
Total:	25.39	26.9

	Number of packs	Price per pack	Total cost
Beech flooring	13	£56.40	£733.20
Beech edging	3	£21.15	£63.45
Oak flooring	75	£61.10	£4582.50
Oak edging	8	£25.85	£206.80
		Total:	£5585.95

Total price exclusive of VAT is: £4754.00

Chapter 19
Really Useful Maths!: Riding stables

Horse	Weight in kg	Feed in kg	Worming paste in tubes
Summer	850	6.1	1.5
Sally	400	4.0	0.75
Skip	550	5.4	1
Simon	500	4.0	1
Barney	350	2.8	0.75
Teddy	650	6.2	1.25

Cost per adult: £28.50

Cost per child: £25.50

Chapter 20
Really Useful Maths!: Garden design

Perimeter of patio	56.55 m	Area of patio	254.47 m²
Perimeter of play area	45.13 m	Area of play area	130.27 m²
Perimeter of one flower bed	13.83 m	Area of one flower bed	7.5 m²
Dimensions of top pond	length = 4 m width = 2 m	Area of top pond	8 m²
Dimensions of second pond	length = 5 m width = 3 m	Area of second pond	15 m²
Dimensions of third pond	length = 6 m width = 4 m	Area of third pond	24 m²
Dimensions of bottom pond	length = 7 m width = 5 m	Area of bottom pond Area of lawn	35 m² 703.26 m²

Chapter 25
Really Useful Maths!: Walking holiday

Day	Distance in km	Height climbed in metres	Time in minutes	Time in hours and minutes	Start time	Time allowed for breaks	Finish time
1	16	270	267	4 h 27 m	9:30 am	2 hours	3:57pm
2	20	210	321	5 h 21 m	9:00 am	$2\frac{3}{4}$ hours	5:06pm
3	15	80	233	3 h 53 m	10:00 am	$2\frac{1}{2}$ hours	4:23pm
4	17	210	276	4h 36 m	10:30 am	$2\frac{1}{4}$ hours	5:21pm
5	18	120	282	4 h 42 m	10:00 am	$2\frac{1}{2}$ hours	5:12pm
6	17	290	284	4 h 44 m	10:30 am	2 hours	5:14pm
7	22	90	339	5 h 39 m	10:00 am	$2\frac{3}{4}$ hours	6:24pm
8	12	300	210	3 h 30 m	10:30 am	$2\frac{1}{4}$ hours	4:15pm

Quick check

1 a 7   **b** 6   **c** 8   **d** 6

Exercise 1A

1 Mode

2 Three possible answers: 12, 14, 14, 16, 18, 20, 24; or 12, 14, 14, 16, 18, 22, 24; or 12, 14, 14, 16, 20, 22, 24

3 53

4 a median (mean could be unduly influenced by results of very able and/or very poor candidates)

   b median (mean could be unduly influenced by pocket money of students with very rich or generous parents)

   c mode (numerical value of shoe sizes irrelevant, just want most common size)

   d median (mean could be distorted by one or two extremely short or tall performers)

   e mode (the only way to get an "average" of non-numerical values)

   f median (mean could be unduly influenced by very low weights of premature babies)

5 The mean is 31.5 which rounds up to 32, so the statement is correct (though the mode and median are 31)

6 a i £18 000   **ii** £24 000   **iii** £23 778

   b A 6% rise would increase the mean salary to £25 204, a £1500 pay increase would produce a mean of £25 278

7 a Median   **b** Mode   **c** Mean

8 11.6   **9** 42.7 kg   **10** 24

Exercise 1B

1 a i 7   **ii** 6   **iii** 6.4   **b i** 8   **ii** 8.5   **iii** 8.2

2 a 668   **b** 1.9   **c** 0   **d** 328

3 a 2.2, 1.7, 1.3   **b** Better dental care

4 a 50   **b** 2   **c** 2.8

5 a Roger 5, Brian 4   **b** Roger 3, Brian 8

   c Roger 5, Brian 4   **d** Roger 5.4, Brian 4.5

   e Roger, smaller range   **f** Brian, better mean

6 a 40   **b** 7   **c** 3   **d** 2   **e** 2.5   **f** 2.5   **g** 2.4

7 a $39 + a$

   b $(0 \times 2) + (1 \times 14) + (2 \times 17) + (3 \times 6) + (4 \times a) = 66 + 4a$

   c 6

Exercise 1C

1 a i $30 < x \leqslant 40$ **ii** 29.5   **b i** $0 < y \leqslant 100$ **ii** 158.3

   c i $5 < z \leqslant 10$ **ii** 9.43   **d i** 7–9   **ii** 8.41

2 a $100 \text{ g} < w \leqslant 120 \text{ g}$ **b** 10.86 kg   **c** 108.6 g

3 a $175 < h \leqslant 200$ **b** 31%   **c** 193.3 hours   **d** No

4 a Yes, average distance is 11.7 miles per day

   b Because shorter runs will be done faster which will affect the average.

   c Yes because the shortest could be 1 mile, the longest 25 miles

5 24

6 Soundbuy; average increases are Soundbuy 17.7p, Springfields 18.7p, Setco 18.2p

Exercise 1D

1 b 1.7

2 b 2.8

3 a i 17, 13, 6, 3, 1   **ii** £1.45

   b ii £5.35

   c Much higher mean. Early morning, people just want a paper or a few sweets, later people are buying food for the day.

4 c 140.4 cm

5 b Monday 28.4 min, Tuesday 20.9 min, Wednesday 21.3 min

   c There are more patients on a Monday, and so longer waiting times, because the surgery is closed at the weekend

Exercise 1E

1 The respective frequency densities on which each histogram should be based are

   a 2.5, 6.5, 6, 2, 1, 1.5   **b** 4, 27, 15, 3   **c** 17, 18, 12, 6.67   **d** 0.4, 1.2, 2.8, 1   **e** 9, 21, 13.5, 9

2 a [histogram] **b** [frequency polygon: Girls, Boys]

   c Girls £4.36, boys £4.81

3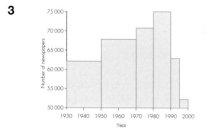

4 a 775   **b** 400

5 a i

Age, *y* (years)	$9 < y \leqslant 10$	$10 < y \leqslant 12$	$12 < y \leqslant 14$	$14 < y \leqslant 17$	$17 < y \leqslant 19$	$19 < y \leqslant 20$
Frequency	4	12	8	9	5	1

   ii 10–12   **iii** 13   **iv** 11, 16, 5   **v** 13.4

b i

Temperature, t (°C)	$10 < t \leq 11$	$11 < t \leq 12$	$12 < t \leq 14$	$14 < t \leq 16$	$16 < t \leq 19$	$19 < t \leq 21$
Frequency	15	15	50	40	45	15

  ii 12–14°C   **iii** 14.5°C   **iv** 12°C, 17°C, 5°C   **v** 14.8°C

c i

Weight, w (kg)	$50 < w \leq 70$	$70 < w \leq 90$	$90 < w \leq 100$	$100 < w \leq 120$	$120 < w \leq 170$
Frequency	160	200	120	120	200

  ii 70–90 kg and 120–170 kg   **iii** 93.33 kg   **iv** 74 kg, 120 kg, 46 kg   **v** 99.0 kg

6 a 7.33 hours   **b** 8.44 hours   **c** 7 hours

7 b 14.3 kg   **c** 14.7 kg   **d** 33 plants

8 a

Speed, v (mph)	$0 < v \leq 40$	$40 < v \leq 50$	$50 < v \leq 60$	$60 < v \leq 70$	$70 < v \leq 80$	$80 < v \leq 100$
Frequency	80	10	40	110	60	60

  b 360   **c** 64.5 mph   **d** 59.2 mph

Exercise 1F

1 Moving averages are: 9.3, 9.1, 9.0, 9.1, 8.7, 8.6, 9.1, 9.0, 9.4, 9.7, 9.7, 9.9, 10.1, 9.7, 9.9, 9.4, 9.9, 10.0, 10.0, 9.9, 10.1, 10.7

2 a Moving averages are: 44.5, 42.3, 41.0, 41.3, 42.3, 44.5, 45.8
  b Amounts raised dip in the middle of the collection period

3 a Moving averages are: 108.10, 107.24, 108.39, 105.89, 109.54, 111.40, 112.55, 118.70, 118.50, 119.80, 120.30, 123.18, 124.33
  b Gradually rises
  c Trend suggests next moving average about £125.50, so estimated first quarter 2006 bill is £137.29

4 b Moving averages are: 80, 81, 82, 83, 82, 85, 87, 90, 94, 92, 91, 89, 86
  c Recent fall may be due to moving to cheaper provider or using e-mail rather than making calls
  d Trend suggests next moving average about 83.5, so first quarter 2006 bill is £78

5 a Moving averages are: 12.3, 13.0, 13.0, 10.0, 10.3, 10.0, 13.7, 13.0, 13.7, 13.0, 13.0, 13.0, 13.0, 13.3, 13.0, 13.7, 13.3, 13.3, 13.7, 14.3, 15.0, 14.7
  b Apart from a blip in June 2004, sales showing slight improvement
  c Trend suggests next moving average about 14.6, so January 2006 sales estimate is 15

6 b Moving averages are: (videos) 3.7, 3.6, 3.3, 2.8, 2.5; (DVDs) 0.6, 1.1, 1.4, 2.1, 2.8
  c Sales of DVD players increasingly strongly, video recorder sales falling
  d Trend suggests next moving averages about 2.3 (videos) and 3.5 (DVDs), so 2006 sales estimates are 2.1 (videos) and 4.0 (DVDs)

Exercise 1H

1 a It is a leading question, and there is no option to disagree with the statement
  b Unbiased, and the responses do not overlap

2 a Responses overlap
  b Give as options: up to £2, more than £2 and up to £5, more than £5 and up to £10, more than £10

Exercise 1I

1 Price 78p, 80.3p, 84.2p, 85p, 87.4p, 93.6p

2 a £1 = $1.80   **b** Greatest drop was from June to July
  c There is no trend in the data

3 a 9.7 million   **b** 4.5 years   **c** 12 million   **d** 10 million

4 £74.73

5 a Holiday month   **b i** 138–144 thousand
                    ii 200–210 thousand

ANSWERS TO CHAPTER 2

Quick check

1 29.0

Exercise 2A

1 b About 328 million   **c** Between 1980 and 1985
  d Rising living standards

2 b Smallest difference Wednesday (7°), greatest difference Friday (10°)

Exercise 2B

1 a
2   8   9
3   4   5   6   8   8   9
4   1   1   3   3   3   8   8
  b 43 cm   **c** 39 cm   **d** 20 cm

2 a
0   2   8   9   9   9
1   2   3   7   7   8
2   0   1   2   3
  b 9 messages   **c** 15 messages

Exercise 2C

1 a Positive correlation, reaction time increases with amount of alcohol drunk.
  b Negative correlation, you drink less alcohol as you get older.
  c No correlation, speed of cars on M1 is not related to the temperature.
  d Weak, positive correlation, older people generally have more money saved in the bank.

2 c $\approx$ 19 cm/s   **d** $\approx$ 34 cm

3 c Greta   **d** $\approx$ 67   **e** $\approx$ 72

4 b Yes, usually (good correlation)

5 b No correlation, so cannot draw a line of best fit

Exercise 2D

1 a cumulative frequency 1, 4, 10, 22, 25, 28, 30
  c 54 secs, 16 secs
2 a cumulative frequency 1, 3, 5, 14, 31, 44, 47, 49, 50
  c 56 secs, 17 secs **d** Pensioners, median closer to 60 secs
3 a cumulative frequency 12, 30, 63, 113, 176, 250, 314, 349, 360
  c 605 pupils, 280 pupils **d** 46–47 schools
4 a cumulative frequency 2, 5, 10, 16, 22, 31, 39, 45, 50
  c 20.5°C, 10°C
5 a cumulative frequency 9, 22, 45, 60, 71, 78, 80
  c 56, 43 **d** 17.5%
6 a cumulative frequency 6, 16, 36, 64, 82, 93, 98, 100
  c 225p, 110p
7 a cumulative frequency 8, 22, 47, 82, 96, 100
  c £1605, £85 **d** 13%

Exercise 2E

1 a
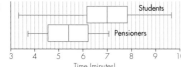

b The students are much slower than the pensioners. Although both distributions have the same inter-quartile range, the students' median and upper quartile are 1 minute, 35 seconds higher. The fastest person to compete the calculations was a student, but so was the slowest

2 a
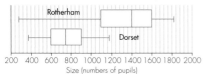

b Schools are much larger in Rotherham than Dorset. The Dorset distribution is symmetrical, but the Rotherham distribution is negatively skewed. This means that most schools in Rotherham are large.

3 a The resorts have similar median temperatures, but Resort B has a much wider temperature range. The greatest extremes of temperature are recorded in Resort B
  b Resort A is probably a better choice as the weather seems more consistent

4 a
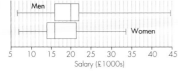

b Both distributions have a similar inter-quartile range, and there is little difference between the upper quartile values. Men have a wider range of salaries, but the higher men's median and the fact that the men's distribution is negatively skewed and the women's distribution is positively skewed indicates that men are better paid than women.

5 b £1605, £85
  c **ii** symmetric
6 a Symmetric   **b** Negatively skewed
  c Negatively skewed **d** Symmetric
  e Negatively skewed **f** Positively skewed
  g Negatively skewed **h** Positively skewed
  i Positively skewed **j** Symmetric

Exercise 2F

1 a Mean 6, standard deviation 2.45 **b** 11.6, 3.77
  c 108, 4.43 **d** 203, 1.41 **e** 73.65, 3.57
  f 1, 2.51 **g** 77.2, 5.19 **h** 35, 3.98
2 a 6 **b** 1.41
3 a 8, 2.61 **b** 18, 2.61 **c** 28, 2.61
4 a 8, 1.94 **b** 8, 4.73
  c Paula because she is more consistent, although Rose occasionally gets high scores

Exercise 2G

1

Time of call	2	3	4	5	6	7	8	9	10	12
Frequency	5	1	1	5	1	3	1	1	1	1

mean 5.4, standard deviation 2.82
2 a Mean 2.15, standard deviation 1.19
  b 24.3, 1.51 **c** 102.15, 1.19 **d** 7.79, 0.47
  e 3.55, 0.88 **f** 0.166, 0.066
3 a i 3.49, 1.73 **ii** 3.0
  b i 6.96, 2.42 **ii** 5.85
  c The mean and the square of the standard deviation is about double that of the result in part a
  d Mean about 10.45, standard deviation about 3
4 a 135.2, 7.44
  b 2.84, 1.49 **i** 135.2 **ii** 7.44
  c Same
  d Smaller numbers

ANSWERS TO CHAPTER 3

Quick check

1 a Perhaps around 0.6 **b** Very close to 1
  c Very close to 0 **d** 1 **e** 1

Exercise 3A

1 a $\frac{1}{5}, \frac{2}{25}, \frac{1}{10}, \frac{21}{200}, \frac{37}{250}, \frac{163}{1000}, \frac{329}{2000}$ **b** 6 **c** 1

  d $\frac{1}{6}$ **e** 1000
2 a $\frac{19}{200}, \frac{27}{200}, \frac{4}{25}, \frac{53}{200}, \frac{69}{200}$ **b** 40
  c No, it is weighted towards the side with numbers 4 and 5
3 a 32 is too high, 20 of the 50 throws between 50 and 100 unlikely to be 5
  b Yes
4 a $\frac{1}{5}, \frac{1}{4}, \frac{38}{100}, \frac{21}{50}, \frac{77}{200}, \frac{1987}{5000}$ **b** 8

5 a 0.346, 0.326, 0.294, 0.305, 0.303, 0.306
  b 0.231, 0.168, 0.190, 0.16, 0.202, 0.201
  c Red 0.5, white 0.3, blue 0.2
  d 1
  e Red 10, white 6, blue 4
6 b 20
7 a 6
8 a Caryl, most throws **b** $\frac{107}{275}, \frac{169}{550}, \frac{91}{550}, \frac{38}{275}$ **c** Yes
9 a Method B **b** B **c** C **d** A **e** B **f** A **g** B **h** B
10 a The table shows percentages rather than actual numbers.
  b i 500 **ii** No. Each percentage should be about 25.

Exercise 3B

1 a Yes **b** Yes **c** No **d** Yes **e** Yes **f** Yes
2 Events a and f
3 $\frac{3}{5}$
4 a i $\frac{3}{10}$ **ii** $\frac{3}{10}$ **iii** $\frac{3}{10}$ **b** All except iii **c** Event iv
5 b i $\frac{1}{10}$ **ii** $\frac{3}{10}$ **iii** $\frac{3}{10}$ **iv** $\frac{7}{10}$ **c** All except iii **d** Event ii
6 a $\frac{3}{8}$ **b** $\frac{1}{8}$ **c** All except ii **d** Outcomes overlap
7 $0.8 - a$
8 Not mutually exclusive events
9 a i 0.25 **ii** 0.4 **iii** 0.7
  b Events not mutually exclusive
  c Man/woman, American man/American woman
  d Man/woman

Exercise 3C

1 25
2 1000
3 a 260 **b** 40 **c** 130 **d** 10
4 5
5 a 150 **b** 100 **c** 250 **d** 0
6 167 **b** 833
7 a $a = 0.2$, $b = 0.4$ **b** 300
8 a Each score expected 10 times **b** 3.5
  c Find the average of the scores, which is 21 (1 + 2 + 3 + 4 + 5 + 6) divided by 6
9 400

Exercise 3D

1 a 23 **b** 20% **c** $\frac{4}{25}$ **d** 480
2 a 10 **b** 7 **c** 14% **d** 15%
3 b 4 **c i** $\frac{1}{4}$ **ii** $\frac{3}{16}$ **iii** $\frac{1}{4}$
4 a 16 **b** 16 **c** 73 **d** $\frac{51}{73}$
5 b 3 **c** $\frac{1}{4}$
6 a The greenhouse sunflowers are bigger on average
  b The garden sunflowers have a more consistent size (smaller range)
7 a 40% **b** 45%
  c No as you don't know how much the people who get over £350 actually earn

Exercise 3E

1 $\frac{2}{5}$
2 a $\frac{1}{6}$ **b** $\frac{1}{6}$ **c** $\frac{1}{3}$
3 a $\frac{1}{4}$ **b** $\frac{1}{4}$ **c** $\frac{1}{2}$
4 a $\frac{2}{11}$ **b** $\frac{4}{11}$ **c** $\frac{6}{11}$
5 a $\frac{1}{3}$ **b** $\frac{2}{5}$ **c** $\frac{11}{15}$ **d** $\frac{11}{15}$ **e** $\frac{1}{3}$
6 a 0.6 **b** 120

7 a 0.8 **b** 0.2
8 a 0.75 **b** 0.6 **c** 0.5 **d** 0.6
  e i Cannot add P(red) and P(1) as events are not mutually exclusive **ii** 0.75
9 a $\frac{17}{20}$ **b** $\frac{2}{5}$ **c** $\frac{3}{4}$
10 Probability cannot exceed 1, and probabilities cannot be summed in this way as events are not mutually exclusive

Exercise 3F

1 a 7 **b** 2, 12
  c P(2) = $\frac{1}{36}$, P(3) = $\frac{1}{18}$, P(4) = $\frac{1}{12}$, P(5) = $\frac{1}{9}$, P(6) = $\frac{5}{36}$, P(7) = $\frac{1}{6}$, P(8) = $\frac{5}{36}$, P(9) = $\frac{1}{9}$, P(10) = $\frac{1}{12}$, P(11) = $\frac{1}{18}$, P(12) = $\frac{1}{36}$
  d i $\frac{1}{12}$ **ii** $\frac{1}{3}$ **iii** $\frac{1}{2}$ **iv** $\frac{7}{36}$ **v** $\frac{5}{12}$ **vi** $\frac{5}{18}$
2 a $\frac{1}{12}$ **b** $\frac{11}{36}$ **c** $\frac{1}{6}$ **d** $\frac{5}{9}$
3 a $\frac{1}{36}$ **b** $\frac{11}{36}$ **c** $\frac{5}{18}$
4 a $\frac{5}{18}$ **b** $\frac{1}{6}$ **c** $\frac{1}{9}$ **d** 0 **e** $\frac{1}{2}$
5 a $\frac{1}{4}$ **b** $\frac{1}{2}$ **c** $\frac{3}{4}$ **d** $\frac{1}{4}$
6 a 6 **b i** $\frac{4}{25}$ **ii** $\frac{13}{25}$ **iii** $\frac{1}{5}$ **iv** $\frac{3}{5}$
7 a $\frac{1}{8}$ **b** $\frac{3}{8}$ **c** $\frac{7}{8}$ **d** $\frac{1}{8}$
8 a 16 **b** 32 **c** 1024 **d** 2^n
9 a $\frac{1}{12}$ **b** $\frac{1}{4}$ **c** $\frac{1}{6}$

Exercise 3G

1 a $\frac{1}{4}$ **b** $\frac{1}{2}$ **c** $\frac{3}{4}$
2 a $\frac{1}{13}$ **b** $\frac{12}{13}$ **c i** $\frac{1}{169}$ **ii** $\frac{25}{169}$
3 a $\frac{2}{3}$ **b** $\frac{1}{2}$ **d i** $\frac{1}{6}$ **ii** $\frac{1}{2}$ **iii** $\frac{5}{6}$ **e** 15 days
4 a $\frac{2}{5}$ **b i** $\frac{4}{25}$ **ii** $\frac{12}{25}$
5 a $\frac{1}{8}$ **b** $\frac{3}{8}$ **c** $\frac{7}{8}$
6 a 0.14 **b** 0.41 **c** 0.09
7 a $\frac{3}{5}$ **c i** $\frac{1}{3}$ **ii** $\frac{7}{15}$ **iii** $\frac{8}{15}$
8 a 1 **b** 1 **c**

	$\frac{1}{4}$		$\frac{1}{4}$	$\frac{1}{10}$
$\frac{3}{5}$	$\frac{1}{3}$	$\frac{3}{5} \times \frac{1}{3}$		
	$\frac{2}{3}$	$\frac{3}{5} \times \frac{2}{3}$	$\frac{2}{3}$	

Exercise 3H

1 a $\frac{4}{9}$ **b** $\frac{4}{9}$
2 a $\frac{1}{169}$ **b** $\frac{2}{169}$
3 a $\frac{1}{4}$ **b** $\frac{1}{2}$
4 $\frac{1}{216}$
5 a $\frac{4}{25}$ **b** $\frac{12}{25}$
6 a 0.08 **b** 0.32 **c** 0.48
7 a 0.336 **b** 0.452 **c** 0.024

Exercise 3I

1 a $\frac{125}{216}$ (0.579) **b** $\frac{91}{216}$ (0.421)
2 a $\frac{1}{16}$ **b** $\frac{15}{16}$
3 a 0.378 **b** 0.162 **c** 0.012 **d** 0.988
4 a $\frac{4}{25}$ **b** $\frac{9}{25}$ **c** $\frac{16}{25}$
5 a i $\frac{1}{216}$ (0.005) **ii** $\frac{125}{216}$ (0.579) **iii** $\frac{91}{216}$ (0.421)
  b i $\frac{1}{1296}$ (0.00077) **ii** $\frac{625}{1296}$ (0.482) **iii** $\frac{671}{1296}$ (0.518)
  c i $\frac{1}{7776}$ (0.00013) **ii** $\frac{3125}{7776}$ (0.402) **iii** $\frac{4651}{7776}$ (0.598)
  d i $\frac{1}{6^n}$ **ii** $\frac{5^n}{6^n}$ **iii** $1 - \frac{5^n}{6^n}$
6 a $\frac{32}{243}$ (0.132) **b** $\frac{1}{243}$ (0.004) **c** $\frac{242}{243}$ (0.996)
7 a $\frac{3}{8}$ **b** $\frac{1}{120}$ **c** $\frac{119}{120}$

Exercise 3J

1 a $\frac{27}{1000}$ **b** $\frac{189}{1000}$ **c** $\frac{441}{1000}$ **d** $\frac{343}{1000}$
2 a $\frac{1}{1296}$ (0.00077) **b** $\frac{625}{1296}$ (0.482) **c** $\frac{125}{324}$
3 a $\frac{1}{9}$ **b** $\frac{7}{18}$ **c** $\frac{7}{18}$ **d** $\frac{1}{9}$ **e** $\frac{8}{9}$
4 a 0.154 **b** 0.456
5 a 0.3024 **b** 0.4404 **c** 0.7428
6 a 0.9 **b** 0.6 **c** 0.54 **d** 0.216
7 a 0.6 **b** 0.6 **c** 0.432 **d** Independent events
8 a $\frac{1}{9}$ **b** $\frac{1}{9}$ **c** $\frac{7}{27}$ **d** $\frac{1}{27}$
9 a 0.126 **b** 0.4 **c** 0.42 **d** 0.054

Exercise 3K

1 a $\frac{1}{60}$ **b** 50
2 a $\frac{1}{6}$ **b** 0 **c i** $\frac{2}{3}$ **ii** $\frac{1}{3}$ **iii** 0

3 a i $\frac{3}{8}$ **ii** $\frac{5}{8}$ **b i** $\frac{5}{12}$ **b ii** $\frac{7}{12}$
4 a i $\frac{5}{13}$ **ii** $\frac{8}{13}$ **b i** $\frac{15}{91}$ **ii** $\frac{4}{13}$
5 a i $\frac{1}{3}$ **ii** $\frac{2}{15}$ **b** $\frac{4}{15}$ **c** $\frac{1}{6}$ **d** 1
6 Both events are independent
7 a $\frac{1}{120}$ **b** $\frac{7}{40}$ **c** $\frac{21}{40}$ **d** $\frac{7}{24}$
8 a $\frac{1}{9}$ **b** $\frac{2}{9}$ **c** $\frac{2}{3}$ **d** $\frac{7}{9}$
9 a 0.000495 **b** 0.00198 **c** 0.000018 **d** 0.00024
10 a 0.54 **b** 0.38 **c** 0.08 **d** 1
11 a RFC, FRC, CFC, CRC **b** $\frac{1}{3}$ **c** $\frac{1}{3}$ **d** $\frac{1}{3}$
  e Probability is the same regardless of which day he chooses

ANSWERS TO CHAPTER 4

Quick check

1 a 3841 **b** 41 **c** 625

2 a any multiple of 7, e.g. 7, 14, 21, …, 70…
  b 11, 13, 17 or 19
  c 1, 4, 9 ,16, 25 ,36 ,49 or 64
  d 1, 3, 9

3 a 17 **b** 25 **c** 5

Exercise 4A

1 a 6000
  b 5 cans cost £1.95, so 6 cans cost £1.95.
    32 = 5 × 6 + 2. cost is £10.53.
2 a 288 **b** 16
3 a 38
  b coach price for adults = £8, coach price for juniors = £4,
    money for coaches raised by tickets = £12 400, cost of
    coaches = £12 160, profit = £240
4 £68.70
5 (18.81…) Kirsty can buy 18 models.
6 (7.58…) Eunice must work for 8 weeks.
7 £8.40
8 £450

Exercise 4B

1 a 18 **b** 140 **c** 1.4 **d** 12 **e** 21.3
  f 6.9 **g** 2790 **h** 12.1 **i** 18.9
2 a 280 **b** 12 **c** 0.18 **d** 450 **e** 0.62
  f 380 **g** 0.26 **h** 240 **i** 12
3 750
4 300

Exercise 4C

1 a 50 000 **b** 60 000 **c** 30 000 **d** 90 000
  e 90 000 **f** 0.5 **g** 0.3 **h** 0.006
  i 0.05 **j** 0.0009 **k** 10 **l** 90
  m 90 **n** 200 **o** 1000
2 a 56 000 **b** 27 000 **c** 80 000 **d** 31 000

  e 14 000 **f** 1.7 **g** 4.1 **h** 2.7
  i 8.0 **j** 42 **k** 0.80 **l** 0.46
  m 0.066 **n** 1.0 **o** 0.0098
3 a 60 000 **b** 5300 **c** 89.7 **d** 110
  e 9 **f** 1.1 **g** 0.3 **h** 0.7
  i 0.4 **j** 0.8 **k** 0.2 **l** 0.7
4 a 65, 74 **b** 95, 149 **c** 950, 1499
5 Elsecar 750, 849, Hoyland 1150, 1249,
  Barnsley 164 500, 165 400

Exercise 4D

1 a 60 000 **b** 120 000 **c** 10 000 **d** 15 **e** 140
  f 100 **g** 200 **h** 0.028 **i** 0.09
  j 400 **k** 8000 **l** 0.16 **m** 45
  n 0.08 **o** 0.25 **p** 4 000 000 **q** 360 000
2 a 5 **b** 50 **c** 25 **d** 600 **e** 3000
  f 5000 **g** 2000 **h** 2000 **i** 400 **j** 8000
  k 4 000 000 **l** 3 200 000

Exercise 4E

The answers will depend on the approximations made.
Your answers should be to the same order as these.
1 a 35 000 **b** 15 000 **c** 960 **d** 5
  e 1200 **f** 500
2 a 39 700 **b** 17 000 **c** 933 **d** 4.44
  e 1130 **f** 550
3 a 4000 **b** 10 **c** 1 **d** 19 **e** 3 **f** 18
4 a 4190 **b** 8.79 **c** 1.01 **d** 20.7 **e** 3.07 **f** 18.5
5 a £3000 **b** £2000 **c** £1500 **d** £700
6 a £15 000 **b** £18 000 **c** £17 500
7 £20 000
8 8p
9 a 40 miles per hour **b** 10 gallons **c** £70
10 a 80 000 **b** 2000 **c** 1000 **d** 30 000
  e 5000 **f** 200 000 **g** 75 **h** 140
  i 100 **j** 3000
11 a 86 900 **b** 1760 **c** 1030 **d** 29 100
  e 3930 **f** 237 000 **g** 84.8 **h** 163
  i 96.9 **j** 2440

12 approx. 500
13 a i 27.57142857 **ii** 27.6
   b i 16.89651639 **ii** 16.9
   c i 704.4198895 **ii** 704

Exercise 4F
You may not have the same approximations. Can you justify your answers?
1 a 1.74 m **b** 5 minutes **c** 240 g **d** 82°C
   e 35 000 people **f** 15 miles **g** 14 m^2
2 82°F, $5\frac{1}{2}$ km, 110 min, 43 000 people, 6.2 seconds, 67th, 1788, 15 practice walks, 5 seconds
   The answers will depend on the approximations made. Your answers should be to the same order as these.
3 40
4 40 minutes
5 60 stamps
6 70 mph
7 270 fans
8 80 000 kg (80 tonnes)

Exercise 4G
1 a 12 **b** 9 **c** 6 **d** 13 **e** 15 **f** 14
   g 16 **h** 10 **i** 18 **j** 17 **k** 8 (or 16) **l** 21
2 4 packs of sausages and 5 packs of buns (or multiples of these)
3 24 seconds
4 30 seconds
5 1 + 3 + 5 + 7 + 9 = 25, 1 + 3 + 5 + 7 + 9 + 11 = 36, 1 + 3 + 5 + 7 + 9 + 11 + 13 = 49, 1 + 3 + 5 + 7 + 9 + 11 + 13 + 15 = 64
6 a −2 **b** −5 **c** −7 **d** −1 **e** −9
   f −11 **g** −12 **h** −20 **i** −30 **j** −13
7 a 1 **b** 3 **c** 4 **d** 2 **e** 10
   f −2 **g** −1 **h** 20 **i** 40 **j** −4
8 a 1, 3, 6, 10, 15, 21, 28, 36, 45, 55, 66, 78, 91, 105
   b Adding consecutive pairs gives you square numbers.
9 a 1, 64, 729, 4096, 15 625
   b 1, 8, 27, 64, 125
   c $\sqrt{a^3} = a \times \sqrt{a}$
   d square numbers
10 a 0.2 **b** 0.5 **c** 0.6 **d** 0.9 **e** 1.2
   f 0.8 **g** 1.1 **h** 1.5
11 The answers will depend on the approximations made. Your answers should be to the same order as these.
   a 60 **b** 1500 **c** 180

Exercise 4H
1 a 84 = 2 × 2 × 3 × 7 **b** 100 = 2 × 2 × 5 × 5
   c 180 = 2 × 2 × 3 × 3 × 5
   d 220 = 2 × 2 × 5 × 11
   e 280 = 2 × 2 × 2 × 5 × 7
   f 128 = 2 × 2 × 2 × 2 × 2 × 2 × 2
   g 50 = 2 × 5 × 5

2 a $84 = 2^2 \times 3 \times 7$ **b** $100 = 2^2 \times 5^2$
   c $180 = 2^2 \times 3^2 \times 5$ **d** $220 = 2^2 \times 5 \times 11$
   e $280 = 2^3 \times 5 \times 7$ **f** $128 = 2^7$
   g $50 = 2 \times 5^2$ **h** $1000 = 2^3 \times 5^3$
   i $576 = 2^6 \times 3^2$ **j** $650 = 2 \times 5^2 \times 13$
3 1, 2, 3, 2^2, 5, 2 × 3, 7, 2^3, 3^2, 2 × 5, 11, $2^2 \times 3$, 13, 2 × 7, 3 × 5, 2^4, 17, 2×3^2, 19, $2^2 \times 5$, 3 × 7, 2 × 11, 23, $2^3 \times 3$, 5^2, 2 × 13, 3^3, $2^2 \times 7$, 29, 2 × 3 × 5, 31, 2^5, 3 × 11, 2 × 17, 5 × 7, $2^2 \times 3^2$, 37, 2 × 19, 3 × 13, $2^3 \times 5$, 41, 2 × 3 × 7, 43, $2^2 \times 11$, $3^3 \times 5$, 2 × 23, 47, $2^4 \times 3$, 7^2, 2×5^2
4 a Double each time
   b 64, 128
   c 81, 243
   d 256, 1024, 4096
   e 3, 3^2, 3^3, 3^4, 3^5, 3^6, 4, 4^2, 4^3, 4^4, 4^5

Exercise 4I
1 a 20 **b** 56 **c** 6 **d** 28 **e** 10 **f** 15
   g 24 **h** 30
2 They are the two numbers multiplied together.
3 a 8 **b** 18 **c** 12 **d** 30
4 No. The numbers have a common factor. Multiplying them together would mean using this factor twice, thus increasing the size of the common multiple. It would not be the lowest common multiple.
5 a 168 **b** 105 **c** 84 **d** 168 **e** 48
   f 54 **g** 75 **h** 144
6 a 8 **b** 7 **c** 4 **d** 14 **e** 12 **f** 9
   g 5 **h** 4 **i** 3 **j** 16 **k** 5 **l** 18
7 a ii and iii **b** iii

Exercise 4J
1 a −15 **b** −14 **c** −24 **d** 6 **e** 14
   f 2 **g** −2 **h** −8 **i** −4 **j** 3
   k −24 **l** −10 **m** −18 **n** 16 **o** 36
2 a −9 **b** 16 **c** −3 **d** −32 **e** 18
   f 18 **g** 6 **h** −4 **i** 20 **j** 16
   k 8 **l** −48 **m** 13 **n** −13 **o** −8
3 a −2 **b** 30 **c** 15 **d** −27 **e** −7
4 a −9 **b** 3 **c** 1
5 a 16 **b** −2 **c** −12
6 Any appropriate divisions.

Exercise 4K
1 a −4 **b** −6 **c** 4 **d** 45 **e** 6 **f** 6
2 a 38 **b** 24 **c** −3 **d** −6 **e** −1 **f** 2
   g −25 **h** 25 **i** 0 **j** −20 **k** 4 **l** 0
3 a (3 × −4) + 1 = −11 **b** −6 ÷ (−2 + 1) = 6
   c (−6 ÷ −2) + 1 = 4 **d** 4 + (−4 ÷ 4) = 3
   e (4 + −4) ÷ 4 = 0 **f** (16 − −4) ÷ 2 = 10
4 a 49 **b** −1 **c** −5 **d** −12

Quick check

1 a $\frac{2}{5}$ **b** $\frac{3}{8}$ **c** $\frac{3}{7}$

2

Fraction	Percentage	Decimal
$\frac{3}{4}$	75%	0.75
$\frac{2}{5}$	40%	0.4
$\frac{11}{20}$	55%	0.55

3 a £23 **b** £4.60 **c** 23p

Exercise 5A

1 a $\frac{1}{3}$ **b** $\frac{1}{5}$ **c** $\frac{2}{5}$ **d** $\frac{5}{24}$ **e** $\frac{2}{5}$ **f** $\frac{1}{6}$ **g** $\frac{2}{7}$ **h** $\frac{1}{3}$

2 $\frac{3}{5}$ **3** $\frac{12}{31}$ **4** $\frac{7}{12}$ **5** $\frac{1}{8}$

6 $\frac{5}{12}$ **7** $\frac{1}{5}$ **8** $\frac{3}{20}$

Exercise 5B

1 a $\frac{8}{15}$ **b** $\frac{7}{12}$ **c** $\frac{3}{10}$ **d** $\frac{11}{12}$ **e** $\frac{1}{10}$ **f** $\frac{1}{8}$

g $\frac{1}{12}$ **h** $\frac{1}{3}$

2 a $\frac{7}{9}$ **b** $\frac{5}{8}$ **c** $\frac{3}{8}$ **d** $\frac{1}{15}$ **e** $3\frac{31}{45}$ **f** $4\frac{47}{60}$

g $\frac{41}{72}$ **h** $\frac{29}{48}$ **i** $1\frac{43}{48}$ **j** $1\frac{109}{120}$ **k** $1\frac{23}{30}$ **l** $1\frac{31}{84}$

3 $\frac{1}{20}$ **4** $\frac{1}{6}$ **5** $\frac{1}{3}$ **6** 260

7 three-quarters of 68 **8** £51 **9** 10 minutes

Exercise 5C

1 a $\frac{1}{6}$ **b** $\frac{1}{10}$ **c** $\frac{3}{8}$ **d** $\frac{3}{14}$ **e** $\frac{7}{20}$ **f** $\frac{16}{45}$

g $\frac{3}{8}$ **h** $\frac{5}{8}$

2 a $\frac{5}{12}$ **b** $2\frac{1}{12}$ **c** $6\frac{1}{4}$ **d** $2\frac{11}{12}$ **e** $3\frac{9}{10}$

f $3\frac{1}{3}$ **g** $12\frac{1}{2}$ **h** 30

3 21 tonnes **4** $\frac{3}{8}$ **5** $\frac{3}{8}$

6 $\frac{2}{5}$ of $6\frac{1}{2}$ **7** £5 **8** £10.40

Exercise 5D

1 a $\frac{3}{4}$ **b** $1\frac{2}{5}$ **c** $1\frac{1}{15}$ **d** $1\frac{1}{14}$ **e** 4 **f** 4

g 5 **h** $1\frac{5}{7}$ **i** $\frac{4}{9}$ **j** $1\frac{3}{5}$

2 40 **3** 15 **4** 16

5 a $2\frac{2}{15}$ **b** 38 **c** $1\frac{7}{8}$ **d** $\frac{9}{32}$ **e** $\frac{1}{16}$ **f** $\frac{256}{625}$

Exercise 5E

1 a 1.1 **b** 1.03 **c** 1.2 **d** 1.07 **e** 1.12

2 a £62.40 **b** 12.96 kg **c** 472.5 g

d 599.5 m **e** £38.08 **f** £90

g 391 kg **h** 824.1 cm **i** 253.5 g

j £143.50 **k** 736 m **l** £30.24

3 1 690 200

4 Bob £17 325, Jean £20 475, Anne £18 165, Brian £26 565

5 575 g

6 60 girls

7 £287.88, £84.60, £135.13, £34.66

8 £540.96

9 Calculate the VAT on certain amounts, and $\frac{1}{6}$ of that amount. Show the error grows as the amount increases. After £600 the error is greater than £5, so the method works to within £5 with prices up to £600.

Exercise 5F

1 a 0.92 **b** 0.85 **c** 0.75 **d** 0.91 **e** 0.88

2 a £9.40 **b** 23 kg **c** 212.4 g **d** 339.5 m

e £4.90 **f** 39.6 m **g** 731 m **h** 83.52 g

i 360 cm

3 £5525 **4** 448 people

5 705 pupils **6** £18 975

7 a 66.5 mph **b** 73.5 mph

8 £39.60 **9** 524.8 units

10 £765 **11** 1.10 × 0.9 = 0.99 (99%)

Exercise 5G

1 a 25% **b** 60.6% **c** 46.3% **d** 12.5%

e 41.7% **f** 60% **g** 20.8% **h** 10%

i 1.9% **j** 8.3% **k** 45.5% **l** 10.5%

2 32% **3** 6.49% **4** 33.7%

5 a 49.2% **b** 64.5% **c** 10.6%

6 17.9% **7** 7.4% **8** 90.5%

9 a Commonwealth 20.9%, USA 26.5%, France 10.3%, Other 42.3%

b 100%, because this is all imports.

Exercise 5H

1 a i 10.5 kg **ii** 11.03 kg **iii** 12.16 kg **iv** 14.07 kg

b 9 days

2 12 years **3 a** £14272.27 **b** 20 years

4 a i 2550 **ii** 2168 **iii** 1331 **b** 7 years

5 a £6800 **b** £5440 **c** £3481.60

6 a i 1.9 million litres **ii** 1.6 million litres

iii 1.2 million litres

b 10th August

7 a i 51 980 **ii** 84 752 **iii** 138 186

b 2010

8 a 21 years **b** 21 years

9 3 years **10** 30 years

11 1.1 × 1.1 = 1.21 (21% increase)

Exercise 5I

1 a 800 g **b** 250 m **c** 60 cm **d** £3075

e £200 **f** £400

2 80

3 T shirt £8.40, Tights £1.20, Shorts £5.20, Sweater £10.74, Trainers £24.80, Boots £32.40

4 £833.33 **5** £300

6 240 **7** £350

8 4750 blue bottles **9** £22

10 less by $\frac{1}{4}$%

11 Calculate the pre-VAT price for certain amounts, and $\frac{5}{6}$ of that amount. Show the error grows as the amount increases. Up to £280 the error is less than £5.

Quick check

1 a $\frac{3}{5}$ **b** $\frac{1}{5}$ **c** $\frac{1}{3}$ **d** $\frac{16}{25}$ **e** $\frac{2}{5}$ **f** $\frac{3}{4}$ **g** $\frac{1}{3}$

2 a £12 **b** £33 **c** 175 litres **d** 15 kg
  e 40 m **f** £35 **g** 135 g **h** 1.05 litres

Exercise 6A

1 $\frac{7}{10}$ **2** $\frac{2}{5}$

3 a $\frac{2}{5}$ **b** $\frac{3}{5}$ **4 a** $\frac{7}{10}$ **b** $\frac{3}{10}$

5 a $\frac{2}{9}$ **b** $\frac{1}{3}$ **c** $\frac{2}{9}$

6 sugar $\frac{5}{22}$, flour $\frac{3}{11}$, margarine $\frac{2}{11}$, fruit $\frac{7}{22}$

Exercise 6B

1 a 160 g : 240 g **b** 80 kg : 200 kg
  c 150 : 350 **d** 950 m : 50 m
  e 175 min : 125 min **f** £20 : £30 : £50
  g £36 : £60 : £144 **h** 50 g : 250 g : 300 g
2 a 160 **b** 37.5%
3 a 28.6% **b** 250 kg
4 a 21 horses **b** 94% (2 sf)
5 a 1 : 400 000 **b** 1 : 125 000 **c** 1 : 250 000
  d 1 : 25 000 **e** 1 : 20 000 **f** 1 : 40 000
6 a 1 : 1 000 000 **b** 47 km **c** 0.8 cm
7 a 1 : 250 000 **b** 2 km **c** 4.8 cm
8 a 1 : 1.6 **b** 1 : 3.25 **c** 1 : 1.125
  d 1 : 1.44 **e** 1 : 5.4 **f** 1 : 1.5
  g 1 : 4.8 **h** 1 : 42 **i** 1 : 1.25

Exercise 6C

1 a 3 : 2 **b** 32 **c** 80
2 a 100 **b** 160
3 1000 g Assam tea **4** 10 125 people
5 5.5 l of tea **6 a** 11 pages **b** 32%
7 Kevin £2040, John £2720
8 20 l lemonade, 0.5 l ginger
9 a 14% (2sf) **b** 75 good apples

Exercise 6D

1 18 mph **2** 52.5 mph **3** 11:50 am

4

	Distance	Time	Av speed
a	150 miles	2 hr	75 mph
b	260 miles	6 hr 30 min	40 mph
c	175 miles	5 hr	35 mph
d	240 km	3 hr	80 km/h
e	544 km	8 hr 30 min	64 km/h
f	325 km	3 hr 15 min	100 km/h
g	215 km	4 hr 18 min	50 km/h

5 a 120 km **b** 48 km/h
6 a 30 min **b** 6 mph
7 a 2.25 h **b** 99 miles
8 a 1.25 h **b** 1 h 15 min
9 a 48 mph **b** 6 h 40 min
10 a 10 m/s **b** $3\frac{1}{3}$ m/s **c** $16\frac{2}{3}$ m/s
  d $41\frac{2}{3}$ m/s **e** $20\frac{5}{6}$ m/s
11 a 90 km/h **b** 43.2 km/h **c** 14.4 km/h
  d 108 km/h **e** 1.8 km/h
12 a 64.8 km/h **b** 27.8 sec (1dp)
  c 8:07 (nearest minute)

Exercise 6E

1 60 g
2 £5.22
3 45 trees
4 a £312.50 **b** 8 textbooks
5 a 56 l **b** 350 miles
6 a 300 kg **b** 9 weeks
7 40 sec

Exercise 6F

1 a large jar as more g per £
  b 600 g tin as more g per p
  c 5 kg bag as more kg per £
  d 75 ml tube as more ml per £
  e large box as more g per £
  f large box as more g per £
  g 400 ml bottle as more ml per £
2 large tin (small £5.11/l, medium £4.80/l, large £4.47/l)
3 a 95p **b** Family size
4 Bashir's
5 Mary
6 Kelly

Exercise 6G

1 a 0.75 g/cm^3
2 $8\frac{1}{3}$ g/cm^3
3 32 g
4 120 cm^3
5 156.8 g
6 3200 cm^3
7 2.72 g/cm^3
8 36 800 kg
9 1.79 g/cm^3 (3 sf)
10 1.6 g/cm^3

Quick check

1 a 0.6 **b** 0.44 **c** 0.375

2 a $\frac{17}{100}$ **b** $\frac{16}{25}$ **c** $\frac{429}{500}$

3 a $\frac{13}{15}$ **b** $\frac{9}{40}$

4 a 5 **b** 4

Exercise 7A

1 a 2^4 **b** 3^5 **c** 7^2 **d** 5^3 **e** 10^7 **f** 6^4
 g 4^1 **h** 1^7 **i** 0.5^4 **j** 100^3

2 a $3 \times 3 \times 3 \times 3$ **b** $9 \times 9 \times 9$ **c** 6×6
 d $10 \times 10 \times 10 \times 10 \times 10$
 e $2 \times 2 \times 2 \times 2 \times 2 \times 2 \times 2 \times 2 \times 2 \times 2$
 f 8 **g** $0.1 \times 0.1 \times 0.1$ **h** 2.5×2.5
 i $0.7 \times 0.7 \times 0.7$ **j** 1000×1000

3 a 16 **b** 243 **c** 49 **d** 125 **e** 10 000 000
 f 1296 **g** 4 **h** 1 **i** 0.0625 **j** 1 000 000

4 a 81 **b** 729 **c** 36 **d** 100 000 **e** 1024
 f 8 **g** 0.001 **h** 6.25 **i** 0.343 **j** 1 000 000

5 a 1 **b** 4 **c** 1 **d** 1 **e** 1

6 Any power of 1 is equal to 1.

7 10^6

8 10^6

9 a 1 **b** –1 **c** 1 **d** 1 **e** –1

10 a 1 **b** –1 **c** –1 **d** 1 **e** 1

Exercise 7B

1 a $\frac{1}{5^3}$ **b** $\frac{1}{6}$ **c** $\frac{1}{10^5}$ **d** $\frac{1}{3^2}$ **e** $\frac{1}{8^2}$

 f $\frac{1}{9}$ **g** $\frac{1}{w^2}$ **h** $\frac{1}{t}$ **i** $\frac{1}{x^m}$ **j** $\frac{4}{m^3}$

2 a 3^{-2} **b** 5^{-1} **c** 10^{-3} **d** m^{-1} **e** t^{-n}

3 a i 2^4 **ii** 2^{-1} **iii** 2^{-4} **iv** -2^3
 b i 10^3 **ii** 10^{-1} **iii** 10^{-2} **iv** 10^6
 c i 5^3 **ii** 5^{-1} **iii** 5^{-2} **iv** 5^{-4}
 d i 3^2 **ii** 3^{-3} **iii** 3^{-4} **iv** -3^5

4 a $\frac{5}{x^3}$ **b** $\frac{6}{t}$ **c** $\frac{7}{m^2}$ **d** $\frac{4}{q^4}$ **e** $\frac{10}{y^5}$

 f $\frac{1}{2x^3}$ **g** $\frac{1}{2m}$ **h** $\frac{3}{4t^4}$ **i** $\frac{4}{5y^3}$ **j** $\frac{7}{8x^5}$

5 a $7x^{-3}$ **b** $10p^{-1}$ **c** $5t^{-2}$ **d** $8m^{-5}$ **e** $3y^{-1}$

6 a i 25 **ii** $\frac{1}{125}$ **iii** $\frac{4}{5}$ **b i** 64 **ii** $\frac{1}{16}$ **iii** $\frac{5}{256}$
 c i 8 **ii** $\frac{1}{32}$ **iii** $4\frac{1}{2}$ **d** 1 000 000 **ii** $\frac{1}{1000}$ **iii** $\frac{1}{4}$

Exercise 7C

1 a 5^4 **b** 5^3 **c** 5^2 **d** 5^3 **e** 5^{-5}

2 a 6^3 **b** 6^0 **c** 6^6 **d** 6^{-7} **e** 6^2

3 a a^3 **b** a^5 **c** a^7 **d** a^4 **e** a^2 **f** a^1

4 a 4^6 **b** 4^{15} **c** 4^6 **d** 4^{-6} **e** 4^6 **f** 4^0

5 a $6a^5$ **b** $9a^2$ **c** $8a^6$ **d** $-6a^4$ **e** $8a^8$
 f $-10a^{-3}$

6 a $3a$ **b** $4a^3$ **c** $3a^4$ **d** $6a^{-1}$ **e** $4a^7$ **f** $5a^{-4}$

7 a $8a^5b^4$ **b** $10a^3b$ **c** $30a^{-2}b^{-2}$ **d** $2ab^3$ **e** $8a^{-5}b^7$

8 a $3a^3b^2$ **b** $3a^2c^4$ **c** $8a^2b^2c^3$

9 $1 = \dfrac{a^x}{a^x} = a^x \div a^x = a^{x-x} = a^0$

Exercise 7D

1 5 **2** 10 **3** 8 **4** 9 **5** 25 **6** 3
7 4 **8** 10 **9** 5 **10** 8 **11** 12 **12** 20
13 5 **14** 3 **15** 10 **16** 3 **17** 2 **18** 2
19 6 **20** 6 **21** $\frac{1}{4}$ **22** $\frac{1}{2}$ **23** $\frac{1}{3}$ **24** $\frac{1}{5}$
25 $\frac{1}{10}$ **26** $\frac{5}{6}$ **27** $1\frac{2}{3}$ **28** $\frac{8}{9}$ **29** $1\frac{4}{5}$ **30** $\frac{5}{8}$
31 $\frac{3}{5}$ **32** $\frac{1}{4}$ **33** $2\frac{1}{2}$ **34** $\frac{4}{5}$ **35** $1\frac{1}{7}$

36 $(x^{\frac{1}{n}})^n = x^{\frac{1}{n} \times n} = x^1 = x$, but
 $(\sqrt[n]{x})^n = \sqrt[n]{x} \times \sqrt[n]{x} \dots n$ times $= x$, so $x^{\frac{1}{n}} = \sqrt[n]{x}$

Exercise 7E

1 a 16 **b** 25 **c** 216 **d** 81

2 a $t^{\frac{2}{3}}$ **b** $m^{\frac{3}{4}}$ **c** $k^{\frac{2}{5}}$ **d** $x^{\frac{3}{2}}$

3 a 4 **b** 9 **c** 64 **d** 3125

4 a $\frac{1}{5}$ **b** $\frac{1}{6}$ **c** $\frac{1}{2}$ **d** $\frac{1}{3}$ **e** $\frac{1}{4}$ **f** $\frac{1}{2}$ **g** $\frac{1}{2}$ **h** $\frac{1}{3}$

5 a $\frac{1}{125}$ **b** $\frac{1}{216}$ **c** $\frac{1}{8}$ **d** $\frac{1}{27}$ **e** $\frac{1}{64}$ **f** $\frac{1}{4}$
 g $\frac{1}{256}$ **h** $\frac{1}{9}$

6 a $\frac{1}{100000}$ **b** $\frac{1}{12}$ **c** $\frac{1}{25}$ **d** $\frac{1}{27}$ **e** $\frac{1}{32}$ **f** $\frac{1}{32}$
 g $\frac{1}{81}$ **h** $\frac{1}{13}$

Exercise 7F

1 a 31 **b** 310 **c** 3100 **d** 31 000

2 a 65 **b** 650 **c** 6500 **d** 65 000

3 a 0.31 **b** 0.031 **c** 0.0031 **d** 0.000 31

4 a 0.65 **b** 0.065 **c** 0.0065 **d** 0.000 65

5 a 250 **b** 34.5 **c** 4670 **d** 346
 e 207.89 **f** 56 780 **g** 246 **h** 0.76
 i 999 000 **j** 23 456 **k** 98 765.4 **l** 43 230 000
 m 345.78 **n** 6000 **o** 56.7 **p** 560 045

6 a 0.025 **b** 0.345 **c** 0.00467
 d 3.46 **e** 0.207 89 **f** 0.056 78
 g 0.0246 **h** 0.0076 **i** 0.000 000 999
 j 2.3456 **k** 0.098 765 4 **l** 0.000 043 23
 m 0.000 000 034 578 **n** 0.000 000 000 06
 o 0.000 000 567 **p** 0.005 600 45

7 a 230 **b** 578 900 **c** 4790 **d** 57 000 000
 e 216 **f** 10 500 **g** 0.000 32 **h** 9870

8 a, b and c

Exercise 7G

1 a 0.31 **b** 0.031 **c** 0.0031 **d** 0.000 31

2 a 0.65 **b** 0.065 **c** 0.0065 **d** 0.000 65

3 a $9\,999\,999\,999 \times 10^{99}$
 b $0.000\,000\,001 \times 10^{-99}$ (depending on number of digits displayed)

4 a 31 **b** 310 **c** 3100 **d** 31 000

5 a 65 **b** 650 **c** 6500 **d** 65 000

6 a 250 **b** 34.5 **c** 0.004 67
 d 34.6 **e** 0.020 789 **f** 5678
 g 246 **h** 7600 **i** 89 700

j 0.008 65 **k** 60 000 000 **l** 0.000 567
7 a 2.5×10^2 **b** 3.45×10^{-1} **c** 4.67×10^4
d 3.4×10^9 **e** 2.078×10^{10} **f** 5.678×10^{-4}
g 2.46×10^3 **h** 7.6×10^{-2} **i** 7.6×10^{-4}
j 9.99×10^{-1} **k** 2.3456×10^2
l $9.876 54 \times 10^1$ **m** 6×10^{-4}
n 5.67×10^{-3} **o** $5.600 45 \times 10^1$
8 2.7797×10^4
9 $2.815 81 \times 10^5$, 3×10^1, $1.382 101 \times 10^6$
10 1.298×10^7, 2.997×10^9, 9.3×10^4

Exercise 7H

1 a 5.67×10^3 **b** 6×10^2 **c** 3.46×10^{-1}
d 7×10^{-4} **e** 5.6×10^2 **f** 6×10^5
g 7×10^3 **h** 1.6 **i** 2.3×10^7
j 3×10^{-6} **k** 2.56×10^6 **l** 4.8×10^2
m 1.12×10^2 **n** 6×10^5 **o** 2.8×10^6
2 a 1.08×10^8 **b** 4.8×10^6 **c** 1.2×10^9
d 1.08 **e** 6.4×10^2 **f** 1.2×10^1
g 2.88 **h** 2.5×10^7 **i** 8×10^{-6}
3 a 1.1×10^8 **b** 6.1×10^6 **c** 1.6×10^9
d 3.9×10^{-2} **e** 9.6×10^8 **f** 4.6×10^{-7}
g 2.1×10^3 **h** 3.6×10^7 **i** 1.5×10^2
j 3.5×10^9 **k** 1.6×10^4
4 a 2.7×10^7 **b** 1.6×10^6 **c** 2×10^7
d 4×10^{-2} **e** 2×10^1 **f** 6×10^{-2}
g 2×10^{-1} **h** 5×10^8 **i** 2×10^5
5 a 5.4×10^5 **b** 2.9×10^9 **c** 1.1×10^{-2}
d 6.3×10^{-4} **e** 2.8×10^2 **f** 5.5×10^{-2}
g 4.9×10^8 **h** 8.6×10^2
6 2×10^{13}, 1×10^{-10}, mass = 2×10^3 g (2 kg)
7 a (2^{63}) 9.2×10^{18} grains
b $(1 + 9.2 \times 10^{18}) \times 32 = 3 \times 10^{20}$ grains
8 a 6×10^7 sq miles **b** 30%
9 1.5×10^7 sq miles **10** 5×10^4
11 2.3×10^5 **12** 3.2×10^8 kg
13 250 **14** 9.41×10^4

Exercise 7I

1 a 0.5 **b** $0.\dot{3}$ **c** 0.25 **d** 0.2 **e** $0.1\dot{6}$
f $0.\dot{1}4285\dot{7}$ **g** 0.125 **h** $0.\dot{1}$ **i** 0.1
j $0.\dot{0}7692\dot{3}$
2 b They all contain the same pattern of digits, starting at a different point in the pattern.
3 $0.\dot{1}$, $0.\dot{2}$, $0.\dot{3}$, etc. Digit in decimal fraction same as numerator.
4 $0.\dot{0}\dot{9}$, $0.\dot{1}\dot{8}$, $0.\dot{2}\dot{7}$, etc. Sum of digits in recurring pattern = 9. First digit is one less than numerator.
5 0.444 ..., 0.454 ..., 0.428 ..., 0.409 ..., 0.432 ..., 0.461 ..., $\frac{9}{22}$, $\frac{3}{7}$, $\frac{16}{37}$, $\frac{4}{9}$, $\frac{5}{11}$, $\frac{6}{13}$
6 $\frac{38}{120}$, $\frac{35}{120}$, $\frac{36}{120}$, $\frac{48}{120}$, $\frac{50}{120}$ $\frac{7}{24}$, $\frac{3}{10}$, $\frac{19}{60}$, $\frac{2}{5}$, $\frac{5}{12}$
7 a $\frac{1}{8}$ **b** $\frac{17}{50}$ **c** $\frac{29}{40}$ **d** $\frac{5}{16}$ **e** $\frac{89}{100}$ **f** $\frac{1}{20}$
g $\frac{27}{20}$ **h** $\frac{7}{32}$
8 a $0.083\dot{3}$ **b** 0.0625 **c** 0.05 **d** 0.04 **e** 0.02
9 a $\frac{4}{3}$ **b** $\frac{6}{5}$ **c** $\frac{5}{2}$ **d** $\frac{10}{7}$ **e** $\frac{20}{11}$ **f** $\frac{15}{4}$
10 a 0.75, $1.\dot{3}$; $0.8\dot{3}$, 1.2; 0.4, 2.5; 0.7, $1.\dot{4}28\dot{57}$; 0.55, $1.8\dot{1}$; $0.2\dot{6}$, 3.75
b no

11 1
12 a 24.242 42 ... **b** 24 **c** $\frac{24}{99}$
13 a $\frac{8}{9}$ **b** $\frac{34}{99}$ **c** $\frac{5}{11}$ **d** $\frac{21}{37}$ **e** $\frac{4}{9}$ **f** $\frac{2}{45}$
g $\frac{13}{90}$ **h** $\frac{1}{22}$ **i** $2\frac{7}{9}$ **j** $7\frac{7}{11}$ **k** $3\frac{1}{3}$ **l** $2\frac{2}{33}$
14 a true **b** true **c** recurring
15 a $\frac{9}{9}$ **b** $\frac{45}{90} = \frac{1}{2} = 0.5$

Exercise 7J

1 a $\sqrt{6}$ **b** $\sqrt{15}$ **c** 2 **d** 4 **e** $2\sqrt{10}$
f 3 **g** $2\sqrt{3}$ **h** $\sqrt{21}$ **i** $\sqrt{14}$ **j** 6
k 6 **l** $\sqrt{30}$
2 a 2 **b** $\sqrt{5}$ **c** $\sqrt{6}$ **d** $\sqrt{3}$ **e** $\sqrt{5}$
f 1 **g** $\sqrt{3}$ **h** $\sqrt{7}$ **i** 2 **j** $\sqrt{6}$
k 1 **l** 3
3 a $2\sqrt{3}$ **b** 15 **c** $4\sqrt{2}$ **d** $4\sqrt{3}$ **e** $8\sqrt{5}$
f $3\sqrt{3}$ **g** 24 **h** $3\sqrt{7}$ **i** $2\sqrt{7}$ **j** $6\sqrt{5}$
k $6\sqrt{3}$ **l** 30
4 a $\sqrt{3}$ **b** 1 **c** $2\sqrt{2}$ **d** $\sqrt{2}$ **e** $\sqrt{5}$
f $\sqrt{3}$ **g** $\sqrt{2}$ **h** $\sqrt{7}$ **i** $\sqrt{7}$ **j** $2\sqrt{3}$
k $2\sqrt{3}$ **l** 1
5 a a **b** 1 **c** $\sqrt{a}$
6 a $3\sqrt{2}$ **b** $2\sqrt{6}$ **c** $2\sqrt{3}$ **d** $5\sqrt{2}$ **e** $2\sqrt{2}$
f $3\sqrt{3}$ **g** $4\sqrt{3}$ **h** $5\sqrt{3}$ **i** $3\sqrt{5}$ **j** $3\sqrt{7}$
k $4\sqrt{2}$ **l** $10\sqrt{2}$ **m** $10\sqrt{10}$ **n** $5\sqrt{10}$ **o** $7\sqrt{2}$
p $9\sqrt{3}$
7 a 36 **b** $16\sqrt{30}$ **c** 54 **d** 32 **e** $48\sqrt{6}$
f $48\sqrt{6}$ **g** $18\sqrt{15}$ **h** 84 **i** 64 **j** 100
k 50 **l** 56
8 a $20\sqrt{6}$ **b** $6\sqrt{15}$ **c** 24 **d** 16 **e** $12\sqrt{10}$
f 18 **g** $20\sqrt{3}$ **h** $10\sqrt{21}$ **i** $6\sqrt{14}$ **j** 36
k 24 **l** $12\sqrt{30}$
9 a 6 **b** $3\sqrt{5}$ **c** $6\sqrt{6}$ **d** $2\sqrt{3}$ **e** $4\sqrt{5}$
f 5 **g** $7\sqrt{3}$ **h** $2\sqrt{7}$ **i** 6 **j** $2\sqrt{7}$
k 5 **l** 24
10 a $2\sqrt{3}$ **b** 4 **c** $6\sqrt{2}$ **d** $4\sqrt{2}$ **e** $6\sqrt{5}$
f $24\sqrt{3}$ **g** $3\sqrt{2}$ **h** $\sqrt{7}$ **i** $10\sqrt{7}$ **j** $8\sqrt{3}$
k $10\sqrt{3}$ **l** 6
11 a abc **b** $\frac{a}{c}$ **c** $c\sqrt{b}$
12 a 20 **b** 24 **c** 10 **d** 24 **e** 3 **f** 6
13 a $\frac{3}{4}$ **b** $8\frac{1}{3}$ **c** $\frac{5}{16}$ **d** 12 **e** 2

Exercise 7K

1 $11 + 6\sqrt{2}$
2 a $2\sqrt{3} - 3$ **b** $3\sqrt{2} - 8$ **c** $10 + 4\sqrt{5}$
d $12\sqrt{7} - 42$ **e** $15\sqrt{2} - 24$ **f** $9 - \sqrt{3}$
3 a $2\sqrt{3}$ **b** $1 + \sqrt{5}$ **c** $-1 - \sqrt{2}$ **d** $\sqrt{7} - 30$
e -41 **f** $7 + 3\sqrt{6}$ **g** $9 + 4\sqrt{5}$ **h** $3 - 2\sqrt{2}$
i $11 + 6\sqrt{2}$
4 a $3\sqrt{2}$ cm **b** $2\sqrt{3}$ cm **c** $2\sqrt{10}$ cm
5 a $\sqrt{3} - 1$ cm^2 **b** $2\sqrt{5} + 5\sqrt{2}$ cm^2
c $2\sqrt{3} + 18$ cm^2
6 a $\frac{\sqrt{3}}{3}$ **b** $\frac{\sqrt{2}}{2}$ **c** $\frac{\sqrt{5}}{5}$ **d** $\frac{\sqrt{3}}{6}$
e $\sqrt{3}$ **f** $\frac{5\sqrt{2}}{2}$ **g** $\frac{3}{2}$ **h** $\frac{5\sqrt{2}}{2}$
i $\frac{\sqrt{21}}{3}$ **j** $\frac{\sqrt{2}+2}{2}$ **k** $\frac{2\sqrt{3}-3}{3}$ **l** $\frac{5\sqrt{3}+6}{3}$

7 a i 1 **ii** –4 **iii** 2 **iv** 17 **v** –44
  b They become whole numbers. Difference of two squares
    makes the 'middle terms' (and surds) disappear.
  c i $\dfrac{5 + 5\sqrt{5}}{-4}$ **ii** $\dfrac{5 + 3\sqrt{3}}{2}$

ANSWERS TO CHAPTER 8

Quick check

1 a i 16 **ii** 4
  b i 20 **ii** 8
  c i 14 **ii** 2
  d i 24 **ii** 0

2 $A(2, 2)$, $B(3, -2)$, $C(-3, -3)$, $D(-2, 1)$

Exercise 8A

1 a Values of y: 27, 12, 3, 0, 3, 12, 27
  b 6.8 **c** 1.8 or –1.8
2 a Values of y: 27, 18, 11, 6, 3, 2, 3, 6, 11, 18, 27
  b 8.3 **c** 3.5 or –3.5
3 a Values of y: 27, 16, 7, 0, –5, –8, –9, –8, –5, 0, 7
  b –8.8 **c** 3.4 or –1.4
4 a Values of y: 2, –1, –2, –1, 2, 7, 14 **b** 0.25
  c 0.7 or –2.7 **e** (1.1, 2.6) and (–2.6, 0.7)
5 a Values of y: 18, 12, 8, 6, 6, 8, 12 **b** 9.75 **c** 2 or –1
  d Values of y: 14, 9, 6, 5, 6, 9, 14 **e** (1, 6)
6 a Values of y: 4, 1, 0, 1, 4, 9, 16 **b** 7.3 **c** 0.4 or –2.4
  e (1, 4) and (–1, 0)
7 a Values of y: 15, 9, 4, 0, –3, –5, –6, –6, –5, –3, 0, 4, 9
  b –0.5 and 3

Exercise 8B

1 a Values of y: 12, 5, 0, –3, –4, –3, 0, 5, 12 **b** 2 and –2
2 a Values of y: 7, 0, –5, –8, –9, –8, –5, 0, 7 **b** 3 and –3
3 c Values of y: 15, 8, 3, 0, –1, 0, 3, 8, 15
  d Values of y: 11, 4, –1, –4, –5, –4, –1, 4, 11
  e 1 and –1, 2.2 and –2.2
4 a Values of y: 5, 0, –3, –4, –3, 0, 5, 12 **b** –4 and 0
5 a Values of y: 16, 7, 0, –5, –8, –9, –8, –5, 0, 7, 16
  b 0 and 6
6 a Values of y: 10, 4, 0, –2, –2, 0, 4, 10, 18 **b** –3 and 0
7 c Values of y: 10, 4, 0, –2, –2, 0, 4, 10
  d Values of y: 6, 0, –4, –6, –6, –4, 0, 6, 14
  e 0 and 3, –5 and 0
8 a Values of y: 9, 4, 1, 0, 1, 4, 9 **b** +2 **c** Only 1 root
9 a Values of y: 10, 3, –2, –5, –6, –5, –2, 3, 10
  b 0.6 and 5.4

10 a Values of y: 19, 6, –3, –8, –9, –6, 1, 12 **b** 0.9 and –3.4
11 a –4, –9, –1, –5, 0, 0, 0, 0, 0, 0
  b (0, –4), (0, –9), (0, –1), (0, –5), (–2, –4), (3, –9), (–1.5, –2.25),
    (1.5, –2.25), (–2.5, –6.25)
12 a $y = (x - 2)^2$ **b** 0
13 a $y = (x - 3)^2 - 6$ **b** –6
14 a $y = (x - 4)^2 - 14$ **b** –14
15 a $y = -(x - 1)^2 - 5$ **b** –5

Exercise 8C

1 a i –1.4, 4.4 **ii** –2, 5 **iii** –0.6, 3.6 **b** 2.6, 0.4
2 a –5, 1 **b i** –5.3, 1.3 **ii** –4.8, 0.8 **iii** –3.4, –0.6
3 a i 0, 6 **ii** 4.3, 0.7 **b i** 4.8, 0.2 **ii** 5.4, –0.4
4 a i –1.6, 2.6 **ii** 1.4, –1.4 **b i** 2.3, –2.3 **ii** 2, –2
5 a 0, 2 **b** 2.5 **c** –0.6, 1, 1.6 **d** 2.8 **e** –0.8, 0.6, 2.2

6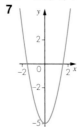
a –0.4, 4.4
b –1, 5

7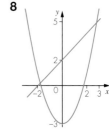
a 1.6, –1.6
b –1.2, 1.2

8
a 2.2, –2.2
b –1.8, 2.8

9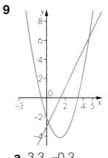
a 3.3, –0.3
b 4.8, 0.2

10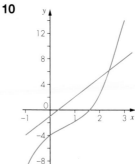
a 2 **b** 2.5

Quick check

1 a 25 **b** 9 **c** 27 **d** 4 **2 a** 48 **b** $\frac{1}{2}$

3 i 2 **ii** 28 **iii** 40 **iv** 30

Exercise 9A

1 a 15 **b** 2
2 a 75 **b** 6
3 a 150 **b** 6
4 a 22.5 **b** 12
5 a 175 miles **b** 8 hours
6 a £66.50 **b** 175 kg
7 a 44 **b** 84 m^2

Exercise 9B

1 a 100 **b** 10
2 a 27 **b** 5
3 a 56 **b** 1.69
4 a 192 **b** 2.25

5 a 25.6 **b** 5
6 a £50 **b** 225
7 a 3.2 °C **b** 10 atm
8 a 388.8 g **b** 3 mm
9 a 2 J **b** 40 m/s
10 a £78 **b** 400 miles

Exercise 9C

1 $Tm = 12$ **a** 3 **b** 2.5
2 $Wx = 60$ **a** 20 **b** 6
3 $Q(5 - t) = 16$ **a** −3.2 **b** 4
4 $Mt^2 = 36$ **a** 4 **b** 5
5 $W\sqrt{T} = 24$ **a** 4.8 **b** 100
6 $gp = 1800$ **a** £15 **b** 36
7 $td = 24$ **a** 3 °C **b** 12 km
8 $ds^2 = 432$ **a** 1.92 km **b** 8 m/s
9 $p\sqrt{h} = 7.2$ **c** 2.4 atm **b** 100 m
10 $W\sqrt{F} = 0.5$ **a** 5 t/h **b** 0.58 t/h

Quick check

1 a 6370 **b** 6400 **c** 6000

2 a 2.4 **b** 2.39

3 a 50 **b** 47.3

Exercise 10A

1 a $6.5 \leqslant 7 < 7.5$ **b** $115 \leqslant 120 < 125$
c $3350 \leqslant 3400 < 3450$ **d** $49.5 \leqslant 50 < 50.5$
e $5.50 \leqslant 6 < 6.49$ **f** $16.75 \leqslant 16.8 < 16.85$
g $15.5 \leqslant 16 < 16.5$ **h** $14\,450 \leqslant 14\,500 < 14\,549$
i $54.5 \leqslant 55 < 55.5$ **j** $52.5 \leqslant 55 < 57.5$
2 a $5.5 \leqslant 6 < 6.5$ **b** $16.5 \leqslant 17 < 17.5$
c $31.5 \leqslant 32 < 32.5$ **d** $237.5 \leqslant 238 < 238.5$
e $7.25 \leqslant 7.3 < 7.35$ **f** $25.75 \leqslant 25.8 < 25.85$
g $3.35 \leqslant 3.4 < 3.45$ **h** $86.5 \leqslant 87 < 87.5$
i $4.225 \leqslant 4.23 < 4.235$ **j** $2.185 \leqslant 2.19 < 2.195$
k $12.665 \leqslant 12.67 < 12.675$ **l** $24.5 \leqslant 25 < 25.5$
m $35 \leqslant 40 < 45$ **n** $595 \leqslant 600 < 605$
o $25 \leqslant 30 < 35$ **p** $995 \leqslant 1000 < 1050$
q $3.95 \leqslant 4.0 < 4.05$ **r** $7.035 \leqslant 7.04 < 7.045$
s $11.95 \leqslant 12.0 < 12.05$ **t** $6.995 \leqslant 7.00 < 7.005$

Exercise 10B

1 a 7.5, 8.5 **b** 25.5, 26.5 **c** 24.5, 25.5
d 84.5, 85.5 **e** 2.395, 2.405 **f** 0.15, 0.25
g 0.055, 0.065 **h** 250 g, 350 g **i** 0.65, 0.75
j 365.5, 366.5 **k** 165, 175 **l** 205, 215
2 a <65.5 g **b** 64.5 g **c** <2620 g **d** 2580 g

Exercise 10C

1 a 38.25 cm^2 $\leqslant$ area < 52.25 cm^2
b 37.1575 cm^2 $\leqslant$ area < 38.4475 cm^2
c 135.625 cm^2 $\leqslant$ area < 145.225 cm^2
2 a 5.5 m $\leqslant$ length < 6.5 m, 3.5 m $\leqslant$ width < 4.5 m
b 29.25 m^2 **c** 18 m
3 79.75 m^2 $\leqslant$ area < 100.75 m^2
4 216.125 m^3 $\leqslant$ volume < 354.375 m^3
5 20.9 m $\leqslant$ length < 22.9 m (3 sf)
6 16.4 cm^2 $\leqslant$ area < 21.7 cm^2 (3 sf)
7 a i 64.1 cm^3 $\leqslant$ volume < 69.6 cm^3 (3 sf)
ii £22 569 $\leqslant$ price < £24 506 (nearest £)
b 23 643 $\leqslant$ price < £23 661 (nearest £)
c Errors in length are compounded by being used 3 times in **a**, but errors in weight are only used once in **b**.
8 a 14.65 s $\leqslant$ time < 14.75 s
b 99.5 m $\leqslant$ length < 100.5 m
c 6.86 m/s (3 sf)
9 a +2.53% (3 sf) **b** +3.82% (3 sf)
10 3.41 cm $\leqslant$ length < 3.43 cm (3 sf)
11 5.80 cm $\leqslant$ length < 5.90 cm (3 sf)
12 14 s $\leqslant$ time < 30 s

Quick check

1 a 90 mm^2 **b** 40 cm^2 **c** 21 m^2

2 120 cm^3

Exercise 11A

1 a 8 cm, 25.1 cm, 50.3 cm^2 **b** 5.2 m, 16.3 m, 21.2 m^2
   c 6 cm, 37.7 cm, 113 cm^2 **d** 1.6 m, 10.1 m, 8.04 m^2
2 a 5π cm   **b** 8π cm   **c** 18π m   **d** 12π cm
3 a 25π cm^2 **b** 36π cm^2 **c** 100π cm^2 **d** 0.25π m^2
4 8.80 m
5 a 440 cm   **b** 4
6 1p : 3.1 cm^2, 2p : 5.3 cm^2, 5p : 2.3 cm^2, 10p : 4.5 cm^2
7 7.96 cm
8 38.6 cm
9 (14π + 14) cm
10 a 18π cm^2 **b** 4π cm^2 **c** 48π cm^2
11 a 16π m^2 **b** 21π cm^2 **c** 9π cm^2
12 a Sue 62.8 cm, Julie 69.1 cm, Dave 75.4 cm, Brian 81.7 cm
   b the difference between the distances round the waists of
     two people is 2π times the difference between their radii
   c 6.28 m

Exercise 11B

1 a 30 cm^2 **b** 77 cm^2 **c** 24 cm^2 **d** 42 cm^2
   e 40 m^2 **f** 6 cm   **g** 3 cm   **h** 10 cm
2 a 27.5 cm, 36.25 cm^2 **b** 33.4 cm, 61.2 cm^2
   c 38.5 m, 90 m^2
3 a 57 m^2 **b** 702.5 cm^2 **c** 84 m^2
4 a 47 m^2 **b** 51 m^2 **c** 86 m^2
5 Any five pairs of lengths that add up to 10 cm.
   For example: 1 cm, 9 cm; 2 cm, 8 cm; 3 cm, 7 cm; 4
   cm, 6 cm; 4.5 cm, 5.5 cm
6 80.2%   **7** 1 100 000 km^2

Exercise 11C

1 a i 5.59 cm   **ii** 22.3 cm^2
   b i 8.29 cm   **ii** 20.7 cm^2
   c i 16.3 cm   **ii** 98.0 cm^2
   d i 15.9 cm   **ii** 55.6 cm^2
2 2π cm, 6π cm^2
3 a 73.8 cm   **b** 20.3 cm
4 a 107 cm^2 **b** 173 cm^2 **c** 18.8 cm^2 **d** 34.9 cm^2
5 (36π − 72) cm^2 **6** 36.5 cm^2 **7** 6π cm
8 i 13.9 cm   **ii** 7.07 cm^2

Exercise 11D

1 i a 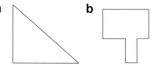   **b**   **c**

   ii a 21 cm^2 **b** 48 cm^2 **c** 36 m^2
   iii a 63 cm^3 **b** 432 cm^3 **c** 324 m^3

2 a 432 m^3 **b** 225 m^3 **c** 1332 m^3
3 525 000 litres   **4** 7650 litres
5 a 21 cm^3, 210 cm^3 **b** 54 cm^2, 270 cm^2
6 146 cm^3 **7** 19 600 m^3
8 327 litres   **9** 1.02 tonnes

Exercise 11E

1 a i 226 cm^3 **ii** 207 cm^2
   b i 14.9 cm^3 **ii** 61.3 cm^2
   c i 346 cm^3 **ii** 275 cm^2
   d i 1060 cm^3 **ii** 636 cm^2
2 a i 72π cm^3 **ii** 48π cm^2
   b i 112π cm^3 **ii** 56π cm^2
   c i 180π cm^3 **ii** 60π cm^2
   d i 600π m^3 **ii** 120π m^2
3 £80   **4** 1.23 tonnes
5 5 cm   **6** 10 cm
7 3 cm   **8** 332 litres
9 1.71 g/cm^3 **10** 7.78 g/cm^3
11 905 g

Exercise 11F

1 a 56 cm^3 **b** 168 cm^3 **c** 1040 cm^3
   d 84 cm^3 **e** 160 cm^3
2 270 cm^3
3 a 73.3 m^3 **b** 45 m^3 **c** 3250 cm^3
4 208 g
5 1.5 g/cm^3
6 a 202 g   **b** 441 g   **c** 47.25 g
7 a 9 cm   **b** 6 cm
8 260 cm^3

Exercise 11G

1 a i 3560 cm^3 **ii** 1430 cm^2
   b i 314 cm^3 **ii** 283 cm^2
   c i 1020 cm^3 **ii** 679 cm^2
2 935 g
3 24π cm^2
4 283 cm^2
5 a 816π cm^3 **b** 720π mm^3
6 140 g
7 2.81 cm

Exercise 11H

1 a 36π cm^3 **b** 288π cm^3 **c** 1330π cm^3
2 a 36π cm^2 **b** 100π cm^2 **c** 196π cm^2
3 65 400 cm^3, 7850 cm^2
4 i 1960 cm^2 **ii** 8180 cm^3
5 125 cm
6 6231
7 a 3.5 cm   **b** 3.3 cm

Quick check

1 5.3   **2** 246.5

3 0.6   **4** 2.8

5 16.1   **6** 0.7

Exercise 12A

1 10.3 cm   **2** 5.9 cm

3 8.5 cm   **4** 20.6 cm

5 18.6 cm   **6** 17.5 cm

7 5 cm   **8** 13 cm

9 10 cm

Exercise 12B

1 a 15 cm   **b** 14.7 cm   **c** 6.3 cm   **d** 18.3 cm

2 a 20.8 m   **b** 15.5 cm   **c** 15.5 m   **d** 12.4 cm

3 a 5 m   **b** 6 m   **c** 3 m   **d** 50 cm

Exercise 12C

1 6.63 m   **2** 2.06 m

3 11.3 m   **4** 19.2 km

5 a 127 m   **b** 99.6 m   **c** 27.4 m

6 4.58 m

7 a 3.87 m   **b** 1.74 m

8 3.16 m   **9** 13 units

10 a 4.74 m   **b** 4.54 m

11 16.5 cm^2 **12** 12.1 m

13 $25^2 = 24^2 + 7^2$: therefore, right-angled

14 7.21 units

Exercise 12D

1 a 32.2 cm^2 **b** 2.83 cm^2 **c** 50.0 cm^2

2 22.2 cm^2

3 15.6 cm^2

4 a

b The areas are 12 cm^2 and 13.6 cm^2 respectively, so triangle with 6 cm, 6 cm, 5 cm sides has the greater area

5 a   **b** 166.3 cm^2

6 259.8 cm^2

7 a 10 cm   **b** 26 cm   **c** 9.6 cm

Exercise 12E

1 a i 14.4 cm   **ii** 13 cm   **iii** 9.4 cm   **b** 15.2 cm

2 No, 6.6 m is longest length

3 a 24 cm and 20.6 cm   **b** 15.0 cm

4 21.3 cm

5 a 8.49 m   **b** 9 m

6 a 11.3 cm   **b** 7 cm   **c** 8.06 cm

7 a 50.0 cm   **b** 54.8 cm   **c** 48.3 cm   **d** 27.0 cm

Exercise 12F

1 a 0.682   **b** 0.829   **c** 0.922   **d** 1   **e** 0.707

   f 0.342   **g** 0.375   **h** 0

2 a 0.731   **b** 0.559   **c** 0.388   **d** 0   **e** 0.707

   f 0.940   **g** 0.927   **h** 1

3 45°

4 a i 0.574   **ii** 0.574   **b i** 0.208   **ii** 0.208

   c i 0.391   **ii** 0.391   **d** Same

   e i sin 15° is the same as cos 75°

      ii cos 82° is the same as sin 8°

      iii sin x is the same as cos (90° − x)

5 a 0.933   **b** 1.48   **c** 2.38   **d** Infinite   **e** 1

   f 0.364   **g** 0.404   **h** 0

6 a 0.956   **b** 0.899   **c** 2.16   **d** 0.999

   e 0.819   **f** 0.577   **g** 0.469   **h** 0.996

7 Has values > 1

8 a 4.53   **b** 4.46   **c** 6   **d** 0

9 a 10.7   **b** 5.40   **c** Infinite   **d** 0

10 a 3.56   **b** 8.96   **c** 28.4   **d** 8.91

11 a 5.61   **b** 7.08   **c** 6   **d** 10

12 a 1.46   **b** 7.77   **c** 0.087   **d** 7.15

13 a 7.73   **b** 48.6   **c** 2.28   **d** 15.2

14 a 29.9   **b** 44.8   **c** 20.3   **d** 2.38

15 a $\frac{4}{5}, \frac{3}{5}, \frac{4}{3}$ **b** $\frac{5}{13}, \frac{12}{13}, \frac{5}{12}$ **c** $\frac{7}{25}, \frac{24}{25}, \frac{7}{24}$

Exercise 12G

1 a 30°   **b** 51.7°   **c** 39.8°   **d** 61.3°

   e 87.4°   **f** 45.0°

2 a 60°   **b** 50.2°   **c** 2.6°   **d** 45.0

   e 78.5°   **f** 45.6°

3 a 31.0°   **b** 20.8°   **c** 41.8°   **d** 46.4°

   e 69.5°   **f** 77.1°

4 a 53.1°   **b** 41.8°   **c** 44.4°   **d** 56.4°

   e 2.4°   **f** 22.6°

5 a 36.9°   **b** 48.2°   **c** 45.6°   **d** 33.6°

   e 87.6°   **f** 67.4°

6 a 31.0°   **b** 37.9°   **c** 15.9°   **d** 60.9°

   e 57.5°   **f** 50.2°

7 Error message, largest value 1, smallest value −1

8 a i 17.5°   **ii** 72.5°   **iii** 90°   **b** Yes

Exercise 12H

1 a 17.5°   **b** 22.0°   **c** 32.2°

2 a 5.29 cm   **b** 5.75 cm   **c** 13.2 cm

3 a 4.57 cm   **b** 6.86 cm   **c** 100 cm

4 a 5.12 cm   **b** 9.77 cm   **c** 11.7 cm   **d** 15.5 cm

5 a 47.2°   **b** 5.42 cm   **c** 13.7 cm   **d** 38.0°

6 a 6   **b** 15   **c** 30

Exercise 12I

1 a 51.3°   **b** 75.5°   **c** 51.3°

2 a 6.47 cm   **b** 32.6 cm   **c** 137 cm

3 a 7.32 cm **b** 39.1 cm **c** 135 cm
4 a 5.35 cm **b** 14.8 cm **c** 12.0 cm **d** 8.62 cm
5 a 5.59 cm **b** 46.6° **c** 9.91 cm **d** 40.1°
6 a 10 **b** 39 **c** 2.5

Exercise 12J
1 a 33.7° **b** 36.9° **c** 52.1°
2 a 5.09 cm **b** 30.4 cm **c** 1120 cm
3 a 8.24 cm **b** 62.0 cm **c** 72.8 cm
4 a 9.02 cm **b** 7.51 cm **c** 7.14 cm **d** 8.90 cm
5 a 13.7 cm **b** 48.4° **c** 7.03 cm **d** 41.2°
6 12, 12, 2

Exercise 12K
1 a 12.6 **b** 59.6 **c** 74.7 **d** 16.0 **e** 67.9 **f** 20.1
2 a 44.4° **b** 39.8° **c** 44.4° **d** 49.5°
  e 58.7° **f** 38.7°
3 a 67.4° **b** 11.3 **c** 134 **d** 28.1° **e** 39.7
  f 263 **g** 50.2° **h** 51.3° **i** 138 **j** 22.8
4 b $\sin\theta \div \cos\theta = \frac{b}{c} \div \frac{a}{c} = \frac{b}{a} = \tan\theta$

Exercise 12L
1 a 65° **2** 2.05–3.00 m
3 44° **4** 6.82 m

5 31° **6 a** 25° **b** 2.10 m
7 a 20° **b** 4.78 m **8** 42.4 m
9 21.1 m **10 a** 4 **b** $\frac{4}{5}, \frac{3}{4}$ **c i** 1.5 **ii** 20 **iii** 30

Exercise 12M
1 10.1 km **2** 22°
3 429 m **4** 156 m
5 a 222 m **b** 42° **6 a** 21.5 m **b** 17.8 m
7 13.4 m **8** 19°

Exercise 12N
1 a 73.4 km **b** 15.6 km
2 a 14.7 miles **b** 8.5 miles
3 120° **4 a** 59.4 km **b** 8.4 km
5 a 15.9 km **b** 24.1 km **c** 31.2 km **d** 052°
6 2.28 km
7 a 66.2 km **b** 11.7 km **c** 13.1 km **d** 170°
8 48.4 km, 100°

Exercise 12P
1 5.79 cm **2** 48.2° **3** 7.42 cm **4** 81.6 cm **5** 9.86 m
6 a 36.4 cm^2 **b** 115 cm^2 **c** 90.6 cm^2 **d** 160 cm^2

ANSWERS TO CHAPTER 13

Quick check
1 $a = 50°$
2 $b = 140°$
3 $c = d = 65°$

Exercise 13A
1 $a = b = 70°, c = 50°, d = 80°, e = 55°, f = 70°,$
  $g = h = 57.5°$

2

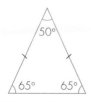

3 a $a = 110°, b = 55°$ **b** $c = e = 105°, d = 75°$
  c $f = 135°, g = 25°$ **d** $e = f = 94°$
  e $f = l = 105°, k = 75°$ **f** $m = o = 49°, n = 131°$
4 40°, 40°, 100°
5 $a = b = 65°, c = d = 115°, e = f = 65°, g = 80°,$
  $h = 60°, i = 60°, j = 60°, k = 20°$
6 a $x = 25°, y = 15°$ **b** $x = 7°, y = 31°$
  c $x = 60°, y = 30°$
7 a $x = 50°$: 60°, 70°, 120°, 110° – possibly trapezium
  b $x = 60°$: 50°, 130°, 50°, 130° – parallelogram or
    isosceles trapezium

c $x = 30°$: 20°, 60°, 140°, 140° – possibly kite
d $x = 20°$: 90°, 90°, 90°, 90° – square or rectangle

Exercise 13B
1 a 1440° **b** 2340° **c** 17 640° **d** 7740°
2 a 150° **b** 162° **c** 140° **d** 174°
3 a 9 **b** 15 **c** 102 **d** 50
4 a 15 **b** 36 **c** 24 **d** 72
5 a 12 **b** 9 **c** 20 **d** 40
6 a 130° **b** 95° **c** 130°
7 a 50° **b** 40° **c** 59°
8 Hexagon
9 a Octagon **b** 89°
10 a i 71° **ii** 109° **iii** Equal
  b If S = sum of the two opposite interior angles,
    then $S + I = 180$ (angles in a triangle), and we know E
    $+ I = 180$ (angles on a straight line),
    so $S + I = E + I$, therefore $S = E$

Exercise 13C
1 a 56° **b** 62° **c** 105° **d** 55° **e** 45°
  f 30° **g** 60° **h** 145°
2 a 55° **b** 52° **c** 50° **d** 24° **e** 39°
  f 80° **g** 34° **h** 30°
3 a 41° **b** 49° **c** 41°
4 a 72° **b** 37° **c** 72°
5 a $x = y = 40°$ **b** $x = 131°, y = 111°$
  c $x = 134°, y = 23°$ **d** $x = 32°, y = 19°$

e $x = 59°$, $y = 121°$ **f** $x = 155°$, $y = 12.5°$

6 $68°$

7 a x **b** $2x$

  c $\angle ABC = (x + y)$ and $\angle AOC = 2(x + y)$

Exercise 13D

1 a $a = 50°$, $b = 95°$ **b** $c = 92°$, $x = 90°$

  c $d = 110°$, $e = 110°$, $f = 70°$

  d $g = 105°$, $h = 99°$ **e** $j = 89°$, $k = 89°$, $l = 91°$

  f $m = 120°$, $n = 40°$ **g** $p = 44°$, $q = 68°$

  h $x = 40°$, $y = 34°$

2 a $x = 26°$, $y = 128°$ **b** $x = 48°$, $y = 78°$

  c $x = 133°$, $y = 47°$ **d** $x = 36°$, $y = 72°$

  e $x = 55°$, $y = 125°$ **f** $x = 35°$

  g $x = 48°$, $y = 45°$ **h** $x = 66°$, $y = 52°$

3 a $x = 49°$, $y = 49°$ **b** $x = 70°$, $y = 20°$

  c $x = 80°$, $y = 100°$ **d** $x = 100°$, $y = 75°$

4 a $x = 50°$, $y = 62°$ **b** $x = 92°$, $y = 88°$

  c $x = 93°$, $y = 42°$ **d** $x = 55°$, $y = 75°$

5 a $x = 95°$, $y = 138°$ **b** $x = 14°$, $y = 62°$

  c $x = 32°$, $y = 48°$ **d** $52°$

6 a $71°$ **b** $125.5°$ **c** $54.5°$

7 a x **b** $360° - 2x$

  c $\angle ADC = \frac{1}{2}$ reflex $\angle AOC = 180° - x$,

  so $\angle ADC + \angle ABC = 180°$

Exercise 13E

1 a $38°$ **b** $110°$ **c** $15°$ **d** $45°$

2 a 6 cm   **b** 10.8 cm   **c** 3.21 cm   **d** 8 cm

3 a $x = 12°$, $y = 156°$ **b** $x = 100°$, $y = 50°$

  c $x = 62°$, $y = 28°$ **d** $x = 30°$, $y = 60°$

4 a $62°$ **b** $66°$ **c** $19°$ **d** $20°$

5 19.5 cm

6 a $\angle AOB = \cos^{-1}\dfrac{OA}{OB} = \cos^{-1}\dfrac{OC}{OB} = \angle COB$

  b As $\angle AOB = \angle COB$, so $\angle ABO = \angle CBO$, so OB bisects $\angle ABC$

Exercise 13F

1 a $a = 65°$, $b = 75°$, $c = 40°$

  b $d = 79°$, $e = 58°$, $f = 43°$

  c $g = 41°$, $h = 76°$, $i = 76°$

  d $k = 80°$, $m = 52°$, $n = 80°$

2 a $a = 75°$, $b = 75°$, $c = 75°$, $d = 30°$

  b $a = 47°$, $b = 86°$, $c = 86°$, $d = 47°$

  c $a = 53°$, $b = 53°$ **d** $a = 55°$

3 a $36°$ **b** $70°$

4 a $x = 25°$ **b** $x = 46°$, $y = 69°$, $z = 65°$

  c $x = 38°$, $y = 70°$, $z = 20°$ **d** $x = 48°$, $y = 42°$

5 a $2x$ **b** $90° - x$ **c** $\angle OPT = 90°$, so $\angle APT = x$

ANSWERS TO CHAPTER 14

Quick check

Trace shape **a** and check whether it fits exactly on top of the others. You should find that shape **b** is not congruent to the others.

Exercise 14A

1 a Yes, SAS   **b** Yes, SSS   **c** No   **d** No

  e Yes, ASA   **f** Yes, RHS   **g** Yes, SSS

  h Yes, ASA

2 a Yes, SSS. A to R, B to P, C to Q   **b** No

  c Yes, SAS. A to R, B to Q, C to P   **d** No

3 i $60°$ **ii** $80°$ **iii** $40°$ **iv** 5 cm

4 i $110°$ **ii** $55°$ **iii** $85°$ **iv** $110°$ **v** 4 cm

5 SSS or RHS

6 SSS or SAS or RHS

Exercise 14B

1 a i $\begin{pmatrix} 1 \\ 3 \end{pmatrix}$ **ii** $\begin{pmatrix} 4 \\ 2 \end{pmatrix}$ **iii** $\begin{pmatrix} 2 \\ -1 \end{pmatrix}$ **iv** $\begin{pmatrix} 5 \\ 1 \end{pmatrix}$

  v $\begin{pmatrix} -1 \\ 6 \end{pmatrix}$ **vi** $\begin{pmatrix} 4 \\ 6 \end{pmatrix}$

 b i $\begin{pmatrix} -1 \\ -3 \end{pmatrix}$ **ii** $\begin{pmatrix} 3 \\ -1 \end{pmatrix}$ **iii** $\begin{pmatrix} 1 \\ -4 \end{pmatrix}$ **iv** $\begin{pmatrix} 4 \\ -2 \end{pmatrix}$

  v $\begin{pmatrix} -2 \\ 3 \end{pmatrix}$ **vi** $\begin{pmatrix} 3 \\ 3 \end{pmatrix}$

 c i $\begin{pmatrix} -4 \\ -2 \end{pmatrix}$ **ii** $\begin{pmatrix} -3 \\ 1 \end{pmatrix}$ **iii** $\begin{pmatrix} -2 \\ -3 \end{pmatrix}$ **iv** $\begin{pmatrix} 1 \\ -1 \end{pmatrix}$

  v $\begin{pmatrix} -5 \\ 4 \end{pmatrix}$ **vi** $\begin{pmatrix} 0 \\ 4 \end{pmatrix}$

 d i $\begin{pmatrix} 3 \\ 2 \end{pmatrix}$ **ii** $\begin{pmatrix} -4 \\ 2 \end{pmatrix}$ **iii** $\begin{pmatrix} 5 \\ -4 \end{pmatrix}$ **iv** $\begin{pmatrix} -2 \\ -7 \end{pmatrix}$

  v $\begin{pmatrix} 5 \\ 0 \end{pmatrix}$ **vi** $\begin{pmatrix} 1 \\ -5 \end{pmatrix}$

2

3 a $\begin{pmatrix} -3 \\ -1 \end{pmatrix}$ **b** $\begin{pmatrix} 4 \\ -4 \end{pmatrix}$ **c** $\begin{pmatrix} -5 \\ -2 \end{pmatrix}$ **d** $\begin{pmatrix} 4 \\ 7 \end{pmatrix}$ **e** $\begin{pmatrix} -1 \\ 5 \end{pmatrix}$

  f $\begin{pmatrix} 1 \\ 6 \end{pmatrix}$ **g** $\begin{pmatrix} -4 \\ 4 \end{pmatrix}$ **h** $\begin{pmatrix} -4 \\ -7 \end{pmatrix}$

4 $10 \times 10 = 100$ (including $\begin{pmatrix} 0 \\ 0 \end{pmatrix}$)

Exercise 14C

1

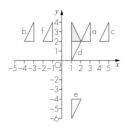

2 a–e

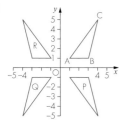

f Reflection in the y-axis

3 b A'(2, −1), B'(5, 0), C'(−3, −3), D'(3, 2)
 c y-value changes sign **d** (a, −b)

4 b A'(−2, 1), B'(0, 5), C'(−3, −2), D'(4, −3)
 c x-value changes sign **d** (−a, b)

5

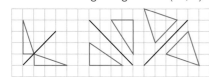

6 a–i

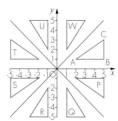

7

j A reflection in y = x

8 c A'(1, 2), B'(0, 5), C'(2, −3), D'(−4, −2)
 d Coordinates are reversed: x becomes y and
  y becomes x **e** (b, a)

9 c A'(−1, −2), B'(−5, 0), C'(2, −3) D'(3, 4)
 d Coordinates are reversed and change sign,
  x becomes −y and y becomes −x **e** (−b, −a)

Exercise 14D

1 a

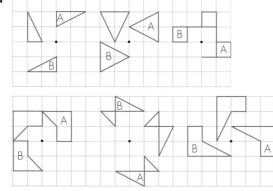

 b i Rotation 90° anticlockwise **ii** Rotation 180°

2

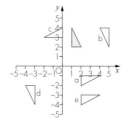

3 a 90° anticlockwise
 b 270° anticlockwise
 c 300° clockwise
 d 260° clockwise

4 c ii A'(2, −1), B'(4, −2), C'(1, −4)
 c iii Original coordinates (x, y) become (y, −x) **iv** Yes
5 ii A'(−1, −2), B'(−2, −4), C'(−4, −1)
 iii Original coordinates (x, y) become (−x, −y) **iv** Yes
6 ii A'(−2, 1), B'(−4, 2), C'(−1, 4)
 iii Original coordinates (x, y) become (−y, x) **iv** Yes
7 Show by drawing a shape or use the fact that (a, b)
 becomes (a, −b) after reflection in the x-axis, and
 (a, −b) becomes (−a, −b) after reflection in the y-axis,
 which is equivalent to a single rotation of 180°
8 Show by drawing a shape or use the fact that (a, b)
 becomes (b, a) after reflection in the line y = x, and (b, a)
 becomes (−a, −b) after reflection in the line
 y = −x, which is equivalent to a single rotation of 180°

9 a

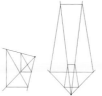

 b i Rotation 60° clockwise about O
  ii Rotation 120° clockwise about O
  iii Rotation 180° about O
  iv Rotation 240° clockwise about O
 c i Rotation 60° clockwise about O
  ii Rotation 180° about O

Exercise 14E

1

2 d All shapes are the same.

3

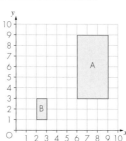

4 a

 b 3:1
 c 3:1
 d 9:1

5 a–c

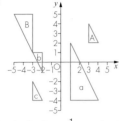

d Scale factor $-\frac{1}{2}$, centre (1, 3)
e Scale factor -2, centre (1, 3)
f Scale factor -1, centre (-2.5, -1.5)
g Scale factor -1, centre (-2.5, -1.5)
h Same centres, and the scale factor are reciprocals of each other

Exercise 14F

1 A translation $\begin{pmatrix} 1 \\ -2 \end{pmatrix}$, B reflection in y-axis,
C rotation 90° clockwise about (0, 0),
D reflection in $x = 3$, E reflection in $y = 4$,
F enlargement by scale factor 2, centre (0, 1)

2 a T_1 to T_2: rotation 90° clockwise about (0, 0)
b T_1 to T_6: rotation 90° anticlockwise about (0, 0)
c T_2 to T_3: translation $\begin{pmatrix} 2 \\ 2 \end{pmatrix}$

d T_6 to T_2: rotation 180° about (0, 0)
e T_6 to T_5: reflection in y-axis
f T_5 to T_4: translation $\begin{pmatrix} 4 \\ 0 \end{pmatrix}$

3 a–d

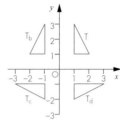

e T_d to T: rotation 90° anticlockwise about (0,0)

4 (-4, -3)
5 a (-5, 2) **b** Reflection in y-axis
6 (3, 1)

7 Reflection in x-axis, translation $\begin{pmatrix} 0 \\ -5 \end{pmatrix}$,
rotation 90° clockwise about (0, 0)

8 Translation $\begin{pmatrix} 0 \\ -8 \end{pmatrix}$, reflection in x-axis,
rotation 90° clockwise about (0, 0)

9 Rotation 180° clockwise or anticlockwise about (0, 0)

ANSWERS TO CHAPTER 15

Exercise 15B

4 a i Construct 60° angle and bisect it
ii Bisect 30° angle
iii Construct 90° angle and bisect it to get 45°, then bisect 45° angle
iv Construct 45° angle on upper arm of 30° angle

8 b AC = 5.1 cm, BC = 6.3 cm
9 b PR = 5.9 cm, RQ = 4.1 cm

Exercise 15C

1 a Circle with radius 2 cm **b** Circle with radius 4 cm
c Circle with radius 5 cm

2 a **b**

c

3 Circle with radius 4 m **4**

5 a b c d e f

6

7

Exercise 15D

1 2

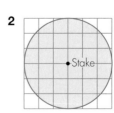

3

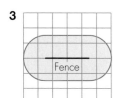

4

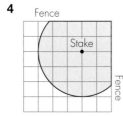

5

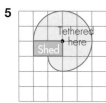

6

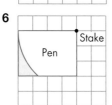

7

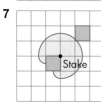

8 a Sketch should show a circle of radius 6 cm around London and one of radius 4cm around Glasgow.
  b No   **c** Yes

9 a Yes
  b Sketch should show a circle of radius 4 cm around Leeds and one of radius 4cm around Exeter. The area where they overlap should be shaded.

10 a This is the perpendicular bisector of the line from York to Birmingham. It should pass just below Manchester and just through the top of Norwich.

b Sketch should show a circle of radius 7cm around Glasgow and one of radius 5 cm around London.
c The transmitter can be built anywhere on line constructed in part **a** that is within the area shown in part **b**.

11 Sketch should show two circles around Birmingham, one of radius 3 cm and one of radius 5cm. The area of good reception is the area between the two circles.

12 Sketch should show a circle of radius 6 cm around Glasgow, 2 circles around York, one of radius 4 cm and one of radius 6 cm and a circle around London of radius 8 cm. The small area in the Irish sea that is between the 2 circles around York and inside both the circle around Glasgow and the circle around London is where the boat can be.

13 Sketch should show 2 circles around Newcastle upon Tyne, one of radius 4 cm and one of radius 6 cm, and two circles around Bristol, one of radius 3 cm and one of radius 5 cm. The area that is between both pairs of circles is the area that should be shaded.

14 Sketch should show the perpendicular bisector of the line running from Newcastle upon Tyne to Manchester and that of the line running from Sheffield to Norwich. Where the lines cross is where the oil rig is located.

15 Sketch should show the perpendicular bisector of the line running from Glasgow to Norwich and that of the line running from Norwich to Exeter. Where the lines cross is where Fred's house is.

16 Sketch should show the bisectors of the angles made by the piers and the sea wall at points A and B. These are the paths of each boat.

ANSWERS TO CHAPTER 16

Quick check

1 Triangles a, c and d are congruent to the triangle in the question

2 a 28   **b** 14

Exercise 16A

1 2, 3
2 a Yes, 4
  b No, corresponding sides have different ratios
3 a PQR is an enlargement of ABC   **b** 1 : 3
  c Angle R   **d** BA
4 a Sides in same ratio **b** Angle P **c** PR
5 a Same angles **b** Angle Q **c** AR
6 a 8 cm **b** 7.5 cm **c** $x = 6.67$ cm, $y = 13.5$ cm
  d $x = 24$ cm, $y = 13$ cm **e** AB = 10 cm, PQ = 6 cm
  f 4.2 cm
7 a Sides in same ratio **b** 1 : 3 **c** 13 cm **d** 39 cm
8 4.8 m

Exercise 16B

1 a 9 cm **b** 12 cm
2 a 5 cm **b** 5 cm **c** $x = 60$ cm, $y = 75$ cm
  d $x = 45$ cm, $y = 60$ cm **e** DC = 10 cm, EB = 8 cm
3 82 m   **4** 220 feet   **5** 15 m
6 3.09 m   **7** 6 m

Exercise 16C

1 5 cm   **2** 6 cm
3 10 cm   **4** $x = 6$ cm, $y = 7.5$ cm
5 $x = 15$ cm, $y = 21$ cm **6** $x = 3$ cm, $y = 2.4$ cm

Exercise 16D

1 a 4 : 25 **b** 8 : 125
2 a 16 : 49 **b** 64 : 343
3 Linear scale factor 2, 3, $\frac{1}{4}$, 5, $\frac{1}{10}$, 7, $\frac{1}{5}$, $\frac{1}{2}$;
  linear ratio 1 : 2, 1 : 3, 4 : 1, 1 : 5, 10 : 1, 1 : 7, 5 : 1, 2 : 1;
  linear fraction $\frac{2}{1}$, $\frac{3}{1}$, $\frac{1}{4}$, $\frac{5}{1}$, $\frac{1}{10}$, $\frac{7}{1}$, $\frac{1}{5}$, $\frac{1}{2}$; area scale factor 4, 9, $\frac{1}{16}$, 25, $\frac{1}{100}$, 49, $\frac{1}{25}$, $\frac{1}{4}$; volume scale factor 8, 27, $\frac{1}{64}$, 125, $\frac{1}{1000}$, 343, $\frac{1}{125}$, $\frac{1}{8}$
4 a 1 : 2 **b** 1 : 8 **c** 8 pints **d** No

5 135 cm^2

6 a 56 cm^2 **b** 126 cm^2

7 a 48 ft^2 **b** 3 ft^2

8 a 2400 cm^3 **b** 8100 cm^3

9 a 3750 cm^3 **b** 3.75 cm^3

10 4 litres

11 91.125 litres

12 a 5.0625 litres   **b** The height of the can

13 a 5.4 m^2 **b** 1.35 m^2

14 1.38 m^3

15 £6

16 6 cm, 8 cm, 10 cm

17 3r cm

18 a 9, 36   **b** 16, 80   **c** 9, 45   **d** 36, 270   **e** Solids b and d

Exercise 16E

1 6.2 cm, 10.1 cm   **2** 4.26 cm, 6.74 cm

3 9.56 cm   **4** 3.38 m

5 35 mins   **6** 8.39 cm

7 26.5 cm   **8** 16.9 cm

9 a 4.33 cm, 7.81 cm   **10** 2478 ml

   b 143 g, 839 g

11 53.8 kg   **12** 1.73 kg

13 92.8 cm   **14** 1.30 m^2, 4.42 m^2

ANSWERS TO CHAPTER 17

Quick check

1 $P = 4l$ **2** $C = \pi d$ **3** $A = \frac{1}{2}bh$

4 $A = \pi r^2$ **5** $V = l^3$ **6** $V = \pi r^2 h$

Exercise 17A

1 $P = 2a + 2b$ **2** $P = a + b + c + d$

3 $P = 4x$ **4** $P = p + 2q$

5 $P = 4x + 4y$ **6** $P = a + 3b$

7 $P = 5x + 2y + 2z$ **8** $P = 2\pi r$

9 $P = 2h + (2 + \pi)r$ **10** $P = 2l + \pi d$

Exercise 17B

1 $A = a^2 + ab$ **2** $A = \frac{1}{2}bh$

3 $A = bh$ **4** $A = \frac{1}{2}(a + b)h$

5 $A = \pi r^2$ **6** $A = 2ad - a^2$

7 $A = \frac{1}{2}bh + \frac{1}{2}bw$ **8** $A = 2rh + \pi r^2$

9 $A = \frac{1}{8}\pi d^2 + \frac{1}{2}dh$ **10** $A = \frac{1}{8}\pi D^2 + \frac{1}{2}(b + D)w$

Exercise 17C

1 $V = 6p^3$ **2** $V = \pi r^2 h$

3 $V = \frac{1}{2}bhw$ **4** $V = \frac{1}{2}bhl$

5 $V = aqt + bpt - apt$ **6** $V = abl + adl + 2cdl$

Exercise 17D

1 a A **b** L **c** L **d** A **e** V **f** V **g** V
   h A **i** L **j** V **k** A **l** L **m** V **n** A
   o V **p** A **q** V **r** A **s** A **t** A **u** L
   v A **w** A **x** A **y** V **z** V

2 a C **b** I **c** C **d** I **e** C **f** I **g** C
   h I **i** C **j** I **k** C **l** C **m** C **n** C
   o C **p** I **q** C **r** C **s** I **t** C **u** C
   v C **w** C **x** C **y** C

3 a C, L **b** I **c** C, V **d** C, L **e** I
   f I **g** C, V **h** C, V **i** C, V **j** C, V
   k C, L **l** I **m** C, V

4 a 2   **b** 2, 3   **c** 2   **d** 2, 2

5 Inconsistent

6 a A is F$_2$, B is F$_4$, C is F$_3$
   b F$_1$ is the total length of the curved edges

ANSWERS TO CHAPTER 18

Quick check

a $\begin{pmatrix} 1 \\ 3 \end{pmatrix}$ **b** $\begin{pmatrix} 3 \\ 0 \end{pmatrix}$ **c** $\begin{pmatrix} 2 \\ -1 \end{pmatrix}$ **d** $\begin{pmatrix} -1 \\ -2 \end{pmatrix}$

Exercise 18A

1 a Any 3 of $\overrightarrow{AC}$, $\overrightarrow{CF}$, $\overrightarrow{BD}$, $\overrightarrow{DG}$, $\overrightarrow{GI}$, $\overrightarrow{EH}$, $\overrightarrow{HJ}$, $\overrightarrow{JK}$ **b** Any 3 of $\overrightarrow{BE}$, $\overrightarrow{AD}$, $\overrightarrow{DH}$, $\overrightarrow{CG}$, $\overrightarrow{GJ}$, $\overrightarrow{FI}$, $\overrightarrow{IK}$
   c Any 3 of $\overrightarrow{AO}$, $\overrightarrow{CA}$, $\overrightarrow{FC}$, $\overrightarrow{IG}$, $\overrightarrow{GD}$, $\overrightarrow{DB}$, $\overrightarrow{KJ}$, $\overrightarrow{JH}$, $\overrightarrow{HE}$ **d** Any 3 of $\overrightarrow{BO}$, $\overrightarrow{EB}$, $\overrightarrow{HD}$, $\overrightarrow{DA}$, $\overrightarrow{JG}$, $\overrightarrow{GC}$, $\overrightarrow{KI}$, $\overrightarrow{IF}$

2 a 2**a**   **b** 2**b**   **c** **a** + **b**   **d** 2**a** + **b**   **e** 2**a** + 2**b**   **f** **a** + 2**b**   **g** **a** + **b**   **h** 2**a** + 2**b**   **i** 3**a** + **b**
   j 2**a**   **k** **b**   **l** 2**a** + **b**

3 a Equal   **b** $\overrightarrow{AI}$, $\overrightarrow{BJ}$, $\overrightarrow{DK}$ **4 a** $\overrightarrow{OJ} = 2\overrightarrow{OD}$ and parallel   **5**
   b $\overrightarrow{AK}$ **c** $\overrightarrow{OF}$, $\overrightarrow{BI}$, $\overrightarrow{EK}$

6 a Lie on same straight line   **b** All multiples of **a** + **b** and start at O
   c H   **d i** $\overrightarrow{OQ} = \mathbf{a} + \frac{1}{2}\mathbf{b}$ **ii** $\overrightarrow{OR} = 3\mathbf{a} + \frac{3}{2}\mathbf{b}$
   e $n\mathbf{a} + \frac{n}{2}\mathbf{b}$

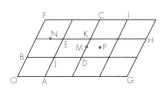

7 a −**b**　**b** 3**a** − **b**　**c** 2**a** − **b**　**d a** − **b**　**e a** + **b**　**f** −**a** − **b**　**g** 2**a** − **b**　**h** −**a** − 2**b**　**i a** + 2**b**
　j −**a** + **b**　　**k** 2**a** − 2**b**　**l a** − 2**b**

8 a Equal but in opposite directions　**b** Any 3 of $\overrightarrow{DA}$, $\overrightarrow{EF}$, $\overrightarrow{GJ}$, $\overrightarrow{FI}$, $\overrightarrow{AH}$

9 a Opposite direction and $\overrightarrow{AB} = -\frac{1}{2}\overrightarrow{CK}$　**b** $\overrightarrow{BJ}$, $\overrightarrow{CK}$　**c** $\overrightarrow{EB}$, $\overrightarrow{GO}$, $\overrightarrow{KH}$

10 a

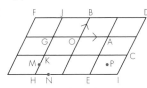

11 a Any 3 of $\overrightarrow{MJ}$, $\overrightarrow{AG}$, $\overrightarrow{HC}$, $\overrightarrow{BD}$, $\overrightarrow{OH}$, $\overrightarrow{NA}$, $\overrightarrow{PO}$, $\overrightarrow{KB}$, $\overrightarrow{IE}$　**b** Any 3 of $\overrightarrow{DG}$, $\overrightarrow{HJ}$, $\overrightarrow{AL}$, $\overrightarrow{EH}$, $\overrightarrow{BA}$, $\overrightarrow{OM}$, $\overrightarrow{FB}$, $\overrightarrow{IO}$, $\overrightarrow{KN}$
　c Any 3 of $\overrightarrow{GD}$, $\overrightarrow{HE}$, $\overrightarrow{BF}$, $\overrightarrow{JH}$, $\overrightarrow{AB}$, $\overrightarrow{OI}$, $\overrightarrow{LA}$, $\overrightarrow{MO}$, $\overrightarrow{NK}$　**d** Any 3 of $\overrightarrow{CH}$, $\overrightarrow{DB}$, $\overrightarrow{EI}$, $\overrightarrow{GA}$, $\overrightarrow{HO}$, $\overrightarrow{BK}$, $\overrightarrow{JM}$, $\overrightarrow{AN}$, $\overrightarrow{OP}$
　e Any 3 of $\overrightarrow{FH}$, $\overrightarrow{EG}$, $\overrightarrow{IA}$, $\overrightarrow{BJ}$, $\overrightarrow{KM}$, $\overrightarrow{OL}$　**f** Any 3 of $\overrightarrow{JD}$, $\overrightarrow{AE}$, $\overrightarrow{OF}$, $\overrightarrow{LH}$, $\overrightarrow{MB}$, $\overrightarrow{NI}$
　g i $\overrightarrow{FG}$, $\overrightarrow{IJ}$ or $\overrightarrow{KL}$　**ii** $\overrightarrow{OC}$, $\overrightarrow{KD}$, $\overrightarrow{NG}$, $\overrightarrow{PH}$　**iii** $\overrightarrow{FJ}$ or $\overrightarrow{IL}$　**iv** $\overrightarrow{FL}$　**v** $\overrightarrow{LF}$　**vi** $\overrightarrow{PC}$　**vii** $\overrightarrow{CP}$
　viii Same as part **d**　**ix** Same as part **a**

12 Parts **b** and **d** could be, parts **a** and **c** could not be

13 a Any multiple (positive or negative) of 3**a**−**b**　**b** Will be a multiple of 3**a**−**b**

Exercise 18B

1 a i −**a** + **b**　**ii** $\frac{1}{2}(-\mathbf{a} + \mathbf{b})$　**iii** 　**iv** $\frac{1}{2}\mathbf{a} + \frac{1}{2}\mathbf{b}$　**b i a** − **b**　**ii** $\frac{1}{2}\mathbf{a} - \frac{1}{2}\mathbf{b}$　**iii**

　iv $\frac{1}{2}\mathbf{a} + \frac{1}{2}\mathbf{b}$　**c** 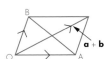　**d** M is midpoint of parallelogram of which OA and OB are two sides

2 a i −**a** − **b**　**ii** $-\frac{1}{2}\mathbf{a} - \frac{1}{2}\mathbf{b}$　**iii** 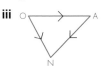　**iv** $\frac{1}{2}\mathbf{a} - \frac{1}{2}\mathbf{b}$　**b i b** + **a**　**ii** $\frac{1}{2}\mathbf{b} + \frac{1}{2}\mathbf{a}$　**iii**

　iv $\frac{1}{2}\mathbf{a} - \frac{1}{2}\mathbf{b}$　**c** 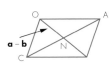　**d** N is midpoint of parallelogram of which OA and OC are two sides

3 a 　**b** 　　**4 a i** −**a** + **b**　**ii** $\frac{1}{3}(-\mathbf{a} + \mathbf{b})$　**iii** $\frac{2}{3}\mathbf{a} + \frac{1}{3}\mathbf{b}$　**b** $\frac{3}{4}\mathbf{a} + \frac{1}{4}\mathbf{b}$
　　5 a i $\frac{2}{3}\mathbf{b}$　**ii** $\frac{1}{2}\mathbf{a} + \frac{1}{2}\mathbf{b}$　**iii** $-\frac{2}{3}\mathbf{b}$　**b** $\frac{1}{2}\mathbf{a} - \frac{1}{6}\mathbf{b}$
　　c $\overrightarrow{DE} = \overrightarrow{DO} + \overrightarrow{OE} = \frac{3}{2}\mathbf{a} - \frac{1}{2}\mathbf{b}$
　　d $\overrightarrow{DE}$ parallel to $\overrightarrow{CD}$ (multiple of $\overrightarrow{CD}$) and D is a common point

6 a 　$\overrightarrow{CD} = -\mathbf{a} + \mathbf{b} = \mathbf{b} - \mathbf{a}$　**b i** −**a**　**ii** −**b**　**iii a** − **b**　**c** 0, vectors return to starting point
　　d i 2**b**　**ii** 2**b** − 2**a**　**iii** −2**a**　**iv** 2**b** − **a**　**v** −**a** − **b**

7 a 　$\overrightarrow{CX} = \sqrt{1^2 + 1^2}\,\mathbf{b} = \sqrt{2}\mathbf{b}$　**b**　$\overrightarrow{YE} = \sqrt{1^2 + 1^2}\,\mathbf{a} = \sqrt{2}\mathbf{a}.$
　　$\overrightarrow{CD} = \overrightarrow{CX} + \overrightarrow{XD} = \sqrt{2}\mathbf{b} - \mathbf{a}$　　$\overrightarrow{DE} = \overrightarrow{DY} + \overrightarrow{YE} = \mathbf{b} - \sqrt{2}\mathbf{a}$

　c i −**a**　**ii** −**b**　**iii a** − $\sqrt{2}$**b**　**iv** $\sqrt{2}$**a** − **b**　**v** $\sqrt{2}$**a** + **a**　**vi** $\sqrt{2}$**b** + **b**　**vii** 2**b** + $\sqrt{2}$**b** − **a** − $\sqrt{2}$**a**
　viii 2**b** + $\sqrt{2}$**b** − 2**a** − $\sqrt{2}$**a**

8 a i −**a** + **b**　**ii** $\frac{1}{2}(-\mathbf{a} + \mathbf{b}) = -\frac{1}{2}\mathbf{a} + \frac{1}{2}\mathbf{b}$　**iii** $\frac{1}{2}\mathbf{a} + \frac{1}{2}\mathbf{b}$　**b i** $\frac{1}{2}\mathbf{b} + \frac{1}{2}\mathbf{c}$　**ii** $-\frac{1}{2}\mathbf{a} + \frac{1}{2}\mathbf{c}$　**c i** $-\frac{1}{2}\mathbf{a} + \frac{1}{2}\mathbf{c}$
　ii Equal　**iii** Parallelogram

9 a i $\frac{1}{2}\mathbf{a}$　**ii c** − **a**　**iii** $\frac{1}{2}\mathbf{a} + \frac{1}{2}\mathbf{c}$　**iv** $\frac{1}{2}\mathbf{c}$　**b i** $-\frac{1}{2}\mathbf{a} + \frac{1}{2}\mathbf{b}$　**ii** $-\frac{1}{2}\mathbf{a} + \frac{1}{2}\mathbf{b}$
　c Opposite sides are equal and parallel　**d** NMRQ and PNLR

Quick check

1 a $2x + 12$ **b** $4x - 12$ **c** $12x - 6$

2 a $5y$ **b** $4x - 3$ **c** $-x - 4$

3 a $6x$ **b** $8y^2$ **c** $2c^3$

4 a $x = 1$ **b** $x = 3$ **c** $x = 9$
  d $x = 8$ **e** $x = 24$ **f** $x = 15$

Exercise 19A

1 a 13 **b** −3 **c** 5
2 a 2 **b** 8 **c** −10
3 a 6 **b** 3 **c** −2
4 a −7 **b** −10 **c** 6.5
5 a −4.8 **b** 48 **c** 32
6 a 1.4 **b** 1.4 **c** −0.4
7 a 13 **b** 74 **c** 17
8 a 75 **b** 22.5 **c** −135
9 a 2.5 **b** −20 **c** 2.5

Exercise 19B

1 $6 + 2m$ **2** $10 + 5l$ **3** $12 - 3y$
4 $20 + 8k$ **5** $6 - 12f$ **6** $10 - 6w$
7 $10k + 15m$ **8** $12d - 8n$ **9** $t^2 + 3t$
10 $k^2 - 3k$ **11** $4t^2 - 4t$ **12** $8k - 2k^2$
13 $8g^2 + 20g$ **14** $15h^2 - 10h$ **15** $y^3 + 5y$
16 $h^4 + 7h$ **17** $k^3 - 5k$ **18** $3t^3 + 12t$
19 $15d^3 - 3d^4$ **20** $6w^3 + 3wt$ **21** $15a^3 - 10ab$
22 $12p^4 - 15mp$ **23** $12h^3 + 8h^2g$ **24** $8m^3 + 2m^4$

Exercise 19C

1 a $7t$ **b** $9d$ **c** $3e$ **d** $2t$ **e** $5t^2$
  f $4y^2$ **g** $5ab$ **h** $3a^2d$
2 a $22 + 5t$ **b** $21 + 19k$
  c $22 + 2f$ **d** $14 + 3g$
3 a $2 + 2h$ **b** $9g + 5$
  c $17k + 16$ **d** $6e + 20$
4 a $4m + 3p + 2mp$ **b** $3k + 4h + 5hk$
  c $12r + 24p + 13pr$ **d** $19km + 20k - 6m$
5 a $9t^2 + 13t$ **b** $13y^2 + 5y$
  c $10e^2 - 6e$ **d** $14k^2 - 3kp$
6 a $17ab + 12ac + 6bc$ **b** $18yw + 6yt - 8wt$
  c $14mn - 15mp - 6np$ **d** $8r^3 - 6r^2$

Exercise 19D

1 $6(m + 2t)$ **2** $3(3t + p)$ **3** $4(2m + 3k)$
4 $4(r + 2t)$ **5** $m(n + 3)$ **6** $g(5g + 3)$
7 $2(2w - 3t)$ **8** $y(3y + 2)$ **9** $t(4t - 3)$
10 $3m(m - p)$ **11** $3p(2p + 3t)$ **12** $2p(4t + 3m)$
13 $4b(2a - c)$ **14** $5bc(b - 2)$ **15** $2b(4ac + 3ed)$
16 $2(2a^2 + 3a + 4)$ **17** $3b(2a + 3c + d)$
18 $t(5t + 4 + a)$ **19** $3mt(2t - 1 + 3m)$
20 $2ab(4b + 1 - 2a)$ **21** $5pt(2t + 3 + p)$
22 a, d, f and **h** do not factorise **b** $m(5 + 2p)$
  c $t(t - 7)$ **e** $2m(2m - 3p)$ **g** $a(4a - 5b)$ **i** $b(5a - 3bc)$

Exercise 19E

1 30 **2** 21 **3** 72 **4** 12 **5** 6
6 $10\frac{1}{2}$ **7** −10 **8** 7 **9** 11 **10** −4
11 7 **12** $2\frac{4}{5}$ **13** 1 **14** $11\frac{1}{2}$ **15** $\frac{1}{5}$

Exercise 19F

1 3 **2** 7 **3** 5 **4** 3 **5** 4
6 6 **7** 8 **8** 1 **9** $1\frac{1}{2}$ **10** $2\frac{1}{2}$
11 $\frac{1}{2}$ **12** $1\frac{1}{5}$ **13** 2 **14** −2 **15** −1
16 −2 **17** −2 **18** −1

Exercise 19G

1 $x = 2$ **2** $y = 1$ **3** $a = 7$ **4** $t = 4$
5 $p = 2$ **6** $k = -1$ **7** $m = 3$ **8** $s = -2$
9 $d = 6$ **10** $x = 11$ **11** $y = 1$ **12** $h = 4$
13 $b = 9$ **14** $c = 6$

Exercise 19H

1 55p **2 a** $1\frac{1}{2}$ **b** 2 **3 a** $1\frac{1}{2}$ cm **b** 6.75 cm^2
4 17 sweets **5** 3 years old **6** 9 years old
7 3 cm **8** 5

Exercise 19I

1 a 4 and 5 **b** 4 and 5 **c** 2 and 3
2 3.5 **3** 3.7 **4** 2.5 **5** 1.5 (or −2)
6 a 2.4 **b** 2.8 **c** 3.2
7 b 7.8 cm by 12.8 cm **8** 5 (or −6)

Exercise 19J

1 $x = 4, y = 1$ **2** $x = 1, y = 4$ **3** $x = 3, y = 1$
4 $x = 5, y = -2$ **5** $x = 7, y = 1$ **6** $x = 5, y = \frac{1}{2}$
7 $x = 4\frac{1}{2}, y = 1\frac{1}{2}$ **8** $x = -2, y = 4$ **9** $x = 2\frac{1}{2}, y = -1\frac{1}{2}$
10 $x = 2\frac{1}{4}, y = 6\frac{1}{2}$ **11** $x = 4, y = 3$ **12** $x = 5, y = 3$

Exercise 19K

1 $x = 2, y = -3$ **2** $x = 7, y = 3$ **3** $x = 4, y = 1$
4 $x = 2, y = 5$ **5** $x = 4, y = -3$ **6** $x = 1, y = 7$
7 $x = 2\frac{1}{2}, y = 1\frac{1}{2}$ **8** $x = -1, y = 2\frac{1}{2}$ **9** $x = 6, y = 3$
10 $x = \frac{1}{2}, y = -\frac{3}{4}$ **11** $x = -1, y = 5$ **12** $x = 1\frac{1}{2}, y = \frac{3}{4}$

Exercise 19L

1 $x = 5, y = 1$ **2** $x = 3, y = 8$ **3** $x = 9, y = 1$
4 $x = 7, y = 3$ **5** $x = 4, y = 2$ **6** $x = 6, y = 5$
7 $x = 3, y = -2$ **8** $x = 2, y = \frac{1}{2}$ **9** $x = -2, y = -3$
10 $x = -1, y = 2\frac{1}{2}$ **11** $x = 2\frac{1}{2}, y = -\frac{1}{2}$ **12** $x = -1\frac{1}{2}, y = 4\frac{1}{2}$
13 $x = -\frac{1}{2}, y = -6\frac{1}{2}$ **14** $x = 3\frac{1}{2}, y = 1\frac{1}{2}$ **15** $x = -2\frac{1}{2}, y = -3\frac{1}{2}$

Exercise 19M

1 Amul £7.20, Kim £3.50
2 a $10x + 5y = 3.45, 8x + 10y = 4.38$ **b** £1.71
3 a $6x + 3y = 4.35, 11x + 7y = 8.80$ **b** £5.55
4 84p **5** 10.3 kg **6** £4.40
7 £62 **8** £195 **9** 2 hr 10 min

Exercise 19N

1 $k = \dfrac{T}{3}$ **2** $y = X + 1$ **3** $p = 3Q$

4 $r = \dfrac{A - 9}{4}$ **5** $n = \dfrac{W + 1}{3}$

15 a $n = \dfrac{W - t}{3}$ **b** $t = W - 3n$

6 a $m = p - t$ **b** $t = p - m$ **7** $m = gv$

16 a $y = \dfrac{x + w}{5}$ **b** $w = 5y - x$ **17** $p = \sqrt{\dfrac{k}{2}}$

8 $m = \sqrt{t}$ **9** $r = \dfrac{C}{2\pi}$ **10** $b = \dfrac{A}{h}$

18 a $t = u^2 - v$ **b** $u = \sqrt{v + t}$

11 $l = \dfrac{P - 2w}{2}$ **12** $p = \sqrt{m - 2}$

19 a $m = k - n^2$ **b** $n = \sqrt{k - m}$ **20** $r = \sqrt{\dfrac{T}{5}}$

13 a $a = \dfrac{v - u}{t}$ **b** $t = \dfrac{v - u}{a}$ **14** $d = \sqrt{\dfrac{4A}{\pi}}$

21 a $w = K - 5n^2$ **b** $n = \sqrt{\dfrac{K - w}{5}}$

ANSWERS TO CHAPTER 20

Quick check

1 a $-3x$ **b** $2x$ **c** $-3x$ **d** $6m^2$
  e $-6x^2$ **f** $-12p^2$

2 a -6 **b** $-\frac{1}{2}$ **c** $\frac{2}{3}$

Exercise 20A

1 $x^2 + 5x + 6$ **2** $t^2 + 7t + 12$ **3** $w^2 + 4w + 3$
4 $m^2 + 6m + 5$ **5** $k^2 + 8k + 15$ **6** $a^2 + 5a + 4$
7 $x^2 + 2x - 8$ **8** $t^2 + 2t - 15$ **9** $w^2 + 2w - 3$
10 $f^2 - f - 6$ **11** $g^2 - 3g - 4$ **12** $y^2 + y - 12$
13 $x^2 + x - 12$ **14** $p^2 - p - 2$ **15** $k^2 - 2k - 8$
16 $y^2 + 3y - 10$ **17** $a^2 + 2a - 3$ **18** $t^2 + t - 12$
19 $x^2 - 9$ **20** $t^2 - 25$ **21** $m^2 - 16$
22 $t^2 - 4$ **23** $y^2 - 64$ **24** $p^2 - 1$
25 $25 - x^2$ **26** $49 - g^2$ **27** $x^2 - 36$

Exercise 20B

1 $6x^2 + 11x + 3$ **2** $12y^2 + 17y + 6$ **3** $6t^2 + 17t + 5$
4 $8t^2 + 2t - 3$ **5** $10m^2 - 11m - 6$ **6** $12k^2 - 11k - 15$
7 $6p^2 + 11p - 10$ **8** $10w^2 + 19w + 6$ **9** $6a^2 - 7a - 3$
10 $8r^2 - 10r + 3$ **11** $15g^2 - 16g + 4$ **12** $12d^2 + 5d - 2$
13 $8p^2 + 26p + 15$ **14** $6t^2 + 7t + 2$ **15** $6p^2 + 11p + 4$
16 $6 - 7t - 10t^2$ **17** $12 + n - 6n^2$ **18** $6f^2 - 5f - 6$
19 $12 + 7q - 10q^2$ **20** $3 - 7p - 6p^2$ **21** $4 + 10t - 6t^2$

Exercise 20C

1 $4x^2 - 1$ **2** $9t^2 - 4$ **3** $25y^2 - 9$
4 $16m^2 - 9$ **5** $4k^2 - 9$ **6** $16h^2 - 1$
7 $4 - 9x^2$ **8** $25 - 4t^2$ **9** $36 - 25y^2$
10 $a^2 - b^2$ **11** $9t^2 - k^2$ **12** $4m^2 - 9p^2$
13 $25k^2 - g^2$ **14** $a^2b^2 - c^2d^2$ **15** $a^4 - b^4$

Exercise 20D

1 $x^2 + 10x + 25$ **2** $m^2 + 8m + 16$ **3** $t^2 + 12t + 36$
4 $p^2 + 6p + 9$ **5** $m^2 - 6m + 9$ **6** $t^2 - 10t + 25$
7 $m^2 - 8m + 16$ **8** $k^2 - 14k + 49$ **9** $9x^2 + 6x + 1$
10 $16t^2 + 24t + 9$ **11** $25y^2 + 20y + 4$ **12** $4m^2 + 12m + 9$
13 $16t^2 - 24t + 9$ **14** $9x^2 - 12x + 4$ **15** $25t^2 - 20t + 4$
16 $25r^2 - 60r + 36$ **17** $x^2 + 2xy + y^2$ **18** $m^2 - 2mn + n^2$
19 $4t^2 + 4ty + y^2$ **20** $m^2 - 6mn + 9n^2$ **21** $x^2 + 4x$
22 $x^2 - 10x$ **23** $x^2 + 12x$ **24** $x^2 - 4x$

Exercise 20E

1 $(x + 2)(x + 3)$ **2** $(t + 1)(t + 4)$ **3** $(m + 2)(m + 5)$
4 $(k + 4)(k + 6)$ **5** $(p + 2)(p + 12)$ **6** $(r + 3)(r + 6)$
7 $(w + 2)(w + 9)$ **8** $(x + 3)(x + 4)$ **9** $(a + 2)(a + 6)$
10 $(k + 3)(k + 7)$ **11** $(f + 1)(f + 21)$ **12** $(b + 8)(b + 12)$
13 $(t - 2)(t - 3)$ **14** $(d - 4)(d - 1)$ **15** $(g - 2)(g - 5)$
16 $(x - 3)(x - 12)$ **17** $(c - 2)(c - 16)$ **18** $(t - 4)(t - 9)$
19 $(y - 4)(y - 12)$ **20** $(j - 6)(j - 8)$ **21** $(p - 3)(p - 5)$
22 $(y + 6)(y - 1)$ **23** $(t + 4)(t - 2)$ **24** $(x + 5)(x - 2)$
25 $(m + 2)(m - 6)$ **26** $(r + 1)(r - 7)$ **27** $(n + 3)(n - 6)$
28 $(m + 4)(m - 11)$ **29** $(w + 4)(w - 6)$ **30** $(t + 9)(t - 10)$
31 $(h + 8)(h - 9)$ **32** $(t + 7)(t - 9)$ **33** $(d + 1)^2$
34 $(y + 10)^2$ **35** $(t - 4)^2$ **36** $(m - 9)^2$
37 $(x - 12)^2$ **38** $(d + 3)(d - 4)$ **39** $(t + 4)(t - 5)$
40 $(q + 7)(q - 8)$

Exercise 20F

1 $(x + 3)(x - 3)$ **2** $(t + 5)(t - 5)$ **3** $(m + 4)(m - 4)$
4 $(3 + x)(3 - x)$ **5** $(7 + t)(7 - t)$ **6** $(k + 10)(k - 10)$
7 $(2 + y)(2 - y)$ **8** $(x + 8)(x - 8)$ **9** $(t + 9)(t - 9)$
10 $(x + y)(x - y)$ **11** $(x + 2y)(x - 2y)$ **12** $(x + 3y)(x - 3y)$
13 $(3x + 1)(3x - 1)$ **14** $(4x + 3)(4x - 3)$ **15** $(5x + 8)(5x - 8)$
16 $(2x + 3y)(2x - 3y)$ **17** $(3t + 2w)(3t - 2w)$ **18** $(4y + 5x)(4y - 5x)$

Exercise 20G

1 $(2x + 1)(x + 2)$ **2** $(7x + 1)(x + 1)$ **3** $(4x + 7)(x - 1)$
4 $(3t + 2)(8t + 1)$ **5** $(3t + 1)(5t - 1)$ **6** $(4x - 1)^2$
7 $3(y + 7)(2y - 3)$ **8** $4(y + 6)(y - 4)$ **9** $(2x + 3)(4x - 1)$
10 $(2t + 1)(3t + 5)$ **11** $(x - 6)(3x + 2)$ **12** $(x - 5)(7x - 2)$

Exercise 20H

1 $-2, -5$ **2** $-3, -1$ **3** $-6, -4$ **4** $-3, 2$
5 $-1, 3$ **6** $-4, 5$ **7** $1, -2$ **8** $2, -5$
9 $7, -4$ **10** $3, 2$ **11** $1, 5$ **12** $4, 3$
13 $-4, -1$ **14** $-9, -2$ **15** $2, 4$ **16** $3, 5$
17 $-2, 5$ **18** $-3, 5$ **19** $-6, 2$ **20** $-6, 3$
21 $-1, 2$ **22** -2 **23** -5 **24** 4
25 $-2, -6$ **26** $5, -3$ **27** 7 **28** $-6, -4$
29 $2, 16$ **30** $-6, 4$ **31** $-9, 6$ **32** $-10, 3$
33 $-4, 11$ **34** $-8, 9$ **35** $8, 9$ **36** 1

Exercise 20I

1 a $\frac{1}{3}, -3$ **b** $1\frac{1}{3}, -\frac{1}{2}$ **c** $-\frac{1}{5}, 2$ **d** $-2\frac{1}{2}, 3\frac{1}{2}$
  e $-\frac{1}{6}, -\frac{1}{3}$ **f** $\frac{2}{3}, 4$ **g** $\frac{1}{2}, -3$ **h** $\frac{5}{2}, -\frac{7}{6}$

i $-1\frac{2}{3}, 1\frac{2}{5}$ **j** $1\frac{3}{4}, 1\frac{2}{7}$ **k** $\frac{2}{3}, \frac{1}{8}$ **l** $\pm\frac{1}{4}$
m $-2\frac{1}{4}, 0$ **n** $\pm 1\frac{2}{5}$ **p** $-\frac{1}{3}, 3$

2 a $7, -6$ **b** $-2\frac{1}{2}, 1\frac{1}{2}$ **c** $7, -6$ **d** $-1, \frac{11}{13}$
e $3, -2$ **f** $-\frac{2}{5}, \frac{1}{2}$ **g** $-\frac{1}{3}, -\frac{1}{4}$ **h** $\frac{1}{5}, -2$
i 4 **j** $-2, \frac{1}{8}$ **k** $-\frac{1}{3}, 0$ **l** ± 5
m $-1\frac{2}{3}$ **n** $\pm 3\frac{1}{2}$ **p** $-2\frac{1}{2}, 3$

Exercise 20J
1 $1.77, -2.27$ **2** $-0.23, -1.43$ **3** $3.70, -2.70$
4 $0.29, -0.69$ **5** $-0.19, -1.53$ **6** $-1.23, -2.43$
7 $-0.41, -1.84$ **8** $-1.39, -2.27$ **9** $1.37, -4.37$
10 $2.18, 0.15$ **11** $-0.39, -5.11$ **12** $0.44, -1.69$
13 $1.64, 0.61$ **14** $0.36, -0.79$ **15** $1.89, 0.11$

Exercise 20K
1 a $(x + 2)^2 - 4$ **b** $(x + 7)^2 - 49$ **c** $(x - 3)^2 - 9$
d $(x + 3)^2 - 9$ **e** $(x - 2)^2 - 4$ **f** $(x + 1.5)^2 - 2.25$
g $(x - 2.5)^2 - 6.25$ **h** $(x + 0.5)^2 - 0.25$ **i** $(x + 5)^2 - 25$
j $(x + 3.5)^2 - 12.25$ **k** $(x - 1)^2 - 1$ **l** $(x + 1)^2 - 1$
2 a $(x + 2)^2 - 5$ **b** $(x + 7)^2 - 54$ **c** $(x - 3)^2 - 6$
d $(x + 3)^2 - 2$ **e** $(x - 2)^2 - 5$ **f** $(x + 1.5)^2 + 0.75$
g $(x - 2.5)^2 - 11.25$ **h** $(x + 0.5)^2 - 1.25$ **i** $(x + 5)^2 - 25$
j $(x + 1)^2 - 2$ **k** $(x - 1)^2 - 8$ **l** $(x + 1)^2 - 10$
3 a $-2 \pm \sqrt{5}$ **b** $-7 \pm 3\sqrt{6}$ **c** $3 \pm \sqrt{6}$ **d** $-3 \pm \sqrt{2}$

e $2 \pm \sqrt{5}$ **f** $-1.5 \pm \sqrt{0.75}$ **g** $2.5 \pm \sqrt{11.25}$
h $-0.5 \pm \sqrt{1.25}$ **i** $-4 \pm \sqrt{22}$
j $-1 \pm \sqrt{2}$ **k** $1 \pm 2\sqrt{2}$ **l** $-1 \pm \sqrt{10}$
4 a $1.45, -3.45$ **b** $5.32, -1.32$ **c** $-4.16, 2.16$

Exercise 20L
1 $52, 2$ **2** $65, 2$ **3** $24, 2$ **4** $85, 2$
5 $145, 2$ **6** $68, 2$ **7** $-35, 0$ **8** $-23, 0$
9 $41, 2$ **10** $40, 2$ **11** $-135, 0$ **12** $37, 2$

Exercise 20M
1 a $1 \pm \sqrt{5}$ **b** $-1 \pm 2\sqrt{2}$ **c** $-2 \pm 4\sqrt{3}$
d $-1 \pm \sqrt{7}$ **e** $4 \pm \sqrt{14}$ **f** $2 \pm \sqrt{2}$
2 a $-1 \pm \dfrac{\sqrt{14}}{2}$ **b** $-1 \pm \dfrac{3\sqrt{2}}{2}$ **c** $\dfrac{-3 \pm \sqrt{19}}{2}$
d $\dfrac{5 \pm \sqrt{89}}{4}$ **e** $\dfrac{-1 \pm \sqrt{61}}{10}$ **f** $\dfrac{-3 \pm \sqrt{33}}{4}$

Exercise 20N
1 $6, 8, 10$ **2** 15 m, 20 m   **3** 29 **4** $6.54, 0.46$
5 $5, 0.5$ **6** 16 m by 14 m   **7** 48 km/h   **8** $45, 47$
9 2.54 m,   **10** 6 cm   **11** 30 km/h   **12** 10p
3.54 m
13 $1.25, 0.8$ **14** 10 **15** 5 h   **16** 0.75 m

ANSWERS TO CHAPTER 21

Quick check

1 A $(3, 0)$, B $((1, 4)$, C $(4, 5)$

2 a 18 **b** 145

Exercise 21A
1 a i 9 am   **ii** 10 am   **iii** 12 noon
  b i 40 km/h   **ii** 120 km/h   **iii** 40 km/h
2 a i 125 km   **ii** 125 km/h
  b i between 2 pm and 3 pm   **ii** about $12\frac{1}{2}$ km/h
3 a i 263 m/min (3 sf)   **ii** 15.8 km/h (3 sf)
  b i 500 m/min   **ii** Paul by 1 minute
4 a Patrick ran quickly at first, then had a slow middle section
    but he won the race with a final sprint. Araf ran steadily all
    the way and came second. Sean set off the slowest,
    speeded up towards the end but still came in third.
  b i 1.67 m/s   **ii** 6 km/h

Exercise 21B
1 a $\frac{15}{2}$ **b** $\frac{25}{8}$ **c** $\frac{15}{16}$ **d** $\frac{2}{25}$ **e** $\frac{6}{35}$ **f** $\frac{1}{2}$ **g** $-\frac{4}{5}$
2 a $2\frac{1}{2}$ km/h **b** 3.75 m/s **c** $2\frac{1}{2}$ km/h
3 a AB: 30 km/h, BC: 6 km/h, CD: 0 km/h,
    DE: 36 km/h (in opposite direction)
  b FG: 4 m/s, GH: 16 m/s, HI: 2 m/s (in opposite
    direction), IJ: 16 m/s (in opposite direction)

Exercise 21C
1 a 20 m/s^2 **b** 7.1 m/s
2 a 3.5 m/s^2 **b** 3.5 m/s^2
3 a between 2 and 4 hours, and between 8 and 10 hours
  b 10 km/h^2, 0 km/h^2, 5 km/h^2, 0 km/h^2, -6.25 km/h^2,
    -3.75 km/h^2

4
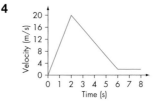

5 a
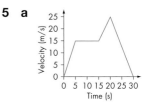
  b 3 m/s^2

Exercise 21D
1 a
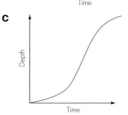
b
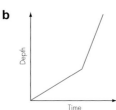
c
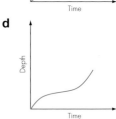
d
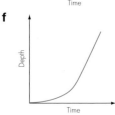
e
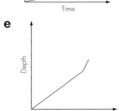
f

2 a 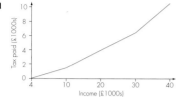 **b**

3 a

End of year	Amount owing (£)	End of year	Amount owing (£)	End of year	Amount owing (£)
1	52 500	6	34 356	11	17 324
2	50 085	7	31 273	12	13 391
3	42 749	8	28 037	13	9260
4	40 087	9	24 639	14	4923
5	37 291	10	21 071	15	369

b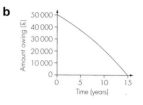

ANSWERS TO CHAPTER 22

Quick check

1 12.96 cm

2 21.6°

Exercise 22A
1 13.1 cm
2 73.7°
3 9.81 cm
4 33.5 m
5 a 10.0 cm **b** 11.5° **c** 4.69 cm
6 63.0°

Exercise 22B
1 a 58.6° **b** 20.5 cm **c** 2049 cm³ **d** 64.0°
2 a 3.46 m **b** 75.5° **c** 73.2° **d** 60.3 m²
3 a 24.0° **b** 48.0° **c** 13.5 cm **d** 16.6°
4 a 32.0° **b** 35.8°
5 a 3.46 m **b** 70.5°

Exercise 22C
1 36.9°, 143.1° **2** 53.1°, 126.9°
3 48.6°, 131.4° **4** 224.4°, 315.6°
5 194.5°, 345.5° **6** 198.7°, 341.3°
7 190.1°, 349.9° **8** 234.5°, 305.5°
9 28.1°, 151.9° **10** 185.6°, 354.4°
11 33.6°, 146.4° **12** 210°, 330°

Exercise 22D
1 53.1°, 306.9° **2** 54.5°, 305.5°
3 62.7°, 297.3° **4** 54.9°, 305.1°
5 79.3°, 280.7° **6** 143.1°, 216.9°
7 104.5°, 255.5° **8** 100.1°, 259.9°
9 111.2°, 248.8° **10** 166.9°, 193.1°
11 78.7°, 281.3° **12** 44.4°, 315.6°

Exercise 22E
1 a 0.707 **b** −1 (−0.9998) **c** −0.819 **d** 0.731
2 a −0.629 **b** −0.875 **c** −0.087 **d** 0.999

3 a 21.2°, 158.8° **b** 209.1°, 330.9°
  c 50.1°, 309.9° **d** 150.0°, 210.0°
  e 60.9°, 119.1° **f** 29.1°, 330.9°
4 30°, 150°
5 −0.755
6 a 1.41 **b** −1.37 **c** −0.0367 **d** −0.138
  e 1.41 **f** −0.492
7 True
8 a cos 65° **b** cos 40°
9 a 10°, 130° **b** 12.7°, 59.3°
10 38.2°, 141.8°

Exercise 22F
1 14.5°, 194.5° **2** 38.1°, 218.1°
3 50.0°, 230.0° **4** 61.9°, 241.9°
5 68.6°, 248.6° **6** 160.3°, 340.3°
7 147.6°, 327.6° **8** 135.4°, 315.4°
9 120.9°, 300.9° **10** 105.2°, 285.2°
11 54.4°, 234.4° **12** 42.2°, 222.2°
13 160.5°, 340.5° **14** 130.9°, 310.9°
15 76.5°, 256.5° **16** 116.0°, 296.0°
17 174.4°, 354.4° **18** 44.9°, 224.9°
19 50.4°, 230.4° **20** 111.8°, 291.8°

Exercise 22G
1 a 3.64 m **b** 8.05 cm **c** 19.4 cm
2 a 46.6° **b** 112.0° **c** 36.2°
3 50.3°, 129.7°
4 2.88 cm, 20.9 cm
5 a i 30° **ii** 40° **b** 19.4 m
6 36.5 m
7 a 36.8 m **b** 22.2 m
8 3.47 m **9** 767 m **10** 26.8 km/h

Exercise 22H
1 a 7.71 m **b** 29.1 cm **c** 27.4 cm
2 a 76.2° **b** 125.1° **c** 90° **d** Right-angled triangle
3 5.16 cm

4 65.5 cm
5 a 10.7 cm **b** 41.7° **c** 38.3° **d** 6.69 cm
e 54.4 cm²
6 72.3°
7 25.4 cm, 38.6 cm
8 58.4 km at 092.5°
9 21.8°
10 a 82.8° **b** 8.89 cm

Exercise 22I

1 a 8.60 m **b** 90° **c** 27.2 cm **d** 26.9°
e 41.0° **f** 62.4 cm **g** 90.0° **h** 866 cm
i 86.6 cm
2 7 cm
3 11.1 km
4 19.9 knots
5 a 27.8 miles **b** 262°

Exercise 22J

1 $\frac{3}{5}$ **2** $\sqrt{\frac{2}{5}}$

3 $\sqrt{19}$, $\sin x = \frac{\sqrt{6}}{\sqrt{19}}$, $\cos x = \frac{\sqrt{13}}{\sqrt{19}}$, $\tan x = \frac{\sqrt{6}}{\sqrt{13}}$

4 a $\sqrt{157}$ **b** $\sin A = \frac{6}{\sqrt{157}}$, $\cos A = \frac{11}{\sqrt{157}}$

5 $9\sqrt{3}$ cm²
6 400 cm²

Exercise 22K

1 a 24.0 cm² **b** 26.7 cm² **c** 243 cm²
d 21 097 cm² **e** 1224 cm²
2 4.26 cm
3 a 42.3° **b** 49.6°
4 103 cm²
5 2033 cm²
6 21.0 cm²
7 a 33.2° **b** 25.3 cm²
9 a $\frac{1}{\sqrt{2}}$ **b** 21 cm²

ANSWERS TO CHAPTER 23

Quick check

1 a 13 **b**

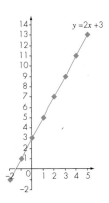

Exercise 23A

1

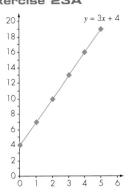

2

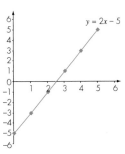

3

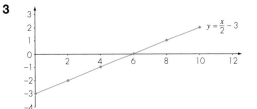

4

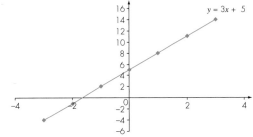

5

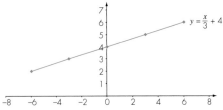

b (3, 7)

6

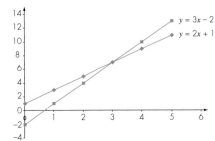

7

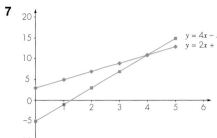

b (4, 11)

8

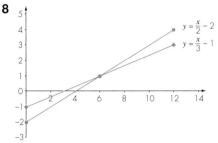

b (6, 1)

9

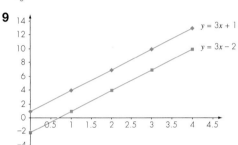

b No, because the lines are parallel.

10

x	0	1	2	3	4	5
y	5	4	3	2	1	0

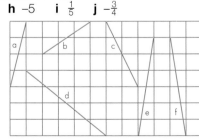

Exercise 23B

1 a 2 **b** $\frac{1}{3}$ **c** –3 **d** 1 **e** –2 **f** $-\frac{1}{3}$ **g** 5
 h –5 **i** $\frac{1}{5}$ **j** $-\frac{3}{4}$

2

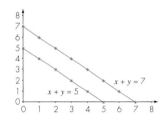

3 a 1
 b –1 They are perpendicular and symmetrical about the axes.

4 a 0.5 **b** 0.4 **c** 0.2 **d** 0.1 **e** 0
5 a $1\frac{2}{3}$ **b** 2 **c** $3\frac{1}{3}$ **d** 10 **e** ∞

Exercise 23C

1

$y = 2x + 6, y = 3x - 4, y = \frac{1}{2}x + 5, y = x + 7$

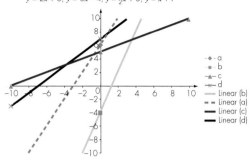

$y = 4x - 3, y = 2x - 7, y = \frac{1}{4}x - 3, y = \frac{2}{3}x + 4$

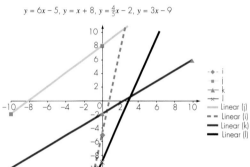

$y = 6x - 5, y = x + 8, y = \frac{4}{5}x - 2, y = 3x - 9$

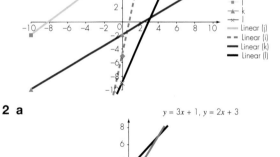

2 a $y = 3x + 1, y = 2x + 3$ **b** (2, 7)

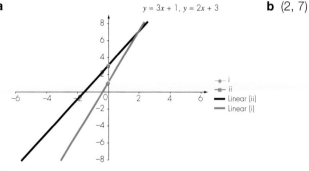

3 a

$y = \frac{x}{3} + 3, y = \frac{x}{4} + 2$

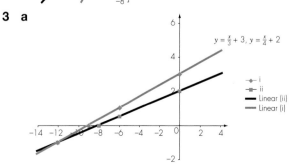

4 a

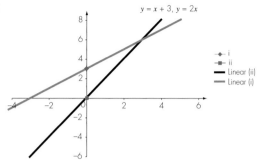

$y = x + 3, y = 2x$

b (3, 6)

3 a

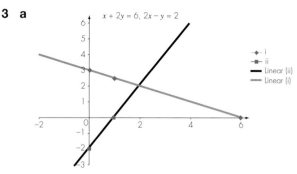

$x + 2y = 6, 2x - y = 2$

b (2, 2)

4 a

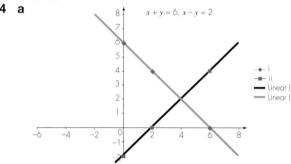

$x + y = 6, x - y = 2$

b (4, 2)

Exercise 23D

1 $3x + 2y = 6, 4x + 3y = 12, 4x - 5y = 20, x + y = 10$

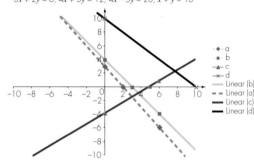

$3x - 2y = 18, x - y = 4, 5x - 2y = 15, 2x - 3y = 15$

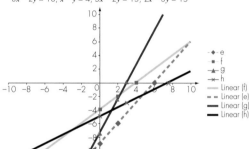

$6x + 5y = 30, x + y = -5, x + y = 3, x - y = -4$

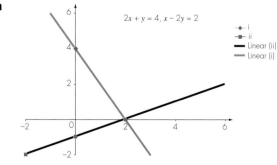

2 a

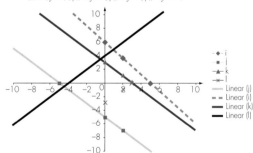

$2x + y = 4, x - 2y = 2$

b (2, 0)

Exercise 23E

1   **a** $y = \frac{4}{3}x - 2$ or $3y = 4x - 6$ **b** $y = x + 1$
   c $y = 2x - 3$ **d** $2y = x + 6$ **e** $y = x$ **f** $y = 2x$
2   **a i** $y = 2x + 1, y = -2x + 1$
      ii reflection in y-axis (and $y = 1$)   **iii** different sign
   b i $5y = 2x - 5, 5y = -2x -5$
      ii reflection in y-axis (and $y = -1$)   **iii** different sign
   c i $y = x + 1, y = -x + 1$
      ii reflection in y-axis (and $y = 1$)   **iii** different sign
3   **a** $y = -2x + 1$ **b** $2y = -x$ **c** $y = -x + 1$
   d $5y = -2x - 5$ **e** $y = \frac{3}{2}x - 3$
4   **a i** $2y = -x + 1, y = -2x + 1$ **ii** reflection in $x = y$
      iii reciprocal of each other
   b i $2y = 5x + 5, 5y = 2x -5$ **ii** reflection in $x = y$
      iii reciprocal of each other
   c i $y = 2, x = 2$ **ii** reflection in $x = y$
      iii reciprocal of each other (reciprocal of zero is infinity)

Exercise 23F

1   **a** 32°F   **b** $\frac{9}{5}$ (Take gradient at C =10° and 30°.)
   c $F = \frac{9}{5}C + 32$
2   **a** 0.07 (Take gradient at U = 0 and 500.)   **b** £10
   c C = £(10 + 0.07U) or Charge = £10 + 7p/unit
3   **a** $\frac{5}{2}$ (Take gradient at D = 0 and 40.)   **b** £20
   c C = £$(20 + \frac{5D}{2})$ or Charge = £20 + £2.50/day
4   **a** $\frac{1}{2}$ (Take gradient at N = 0 and 500.)   **b** £50
   c C = £$(50 + \frac{N}{2})$ or £50 + 50p/person
5   **a** $\frac{4}{10}$ **b** 24.5 cm   **c** 0.1 cm or 1 mm
   d $\angle = 24.5 + \frac{W}{10}$ or Length = 24.5 + 1 mm/kg

Exercise 23G

1 (4, 1) **2** (2, 3) **3** (3, 10)
4 (5, 5) **5** (1, 5) **6** (3, 16)
7 (−2, 6) **8** (−6, −9) **9** (1, −1)
10 (2, 6) **11** (2, 8) **12** $(7\frac{1}{2}, 3\frac{1}{2})$

Exercise 23H

1 a $-\frac{1}{2}$ **b** $\frac{1}{3}$ **c** $-\frac{1}{5}$ **d** 1 **e** −2 **f** −4
  g 3 **h** $\frac{3}{2}$ **i** $-\frac{2}{3}$ **j** $-\frac{1}{10}$ **k** $\frac{1}{6}$ **l** $-\frac{3}{4}$
2 a $y = -\frac{1}{2}x - 1$ **b** $y = \frac{1}{3}x + 1$ **c** $y = -x + 2$ **d** $y = x + 2$
  e $y = -2x + 3$ **f** $y = -4x - 3$ **g** $y = 3x$ **h** $y = 1.5x - 5$
3 a $y = 4x + 1$ **b** $y = \frac{1}{2}x - 2$ **c** $y = -x + 3$

4 a $y = -\frac{1}{3}x - 1$ **b** $y = 3x + 5$ **c** $y = -x + 1$
5 a $y = -x + 14$ **b** $y = x + 2$
6 $y = 2x + 6$
7 $y = -\frac{1}{4}x + 2$
8 a (0, −20) **b** $y = -\frac{1}{5}x + 6$ **c** $y = 5x - 20$
9 $y = -\frac{1}{2}x + 5$
10 a $y = 3x - 6$
  b Bisector of AB is $y = -2x + 9$, bisector of AC is
     $y = \frac{x}{2} + \frac{3}{2}$, solving these equations shows the lines
     intersect at (3, 3)
  c (3, 3) lies on $y = 3x - 6$ because $(3 \times 3) - 6 = 3$

ANSWERS TO CHAPTER 24

Quick check

−1, 2

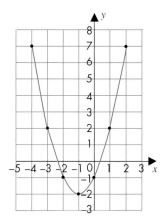

Exercise 24A

1 a Values of y: 10, 5, 4, 2.5, 2, 1.33, 1, 0.67, 0.5
  b i 0.8 **ii** −1.6
2 a Values of $5\sqrt{x}$: 0, 5 and −5, 7.1 and −7.1,
     8.7 and −8.7, 10 and −10, 11.2 and −11.2
  b i 9.4 and −9.4 **ii** 2.6
3 a Values of $\frac{1}{2}\sqrt{x}$: 0, $\frac{1}{2}$ and $-\frac{1}{2}$, 0.71 and −0.71, 0.87 and
     −0.87, 1 and −1, 1.1 and −1.1
  b i 0.8 and −0.8 **ii** 2.25
4 a Values of y: 10, 5, 2.5, 2, 1, 0.5, 0.4, 0.25, 0.2
  c 4.8 and 0.2
5 a Values of y: 25, 12.5, 10, 5, 2.5, 1, 0.5, 0.33, 0.25
  c 0.48 and −10.48

Exercise 24B

1 a Values of y: −24, −12.63, −5, −0.38, 2, 2.9, 3, 3.13, 4,
     6.38, 11, 18.63, 30 **b** 4.7

2 a Values of y: −54, −31.25, −16, −6.75, −2, −0.25, 0,
     0.25, 2, 6.75, 16, 31.25, 54 **b** 39.4
3 a Values of y: 27, 15.63, 8, 3.38, 1, 0.13, 0, −0.13, −1,
     −3.38, −8, −15.63, −27 **b** 0.2
4 a Values of y: −36, −23.13, −14, −7.88, −4, −1.63, 0,
     1.63, 4, 7.88, 14, 23.13, 36 **b** 0.6
5 a Values of y: −45, −26.88, −14, −5.63, −1, 0.63, 0,
     −2.13, −5, −7.88, −10, −10.63, −9 **b** −9.3
6 a Values of y: −16, −5.63, 1, 4.63, 6, 5.88, 5, 4.13, 4,
     5.38, 9, 15.63, 26 **c** −1.6, −0.4, 1.9
7 a Values of y: −20, −9.63, −3, 0.63, 2, 1.88, 1, 0.13, 0,
     1.38, 5, 11.63, 22 **c** −1.9, 0.4, 1.5
8 a Quadratic **b** Linear **c** None
  d Reciprocal **e** None **f** Cubic
  g Linear **h** None **i** Quadratic

Exercise 24C

1 a Values of y: 0.01, 0.04, 0.11, 0.33, 1, 3, 9, 27
  c 15.6 **d** −0.63
2 a Values of y: 32, 16, 8, 4, 2, 1, 0.5, 0.25, 0.13, 0.06, 0.03
  c 0.18 **d** 0.42
3 b Values of y: 1, 2, 4, 8, 16, 32, 64, 128, 256, 512
  c 9.2×10^{18} **d** £4.61×10^{14}
4 a Number of pieces: 2, 4, 8, 16, 32, 64, 128, 256
  b number of pieces = 2^n **c** 1.1×10^{15} pieces
  d 1.1×10^8 km

Exercise 24D

1 115° **2** 327°
3 324° **4** 195°
5 210°, 330° **6** 135°, 225°
7 a 64° **b** 206°, 334° **c** 116°, 244°

ANSWERS TO CHAPTER 25

Quick check

1 a 17, 20, 23 **b** 28, 36, 45 **c** 15, 10, 5
  d 49, 64, 81
2 a 1 **b** 4 **c** 7

3 a $2(x + 3)$ **b** $x(x - 1)$ **c** $2x(5x + 1)$
4 a $x^2 + 8x + 12$ **b** $2x^2 - 5x - 3$ **c** $x^2 - 4x + 4$
5 a $x = 3 - 2y$ **b** $x = 4 + 3y$ **c** $x = 4y - 3$

Exercise 25A

1 a $\dfrac{5x}{6}$ **b** $\dfrac{19x}{20}$ **c** $\dfrac{23x}{20}$ **d** $\dfrac{3x+2y}{6}$ **e** $\dfrac{x^2y+8}{4x}$

  f $\dfrac{5x+7}{6}$ **g** $\dfrac{7x-3}{4}$ **h** $\dfrac{13x-5}{15}$ **i** $\dfrac{3x-1}{4}$

  j $\dfrac{12x-23}{10}$

2 a $\dfrac{x}{6}$ **b** $\dfrac{11x}{20}$ **c** $\dfrac{7x}{20}$ **d** $\dfrac{3x-2y}{6}$ **e** $\dfrac{xy^2-8}{4y}$

  f $\dfrac{x-1}{6}$ **g** $\dfrac{x-1}{4}$ **h** $\dfrac{-7x-5}{15}$

  i $\dfrac{x-1}{4}$ **j** $\dfrac{-8x+7}{10}$

3 a 3 **b** 6 **c** 2 **d** 5 **e** 0.75 **f** 3

4 a $\dfrac{x^2}{6}$ **b** $\dfrac{3xy}{14}$ **c** $\dfrac{8}{3}$ **d** $\dfrac{2xy}{3}$ **e** $\dfrac{x^2-2x}{10}$

  f $\dfrac{1}{6}$ **g** $\dfrac{6x^2+5x+1}{8}$

  h $\dfrac{2x^2+x}{15}$ **i** $\dfrac{2x-4}{x-3}$ **j** $\dfrac{1}{2x}$

5 a $\dfrac{3}{2}$ **b** $\dfrac{x}{y}$ **c** $\dfrac{8}{3}$ **d** $\dfrac{2xy}{3}$ **e** $\dfrac{5x}{2x-4}$

  f $\dfrac{2x^2-12x+18}{75}$ **g** 1 **h** $\dfrac{1}{4x+2}$

  i $\dfrac{x^2-5x+6}{48}$ **j** $\dfrac{1}{2x}$

6 a x **b** $\dfrac{x}{2}$ **c** $\dfrac{3x^2}{16}$ **d** 3

  e $\dfrac{17x+1}{10}$ **f** $\dfrac{13x+9}{10}$ **g** $\dfrac{3x^2-5x-2}{10}$

  h $\dfrac{x+3}{2}$ **i** $\dfrac{2}{3}$ **j** $\dfrac{2x^2-6y^2}{9}$

8 a 3, −1.5 **b** 4, −1.25 **c** 3, −2.5 **d** 0, 1

  i $\dfrac{x-1}{4}$ **j** $\dfrac{-8x+7}{10}$

9 a $\dfrac{x-1}{2x+1}$ **b** $\dfrac{2x+1}{x+3}$ **c** $\dfrac{2x-1}{3x-2}$

  d $\dfrac{x+1}{x-1}$ **e** $\dfrac{2x+5}{4x-1}$

Exercise 25B

1 a (5, −1) **b** (4, 1) **c** (8, −1)
2 a (1, 2) and (−2, −1) **b** $x = -4, y = 1$; $x = -2, y = 2$
3 a (3, 4) and (4, 3) **b** (0, 3) and (−3, 0) **c** (3, 2) and (−2, 3)
4 a (2, 5) and (−2, −3) **b** (−1, −2) and (4, 3) **c** (3, 3) and (1, −1)
5 a (2, 4) **b** (1, 0) **c** The line is a tangent to the curve

Exercise 25C

1 a 21, 34: add previous 2 terms **b** 49, 64: next square number **c** 47, 76: add previous 2 terms

2 15, 21, 28, 36   **3** 61, 91, 127   **4** $\frac{1}{2}, \frac{3}{5}, \frac{2}{3}, \frac{5}{7}, \frac{3}{4}$
5 a 6, 10, 15, 21, 28
  b It is the sums of the natural numbers, or the numbers in Pascal's Triangle.
6 a 2, 6, 24, 720 **b** 69!

Exercise 25D

1 a 13, 15, $2n + 1$ **b** 25, 29, $4n + 1$
  c 33, 38, $5n + 3$ **d** 32, 38, $6n - 4$
  e 20, 23, $3n + 2$ **f** 37, 44, $7n - 5$
  g 21, 25, $4n - 3$ **h** 23, 27, $4n - 1$
  i 17, 20, $3n - 1$ **j** 42, 52, $10n - 8$
  k 24, 28, $4n + 4$ **l** 29, 34, $5n - 1$
2 a $3n + 1$, 151 **b** $2n + 5$, 105 **c** $5n - 2$, 248
  d $4n - 3$, 197 **e** $8n - 6$, 394 **f** $n + 4$, 54
  g $5n + 1$, 251 **h** $8n - 5$, 395 **i** $3n - 2$, 148
  j $3n + 18$, 168 **k** $7n + 5$, 355 **l** $8n - 7$, 393
3 a 33rd **b** 30th **c** 100th = 499
4 a i $4n + 1$ **ii** 401 **iii** 101, 25th
  b i $2n + 1$ **ii** 201 **iii** 99 or 101, 49th and 50th
  c i $3n + 1$ **ii** 301 **iii** 100, 33rd
  d i $2n + 6$ **ii** 206 **iii** 100, 47th
  e i $4n + 5$ **ii** 405 **iii** 101, 24th
  f i $5n + 1$ **ii** 501 **iii** 101, 20th
  g i $3n - 3$ **ii** 297 **iii** 99, 34th
  h i $6n - 4$ **ii** 596 **iii** 98, 17th
  i i $8n - 1$ **ii** 799 **iii** 103, 13th
  j i $2n + 23$ **ii** 223 **iii** 99 or 101, 38th and 39th
5 a $\dfrac{2n+1}{3n+1}$ **b** Getting closer to $\frac{2}{3}$ (0.$\dot{6}$)
  c i 0.667 774 (6dp) **ii** 0.666 778 (6dp)
  d 0.666 678 (6dp), 0.666 667 (6dp)
6 a $\dfrac{4n-1}{5n+1}$ **b** Getting closer to $\frac{4}{5}$ (0.8)
  c i 0.796 407 (6dp) **ii** 0.799 640 (6dp)
  d 0.799 964 (6dp), 0.799 9996 (7dp)
7 a 64, 128, 256, 512, 1024 **b i** $2^n - 1$ **ii** $2^n + 1$ **iii** 3×2^n
8 a The number of zeros equals the power. **b** 6
  c i $10^n - 1$ **ii** 2×10^n
9 a Even, **b** Odd,

+	**Odd**	**Even**
Odd	Even	Odd
Even	Odd	Even

×	**Odd**	**Even**
Odd	Odd	Even
Even	Even	Even

10 a 36, 49, 64, 81, 100 **b i** $n^2 + 1$ **ii** $2n^2$ **iii** $n^2 - 1$
11 $1 + 3 + 5 + 7 = 16 = 4^2$, $1 + 3 + 5 + 7 + 9 = 25 = 5^2$
12 a 28, 36, 45, 55, 66 **b i** 210 **ii** 5050 **c** You get the square numbers.
13 a Even **b** Odd **c** Odd **d** Odd **e** Odd
  f Odd **g** Even **h** Odd **i** Odd
14 a Odd or even **b** Odd or even **c** Odd or even
  d Odd **e** Odd or even **f** Even

Exercise 25E

1 b $4n - 3$ **c** 97 **d** 50th diagram
2 b $2n + 1$ **c** 121 **d** 49th set
3 a 18 **b** $4n + 2$ **c** 12
4 a i 24 **ii** $5n - 1$ **iii** 224 **b** 25

5 a i 20 cm **ii** $(3n + 2)$ cm **iii** 152 cm **b** 332
6 a i 20 **ii** 162 **b** 79.8 km
7 a i 14 **ii** $3n + 2$ **iii** 41 **b** 66
8 a i 5 **ii** n **iii** 18 **b** 20
9 a 2^n **b i** $100 \times 2^{n-1}$ ml **ii** 1600 ml

Exercise 25F

1 a i 35, 48 **ii** $n^2 - 1$ **b i** 38, 51 **ii** $n^2 + 2$
c i 39, 52 **ii** $n^2 + 3$ **d i** 34, 47 **ii** $n^2 - 2$
e i 35, 46 **ii** $n^2 + 10$
2 a i 37, 50 **ii** $(n + 1)^2 + 1$
b i 35, 48 **ii** $(n + 1)^2 - 1$
c i 41, 54 **ii** $(n + 1)^2 + 5$
d i 50, 65 **ii** $(n + 2)^2 + 1$
e i 48, 63 **ii** $(n + 2)^2 - 1$
3 a i $n^2 + 4$ **ii** 2504 **b i** $3n + 2$ **ii** 152
c i $(n + 1)^2 - 1$ **ii** 2600 **d i** $n(n + 4)$ **ii** 2700
e i $n^2 + 2$ **ii** 2502 **f i** $5n - 4$ **ii** 246
4 a $2n^2 - 3n + 2$ **b** $3n^2 + 2n - 3$ **c** $\frac{1}{2}n^2 + \frac{5}{2}n + 1$

Exercise 25G

1 $-8y$ **2** $\dfrac{-x}{8}$ **3** $\dfrac{b + 5c}{4}$

4 $\dfrac{b(q + p)}{q - p}$ **5** $\dfrac{a(q - p)}{q + p}$ **6** $\dfrac{A}{\pi(2h + k)}$

7 $\dfrac{u}{\sqrt{(1 - a)}}$ **8** $\dfrac{3 + st}{2 + s}$ **9** $\dfrac{6 + st}{2 + s}$

10 $\dfrac{2R - 3}{R - 1}$ **11 a** $\dfrac{P}{\pi + 2k}$ **b** $\sqrt{\dfrac{2A}{\pi + \sqrt{(k^2 - 1)}}}$

12 $\dfrac{100A}{100 + RY}$ **13 a** $b = \dfrac{Ra}{a - R}$ **b** $a = \dfrac{Rb}{b - R}$

14 a $\dfrac{2 + 2y}{y - 1}$ **c** $x = \dfrac{2W + 2zy}{z + y}$
d Same formula as in **a**
15 a Cannot factorise the expression.
b $\dfrac{3V}{r^2(2r + 3h)}$ **c** Yes, $\sqrt[3]{\dfrac{3V}{5\pi}}$
16 $x = \dfrac{2W - 2zy}{z + y}$

ANSWERS TO CHAPTER 26

Quick check

1 a 8 **b** 10

2 a 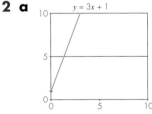 **b**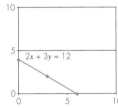

Exercise 26A

1 a $x < 3$ **b** $t > 8$ **c** $p \geqslant 10$ **d** $x < 5$
e $y \leqslant 3$ **f** $t > 5$ **g** $x < 6$ **h** $y \leqslant 15$
i $t \geqslant 18$ **j** $x < 7$ **k** $x \leqslant 3$ **l** $t \geqslant 5$
2 a 8 **b** 6 **c** 16 **d** 3 **e** 7
3 a 11 **b** 16 **c** 16
4 a $x \geqslant -6$ **b** $t \leqslant \frac{8}{3}$ **c** $y \leqslant 4$ **d** $x \geqslant -2$
e $w \leqslant 5.5$ **f** $x \leqslant \frac{14}{5}$
5 a $x \leqslant 2$ **b** $x > 38$ **c** $x < 6\frac{1}{2}$ **d** $x \geqslant 7$
e $t > 10$ **f** $y \leqslant \frac{7}{5}$
6 a $3 < x < 6$ **b** $2 < x < 5$ **c** $-1 < x \leqslant 3$
d $1 \leqslant x < 4$ **e** $2 \leqslant x < 4$ **f** $0 \leqslant x \leqslant 5$

Exercise 26B

1 a $x > 1$ **b** $x \leqslant 3$ **c** $x < 2$ **d** $x \geqslant -1$
e $x \leqslant -1$ **f** $x \geqslant 1$
2 a 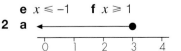 **b**

c 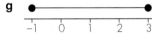 **d**

e 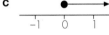 **f**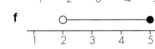

g

h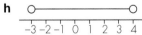

3 a $x \geqslant 4$

b $x < -2$

c $x \geqslant 3\frac{1}{2}$

d $x < -1$

e $x < 1\frac{1}{2}$

f $x \leqslant -2$

g $x > 50$

h $x \geq -6$

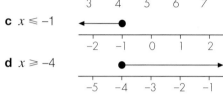

4 **a** $x > 2$

b $x \geq 6$

c $x \leq -1$

d $x \geq -4$

16 $x \geq 10, x \leq -10$

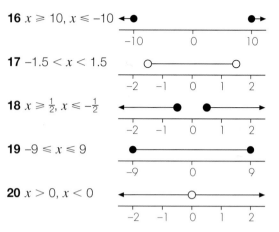

17 $-1.5 < x < 1.5$

18 $x \geq \frac{1}{2}, x \leq -\frac{1}{2}$

19 $-9 \leq x \leq 9$

20 $x > 0, x < 0$

Exercise 26C

1 $-2 \leq x \leq 2$

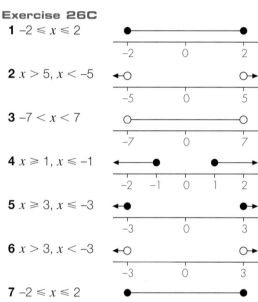

2 $x > 5, x < -5$

3 $-7 < x < 7$

4 $x \geq 1, x \leq -1$

5 $x \geq 3, x \leq -3$

6 $x > 3, x < -3$

7 $-2 \leq x \leq 2$

8 $-4 < x < 4$

9 $x > 1, x < -1$

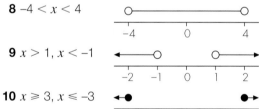

10 $x \geq 3, x \leq -3$

11 $x > 2, x < -2$

12 $-3 < x < 3$

13 $-1 \leq x \leq 1$

14 $-4 < x < 4$

15 $x \geq 5, x \leq -5$

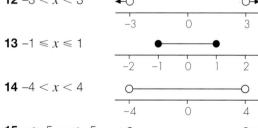

Exercise 26D

1

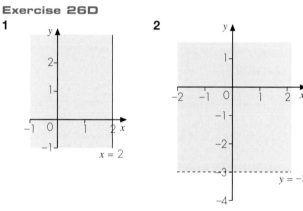

2

3

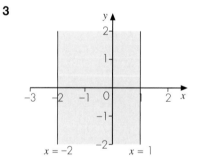

4

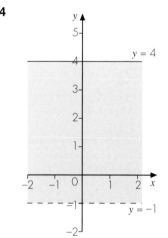

5 a

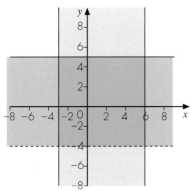

b i Yes
ii Yes
iii No

6

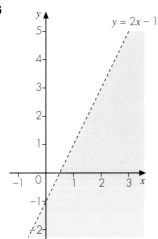

7

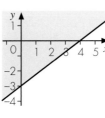

8

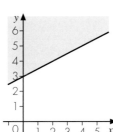

9

10 a–d

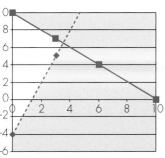

e i No
ii No
iii Yes

11 a–f

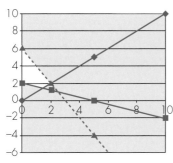

g i No
ii No
iii Yes

12

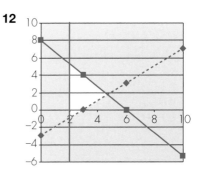

b i No **ii** Yes
iii No **iv** No

Exercise 26E

1 a £148x **b** £125y **c** £(148x + 125y)
2 a £(Ax + By) **b** £(Ax + 2Bx) **c** £(9A + (9 + y)B)
3 a May be true **b** Must be false
c May be true, e.g. x = 30, y = 20
d May be true, e.g. x = 3, y = 40
4 a May be true **b** May be true
c Must be false
5 E Excels hold 40E; S Storms hold 50S. There must be at least 1500 seats, so 40E + 50S ⩾ 1500. Cancelling through by 10 gives 4E + 5S ⩾ 150
6 a W rides cost £1.50W. This cannot exceed £6.00, so 1.50W ⩽ 6.00. Cancelling through by 1.5 gives W ⩽ 4
b Likewise 2D ⩽ 6, giving D ⩽ 3
c Total cost is 1.50W + 2D ⩽ 6.00. Multiplying through by 2 gives 3W + 4D ⩽ 12
d D ⩽ 2 **e i** Yes **ii** No **iii** No **iv** Yes
7 a 45x + 25y ⩽ 200 ⟹ 9x + 5y ⩽ 40 **b** y ⩾ x + 2
8 a i Cost 30x + 40y ⩽ 300 ⟹ 3x + 4y ⩽ 30
ii At least 2 apples, so x ⩾ 2
iii At least 3 pears, so y ⩾ 3
iv At least 7 fruits, so x + y ⩾ 7
b i No **ii** No **iii** No **iv** Yes
9 a i Space 4x + 3y ⩽ 48
ii Cost 300x + 500y ⩽ 6000 ⟹ 3x + 5y ⩽ 60
b i Yes **ii** No **iii** No **iv** Yes
10 a i Number of seats required is 40x + 50y ⩾ 300 ⟹ 4x + 5y ⩾ 30
ii Number of 40-seaters x ⩽ 6
iii Number of 50-seaters y ⩽ 5
b i Yes **ii** Yes **iii** Yes **iv** Yes
c Combination iii, which costs £760
d Five 40-seaters and two 50-seaters cost £740

Quick check

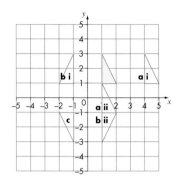

Exercise 27A

1 a–d

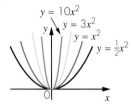

$y = 10x^2$
$y = 3x^2$
$y = x^2$
$y = \frac{1}{2}x^2$

e Stretch sf in y-direction: $3, \frac{1}{2}, 10$

2 a–d

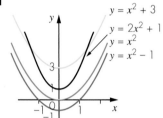

$y = x^2 + 3$
$y = 2x^2 + 1$
$y = x^2$
$y = x^2 - 1$

e *b* Translation $\begin{pmatrix} 0 \\ 3 \end{pmatrix}$ *c* Translation $\begin{pmatrix} 0 \\ -1 \end{pmatrix}$ *d* Stretch sf 2 in y-direction, followed by translation $\begin{pmatrix} 0 \\ 1 \end{pmatrix}$

3 a–d

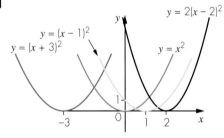

$y = 2(x - 2)^2$
$y = (x - 1)^2$
$y = (x + 3)^2$
$y = x^2$

e *b* Translation $\begin{pmatrix} -3 \\ 0 \end{pmatrix}$ *c* Translation $\begin{pmatrix} 1 \\ 0 \end{pmatrix}$

d Stretch sf 2 in y-direction, followed by translation $\begin{pmatrix} 2 \\ 0 \end{pmatrix}$

4 a–c

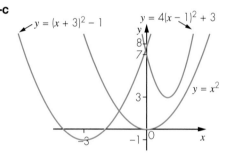

$y = (x + 3)^2 - 1$
$y = 4(x - 1)^2 + 3$
$y = x^2$

d *b* Translation $\begin{pmatrix} -3 \\ -1 \end{pmatrix}$

c Translation $\begin{pmatrix} 1 \\ 3 \end{pmatrix}$ followed by stretch sf 4 in y-direction

5 a–d

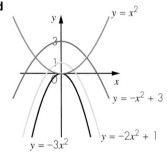

$y = x^2$
$y = -x^2 + 3$
$y = -2x^2 + 1$
$y = -3x^2$

e *b* Reflection in x-axis, followed by translation $\begin{pmatrix} 0 \\ 3 \end{pmatrix}$

c Reflection in the x-axis, followed by stretch sf 3 in y-direction
d Reflection in x-axis, followed by stretch sf 2 in y-direction and translation $\begin{pmatrix} 0 \\ 1 \end{pmatrix}$

6 a–d

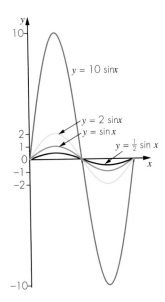

7 a–d

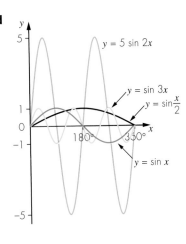

e *b* Stretch sf $\frac{1}{3}$ in *x*-direction
 c Stretch sf 2 in *x*-direction
 d Stretch sf 5 in *y*-direction, followed by stretch sf $\frac{1}{2}$ in *x*-direction

e Stretch sf in *y*-direction: 2, $\frac{1}{2}$, 10

e *b* Translation $\begin{pmatrix} -90 \\ 0 \end{pmatrix}$ *c* Translation $\begin{pmatrix} 40 \\ 0 \end{pmatrix}$

 d Stretch sf 2 in *y*-direction followed by translation $\begin{pmatrix} 90 \\ 0 \end{pmatrix}$

8 a–d

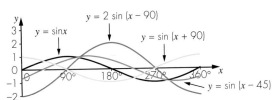

e *b* Translation $\begin{pmatrix} 0 \\ 2 \end{pmatrix}$ *c* Translation $\begin{pmatrix} 0 \\ -3 \end{pmatrix}$

 d Stretch sf 2 in *y*-direction followed by translation $\begin{pmatrix} 0 \\ 1 \end{pmatrix}$

9 a–d

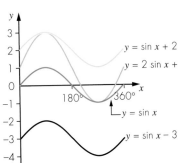

e *b* Reflection in *x*-axis *c* Reflection in *y*-axis *d* This leaves the graph in the same place and is the identity transform

10 a–d

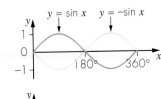

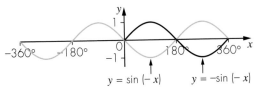

e *b* Stretch sf 2 in *y*-direction *c* Translation $\begin{pmatrix} 60 \\ 0 \end{pmatrix}$

 d Translation $\begin{pmatrix} 0 \\ 2 \end{pmatrix}$

11 a–d

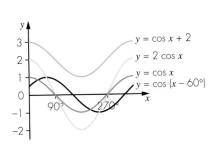

12 **a i** Stretch sf 4 in *y*-direction **ii** Stretch sf 9 in *y*-direction
 iii Stretch sf 16 in *y*-direction **b i** Stretch sf $\frac{1}{2}$ in *x*-direction
 ii Stretch sf $\frac{1}{3}$ in *x*-direction **iii** Stretch sf $\frac{1}{4}$ in *x*-direction
 c Stretch sf a^2 in *y*-direction, or stretch sf $\dfrac{1}{a}$ in *x*-direction

13 a 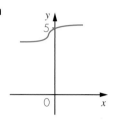 **b** 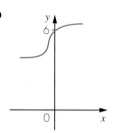 **c** 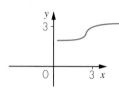 **d**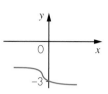

e  **f**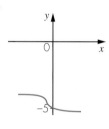

14 a $y = 5x^2$ **b** $y = x^2 + 7$ **c** $y = (x + 3)^2$
   d $y = 3x^2 + 4$ **e** $y = (x + 2)^2 - 3$ **f** $y = -3x^2$

15 a $y = 6\cos x$ **b** $y = \cos x + 3$ **c** $y = \cos(x + 30°)$ **d**
$y = 3\cos x - 2$ **e** $y = \cos(x - 45°) - 2$

16 a 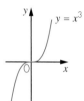 **b i** 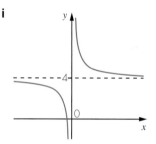   **ii** 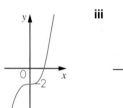   **iii** 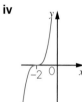   **iv**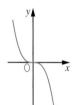

c i $y = -x^3$ **ii** $y = x^3 - 2$ **iii** $y = 3x^3$ **iv** $y = (x + 2)^3$

17 a 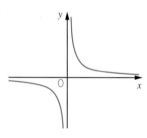 **b i** 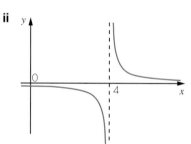   **ii**

iii 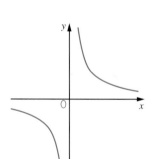   **iv**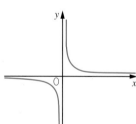

c i $y = \dfrac{1}{x} + 4$ **ii** $y = \dfrac{1}{x - 4}$

   iii $y = \dfrac{3}{x}$ **iv** $y = \dfrac{1}{2x}$

18 a $y = x^2 + 2$ **b** $y = (x - 2)^2$
   c $y = 2x^2$ **d** $y = -x^2 + 4$

19 a $y = 2\sin x$ **b** $y = \sin(x - 30°)$
   c $y = 2\sin(x - 60°)$ **d** $y = \sin 2x$

20 a Translation $\begin{pmatrix} 0 \\ -90 \end{pmatrix}$ **b i** Equivalent   **ii** Equivalent   **iii** Not equivalent   **21 i** A   **ii** D   **iii** E   **iv** C   **v** B

ANSWERS TO CHAPTER 28

Quick check

1 $z = x + y$ **2** $p^2 = q^2 + r^2$

3

+	Even	Odd
even	even	odd
odd	odd	even

Exercise 28A

6 a 3, 5, 8, 13, 21, 34, 55
   b $3a + 5b$, $5a + 8b$, $8a + 13b$, $13a + 21b$,
     $21a + 34b$

8 a i 40°

9 a i 10

Index

Index